MCSE Guide to

Microsoft Exchange 2000 Server Administration

Shawn Porter
Evan Benjamin

Australia • Canada • Mexico • Singapore • Spain • United Kingdom • United States

MCSE Guide to Microsoft Exchange 2000 Server Administration

by Shawn Porter and Evan Benjamin

Associate Publisher:
Steve Elliot

Product Manager:
Amy M. Lyon

LANWrights Project Editor:
Karen Annett / Kim Lindros

Developmental Editor:
Lisa M. Lord

Production Editor:
Kristen Guevara / Elena Montillo

Technical Editor:
Emmett Dulaney,
Mercury Technical Solutions

Contributing Authors:
Kevan Smith,
Alan Simpson,
Tony Krajnc

Manufacturing Coordinator:
Alexander Schall

Quality Assurance Technical Lead:
Nicole Ashton

Marketing Manager:
Toby Shelton

Associate Product Manager:
Tim Gleeson

Editorial Assistant:
Nick Lombardi

Marketing Manager:
Toby Shelton

Text Designer:
GEX Publishing Services

Compositor:
GEX Publishing Services

Cover Design:
Joseph Lee,
Black Fish Design

Printed in Canada

1 2 3 4 5 6 7 8 9 WC 05 04 03 02 01

For more information, contact Course Technology, 25 Thomson Place, Boston, Massachusetts, 02210.

Or find us on the World Wide Web at: www.course.com

ISBN 0-619-06218-5

BRIEF

Contents

PREFACE xv

CHAPTER ONE
An Overview of Microsoft Exchange 2000 Server 1

CHAPTER TWO
Planning for Windows 2000 39

CHAPTER THREE
Planning an Exchange 2000 Server Design Scenario 77

CHAPTER FOUR
Preparing to Deploy Exchange 2000 Server 113

CHAPTER FIVE
Installation of Exchange 2000 Server in New Environments 169

CHAPTER SIX
Upgrading or Migrating from Exchange 5.5 to Exchange 2000 211

CHAPTER SEVEN
Configuring MAPI Clients in Exchange 2000 Server 259

CHAPTER EIGHT
Configuring Internet Clients in Exchange 2000 Server 307

CHAPTER NINE
Exchange 2000 Server Management 357

CHAPTER TEN
Connector and Routing Management in Exchange 2000 Server 403

CHAPTER ELEVEN
Configuring Real-Time Collaboration in Exchange 2000 Server 463

CHAPTER TWELVE
Security and Encryption in Exchange 2000 Server 505

CHAPTER THIRTEEN
Exchange 2000 Server Public Folders 543

CHAPTER FOURTEEN
Maintaining and Monitoring Exchange 2000 Server 575

CHAPTER FIFTEEN
Exchange 2000 Server Disaster Recovery 611

APPENDIX A
Exam Objectives Tracking for MCSE Certification Exam #70-224: Installing, Configuring, and Administering Microsoft Exchange 2000 Server 645

APPENDIX B
Exchange Resources 651

APPENDIX C
Common Troubleshooting Scenarios 657

APPENDIX D
Outlook 2002, Outlook Express 6, and Exchange 2000 Server 665

GLOSSARY 689

INDEX 701

TABLE OF

Contents

PREFACE **xv**

CHAPTER ONE
An Overview of Microsoft Exchange 2000 Server **1**
Overview of Messaging System Behavior 2
Components of Messaging Systems 2
Comparing Various Messaging Servers 2
The Exchange Server Messaging Model 5
Integration of Essential Exchange 2000 Server Components 5
Essential Components of Exchange 2000 Server 8
Optional Components of Exchange 2000 Server 10
How Components Produce Message Flows in Exchange 2000 Server 11
Comparing Exchange Server 5.5 to Exchange 2000 Server 14
Basic Components Used in Exchange Server 5.5 15
The New and Improved Exchange 2000 Server 17
Administrative Groups 17
Routing Groups 18
Simple Mail Transport Protocol 18
Storage Groups 19
Real-Time Collaboration Services 19
Workflow and Workgroup Management 21
The Future of Messaging 21
Chapter Summary 22
Key Terms 23
Review Questions 27
Hands-on Projects 30
Case Projects 37

CHAPTER TWO
Planning for Windows 2000 **39**
The Microsoft Solutions Framework 40
The Four Phases of the MSF Model 40
Active Directory Planning and Design 50
The NT 4.0 Domain Structure 50
Active Directory Domain Structure 51
All About Forests 52
Trust Relationships 56
The Active Directory Schema 58
Global Catalog Servers 59
Organizational Units 59
Naming Contexts 61
Optimal Domain Design 62
Domain Name System Planning and Design 63
DNS Overview 63
DNS Zones 64
DNS Records 64
Reliance on DNS 65
Using Non–Windows-Based DNS Systems 66

Chapter Summary 67
Key Terms 68
Review Questions 69
Hands-on Projects 72
Case Projects 76

CHAPTER THREE
Planning an Exchange 2000 Server Design Scenario 77
The Microsoft Solutions Framework Revisited 78
Understanding the Current Requirements for Exchange 2000 Server 79
User Requirements 79
Company Requirements 80
Current Network Infrastructure Requirements 81
Understanding the Architecture of Exchange 2000 Server 85
The Components of Exchange 2000 Server 85
Understanding Exchange 2000 Server Site Design 89
Establishing Bridgehead Servers 89
Establishing Connector Servers 92
Establishing Cluster Configurations 93
Establishing Front-End and Back-End Configurations 95
Establishing Mailbox Servers 97
Establishing Public Folder Servers 98
Understanding Coexistence and Migration Issues 99
Maintaining Existing Users 100
Chapter Summary 102
Key Terms 103
Review Questions 104
Hands-on Projects 107
Case Projects 110

CHAPTER FOUR
Preparing to Deploy Exchange 2000 Server 113
Developing and Deploying Your Exchange 2000 Server Project Plan 114
The Developing Phase 114
The Deploying Phase 121
Deploying Active Directory with Exchange Server 5.5 and Exchange 2000 Server 122
Deploying Active Directory 122
Deploying the Active Directory Connector 126
Deploying Administrative Groups and Routing Groups 133
Administrative Groups 133
Routing Groups 136
Deployment in Mixed-Mode Environments and Legacy Windows NT 4.0 Domains 140
Deployment Guidelines for Mixed-Mode Environments 140
Migration Issues 140
Managing Resources in Mixed-Mode Environments 141
Using Front-End and Back-End Deployments 142
Guidelines for Front-End/Back-End Servers 143
Chapter Summary 144
Key Terms 146
Review Questions 147
Hands-on Projects 151
Case Projects 167

CHAPTER FIVE
Installation of Exchange 2000 Server in New Environments 169
Reviewing Windows 2000 Integration 170
Windows 2000 Protocols 170
Windows 2000 Services 171
Preinstallation Steps 172
Gather Information for the Exchange 2000 Installation 173
Verify That Hardware Meets Necessary Requirements 173
Apply Patches, Security Hot Fixes, and Service Packs 174
Optimize Current System Settings for Performance 174
Verify That Appropriate System Protocols and Services Are Available 176
Create Any Special Accounts Required for Installation 178
Optional Preinstallation Steps 179
Installation of the First Exchange 2000 Server 179
Starting the Installation 180
Installation of Subsequent Exchange 2000 Servers 184
Postinstallation Steps 185
Troubleshooting Failed Installations 187
Resources for Troubleshooting 187
When to Perform an Uninstall of Exchange 2000 190
Performing an Unattended Installation 192
Chapter Summary 193
Key Terms 194
Review Questions 195
Hands-on Projects 198
Case Projects 208

CHAPTER SIX
Upgrading or Migrating from Exchange 5.5 to Exchange 2000 211
Understanding How Migration to Windows 2000 Server Affects Exchange 2000 Migration 212
Upgrading Versus Migrating 212
A Sample Upgrade Scenario 215
Upgrading Exchange Server 5.5 to Exchange 2000 Server 219
Preparing the Windows 2000 Forest and Domain Structure 221
Managing Coexistence in a Mixed-Mode Environment 227
Using the Active Directory Connector in a Mixed-Mode Environment 228
A Review of the Active Directory Connector 228
Populating Active Directory Using the Active Directory Connector 231
Troubleshooting Exchange Upgrading and Migrating Issues 234
Troubleshooting Setup Issues 234
Troubleshooting Active Directory Connector Issues 236
Network and DNS Issues Affecting Active Directory 237
Chapter Summary 237
Key Terms 239
Review Questions 239
Hands-on Projects 244
Case Projects 256

CHAPTER SEVEN
Configuring MAPI Clients in Exchange 2000 Server 259
Reviewing Different Types of Clients 260
Messaging Application Programming Interface and E-Mail Clients 262
Outlook 2000 262
Outlook 97/98 266

Outlook Express 267
Outlook Web Access 270
Older 16-Bit Clients 272
Selecting Your Client Software 273
Installation of Outlook 2000 274
Command-Line Switches 278
Setup Information File 279
Office Custom Installation Wizard 280
Configuring Outlook 2000 280
Remote Access Using Outlook 2000 283
Configuring Messaging Profiles 284
Troubleshooting Common Outlook 2000 Problems 288
Recovery of Deleted Items 288
Permissions-Related Issues 290
Problems Synchronizing Data 290
Chapter Summary 291
Key Terms 293
Review Questions 293
Hands-on Projects 296
Case Projects 305
Case Projects Background 305

CHAPTER EIGHT
Configuring Internet Clients in Exchange 2000 Server 307
Overview of Internet Protocols 308
Virtual Protocol Servers 308
Simple Mail Transport Protocol 309
Post Office Protocol 3 313
Internet Messaging Access Protocol Version 4 314
Lightweight Directory Access Protocol 317
Hypertext Transfer Protocol with Web Distributed Authoring and Versioning Extensions 319
Network News Transport Protocol 320
Introduction to Internet Information Server 322
The Web Storage System 323
The Exchange Interprocess Communication Layer 324
Outlook Web Access 324
Installing Outlook Web Access 325
Configuring Outlook Web Access 330
Security and Outlook Web Access 334
Outlook Web Access in Front-End and Back-End Environments 335
Chapter Summary 337
Key Terms 339
Review Questions 339
Hands-on Projects 342
Case Projects 354
Case Projects Background 354

CHAPTER NINE
Exchange 2000 Server Management 357
Using Exchange 2000 Server Tools for Server Management 358
The System Manager Console and Its Components 358
Configuring Servers Using System Policies 361

Using Windows 2000 Tools for Exchange Server Management 365
- Active Directory Users and Computers 365
- Computer Management 366
- Registry Editor 368
- Performance Console 370
- Event Viewer 370
- Task Manager 371

Managing Exchange 2000 Server Resources 372
- Managing Administrative Groups 372
- Managing Storage Groups 374
- Managing Growth of Message Stores and Messaging Traffic 376

Managing Exchange 2000 Recipients 379
- Managing Exchange 2000 Using Recipient Policies 380
- Managing Address Lists 381
- Managing Full-Text Indexing in Exchange 2000 382

Chapter Summary 385
Key Terms 386
Review Questions 386
Hands-on Projects 389
Case Projects 400

CHAPTER TEN
Connector and Routing Management in Exchange 2000 Server 403

Exchange 2000 Connectivity Overview 404
- Simple Mail Transport Protocol Virtual Servers 404

Message Routing Concepts 407
- Technical Overview of Message Routing 407

Exchange 2000 Transport Architecture 410
- Message Storage and Retrieval 412
- Message Routing 413
- Event Handling and Event Sinks 415

Planning Routing Groups 417
- Administering Routing Groups in Administrative Groups 419
- Creating Routing Groups 420
- Connecting Routing Groups 420

Using Exchange 2000 Connectors 424
- The Routing Group Connector 425
- The SMTP Connector 427
- The X.400 Connector 427
- The Lotus Notes Connector 428
- The Lotus cc:Mail Connector 428
- The Novell GroupWise Connector 429
- The MS Mail and Schedule+ Free/Busy Connectors 430
- Legacy Exchange 5.5 Connectors 432

Managing Link State Information 433

Troubleshooting Messaging Connectivity 437
- Using Delivery Status Notifications to Pinpoint Problems 437
- Resolving Routing Problems 439

Chapter Summary 443
Key Terms 444
Review Questions 445
Hands-on Projects 450
Case Projects 458

CHAPTER ELEVEN
Configuring Real-Time Collaboration in Exchange 2000 Server 463
Introduction to Real-Time Collaboration in Exchange 2000 464
A Detailed Look at Instant Messaging 465
Protocols Used for Instant Messaging 466
Comparing Microsoft Instant Messaging with Third-Party Instant Messaging Products 468
Installing the Instant Messaging Service 470
Determining Instant Messaging Naming and Addressing 471
Configuring and Managing the Instant Messaging Service 472
Troubleshooting Instant Messaging Problems 473
A Detailed Look at Chat Services 475
Chat Services Nomenclature 475
Installing Chat Services 476
Configuring Chat Services 477
Troubleshooting Chat Services 484
A Detailed Look at the Exchange 2000 Conferencing Server 485
Installing the Exchange 2000 Conferencing Server 486
The Future of Collaboration 488
Chapter Summary 488
Key Terms 489
Review Questions 490
Hands-on Projects 492
Case Projects 502
Case Projects Background 502

CHAPTER TWELVE
Security and Encryption in Exchange 2000 Server 505
Introduction to Security Issues in Exchange 2000 506
Auditing and Logging Exchange 2000 Server 506
Controlling Access to Exchange 2000 Server 509
Public Key Infrastructure 510
Certificate Services 513
Overview of Key Management Services 516
The Basics of Key Management Services Architecture 516
Overview of Installing Key Management Services 518
Troubleshooting Security Issues in Exchange 2000 Server 518
Firewalls and Exchange 2000 519
Advanced Security Issues 520
Internet Security Issues 520
Potential Security Attacks Against Windows 2000 and Exchange 2000 521
Exchange 2000 Server Security Bulletins 523
Chapter Summary 525
Key Terms 526
Review Questions 527
Hands-on Projects 529
Case Projects 540
Case Projects Background 540

CHAPTER THIRTEEN
Exchange 2000 Server Public Folders 543
Introduction to Public Folders 544
The Public Folder Hierarchy 545
Creating Public Folders 546

Configuring Public Folder Properties 548
Securing Public Folder Access 549
Managing Public Folders 550
Replicating Public Folders 551
Mail-Enabling Public Folders 554
Monitoring Public Folder Usage 555
Creating Public Folder Items Offline 557
Using Public Folders with Outlook Web Access 557
Chapter Summary 559
Key Terms 560
Review Questions 560
Hands-on Projects 563
Case Projects 573
Case Projects Background 573

CHAPTER FOURTEEN
Maintaining and Monitoring Exchange 2000 Server 575
Maintenance Concepts 576
Preventive Maintenance and Optimization 576
Maintaining Exchange 2000 Server Databases 577
Maintenance of Exchange 2000 Databases 578
Recovering Space in Exchange 2000 Information Store Databases 580
Maintaining Log Files with Circular Logging 582
Other Maintenance and Monitoring Tasks 582
Windows 2000 Event Viewer 583
Configuring Notifications in Exchange System Manager 583
Using Message Tracking in Exchange System Manager 585
Monitoring Message Queues and System Resources 587
Using the Performance Console 588
Network Monitor 593
Troubleshooting and Maintenance Utilities for Exchange 2000 594
Chapter Summary 595
Key Terms 597
Review Questions 597
Hands-on Projects 600
Case Projects 609
Case Projects Background 609

CHAPTER FIFTEEN
Exchange 2000 Server Disaster Recovery 611
Developing a Disaster Recovery Plan for Your Organization 612
Designing an Effective Backup Strategy 615
Selecting the Type of Data to Back Up 616
Backing up Exchange 2000 Database Information 617
Online and Offline Backups 618
Backing up Exchange 2000 Configuration and System State Information 619
Restoring and Recovering Exchange 2000 Data 620
Prerequisites for Restoration 620
Restoring a Full Backup to the Production or Recovery Server 622
Restoring a Single Mailbox 623
Restoring Online and Offline Backups 623
Additional Exchange 2000 Recovery Options 624

Chapter Summary 625
Key Terms 626
Review Questions 627
Hands-on Projects 629
Case Projects 642
Case Projects Background 642

APPENDIX A
Exam Objectives Tracking for MCSE Certification Exam #70-224: Installing, Configuring, and Administering Microsoft Exchange 2000 Server 645
Installing and Upgrading Exchange 2000 Server 645
Configuring Exchange 2000 Server. Types of Servers Include Mailbox, Public Folder, Gateway, Virtual, Chat, and Instant Messaging 646
Managing Recipient Objects 647
Monitoring and Managing Messaging Connectivity 648
Managing Exchange 2000 Server Growth 649
Restoring System Functionality and User Data 650

APPENDIX B
Exchange Resources 651
Printed Materials 651
Online/Electronic Materials 651
Chapter 2 Web References 651
Chapter 4 Web References 652
Chapter 5 Web References 652
Chapter 6 Web References 652
Chapter 7 Web References 653
Chapter 8 Web References 653
Chapter 9 Web References 653
Chapter 10 Web References 654
Chapter 11 Web References 654
Chapter 12 Web References 654
Chapter 14 Web References 654
Chapter 15 Web References 655
Other Exchange Resources 655
Outlook 2002 Resources 655

APPENDIX C
Common Troubleshooting Scenarios 657
Scenario 1 657
Situation 657
Problem 657
Suggested Answer 657
Scenario 2 658
Situation 658
Problem 658
Suggested Answer 658
Scenario 3 658
Situation 658
Problem 659
Suggested Answer 659

Scenario 4 659
Situation 659
Problem 659
Suggested Answer 659
Scenario 5 660
Situation 660
Problem 660
Suggested Answer 660
Scenario 6 660
Situation 660
Problem 661
Suggested Answer 661
Scenario 7 661
Situation 661
Problem 661
Suggested Answer 661
Scenario 8 662
Situation 662
Problem 662
Suggested Answer 662
Scenario 9 662
Situation 662
Problem 662
Suggested Answer 663
Scenario 10 663
Situation 663
Problem 663
Suggested Answer 663
Scenario 11 664
Situation 664
Problem 664
Suggested Answer 664

APPENDIX D
Outlook 2002, Outlook Express 6, and Exchange 2000 Server 665
Overview of Outlook 2002 Improvements 666
New and Improved Security and Virus Protection 666
Installing and Registering Security Components 670
Creating a Public Folder for Security Settings 670
Defining Security Settings 670
Outlook 2002 Calendaring Enhancements 675
Using MSN Messenger 680
Workflow Enhancements 682
Mailbox Manager Improvements 683
Improvements to Remote Access 684
Synchronization Performance Improvements 685
Full-Text Indexing and Searching 686
Outlook Express 6 687
Chapter Summary 687

GLOSSARY 689

INDEX 701

Preface

Welcome to the *MCSE Guide to Microsoft Exchange 2000 Server*! This book provides in-depth coverage of the knowledge and skills required to pass Microsoft Certification Exam #70-224: *Installing, Configuring, and Administering Microsoft Exchange 2000 Server.* In addition to exam preparation, this book will provide you with practical hands-on learning by taking you through projects in each chapter. These projects are geared toward real-world activities that will give you the knowledge you need to administer and configure an Exchange 2000 server, including other services such as Instant Messaging and Outlook Web Access. You will also be provided with references and information straight from the authors' experiences in the industry and with Exchange 2000.

The Intended Audience

This book is intended to serve anyone interested in learning more about Microsoft Exchange 2000 Server, particularly those who are interested in earning Microsoft certification on this topic. This book guides you through the planning, setup, configuration, and troubleshooting of Exchange 2000 Server. When you finish the book, you should be able to deploy and administer Exchange 2000 Server, including its advanced features, such as user collaboration.

Chapter Descriptions

Chapter 1, "An Overview of Microsoft Exchange 2000 Server," gives an overview of Exchange 2000 Server and the various features in this version.

Chapter 2, "Planning for Windows 2000," lays the foundation material necessary to understand the planning involved with Exchange 2000, including the first two phases of the Microsoft Solutions Framework.

Chapter 3, "Planning an Exchange 2000 Server Design Scenario," continues the foundation laid out in Chapter 2 and outlines the last two phases of the Microsoft Solutions Framework.

Chapter 4, "Preparing to Deploy Exchange 2000 Server," describes the steps required to prepare your servers for an Exchange 2000 installation, including what you should consider when upgrading from Exchange Server 5.5 and what configuration steps you must take when installing to a Windows 2000 server.

Chapter 5, "Installation of Exchange 2000 Server in New Environments," details the steps in installing Exchange 2000 on a new Windows 2000 server, including the exact preliminary configuration to expedite the installation process and make it go more smoothly.

Chapter 6, "Upgrading or Migrating from Exchange 5.5 to Exchange 2000," describes how to upgrade an existing Exchange 5.5 server to Exchange 2000, including how to perform the installation and the different upgrade options available to you.

Chapter 7, "Configuring MAPI Clients in Exchange 2000," discusses the different clients you can use with Exchange 2000 services. The focus of this chapter is installing, configuring, and using Outlook 2000—the main client used with Exchange 2000 Server.

Chapter 8, "Configuring Internet Clients in Exchange 2000 Server," shows you how to configure Exchange 2000 to support the variety of protocols used for messaging. In addition to learning how to configure these protocols, you will learn about installing and configuring Outlook Web Access, a free Web client included with Exchange 2000.

Chapter 9, "Exchange 2000 Server Management," covers the utilities and methods that you can use to effectively manage your Exchange 2000 server. In addition to these tools, you will learn more about managing Exchange 2000 Server resources and recipients.

Chapter 10, "Connector and Routing Management in Exchange 2000 Server," discusses message routing and the management of connectors in Exchange 2000 Server. In addition, you will learn about routing groups and how to plan, create, and administer them.

Chapter 11, "Configuring Real-Time Collaboration in Exchange 2000 Server," covers the advanced collaboration features included with Exchange 2000, including Instant Messaging, Chat, and the optional Conferencing Server that can be used to complement an Exchange 2000 server.

Chapter 12, "Security and Encryption in Exchange 2000 Server," discusses the main security issues you should be concerned about with Exchange 2000. In addition, you will learn about Key Management Services and how they can help secure your user's e-mail messages.

Chapter 13, "Exchange 2000 Public Folders," explains creating and managing the public folder implementation in Exchange 2000 and how you can use it to improve your users' productivity.

Chapter 14, "Maintaining and Monitoring Exchange 2000 Server," covers maintenance concepts related to Exchange 2000, the operating system, and the server. You will also learn about maintaining the Exchange 2000 databases and how to monitor Exchange 2000 for problems.

Chapter 15, "Disaster Recovery in Exchange 2000 Server," discusses the importance of a good disaster recovery plan for your organization and how to implement and perform backups and restores of your critical Exchange 2000 data.

Features

To ensure a successful learning experience, this book includes the following pedagogical features:

- **Chapter Objectives.** Each chapter in this book begins with a detailed list of the concepts to be mastered. This list gives you a quick reference to the chapter's contents and is a useful study aid.
- **Illustrations and Tables.** Numerous illustrations of server screens and components aid you in visualizing common setup steps, theories, and concepts. In addition, many tables provide details and comparisons of both practical and theoretical information and can be used for a quick review of certain topics.
- **End-of-Chapter Material.** The end of each chapter includes the following features to reinforce the material that's been covered:
  - *Chapter Summary*—A bulleted list gives a brief but complete summary of the chapter to revisit and reinforce concepts introduced and covered.
  - *Key Terms List*—A list of all new Exchange 2000 terms and their definitions provides a helpful reference and ensures your understanding of the chapter's key concepts.
  - *Review Questions*—A set of review questions tests your knowledge of the concepts covered in the chapter and can be used to help prepare you for the Microsoft certification examination.

Hands-on Projects—A set of step-by-step exercises helps you apply the knowledge from the chapter to hands-on implementations to give you real-world experience.

Case Projects—A set of case projects takes you through real-world scenarios to sharpen your troubleshooting and decision-making skills by asking you to evaluate situations and determine a course of action to solve the problem.

- **On the CD-ROM.** On the CD-ROM, you will find **CoursePrep®** exam preparation software, which provides 50 sample MCSE exam questions that mirror the look and feel of the MCSE exams.

Text and Graphic Conventions

Wherever appropriate, additional information and exercises have been added to this book to help you better understand what is being discussed in the chapter. Icons throughout the text alert you to additional materials. The icons used in this book are as follows:

Tips from the authors' experience are included and offer extra information on installation, how to attack problems, time-saving shortcuts, or what to do in certain real-world situations.

The Note icon is used to indicate additional helpful material related to the subject being discussed.

The Caution icon identifies important information about potential mistakes or hazards.

Each hands-on project in this book is preceded by the Hands-on icon.

Case project icons mark the case projects, which are more involved, scenario-based assignments. In these extensive case examples, you are asked to independently apply what you've learned.

Instructor's Materials

The following supplemental materials are available when this book is used in a classroom setting. All of the supplements are provided to the instructor on a single CD-ROM.

Electronic Instructor's Manual. The Instructor's Manual that accompanies this textbook includes:

- Additional instructional material to assist in class preparation, including suggestions for classroom activities, discussion topics, and additional projects.
- Solutions to all end-of-chapter materials, including the review questions, hands-on projects, and case projects.

ExamView®. This textbook is accompanied by ExamView, a powerful testing software package that allows instructors to create and administer printed, computer (LAN-based), and Internet exams. ExamView includes hundreds of questions that correspond to the topics covered in this text, enabling students to generate detailed study guides that include page references for further review. The computer-based and Internet testing components allow students to take exams at their computers and also save the instructor time by grading each exam automatically.

PowerPoint presentations. This book comes with Microsoft PowerPoint slides for each chapter. These are included as a teaching aid for classroom presentation, to make available to students on the network for chapter review, or to be printed for classroom distribution. Instructors, please feel at liberty to add your own slides for additional topics you introduce to the class.

Acknowledgments

Shawn Porter: I would first and foremost like to thank Karen Annett at LANWrights for helping me remain sane and keep on track throughout this entire book; it has been a long but rewarding road to travel down. I would also like to thank Ed Tittel at LANWrights for the opportunity to work on this project and his advice and support to all of us during the entire process. As well, I would like to thank the Course Technology staff who worked on this project for helping provide the insights necessary to make this a great title. I would also like to thank my fellow authors on this book—Evan, Kevan, Alan, and Tony—for your help and information as we worked on this book. Finally, I would like to thank my family (especially my wife, Nicole) for listening to my terribly interesting stories about writing this book and their encouragement, help, and patience in putting up with my long hours and me in general!

Evan Benjamin: To my co-author, Shawn, your contributions are deeply appreciated and acknowledged. This book could not have been done without your words. To Karen Annett and Ed Tittel at LANWrights whose constant concerns and hopes kept this project moving along even though I was too weak to type (thanks, Karen, for all your interventions). To the wonderful folks at Course Technology and the rest of the staff who cared about this book, I'm much obliged that all of you cared so much about detail because you wanted a first-rate book as a result. It does take a village to write a book, and even though I keep telling myself "no more," I find myself back at the drawing board once again. Thank you, everyone.

Collectively: Our sincere thanks goes to the ever-capable staff at Course Technology, including (but not limited to) Amy Lyon, our Product Manager who so efficiently kept us on track from beginning to end; Lisa Lord, our Developmental Editor, who read and edited each and every word and helped us turn our words into this wonderful book; Emmett Dulaney, our Technical Editor, who helped ensure the technical accuracy; and Kristen Guevara and Elena Montillo, our Production Editors, who helped manage the production process and made our pages look so pretty! We also want to thank all other members of the Course Technology team who contributed to this project, either directly or indirectly, and a special thanks to the peer reviewers who offered helpful feedback: Sheldon Bartel, Amanda Hart, Greg Kolisnyk, and Dwight Watt.

Dedication

Shawn Porter: I would like to dedicate this book to my father, Wayne, and my wife, Nicole. My father for coughing up the dough for that Commodore 64 (which I adored) and then eventually the 286. I guess all those years that I didn't want to do anything but muck around on my computers have finally paid off; thanks for foreseeing and supporting that! And to my wife, Nicole, for the constant support and for lending an ear to my troubles—even if you didn't understand a single word I was saying, you were always there for me!

Read This Before You Begin

The hands-on projects in this book have been written to function in a classroom with the minimum required lab equipment and network connections. Although it is possible to work through nearly all the hands-on projects with the minimum required lab equipment, you (or your students) will have a better experience if you can meet the requirements for recommended standard equipment.

Minimum Lab Requirements

Hardware:

- Each student requires one server equipped with at least 128 MB of RAM, an Intel Pentium or compatible processor running at 166 Mhz or higher, 10 MB of free space on the hard disk where Exchange 2000 is installed, and 5 MB of free space on the system drive. Higher than minimum specifications are always recommended for the student servers.
- A CD-ROM drive is required for each server
- A modem or other source of Internet access is required for each server

Software:

- You need a copy of Exchange 2000 Server (Enterprise edition) and Windows 2000 Server for each student server. You also need Windows 2000 Service Pack 1 available to install on each student's server and access to Exchange Server 5.5, preferably one for every three Exchange 2000 servers minimum. These Exchange 5.5 servers must be installed on Windows NT 4.0 and have Exchange 5.5 Service Pack 3 installed. Servers shouldn't be installed or configured until you are ready to use them in the book's hands-on projects. As well, you will need a copy of Exchange 2000 Enterprise Server on CD-ROM and Outlook 2000 on CD-ROM or as part of Office 2000.

Configuration:

- Each server should have Windows 2000 Server installed. During the installation, choose to create a single partition on the hard disk and format it with the NTFS file system. Following the installation, install the latest Windows 2000 service pack (at least Service Pack 1). Students can emulate either one or both required network cards by using the Microsoft Loopback Adapter, but each server should preferably have at least one network card. You can create your own IP addressing scheme for the classroom; creating an address range in the 192.168.x.x network is recommended, with each student having 5 to 10 IP addresses.

Recommended Lab Requirements

Hardware:

- To improve the productivity of your students in working through the hands-on projects, the authors recommend the following increases from the minimum requirements: Increase RAM to at least 256 MB, processor speed to 400 Mhz or higher, free space on the Exchange 2000 installation drive to 3 GB, and free space on the system drive to 1 GB. High-speed Internet access, preferably cable, DSL, or faster, would also be beneficial.

Configuration:

- The authors also recommend the following enhancements to the minimum configuration to improve students' experiences: In addition to the single NTFS-formatted partition, a second smaller NTFS partition may be useful for students to store downloaded software or other utilities for later use. Also, two network cards, each with its own IP address, for each server is recommended as well as the other minimum recommendations for IP addressing schemes.

CHAPTER

1

An Overview of Microsoft Exchange 2000 Server

After reading this chapter and completing the exercises, you will be able to:

- Understand the general behavior of a messaging system
- Recognize the way Exchange 2000 and Windows 2000 are integrated and see how Exchange 2000 Server depends on the architecture of Windows 2000
- Relate features in Exchange Server 5.5 to those in Exchange 2000 Server
- Identify components new to Exchange 2000 Server and understand how these components work together as a single unit
- Understand the exciting trends in messaging in Exchange 2000 Server so you can plan long-range implementations for your organization

This chapter introduces you to the concept of messaging systems, specifically the messaging platform developed by Microsoft, known as Exchange Server. Messaging systems have been evolving ever since the Advanced Research Projects Agency (ARPA), an arm of the U.S. Department of Defense, funded a special networking project that resulted in the inception of the Internet known as the ARPANET. Over the years, we have witnessed a rapid progression toward sophisticated messaging systems that are focused almost totally on the most current Internet technology. Messaging in general, and e-mail in particular, are changing the way we communicate with each other, so it is important to understand the history and future of messaging systems, including the one that strives to provide the most complete messaging solution: Exchange 2000 Server.

Overview of Messaging System Behavior

The concept of messaging is not a new one. In fact, messaging is now one of the most pervasive applications used throughout the world, regardless of industry or culture. The question to ask is not "Are organizations using some type of messaging application?" but "What is the best messaging application to use given the current organizational climate?" Not all messaging systems are created equal, however, so it is just as important to select the right messaging system as it is to correctly administer it. One of the best ways to evaluate a particular messaging system is to understand how these systems behave in general and see the subtle differences between products. This book focuses on Microsoft Exchange 2000 Server; a stable, secure messaging platform that offers the functionality and security that most e-mail administrators are looking for. After completing this chapter, you will have a better picture of how a messaging system is designed to operate and how messaging systems are evolving into increasingly sophisticated systems.

Components of Messaging Systems

Analyzing the behavior of a system implies an understanding of that system's components; therefore, to understand how a messaging system behaves, you have to first understand what components make up a messaging system. Before you get into higher-level concepts, such as message flows and message transport mechanisms, you need a clear idea of a messaging system's basic components: a message and a messaging server. A **message** is nothing more than a string of data specially formatted to represent a request or a reply sent to a **messaging server**, which is a message exchange application used to process these messages. A messaging system creates, stores, or exchanges data (text, images, e-mail, and so forth) in the form of messages over some form of communications network.

Comparing Various Messaging Servers

Many outdated texts refer to different models of messaging servers. You may see terms such as "point-to-point" or "publish/subscribe" when referring to these servers. However, the more appropriate terms to learn are *shared-file messaging systems* and *client-server messaging systems.* A **shared-file messaging system** dedicates file servers as "post offices" and gives users access to messaging services via mailboxes inside the post office. A **client-server messaging system** uses an active server (implying that most e-mail processing is done by the server itself, not the client) that interacts with clients or users to process their messaging requests. The differences between these two systems are quite clear-cut, as shown in Figures 1-1 and 1-2.

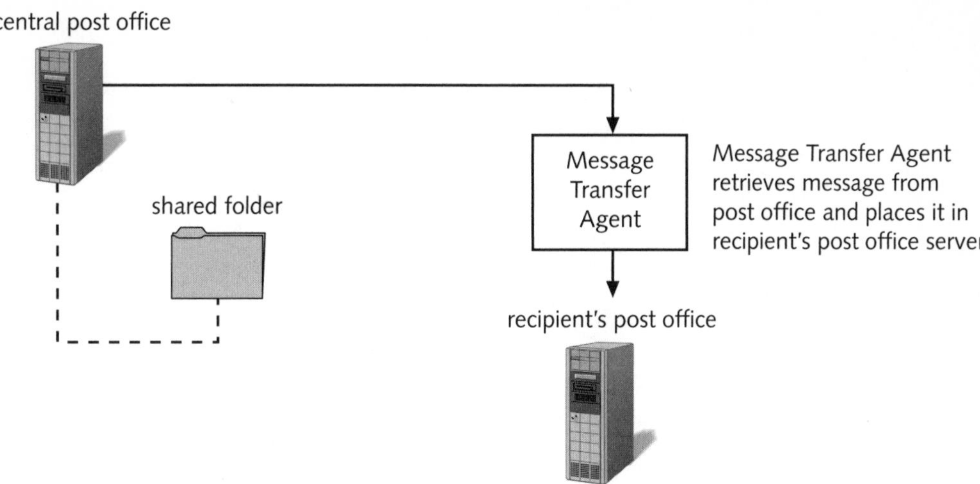
central post office
shared folder
Message Transfer Agent
Message Transfer Agent retrieves message from post office and places it in recipient's post office server
recipient's post office

Figure 1-1 Shared-file messaging system with multiple mailboxes for each user

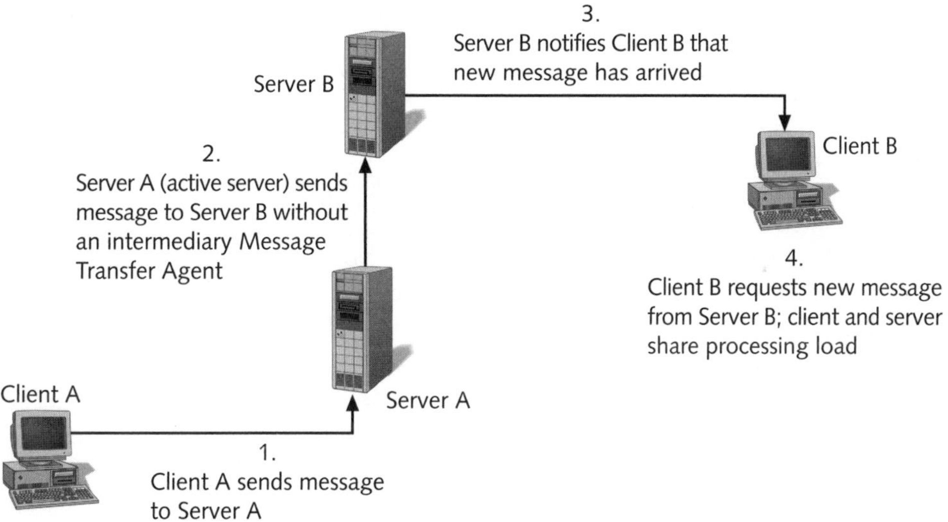
3.
Server B notifies Client B that new message has arrived
Server B
Client B
2.
Server A (active server) sends message to Server B without an intermediary Message Transfer Agent
4.
Client B requests new message from Server B; client and server share processing load
Client A
Server A
1.
Client A sends message to Server A

Figure 1-2 A client-server messaging system

Note

The terms *active* and *passive* are applied to the server, not the client. If a file system is active, then the server is capable of manipulating this file system. A passive file system resides on the server, but cannot be manipulated in any way by the server's operating system.

A shared-file system, such as Microsoft Mail for PC networks, uses a passive file structure so that the burden of processing messages is placed on the client application. Clients or users actually poll or query their post office at specified intervals to determine the status of pending mail. On the other hand, in a client-server system, such as Microsoft Exchange 2000 Server, the server takes an active role in checking for, receiving, and sending new mail to clients. All processing is considered to be server-side, not client-side.

Given the requirements of these two systems, you can compare the advantages and disadvantages of the two systems. You cannot assume that one system will always prevail in every organization. The choice of a messaging system depends on many factors, including the number of clients involved, the hardware used to support the messaging platform, and the level of security needed.

Advantages of shared-file messaging systems include:

- Simple installation with minimal configuration needed
- Minimal hardware requirements because processing is concentrated on the client side

Disadvantages of shared-file messaging systems include:

- Clients have to poll their post offices at regular intervals, possibly creating a large volume of unnecessary network traffic.
- Clients might accidentally delete files while accessing the shared-file structure of the post office on the server because they have read and write access to this structure.
- Certain shared-file systems (such as Microsoft Mail) are limited in the number of users they can service simply because an increase in users tends to drain limited system resources.
- Shared-file systems are limited in the functionality they offer. For instance, they might not offer advanced user interfaces in the client application as their client-server counterparts do, or allow recovery of deleted items.

As you can see, the disadvantages of shared-file systems seem to outweigh the advantages, so now try examining the advantages and disadvantages of client-server systems.

Advantages of client-server messaging systems include:

- Clients do not have to query their host server at regular intervals because the server can inform clients when new mail has arrived. This eases network traffic.
- Client-server systems can handle more users than shared-file messaging systems because shared-file systems were designed to host a limited number of mailboxes per server post office. A check has to be placed on the number of clients who can poll a central post office at one time; otherwise, network traffic would increase to unmanageable levels.

- Only services directly related to the server have direct access to messaging databases or stored messages; this feature enhances security within a network because clients cannot modify the messaging infrastructure.

Disadvantages of client-server messaging systems include:

- Increased centralized administration, especially if several servers are involved
- Investment in server hardware designed to meet the organization's current user needs and maintenance of an upgrade schedule as current technology becomes obsolete

Comparing advantages and disadvantages highlights the importance of choosing an appropriate messaging model for a given environment. You have to decide if an increase in network traffic caused by excessive client polling of a centralized post office is better than keeping hundreds of mailboxes on a centralized server and not giving users access to stored messages. There is always a trade-off involved in any planning decision; it may help to list a worst-case scenario and a best-case scenario for every decision that is made.

THE EXCHANGE SERVER MESSAGING MODEL

Microsoft designed Exchange 2000 Server with modularity and complexity in mind. This complexity adds to the overall power and robustness of Exchange, compared to previous versions. Many active components reside on the server that simultaneously perform specific tasks, such as storing and retrieving e-mail messages or monitoring the state of connections among different servers. These components establish regular communication not only among themselves, but also with services integrated within the Windows 2000 operating system, such as Active Directory. The messaging model supports basic functions for users—sending messages or accessing information contained in a database of some type. The Exchange components can be separated into two distinct groups: those that are considered basic or essential, and those that are considered optional or accessory (though not trivial). After reviewing the characteristics of these components in the upcoming section "The New and Improved Exchange 2000 Server," you'll see how components communicate with each other to produce transparent message flows in any organization.

Integration of Essential Exchange 2000 Server Components

Exchange 2000 Server comes with predefined components and modules that organizations can use to set up a client-server infrastructure for transferring messages between end users. However, message flow also depends on essential services provided by Windows 2000. This integration with Windows 2000 is so tight that some people might mistake Exchange 2000 Server components for Windows 2000 Server components. This integration is discussed in more depth in Chapter 2, "Planning for Windows 2000." For now, however, it's more important to highlight the areas of integration that are discussed in detail in later chapters. The total number of components, combined with the degree of integration with Windows 2000, seems daunting to most administrators at first glance.

It's simpler, however, if you realize that two of the most vital components needed for successful messaging are a directory service and a few access protocols. Figure 1-3 shows this relationship.

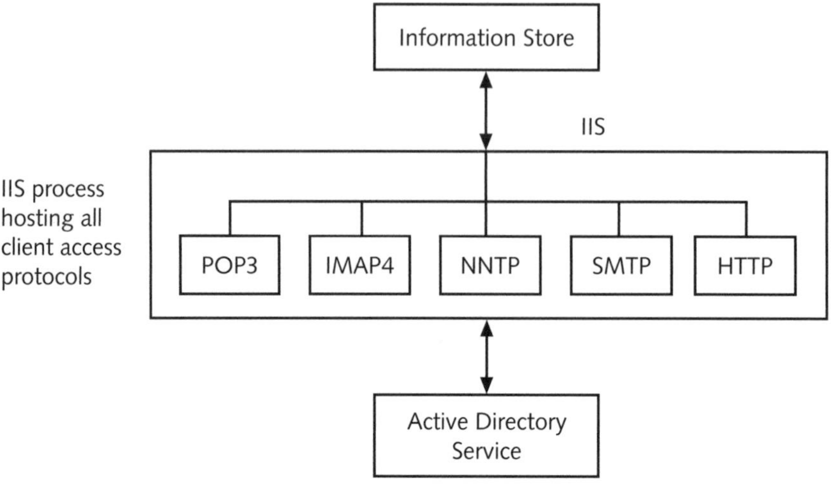

Figure 1-3 The integration of AD with Internet Information Server

Directory Service Integration

There are many areas of integration between Windows 2000 and Exchange 2000, especially in the Active Directory (AD) service; this service makes it easy to manage large amounts of directory information and makes it possible for users to search for objects, such as other users, groups, or contacts. AD, a directory database found in a local file named Ntds.dit, integrates with Exchange 2000 by acting as a central storehouse for mailbox information for Exchange 2000; therefore, making sure its structure matches the design of your organization can help reduce total system administration for both Windows 2000 and Exchange 2000.

The Windows 2000 Active Directory stores attributes, or property information, specific to Exchange 2000 Server. In fact, an installation of Exchange 2000 automatically extends the AD schema by adding new classes or new attributes to existing classes of objects within AD.

The AD schema holds formal definitions of the Active Directory contents, including all attributes and object classes. When you install AD on a domain controller in your network, a default schema is automatically created, and contains definitions of some common objects, such as users and computers in your domains.

Most object classes or attributes can be displayed in Windows 2000 by using tools such as ADSI Edit, provided on the Windows 2000 Server CD in the \Support\Tools directory.

This operating system integration can even be seen with respect to Exchange Server clients. For instance, when users use Outlook 2000 to search for directory information from an Exchange 2000 server, they are forwarded to a Windows 2000 component known as the **Global Catalog (GC)** server, which is a central physical storage location for attributes of every object in AD. This forwarding takes place through an Exchange 2000 service known as **Directory Service Proxy (DSProxy)**, which helps ensure that all responses from a GC server are sent to the client who made the initial request.

Transport Protocol Integration

The final area of integration between Windows 2000 and Exchange 2000 centers on transport protocols, which are used to deliver data from one computer to another computer along transmission media such as Category 5 cable. Exchange 2000 relies on **Transmission Control Protocol/Internet Protocol (TCP/IP)**, an industry-standard communications protocol, and the **Remote Procedure Calls (RPC)** protocol. RPC is administered using the **Windows Sockets Application Programming Interface (API)**, which is used to manage server-to-server communication processes. The RPC protocol is used by Exchange 2000 when it connects to another Exchange server in the same site or routing group.

Microsoft **Internet Information Server (IIS)** is the built-in Web server component of Windows 2000 Server. It allows you to host Web sites and take advantage of designing interactive applications on your network. IIS provides two services in particular that Exchange 2000 relies heavily on: **Simple Mail Transport Protocol (SMTP)** and **Network News Transport Protocol (NNTP)**, which Exchange 2000 extends for enhanced functionality. SMTP is used to transfer e-mail messages from one computer to another, and NNTP is the standard Internet protocol used in retrieving and posting Usenet newsgroup articles on the Internet. Keep in mind that IIS version 5.0 is installed automatically when you perform a default installation of Windows 2000 Server or Windows 2000 Advanced Server.

The IIS process is vital to Exchange 2000 because it hosts all Exchange 2000 protocols, such as SMTP or **Post Office Protocol version 3 (POP3)**, but IIS version 5.0 is not as interwoven with AD as Exchange 2000 is. Exchange 2000, however, stores IIS configuration information in Active Directory on its own. The IIS process is also important to the operation of other essential Exchange 2000 services and protocols, including the **Internet Messaging Access Protocol version 4 (IMAP4)** service, which can be used to directly manipulate an e-mail message on a server.

POP3 enables an e-mail client, such as Microsoft Outlook 2000, to download e-mail from an Exchange server, but it does not allow clients to manipulate messages directly on the server, as IMAP4 does.

The IIS executable file in Windows 2000 Server (formally known as Inetinfo.exe) communicates with another essential element of Exchange 2000: the **Web Storage System**. This system allows you to store items and control information about them (for example, security information). Protocols such as SMTP communicate and exchange information with the Web Storage System using a special communication layer, the **Exchange Interprocess Communications (ExIPC) layer**. The ExIPC is part of the Information Store service and helps access protocols, such as HTTP or POP3, exchange information with the Information Store. The Web Storage System was designed with collaboration and document management features in mind. It works similarly to traditional file systems (such as the Win32 file system or NT File System in Windows 2000) in that it stores an object in a folder structure. The Web Storage System contains schemas (which can be extended) that help establish definitions for the stored contents and plays an important role in application development for Exchange 2000. It even supports an emerging protocol known as the **Web Distributed Authoring and Versioning (DAV)** protocol, which allows users to access Web Storage System content over the Internet using common **Uniform Resource Locators (URLs)**.

Essential Components of Exchange 2000 Server

All server-centered user information (e-mail messages, public folder information) is stored centrally in an essential component known as the **Information Store**, or simply "the store."

Public folders, available to every user in your Exchange organization, are used to share information and applications across a private or public network. They contain a variety of information, including message items, Microsoft Office documents, and even contact objects.

It is referred to as "the store" because the service runs as Store.exe in the default installation directory of Exchange 2000 Server (usually C:\Exchsrvr\Bin). The Information Store service maintains two different types of stores: one for private e-mail messages, called a **mailbox store**, and one for data stored in public folders, known as a **public folder store**. Each store possesses database files distinct from the other. A **Messaging Application Programming Interface (MAPI)** client, such as Outlook 2000, communicates with the Information Store to gain access to messages or public folders.

The Information Store can be further organized into formal structures known as **storage groups (SGs)**. These groups are nothing more than combinations of mailbox stores and public folder stores. All mailbox and public folder stores in a storage group share one set of **transaction log** files. These log files, normally found in the \Exchsrvr\Bin\Mdbdata directory on your local hard drive, contain records of transactions for all mailbox and public folder stores written sequentially. A single Exchange 2000 Server machine can hold up to four differently named SGs, each containing up to five mailbox stores, five public stores, or a combination of both. Each mailbox store is capable of hosting multiple e-mail accounts, which means that different users can be placed in different mailbox stores or different SGs within the same Exchange 2000 server. Whatever the combination, you cannot exceed a total of five stores in a specific SG.

The Information Store depends on another essential component of Exchange 2000 Server, the **System Attendant (SA)**. This small executable service can be found with Store.exe, in the default installation directory of Exchange 2000 Server, or C:\Exchsrvr\Bin (if C: is the partition selected during the installation). The SA performs the following functions:

- Cleans users' mailboxes
- Generates e-mail addresses
- Monitors critical server services
- Moves mailboxes
- Assigns public folders to new servers for various e-mail clients
- Configures replication between servers
- Generates routing tables for message delivery
- Regulates password changes for the service account
- Gathers important system statistics
- Defragments the Information Store
- Supports direct Active Directory queries by MAPI-based clients, such as Outlook 2000

Two important facts about the System Attendant must be noted. First, the SA can be used to shut down all other vital Exchange 2000 Server services, such as the Information Store or the POP3 service. However, certain services, such as SMTP or NNTP, are not shut down because they are hosted by another process, Inetinfo.exe. Second, certain services cannot be *started* unless the SA is running. If you accidentally stop the SA, for instance, then the Information Store does not run correctly. Because the SA is so critical in this circumstance, starting the Information Store by itself automatically starts the SA. Again, this scenario does not affect the SMTP or NNTP services.

A final essential component to consider is SMTP, which is now the primary protocol used between computers hosting Exchange 2000 Server. It is used to transfer Internet e-mail and also defines message formats. Exchange 2000 Server extends the functionality of the basic SMTP Service in the Windows 2000 operating system by adding new components, such as an advanced queuing engine and a message categorization agent. The advanced queuing engine manages queues for all messages and relays messages to a categorizer, which performs address resolution to determine the proper destination for every message and also aids in expanding distribution lists. The SMTP Service, hosted by the IIS process in Windows 2000, has also replaced the Internet Mail Service used in previous versions of Exchange Server. Windows 2000 includes its own SMTP component as part of a basic installation, but Exchange 2000 extends SMTP by providing enhanced delivery functions.

Optional Components of Exchange 2000 Server

Optional components used for message flows in Exchange 2000 sometimes include services that help sustain backward-compatibility with Exchange Server 5.5 (for example, the Site Replication Service and the Active Directory Connector) for organizations that are using both Exchange 5.5 and Exchange 2000. Other components are considered optional not for backward-compatibility, but to support a new technology, such as video or data conferencing services.

You should become familiar with these optional services and components because you don't want to arbitrarily run them on every Exchange server in your organization. You want to be selective and run specific services on specific machines so that one machine's processor does not become overloaded or overtasked managing unnecessary processes. For instance, you would not want to enable video or data conferencing for an organization with no remote offices that is running only one Exchange 2000 server.

The following list describes the most common components that are usually installed in a typical Exchange organization. ("The New and Improved Exchange 2000 Server" section later in this chapter gives more detailed coverage of some of these components.) It is the right mixture of essential components and optional components that produces optimal message flows in your organization.

- *The Exchange 2000 Conferencing Server*—Is new to the Exchange Server family and should be purchased independently of Exchange 2000 Server or Exchange 2000 Enterprise Server. This component provides one interface for meetings of any type and allows an administrator to dictate how many conferences can be scheduled at one time. It can even be used to manage remote servers. The Exchange 2000 Conferencing Server contains both the Data Conferencing Provider, used to manage the conference process from start to finish and to support chat services, and the Video Conferencing Provider, which allows clients to engage in various forms of video conferencing. The components that make all this possible include a resource reservation agent and the Conference Management Service.
- *Chat and Instant Messaging services*—Allow Exchange 2000 Server to transfer dynamic data when users need it most. Instant Messaging gives users the ability to engage in instantaneous and immediate dialogue with their co-workers. This technology can be invaluable for a team project or a session requiring feedback from multiple parties within seconds of each other. However, if one-to-one

communication is not appropriate, then Exchange 2000 Server provides Chat Services, which allow a user to join a community and participate in discussion forums focusing on one or more topics.

- *Message Transfer Agent (MTA)*—Is now considered optional only because it has been primarily replaced by the native SMTP of Windows 2000. The MTA was the central routing engine for Exchange Server 5.5, but is now considered an optional component that connects Exchange 2000 Server to external messaging systems. It still has a role, but is used more to configure an X.400 route between routing groups (explained later in the section "Routing Groups"). It can even be used to configure a route between a routing group and an external X.400 messaging system.
- *Active Directory Connector and* ***Site Replication Service (SRS)***—Enable directory replication and integration between the Exchange Server 5.5 directory and Exchange 2000 Server, which is dependent on the Active Directory structure of Windows 2000 Server. SRS uses the familiar RPC protocol to talk to the directory service structure in Exchange Server 5.5.
- *Various connectors*—Used to connect to messaging systems besides Exchange 2000 Server, including the connectors for Lotus Notes, Lotus cc:Mail, and Novell GroupWise. Microsoft recognizes that many companies retain legacy messaging systems because of cost constraints or simple resistance to change. No matter how complex a connector may seem in terms of installation or configuration, it is worth remembering that most of these tasks occur in the background and do not disrupt sending or receiving mail.
- *Key Management Service*—Uses Windows 2000 Certificate Services to provide a protected messaging environment, using the art and science of cryptography, for organizations concerned with advanced security. (Security and encryption technologies are discussed in Chapter 12, "Security and Encryption in Exchange 2000 Server.") The functionality of the Key Management Service has been somewhat enhanced since the days of Microsoft Exchange Server 5.5.

How Components Produce Message Flows in Exchange 2000 Server

Successful receipt and delivery of messages in Exchange 2000 depends on successful communication between essential components and optional components. When you look at the architecture, or model, of messaging with Exchange 2000, you have to understand how all these components interact with each other and how often. A big part of troubleshooting this product is understanding and following all the interdependencies to see where the kink might be. It is similar to figuring out why someone cannot log on to a network, a seemingly simple task that invariably fails for some reason. When troubleshooting logon problems, you need some kind of mental picture of how all the network components interact. If one component fails or refuses to communicate, then all communication between two machines fails. However, you still have to know what component to start testing before you randomly replace components that might still be functional.

Example of Inbound Message Flow Using Simple Mail Transport Protocol

What happens when Client A sends a message to Client B in the same Windows 2000 domain? The following steps outline the process:

1. Client B opens a connection to Client A on SMTP port 25.
2. The IIS process that hosts the SMTP Service also listens on port 25.
3. The SMTP Service on Client B receives the first command concerning the message that was sent (for instance, it receives the HELO command from Client A).
4. The SMTP Service on Client B creates a special object known as IMAILMSG, which the SMTP Service uses to store message properties.
5. The SMTP Service on Client B receives a DATA command from Client A. Then the IMAILMSG object on Client B communicates with an Information Store driver file to store the message content.
6. The Information Store driver writes the message body into a local \Queue directory on the hard drive (found in the \Exchsrvr\Mailroot directory).
7. The IMAILMSG object is then handed over to the advanced queuing engine component of IIS, where it can be categorized according to priority and destination domain.
8. The advanced queuing engine then passes the message to the routing engine. If the message is intended to be delivered locally, it is placed inside a local delivery queue. If it's remote, then SMTP is used to transport the message to a remote queuing process. Local messages are picked up by a store driver and submitted to the Web Storage System in Exchange 2000.

Exchange 2000 uses highly defined mechanisms and paths to define a session, or communication stream. This stream, called an Interprocess Communication (IPC) path, uses various protocols known as RPC or Windows Sockets. Many components can talk among themselves using shared memory or even e-mail messages. Also, clients need to talk to server-side components to accomplish their objectives. Both RPC and the **Lightweight Directory Access Protocol (LDAP)** are used for this purpose.

Exchange 2000 Server relies on many new and different file system components to guarantee message delivery, including Inetinfo.exe, Store.exe, Smtpsvc.dll, Ntfsdrv.dll, Drviis.dll, and Phatcat.dll. The main component is the IIS process (Inetinfo.exe), which is host to all the Internet protocols used by clients, including HTTP, POP3, and SMTP. It also hosts components such as the routing engine and the advanced queuing engine. As mentioned previously, Inetinfo.exe communicates with the Information Store (Store.exe) through the Exchange Interprocess Communication (ExIPC) layer.

The Store.exe file is in the \Exchsrvr\Bin directory on the local hard drive, and ExIPC is represented by a dynamic link library called ExIPC.dll in the \Winnt\System32 directory.

The SMTP engine (Smtpsvc.dll), located in the \Winnt\System32\Inetsrv directory, initiates all outbound connections. This dynamic link library is really the centerpiece of SMTP and is responsible for issuing all commands between hosts. SMTP is also used to store incoming messages to the hard drive, using the store driver Ntfsdrv.dll (found in \Winnt\System32\Inetsrv). The actual messages can be found in the \Exchsrvr\Mailroot\Vs1\Queue directory on the hard drive.

Another store driver in \Winnt\System32\Inetsrv, called Drviis.dll, communicates with the Web Storage System using the ExIPC. In other words, Exchange 2000 delivers a message either to the Web Storage System using one store driver—Drviis.dll—or to the local file system using a second store driver—Ntfsdrv.dll. The advanced queuing engine component of SMTP works with these store drivers and manages all queues for message delivery. After finding the proper destination, the advanced queuing engine queues this message for delivery before delivering it to the Web Storage System or the local file system.

Finally, Phatcat.dll is actually an add-on to the advanced queuing engine. Although the advanced queuing engine is a .dll file in the \Winnt\System32\Inetsrv directory (part of the IIS process in Windows 2000), Phatcat.dll is in the \Exchsrvr\Bin directory. It is the message categorizer component of the advanced queuing engine and performs name resolution on all messages that pass through the advanced queuing engine. It also expands distribution lists if needed. However, this message categorizer is disabled by default in Windows 2000 Server; Exchange 2000 is needed to activate and enable it, so Phatcat.dll is located in the main Exchange Server directory, \Exchsrvr\Bin.

The main point to garner from all this is that Exchange 2000 depends heavily on SMTP, which allows all messages destined for local recipients to be delivered directly to the Web Storage System. The Exchange System Manager snap-in configures the SMTP Service, whereas the Exchange 2000 System Attendant component applies all SMTP configuration changes directly to the IIS process of Windows 2000. See Figure 1-4 for an overview of the SMTP architecture.

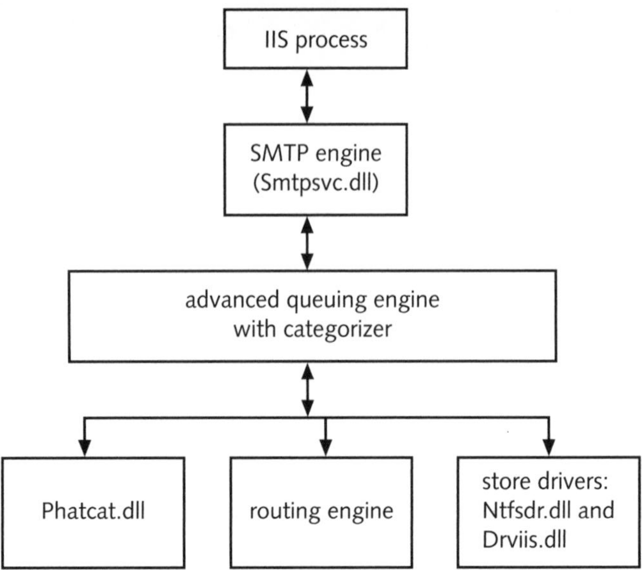

Figure 1-4 The SMTP architecture in Exchange 2000 Server

Comparing Exchange Server 5.5 to Exchange 2000 Server

What convinces an organization to suddenly switch over to Exchange 2000 Server, given that it has been successfully using Exchange Server 5.5 for some time? Is it a matter of time before all companies are forced to switch over to this new messaging system? Although Chapter 6, "Upgrading or Migrating from Exchange 5.5 to Exchange 2000 Server," discusses migrations and upgrades from Exchange Server 5.5 to Exchange 2000 Server, it is helpful to get an overview of the direction Microsoft wants to take with its new messaging product. Chapter 6 reinforces this direction and provides more in-depth explanations of the new designs.

Microsoft never intended for administrators to discard previous versions of Exchange Server. In fact, without an understanding of the previous messaging architecture, it becomes almost impossible to appreciate the new messaging architecture. You should never forget the object-oriented concepts in earlier versions of Exchange Server. This orientation gave rise to such concepts as the **organization**, the **site**, and the user mailbox. In its simplest form, the organization defined your ultimate boundary for Exchange Server 5.5, and you were allowed to place sites within this organizational structure. Every site contained one or more Exchange 5.5 servers, and you could then connect multiple sites together using a single Site Connector.

Basic Components Used in Exchange Server 5.5

Exchange 5.5 relied on four basic services to function as a large-scale messaging provider: the Directory Service (DS), the Information Store, the Message Transfer Agent, and the System Attendant. Figure 1-5 shows the basic Exchange 5.5 architecture and where the transaction logs were originally maintained for the Information Store and the DS. The DS contained the global address list (GAL) and replicated information to other Exchange servers within the same site or between sites.

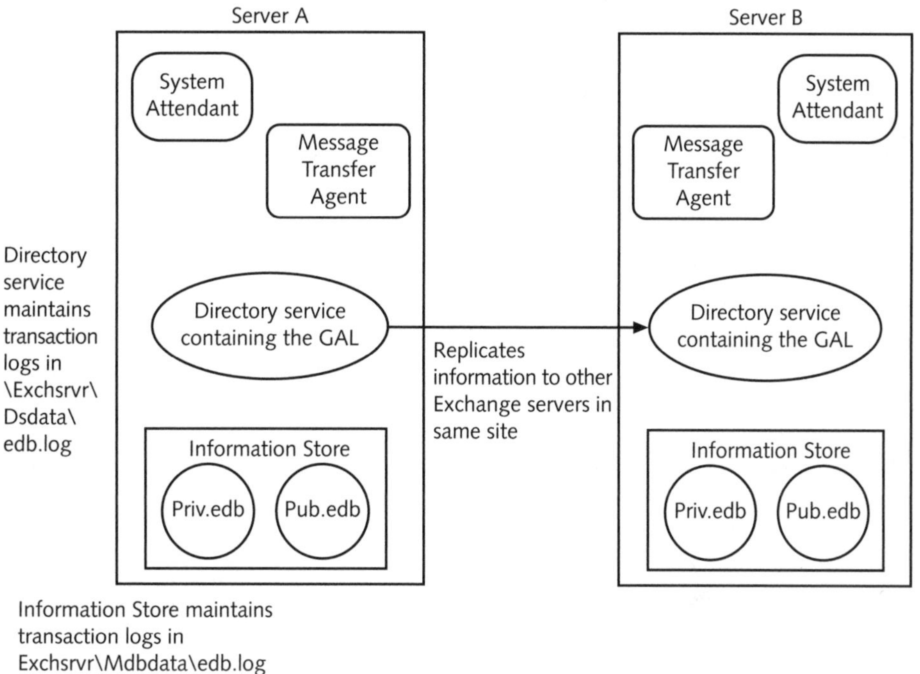

Figure 1-5 Exchange Server 5.5 components

Other components communicated with the DS to get information about mailboxes, public folders, or even configuration data. The SA was responsible for management services in Exchange Server 5.5, including generating e-mail addresses for new users, building routing tables for a site, controlling server and link monitors between sites, and enabling encryption within a server. The Information Store consisted of both a private information store and a public information store and handled local message delivery if the sender and recipient existed on the same server. It was responsible for mailbox and public folder information and worked closely with the MTA. The MTA routed messages for users on remote servers and also informed the SA if it was going to send or receive a message from an external messaging system. All four components worked in perfect harmony to ensure that messages flowed inside and outside an Exchange Server 5.5

machine, and it was possible to troubleshoot each component individually so that service to end users was not disrupted.

The other area of importance in Exchange Server 5.5 centered on transaction log files. Recall that all messages were written to log files before being committed to the Information Store databases known as Priv.edb and Pub.edb. Transaction logs were used to record changes made to these and other databases used by Exchange Server. Any changes to a database were written immediately in sequential order. Transaction logs were usually kept on a separate disk or partition from the database files, and they were always 5 MB.

You will definitely see some changes when working with Exchange 2000 Server, but it's interesting to note that all former Exchange Server 5.5 components coexist peacefully with all Exchange 2000 Server components. In other words, you don't have to manually transform any of the components you just read about to communicate with Exchange 2000 Server. You do, however, have to optimize the components that are most often used in Exchange 2000 Server so that you can experience the best of both worlds—a functioning legacy environment that does not need extra administrative effort to maintain, and a functioning new environment that supports advanced technologies previous versions of Exchange are incapable of handling.

The next section in this chapter discusses what's new in Exchange 2000 Server, but you will soon discover that Exchange 2000 Server is no longer a self-contained messaging system because it has been so integrated into Windows 2000 Server. The following list of the ways Exchange 5.5 differs from Exchange 2000 helps you answer the question, "How can you easily tell the difference between an Exchange Server 5.5 and an Exchange 2000 Server machine?"

- Exchange 5.5 computers all contain an independent directory database.
- Exchange 5.5 servers are all located within sites defined by an administrator.
- Every Exchange 5.5 site possesses a unique SMTP address in the Exchange Server organization.
- Every Exchange 5.5 site contains a directory replication bridgehead server that connects different sites and replicates Exchange directory information between the sites.
- Exchange 5.5 is dependent on connectors such as the Professional Office System (PROFS) Connector and the Systems Network Architecture Distribution System (SNADS) Connector for connectivity to external systems, such as IBM mainframes.

As you can tell from the previous list, some of the differences between the two versions of Exchange are subtle, so it's not always easy to tell the two apart. Many connectors that work with Exchange Server 5.5 also work well with Exchange 2000 Server, and there is now one service in Exchange 2000 that emulates an Exchange 5.5 server. In fact, Exchange 2000 can sit peacefully inside an Exchange 5.5 site and replicate directory information with Exchange 5.5 servers (Chapter 6 shows how this occurs.)

THE NEW AND IMPROVED EXCHANGE 2000 SERVER

Exchange 2000 Server is the first application (in the BackOffice suite of Microsoft applications) that makes widespread use of Active Directory, but where did AD come from? Surely other operating systems have attempted this innovative directory design. Novell NetWare, for example, incorporates Novell Directory Services (NDS) to store all network-related objects, such as users and groups. However, Microsoft is not merely repeating the success of NDS in Exchange 2000 Server. AD as an operating system service originated with the Exchange 5.5 Directory Service database. So even though AD can offer advanced functionality for both Windows 2000 and Exchange 2000, it still has to offer all the functionality of previous Exchange versions. To say that Exchange 2000 is the first application to make use of AD is to imply that Windows 2000 is the first operating system that makes use of the Exchange 5.5 Directory Service.

You cannot afford to make mistakes when planning your initial AD design because you will be affecting more than your messaging system. It was relatively easy to fix directory service mistakes in previous versions of Exchange Server, but this is not true in the current version. If you have to completely reinstall AD, your underlying Windows 2000 infrastructure is immediately and negatively affected. The following sections review some of the new features in Exchange 2000 Server.

Administrative Groups

The Exchange 5.5 concept of sites has been replaced with the Exchange 2000 concept of administrative and routing groups. **Administrative groups** are graphical representations of a company's organizational structure (but not related to a company's physical network topology), and are helpful for companies with many different departments running multiple Exchange servers. They describe a collection of servers managed by different groups of administrators. You can, for instance, define all mailbox servers as belonging to one particular administrative "group," even though these servers might be geographically dispersed throughout the world.

These groups simplify departmental management when assigning rights or permissions to resources. Microsoft designed Exchange 2000 so that administration can be customized according to your needs. The key to deploying these groups is to assign servers to them without even worrying about message routing between servers. There is one caveat, which pertains to managing a **mixed-mode environment** of Exchange 5.5 and Exchange 2000 servers (discussed in more depth in Chapter 6). If you are designing a mixed-mode environment, any administrative groups you have will mirror your

Exchange 5.5 site; you also have to understand the consequence of a routing group, discussed in the following section. Mixed-mode environments also affect how you move users' mailboxes to other servers within your site or how you move entire servers to other locations.

Routing Groups

A **routing group** is a group of servers connected with each other using permanent and high-speed local area network (LAN) links. SMTP manages the communication process within these groups. The benefit of routing groups is that you can create or delete them as you see fit, and you can even change membership in these groups at will. This scalability option is beneficial for companies that face constantly changing network requirements. It is not uncommon for new departments to form or new network infrastructures to be devised over relatively short timeframes (six months to one year, perhaps). Exchange 2000 can now help handle sudden or unforeseen changes in your company and adapt rather easily through the use of routing groups. However, you have to maintain a **native-mode environment** so that all your routing groups can be part of the same administrative group. A native-mode Exchange organization runs only Exchange 2000 Server and does not interoperate or coexist with any Exchange Server version prior to Exchange 2000.

Simple Mail Transport Protocol

SMTP is the only protocol used between any two servers in the same routing group. You might wonder why protocols are so important to a messaging infrastructure, but choosing the appropriate transport protocol or routing mechanism for your messaging system is a critical choice indeed. You are dealing with a highly structured core component that determines the success or future of your messaging operations. Microsoft has realized this by offering SMTP, a flexible transport and routing protocol. Previous versions of Exchange Server relied on high-speed and permanent network connections being available for one server to communicate with another, but used RPC as the transport protocol. However, RPC presented some limiting deployment issues, especially with slow bandwidth links; RPC requires synchronous high-speed connectivity between hosts, and slow bandwidth connections caused excessive network traffic when attempting to reestablish links that could not cross a slow connection path. With Exchange 2000, administrators can enjoy a more flexible approach to site design because they are not limited to permanent or high-bandwidth connectivity. SMTP also happens to be an Internet standard protocol used to transport or deliver all forms of electronic data. It contains a highly developed queuing engine that acts as an information dispatcher for all other services involved so that every message presented to an Exchange 2000 server passes through this engine. SMTP works in tandem with Active Directory to resolve and identify recipient names and expand distribution lists. It also communicates directly with the Information Store to retrieve or distribute messages.

Storage Groups

Storage groups are new to Exchange 2000 and represent a modification to the Extensible Storage Engine (ESE) component of Exchange Server 5.5. A storage group architecture is a drastic departure from the previous "fixed database" format in Exchange Server and is considered a separate instance of the ESE architecture with its own set of transaction log files. There is a current limit of four storage groups per Exchange 2000 server, with each storage group containing up to five separate databases. That means every single Exchange 2000 server is capable of holding a maximum of 20 separate databases. What you have to determine is the makeup of these databases; they will be either mailbox stores for users' mailbox data or public folder stores, holding information used by collaborative applications or information meant to be shared across your network, such as calendar information. The key point to remember is that all storage groups share one transaction log file by design; Microsoft wanted to make it easy to back up individual storage groups and messaging databases without having to back up the entire server. This feature becomes important for disaster and recovery procedures, which are discussed in Chapter 15, "Disaster Recovery in Exchange 2000 Server." You could, for instance, back up and restore one single database within a storage group without disabling other databases running inside that storage group.

Real-Time Collaboration Services

Many organizations keep an eye on future developments and try to be on the cutting edge. This stance can be a double-edged sword, however, because some companies do not want to be the first to adopt new technology; they would rather wait and see how the new technology is incorporated into other, similar companies or industries. However, a new type of technology is emerging that companies should consider for certain types of communication within their organizations. These are collaborative technologies, such as instant messaging or real-time chat services. Microsoft has found this area to be so promising that it has invested almost $1 billion in research and development expenses to further this cause (according to its Web site at *http://www.microsoft.com/exchange*). The following sections describe three real-time services briefly; more detailed information is given in Chapter 11, "Configuring Real-Time Collaboration in Exchange 2000 Server."

Chat Services

Chat Services existed in Exchange Server 5.5, but have been enhanced in Exchange 2000 Server. These services can be useful for companies with geographically dispersed branches, for example, or contract employees who work from home. Many people are already accustomed to using the **Internet Relay Chat (IRC)** service with their regular Internet service provider account and will find similar functionality in Exchange 2000. Using Chat Services allows a group of people to communicate in real-time under moderated or unmoderated conditions. This service uses Active Directory to store information on chat communities and chat channels (described in Chapter 11). The new Chat Services in Exchange 2000 use the original IRC protocol, defined in Request for Comment (RFC) 1459, as well as the extended IRC protocol, IRCX. Your goal in using this tool is to create channels, which allow multiple users to communicate using text-based messaging standards. The Exchange 5.5 Chat Services depended on establishing gateways between multiple chat servers to add connections. Exchange 2000 Server can host many users on a single machine, so it's possible to aggregate channels and users on a single Exchange 2000 computer. Estimates of up to 20,000 users per server have been reported on the Microsoft Web site.

Instant Messaging Services

Exchange 2000 has introduced a feature that many claim is similar to basic e-mail messaging, but it is not. Instant Messaging (IM) is a relatively new technology that allows users to exchange simple text or graphic messages using Hypertext Transfer Protocol (HTTP). IM, like Chat Services, is a client-server tool, which uses a server extension that runs on a machine configured with Internet Information Server version 5.0. IM is similar to e-mail in that it can send text messages, pictures, and even links to Web sites. However, unlike e-mail, an instant message is not saved after it has disappeared from a user's screen or monitor. The most important development in IM is presence information, which allows you to know precisely when another user has logged on to the IM server so you can communicate with him or her. You can allow other users to get status information when you are online, and available users are shown in a screen known more commonly as a "buddy list." The essence of IM is HTTP version 1.1, which uses a simple address to identify users who are logged on to the system. Chapter 11 explains in more detail how IM is used in most organizations; you'll see how to configure IM home servers that host all user accounts, IM routers that route all IM requests from a client to a home server, and the IM clients themselves. Even though IM Server is used on a computer that runs Windows 2000 Server or Windows 2000 Advanced Server, you can use it as an enhancement or supplement to an existing Exchange 5.5 organization. In any case, the use of IM Server requires that AD and the Windows 2000 OS be installed on at least one system.

Data Conferencing Services

A new member of the Exchange 2000 Server family has arrived: the Exchange 2000 Conferencing Server, which is purchased independently of Exchange 2000 Server or Exchange 2000 Server Enterprise Edition. The goal of this Exchange component is to allow data conferencing, voice conferencing, and video conferencing using the public space of the Internet (or even within the private confines of your organization). There are basically two standards or protocols at work in this component: the T.120 standard, used for data conferencing services, and the H.323 protocol suite, used for video conferencing services. T.120 is used for applications such as Microsoft's NetMeeting, which allows textual chat with multiple users (up to eight under the current version), the ability to draw or work with images on a shared "whiteboard," the use of IP telephony with one other user, and video conferencing with one other user (which requires a video capture card or PC camera). H.323 defines enhanced video conferencing services based on the H.323 protocol, a standard approved by the International Telecommunication Union to help promote compatibility in video transmissions for IP-based networks. H.323 also supports the emerging technology Voice-over-IP (VoIP), which provides predictable real-time voice and fax communication over your existing IP data network or the Internet.

Workflow and Workgroup Management

Workgroup and workflow technologies revolve around programmable objects in Windows 2000 Server and Exchange 2000 Server.You may hear that Collaboration Data Objects (CDO) is one method of adding functionality to business applications. First seen in Exchange Server 5.5, CDO is Microsoft's official technology for building messaging applications or adding these capabilities to an existing application. It was formerly known as object linking and embedding (OLE) messaging in Exchange Server 4.0 and Active Messaging in Exchange Server 5.0. Seen from another perspective, CDO is a scripting interface to the MAPI. Web page designers can even use CDO with Active Server Pages technology to write scripts that exchange text-based e-mail with remote users or remote Web sites.

CDO is usually discussed in the context of developing applications using the Microsoft Outlook 2000 client. An in-depth study of it is outside the scope of this book, but you should know that CDO is a technology used to build custom solutions for an enterprise. In this book, you will be concentrating more on workflow applications for Exchange 2000 Server, which are special types of collaborative solutions, such as moderating a public folder or document review and publishing. All these applications are modeled as "business processes."The task of developing these applications is simplified in Exchange 2000 Server through the use of a workflow engine and workflow modeling tools. Exchange 2000 also offers a new tool known as Workflow Designer for Exchange, which allows you to create workflow processes easily. These processes show a series of actions to be taken and the order in which they will be performed in a graphical format that you can easily edit.

The Future of Messaging

Electronic messaging is a concept that is definitely here to stay. Exchange Server has embraced this concept from the first day it appeared on the public scene in 1996 with Exchange 4.0 Server. Since then, there have been monumental changes in the architecture of this messaging system almost every year. Exchange Server has continued to show that there is no real limit to designing a stable and efficient means of delivering communication on a global scale. Do not be surprised at the breadth or depth of Exchange 2000 as it continues to incorporate more advanced features. For example, many people were surprised to see the introduction of active-active clustering in Exchange 2000 (supported with Windows 2000 Advanced Server Edition). Also, scalability has increased with each version of Exchange Server, and Exchange 2000 is no exception to this rule. In fact, in a study commissioned by Microsoft in January 2001, eTesting Labs (a division of Ziff-Davis Media) compared the scalability of Exchange 2000 running on Windows 2000 Advanced

Server with Exchange Server 5.5 running on Windows NT 4.0 Enterprise Edition. Given equivalent machine types, processors, and network adapter cards, Exchange 2000 Server was found to be 66% more scalable than Exchange Server 5.5 (meaning it could deliver e-mail to 66% more users than the previous version). Server response times in Exchange 2000 were also about 20% faster than in Exchange 5.5.

Most people see the addition of conferencing services or multiple databases as the "icing on the cake" for Exchange Server, but the end is not in sight. We are ready to start tackling some of the details that underlie these topics in the chapters that follow, highlighting the features and tasks that are common to everyday administration. We hope that in the process you gain a new appreciation for this magnificent messaging system.

Chapter Summary

- Messaging systems have been around since the early days of the Internet, and they have continued to increase in complexity and improve in design.
- A messaging server, such as Exchange 2000, is an application that creates and stores data on some type of communications network. This is an example of a client-server technology in which most of the processing is taken away from the messaging client.
- A shared-file system dedicates file servers as centralized post offices and gives all users access to messaging services via mailboxes inside these post offices. This setup puts the burden on client systems, but also increases network traffic unnecessarily.
- A shared-file system is simple to install and requires less hardware than a client-server system. However, because clients have access to files, they could delete files accidentally in the centralized post office. In addition, many shared-file systems are limited in the total number of users that can be supported.
- Client-server systems are spared from querying a centralized host server because the server component notifies clients when new mail has arrived. Also, client-server systems handle larger user populations than their shared-file counterparts. More server hardware is needed, however, which results in increased administration tasks.
- Exchange 2000 Server is composed of both essential and optional components, which together provide the overall framework for messaging functionality. All components eventually communicate with each other to produce the overall messaging model that is used.
- Message flow in Exchange 2000 also depends on services provided by Windows 2000 Server because of the integration between Exchange 2000 and Active Directory services. Besides AD, Exchange 2000 depends heavily on protocols hosted within the IIS process (Inetinfo.exe).

- The most common optional components installed with Exchange 2000 Server include the Chat Services, IM Services, and Data Conferencing/Video Conferencing Services. These components show a trend toward developing a virtual office where users can hold "meetings without walls" and use the Internet for collaborative purposes on a global scale.
- Exchange 2000 Server can coexist in an Exchange Server 5.5 mixed-mode environment, but there are many coexistence issues to consider. Exchange 2000 uses many features not available in previous versions, such as administrative groups and routing groups. It also uses a new native protocol, SMTP, to communicate with other servers, and is capable of supporting many more users because of the new storage group architecture. Each storage group can now contain up to five separate databases for mailbox stores or public folder stores.

Key Terms

administrative group — A group that helps define your company's organizational structure and helps define separate groups of administrators who are responsible for distinct servers spread throughout the organization. This group is equivalent to an Exchange 5.5 site in a mixed-mode organization.

client-server messaging system — A network architecture that involves processing work on a dedicated machine, known as the server, which processes client requests. Clients normally talk to servers by using translation mechanisms called protocols.

Directory Service Proxy (DSProxy) — A dynamic link library in Exchange 2000 Server that allows a MAPI client, such as Microsoft Outlook 2000, to access the Active Directory database on a Windows 2000 Server computer. It sends all client directory requests using a Name Service Provider Interface (NSPI).

Exchange Interprocess Communication (ExIPC) layer — A message-queuing layer between the IIS process (Inetinfo.exe) and the Web Storage System in Exchange 2000 Server that facilitates fast data exchange between these two components. The IIS process hosts all Exchange 2000 protocols, whereas the Web Storage System is a structured database that manages items such as e-mail messages or Web pages.

global catalog (GC) — A centralized clearinghouse of information, similar to a phone book, that stores information about every object that could exist in a Windows 2000 domain or forest. Users query the global catalog when searching for objects stored in Active Directory. At least one server in each Windows 2000 domain must function as the Global Catalog server, which holds a copy of the global catalog.

Information Store — The Exchange 2000 component that maintains information on user data, such as e-mail messages or public folder information. It is run as one file, known as Store.exe, and separates mail messages into private mailbox stores and public data into public folder stores.

Internet Information Server (IIS) — A set of services included with Windows 2000 that provides various Internet services, including the ability to host FTP and Web sites. Exchange 2000 uses IIS to provide Outlook Web Access services.

Internet Messaging Access Protocol version 4 (IMAP4) — A messaging protocol that allows users to retrieve e-mail from a server without directly downloading it to their local disks. Users access e-mail information or public folder information as though it were stored locally on their computers.

Internet Relay Chat (IRC) — A system for chatting over the Internet that uses a set of rules and conventions. It is one form of client-server communication and uses TCP/IP on port 6667.

Lightweight Directory Access Protocol (LDAP) — A distributed directory services protocol that can be used to gain access to directory services residing on other operating systems. It is an industry standard described in RFC 1777 and uses TCP/IP for client-server communication to build directories based on object information.

mailbox store — A part of the Information Store that holds user mailboxes or provides mailbox information to clients using a protocol such as the MAPI specification. You can have up to five mailbox stores per storage group.

message — Also known as electronic messaging, it refers to the creation, storage, and management of various forms of data, including text, images, voice, and e-mail, over some form of communications network. It is an exchange of specially formatted data describing some event or a request to a messaging server.

Messaging Application Programming Interface (MAPI) — An industry standard used to write e-mail messages used by Exchange 2000 and other similar messaging systems. It is also the interface that allows you to attach a Windows application to an e-mail note.

messaging server — A message exchange program for client programs. It is a middleware program that handles messages sent for use by other programs using a MAPI. Messaging servers usually prioritize and queue messages sent to them.

mixed-mode environment — The condition that exists when an Exchange 5.5 server is used in an Exchange 2000 Server organization or an Exchange 2000 server is introduced into an Exchange Server 5.5 organization. In this setting, the Exchange 5.5 server cannot distinguish between separate administrative groups or routing groups, so each Exchange 2000 administrative group appears as an Exchange 5.5 site.

native-mode environment — The optimal state of operations for Exchange 2000 Server. All servers are running Exchange 2000 Server, with no communication whatsoever with previous versions of Exchange. You have full flexibility in using routing and administrative groups, so that routing groups can now contain servers from different administrative groups. This setup cannot happen in a mixed-mode environment.

Network News Transport Protocol (NNTP) — The main protocol used by computers for administering messages posted on Usenet newsgroups on the Internet; it is slowly replacing the UNIX-to-UNIX Copy Protocol (UUCP). The protocol allows distribution, retrieval, and posting of news articles using a stream-based transmission of news among the Internet community. NNTP is a client-server protocol. An NNTP server manages all Usenet newsgroups, and an NNTP client is included with most browsers so that users can download messages posted to newsgroups.

organization — A logical object used in Exchange 5.5 and Exchange 2000 to represent the highest level in a hierarchy of objects. This object defines a boundary for other objects used by Exchange (such as server objects).

Post Office Protocol version 3 (POP3) — A standard Internet protocol allowing a client to download e-mail from a server. It differs from IMAP4 in that messages are managed locally on the client's computer, not on the server, as with IMAP4. Users cannot directly manipulate messages stored on a server, nor can they access public folders on a server using POP3. POP3 offers much less functionality than IMAP4.

public folder store — A database residing on an Exchange 2000 server that holds information stored in public folders, which become accessible to entire communities of users at one time. Users can access public folders using a MAPI client, such as Outlook 2000, or using Internet protocols, such as HTTP and IMAP4. It is possible to replicate information in public folder stores, which are part of the Information Store in Exchange 2000.

Remote Procedure Calls (RPC) — A communication mechanism operating at the Application layer of the Open Systems Interconnect (OSI) model and used by Exchange 2000 Server components for Interprocess Communication. A machine uses RPC to request a service from a program found on another machine. It represents a synchronous operation, which suspends the requesting program until all results of the remote procedure have been returned.

routing group — A group of Exchange 2000 servers that share permanent and high-bandwidth connections and communicate via SMTP. In a default installation of Exchange 2000 Server, all servers are added to a default routing group known as the First Routing Group. Servers in one routing group can belong to more than one administrative group.

schema — An object or component, such as a user object, that controls the attributes maintained by the Active Directory service in Windows 2000 Server. The schema is the group of classes that represent directory objects, such as computers and groups. Installing Exchange 2000 Server automatically adds new object classes to the existing schema structure.

shared-file messaging system — A system that uses a centralized location to process incoming mail for users. The centralized location is referred to as a post office, and each user has one mailbox in the post office. An example of a shared-file system is Microsoft Mail for PC Networks. The alternative to a shared-file system is a client-server architecture.

Simple Mail Transport Protocol (SMTP) — A protocol used for sending e-mail messages. It is often used with POP3 and IMAP4 because it is limited in its ability to queue messages at the receiving station. These other protocols allow users to download mail from a server. SMTP, described in RFC 821, is implemented over TCP/IP port 25. SMTP can transfer messages across low-speed connections and is used to transfer messages between servers in a routing group.

site — A logical representation of a collection of Exchange 5.5 servers that may or may not be in close proximity. All servers in a site use Remote Procedure Calls to communicate with each other.

Site Replication Service (SRS) — A component that works with the Active Directory Connector to provide interoperability with legacy Exchange sites running Exchange Server 5.5. It directly communicates with the Exchange Server 5.5 directory service using Remote Procedure Calls. SRS contains some of the same executable code that ran previous versions of the Exchange Directory Service. This helper service is activated when you install your first Exchange 2000 server in a site or when you upgrade a directory replication bridgehead server. It consists of the Srsmain.exe executable, a site consistency checker that creates replication links, and the Srs.edb database, which contains Exchange Server 5.5 directory data.

storage group — An instance of the Extensible Storage Engine database architecture used in Exchange 2000 Server. It describes the organizational unit of the Information Store (Store.exe) and can consist of mailbox stores or public folder stores. Each storage group is capable of holding up to five separate databases that all share one common transaction log file. Up to four storage groups can run simultaneously on a single Exchange 2000 computer.

System Attendant (SA) — The service that controls the Information Store in Exchange 2000. This component (Mad.exe, in the \Exchsrvr\Bin directory by default) is responsible for monitoring services and connectors. The SA communicates directly with Active Directory to generate e-mail addresses for new users and also updates the configuration repository for IIS known as the metabase.

Transmission Control Protocol/Internet Protocol (TCP/IP) — This basic communication language of the Internet is a suite of protocols broken down into two basic layers. The upper layer manages assembling packets for transmission over the Internet or a private network, and the lower layer manages the addressing of each data packet to ensure that it reaches its intended destination. TCP/IP is an example of the client-server model of communication and uses a point-to-point mechanism so that each communication between computers is from one distinct host computer to another distinct host computer. As a suite, TCP/IP contains other higher-layer protocols, such as HTTP, FTP, and SMTP.

transaction logs — The files on the hard disk that store all changes made to Exchange 2000 Server database files. These files store a history of all operations performed in memory and are used in case of disaster to restore transactions that have already been committed to disk. The log files should never exceed 5 MB because this is a sure sign of corruption. Log files and database files should always remain on separate physical hard drives for optimum performance of Exchange 2000 Server.

Uniform Resource Locator (URL) — The address of a resource that is accessible over the public Internet. It contains the name of the protocol used to access the resource, a domain name specifying a unique computer on the Internet, and the path description of the file location on the computer. For example, the following is a valid example of a URL: *http://www.microsoft.com/exchange*. The protocol used is HTTP, the domain name specifying the computer name is *www.microsoft.com*, and the directory or file path for the requested files is */exchange*.

Web Distributed Authoring and Versioning (DAV) Protocol — An extension to HTTP version 1.1, WebDAV is a communications-related protocol that provides an interface to the Web Storage System in Exchange 2000 Server. It allows access to all databases in Exchange 2000 Server.

Web Storage System — A file-based system that integrates the Store.exe service of Exchange 2000 Server with the protocols hosted by the IIS process (Inetinfo.exe) of Windows 2000 Server. Many features of Exchange 2000, including Outlook Web Access, are based on this new system of accessing information in the Information Store. Most items in the Web Storage System can be accessed using common URL notation.

Windows Sockets Application Programming Interface (API) — The Microsoft implementation of a communication mechanism that was instituted by BSD UNIX; it is an interface for accessing underlying protocols used for network communications, such as TCP/IP. A socket is normally thought of as the endpoint in a network connection, but it can also be used for communication between processes within the same computer.

Review Questions

1. What are the two types of messaging systems in existence today?
   a. shared-file messaging systems
   b. multipoint messaging systems
   c. client-server messaging systems
   d. published messaging systems
2. Microsoft Mail for PC Networks is one example of a client-server messaging system. True or False?
3. How do clients check for new mail in a shared-file messaging system?
   a. They synchronize their system clocks with the mail server.
   b. They use IMAP4 to retrieve new mail from the server.
   c. They use HTTP 1.1 for automatic mail retrieval from the server.
   d. They poll the post office at regular intervals to check for new mail.

4. Which of the following represent advantages of a shared-file messaging system? (Choose all that apply.)
   a. Clients poll their post office on a regular basis.
   b. They involve simple installations with minimal configuration.
   c. Minimal hardware is required because processing is performed on the client side.
   d. There is a decrease in total network traffic because the server handles most of the processing activity.
5. What is an advantage of using a client-server messaging system?
   a. It can handle more users than shared-file systems can.
   b. It can handle fewer users than shared-file systems can.
   c. Clients have to query their host server at regular intervals.
   d. The centralized post office is limited to 500 connections at any given time.
6. Which of the following describes a disadvantage of the client-server messaging architecture?
   a. Increased administration is needed, especially for large server farms.
   b. Less centralized administration is needed compared to shared-file messaging systems.
   c. Clients have to query their host server at regular intervals.
   d. These systems can handle more users than shared-file messaging systems can.
7. Exchange 2000 Server is most integrated with which of the following services?
   a. Internet Information Server 5.0
   b. Microsoft Windows 2000 Active Directory Service
   c. the POP3 Service
   d. the HTTP Service
8. Which component of Windows 2000 Server hosts all Internet Protocols for Exchange 2000 Server?
   a. DHCP Manager
   b. My Network Places
   c. Inetinfo.exe
   d. Routing and Remote Access Engine
9. Where can you now find attributes for objects stored in Exchange 2000 Server?
   a. in the Web Storage System
   b. in the Information Store
   c. in a storage group that hosts a mailbox store
   d. in the schema for Active Directory

10. You install Exchange 2000 Server on a machine running Windows 2000 Advanced Server. What has Exchange done to the structure of Windows 2000?
    a. It has extended the number of classes but not the number of attributes.
    b. It has extended the AD schema of Windows 2000.
    c. It has configured four empty storage groups by default in Windows 2000.
    d. It has created four databases in the First Storage Group by default.
11. Which two services provided by the IIS process are relied on exclusively by Exchange 2000 Server?
    a. SMTP
    b. POP3
    c. IMAP4
    d. NNTP
12. Which component does the IIS process communicate with so that you can dedicate specific servers for specific tasks using Exchange 2000 Server?
    a. the Web Storage System
    b. the Information Store System
    c. the WebDAV System
    d. the SMTP process
13. How does the IIS process communicate with the Web Storage System in Exchange 2000 Server?
    a. by using a queuing layer known as the Exchange Queue Layer
    b. by using a queuing layer known as the ExIPC
    c. by using a process known as Inetinfo.exe
    d. by using a process known as Webstore.exe
14. How do users access information in the Information Store using the Web Storage System?
    a. through a protocol called HTTP 1.0
    b. through a protocol called SMTP 1.1
    c. through a protocol called WebDAV
    d. through a protocol called NNTP 1.1
15. Which of the following protocols can be used to directly manipulate an e-mail message residing on a server?
    a. POP3
    b. SMTP
    c. NNTP
    d. IMAP4

16. In which directory can you find the default installation directory for the Information Store in Exchange 2000 Server?
    a. in the \Program Files\Exchange directory
    b. in the \Exchsrvr\Bin directory
    c. in the \Exchsrvr\Exchange directory
    d. in the \Exchsrvr\IS\Bin directory
17. Which component of Exchange 2000 Server helps replicate IIS configuration changes into a remote IIS server?
    a. the System Attendant
    b. the Directory Service
    c. the Message Transport Agent
    d. the Information Store
18. Which of the following Exchange 2000 Server services are not responsible for generating proxy e-mail addresses? (Choose all that apply.)
    a. the Directory Service
    b. the System Attendant
    c. the Information Store
    d. the Inetinfo.exe process
19. Which is true regarding routing groups for an Exchange 2000 Server organization in native mode?
    a. A routing group can contain servers from multiple administrative groups.
    b. An administrative group must belong to multiple routing groups.
    c. You can move a server between administrative groups.
    d. Servers in a routing group use RPC to communicate with each other.
20. Every Exchange 2000 server you configure will have a maximum of __________ transaction log files associated with it.

HANDS-ON PROJECTS

Project 1-1

To review the Windows 2000 Administrative Tools:

1. Log on to the Windows 2000 Server computer.
2. Click **Start**, point to **Programs**, and point to **Administrative Tools**. The Administrative Tools menu items are displayed.

If Administrative Tools is not listed under Programs, click **Start**, point to **Settings**, click **Taskbar & Start Menu**, and then click the **Advanced** tab. Click to mark the **Display Administrative Tools** check box, as shown in Figure 1-6, and then click **OK**.

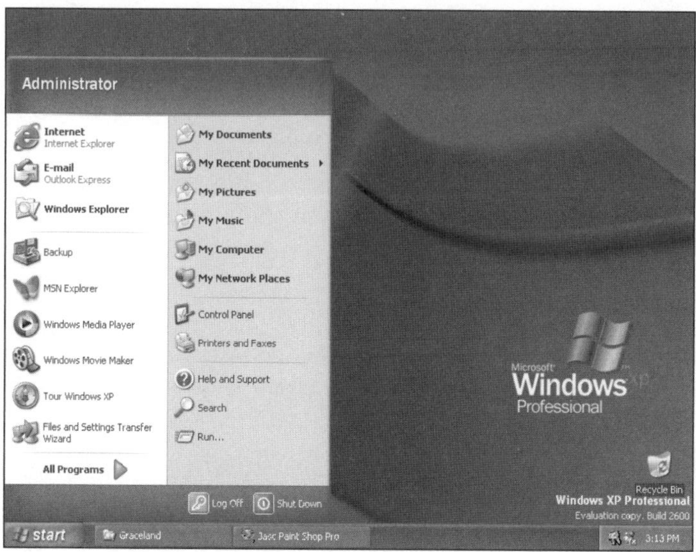

Figure 1-6 Enabling the display of Administrative Tools in the Start menu

3. Click the first menu item and explore the various menus in the resulting window to become familiar with the tool. Do not save any changes. Close the window when you're done exploring the tool.
4. Repeat Steps 2 and 3 for all Administrative Tools menu items, and then close any open windows or applications.

Project 1-2

In this project, you will analyze a scenario involving a fictitious organization, MintLotus. It is a financial service company consisting of twenty offices across the United States and four offices overseas (in Paris, London, Munich, and Rome). The U.S. headquarters in Dallas consists of the following departments:

- Accounting—300 users who regularly transfer important and confidential data between offices, but do not require Internet access to e-mail.
- Finance—Five users who do not require high-speed connections, but must be able to enjoy full read-write access to their messaging databases.
- Vice Presidents—75 users who need to be notified of important messages arriving from overseas offices. This group spends a lot of time away from the office.
- Marketing—110 users in Atlanta, Georgia who need basic but reliable messaging functionality without having to worry about continually purchasing new hardware.

All users in the company use a mixture of Windows NT Workstation and Windows 98 computers to connect to their current messaging server. The company is using a 128-Kbps ISDN connection to transfer files between Atlanta and Dallas.

The company is currently using a Microsoft Mail for PC Networks–based messaging system. Each department listed previously has its own requirements and needs for messaging and collaboration. These needs and requirements are summarized in the following list:

- *Priority levels*—Indicates whether the department produces material that's considered mission-critical. For example, a weekly financial forecast is of higher priority than a press release announcing an upcoming financial seminar.
- *Security*—Ensures that all message transmissions and receipts are secure from prying eyes and cannot be tampered with easily, without some form of administrative alert being generated.
- *Customization*—Refers to how easily the current messaging system can be customized. For example, you may want to customize error messages produced by the operating system. You may also want your system to support processing messaging rules, such as sending "out-of-office" messages when you cannot respond to requests in a timely fashion.

To evaluate different types of messaging systems and select the one that is best for an organization:

1. Review Table 1-1 to determine what type of messaging system is best for each department, depending on its needs and requirements.
2. In the final column, write down the type of system you think best serves each department (either a shared-file system or a client-server system).

Table 1-1 Selecting the Best Messaging System for Each Department

Department	Priority Level for Messaging Services	High Availability	Security Necessary	Server Hardware	Type of System You Would Select
Accounting	Medium priority	Needed only during the day (normal working hours 9 a.m. to 5 p.m.)	High security	Wants reliable hardware to support messaging system	
Vice Presidents	High priority	Medium levels needed	Medium security	Wants to upgrade existing hardware to meet increased messaging levels	
Marketing	Low priority	Low to medium access to messaging needed	Low security	Can work with existing messaging infrastructure	
Finance	Low priority	Low access to messaging services needed	Low security	Does not care about the type of hardware used	

Project 1-3

To establish the existence and operation of SMTP in Windows 2000 in preparation for Exchange 2000:

1. To verify that the SMTP Service is operational (SMTP is installed by default in a typical Windows 2000 installation), click **Start**, point to **Programs**, point to **Administrative Tools**, and then click **Services**.
2. When the Services dialog box opens, locate SMTP in the Details pane. (It might help to maximize all windows and expand columns in the window to get a better view.) The third column should read "Started". If not, right-click **Simple Mail Transport Protocol (SMTP)**, and then click **Start** on the shortcut menu. Wait for "Started" to appear in this column, and then close the Services window.

3. Now open a command prompt by clicking **Start**, clicking **Run**, and then typing **cmd** in the Open text box. Click **OK** to open a DOS command-prompt window. Then type **cd** at the current command prompt to change your current directory to C:\>. This process is known as changing to the root directory.

Although changing to the root directory is not an absolute requirement for checking the existence of SMTP, it's best to start from the root directory for readability purposes. Start from a root directory path, such as C:\>, unless you are specifically told to navigate to another directory location, such as C:\Winnt\System32.

4. At the current command prompt (which should be C:\>), type the command **telnet**. Your screen should look similar to Figure 1-7, and the command prompt will change to **Microsoft Telnet>**. At this command prompt, type the command **set local_echo**, and then press **Enter** so that the screen will display all the text you type.

```
C:\WINNT\System32\cmd.exe - telnet
Microsoft (R) Windows 2000 (TM) Version 5.00 (Build 2195)
Welcome to Microsoft Telnet Client
Telnet Client Build 5.00.99203.1

Escape Character is 'CTRL+]'

Microsoft Telnet> set local_echo
Microsoft Telnet> _
```

Figure 1-7 The Microsoft Telnet command prompt

5. Type the command **open *computername* 25** at the **Microsoft Telnet>** command prompt, and then press **Enter**. (Replace ***computername*** with the name you have specified for your machine; for example, the command **open computer1 25** would open port 25 on a machine named computer1.)
6. After pressing Enter in Step 5, your screen changes to display two lines of text at the top of the screen, as shown in Figure 1-8. The text "220 *computername.domain* Microsoft ESMTP MAIL Service, Version: 5.0.2195.*x*" indicates the Microsoft Windows 2000 SMTP Service.

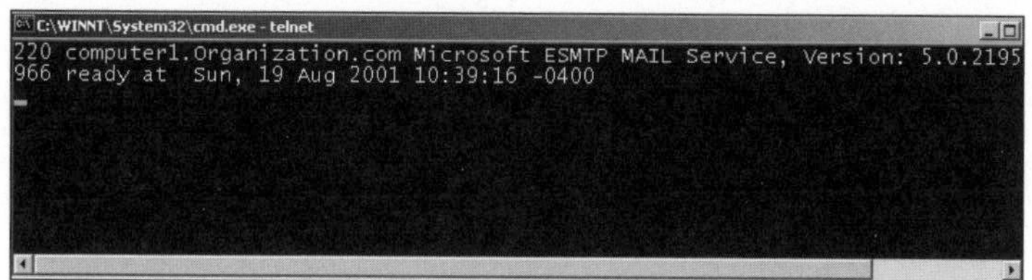

Figure 1-8 The Microsoft Windows 2000 SMTP Service version

The "x" after the Version: 5.0.2195 in Step 6 refers to the service pack that may be installed on your system. If "x" equals 1600, you have Service Pack 1 for Windows 2000 installed. If "x" equals 2966, you have Service Pack 2 for Windows 2000 installed on your system.

7. Type the command **ehlo**, and then press **Enter** to start communicating with the SMTP Service on your local machine. You will see a list of replies that start with 250- . This indicates that queuing for your computer has started and any requested mail action has been completed without errors.

The EHLO command is an extension to the standard SMTP HELO command, which identifies an SMTP client to an SMTP server. A client SMTP should always start an SMTP session by issuing the EHLO command. If the SMTP server supports SMTP Service extensions, such as EHLO, it gives a successful response, a failure response, or an error response. If the SMTP server does not support any SMTP Service extensions, it generates an error response. Older SMTP systems may use HELO (as specified in RFC 821) instead of EHLO, and servers must support the HELO command and reply to it. In any case, a client must issue HELO or EHLO before starting any mail transaction. A "250 OK" reply to these commands indicates that the SMTP client and SMTP server are in the initial state of communications.

8. Type **quit** to terminate your current connection, and then press **Enter**. You will see the message "Connection to host lost. Press any key to continue." Press any key to return to the Microsoft Telnet> command prompt. Then type **q** and press **Enter** to return to the root directory prompt C:\>.

Project 1-4

Even though Exchange 2000 services differ from those in Exchange 5.5, these two versions still share common elements.

To identify components unique to Exchange 2000 and common to both Exchange 2000 and Exchange Server 5.5:

1. Using the following list of components, write the letter corresponding to a component in the proper column in Table 1-2. Each component should be assigned to the

Exchange Server 5.5 column, the Exchange 2000 Server column, or, if the component can be associated with both Exchange versions, the Common to Both column.

If you have any questions or problems completing Table 1-2, you can research these topics or components at *http://search.support.microsoft.com/kb*. This is the Microsoft Knowledge Base, where you can search for information on various products and features.

a. Message Transfer Agent (MTA)
b. Simple Mail Transport Protocol (SMTP) Service
c. Network News Transport Protocol (NNTP) Service
d. Directory Service (DS)
e. System Attendant (SA)
f. Private Information Store
g. Public Information Store
h. streaming data file (.stm file)
i. storage groups
j. IIS Admin Service (Inetinfo.exe process)
k. Active Directory (AD)
l. global catalog
m. Exchange Interprocess Communication (ExIPC) Layer
n. Instant Messaging (IM)
o. Active Directory Connector (ADC)
p. administrative groups

Table 1-2 Comparing Exchange Server 5.5 with Exchange 2000 Server

Exchange Server 5.5	Exchange 2000 Server	Common to Both Exchange 5.5 and Exchange 2000

Case Projects

Case 1

You have been asked to devise a new messaging system for a local pet store in your city. They have been using Microsoft Mail for PC Networks, but have found that some clients have been accidentally deleting information in the post office. What recommendations can you make so that their messaging services become more reliable and efficient?

Case 2

A good friend calls you at work asking for your opinion. His company wants to incorporate Exchange 2000 Server into an existing Exchange 5.5 organization. He is unsure whether to retain his Exchange 5.5 server or upgrade it completely to Exchange 2000 Server. You want to suggest the best option to him, knowing that his company uses legacy mainframe computers and maintains connections to external messaging systems. How should you advise your friend?

Case 3

Your organization has decided to purchase new computers running Exchange 2000 Server. No previous versions of Exchange Server will be running in your company. You have been asked to design an administrative topology that mirrors the company's current organizational structure with specific servers dedicated to specific tasks (for example, one server will host only public folder information). The company is concerned about the scalability and flexibility of the new and untested Exchange 2000 Server. How can you assure them that they are making the right choice concerning Exchange 2000 Server?

CHAPTER

2

PLANNING FOR WINDOWS 2000

After reading this chapter and completing the exercises, you will be able to:

- Identify the four phases of the Microsoft Solutions Framework model to help plan for an effective implementation of Exchange 2000 Server
- Plan and design Active Directory to ensure a better installation and management of Exchange 2000 Server
- Understand Domain Name System planning and how important its proper setup and operation is to Exchange 2000 Server

In Chapter 1, "An Overview of Microsoft Exchange 2000 Server," you learned about the fundamentals of Exchange 2000, including the Exchange messaging server model and new features that have been added since Exchange 5.5. In this chapter, you continue to learn about new features of Exchange 2000. First, you look at the Microsoft Solutions Framework model and see how it can help you effectively plan an Exchange 2000 environment using Windows 2000 and Active Directory. Next, you learn how to properly plan and design AD, including how to use appropriate naming conventions. Finally, you learn how to plan and deploy the Domain Name System and see how Exchange 2000 depends on this service.

Given today's fast-growing corporate landscape, using Windows 2000, Active Directory, and Exchange 2000 can help you manage an organization's network communication needs if they are properly designed and applied. With the information in this chapter, you will be able to take the first step toward designing an efficient Exchange 2000 environment.

THE MICROSOFT SOLUTIONS FRAMEWORK

Microsoft came up with the Microsoft Solutions Framework in 1994 as a result of combining common best-practice scenarios with standardized training methods to help promote a reliable and consistent approach in infrastructure development. The **Microsoft Solutions Framework (MSF)** is a set of guidelines to help establish a reliable development path for implementing infrastructure projects efficiently and in a disciplined manner. Corporate infrastructures are growing at a remarkable rate, and many of them are experiencing difficulties caused by a poor initial organizational design. Because many of these networks were first created long before widespread Internet use, organizations must now struggle to adapt and include these technologies in networks that often were not designed with future expansion in mind.

The MSF can be useful in expansion situations, when organizations are planning an effective technology rollout. By providing a set of specific steps, the MSF can help you lay out project duties and responsibilities clearly, plan proactively for risk management, and ensure that the organization has the ability to adapt to changes in project requirements.

The Four Phases of the MSF Model

There are four major phases in the MSF model:

- Envisioning
- Planning
- Developing
- Deploying

Each phase is an important component in the overall implementation of the MSF model and needs to be completed to ensure continuity throughout the entire process.

The real benefit to the MSF model is its ability to help planners and implementers assess project risks and requirements. By allowing you to assess the risks in a clear and realistic manner, the MSF enables you, as an Information Technology (IT) implementer or planner, to mitigate the project's level of risk. To create your plan effectively, you need to spend some time assessing the product's minimum and recommended requirements, both of which can affect your project. For instance, if your servers can handle the minimum specifications but cannot support a required feature, you might have to upgrade the existing hardware before implementing the software in your project plan.

As you move through the project, you will likely find that the initial plan used to assess risk and requirements changes several times. New issues arise or old ones come back to the forefront; with a clear plan, however, these issues are easier to handle.

The Envisioning Phase

In the envisioning phase of the MSF, you must look at the project as a whole while outlining its goals and basic design. You should keep the following main points in mind:

- Organization of the project's team
- Project requirements
- Project vision, project scope, and any assumptions about the project
- Conceptual design layout of the project

A hazard of this phase is that people sometimes like to jump right into implementing new systems without spending the time to outline the project's goals, determine current and future requirements, or assess potential risks. If the project team doesn't pay enough attention to these issues, the project could become unmanageable, and the end result will likely be a mess.

Organization of the Project's Team The first step during the envisioning phase is to organize and assemble the project team. This step allows you to delegate responsibilities and tasks to people who specialize in certain areas. In the MSF model, it is usually this assembled team that lays out the project and makes it a reality. Table 2-1 outlines a potential project team.

Table 2-1 Project Member Roles and Duties

Team Member	Description of Role
Project manager	Works with the client to determine the requirements, objectives, and budget for the project. The manager doesn't need to be technically knowledgeable, but should be good at communicating issues to the client and team.
Program manager	Manages the Exchange design and rollout
Executive advisory member	Assumes an advisory role from a management level for the duration of the project. This person can be, for example, a director or vice president, but doesn't necessarily need to be directly involved with the team.
Project advisory member/group	Monitors progress throughout the project and can be a single team member or a small group that represents key stakeholders in the organization. Like the executive advisory member, this person or group need not be directly involved with the team, but should receive updates from the team or project manager.
Development/ engineering group	Plans all technical configuration and implementation for the project. For Exchange 2000, this could include servers, clients, and any external connections required to meet the project needs. This group of people will likely be the largest and most diverse of the team, and could include departments such as Messaging, Network Connections, Internet, Workstation, User Accounts, Security, and Operations.

Table 2-1 Project Member Roles and Duties (continued)

Team Member	Description of Role
Testing/quality assurance manager	Assumes the role of detective and is responsible for testing the various system functions to ensure that the final configuration works as it should
User training team	Generates documentation and training outlines for clients using the new service. Members of this team should have a good knowledge of the product and good communication skills.
Logistics manager	Analyzes the project and determines the best way to deploy the product and plan an effective transition from an older product if required

Depending on the size of the project, you might need to assign several people to the same role or give one person multiple roles. When assigning duties to the team, keep in mind that the team members should have a working knowledge of and the ability to work with Exchange 2000 and Windows 2000, except for the roles in Table 2-1 that indicate otherwise. This way, each member can effectively contribute to the overall project.

Project Requirements The second step of the envisioning phase is to generate the project requirements. During this step, you add details to fill out the goals and basic design you have been working on during this phase. The methods you choose for determining project requirements depend on your organization and its preferences for handling technology rollouts. At a minimum, it is a good idea to hold regular meetings with the team members and keep all pertinent documents in an accessible place, such as on the network or company intranet, so that anyone taking part in the project has immediate access to the latest available information.

Because Exchange 2000 can result in a dramatic infrastructure change, gathering suggestions for requirements from the entire organization is vital. These suggestions should include business, user, and network infrastructure requirements. As you gather information from various groups and departments, you should categorize the requests for features into levels of importance, asking the team to help determine the most important requests, especially if the time available to implement the project is limited.

Project Vision, Project Scope, and Assumptions The third step of the envisioning phase is to define the project vision, project scope, and assumptions. Defining the project vision helps the team direct its attention to what's needed to carry out the plan successfully. Like a company vision statement, the project vision should outline what the team sees as the end result of the project. Look at the following brief example of a project vision:

XYZ Company will replace its existing messaging infrastructure with a new enterprise-messaging product. The new messaging infrastructure will include Microsoft Exchange 2000, which will allow XYZ Company to communicate in a more efficient manner and help lower personnel and operational costs. This new infrastructure will be implemented company wide, will start in one month, and will be completed in 12 months.

The project scope takes the project vision a step further and actually defines what features need to be implemented given the time allowed for the project, rather than what you want to see in a best-case scenario, as in the example of a project vision. Some factors that might affect the project scope could be:

- *Resources*—Available personnel and funding
- *Schedule*—Available time for implementation
- *Features*—Desired feature set and requirements to include them

Any assumptions the team might have about the project should be laid out as early as possible in the envisioning phase. With the assumptions defined, the team can better determine whether the assumptions are in fact correct and whether they fit in with the project as a whole. For instance, the team in charge of supporting and training the staff might assume that users are already familiar with Outlook 98 and need very little training to use Outlook 2000. The assumption might indeed be correct, but it should be noted and confirmed or denied.

Conceptual Design Layout of the Project The fourth step in the envisioning phase is to lay out the conceptual design of the project. In most projects, you have an idea of the end result, which is usually a mix of your project vision and your requirements. When creating a conceptual design, a broad outline of the optimal solution is the best starting point. Including this information in your project vision and project requirements can help the team keep the project vision in mind, but not lose sight of the obtainable goal specified in the project scope. You shouldn't spend too much time on this step because you will spend more time developing the design during the project's planning phase. The conceptual design is akin to the project vision, except that, instead of saying what you plan to achieve, you outline what actually will be achieved. For instance, the conceptual design for XYZ company would be "Implement a fully featured Exchange 2000 Server implementation running on Windows 2000 Server with Active Directory configured for our domain, xyz.com."

The Planning Phase

The planning phase can make or break your project. Without proper planning, your Exchange 2000 deployment can run into problems or unnecessary delays. During the planning phase, the team finalizes the concepts generated during the envisioning phase and begins to develop the detailed plans and engineering requirements for the project. The planning phase helps define three main goals for the project:

- *Functional specification*—Final solution that will be delivered
- *Master project plan*—Plan that outlines how the project is designed, tested, and implemented
- *Project schedule*—Actual plan that shows how the project will begin and gives deadlines for each stage of the implementation, including when the project will be tested and completed

To define these three main goals, the team must complete several important steps during the project's planning phase. Assigning planning tasks helps the team gain a better understanding about the existing environment (if any) and what the new project will be like. Some of the general planning tasks (explained in more detail in the following sections) that should be assigned to team members during the planning phase are as follows:

- Information gathering
- Functional specification design
- Proof of concept testing
- Resource identification (personal and otherwise)
- Project plan generation
- Project schedule generation

When installing or upgrading to Exchange 2000, you should assign the following specific planning tasks to team members to ensure a smooth rollout:

- Understand the current Windows environment, whether it is Windows NT or Windows 2000. If Windows NT is currently being used, then the team must first understand how Windows 2000 will be implemented.
- Design a plan that allows for interoperability, integration, and user migration to Exchange 2000 if Exchange 5.5 is currently in use.
- Assign an Active Directory manager for planning and operational stages of the project. By taking care of this task early in the project, you can avoid potential personnel conflicts caused by changes in roles resulting from Exchange 2000 integration with Active Directory. For example, system administrators, not e-mail administrators, might control e-mail accounts under Exchange 2000, and Exchange administrators might not appreciate someone else handling tasks they previously handled.

Information Gathering It can be critical for the team to have a good idea of the current infrastructure before deploying a new messaging system such as Exchange 2000. Knowing what the old environment was like can help the team predict and prevent possible pitfalls before they happen. Table 2-2 describes the type of information that should be gathered during this step.

Functional Specification Design The information your team gathered in the previous step is then combined with the project requirements, your project vision and scope, and the project's conceptual design layout to generate a functional specification design. This design helps give the team the details it needs to start working on the various projects that have been assigned to them.

Table 2-2 Type of Information to Gather

Information	Details
Organizational structure and location of important data	Find out how the company operates, including departmental divisions and geographical locations (if the company has branch offices). This helps you get a better idea of how messages should be handled. At this stage, determining the number of clients is necessary to assess user requirements.
Network infrastructure	Lay out how the network is constructed, including how much of the network is used. Current remote access capabilities should be determined.
Messaging and directory structure	Establish how the existing messaging system operates and figure out how the new system will integrate with existing systems.
Desktop and server configurations	Inventory the types of systems and servers the network is currently populated with. This inventory helps determine if any systems will have to be replaced or upgraded.
Existing organizational standards	Document any existing organizational standards, such as those for network security or administration, and how the changes may affect them.
Project requirements	Gather information from users and the IT Department as to the features they expect the new messaging system to have.

When the functional specification design starts to take shape, it might become apparent that there is not enough time to include everything that was suggested for the project's end result. During this step, you might need to focus on the most important features and leave the less important ones until later in the schedule or when there is more time, so the project can meet its minimum requirements for functionality. Most features can be added later when the time and resources are available.

During this phase, establishing realistic goals for functionality is important. Sit down with the team and the end users and decide which features are considered a minimum for the project, so that you have an obtainable goal that also satisfies everyone. Also, consult managers from each department to get their opinions on project requirements and what they feel will make the project an overall success. This step provides valuable feedback from the point of view of management and the departments the project will support.

Proof of Concept Testing At this point in the planning phase, you might need to assemble a test system to test functionality or the ability to meet requirements. During this proof of concept testing step, you can get a better idea of how the system or components work. Generally, this is not a nitty-gritty test of the system, but a quick test to see if the product reacts the way you expect and need it to. For instance, you can try testing how SMTP forwarding works between two different Exchange 2000 servers or even test how the layout of public folders works from a usability standpoint.

Resource Identification Organizing and determining what resources are required for the project, such as personnel, hardware, and software is a crucial step in the MSF's planning phase. After you have specified what you require for the project, you can then decide what the project plan and schedule will look like.

When determining resources necessary for the project, some potential problems to consider are:

- Do you need to find someone to cover a team member's position during the project if he or she is on vacation or temporary leave?
- Are the members of the team appropriately trained or experienced for their tasks?
- Are there any hardware and software resources that might need to be obtained, such as new servers, operating systems, and software licenses for Exchange 2000?
- Are any additional tools or utilities needed to facilitate other areas of the project, such as moving mailboxes from the old system to Exchange 2000?

All of these questions must be addressed to help the project move along smoothly and on time.

Project Plan Generation Every project typically has several smaller projects contained within it. Usually, each set of tasks assigned to a team member can be considered a project; important tasks generally included in an Exchange 2000 rollout are system architecture, security, end-user testing, budget, deployment, and risk management. After you bring together the smaller individual project plans, you can generate the final plan that encompasses the entire project. By outlining these individual projects, you can better lay out the final project plan. Remember that during the generation of the project plan, all of the smaller projects must come together and take the other projects into account. The final creation of the project plan is a lot like putting together a jigsaw puzzle. Some pieces may fit correctly, but others are just not right.

For instance, all the different components of the project plan might fit together perfectly, but a company security policy does not allow the whole project to come together because the project's security implementation does not meet the company policy's requirements. One of two things needs to be done: Either the policy has to be updated to take into account the changes needed, or the project needs to be modified to suit the policy. The path you choose depends on the circumstances involved and which choice is most beneficial to the organization and to the project as a whole.

Project Schedule Generation After the draft of the final project plan has been generated, the team can now move ahead and create a project schedule. During this step, the team can finally determine the actual deployment date for the new infrastructure. In addition, the team must outline the due dates for the individual tasks assigned to the team members to determine when the smaller projects need to be finalized. This is the best time for the team to reassess the information they have gathered up to this point and approximate the time needed for the project. Using a project management software package, such as Microsoft Project, can be a great aid during this step because it can help the team manage timelines and due dates and check how the members are proceeding with their respective projects. More information on Microsoft Project can be found at *http://www.microsoft.com/office/project/default.htm.*

When the team is meeting to finalize the project schedule, the entire team needs to understand and agree to the proposed project schedule. If it does not, this can cause problems down the road, when team members drop the ball or realize they have misjudged the time needed to perform their tasks. The project schedule can also help team members gauge their progress based on other members' project status.

The Developing Phase

The developing phase of the project is when the team actually performs the testing and determines whether the project design and plans fleshed out during the planning phase are correct. During the developing phase, the teams set up the infrastructure they planned and follow the design through to duplicate the final environment as closely as possible. Also during this phase, the team initiates a series of checks and tests to validate the design and check for usability.

Validating the Design After the hardware and software are available for testing, the team then needs to set up the design they created in the planning phase to validate that the design does in fact do what it is supposed to do. Also during this step, the team can confirm the installation procedures, assess the functionality of the required features, and determine whether time is available for optional or less-important features. During this step, a systematic approach to testing the systems gives you a clearer picture of the end result.

The first step of testing is to validate the individual servers and system components to verify that they work according to the specifications the team determined. After validating that the servers and components work properly, the team should move on to testing the implementation on the end-user system level, which can help test the entire system as a whole.

Keep in mind that these tests are still preliminary and are usually performed in a controlled environment. Final testing is not finished until end users test the product. The validation tests are used only to determine whether the project is ready to be implemented on production-level systems.

After the system has been successfully tested, it is time to test the software on what will become the final production systems and servers. After this testing has been done, the project is ready to move to the final stages of testing.

Technical User Testing After the project has been installed on production servers following the validation step, it is advisable to have a selection of technical users test the system before the project team has end users try out the product. This step allows you to have relatively experienced people track down any problems that might not have been noticed during the validation step of testing, such as a setting on the server that does not keep a record of the user's mailbox information for data redundancy. As in the validation step, following a set testing plan gives you the most benefit from the time spent testing. After you have the results from the technical user testing, the team can then address any issues that arose and move on to the user testing step.

User Testing The most important part of the testing process is when the actual users use the product in the way they use the existing system. This step gives the team the best idea of how the product is operating before the project's deployment phase begins. The best users for this step are volunteers because they will, you hope, give constructive feedback even though they are testing a less-than-perfect setup. During the user-testing step, all components and features that will exist during the full rollout should be in place, including support, training, and operations/administration so that the team can determine their effectiveness as well. During the user-testing step, make sure you have the following items in place:

- End-user training
- Documentation (administrative and end user)
- End-user installation processes
- End-user support
- Access to public folders for user feedback
- User evaluation forms

After the user-testing step is finished, the team should then assess how the developing phase went and determine whether the project is ready to move forward or whether it requires changes. It is important to build in time to make adjustments to or change the configuration of the servers in the planning phase. Then if problems arise (and they likely will) during the developing phase, the team has time to address them before the project is due to go live in the production environment. After the testing is finished and the necessary changes have been made, the team is ready to move into the final deploying phase of the project.

At some point during the developing phase, especially during the user-testing step, there will probably be some requests for features that were not initially included in the project plan. Although it may be feasible to include some of these features, any major changes should wait until a future update of the system so that the project can finish on time.

The Deploying Phase

The final phase of the project is the deployment of the final product. During this phase, all end users are moved from the old messaging system to the new one using the steps outlined in the planning phase. Also during this phase, end users receive their training and the team moves into an observation mode to monitor how the new infrastructure is performing. Ultimately, the deployment team controls this phase entirely, but they can call upon the other teams to assist in resolving problems or determining when future updates to the product might be needed.

User Migration After the components important to the infrastructure have been moved into place (gateways, servers, Internet, and so forth), the end users can be migrated to the new system. Users should be trained in using the new infrastructure and then moved over, preferably in batches to minimize support headaches, so that eventually all the users are moved off the old system. Properly training your employees can make or break your project because if users get frustrated, they could become resistant to fixes or additional assistance you offer. Moving everyone over in one fell swoop is not recommended (unless it's a small deployment) because some problems or issues could still arise after the migration. After all the users have finally moved over and everything is running smoothly, the management of the system can be turned over to the operations team, and the project can be considered to be in full production.

Project Completion and Evaluation When the new system is in place and working as intended based on the results of the user testing and final user migration steps, the project team can officially end the project. After the project has ended, the entire team should meet to discuss what happened during the project (both good and bad) and to discuss the different components of the deployment and whether project requirements were met. After determining that all the project's required facets have been addressed, the team should evaluate the project to review whether anything can be improved and then document these findings for future projects.

In many cases, a review of the entire project and of user and management input can help resolve issues for future projects. You should gather user and management feedback on how they felt the project progressed by using questionnaires or other types of forms; make sure to ask questions such as "Did any step of the process adversely affect your productivity?" Keep the questionnaire brief and highlight the most important information because most users and managers will not take the time to answer a 20-question survey. Also, inform them that the survey is intended to ensure that all their needs were met and to make sure future projects achieve the same level (or better) of end-user and management satisfaction. To conclude your questionnaire, tell them that, if necessary, you might contact them directly for more information.

Properly planning a project of this size is important to the success of a large-scale infrastructure change, such as implementing Exchange 2000, and can mean the difference between a smooth rollout of the technology and a rocky one. To best benefit from a structured approach such as the MSF, you should allow for flexibility yet still maintain a realistic schedule that everyone on the team can follow. A structured approach makes it much easier to enjoy a successful rollout of Exchange 2000 technology. In addition to a realistic schedule and a structured plan, proper testing of your implementation by team members and technically minded volunteer users can provide insights and detect errors that might crop up during daily use. Feedback from these users and other department managers provides valuable information that can be used to adjust the project accordingly and fix any problems that might arise before finally deploying the project.

ACTIVE DIRECTORY PLANNING AND DESIGN

Active Directory (AD), is a Windows 2000 network directory structure used to organize users, data, and other objects into a scalable tree architecture for easier management and expandability. AD is a major step forward in domain management and design for a Microsoft operating system. AD can allow for a larger installed base, and scales well, from a single server to a worldwide network with thousands of servers and millions of users. To help manage this new scalability, AD includes a bevy of improvements to centralized management of resources on the network. Among the major changes made to facilitate these improvements are a completely new domain structure and an entirely new namespace convention. Veterans of Novell Network Directory Services (NDS)—the Novell network directory structures that allows for a tree-structured network design—find many of the features or structure of AD familiar, as it appears Microsoft drew heavily from this previously established design.

The NT 4.0 Domain Structure

It is difficult to move forward without first looking back to see where you came from. The NT 4.0 domain structure could be called archaic at best, but it is still a serviceable implementation. The main problem with the old structure is that it becomes difficult to effectively manage users and their respective rights when domains grow larger. Often, for the sake of management, it becomes necessary to segment networks into multiple domains to take some burden off administrators and servers.

An NT 4.0 domain is typically very flat, with a single **primary domain controller (PDC)** and a number of **backup domain controllers (BDCs)** managing logons and rights to network resources. This single point of management works well on small to midsize networks, but bogs down on larger networks because there is no way to organize users and resources effectively. This can be especially true when the domain is spread over several different geographical locations. It can become downright impossible to administer resources and users for these different locations when they aren't even in the same time zone as the network administrators.

There are some more complex domain configurations for Windows NT 4.0, such as multi-master, which allows for a slightly more segmented domain structure and a slightly better management scheme, in which resources are controlled on a domain-by-domain basis but users are still centrally managed. Ultimately, Microsoft has moved toward the complete trust model of domain structure, which is what AD represents. The complete trust model allows for multiple domain administrators and varied organizational units under one central root domain. You will learn more about the different trust models later in this chapter in the section "Transitive and Non-Transitive Trusts."

Active Directory Domain Structure

Like Windows NT 4.0, AD is organized into units called domains; however, multiple domains can be contained within one domain. AD can group and manage multiple resources in different networks within one domain structure. In this structure, the domain boundaries are defined by the namespace and can include more than one domain controller.

In Windows 2000, AD uses what's known as a multi-master peer controller model called the domain controller. Every domain controller with authority in a given domain can send and receive changes to the domain and spread them around; this ability allows updates to be propagated to domains even if one domain controller is not operating.

Domain Modes

An AD domain can operate in two different modes: mixed mode or native mode. In a mixed-mode domain, the domain is restricted by certain limitations caused by the Windows NT 4.0 servers active in the domain. A Windows 2000 domain controller can be used in a Windows NT 4.0 domain, but it must take over the PDC duties in the domain. The downside is that the Windows 2000 domain controller takes on the same limitations that a Windows NT 4.0 domain controller would have (that is, 40,000 objects). Any BDCs on the network view the Windows 2000 server as a PDC; if more than one Windows 2000 domain controller is active in a Windows NT 4.0 domain, it is possible to manage which server takes on the PDC role.

If you want to fully appreciate the scalability and other benefits an AD domain brings with it, you must run your Windows 2000 domain in native mode, which refers to running a pure Windows 2000 domain with no remaining NT 4.0 domains or servers. After you have converted to native mode, you cannot back out, and any domain controllers must be upgraded to or be running Windows 2000. AD can then handle more than a million objects and allows for better management because you can group and nest objects and users, which is beneficial to Exchange 2000. It is impossible for a Windows 2000 native-mode domain to contain Windows NT 4.0 domain controllers, but you can still have Windows NT 4.0 member servers and workstations in the domain with no problems. Native mode is highly recommended for your AD configuration because it not only increases the domain's capabilities, but it also makes installing and managing Exchange 2000 a much easier task.

All About Forests

A Windows 2000 domain is broken up into forests and trees. A **forest** is essentially a collection of one or more Windows 2000 AD domain trees connected by transitive-trust relationships between the root domains of each tree domain. Every tree that inhabits a single forest has the same configuration as the others. As explained later in the section "Domain Tree," when naming between domains isn't in line with the child-parent configuration, multiple trees exist within the forest.

Remember that for Exchange 2000 implementations, the AD domain forest represents the boundary for the organization because Exchange 2000 cannot cover more than one Windows 2000 forest. If there is more than one forest in an organization, more than one Exchange 2000 organization is necessary.

When migrating your domains over to native-mode domains, it is not necessary to migrate all the domains at once. You can change over parent and child domains one by one as required. The best explanation of what makes a domain forest is that when a group of domain trees are under a single root domain encompassing all the subdomains into the same namespace under AD, they become a forest. This forest outlines a single configuration that every domain tree in the forest replicates to the others, thus providing consistency between all the domain trees in the domain forest.

Exchange 2000 and Forests

A forest is the boundary that Exchange 2000 must live by. It is impossible to have multiple Exchange 2000 servers in the same Exchange 2000 organization but in different forests. There are two different ways to plan an Exchange 2000 deployment: in a single forest using AD with all domains trusting each other and using a single Exchange organization; or in multiple AD forests using earlier versions of Exchange to coexist and connect with the other forests and Exchange organizations.

With a multiple-forest infrastructure, you must set up a different Exchange 2000 organization for each forest. After this setup has been carried out, you can expect to run into some of the following issues:

- Multiple Exchange 2000 organizations to administer and manage
- Inability to use automatic AD replication between the forests; as a result users have only half the organization's addresses in the **global address list**, the central "address book" for users in an AD forest
- Inability to use Routing Group Connectors between the Exchange 2000 organizations; instead, SMTP or X.400 connectors are required
- Lack of status updates between the organizations because there are no Routing Group Connectors to transfer the information

As soon as you attempt a multiple-forest Exchange 2000 implementation, you generate a lot of additional administration and maintenance. It is possible to keep this setup working; however, you have to establish manual trusts between the domains, which is rather counterproductive because it is more or less the same as having a Windows NT 4.0 domain setup.

If the setup mandates a multiple-forest, multiple-Exchange 2000 deployment, some data will probably need to be synchronized regularly to make sure the overall system works as it should. A bevy of third-party software packages are on the market, such as Compaq LDAP Synchronization Utility, that can help replicate the data from one Exchange 2000 organization to another.

Numerous other issues can arise when running multiple forests, such as not being able to synchronize calendars between organizations or to see the complete global address list without extra configuration and administrative headaches. Make every effort to implement a single forest with Exchange servicing that one forest.

Domain Tree

Windows 2000 domain nomenclature includes the use of the terms *tree* and *forest* to refer to domain topology. A Windows 2000 domain is a parent-child design called a **domain tree**. A domain tree consists of more than one Windows 2000 domain; these domains are members of the same root domain (the domains are collectively referred to as a forest). Figure 2-1 illustrates a single root domain tree with four total domains.

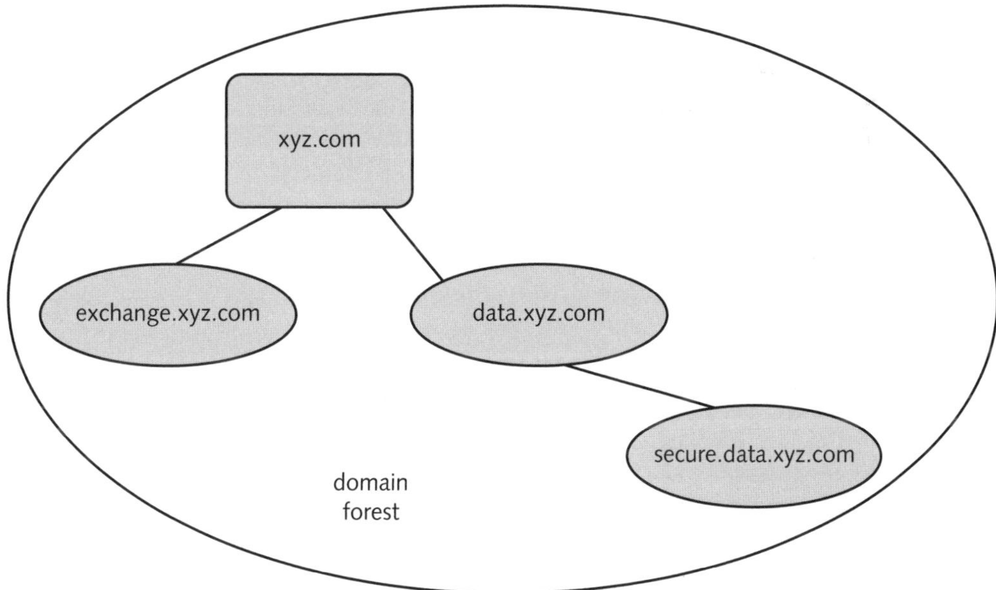

Figure 2-1 A single root domain tree with four total domains

The Windows 2000 domain name structure uses regular Domain Name System names, such as "data.xyz.com," as shown in Figure 2-1. In this example, the domain "data" is a child in the parent domain "xyz.com." Following the child domain is the grandchild domain "secure.data.xyz.com," with the "secure" domain being a child to the "data" domain and a grandchild to the "xyz.com" root domain. The design is both simple and complex, and allows for incredible flexibility in design and organization. The only issue occurs when a domain doesn't share the same basic domain name, "xyz.com," as the parent above it. For instance, "secure.xyz.com" (not "secure.data.xyz.com") would be considered its own tree domain under the "xyz.com" root forest, not a child of the "data.xyz.com" tree. Figure 2-2 illustrates multiple domain trees within one forest.

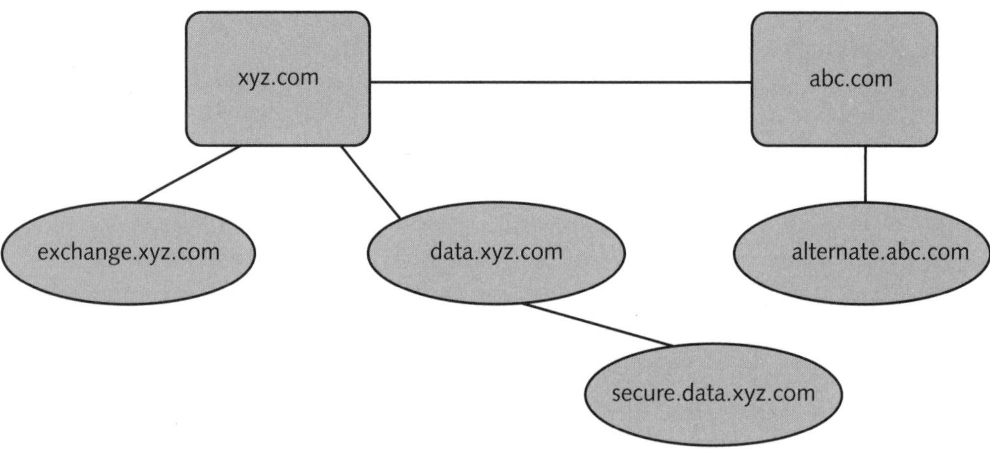

Figure 2-2 Multiple domain trees within one forest

Domain Controller

In a Microsoft domain setup, the system that can authenticate users to the domain is known as a domain controller. Naturally, for a domain to exist, at least one domain controller must be available. Every domain controller that participates in a network keeps a copy of the current domain configuration, including users and other resources, such as files and folders.

Under Windows 2000, it is possible to promote a regular member server to a domain controller with the standard Windows 2000 Server utility Dcpromo.exe. In Windows NT 4.0 domains, once a system has become a domain controller, you can't force the system to stop being a domain controller; you are forced to reinstall the operating system if you do not want that system to act as a domain controller anymore. Obviously, this limitation is frustrating; however, with Windows 2000 AD, you can use the same utility to demote a current domain controller back to a regular member server, which is a great timesaver.

Initial Domain Configuration The very first domain configured for an AD forest is the key point in the entire domain. When the domain is first created, the AD forest name is based on the Domain Name System name of the first domain controller configured, so choose your systems' names wisely so that management of the names is not confusing. For instance, a good domain name, such as xyz.com, represents the name of the company; child domains can then be added with names that relate to the domain's purpose, such as a service (Exchange) or location (Calgary). With a poorly chosen domain name, such as 77clg00.com, only the domain's creator can understand the meaning of such a cryptic name. When first creating the AD forest, remember that the first domain created as part of a forest cannot be removed from that forest. Also, any domains created after the first root domain cannot appear higher in the domain forest than the original domain. It is possible to create new domains as their own forest, but they cannot replace the initial root domain in any given forest.

Remember to pay special attention to naming any systems in your domain, even the initial domain controller. If the AD forest is going to interact directly with the Internet, it is important to name the domain appropriately (such as my.domain.com). Even if the AD forest doesn't currently interact with the Internet, preparing for that possibility by following proper domain-naming conventions is wise.

Adding More Domain Controllers The number of domain controllers you add to a domain depends entirely on the network's requirements for fault tolerance (the ability of the domain and network to handle hardware or software failure) and the amount of network resources that need to be load-balanced between servers to distribute processing. Use the following points to assess the network's needs for additional controllers:

- There should always be at least two domain controllers in the same physical network for fault tolerance.
- If there is only one domain controller in a particular location, make sure the WAN connection to other domain controllers (if there are any) is reliable so that other connected domain controllers can still authenticate users.
- If you have a large network configuration, additional domain controllers can help other domain controllers handle the user authentication and resource access needs.

The number of users and connections a domain controller can manage is, of course, entirely dependent on the server's physical resources, including memory, processor speed, and network hardware configuration.

Trust Relationships

When you require security across domains, AD uses trust relationships between different domains. AD uses an authentication method for users on each domain separately, but trusts the authentication method used for all the trusted domains. So if a user has already logged on to one domain, all other domains that have established trust with that domain automatically accept the user. This allows the user unfettered access to data and resources that he or she has rights to in the trusting domain. Figure 2-3 illustrates a simple one-way trust relationship.

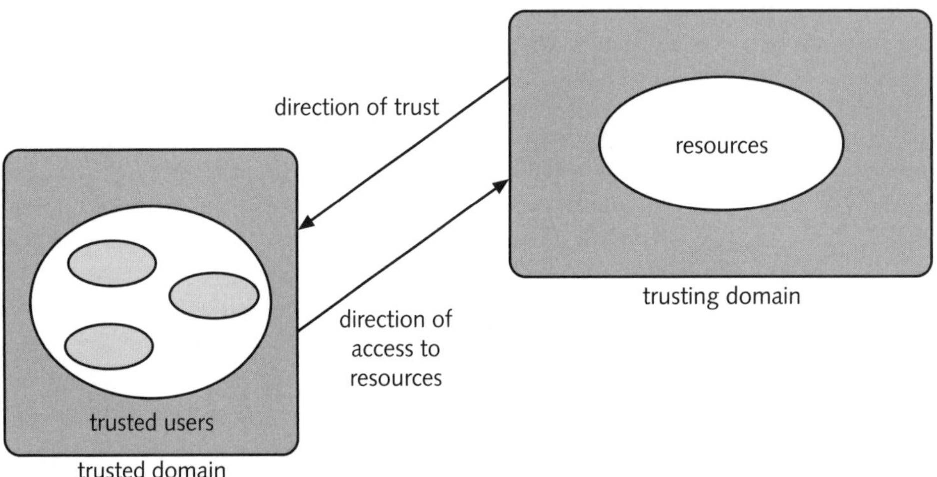

Figure 2-3 A simple one-way trust relationship between two domains

When a user logs on to another domain that trusts his source domain, he is always subject to the limitations of the **access control list (ACL)**, which determines the rights for an item, group, or other resource in AD. The ACL is modified any time you set the rights to a network share or adjust a user's permissions; when those shares, items, or objects are accessed, the ACL is referenced to see if the user trying to get access has permission to do so. Keep in mind that even if the user can log on to the domain, it doesn't necessarily mean he or she can do anything once inside.

Transitive and Non-Transitive Trust

Windows 2000 domains can be connected to a domain tree or forest, and each child domain under the root has an automatic two-way trust relationship with the main parent domain. Not only that, but the domain also has a transitive trust. In a transitive trust, Domain A trusts Domain B, and essentially inherits any trusts that Domain B had. When a transitive trust is established, it is applied automatically for all domains that are members of that particular forest or tree, saving administrative time by eliminating the need to apply trusts on a system-by-system basis.

For instance, Domain2 has a two-way transitive trust with Domain A, and both domains have several child and grandchild domains underneath them. If users log on to Domain1, the parent of Domain2, they have access to resources in Domain2 that might not be trusted directly by Domain1, but are trusted by another child domain in the Domain2 hierarchy. Therefore, because a child domain trusts not only Domain1, but also the grandchild domain under the child domain, Domain1 automatically trusts the grandchild domain—even though no direct trust has been established between the two. This trust process works in reverse as well: It is possible for the same user to log on to the grandchild domain and access resources in the parent domain, even though there isn't a direct trust between the two. It's a complex concept, but allows a great deal of flexibility in accessing resources.

The end result of transitive trusts on a Windows 2000 domain is that there is now a complete trust between all domains in the AD forest because every domain has a transitive trust with its parent domain. Having all domains completely trust each other makes handling multiple domains under Windows 2000 much easier than it was under the Windows NT 4.0 domain structure.

As mentioned earlier, a popular Windows NT 4.0 domain structure is called the multiple-master domain model. In this model, the domain that controls the primary user accounts is called a master user domain, and the domain that contains the computer accounts and resources is called the master resource domain. However, a problem arises when you want to add another domain; you must generate a series of new trusts, which in larger networks can often be confusing and difficult to manage. Windows 2000 AD takes care of this problem by setting up transitive trusts by default when a new domain is added.

Limiting Trust Relationships

The only downfall to the automatic transitive-trust setup is that you might have a situation in which you do not want one domain to trust another. Unfortunately there is no way to break the trust, and there are accounts and groups in the forest that can manipulate the forest, such as Exchange administrators who must be able to administer users' message settings across the domain. To avoid this problem, you might have to establish more than one domain forest to segment the domain and "isolate" a particular domain or group of domains. The following list outlines some reasons for limiting trust relationships:

- Administrators from one domain don't trust administrators from another domain, which can happen when there are disagreements on how to handle the administration of shared elements or the domain itself. This lack of trust can also happen during joint ventures, when companies have to work together on a project, and each company doesn't want another company to gain access to sensitive information.
- Separate organizations cannot agree on domain change policies. This situation can arise when changes to the domain, especially ones that could affect the entire forest, need to be made, and an organization that participates in this domain cannot agree how to manage or implement the changes that might affect the others.

- Limiting the trust relationship is required. In this situation, if certain users or domains must not have access to information on one domain or the other (be it accounts or other resources), it might become necessary to move them to another forest and grant access on a resource-by-resource basis.

Resources in a multiple-domain AD model have transitive trusts with each other for user and resource access by default; however, the transitive trust does not extend to administrators. This increases security on the domain by not allowing any domain administrator to manage another domain unless access is granted beforehand.

Using Shortcut Trusts to Optimize Authentication

Depending on the size and physical configuration of your network, when a user requests access to a resource in a domain other than his own, the user's domain controller might have to get access for the user. If the user's domain is not in a parent-child direct trust, the user's domain might need to communicate with every domain controller in each domain between the user's domain and the target domain until access has been established.

If the network is separated geographically, this can take quite a while or not succeed at all. Networks can slow down or fail to deliver packets properly and the worldwide networks have a tendency to drop packets. In an effort to curb this problem, it is possible to connect any two domains together with a shortcut trust relationship. In this type of trust, a domain administrator can connect a group of domains in a complete trust with each other, instead of everyone trusting each other in a long line of trusts that requires any authentication traffic to eventually go through the root of the domain. This direct trust can help speed up resource access and limit the amount of authentication traffic burdening the network and domains.

The Active Directory Schema

The AD schema is basically an extensible, programmable catalog of all the objects and settings in AD. When Exchange 2000 is installed, AD must get configuration data from Exchange 2000. At this point, Exchange 2000 must extend the Active Directory schema to include Exchange 2000 objects, classes, and other settings that are carried out to all other domain controllers across the entire forest. This extension creates new objects in AD for all the domains, which include information on things like users, the Exchange 2000 configuration, and public folder objects.

Making a change to the schema, especially when expanding it as Exchange 2000 does, requires some preplanning to ensure the transition goes smoothly. A schema expansion can burden the network and potentially inconvenience many users, so you might want to consider using the Exchange 2000 ForestPrep utility to expand the schema at a better time (such as during non-business hours), but have this major step completed when you want to deploy Exchange 2000, which requires the expanded schema. You will learn more about the Exchange 2000 ForestPrep utility in Chapter 5, "Installation of Exchange 2000 Server in New Environments."

Global Catalog Servers

In AD, a global catalog is a complete copy of all objects in the domain and a partial copy of all objects in the forest; it's what Exchange 2000 clients use to access the contents of the global address list. Physical location can affect the performance of a Global Catalog server's response to client requests. For instance, if a remote domain is accessing the global address list over a slow WAN connection such as ISDN, responses to requests for information from the global address list could be slower because of limited bandwidth. For that reason, it's recommended that there be at least one GC server at every physical Windows 2000 site.

There are a few things to consider when implementing GC servers, such as:

- Has the AD schema been updated for Exchange 2000? If not, it needs to be.
- Which attributes from the domain need to be replicated to the global catalog?
- Is there at least one GC server at each Windows 2000 site?

By performing the tasks necessary to address the previously listed items, you will see how much preparation work is required to configure the AD schema, including the number of settings and attributes that must be carried over and the availability requirements of GC servers to maintain optimal performance.

Organizational Units

AD has several features to help make management of your domains much easier. One such feature is organizational units (OUs). An OU can help define where objects are located in your forest domain and how administration of those objects is handled, whereas the domain defines the replication and security requirements. An OU can be thought of in terms of how the domain is configured and laid out. If you have a domain forest with each of its domain trees as individual offices based on location, such as a particular city, it wouldn't make sense to have resources for one domain based on a city in another domain (for example, having resources for the L.A. office in the New York office domain). OUs are also a good way to implement group policies (GPs) for groups of objects. GPs determine rights to resources and objects for groups of users who need access. Instead of setting access rights on a user-by-user basis, you add the user to the group.

OUs have certain characteristics that you should keep in mind when organizing and planning the structure of your domains:

- OUs can be nested and can include child OUs, allowing for a hierarchical OU structure within a domain.
- The administrator can use OUs to delegate administrative access control to AD objects. By using nesting and delegation of access control, you can have detailed object administration.

- OUs cannot be used to define security or access rights. In AD, you can specify that a group has rights to a certain object, but you cannot do the same with OUs. OUs are intended to make management of objects easier, not to provide access authentication.
- The administrator can use GPs and associate them with OUs. A GP can be associated with sites, domains, and OUs, and can enable different policies to be used in the same domain structure.
- Users do not need to navigate the OU using Windows Explorer or a similar method of accessing files and directories. Although users can use the OU to find what they are looking for on the network, they should use AD and global catalogs to find the resources they need.

When implementing an OU in the domain, make sure you plan ahead and document why each OU is where it is and what its purpose is. After you have this setup planned, it is much easier not only for you but also for users and other administrators to make heads or tails of your OU layout and what it does. Some examples of purposely built OUs are OUs for delegating administrative duties, for obscuring objects (to limit viewing by users who do not need to see the objects, thus cleaning up the OU structure they use and see) in the domain, and for setting group policies.

Delegating administrative duties is much more flexible in Windows 2000 than in Windows NT 4.0. In Windows 2000 domains, you can decide how you want to delegate administrative duties for specific objects or types of objects by using access control lists and OUs. Under Windows NT 4.0 domains, you were limited by predefined delegated roles that could not offer a wide range of capabilities, but were instead limited to one task, such as account administration. By delegating duties to other administrators, your company can benefit by minimizing the number of users who must have administrative access to do the job one person could do across several systems, which also helps limit potential problems that occur from human error.

OUs require a lot of administrative overhead, and many steps are needed to create a well-designed OU. If you plan on using an OU to its fullest potential, you should review some of the technical documents on AD and OUs on the TechNet Web site at *http://www.microsoft.com/technet*.

Exchange 2000 and Organizational Units

OUs for the most part have no direct impact on the management and use of Exchange 2000 because it does not matter where a user or server is located in relation to the Exchange 2000 server. Exchange 2000 is flexible enough that the mailbox doesn't even have to exist in the same OU or domain as the object it services. This makes it much easier to move mailboxes or objects without affecting one or the other, which was much more difficult in Exchange 5.5.

It does not matter to Exchange 2000 how the domain or OU is set up before upgrading or when they are first set up (if doing a clean install), so no OU setup is seen in the Exchange 2000 address book.

Naming Contexts

Under Windows 2000, AD uses **naming contexts** to outline what information is stored in the naming databases used to organize the domain. Naming contexts help separate the AD information into three different sections—domain, configuration, and schema—and handle the replication for these sections of data. If the domain controller is also a GC server, there is a fourth section of data containing the necessary information for the GC server within the naming context. Naming contexts for configuration and schema data are common between domains that are members of the same forest, but forests hold their own unique domain naming context.

Domain Data in Naming Contexts

A domain naming context contains every object particular to that domain. This data is replicated to every domain controller in that domain, but not to any other domains in AD, other than the original domain.

Configuration Data in Naming Contexts

AD configuration data is replicated across the entire AD forest to every domain in that forest. Configuration context data can include data on the physical network that assists the domains in setting up data replication with other domain controllers. With Exchange 2000, configuration naming contexts hold Exchange 2000 organizational information that is replicated to every domain, and inform the other domains of the organizational layout, protocols, and services. The Enterprise Administrators group has full control over the configuration naming context and can help apply a consistent configuration across every domain. The configuration naming context, an important part of how AD operates, helps apply common domain configuration data across the entire AD forest.

Schema Data in Naming Contexts

Schema naming contexts outline the object classes and settings for the objects under AD. The schema context data is replicated by AD to every domain in the forest and does not change from domain to domain. The Schema Administrators group maintains full control over the schema naming context.

Exchange 2000 and Naming Contexts

The AD schema is expanded to include the additional Exchange 2000 settings when Exchange 2000 is first installed to the forest. The attributes added to the schema start with the msExch attribute, and other AD attributes are modified to adjust how Outlook users see this information. As you have learned, the entire process takes a considerable amount of time the first time around. This is time well spent, however, because any and all Exchange-related objects and configuration data are contained in AD, including recipients, configuration data, schema, and the global address list. Thanks to AD and replication of the configuration naming contexts, Exchange information is sent to every domain, which helps make administering Exchange 2000 content that much easier across the domains in the forest.

It is important to understand the Windows 2000 AD naming structure and how it affects Exchange 2000 configuration and administration. Administrators of different domains in a forest domain must agree on a common naming context because it is difficult later to go back and change some naming contexts, such as e-mail addresses.

Optimal Domain Design

There are many things to keep in mind when laying out an optimal domain design. It is most important to ensure advance planning time. Planning ahead when designing your domains makes the difference between an optimal or broken design. Here are some pointers to help plan your domain:

- Ensure that there is appropriate bandwidth to support the infrastructure you want. Quite often when dealing with WANs, for example, organizations try to do too much with the connections and physical network equipment they have, forcing upgrades down the line.
- If a location in your organization does not have a direct connection with the rest of your network, set up an individual site, and use Exchange 2000 to communicate between the networks utilizing SMTP.
- If you have sites that don't have a local domain controller, try to group them with other sites that do have one. When grouping, do it logically to promote efficient routing of replication data. Recall the earlier example of a forest with multiple domains that correspond to the cities where the domains are located. Assume you have a small branch office just outside Calgary in Red Deer, but no domain controller in Red Deer; you would group that branch office with the Calgary domain, not (for instance) with the Chicago domain.
- If there are multiple domains, and you have the network bandwidth to support them as a group, consider those domains as one site and group them together to help ease administrative burdens.
- If there is limited bandwidth between two different networks during peak times, set those networks up as separate sites and set up replication to send data between sites during off hours.

When deciding how the forest will be structured, make sure you include such details as the number of domains in the forest, what the root domain of the forest is, and what might happen if you make result changes to the domain. Also, before you decide to create several domains to occupy your forest, consider using only one domain to minimize administrative headaches. Additional domains are often created when one is more than enough to handle the network's needs. When implementing or planning for additional domains, try to outline the additional costs for not only the hardware required, but also the personnel needed to install extra domains. If you cannot justify the costs or gain sufficient benefits, it is probably best to stick with your current configuration.

DOMAIN NAME SYSTEM PLANNING AND DESIGN

Many people think of the **Domain Name System (DNS)** as the Internet service that resolves IP addresses to readable Web site addresses, when in fact DNS can perform name resolution for networks other than the Internet. AD and Exchange 2000 rely on DNS for their naming conventions, so you need a good idea of how DNS works and what is needed to properly set up and operate DNS. The following sections outline DNS and explain how Exchange 2000 relies on it.

DNS Overview

A DNS namespace is a distributed hierarchical tree design. Every individual component of the tree is a domain and has a name representing it in the tree. The first domain in the tree is called the root and does not have a name preceding the domain name (for example, xyz.com). Each domain can have at least one other subdomain.

The DNS database holds a set of resource records that associate a value with an entry in this database. Each resource has an identifier that allows you to determine what type of host it is. For instance, an Exchange 2000 server has an MX record because it is a mail exchanger host. Another type of record is a PTR record that associates IP addresses with hostnames, allowing for reverse DNS lookups. More on DNS and its role in AD and Exchange 2000 is covered later in this chapter in the section "Reliance on DNS."

DNS enables you to resolve readable names to IP addresses. DNS servers can be used for networks other than the Internet to resolve names, an efficient method of providing network-naming services. Microsoft has its own DNS server options; for the most part, they work just fine for any implementation people need. However, there is a more widely used DNS server that could be considered the DNS backbone of the Internet, **Berkley Internet Name Domain (BIND)**.

Created at Berkley University, BIND is considered a more reliable set of DNS services than most that are currently in use. BIND is open source and commonly found under Linux, but it can, and is, ported to other operating systems by intrepid open source programmers. BIND can be used with Windows 2000 AD and Exchange 2000 configurations, and if a BIND configuration already exists as part of your DNS solution, there is little need to change to another DNS server, such as Microsoft, unless you want some of the following benefits of the Microsoft DNS services:

- Increased fault tolerance
- Easier management (integration with Windows 2000)
- Easier security management
- Efficient replication or larger zones

Keep the following tips in mind when planning your DNS domain-naming conventions:

- Use names that relate to registered Internet DNS names (if any).
- Use Internet-acceptable characters (A–Z, a–z, 0–9, and -).
- Never use the same name more than once.
- Use distinct names that are relevant to the domain.
- Use the smallest number of separate domain trees possible.
- Make the first part of the DNS name the same as the system name.
- If you are dealing with an international domain-naming convention, make sure your domain names don't mean something offensive in another language.
- Use easy-to-remember names, not a jumble of characters.
- Ensure that domain names are not related to computer names; for instance, do not make the domain name calgary.calgary.com.

DNS Zones

For the best operation, a DNS server should include the requisite information for the entire tree it covers. However, the amount of DNS information might be more than a single DNS server can handle. Therefore, you might need to delegate authority for a portion of the domain namespace to another DNS server. When this happens, there is an entry for the forwarded domain name in the first DNS server that points to the second DNS server. This second DNS server contains the information needed to complete the request. The set of records that a DNS server manages is called a zone. The DNS server that contains a zone is authoritative for the names held in that zone; it's the zone that handles record requests for that domain.

DNS Records

DNS servers are basically databases that contain three pieces of information for each record: name, address, and type. The record's name is its DNS name, which is resolved to the record's address (IP address), and the type is the category of record (for example, MX for mail exchanger). Figure 2-4 shows an example of the nslookup utility in Windows 2000, which supplies DNS information for servers on your network and on the Internet.

```
C:\WINNT\System32\cmd.exe - nslookup
C:\>nslookup
Default Server:  edtnps01.telusplanet.net
Address:  199.185.220.36

> set type=MX
> microsoft.com
Server:  edtnps01.telusplanet.net
Address:  199.185.220.36

Non-authoritative answer:
microsoft.com   MX preference = 10, mail exchanger = mail4.microsoft.com
microsoft.com   MX preference = 10, mail exchanger = mail5.microsoft.com
microsoft.com   MX preference = 10, mail exchanger = mail1.microsoft.com
microsoft.com   MX preference = 10, mail exchanger = mail2.microsoft.com
microsoft.com   MX preference = 10, mail exchanger = mail3.microsoft.com

microsoft.com   nameserver = DNS2.CP.MSFT.NET
microsoft.com   nameserver = DNS1.CP.MSFT.NET
microsoft.com   nameserver = DNS1.TK.MSFT.NET
microsoft.com   nameserver = DNS2.TK.MSFT.NET
microsoft.com   nameserver = DNS3.UK.MSFT.NET
microsoft.com   nameserver = DNS4.UK.MSFT.NET
microsoft.com   nameserver = DNS3.JP.MSFT.NET
microsoft.com   nameserver = DNS4.JP.MSFT.NET
microsoft.com   nameserver = DNS1.DC.MSFT.NET
microsoft.com   nameserver = DNS2.DC.MSFT.NET
microsoft.com   nameserver = DNS1.SJ.MSFT.NET
microsoft.com   nameserver = DNS2.SJ.MSFT.NET
mail4.microsoft.com     internet address = 131.107.3.122
mail5.microsoft.com     internet address = 131.107.3.121
mail1.microsoft.com     internet address = 131.107.3.125
mail2.microsoft.com     internet address = 131.107.3.124
mail3.microsoft.com     internet address = 131.107.3.123
DNS2.CP.MSFT.NET        internet address = 207.46.138.21
DNS1.CP.MSFT.NET        internet address = 207.46.138.20
>
```

Figure 2-4 The output of the nslookup utlitity and a DNS record

It is possible for someone to deliberately or accidentally poison DNS records by inserting incorrect DNS record information in a DNS server, which is then replicated across other DNS servers. After the incorrect data is spread, it can be downright impossible for systems serviced by the affected DNS servers to access the modified sites by domain name. However, if they know the IP address, connections are still possible. The real purpose of DNS, however, is so that people do not need to know an exact address, just a typically easy-to-remember name.

There can be some confusing steps in configuring DNS records for your required services. For more information on DNS and Windows 2000, visit *http://www.microsoft.com/TechNet/win2000/dnsover.asp*.

Reliance on DNS

AD clients rely on DNS services being available because they use DNS to get the IP addresses of the **Lightweight Directory Access Protocol (LDAP)** and **Kerberos** services, which are used to access directory information for AD and connect securely to Exchange 2000, respectively. You will learn more about LDAP in Chapter 5 and more about Kerberos in Chapter 12, "Security and Encryption in Exchange 2000 Server." When a client needs to log on to a local domain controller, it sends its request to the DNS server; the DNS server holds a list of the domain controllers and their addresses and sends that information back to the client, allowing the client to connect to and log on to the fastest responding domain controller. Therefore, having a functional DNS server and ensuring high availability standards for clients accessing the DNS services help performance across the entire network.

Windows 2000 DNS services can provide a more secure method of DNS updates, called secure dynamic updates. This method enables automatic updates and replication to all the DNS zone databases in the forest, thus taking the burden of DNS maintenance off the administrator's hands. Administrators can delegate and set rights for users and computers that are making changes to the DNS records by using ACLs to manage security on them. Dynamic updating and applying ACLs on zone database entries are functions of Windows 2000 DNS services, and, as of this writing, aren't available in other DNS services. Windows 2000 offers DNS setup checklists and information, as shown in Figure 2-5.

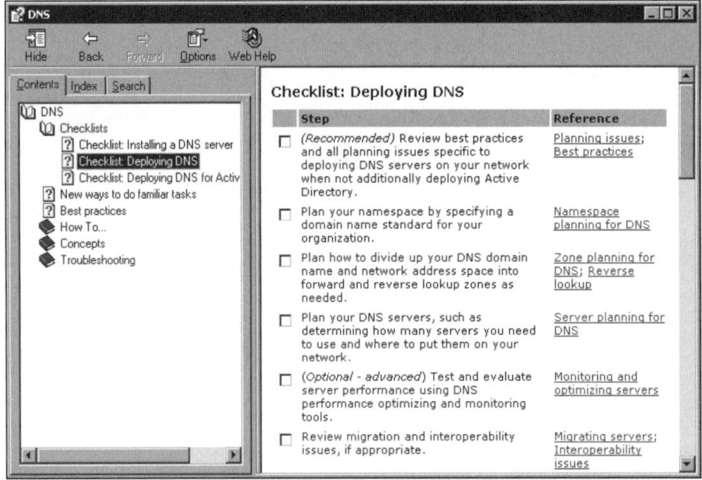

Figure 2-5 An example of the DNS setup checklists and information

Windows clients do not support dynamic DNS updating, so they must be manually updated to keep their DNS records current. If a dynamic host configuration protocol (DHCP) server is installed on the network, an administrator can specify what should happen if a name conflict occurs on the network. Usually, the client overrides the entry in the database to resolve a name conflict.

Using Non–Windows-Based DNS Systems

It is not necessary for AD to use a Windows 2000 DNS server, but it can make administration of AD and the network much easier. As you have learned, if there is already another DNS in place, such as BIND, it is usually recommended that you continue using that system unless you want to take advantage of some of the features mentioned earlier.

If you choose not to use the Windows 2000 DNS services, you must plan ahead to ensure fault tolerance. One way to ensure this is to enable zone transfers between different DNS zones. However, keep in mind that having zone transfers enabled can be a security risk and should be limited to trusted DNS servers only. The risk is that someone could transfer faulty DNS information to you using zone transfers, and poison your DNS records.

Some new features help reduce network traffic and the amount of data transferred across networks when DNS servers are synchronizing data with each other. Incremental zone transfers is a feature that transfers only the data that has changed in the DNS zone is transferred, instead of all the data in the zone, which is how zone transfers are typically done. Check Microsoft TechNet at *www.microsoft.com/technet* to read more about this DNS innovation. Regardless of the improvements in DNS transfers, careful planning remains important.

If you do implement a Windows 2000 DNS service, you will also benefit from not having to set up primary and secondary zones and incremental zone transfers. You can interconnect DNS servers with AD and use AD replication to synchronize DNS data. By doing so, you can minimize DNS administration and still offer better fault tolerance.

Chapter Summary

- The Microsoft Solutions Framework gives your organization a well-thought-out plan to carry out infrastructure changes such as implementing Exchange 2000. If you follow the phases outlined in the MSF—envisioning, planning, developing, and deploying—you and your team will effectively implement Exchange 2000 in a cost-effective and timely fashion.
- Active Directory planning can be time-consuming, but when your AD structure is properly planned and designed, it can offer tangible rewards, such as easing overall administrative effort, and help implement and maintain an AD-enabled network. Proper planning also assists in implementing other AD-enabled services, such as Exchange 2000.
- The Domain Name System can be a complex technology to understand, but time spent planning your DNS implementation improves not only how Exchange 2000 performs, but also how your whole AD forest functions. With properly assigned domain names and a thoughtfully designed layout of the domains in the forests and trees, an AD network can be much easier to maintain and administer—a task that was much more difficult before the advent of AD and its reliance on DNS.

KEY TERMS

access control lists (ACLs) — Security settings placed on objects that dictate what users and other systems can do in relation to the object.

Active Directory (AD) — A new domain management structure introduced with Windows 2000. AD uses the Domain Name System to perform naming resolution and is much more flexible and expandable than previous Windows domain management methods.

backup domain controllers (BDCs) — For redundancy and network performance, BDCs can perform backup authentication on the network in case the primary domain controller fails, or if the PDC is busy, the BDC can authenticate requests.

Berkley Internet Name Domain (BIND) — A set of services that is considered a very reliable set of Domain Name System services and is open source. It is commonly found under Linux, but can be used with Windows 2000 and Exchange 2000.

Domain Name System (DNS) — A commonly used service that translates IP addresses into readable English names. Active Directory uses DNS to handle all name translation requests from the clients and other services that use DNS.

domain tree — A grouping of domains, usually by a common organizational structure or naming scheme.

forest — The collection of domain trees that is usually the boundary of the main domain structure. Exchange 2000 can work only within its own forest, not with domains outside that forest.

global address list — A central depository for all objects and users in the Active Directory domain. For instance, users access the global address list when sending an e-mail to someone else in the domain; they can type a name instead of a full e-mail address. Active Directory searches for the name entered and sends it to the appropriate user if possible.

Kerberos — Named after the three-headed dog from Greek mythology, this authentication protocol has three main components to its design: the key distribution center, the client user, and the server.

Lightweight Directory Access Protocol (LDAP) — An open network protocol used to provide access to directory services and enable queries and modifications to the directory information structure.

Microsoft Solutions Framework (MSF) — A set of guidelines developed by Microsoft to help establish a reliable path for implementing infrastructure projects efficiently and properly.

naming contexts — Components that outline which naming information is stored in the naming databases Active Directory uses to organize the domain.

primary domain controller (PDC) — The main domain controller on the network. The PDC contains the master list of users and their rights on the network and replicates the data as necessary. PDCs are used only in Windows NT 4.0 domains, but can still be present in Active Directory mixed-mode networks.

Review Questions

1. When your organization wants to implement Exchange 2000, what is a potential benefit of using the Microsoft Solutions Framework? (Choose all that apply.)
   a. helps lay out clear project duties
   b. provides proactive risk management
   c. outlines an unbreakable schedule to follow
   d. gives you an easy way to extract more budgetary funding
2. What are the four phases of the MSF model?
   a. planning, scheduling, testing, deploying
   b. budgeting, scheduling, deploying, testing
   c. envisioning, planning, developing, deploying
   d. envisioning, developing, testing, deploying
3. Which of the following items should you outline during the envisioning phase of the MSF? (Choose all that apply.)
   a. organize the project's team
   b. plan the budget
   c. lay out the conceptual design
   d. perform preliminary research and development
4. Of the following job descriptions, which best describes the logistics manager's function in the team?
   a. gathers hardware and software for the project
   b. gets supplies needed for the team, such as office supplies
   c. provides an advisory function and acts as a liaison between management and the team
   d. determines the best way to deploy the product and plan an effective transition if required
5. When implementing Exchange 2000, it is necessary to gather ______________ from the entire company to help generate requests for the project's features.
6. Every project starts with a concept of what the final project will be. The concept is derived from ______________.
   a. the project vision and project requirements
   b. the project budget and project requirements
   c. the project vision and project planning
   d. the project planning and project timeline

7. Which of the following functions should be assigned during the planning phase?
   a. information gathering
   b. project budget
   c. proof of concept testing
   d. final testing
   e. both a and c
   f. both c and d
8. The finalized project plan and schedule can't really be determined until the project resources have been planned. True or False?
9. The first step in validating the operation of servers and other project components is to test the functionality of the core set of specifications laid out in the ______________ phase.
10. It is important to have ______________ available during the end-user testing phase.
    a. management approval
    b. end-user training
    c. documentation
    d. research and development staff
    e. both a and d
    f. both b and c
11. When users access resources on other trusted domains, they have unlimited access to the files on those domains. True or False?
12. An example of a(n) ______________ is a root domain trusting another domain that has an established trust with another domain, effectively implying trust with the original root domain.
13. What is a common reason for isolating a particular domain from other domains, and limiting the trusts established with that domain? (Choose all that apply.)
    a. Separate domain administrators cannot agree on a common way to manage domains.
    b. There is a corporate takeover and the administrators want to protect sensitive data.
    c. There has been a problem with rival companies accessing files on that domain.
    d. An administrator wants to practice resource management without affecting the rest of the network.
14. With Windows 2000, a single domain cannot efficiently contain multiple physical locations. True or False?

15. As in Windows NT 4.0, you cannot demote domain controllers under Windows 2000 Active Directory without removing them from the network and reinstalling the operating system. True or False?
16. When adding domain controllers to your domain tree, it is important to look at which of the following issues?
    a. fault-tolerance requirements
    b. network performance between separate physical networks
    c. type of software being run for network services
    d. number of files being shared between users
    e. both a and b
    f. both b and d
17. In the domain name Calgary.exchange.xyz.com, which part of the domain name is the parent domain?
    a. Calgary
    b. exchange
    c. xyz
    d. com
18. Exchange 2000 clients use the ________________ to look up Active Directory objects and mailboxes.
19. When creating organizational units in a domain, which of the following tasks is most important?
    a. Create backups of user objects.
    b. Set object access control using the organizational units.
    c. Document what each organizational unit does.
    d. Ensure that you have the software and hardware to create.
20. After you have installed Exchange 2000, you cannot make further changes to your domain naming contexts because the schema has permanently changed them. True or False?
21. Which of the following features is the main reason that BIND is commonly used for DNS services?
    a. It has a faster response to client requests.
    b. BIND is optimized for Microsoft platforms.
    c. Entries cannot be tampered with by anyone but administrators.
    d. It's reliable.
    e. It cannot perform zone transfers; therefore, it is more secure.

22. What has happened when a DNS server has been poisoned?
    a. Someone has installed a mirrored DNS server to hijack requests.
    b. DNS requests have outstripped the server's ability to process requests, thereby shutting down the server.
    c. Someone purposefully or accidentally inserts faulty DNS information in the server.
    d. The DNS server loses the proper name for site entries in the server.
23. An alternative to the Microsoft DNS service is ______________, but this service is not recommended unless necessary.

HANDS-ON PROJECTS

Project 2-1

Verifying DNS functionality can be useful when troubleshooting DNS-related issues. The utility you will use in this project, nslookup, is also handy for confirming DNS information for a particular server or network, such as your Internet service provider. This project assumes that an operating DNS service has been set up on a Windows 2000 server.

To verify DNS functionality:

1. If necessary, log on to your system. After the system has finished booting to the desktop, click **Start**, and then click **Run**.
2. Type **nslookup** in the Open text box, and then press **Enter**. You should see the active DNS server listed, including its IP address.
3. At the prompt, type **127.0.0.1**, and then press **Enter**. If the DNS service is responding, you should see localhost with the address you entered listed. See Figure 2-6 for a sample confirmation of DNS operability using the nslookup utility.

```
C:\WINNT\System32\cmd.exe - nslookup
Microsoft Windows 2000 [Version 5.00.2195]
(C) Copyright 1985-2000 Microsoft Corp.

C:\>nslookup
Default Server:  edtnps01.telusplanet.net
Address:  199.185.220.36

> 127.0.0.1
Server:  edtnps01.telusplanet.net
Address:  199.185.220.36

Name:    localhost
Address:  127.0.0.1

>
```

Figure 2-6 Using nslookup to verify that DNS is working

4. Type **exit**, and then press **Enter** to close the nslookup utility.

Project 2-2

2

ForestPrep is run only once at the start of the Exchange 2000 installation process to extend the domain schema to include Exchange AD objects. This project assumes that you have a copy of Exchange 2000 to install, and that there are no previous versions of Exchange on the domain.

To install ForestPrep:

1. Insert the Exchange 2000 CD into your CD-ROM drive, or locate the setup files (if placed on a hard drive).
2. Click **Start**, click **Run**, and then type ***X:\setup*****\i386\setup /ForestPrep** in the Open text box. Replace *X:* with the location of the Exchange 2000 CD-ROM or the location of the Exchange 2000 installation files (make sure you have typed the command correctly or ForestPrep will not install), and then press **Enter**.

If you don't find the setup file in this directory, ask your instructor or technical support person for help. The pathname could be different, depending on the CD you are using.

3. The Exchange 2000 Installation Wizard appears. In the welcome window, click the **Next** button to proceed with the wizard. Continue clicking the **Next** button, if necessary, until you get to the Component Selection window.
4. The Component Selection window opens with ForestPrep in the Action column. Click the **Next** button to proceed.
5. The Installation Type window opens, where you must specify what type of Exchange organization you will use. You are either creating a new Exchange 2000 organization or upgrading from an existing Exchange 5.5 organization. Leave this selection at its default (Create a new Exchange Organization), as shown in Figure 2-7 on the next page, and then click the **Next** button to proceed.
6. The Organization Name window opens. Enter the name for your Exchange organization in the Organization Name text box. Remember, this name cannot be changed without reinstalling Exchange, so choose carefully. After you have entered the name, click the **Next** button.
7. The Exchange 2000 Administrator Account window opens. In the Account text box, enter the name of the account you want to use for administering Exchange, and then click the **Next** button.
8. The wizard starts the ForestPrep process. You can watch the progress as the Active Directory schema expand. This can take 20 minutes or longer. When the installation completion window appears, click the **Finish** button to complete the wizard.

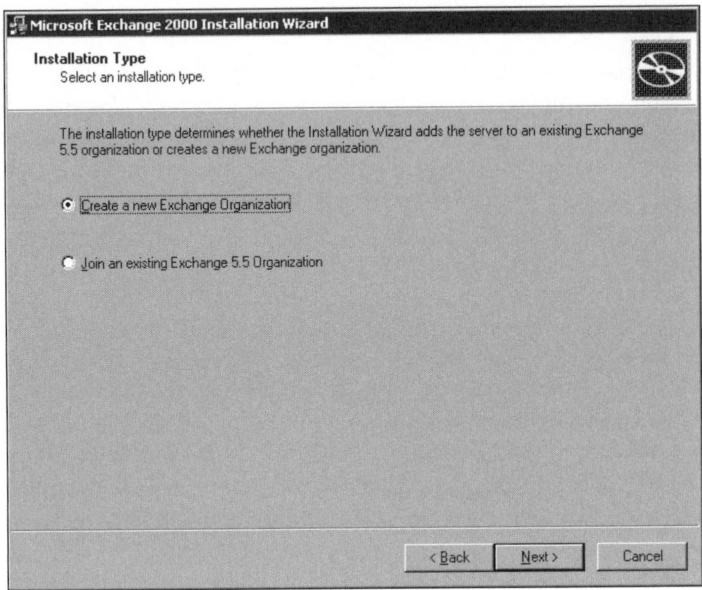

Figure 2-7 Selecting an installation type

Project 2-3

This lab helps reinforce the different steps of the MSF.

To match steps of the MSF with the appropriate phases:

1. Create a two-column table similar to Table 2-3, but allow for additional entries beyond the two listed here.

Table 2-3 Matching Steps of the MSF with the Appropriate Phase

Step	Phase
Organize the project team	Envisioning
Establish the project schedule	Planning

2. Enter at least 10 different main steps used in the MSF process in the Step column. Do not count the two listed already!
3. In the Phase column, enter the corresponding phase for the steps you listed in Step 2.

Project 2-4

This project shows you how to refresh your client system's DNS configuration information. This procedure can help confirm that your DNS servers are working properly before installing Exchange 2000 Server. This project requires a Windows 2000 Server, with DNS installed and active, that is connected to a network with at least one other workstation. The workstation can use any operating system, but Windows 2000 Professional is preferred and must be configured to exist on the same network as the server.

To renew DNS configuration information:

1. Power on your server and allow it to boot normally. Next, power on your workstation and allow it to boot normally. If the workstation requires you to log on, do so.
2. Open a command-prompt window. To do this, click **Start**, and then click **Run**. In the Open text box, type **cmd**, and then press **Enter**. A new command-prompt window opens.
3. Type **Ipconfig /registerdns**, and then press **Enter**.
4. Windows returns a message stating that the registration of DNS records has been initiated and the results of the registration will be recorded in the Event Viewer in 15 minutes.
5. After you see the response in Step 4, close the command-prompt window and any open windows. After 15 minutes, view the logs in Event Viewer to see if there are any stop errors that indicate a failed client DNS registration. Close any open windows and applications.

Project 2-5

This project helps you understand where the DNS configuration information is stored and determine what DNS servers you have installed and configured. This project requires a Windows 2000 Server with DNS installed and active.

To look at the DNS configuration console in Windows 2000:

1. If necessary, power on your server and allow it to boot normally. Next, power on your workstation and allow it to boot normally. If the workstation requires you to log on, do so.
2. Open the DNS console. To do this, click **Start**, point to **Programs**, point to **Administrative Tools**, and then click **DNS**.
3. Locate the server entry for the server you are on. Click the + next to the various branches of the tree that allow expansion. After you have expanded all the different trees, take note of the servers listed under the Forward Lookup Zones folder and the Reverse Lookup Zones folder.

4. Look at the configuration information under each server by right-clicking the server entry and clicking **Properties** on the shortcut menu. Be sure not to change anything you see. It is worthwhile to note the different tabs and the information they contain. This information can be used for future reference should you need to add more servers or perform a restoration or maintenance on your DNS services.
5. After you finish analyzing the information, close any open windows or applications.

CASE PROJECTS

Case 1

XYZ Company wants to install Exchange 2000. The company is already using Active Directory with an efficient domain naming structure that had a rocky transition and deployment. Now they want your consulting firm to deploy Exchange 2000 in an efficient manner. What four phases of the MSF model should you use, and why? What is the first step in using the MSF that will form the basis of the project? What information must you gather before starting the planning phase?

Case 2

XYZ Company has been taken over by ABC Ltd. Although it is a friendly takeover, the two head administrators at these companies disagree on how to effectively manage the domains for the companies. In this situation, what is the best plan of action?

Case 3

LMN Inc. has started to grow quite quickly and has added a new Finance Department on a different floor of its building. This new Finance Department is connected to the same physical network backbone, but has sensitive data and requires focused administration to handle the management of users and data. You have been asked to determine the best way to add this new department to the domain with the best organization possible. What can be done to take some of the administrative burden off your hands? How should security between domains be handled? Will Exchange 2000 work with what you propose?

CHAPTER

3

PLANNING AN EXCHANGE 2000 SERVER DESIGN SCENARIO

After reading this chapter and completing the exercises, you will be able to:

- Review the Microsoft Solution Framework envisioning and planning phases to assess requirements for deploying Exchange 2000 Server
- Understand user, company, and network requirements to plan for a successful Exchange 2000 Server deployment
- Understand the Exchange 2000 Server architecture to make full use of its features in your design scenario
- Understand Exchange 2000 Server site design to determine the proper server configuration and types of connectors
- Understand coexistence and migration issues with Exchange Server 5.5 and Exchange 2000 Server to plan for a successful upgrade

In Chapter 2, "Planning for Windows 2000," you learned about the Microsoft Solutions Framework (MSF) and the four main phases of this project management tool. You also learned about fundamental Active Directory (AD) layout and design considerations as well as Domain Name System (DNS) planning and design.

In this chapter, you revisit the envisioning and planning phases of the MSF to better understand how to assess user, company, and network infrastructure requirements when planning an Exchange 2000 upgrade. You also learn about the Exchange 2000 architecture and the major factors in Exchange Server site design to best prepare you to design your own Exchange 2000 deployment. Finally, you look at migration and coexistence issues when moving from Exchange 5.5 to Exchange 2000 or running your network in a mixed-mode environment to understand how a migration from an existing Exchange 5.5 organization works with Exchange 2000 Server.

THE MICROSOFT SOLUTIONS FRAMEWORK REVISITED

As you learned in Chapter 2, the MSF can be a very useful tool to help you plan and implement large-scale infrastructure changes such as putting Exchange 2000 or Active Directory into action. The MSF is divided into four main phases: envisioning, planning, developing, and deploying. In this chapter, you take an in-depth look at the envisioning and planning phases to develop an understanding of how to assess user, company, and network requirements when planning for an upgrade; in Chapter 4, "Preparing to Deploy Exchange 2000 Server," you will delve into the developing and deploying phases. Reviewing the different phases helps put you into the right mindset while you learn about the related steps in those phases.

The envisioning and planning phases help you assess requirements for deploying Exchange 2000 Server. Refer to Chapter 2 for more detailed information on the specific steps in these phases, but as a quick refresher, the envisioning phase consists of organizing the project's team, generating the project requirements, defining the project vision, project scope, and any assumptions about the project, and creating the project's conceptual design layout. The planning phase involves creating the functional specification plan, which lays out the final solution to be delivered to the client; the master project plan, which outlines how the project is designed, tested, and carried out; and the project schedule, which gives dates for beginning and completing steps in the project.

Each of these phases must be completed to benefit from the MSF process. If the steps in all phases are performed properly, you stand a good chance of encountering fewer issues and avoiding common problems when deploying an infrastructure change such as implementing Exchange 2000. (However, as with any technology deployment, you should be prepared for an issue or two to crop up that needs resolving.) The last thing you want is to deploy a partially working or poorly planned Exchange 2000 server and be constantly adjusting, fixing, or inevitably rebuilding the system, which is troublesome, wastes time, and costs money.

The MSF has some room for flexibility; although it is designed to be a complete process, many smaller sites might not need to use all the steps. In a smaller Exchange rollout, you should still use the MSF, but perhaps use only the steps that provide the most benefit to your organization. For instance, if your organization is small and the only people who will use Exchange 2000 Server are the people on the project team, there is likely no need to have multiple stages of testing before finally rolling out the installation.

UNDERSTANDING THE CURRENT REQUIREMENTS FOR EXCHANGE 2000 SERVER

3

Determining the requirements for Exchange 2000 Server encompasses more than simply knowing what the hardware requirements are for the software to run. Requirements run the gamut from hardware and software to users' needs, the organization's needs, and the network infrastructure's needs.

User Requirements

User requirements consist of what users must have to perform their jobs and what features would help make their jobs easier or more efficient. When users communicate their needs to the project team (see Chapter 2 for more details on the project team members), it is important to separate actual requirements from an unnecessary "wish list." Often users have a tendency to ask for features that sound interesting, rather than those which are actually useful.

After the team members have collected feedback on user requirements, they might have to translate requirements from users who are technically less savvy into actual technical features or specifications. This translation step not only helps the team plan which features must be installed or enabled for the rollout, but also helps the team carefully assess the features to make sure they function in the way users need. Table 3-1 shows some examples of translating possible user requirements to actual technical requirements.

Table 3-1 Comparing User Requirements to Technical Requirements

User Requirements	Technical Requirements
Ability to have several people collaborating on documents and projects	Install and set up Instant Messaging and NetMeeting Services
Ability to publish HTML-type documents from Microsoft Word or FrontPage to Exchange public folders	Install and set up the Exchange 2000 Web Storage System
Ability to find messages and documents quickly	Configure full-text indexing in mailbox stores

Other user requirements must be determined, including what the organization considers necessary for users, beneficial features they want the users to have, and features the organization does not allow. For example, some companies may have strict rules against instant messaging, so even if all the users want it, the organization might not allow it because of possible security risks or because it fears a drop in productivity if employees use instant messaging inappropriately. It is a good idea to compare what the users want and what the organization allows and wants, and then work with management to hammer out the final list of user requirements to be implemented during the initial rollout.

If there's a particular feature management doesn't know about that could improve productivity, suggest it at this point. Offer to demonstrate it during the project's initial testing or installation phases so management can get a better idea of whether it should be included.

Company Requirements

A company's needs are often varied and can include critical features, rules and regulations, security concerns, budgetary concerns, or physical space limitations (for instance, not enough room for a new server if required). Company requirements ultimately shape the guidelines for the core features to be included in the project plan. User requirements are important to include in the plan, but the company requirements likely form the basic services that Exchange 2000 must include for the service to interact with other services or networks.

Most companies consider e-mail a critical Internet application because of its advantages in allowing people to communicate quickly and concisely. However, it can also generate more requirements when users and companies want additional e-mail features, such as Outlook Web Access, or when varied storage options are needed, such as public folders.

The company requirements usually go hand in hand with the organization's rules and regulations for conduct, legal issues, and security risks. For instance, company rules and regulations might outline appropriate e-mail usage (for example, no personal or lewd e-mail) or address e-mail retention and security issues (such as being required by law to keep messages for a set amount of time or being concerned that e-mail held on the servers could allow someone to gain access to sensitive company information).

Budgetary concerns and physical space limitations can also limit what the company requirements allow. For instance, if the company simply does not have the necessary cash to purchase additional hardware that a particular feature requires or if there isn't room to add a new piece of equipment, such as a server, the company might decide that feature is not necessary or feasible at this time.

After the project team has collected feedback to outline the user and company requirements for messaging services, you can then look at the features and functions Exchange 2000 brings to the table and assess how to meet those user and company requirements. To do that, review the features Exchange 2000 offers and what services and components are needed to implement those features. After outlining the required services and components, determine whether additional hardware and configuration is necessary to implement these services and components. Take this information and compare it with the company requirements and the budgetary and physical space concerns to assess whether the requirements will be met. After determining how to meet the requirements, you should consider how to improve on the implementation by using other features designed to simplify or expand on Exchange 2000 Server abilities.

Company guidelines on inappropriate e-mail usage are becoming more common these days, so it is important to not ignore any guidelines addressing that issue. With companies' growing concerns about sexual harassment through e-mail and leakage of sensitive company information, they must protect themselves through these guidelines. Make sure you adhere to any that are in place.

Current Network Infrastructure Requirements

Just as understanding requirements from the user and company perspectives is important, it is also important to understand what the current network consists of. Once you have an understanding of the current network and services infrastructure, you can then determine how it will work with your Exchange 2000 Server deployment and what modifications might have to be made to accommodate the network infrastructure change. The minimum requirements for Exchange 2000 Server are discussed in Chapter 5, "Installation of Exchange 2000 Server in New Environments."

How the network is designed can make or break the project because if the network is not organized properly or doesn't perform well, installing another product such as Exchange 2000 Server makes the network even more difficult to manage and potentially causes more performance issues. It is not unusual for changes to be required. However, if the network's design makes deploying Exchange 2000 difficult because of improper organization or poor performance, additional planning and implementation of other services could become necessary for the project to move forward. For instance, the type and design of the Domain Name System (DNS) and the performance of a wide area network need to be understood to best prepare the team to develop an effective plan.

Creating network diagrams (as well as server equipment diagrams) can help IT departments plan the proper organization of their networks and thus their Exchange installation. Network diagrams are also useful when it comes time to troubleshoot, move equipment, or make changes to wiring. When planning network diagrams, include as much information as possible to help anyone not familiar with your site, but not so much as to compromise security.

The Existing Domain Name System

As you learned in Chapter 2, Exchange 2000 relies on Windows 2000 Active Directory, and in turn AD relies on the DNS to provide name resolution services. Exchange 2000 is capable of using any standard DNS service, such as Berkeley Internet Name Domain (BIND). However, the alternative DNS service should be stable and operate properly to get the optimum performance from AD and, consequently, Exchange 2000. As the old adage says, "You are only as strong as your weakest link"—and you certainly don't want that weak link to be your DNS service.

Older DNS services, such as those in Windows NT 4.0, used **Windows Internet Naming Service (WINS)** as the naming service; DNS was used only for Internet name resolution, Simple Mail Transport Protocol (SMTP), and **Outlook Web Access (OWA)**.

(OWA enables remote clients to connect to Exchange 2000 via a compliant Web browser to read e-mail and other Exchange 2000 services without the need for another client software package, such as Outlook 2000.) For best performance and compatibility, it is usually a good idea to have your Exchange 2000 server(s) occupying a DNS server that's handled by a Windows 2000 DNS service because any name-resolution requests are fulfilled more quickly.

When clients are trying to locate the closest Global Catalog server, their client software, such as Outlook 2000, uses DNS services to find it. Also, Exchange 2000 uses DNS services to locate additional Exchange servers in the forest domain. With such critical DNS services in use, Exchange 2000 must have a fully functioning DNS service. When you are planning for your Exchange 2000 implementation, you should spend some time assessing the organization's current DNS services. Here are some issues that should be discussed during your assessment:

- Is there an existing DNS service?
- What operating system is hosting the existing DNS service?
- What type and version of DNS service is it?
- Is AD in place and utilizing this DNS service?
- Are there any DNS namespaces already in place that need to be integrated?
- Do the client systems use this DNS service, another service, or none at all?

Determining the answers to these questions gives you the best idea of how DNS is set up and used. If the network is utilizing WINS and not DNS, the organization should move from WINS to DNS so that Exchange 2000 Server can operate properly.

If you do decide to implement BIND as your DNS of choice, you should run version 8.1.2 or later because it supports service records and dynamic updates. These two features, used by Exchange 2000 and AD, improve the way DNS performs.

Wide Area Network Requirements and Structure

Many larger businesses make use of a wide area network (WAN) to connect offices in different locations. WANs can be different sites linked by some type of network connection anywhere around the globe or just across town. Most agree that a WAN is basically a network that's not connected to the same direct LAN you have in your office by means of a common switch or hub; instead, WANs are a few local LANs linked via network connections over a distance.

Although many companies cannot afford or manage a WAN, let alone many WANs, if you do work for an organization with WANs, you need to see how WAN requirements can affect your Exchange 2000 installation. Quite often, IT departments make system and infrastructure changes without considering the possible ramifications to the network and WAN structure and operation. After determining the current network design and WAN structure, you should decide how routing groups should be set up for Exchange 2000 to achieve the best possible performance and network redundancy (the ability for the network connection to still function when a segment of the network fails or the connection is lost). Depending on the network design, extra routing groups can be created so that data has more than one path to follow between other servers in the network. In some cases, grouping similar servers and networks in one routing group can improve performance; creating additional connections to that system or group of systems provides redundancy in case one of the network links goes down.

If the organization or WAN is large, determining the network's scope and design could take a lot of time and research. However, the project team might have already gathered much of this information during the envisioning and planning phases, especially if the organization has gone through a Windows 2000 AD rollout before taking on an Exchange 2000 installation. Many of the same issues affect both Exchange 2000 and Windows 2000 AD, so consult with the team members who oversaw the Windows 2000 AD rollout and review the documentation they generated during and after the project.

If you want to get the best overall overview of a WAN, it's a good idea to design a basic network architecture diagram. (A sample WAN configuration is shown in Figure 3-1.) This diagram should include the major network connections, servers, and other essential network resources, including the bandwidth availability between connections (if laying out a WAN). By creating a basic network diagram, you get an overview of where potential problems might crop up. For instance, when analyzing your network diagram, you notice that the network connection between two sites is only a slow dial-up modem connection. You would then take the appropriate steps to increase the connection's speed or make the necessary changes in Exchange 2000 to make sure data is sent over this connection in a timely fashion. Users and servers would then have the appropriate up-to-date directory synchronization for data and e-mail messages. An alternative fix in this situation would be installing an additional connection to another server on the network that has a faster connection with your other servers. Instead of relying on the one slow connection, you would need to use routing through faster connections to transfer data.

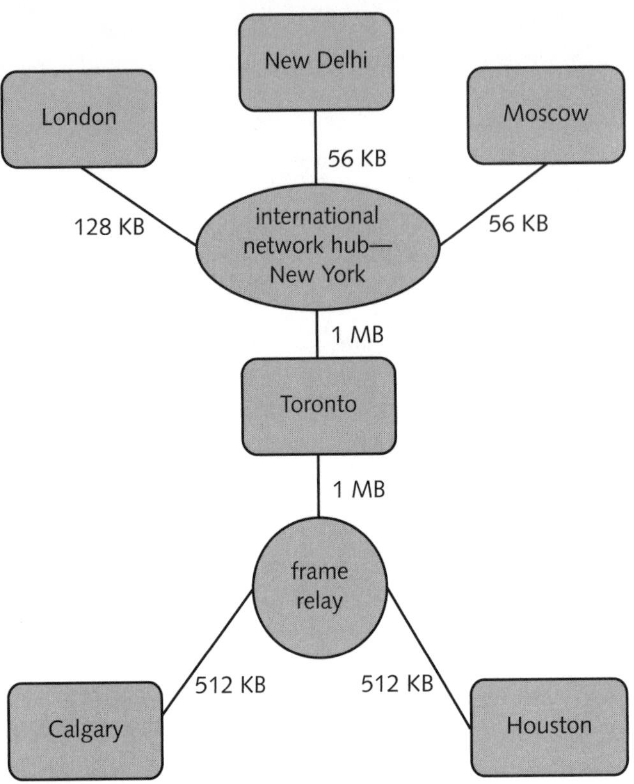

Figure 3-1 Diagram of a WAN configuration

On the network diagram, each location and connection on the network or WAN should have more detailed, real-world connection information, such as typical connection reliability issues. With this information, you can review the big picture and then take a closer look at each location as necessary. This overview of the network at large allows you to plan how the deployment will go and ensure proper placement of routing groups by showing where servers should be grouped and linked to get the best possible network performance when synchronizing and transferring data between servers. When designing these more detailed outlines of each connection, try to include the following information:

- Connection origin
- Connection destination
- Connection speed (or average speed if shared line)
- Connection type (T1, DSL, modem, and so on)
- Alternative connection paths to the network
- Available bandwidth

- Type of protocols active on the connection
- Internet information associated with the connection (IP address, domain, and so on)

When dealing with large WAN deployments of Exchange 2000 Server with many network connections and sites, it can be a lot of work to properly plan for and implement an effective solution.

WANs that span large bodies of water or territories with uncertain political status can muddy the situation when you're trying to plan your WAN connectivity solutions, especially if a certain level of uptime is expected. For example, if the new ruling party in a territory your connection spans decides to disable your network connection because it doesn't agree with your organization's type of business, you should have a few back-up plans to ensure that your network data flow remains intact. Make sure to address these types of difficulties when outlining your plan.

UNDERSTANDING THE ARCHITECTURE OF EXCHANGE 2000 SERVER

Like anything else in this world, knowing how something works internally gives you a better grasp of how to work with it. Take, for instance, an automotive engine: A mechanic who doesn't know how an engine works will have a much harder time figuring out why it won't run. Knowing how the architecture and major components of Exchange 2000 Server come together helps you and your team during the planning and deploying phases. This knowledge also proves invaluable when performing troubleshooting before or after the deployment. To understand the architecture of Exchange 2000 Server, you need to examine its components, each of which performs a different task. Independently, they don't do much, but together they provide a seamless service that, if set up properly, allows user interaction with a minimum of effort.

The Components of Exchange 2000 Server

Exchange 2000 Server is made up of different components: stores, groups, and services. The following sections focus on two Exchange 2000 stores and Exchange 2000 storage groups. Each of these components serves an important function in Exchange 2000; learning what these components do gives you a better idea of how to plan your organization's Exchange 2000 deployment strategy.

The Information Store

At the heart of Exchange 2000 lies the **Information Store**. This component is basically a relational database technology that stores information in tables and then matches those tables to other tables to relate information. Each major system in Exchange 2000 is basically a database; mailbox stores and public folder stores, for example, are simply databases.

The Information Store is further organized into storage groups, which are combinations of mailbox stores and public folder stores, and manages these databases and transfers the data back and forth accordingly, as shown in Figure 3-2. The Windows 2000 service called Store.exe manages these databases, which come together to form the Information Store.

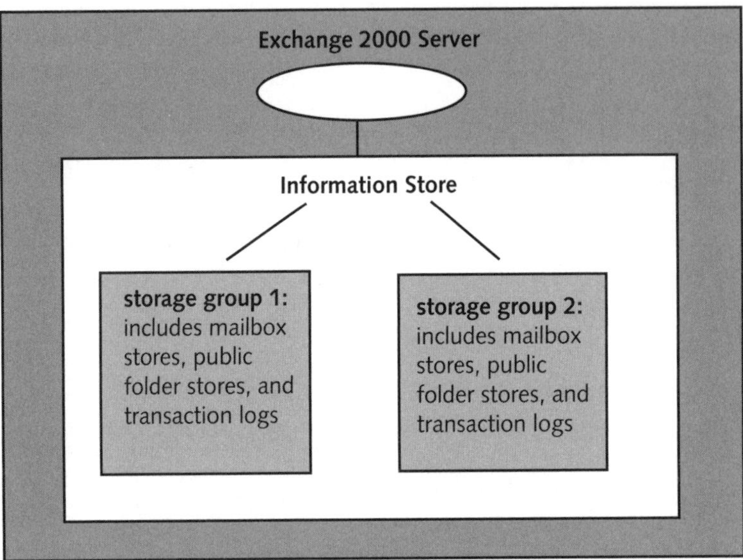

Figure 3-2 Structure of the Information Store and storage groups in Exchange 2000

The Information Store uses a single-instance storage design that enables Exchange to more efficiently transfer mail to recipients. It works by taking a message destined for multiple users and storing it in the Information Store, and then sending the message recipients a pointer (a shortcut) to the message stored in the Information Store. This method makes delivering multiple messages much faster than other commonly used designs, which send out an exact copy of the message to every person specified in the message's intended recipient list. Sending out multiple copies can be rather cumbersome, and it consumes a lot of network bandwidth if several people are receiving the same message, especially if there is a file attachment.

The Information Store also handles any transaction logging for activity within and between the databases, including clients' requests for information and mail transfer between the Information Store and mail delivery services, such as logging a user's request to open an e-mail stored on the server. The Information Store is not without fault, though; as it grows in size, it can be a real drain on resources and requires a bit of maintenance (like any database) to keep running in an orderly fashion. With the Informatioin Store handling all the actual storage of mail, transaction logs, and directory configuration information, it can expand rather quickly, even in small installations. Proper planning and maintenance, however, keep the Information Store and, therefore, Exchange 2000 running smoothly. For example, dividing the mailbox stores, transaction logs, and public folders into more streamlined storage groups (the section "The Storage Group" later in this chapter covers this in more detail) can decidedly reduce the overall size of the Information Store.

The Mailbox Store

The **mailbox store** is an Exchange database that contains the message information and settings for each Exchange user's mailbox. Exchange 2000 Server brings about a few improvements over Exchange 5.5 and earlier designs in that it can handle more than one mailbox and public folder store. With earlier versions, the entire mailbox was located under one big list with no features for organizing it, which made the mailbox store large and difficult to back up and restore efficiently.

Exchange 2000 changes all of that with its improved database-management features. Because you can now have multiple databases, you can have multiple mailbox stores and organize them any way you like. These new organized mailboxes are smaller than the one large mailbox, which makes backing up and restoring the mailbox stores much quicker and easier.

Even though the new database design of Exchange 2000 Server does allow for more flexibility and multiple mailbox stores, keep in mind that additional mailbox stores inevitably cause more administrative work in setting up backups, replication, and other tasks that need to be handled for each mailbox store.

In addition to these improvements, the new mailbox store design allows you to independently stop and start a mailbox store without affecting any other mailbox store operations. The same holds true for restoring mailbox stores, which can be done without affecting users in another mailbox store. This feature aids administration because in Exchange 5.5, the entire mailbox store had to be stopped, which affected all the other users while a mailbox was being restored. When you are upgrading from an Exchange 5.5 installation, you should consider the following factors when assessing the best plan for migrating user mailboxes:

- What is the default mailbox size limit?
- How long does the system keep deleted mail?
- Are there any special-needs mailboxes (such as one mailbox shared by several users)?
- Is there more than one company on the Exchange server? Some companies called **application service providers** provide server space-sharing for organizations.

After assessing these factors, you should have a better idea how to approach migrating or implementing your new Exchange 2000 Server mailbox layout for the best possible organization and ease of administration.

Creating a specific mailbox store for just the president of the company or the management committee can make it much more efficient to quickly back up and restore this typically critical mailbox. Because of the extra administrative effort, however, you should avoid setting up too many of these separate mailbox stores for "special" users.

The Storage Group

The **storage group (SG)** is a new Exchange 2000 feature that gives you more customization options for organizing Exchange 2000 components. SGs are databases used to organize the mailbox store, public folders, and related transaction logs into a singular administrative unit. Every SG is handled by Exchange 2000 Server in its own process, thus providing better overall reliability by not allowing the other SGs access to the system resources it needs; also, if one storage group fails, it doesn't bring down the others. In addition, the transaction logs associated with the SGs should keep their respective records on separate drive partitions to provide fault tolerance if data needs to be restored in an SG; you can improve this design by using a redundant array of independent disks (RAID) to add an additional level of fault tolerance and, in some cases, improved performance. An example of optimal transaction log configuration for storage groups is shown in Figure 3-3.

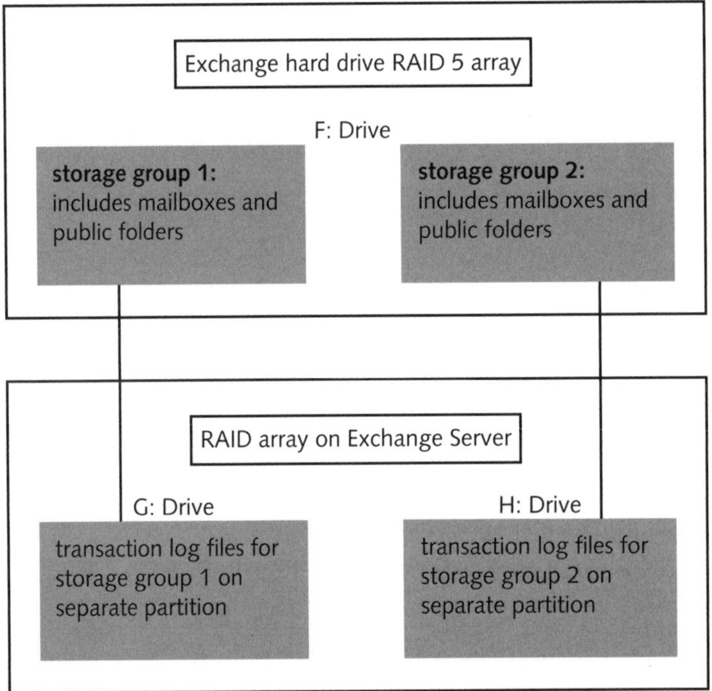

Figure 3-3 An optimal transaction log configuration for storage groups

The level of organization that SGs provide also makes allocating resources (hardware or personnel) easier. Being able to organize SGs into company-, department-, or even location-specific designs is an advantage when your Exchange 2000 implementation encompasses more than one company or location because you can dedicate Exchange 2000 SGs for each location, instead of installing one large SG for the entire company. For instance, users in one remote location might not be able to access information in SGs stored a great distance away because performance is slow over your WAN connection to the remote site. By using this feature of location-specific design, application service providers, for example, can tailor SGs for individual needs and provide the reliability and uptime companies want. In addition, when application service providers need to perform maintenance on a particular mailbox store, they don't have to worry about affecting the rest of their customers. As you learned in Chapter 1, "An Overview of Microsoft Exchange 2000 Server," you are limited to four different storage groups per Exchange 2000 Server installation. If you add more Exchange 2000 Server installations to your network, you can then have additional SGs if needed.

Understanding Exchange 2000 Server Site Design

For many organizations, deploying Exchange 2000 Server is often not as simple as installing Exchange 2000 and plugging it into the network. There can be many different configurations, duties, and servers that are part of an organization's Exchange deployment. Some types of Exchange 2000 server configurations can help direct mail between domains; others can help provide redundancy or even determine how Exchange 2000 performs.

To better understand how you can optimize the performance and functionality of your Exchange 2000 installation, the information in the following sections about different types of servers and configurations will be quite helpful. For instance, bridgehead servers can be used to provide dedicated replication services between other servers for message transfer. Also, you can use connector servers as dedicated servers to provide various types of site connectors between other e-mail servers and Exchange servers. Using servers in this fashion can help alleviate strain on an Exchange server, especially if the network is large.

Establishing Bridgehead Servers

Bridgehead servers in Exchange 2000 are slightly different from previous designs in earlier versions. Previously, bridgehead servers were any servers that had one or more connectors linking multiple Exchange sites or providing connections to the Internet for Exchange servers. Bridgehead servers also handled mail transfer between the servers they connected and replicated public folder and directory information as necessary. An Exchange 5.5 bridgehead server design is shown in Figure 3-4.

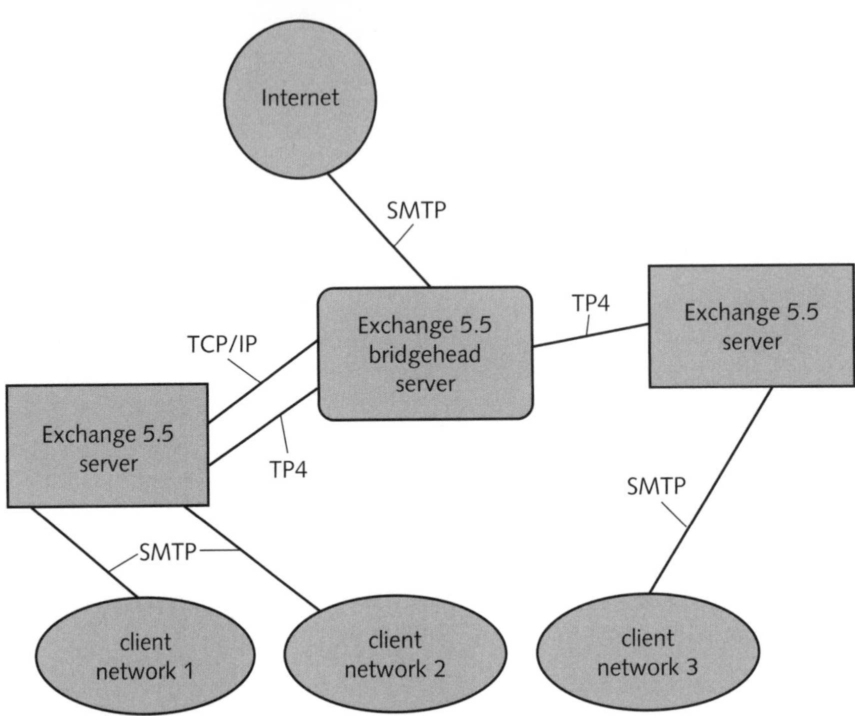

Figure 3-4 Exchange 5.5 bridgehead server design

For Exchange 2000, bridgehead servers still exist and perform the same basic functions; however, the way they perform them has changed. Instead of transferring data, such as mail, public folder, and directory information, Exchange 2000 bridgehead servers replicate the data between sites using the global catalog as a central point of data. Although the global catalog can be replicated to other servers, the data in the global catalog is the same for every domain in the domain forest, making replication as easy as comparing the current global catalog to the information on the other servers and updating the global catalog with the information held on other servers to produce one unified address book. This is a much more efficient method of supplying the necessary information for Exchange servers and clients because Exchange 2000 bridgehead servers are dedicated to replicating the information; they have to update only the information that has changed. Figure 3-5 illustrates an Exchange 2000 bridgehead server design. Use Table 3-2 to determine the key elements for each bridgehead server connection in the network.

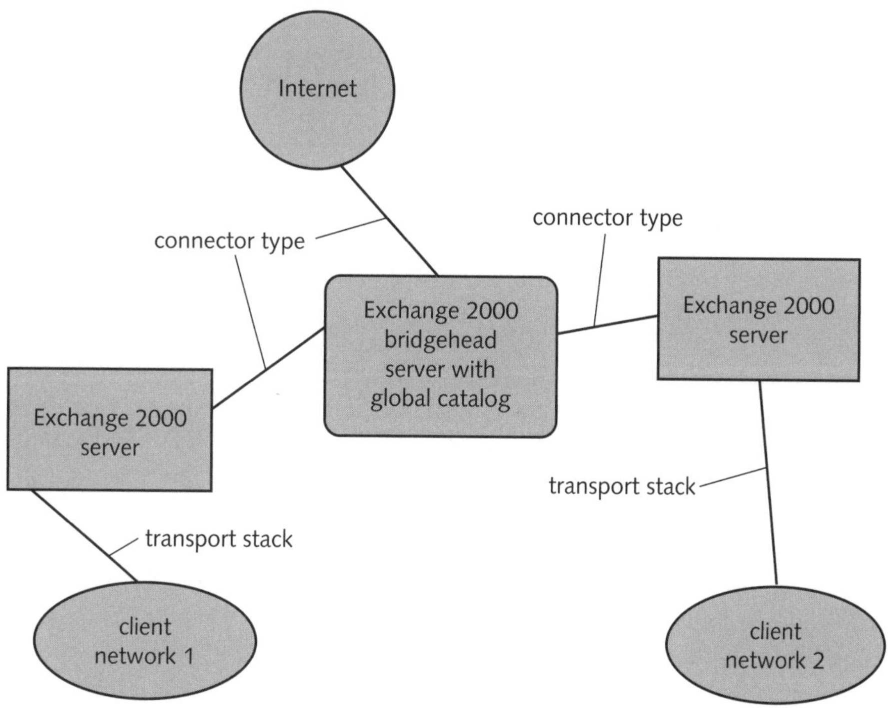

Figure 3-5 Exchange 2000 bridgehead server design

Table 3-2 Exchange Connector Issues for Bridgehead Servers

Connector Issues	Information/Responses
Type of transport stack	TCP
Type of connector in use	SMTP Connector, X.400 Connector, other site connectors
Destination of connector	For example, the head office in Brazil, the Accounting Department
Available network bandwidth for above connector	For example, fractional T1 (512 KB)
Frequency of mail transmission	For example, every 30 minutes, every day, and so forth
Utilization of Exchange directory replication	Yes/No
Exchange directory replication frequency	For example, every 30 minutes, every day, and so forth
List any pertinent connector limitations	For example, transmissions can take place only in evening hours to reduce network traffic during the day when the network is busier and thus slower

Once you have reviewed Table 3-2 to determine the information needed to plan your bridgehead server installation or upgrade, take a look at what type of transport stack is currently in place. If the current bridgehead transport stack is TP4, these bridgehead servers must be changed over to TCP to ensure complete compatibility between older Exchange servers and newer Exchange 2000 servers in mixed-mode environments because Windows 2000 Server does not support TP4.

Establishing Connector Servers

Exchange 2000 has eliminated support for some of the connector types previously available in Exchange 5.5 and earlier versions. However, if the Exchange 5.5 server has been set up with connectors supported under Exchange 2000—Lotus cc:Mail, Lotus Notes, Microsoft Mail, and Novell GroupWise, among others—it can still migrate the connector information to Exchange 2000 servers for the sake of backward-compatibility. In some cases, administrators might want to install dedicated connector servers with the sole function of connecting different types of servers. This installation can produce the best possible connector performance because the server isn't performing other duties, such as archiving mail or processing user requests. You will learn more about connector servers and connector groups in Chapter 10, "Connector and Routing Management in Exchange 2000 Server."

In addition to the aforementioned supported connectors, other Exchange 2000 servers fall under the list of supported connectors because other Exchange 2000 servers must communicate with each other. Exchange 5.5 supports several additional connector types, but the ones for antiquated or infrequently used mail systems were eliminated in Exchange 2000 Server.

When planning Exchange 2000 deployments and determining whether to upgrade existing Exchange 5.5 servers, the types of connectors currently in use have a major impact on the decision to upgrade or use existing services. If the existing connectors are not supported in Exchange 2000, but are still required for your network, then you might want to consider leaving the current Exchange 5.5 servers as is. However, if the connectors are supported in Exchange 2000, upgrading all servers improves performance because the servers are all running Exchange 2000 and taking advantage of its improved overall design. Performing common administrative tasks is easier, too, by not having to maintain a mixed-mode Exchange environment with separate connectors to transfer information from Exchange 5.5 to Exchange 2000. A sample Exchange connector configuration in a mixed-mode environment is shown in Figure 3-6.

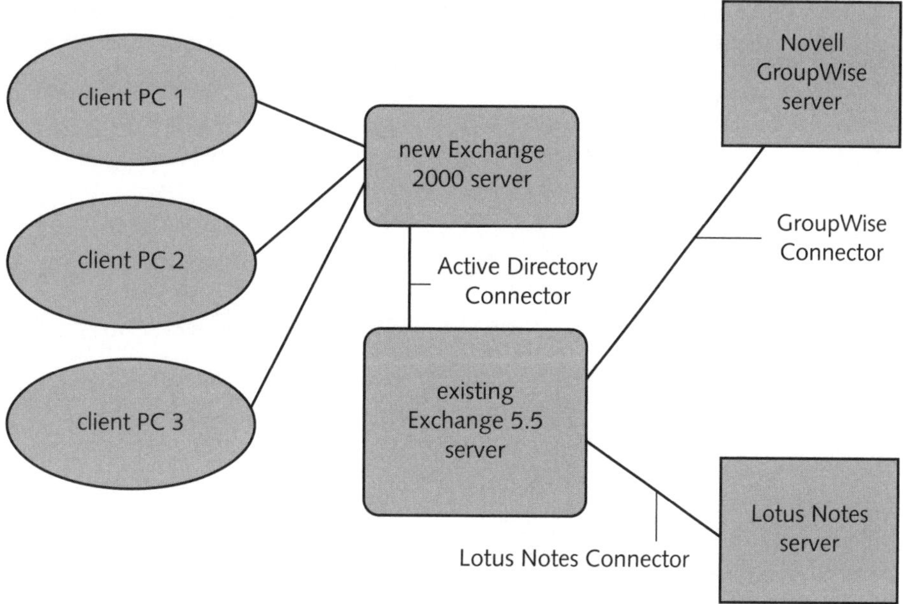

Figure 3-6 Sample Exchange connector configuration

Microsoft has done its homework in deciding which previously supported connectors to remove in Exchange 2000. The e-mail service connectors that are no longer supported are rarely in use and likely will be removed in the near future. Therefore, you probably don't need to worry about continuing to use Exchange 5.5 servers to support those connectors because in many cases you will want to remove unsupported connectors if possible.

Establishing Cluster Configurations

For almost any organization, redundancy and uptime issues need to be addressed. Because e-mail is a vital component in how companies do business, uptime—the period during which a service is working and available to use—is critical for e-mail services. Like any other service on your network, however, e-mail servers must undergo maintenance procedures, whether it's applying new software patches, performing security fixes, changing defective hardware, or simply rebooting the operating system because of an error. Inevitably, the server has to come down at one point or another.

The way around the problem of downtime is redundancy—that is, setting up a cluster of servers. **Server clusters** are made up of two or more physical servers that typically use the same shared disk subsystem (they maintain their own disk subsystem for the operating system) and behave as a single computer even though they are separate physical systems. Server clusters also share the same network name and IP address. Although this sounds like it shouldn't work, it does. However, the trick is that only one server in the cluster—the **active server**—is actually performing the duties; the rest are there only in case the active server goes down. Figure 3-7 illustrates a sample server cluster.

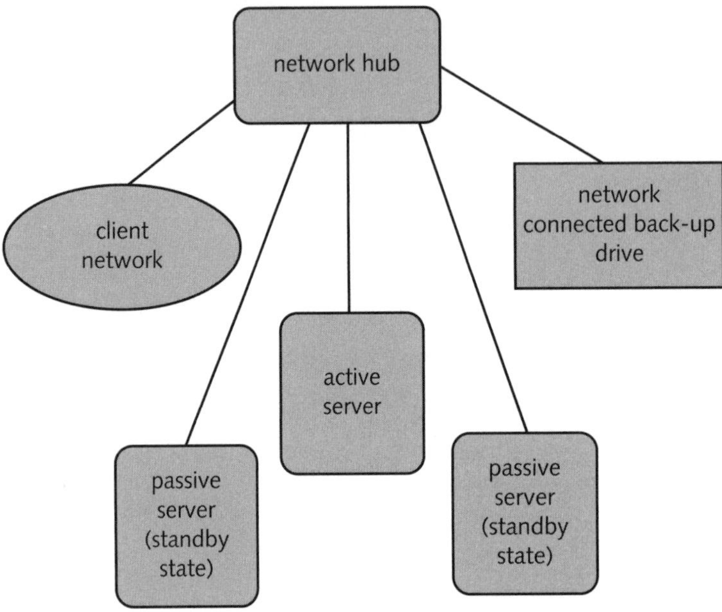

Figure 3-7 An example of a server cluster

The active server in the cluster maintains complete control over the shared disk subsystem and anything else managed by the cluster. The other members of the cluster are called **passive servers**. These passive servers run only in a standby state, ready to take control if the active server crashes or is taken down for maintenance. Because server clustering happens seamlessly, users should not see any change or slowdown in performance. By having a cluster setup, an administrator can take down passive servers as needed and apply patches, repair hardware, or replace systems entirely. The administrator can then change the current active server and perform the changes on the other remaining passive servers without affecting the users or causing service downtime.

Think of clustering as a type of RAID, except that instead of hard drives, servers are used. In a common RAID implementation, if one drive fails, the system can keep running so that the failed part can be replaced, thus maintaining uptime. In almost every server, RAID is considered mandatory; however, server clustering is not as common. If constant uptime is required, however, server clustering should be a serious consideration.

As you can see, clustering your servers can be a great aid in high-uptime environments. Out of the box, Windows 2000 Advanced Server offers dual-node active clustering, but this feature is more of a load-balancing one because each server takes on some of the workload as necessary. If one of the servers goes down, the others pick up all the slack. This type of clustering technology has a minimal impact on regular system operation, so users don't notice the changeover, and you have the added bonus of getting twice the processing capability instead of having idle equipment sitting around gathering dust. Figure 3-8 illustrates an example of a load-balanced cluster.

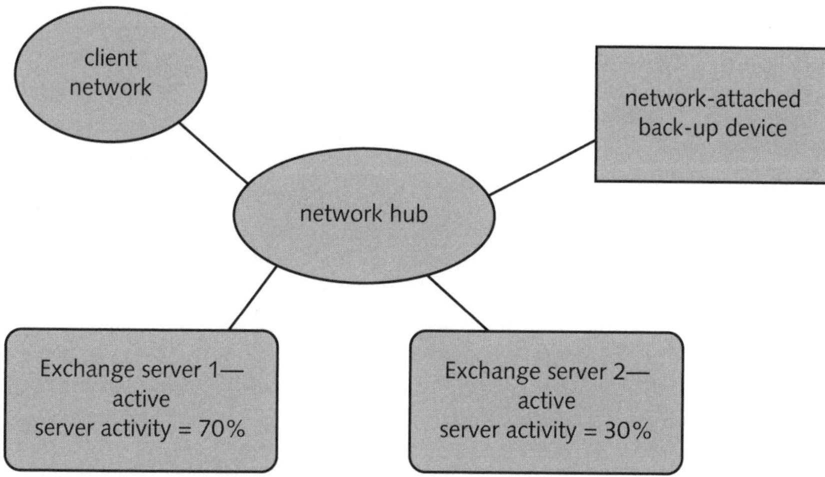

Figure 3-8 An example of a load-balanced cluster

Establishing Front-End and Back-End Configurations

The concept of **front-end** and **back-end** architecture is a new one to users of previous versions of Exchange. Front-end servers provide the connection to the outside; for example, an OWA server is a front-end server to which the clients connect. A front-end server does not perform any of the processing. Any requests made by the client through the front-end server are relayed to the appropriate back-end server that does the actual processing, such as processing e-mail. These server configurations offer improved scalability and availability of network services by providing a true multitiered approach. An example of a front-end/back-end configuration can be seen in Figure 3-9. The service that mainly benefits from front-end and back-end server configurations is Outlook Web Access (OWA), a Web-based client that can be accessed through a network (such as the Internet) and that provides much of the same functionality as Microsoft Outlook.

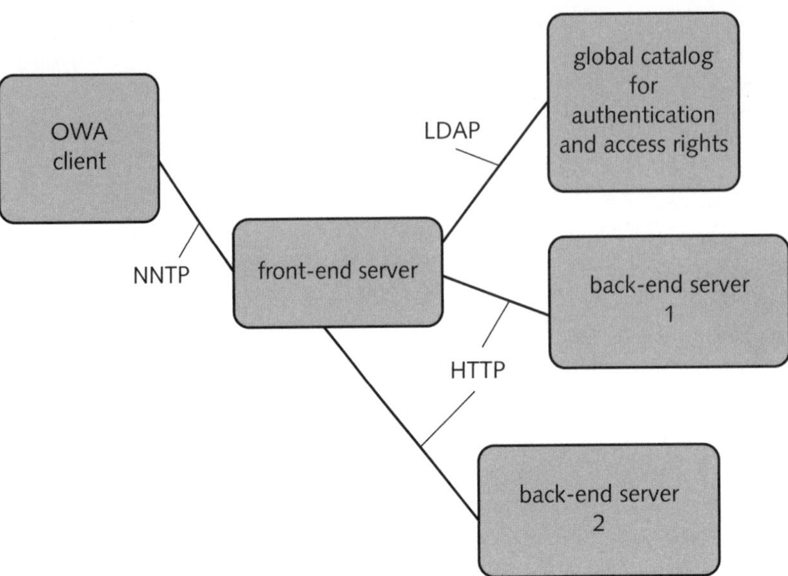

Figure 3-9 A front-end/back-end server configuration

For many organizations, a single Exchange 2000 server that handles any and all activity on the network is fine, including hosting a single OWA server for users. The need for front-end servers arises when an organization has multiple Exchange 2000 servers, and you want to have only one Web site address to handle all inbound OWA requests. By running multiple front-end servers all directed to the same Web site, many more users can log on and use OWA. Think of the design as similar to a grocery store that has 20 people in line for one checkout counter; the more checkout counters you open, the more people get served quickly. Front-end and back-end servers can also provide additional security by establishing a front line of defense between the front-end server and the Exchange 2000 server; in other words, you have another system between the outside and the Exchange 2000 server itself. A front-end/back-end arrangement basically sets up a Hypertext Transfer Protocol (HTTP) filter, allowing you to limit and direct flow from the front-end servers sending requests to the back-end Exchange 2000 servers filling the requests. Back-end servers are designed and specifically configured to support the front-end server they work with. A common misconception is that to access a back-end server, all requests, including replication, must go through the front-end server first. However, this is not so; requests for data transfers and public folder replication can be configured to transfer directly to and from the back-end server.

The basic rule of thumb for creating a front-end/back-end server configuration is to create at least one front-end server per four mailbox servers. This guideline doesn't, however, take into account redundancy requirements (you might want to run two front-end OWA servers in case one fails) and network usage of the front end. If your primary e-mail client is OWA, you might have a higher load of network traffic directed toward the front-end servers, so you might need to create more front-end servers than the basic design requires. Only by assessing your usage patterns can you determine what is required for your network's hardware and server configurations.

To make it easier to manage a group of front-end servers that share a common namespace (for instance, xyz.com.bz and xyz.com.uk fall under the xyz.com namespace), you could have all the namespaces for the front-end servers point toward the single namespace (xyz.com) and have a single back-end server set up to manage that one namespace. To do that, you use a virtual server for the namespace instead of setting up three separate back-end servers. A virtual server can be configured on the one back-end server and provide the necessary connectivity and configuration options each site requires and can have a setup identical to the front-end server, including folders on the back-end server. You will learn more about front-end and back-end servers in Chapter 4, and more about virtual servers in Chapter 8, "Configuring Internet Clients in Exchange 2000 Server."

Details such as SMTP domain information, IP address, and where the mailboxes reside must match on both the front-end and back-end servers.

Working out a front-end and back-end design can take a lot of setup and configuration time, but the benefits can be quite worthwhile, especially if the site handles several different segments of an organization, or the server plays host to several different companies with varying needs. On the other hand, there are some downfalls to using a front-end and back-end configuration. The extra servers you need for this configuration mean added expense and administration, and the network architecture can become more complex and harder to manage.

Establishing Mailbox Servers

Exchange 2000 handles mailboxes quite efficiently, and for most companies, the default mailbox server is usually quite adequate. Depending on the number of mailboxes and the company's organizational structure, however, you might need to set up Exchange servers dedicated to providing only mailbox services. As you learned earlier, grouping multiple mailbox stores can make administration easier (to a degree, of course); this grouping also allows for a host of other benefits, including:

- Faster backups and restores
- VIP mailbox stores for select people or small groups for the fastest possible restores
- Fewer resources needed to perform indexing on mailboxes
- Lower disk space usage requirements because users or departments that often send attachments to each other can be grouped

Mailbox services are pretty straightforward; they become complex only when you attempt to set up multiple mailbox stores to achieve some of the benefits in the preceding list. When making these changes, do not go overboard with the division of mailbox stores to help minimize administrative effort; it is usually not a good idea to put only one mailbox in its own mailbox store because you have to spend more administrative time and effort configuring settings, including global catalog synchronization, when each mailbox is in a separate mailbox store. You should analyze your current mailbox setup and assess how you want your mailboxes to be organized. Mirroring your company's organizational structure when grouping mailbox stores is a good idea, but ultimately, forethought and planning benefit you the most.

Establishing Public Folder Servers

Much like mailbox servers, you can have dedicated public folder servers. **Public folders** are directories on the Exchange server where security can be set on particular files, folders, or the entire public folder. Users can place files, contact lists, calendars, and more in the public folder for other users to access. The possibilities for public folders are endless, and they can become valuable access points for departments such as Human Resources, which often needs to consult contact lists, or teams trying to book meeting times in a common board room. Because of their usefulness, you should give some attention to how to incorporate them into your Exchange 2000 rollout plans.

When you install Exchange 2000, there is one default public folder store with a basic hierarchy in place (the same principle as an AD tree, with the root folder at the top and other folders expanding out from there). Exchange 2000 supports multiple public folders and public folder hierarchies, giving you more customization options when planning your public folder setup. You can, for example, establish your public folder configuration on just one server or spread it out over several servers and have Exchange replicate the data to all the servers. Using several servers is sometimes preferable if you have a spread-out organization (such as a WAN) or a heavily used public folder system that could tax your existing server setup.

If you do decide to set up more than one public folder configuration, keep in mind that only the original public folder hierarchy is accessible from Internet Messaging Access Protocol (IMAP) or Messaging Application Programming Interface (MAPI) clients (such as OWA). Any folder that comes after the root in the hierarchy is accessible only from conventional client software, such as Microsoft Outlook or another application that supports the Installable File System.

Should users need to access shared company information from a Web browser, the public folder component also supports publishing documents as Web pages in public folders. To publish documents and Web pages to public folders, you can use any standard HTML markup software, such as Microsoft FrontPage, making it easy for any user to add content to a company Web site.

With the Exchange 2000 support for publishing Web sites from the content in public folders, users can also make use of additional special Exchange content, such as calendars or documents stored in public folders. This feature enables project collaboration or data access from just about anywhere there is an Internet connection.

Installable File System

Even though it is called a file system, the **Installable File System (IFS)** is more of a storage technology that doubles as a filing system. It's a service that allows for direct access to Exchange data, including mailboxes and public folders. IFS enables Exchange to make mailboxes and public folders available to non-e-mail client software, such as Internet Explorer, or even the Windows command prompt, instead of having to use a client software package, such as Outlook 2000. IFS also creates a common interface for users to access files with, similar to Windows Explorer. With IFS, it is even possible to map Exchange folders to a shared network drive, allowing users to access the folders as they do files on their own hard drive, without necessarily having to use a client software package.

The IFS can really shine when you use it with other features the Information Store offers. One such feature is the ability to turn Exchange into a custom file repository that has advanced search capabilities when you combine IFS with full-text indexing and HTTP client support. By using OWA or Microsoft Outlook 2000 or later, users can perform custom searches much faster than they could with Windows, making IFS that much more useful. Because IFS enables you to share public folders and improve file searches, you can create a network share to a common data directory, have users map to it, and be able to interact with it like any other drive on the network.

If you are considering the benefits of using IFS to share public folders, you'll find that file searches are typically faster than standard Windows NT File System (NTFS) file searches. This benefit alone makes IFS worthwhile, especially in folders with a substantial amount of data to be sorted.

When an initial IFS hierarchy is set up, it contains two folders: one called Public Folders and the other called Mbx. In the Public Folders folder, you can store documents that can be manipulated like any other files by copying, deleting, and so on. The Mbx folder is the root for every mailbox in the Exchange server. As long as you have the permissions to do so, you can access every mailbox in this folder.

Understanding Coexistence and Migration Issues

Planning a coexistence or migration with Exchange 5.5 and Exchange 2000 can be time-consuming at the best of times. As you can imagine, a migration from Exchange 5.5 to 2000 is not as simple as installing Exchange 2000 and connecting it to the network. Existing mailboxes must be transferred, as well as public folder information, and more.

Also, as mentioned previously, you might need to keep Exchange 5.5 active if you're currently using a type of mail connector that's not supported in Exchange 2000. Microsoft has built some utilities and design features into Exchange 2000 that allow for a smooth migration or coexistence between the two mail systems.

One of the more important utilities included with Exchange 2000 is the **Active Directory Connector (ADC)**. The ADC allows Active Directory and Exchange 5.5 to synchronize and replicate data between their directory structures. Because AD has increased capabilities for storing all pertinent account information, including security and messaging information, Exchange 2000 doesn't need to have its own directory structure, as Exchange 5.5 does. ADC, which is installed after the initial Exchange 2000 deployment, uses Lightweight Directory Access Protocol (LDAP) to replicate and synchronize objects and settings from Exchange 5.5 to Exchange 2000 and continues to keep the data synchronized to ease coexistence between the two systems. ADC also offers the following functions:

- Manages active replication of data from AD, rather than Exchange 5.5, taking some administrative effort off your hands
- Replicates changes only between Exchange 5.5 and AD, if possible, to minimize data transfer and the amount of synchronization required
- Maintains object unity between the two directories (that is, matches an AD group to the appropriate Exchange 5.5 distribution list) to cut down on administrative overhead
- Manages multiple connections from one AD server

After the ADC has been installed, it can be started and stopped like a regular Windows service and is managed with the Active Directory Connector Management console. Active Directory Connector Management can be used to configure the relationships between Exchange 5.5 directory structures and their related AD targets, such as an Exchange 5.5 mailbox and the corresponding Active Directory user object.

In Chapter 4, you learn more about using the ADC to enable coexistence and migration between Exchange 5.5 and Exchange 2000.

Maintaining Existing Users

In any Exchange upgrade scenario, you will undoubtedly encounter existing users and their mailboxes. Knowing how to handle the mailbox transition to Exchange 2000 is an important part of your migration strategy. The waters are muddied somewhat by having three different ways to handle upgrading and migrating mailboxes from Exchange 5.5 to Exchange 2000, meaning your choices require a little more thought.

With the flexibility of Exchange 2000 of being able to use more than one storage database, you have some choices when it comes time to decide if you want to move mailboxes one by one from an existing Exchange 5.5 environment or if you want to upgrade all the mailboxes to Exchange 2000. This flexibility gives you the best possible opportunity to plan the migration the way your organization wants it.

Of the three major ways to make the transition from Exchange 5.5 to Exchange 2000, no single one is the "right way" to do it. Each offers its own benefits and drawbacks, and it is up to you to decide which is best for your deployment. The advantages and disadvantages of the three methods are outlined in the following list (these methods are explained in more detail in Chapter 6, "Upgrading or Migrating from Exchange 5.5 to Exchange 2000 Server"):

- *In-place upgrade*—Typically, if you have performed the requisite testing beforehand, your Exchange server is sparsely populated, or you are not concerned about possible failures during the upgrade, this is a viable method to upgrade the user mailboxes. It's also the most economical of the upgrade options. If the server is mission critical, however, this is definitely not the recommended upgrade method because of the potential loss of mailbox or other important information. Also, a failed installation usually means additional downtime when the server is being upgraded. If it's the only server that provides e-mail and other services on the network, users won't be able to do their work until the server upgrade is finished or repaired, if it has failed.
- *Move mailbox upgrade*—This type of mailbox upgrade requires an existing Exchange 2000 server running in the same site as the Exchange 5.5 server the mailboxes will be moved from. After the two servers are in the same site and the ADC is in use, you can then migrate mailboxes at your leisure. With this method, you can make sure the servers are working correctly and then bring down the Exchange 5.5 server when the transition has been successful.
- *Leapfrog upgrade*—This type of mailbox migration can be useful if you have several Exchange 5.5 servers to move; it helps limit additional server hardware to only one other system. In this type of migration, an Exchange 2000 server is built, and mailboxes are moved to it from the first Exchange server. After a successful upgrade, the first Exchange 5.5 server is rebuilt with Exchange 2000 and the process is performed again on the next Exchange 5.5 server. This type of upgrading can take a while, but it helps limit the hardware resources used and ensures that each server is working properly before moving forward.

Migrating users with any of these methods can commence after you have established the ADC and, obviously, established a working Exchange 2000 server on the network (except in the in-place upgrade option). One important thing to note about performing migrations is that Exchange 5.5 servers cannot be moved between different Exchange sites. When Exchange is running in mixed mode (both Exchange 5.5 and Exchange 2000 active with AD), an Exchange 5.5 server has a matching Exchange 2000 administrative group, which also matches up with an Exchange 2000 routing group. This relationship between Exchange 5.5 and Exchange 2000 enables the two to synchronize data, migrate mailboxes, and transfer messages, and allows each to have the appropriate rights and server configuration information for the other server. This information is critical to the ADC and required for mixed-mode operation and migration. If this setup is changed, message transfer between the two servers can become unreliable because the servers might not have the necessary administrative rights or server information. When performing your mailbox migrations in a live environment, you can ensure reliable message transfer by not altering the configuration between the two servers before you have finished the migration or reached the point where you can take the old Exchange 5.5 servers offline and out of the Exchange organization.

You will learn more about upgrading Exchange 2000 from Exchange 5.5, including connectors, users, and mailboxes, in Chapters 6 and 10.

Chapter Summary

- The Microsoft Solutions Framework mates well with Exchange 2000 deployments because Exchange can represent a rather large change to an organization's infrastructure. The MSF can help ease infrastructure changes by promoting a solid, repeatable, well-documented process that can enable any organization to develop and properly implement an infrastructure change such as putting Exchange 2000 into operation.
- When looking at the requirements for Exchange 2000, remember that there are more than simply hardware requirements to keep in mind. User and company requirements must also come into play in any project plan to ensure that the needs of the users and requirements of the company are being taken into account.
- The current infrastructure and Exchange environment is a major issue when considering an upgrade or migration to Exchange 2000. Such issues as current DNS services, WAN structure, and Exchange 5.5 connectors and organization all must figure into the big picture.
- Exchange 2000 brings about some improvements in how key components of Exchange operate. The ability of Exchange 2000 to handle multiple databases allows for greater flexibility and organization when implementing mailbox stores, public folders, and storage groups. These improvements in particular can help organizations that provide hosting for multiple companies. In addition, these improvements help improve backup and restore performance, with the side benefit of not interfering with other users' mailboxes when maintenance is required.
- Coexistence and migration are made easier by the use of the Microsoft Active Directory Connector. The ADC can help connect Exchange 5.5 directories to AD and allow for smoother migration of mailboxes and public folders. In addition, the ADC allows Exchange 5.5 servers to coexist with Exchange 2000 servers if there's a need to keep up older site connectors, thus preserving support for older or different mail services.

Key Terms

Active Directory Connector (ADC) — A Microsoft utility that helps provide temporary coexistence between Exchange 5.5 and Exchange 2000 and then helps ease the migration to the final Exchange 2000 deployment. Basically, the ADC enables Active Directory to support the older directory design in Exchange 5.5.

active server — The server in a cluster that maintains complete control over the shared disk subsystem and anything else managed by the cluster. The active server performs all necessary processing; if it fails, a passive server switches to an active server to fill this role.

application service providers — A new type of business service in which a provider operates a server farm that hosts published applications for a company, which connects to the service using client software. None of the software is managed from the client end, and data is typically stored at the provider's site. The application service providers also ensure that the services remain up and are maintained and backed up, relieving the cost and burden of maintenance for the client.

back-end — Represents the actual Exchange 2000 servers that provide the bulk of the processing. The front-end server forwards requests from the client software to the back-end servers for processing.

bridgehead servers — Exchange 2000 servers that have one or more connectors linking multiple Exchange sites or providing connections to the Internet for Exchange servers. These servers are typically set to be bridgehead servers by the Exchange administrator.

front-end — The server that the client software typically connects to. A common example of a front-end server is OWA. The front-end server rarely controls information or fulfills requests for the client; rather, it sends the users' requests to the back-end servers.

Information Store — A database responsible for data storage and management that performs lookups of information when requests are made for data in mailboxes or public folders.

Installable File System (IFS) — A service that enables for direct access to Exchange data, including mailboxes and public folders. With this direct access, a user can map a shared folder to a mailbox or public folder and access it as though it were a directory on a server's hard drive.

Internet Mail Service (IMS) — The system-level service that Microsoft Exchange uses to transfer information to and from external message systems that use SMTP. IMS dictates how the server uses SMTP, DNS, and TCP/IP to perform the required message transfer services.

mailbox store — A database containing all e-mail, mailbox data, and settings for mailboxes managed by a particular mailbox store. You can have multiple mailbox stores on an Exchange 2000 server to provide the level of customization and optimization you need.

Outlook Web Access (OWA) — An Exchange service that enables Internet Explorer users to connect to their Exchange mailboxes and any public folders for which they have access, using their Web browser in an interface similar to Microsoft Outlook client software.

passive servers — Servers that are members of a server cluster but are not currently active. Passive servers sit in a standby state, waiting for the active server in the cluster to fail or go offline; when one goes down, one of the passive servers in the cluster activates and becomes the active server.

public folders — A separate file system in Exchange where users can create folders and place documents, such as calendars and contact lists, that can be accessed by anyone in the network. Although these folders are called "public," security settings are available for the data if needed.

server clusters — A pair or group of servers used for load balancing or for providing redundancy for your servers. In a server cluster, if one server goes down, another member of the cluster should automatically pick up where the other left off, allowing functionality to continue uninterrupted.

storage groups (SGs) — A new Exchange feature used to organize a collection of mailbox stores, public folder stores, and transaction log files into one group. This grouping feature can ease management and offer better organizational control.

Windows Internet Naming Service (WINS) — A Windows naming service that allows for NetBIOS name translation to TCP/IP addresses. Typically, a WINS server helps cut down on TCP/IP traffic by providing name-resolution services with less broadcast traffic on the network.

Review Questions

1. You have some flexibility in using the MSF because not every Exchange 2000 installation requires as much development or even testing as other installations. True or False?
2. Which two of the following features and services would you choose if your users needed to collaborate on documents and projects?
   a. Instant Messaging
   b. NetMeeting
   c. public folders
   d. storage groups
3. User and company requirements are different for which of the following reasons? (Choose all that apply.)
   a. Users sometimes ask for features that are not realistic.
   b. Users sometime ask for features that management doesn't want them to use.
   c. The organization might have legal concerns that prohibit including some user requirements.
   d. The user-mandated features cost too much.

4. Poor or inadequate WAN design can dictate changes to the current organization infrastructure to facilitate an Exchange 2000 implementation. True or False?
5. Windows Internet Naming System is an important feature to have installed for optimum DNS performance under Exchange 2000 Server. True or False?
6. Which of the following should be included in a network architecture diagram? (Choose all that apply.)
   a. the date the routers were installed
   b. IP addresses of all connections
   c. connection type, including available bandwidth
   d. protocols active on the connection
7. A component of Exchange 2000 Server that contains all the data and configuration information for mailboxes and public folders is called the ________________.
8. Which of the following improvements does Exchange 2000 bring about because of its new mailbox store database-management abilities? (Choose all that apply.)
   a. the ability to handle multiple mailbox stores
   b. faster backups because of a smaller overall Information Store size
   c. ability to restore individual mailboxes created in their own mailbox store instead of all or nothing
   d. ability to use Exchange for Application Service Providers
9. What are the three Exchange components that you can organize into storage groups?
10. When bridgehead servers transfer data between sites, they use which one of the following items?
    a. SMTP
    b. ADC
    c. Information Store
    d. global catalog
11. Under Windows 2000, the recommended protocol for use with bridgehead servers is ________________.
12. Leaving Exchange 5.5 servers up is often the only way to continue supporting some mail connectors. True or False?
13. Which two of the following benefits are the results of using a server cluster configuration in Exchange?
    a. improved performance
    b. ease of maintenance
    c. continued uptime
    d. expanded public folder database size

14. If your primary e-mail software client of choice is OWA, the best way to handle the increased load is to:
    a. implement an Exchange server cluster
    b. set up multiple back-end servers
    c. set up multiple front-end servers
    d. upgrade to Windows 2000 Advanced Server
15. Public folders are a useful Exchange component that can help users collaborate with each other and give departments, such as Human Resources, a central place to post documents that can be used by anyone. True or False?
16. The ______________ enables mapping of mailboxes and public folders and gives users the ability to access them like a regular directory on their hard drive.
17. Which two folders are created when IFS is first implemented?
    a. Mbx
    b. Pbx
    c. mailbox
    d. Public Folders
18. Which utility helps synchronize data between Exchange 5.5 and Exchange 2000?
19. Of the following choices, which is the single best method of migrating mailboxes and public folders from a multiserver Exchange 5.5 environment to an Exchange 2000 environment?
    a. leapfrog upgrade
    b. in-place upgrade
    c. manual mailbox move
    d. none of the above
20. When designing a front-end/back-end server configuration, what is the recommended ratio of front-end servers to mailbox servers?
    a. two front-end to three mailbox servers
    b. one front-end to four mailbox servers
    c. one front-end to one mailbox server
    d. three front-end to two mailbox servers
21. When you implement a dual-node active cluster, what are you actually doing?
    a. running one server as the active server and one as a system that constantly mirrors the first
    b. providing two active backup servers in a three-member cluster configuration
    c. server load-balancing between two systems
    d. running one server parallel to another that exists on another network
22. The method used by the Exchange 2000 Information Store to transfer mail to local mailbox recipients is called ______________.

HANDS-ON PROJECTS

Project 3-1

This project helps you learn the basic information that must be included in an Exchange Server proposal. The basic outline you create can serve as the basis for plugging in the information you glean during the envisioning and planning phases of the Microsoft Solutions Framework.

The company you are generating this Exchange Server proposal for is Canadian Skates Ltd. Canadian Skates has 500 employees; many of them are salespeople who access their e-mail and other scheduling information through the Internet from a remote site. These users need to have a quick method of searching for messages and files posted to the public folders. Other members of Canadian Skates's IT Department will join you to help with the project; they are Janet, Kent, Doug, Kiara, Nicole, Stuart, and Peter. Of these employees, only Janet and Doug have previous Exchange 5.5 experience, but the rest have various levels of troubleshooting and implementation skills.

To draft an Exchange Server proposal:

1. Every good project needs a vision of what the project will accomplish when it is finished. Begin your proposal by writing down the project vision.
2. The next addition to your project plan is the project requirements. They stipulate what features and functions you need for the project to be considered a success. Write down the main requirements for your project (bullet points or brief sentences are usually adequate).
3. Keeping in mind that this is simply a proposal and not a complete plan, prepare a rough outline of the project's schedule. It does not have to be that detailed, but should include a start date and a rough estimate of how long it will take to complete. Remember, at this point it is only an estimate.
4. Write down a description of the key members of the project team (including yourself) and what resources are initially required.
5. Write down a list of user requirements and features, based on the typical user requests listed in the company profile above.
6. Try to lay out the project plan in a clean and simple document that includes the aforementioned information and any project-specific notes that may be of use. Because this project proposal will be presented to a management committee, make sure the proposal is easy to read and focus on pertinent information so that the committee members can understand the project.

Project 3-2

This project helps you determine user requirements for the migration to Exchange 2000. This information is used to create the overall requirements for the migration.

To establish user requirements for a proposed migration:

1. Before polling the users, determine what features are mandatory (for example, e-mail and calendars). After you have established the mandatory features, generate an e-mail or typed document that briefly explains the migration and the benefits to the users. Ask the users to inform you by letter, phone, or e-mail what features they need and want to see implemented, as well as the importance and potential usage levels of those features (for example, ask them to rate the feature as being used often, occasionally, or rarely). For this step, generate a mock letter to be sent out to the users and give it to a lab partner. Have your lab partner do the same. After you have your mock letters, each lab partner should then come up with his or her own list of required features, including their importance and how much those features would be used (guesstimate a usage rate).
2. After you have gotten the user responses from your partner, the next step is to group common requirements and optional features. You can then start to weed out unrealistic requests or features that Exchange doesn't support. After you have an edited list of requirements and optional features, decide which features you should implement and what additional training is required (for example, sending e-mail typically does not require training).
3. After you have established a rough draft of requirements, write another letter explaining which requested features were cut from the proposal and why. Exchange these letters with your lab partner; then each of you should review your letters to make sure nothing was missed from the first round of correspondence. If necessary, make additional requests for changes, or approve the proposal as written. Exchange letters with your partner again and review the approval or requested changes, incorporating any changes that might be needed at this point.
4. Review your proposal and sort requested features based on level of importance to job performance, the number of users for a particular feature, and any information you received on how frequently users will use the features (often, occasionally, rarely). For the purposes of this step, determine whether additional resources will be required (for example, heavy use of public folders could dictate additional Exchange servers to handle the additional folders) and write them down in your proposal. Normally, it is necessary to schedule time to implement these features and note the cost of additional resources on this requirements list; however, for this project, you will skip that step.
5. The last step is to take the completed list to the management committee for final approval, based on organizational policies, budget constraints, and time required to implement the project. For this step, give the list to your instructor for approval.

Project 3-3

This project gives you an opportunity to estimate the server resources and services you need to incorporate the user-requested requirements.

To calculate the number of servers based on requested user requirements:

1. First, take the information you gathered from Project 3-2 and write down each individual feature users have requested.
2. Assess which services must be implemented for each feature. For example, if users need fast searches in a centralized filing system, you have to implement the IFS to meet that requirement.
3. Take the number of users on the proposed Exchange server (for the purposes of this project, use 100) and determine the workload (light, medium, heavy) for each requested feature, based on the information gathered in Project 3-2.

Project 3-4

This project requires you to lay out a front-end/back-end configuration that supports the following features and requirements:

- 100 users (light workload)
- Outlook Web Access as the primary client
- Separate storage groups for four departments (Research, Sales, Management, and IT)

To establish a front-end/back-end configuration on paper:

1. Based on what you learned about front-end/back end configurations and storage groups, lay out a basic Exchange 2000 Server design that takes into account the above specifications, including how many Exchange installations are required.
2. As an optional step in this project, lay out the same network, but design it with performance and redundancy in mind.

Project 3-5

For this project, you will be laying out an Exchange dual-node cluster configuration on paper. This plan includes all pertinent information so that you can see how the cluster is configured and outlines the basic steps you must take when the time comes to implement the cluster. This project assumes that Windows 2000 Advanced Server has already been set up in a cluster configuration in its own domain with the appropriate settings for the cluster to work.

To establish server cluster configurations on paper:

1. The first step is to outline which account Exchange 2000 uses to install to the cluster. Make sure you use the same account used to create the cluster in the first place for Windows 2000 Advanced Server. Write down which account was used; typically, it is called SvcCluster.

2. The next step is to prepare AD for the impending Exchange 2000 installation. The logical thing here is to log on as SvcCluster and then proceed to run ForestPrep (as discussed in Chapter 2). Document the basic steps you use to complete this task.
3. Next, you must install Exchange 2000 with a typical installation. Make sure you run the Exchange setup logged on as the same account specified as Exchange Administrator during the ForestPrep installation. During the installation, you must specify to which partition and directory you are installing (for example, c:\exchsrv). On both installations, the directory absolutely *must* be the same for the cluster to work properly. Document which folder you will install to, the steps used to start the installation, and what Exchange Administrator account must be logged on for this step to succeed.
4. After the server has been installed, the next step is to create virtual Exchange servers. To do this, you must use Windows 2000 Cluster Administrator to create two virtual Exchange servers. Each must have its own name but should have a consistent theme that lends itself to easy identification. For this step, select the names for the two virtual Exchange Servers.
5. When you are actually configuring the virtual Exchange servers, you will be required to create an IP address resource for each virtual server. Select an appropriate IP address from the network's available addresses and write one down for each server. These IP addresses must be different from the IP addresses assigned for the cluster nodes.
6. There are many steps to reach a fully functional Exchange 2000 server cluster; however, the information you decided on will apply when it comes time to implement your cluster plan.

CASE PROJECTS

Case 1

Widget Express, Inc. is migrating from its existing Exchange 5.5 server setup to Exchange 2000. Management wants you to poll the users and determine what features they want from the new system. After gathering user opinions, you determine that the most important single feature users need is the ability to publish documents to a common company intranet for remote user access. Management approves the feature, and it is up to you to implement the service. Which services and common software package do you install to make it easier for users to use this feature?

Case 2

SuperZip Ltd. has hired you as an Exchange consultant. It is planning a migration from Exchange 5.5 to Exchange 2000; however, the Active Directory implementation hasn't been working well, and management wants you to look at it before deploying Exchange 2000.

The current setup consists of Windows 2000 with WINS installed and operating (upgraded from Windows NT 4.0 Server). Due to some of the naming problems they were having, the network administrator decided to replace WINS with DNS services but was not able to get it operating properly because of inexperience with the product. The DNS service installed is BIND 8.1, and it has been operating unreliably since it was first installed. Even with these unreliability problems, the network administrator is a devout Linux user who does not want to stop using BIND for DNS services. What recommendations should you make to adjust the company's setup to have its DNS services operate properly while still accommodating the network administrator's preferences?

Case 3

ABC Toy Company has just finished its Exchange 2000 migration, and everything is working in more or less the same fashion as it was with Exchange 5.5. The company now wants to take advantage of some of the new organizational features of Exchange 2000, which is why you were called in to make some recommendations. The first issue is that this company has large mailboxes that need regular backups; in the current setup, the backups are taking too long. The next issue is that the mail server is quite busy whenever departments e-mail files to people in their own department; this intradepartmental e-mailing causes systemwide sluggishness and has been contributing to the overall bloated Information Store problem. The final issue is that the absent-minded company president quite often deletes e-mails and doesn't realize he needs them until later, so e-mails have to be restored on a regular basis.

For ABC Toy Company, what can you recommend doing to minimize the effect on other users while speeding up the restore process so that the president can get back to work as quickly as possible? And what should be done about backups for the company's large mailboxes and the intradepartmental e-mail contributing to the systemwide sluggishness? Outline the suggestions you would present to ABC Toy Company.

Case 4

You work for an organization that offers application and data hosting for users on a network who regularly do business 20 hours a day because of the activity on world stock markets. Typically, people are working in the clients' offices almost every hour of the day, so you rarely have an opportunity to bring down Exchange servers for updating or maintenance; having a server crash in the middle of active trading hours would be a definite problem. What should your organization do to give these users the most uptime? Also, what would you do if the organization is on a tight budget but wants high uptime with little to no wasted equipment?

Case 5

Your company has had a successful Exchange 2000 rollout some time ago and everything has been running fine. Your public folder organization has gone over well, and almost every department has started storing vast amounts of information in it. The company also has some general-use mailboxes for receiving information on the competition and industry news updates that the Research and Sales Departments read on a regular basis. What service can you implement that improves on the already well-organized public folder setup and allows users to quickly find specific e-mails?

Case 6

You are the network administrator at a midsized company migrating from Exchange 5.5 to Exchange 2000, and you have been tasked with finding the best way to migrate while minimizing potential problems and utilizing the fewest resources. Your Exchange environment consists of six Exchange 5.5 servers, five of which will carry over to Exchange 2000 and one that will be retired after the migration has been completed. You have a limited budget but have plenty of time to finish the migration. What is the best plan of action to ensure that all the servers are upgraded, the budget stays in check, and you have a way to back out of a failed migration?

CHAPTER

4

PREPARING TO DEPLOY EXCHANGE 2000 SERVER

After reading this chapter and completing the exercises, you will be able to:

- Implement the Microsoft Solutions Framework by developing and deploying an Exchange 2000 Server project plan within your own organization
- Deploy Active Directory in a mixed-mode environment to implement gradual migrations to Exchange 2000 Server
- Develop plans for setting up administrative groups and routing groups that reflect your current organizational structure
- Understand how to work with legacy Windows NT domains and earlier versions of Exchange Server when migrating an organization to Exchange 2000 Server and Windows 2000 Server
- Optimize your network by planning a front-end/back-end configuration

Deploying Exchange 2000 Server is part of the overall phased approach—the Microsoft Solutions Framework—that has been discussed in previous chapters. Deploying Exchange 2000 is a rather complex undertaking, and adhering to the precepts of the MSF model ensures that you have considered all aspects of your current messaging infrastructure, and that you have seen how it can be transformed into a fully functioning Exchange 2000 Server environment. Chapter 3, "Planning an Exchange 2000 Server Design Scenario," addressed the model's first two phases, envisioning and planning, in depth. This chapter focuses on the final two phases of the model: developing a final system by using information gathered in the planning phase, and deploying a system by taking a project from a pilot stage to a final production stage.

DEVELOPING AND DEPLOYING YOUR EXCHANGE 2000 SERVER PROJECT PLAN

The MSF describes best practices that help you plan and deploy technology projects, including Exchange 2000 Server. The MSF model—or, more formally, the MSF Infrastructure Deployment Process Model—is milestone-driven and based on a team approach to problem solving and design. The focus in Chapter 3 was on defining the scope of your project design and identifying all relevant risks you might face in your project plans. It also concentrated on assessing user, company, and network infrastructure requirements for implementing Exchange 2000 Server. This chapter focuses more on developing your final system and actually deploying a production server. You have moved beyond the "paper" stages and are ready to select the physical hardware that will house your messaging databases and Information Stores. You must have a thorough understanding of all the necessary Windows 2000 components, but you should also have a detailed understanding of what Exchange 2000 needs independently of Windows 2000 Server. Windows 2000 gives you the foundation, or the skeleton structure, but Exchange 2000 offers enhancements to this skeleton architecture.

The Developing Phase

Remember the phrase "First you develop, then you deploy." Adhering strictly to this Microsoft framework of best practices helps you lay the groundwork for successful implementations of Exchange 2000 Server. It is easy to rush into an overnight implementation of Exchange 2000 on production servers; however, the consequences of doing this can be quite damaging. For example, if you don't take the time to go through the envisioning and planning phases of the MSF, you might wind up using a connector that serves only to contribute unnecessary network overhead, or your distribution of users into storage groups or administrative groups might not be the most efficient for your company. Envisioning and planning help you produce specific, detailed designs and plans that are ready to be implemented. The third phase of your project—developing—involves validating or verifying these designs, building a test system, and setting up teams that are responsible for conducting pre-pilot tests on users and systems. There is no standard time frame for this phase. You will know you're ready for production when all "pilot tests" have been performed to your satisfaction. A successful deployment depends on your existing hardware and network infrastructure and whether you have prepared this existing infrastructure for the new messaging environment. For this reason, some upgrade scenarios have been included in the section "Testing Upgrade Scenarios" later in this chapter to illustrate deployment issues.

Validating the Design

The first step in the developing phase is validating the planned project design, when the team sets up a test environment to confirm installation procedures, assess how well required features are working, and basically test all aspects of the implementation to ensure that it will provide the services your organization needs (see Chapter 2, "Planning for Windows 2000," for introductory details on this phase of the MSF model). When developing your test environment, you should try to simulate your original network environment by duplicating the production environment's hardware, software, and network connectivity. Even though you will not duplicate exact levels of messaging traffic, you do gain insight into how the various components work with your simulated Exchange 2000 server. You should re-create situations that occur on a daily basis, such as instant messaging between users. You should make sure to test features you know will be used, as well as features that should be used. Many features of Exchange 2000 Server (for instance, the Chat Service) can offer benefits to users that weren't possible before. For instance, with the Chat Service, users can collaborate on organizational projects with remote users, thus increasing productivity for the company. The Exchange 2000 Conferencing Server also provides time and cost savings in the form of centralized, real-time collaboration for all users. During this step of the developing phase, you can verify installation procedures as well as functional specifications derived during the envisioning and planning phases.

User Testing

Validating and verifying your design plans are only part of the total development package. The developing phase of the MSF model also incorporates system tuning and pilot projects, and these activities can help you design more refined deployment plans for the final MSF phase (see "The Deploying Phase" later in this chapter). As mentioned in Chapter 2, a systematic approach to testing gives you a clearer picture of the end result you want to achieve. Testing should be done both with technical users who are experienced in system-level operations and with end users who will use this product on a daily basis in the organization. The following sections cover proper testing methodologies that can be applied to both technical and nontechnical users in the organization.

The Test Environment

While still in the developing phase, you need to make sure your production hardware is in place and ready for user testing. You should verify that the server on which you'll be running Exchange 2000, in a test or production environment, meets all minimum hardware and software requirements. Sufficient processing power, memory, and hard drive space are needed to support all the functionality of Exchange 2000. Consider the use of multiple processors if using Windows 2000 Server—which supports one- to four-processor Symmetric Multiprocessing (SMP) systems and up to 4 GB of physical memory—or Windows 2000 Advanced Server edition, which supports configurations with up to eight processors and two-way clustering. You should document each server's configuration with respect to the number and type of CPUs installed, the amount of RAM, the number and type of physical storage systems, and the location and number of paging files.

To support a minimum Exchange 2000 configuration, Microsoft recommends a minimum hardware configuration of a Pentium 166 MHz processor with 128 MB of physical memory. However, this configuration depends on the *role* your servers are playing. For example, will they act as connector servers, mailbox servers, or front-end servers that proxy client requests to a back-end server?

Because of administrative requirements or budget constraints, many organizations deploy Exchange 2000 Server on one dedicated piece of hardware; however, be aware that you will see faster response times and have less downtime for maintenance if you deploy Exchange 2000 Server on dedicated multiple servers. For example, one server can be used exclusively for mailbox stores, another server can be used to host only public folder stores, and a third server can be used simply to route messages. You must also make sure that all hardware being used is on the Hardware Compatibility List provided by Microsoft, available at *http://www.microsoft.com/hcl.*

Cost always plays a major role in choosing hardware for your test environment. If you try to emulate your production network exactly, you end up purchasing hardware that is too expensive to be used just for testing purposes. If you purchase only low-end hardware, however, you run the risk of not fully testing the Exchange 2000 Server scalability features because scalability is a direct function of hardware that can support large amounts of storage space and memory. If you are testing just a sample population of your total user base, you can select hardware that represents a smaller version of your production servers. (For instance, if normal production servers use a 10 GB hard drive for storage, you might need only a 2 or 3 GB hard drive to test a smaller portion of users in a test environment, using fewer storage groups or mailbox stores.) Microsoft publishes information on its Web site about server scalability and messaging benchmarks you can use to choose appropriate hardware. Check *http://www.microsoft.com/exchange/techinfo/planning/2000/mmb2desc.asp* for details.

Finally, because your goal is to create a miniature version of your production network, make sure you include all relevant software or operating systems in your test network. For example, you might want to include computers running Windows NT 4.0 and Exchange Server 5.5 or computers running the DHCP service. You might even be using a mixture of other messaging systems (such as Novell's GroupWise or the UNIX-based sendmail messaging system) and want to duplicate these external mail systems as well. You should also include third-party applications running in your production network, such as fax connectors or back-up software specially designed for Exchange 2000 Server, and include as many e-mail clients as possible to validate the use of all relevant Internet access protocols, such as POP3, IMAP4, and NNTP.

Testing All Possible Scenarios

Performing a thorough evaluation of any new product gives you valuable insight into that product and how it will work under varying conditions in your organization. For this reason, when testing Exchange 2000 in your organization, you should test all possible scenarios that could occur during normal operations. Before fully deploying Exchange 2000 (which is covered in the next section), try to determine how certain features will affect your enterprise. For example, test how many users can be created on your test system or how many messages with large attachments can be sent at one time to see how these procedures affect server memory. You might not be able to successfully test every single Exchange 2000 Server feature in your test environment because certain services or protocols may not be able to coexist as they do in a production network. A production network offers benefits such as connectivity to routers and switches that a test network might not be able to take advantage of; however, you can test a specific feature to see how it behaves in a production setting. You can, for example, configure multiple storage groups on your test server and see what happens if you create more than five databases per storage group. It helps to see the effect of certain actions, even those that aren't recommended for production environments, in case they happen unintentionally in a production network. Preparing for errors and knowing what to do when they happen are important aspects of system administration for any Exchange server network. You can also experiment with different back-up strategies, such as daily backups, full backups, or incremental backups, to see which method is appropriate for your network in terms of server response time and data accuracy.

The following sections cover some features of Exchange 2000 Server that should be tested thoroughly in a test environment before fully deploying Exchange 2000 Server in a production environment. The focus in these sections is on connectors, e-mail clients, storage groups, routing groups, and upgrade scenarios.

Testing Third-Party Connectors Exchange 2000 Server uses connectors called **routing connectors** to establish connectivity between routing groups. (Routing groups are covered in more detail later in this chapter in the section "Routing Groups.") You should plan on configuring these connectors so that you can test the routing functionality between routing groups. You can also test the creation and use of connectors such as the SMTP or X.400 Connector if you deal with external messaging systems. Because there is a strong relationship between connectors in Exchange 2000 Server and Exchange Server 5.5, you might want to include a legacy Exchange server in your test environment (although this is not essential to optimal design for an Exchange 2000 organization). You will discover, for instance, that the Routing Group Connector corresponds closely to the Site Connector in Exchange Server 5.5, especially in a mixed-mode environment, and the SMTP Connector corresponds closely to the Internet Mail Connector in Exchange Server 5.5.

It is easy to test routing connectors because of the compatibility between all versions of Exchange Server, but it is difficult to test another type of connector, known as a **gateway connector**, because this compatibility is not as strong. Gateway connectors are not used to connect routing groups; rather, they are used to connect Exchange Server to other systems or applications. For instance, Exchange Server 5.5 supported the Professional Office System (PROFS) Connector for connectivity to IBM mainframe systems, but Exchange 2000 Server does not. So if you need IBM connectivity, your deployment must include a downlevel Exchange 5.5 server that already runs this PROFS Connector. There are other gateway-type connectors that support fax or virus-scanning capabilities, but most of them depend heavily on the Exchange Server 5.5 directory database. Because Exchange 2000 Server depends on the Windows 2000 Active Directory database for object information, these connectors may no longer be viable, meaning you'll need to purchase upgraded software or connectors.

Testing E-Mail Clients When testing e-mail clients, you should always be cognizant of the server load caused by different access protocols. Some protocols, such as IMAP4, require more server overhead and processing power than others, such as POP3. You should take this factor into consideration when planning the types and numbers of clients that will be accessing your Exchange 2000 Server.

If you're configuring MAPI-based clients, such as Outlook 2000 or Outlook 97, you should be aware that they can directly access information stored on a Global Catalog (GC) server, which means they can directly access the Active Directory database. However, other clients (for example, POP3 clients) are usually *referred* to a GC server, which could cause additional network traffic, especially when accessed over the Internet.

If you regularly analyze client network traffic in your production network, you will have a better sense of what types of clients to use and what types of client-server configurations best meet your needs. For instance, Outlook Web Access could provide standard e-mail access for your users if most of them are accessing mail remotely over the Internet. Knowing that OWA will be heavily deployed, you can then begin to make decisions related to its deployment, such as standardizing the Internet browser used for this client (either Microsoft Internet Explorer or Netscape Navigator, for example). You can deploy the OWA client for Exchange Server 5.5 or the one for Exchange 2000 Server. However, the Exchange 2000 OWA client is not compatible with the Exchange 5.5 OWA client, so you cannot access an Exchange 5.5 server using the Exchange 2000 OWA. However, you can access an Exchange 2000 Server computer using the Exchange Server 5.5 OWA. Upgrading an Exchange 5.5 OWA to an Exchange 2000 OWA causes you to lose all previously configured property settings.

You should test the Internet browsers currently used in your organization to check for compatibility with the OWA client. If your organization is using different browsers for different purposes, you should suggest using on one specific browser, especially if the OWA client will be used frequently. Standardization of most components (including hardware components and software packages) eases the management burden and makes it easier to troubleshoot problems. Because older browsers supported fewer frame features than the preferred browser for Exchange 2000 (Internet Explorer 5.0), it is no surprise that IE version 5.0 is considered the "best" OWA client by Microsoft because it supports all HTML 3.2 features and JavaScript, thus enabling you to manipulate data directly on the server using WebDAV, an extension of HTTP. Microsoft recommends using IE version 5.0

because only this browser supports context menus, eXtensible Markup Language (XML)-based viewing of data, and **Kerberos version 5 authentication** schemes.

Kerberos is a secure method of authenticating clients' requests for services in many computer networks, especially those networks using the Windows 2000 Server operating system. Users request an encrypted ticket from an authentication process, which is then used to request services such as authentication or security access from a server.

Other tasks you should consider performing for e-mail clients include the following:

- Verify that clients can send, receive, reply to, and forward all mail formats, including attachments.
- Verify that personal folder stores, mailbox stores, and public folder stores have been created and are working correctly. Also, make sure that users can copy messages to and from their personal folders (.pst files).
- Make sure users can work effectively with personal address books.
- Enable and test **full-text indexing**, an Exchange component integrated with the Windows 2000 Search service in Exchange 2000 so that users can perform fast searches for specific data in their mailbox stores or public folder stores.
- Test permissions on public folder stores to make sure distribution list members cannot access public folders containing sensitive information.

Testing Storage Groups Exchange 2000 has expanded the concept of database storage to new heights with the introduction of the storage group feature. During the developing phase, it's a good idea to test this feature by creating new storage groups on one server and seeing how many databases or mailbox stores it can support. You should also test an optimal distribution of users among these storage groups so that all users are not accessing a single storage group residing on a single volume or partition in the server. To determine an optimal distribution, you can move users between mailbox stores or even between storage groups themselves.

You can also plan backup schedules according to the number of storage groups you create because Exchange 2000 allows you to back up multiple individual storage groups or databases simultaneously, without disrupting other storage groups or messaging databases. For example, you can perform full backups on one storage group and incremental backups on the other storage groups. You can also restore one storage group while other storage groups are still operational. Because every storage group contains only one set of transaction log files, you can test the backup of multiple databases within a single storage group or the backup of multiple storage groups at the same time.

Testing Routing Groups Deploying routing groups within your test environment allows you to concentrate a group of Exchange 2000 servers that all share a permanent and high-bandwidth connection. Every server in a routing group communicates with the others using native SMTP. Your goal in deploying routing groups is to control the flow of messages between all servers in your organization.

First, you have to determine how many routing groups are needed. If you don't plan on having multiple external WAN connections, a single routing group will suffice. In any case, a default routing group named First Routing Group is created during a standard Exchange 2000 Server installation. Servers within a routing group can still belong to multiple administrative groups. You can think of routing groups as being equivalent to an Exchange Server 5.5 site. They are more flexible, however, because you can move servers between routing groups as long as they are in the same administrative group.

Second, you need to test all aspects of routing group functionality so you can understand how messages can be transferred in a production network. Messages are transferred not only between servers in a routing group, but also between servers and other messaging hosts in external networks. Connectors are used to transfer messages between routing groups, and you should test each type of connector that can be used in your test environment: the Routing Group Connector, the SMTP Connector, and the X.400 Connector. For example, you can test the application of the Routing Group Connector by creating two different routing groups, each containing one or more servers. You can then create multiple users and place them in different routing groups. Finally, you need to configure a Routing Group Connector between the two routing groups and verify that messages can be sent from one recipient to another. Another test situation consists of creating two different routing groups within one administrative group and then attempting to move servers between routing groups. These tests confirm the relationship between administrative groups and routing groups so you can better manage these objects in your production network. (This relationship is explained further in the section, "Deploying Administrative Groups and Routing Groups.")

Testing Upgrade Scenarios Exchange 5.5 servers are still used in many networks, so upgrades are both common and necessary. An upgrade by itself is not a complex process; however, it can be prone to failures and technical difficulties if you do not plan for it properly. You have to know *how* you will be upgrading to Exchange 2000 Server. For example, you can perform an in-place upgrade using the same hardware used for Exchange Server 5.5, or you can use more powerful server hardware by moving mailboxes and public folders to a new Exchange 2000 server. Regardless of the upgrade method used, you must deploy the Active Directory Connector (ADC). To plan for the upgrade process, you should test the following upgrade scenarios in your test environment:

- You can perform an in-place upgrade on existing hardware and then install the ADC.
- You can install Windows 2000 Server and populate its Active Directory database using the ADC before upgrading to Exchange 2000 Server.
- You can use the Active Directory Migration Tool (ADMT) after installing Windows 2000 Server, and then install the ADC.

Trying out different migration scenarios helps you discover what works best for your company. The ADC is covered in detail in the section "Deploying the ADC," later in this chapter. The Exchange 2000 Help menus also give more information on this topic.

The Deploying Phase

To avoid confusing "developing" with "deploying," remember that when you actually deploy Exchange 2000 Server, you have already conducted all the previous phases of planning, envisioning, and developing. That means all your users are physically ready for migration to Exchange 2000 Server because they have been previously educated regarding the change that's about to occur. It also means all testing has been completed successfully in a test network and any major errors have been addressed and corrected before they can affect your production network.

When introducing and implementing a new Exchange 2000 server (upgrading from an Exchange 5.5 server is addressed in Chapter 6, "Upgrading or Migrating from Exchange 5.5 to Exchange 2000 Server"), you should be concerned with taking your project to a state of full production. In this phase, normal operations personnel closely monitor your production servers while users take advantage of all the features in Exchange 2000. Some isolated features might still need testing for problem resolution. For example, users could suddenly discover new features, such as video conferencing, in the Exchange 2000 Conferencing Server, but these features might not have been given high priority during the developing phase of the implementation.

The Steps in Deploying: Completing the Project

The deploying phase has its own steps or hierarchy of activity. Deploying is not an act, but a process, and one that should be proactively monitored. For example, the decision to deploy a routing topology through the use of connectors should be considered before the decision to deploy a feature such as Instant Messaging. You want to deploy core components and technologies before deploying "peripheral" ones. Core components include external connectors and gateways, such as the SMTP Connector or the Routing Group Connector. These core components can help manage basic message flows throughout your organization and form the backbone of any Exchange 2000 implementation. Peripheral components include those that do not contribute to the messaging backbone or your network's physical topology, such as Instant Messaging services and public folders. Although these items are useful, they do not represent core architectural elements as the other components do. In summary form, the steps of the deploying phase include the following:

- *Migrating users*—Identify and place servers in various locations throughout your enterprise, and then migrate users to these new systems according to your mailbox store and public folder store designs.
- *Formally assign control*—Turn over control of this implementation project to a formal network or messaging team who will be fully responsible for all events related to Exchange 2000 operation in your organization. Usually the person

who has physically placed the servers and migrated the users is not responsible for managing the daily operations of Exchange 2000 (although many smaller firms grant all rights to only one or two people for budgetary and administrative reasons).

- *Formally completing all stages*—The team that has managed the implementation up to this point is now ready to close this project for good. In some organizations, this process is known as "signing off" on the project. The key to formally closing any project is total agreement by all people involved in the project that the necessary steps have been completed and that this project has received a fair evaluation from management.

Deploying Active Directory with Exchange Server 5.5 and Exchange 2000 Server

In any deployment of Exchange 2000 Server, problems can arise simply because you have incorrectly configured the Active Directory services in Windows 2000 Server. AD plays a major role in managing directory services and acts as a bridge between the Windows 2000 Server operating system and the Exchange 2000 Server software interface. When you deploy Exchange 2000 Server, you must always remember that AD is providing the structure for all objects and configuration information that Exchange 2000 needs. Managing Exchange means managing Active Directory.

The importance of certain AD objects to Exchange 2000, such as sites, organizational units, and the schema, is covered in the following sections, as well as the importance of the Active Directory Connector for mixed-mode Exchange environments.

Deploying Active Directory

When you initially deploy Exchange 2000 Server, you should have already defined your Windows 2000 physical and logical network topologies. Your sites and domains should be separate, properly defined structures, and you should probably start with a small but manageable number of domain structures. Your site design becomes important during deployment because Windows 2000 Server tries to locate domain controllers that exist in the same site in which users are created.

Microsoft suggests that you limit the total number of domains and subdomains to five or less. Any more than that increases your administrative burden, unless you assign this task to other administrators.

Organizational Units and Domain Structures

You must also make sure you have correctly planned your organizational unit (OU) structure. An organizational unit is not equivalent to a domain; an OU is an administrative structure created in the Windows 2000 Active Directory Users and Computers snap-in to group objects according to a logical design. Domains are also groupings of computers, but are created on a higher level. That is, a domain contains organizational units, not vice versa. Domains are parent containers for all other logical structures you create, including organizational units, groups, and users. An OU should be used to adapt to changes in your organizational structure because it's easier to move users between OUs than between domains. There are no known limitations on how deep an OU hierarchy can become, although Microsoft recommends a simple domain structure containing a limited number of child domains. In any case, you should attempt to design a small and easily managed OU structure because it's hard to manage an extensive number of OU structures unless you assign this role to separate administrators in your organization.

Replication and Synchronization

Domain structures also affect Active Directory synchronization and replication in your Windows 2000 forest. Because many domain controllers can exist in one domain (or even one forest), they must have some way of communicating changes to their individual directories. Most domain controllers hold only a *replica* of the master database of information found in the entire forest. The AD structure holds a complete replica of all domain information from every domain in the forest. Whether you are working with a native-mode Exchange 2000 environment or a mixed-mode Exchange 5.5/Exchange 2000 environment, you will always have directory replication and synchronization.

Active Directory replicates directory information between all domain controllers in a Windows 2000 forest. This process is known as **multi-master replication**, and is contrasted with the single-master replication process used by Windows NT 4.0 Server. Ultimately, all information in Windows 2000 is categorized into a global catalog, or index of information. This multi-master replication is similar to Exchange 5.5 directory synchronization procedures; however, that does not mean AD behaves in the same way as an Exchange 5.5 directory. Object replication in AD and Exchange 5.5 has many differences, listed in Table 4-1, so you need the Active Directory Connector (ADC) as an intermediary tool to synchronize directory information between AD and Exchange Server 5.5.

Table 4-1 Replication Differences Between Active Directory and Exchange Server 5.5

Active Directory	Exchange 5.5 Directory
Uses an object's globally unique identifier (GUID) for replication purposes, allowing objects to be safely renamed	Uses distinguished names for replication. Directory names become permanent once chosen, which makes it hard to rename objects in the directory database in the future
Replicates information using only data that has changed	Replicates information using all attributes of an object, not just changed information
Supports intersite replication using either SMTP or RPC	Supports intersite replication using only SMTP
Produces a flexible replication topology or structure between Windows 2000 sites	Produces a somewhat limited replication topology or structure between sites and uses only e-mail as a transport mechanism

Windows 2000 Server is more efficient than Windows NT 4.0 in terms of replicating directory information because you can select the types of attributes that are replicated to the global catalog within the forest structure. Being selective about the type of information that's replicated means less replication traffic in your network. When replicating directory information between different versions of Exchange, you should be concerned about replication traffic. An Exchange 5.5 site generates much more replication traffic than an AD site because every Exchange 5.5 server you run contains a complete copy of the entire Exchange Server directory database. AD, on the other hand, replicates information only to a domain controller or GC server, which reduces replication traffic. Earlier versions of Windows dealt with increasing levels of replication traffic because two levels of replication were taking place in these networks. In networks consisting of Exchange 5.5 servers running on Windows NT 4.0 primary domain controllers or backup domain controllers, two databases need replication: the Exchange 5.5 directory database and the Windows NT 4.0 Security Accounts Manager database (consisting of all users created in the Windows NT 4.0 domain). Windows 2000 has alleviated this replication overhead by consolidating all directory databases into one single directory component: Active Directory.

Global Catalog Servers

In deploying Exchange 2000 Server, you have to be concerned with how your end users access directory information when performing queries or searches using their Exchange client (usually a version of Microsoft Outlook, but it can be a POP3 or IMAP4 client, such as Outlook Express). Global Catalog servers are a vital component of an Exchange 2000 deployment because they give users access to directory information. In fact, anyone using a MAPI-based client, such as Microsoft Outlook 2000 or Outlook 97, can view directory information for any user in any domain in the forest simply because MAPI attributes are replicated to a GC server. Make sure you have, at a minimum, one

GC server for every Windows 2000 site. Sometimes a site can cover multiple domains in a forest; in this case, you may want to add a GC server for every domain containing an Exchange 2000 server and its associated clients. You have to monitor your GC servers and domain controllers in the first few weeks of your deployment to determine whether the current setup can support your user population and message traffic levels. Also, keep in mind that although you have the option of selecting or "tagging" many object attributes for replication to the global catalog, you don't want to consume a lot of network bandwidth with excessive replication requests.

You can visit the Microsoft site at *http://support.microsoft.com/support/kb/articles/Q244/3/68.asp* for information about optimizing resources on domain controllers or GC servers.

Even though you should always have one GC server per Windows 2000 site, it is a good idea to exceed this minimum to give users more efficient, accurate directory searches. A rule of thumb is to have one GC server for every four mailbox servers in your organization.

The DSProxy Service

The Directory Service Proxy DLL function (or DSProxy, as described in Chapter 1, "An Overview of Microsoft Exchange 2000 Server") is an Exchange 2000 service that helps users access information in Active Directory. A DSProxy server promotes compatibility with previous versions of Exchange Server and enables directory communications between different Exchange Server versions by using the ADC. (More details are given in the section "Deploying the Active Directory Connector.")

An e-mail client accesses one of two different computers when performing a search for an object: It accesses AD directly on the Windows 2000 domain controller or GC server, or it queries an Exchange 2000 server and is referred to a GC server to access AD. If a client cannot access AD directly because it doesn't support Lightweight Directory Access Protocol (LDAP), it uses the DSProxy service to perform name resolution services against AD. DSProxy refers requests from MAPI clients (such as Microsoft Outlook) to Active Directory whenever these MAPI clients are searching for a GC server, and then provides name resolution services by supplying the name of the nearest GC server. It finds the nearest GC server by using the DSAccess service, which is part of the Exchange Server System Attendant component. You can use any network protocol to communicate with DSProxy, except the NetBIOS protocol used in Windows NT 4.0 or Windows 2000 Server. DSProxy can be used to help clients that run any version of Outlook. For recent clients, such as Outlook 2000, DSProxy offers valuable assistance in locating the next available GC server should a primary GC server fail.

Deploying the Active Directory Connector

The ADC, used primarily in mixed-mode environments running both Exchange Server 5.5 and Exchange 2000 Server, synchronizes directory information between AD and Exchange Server 5.5. Being able to replicate objects from Exchange Server 5.5 to AD means that these objects can be made accessible to Exchange 2000 Server. You can specify replication or synchronization of objects from AD to Exchange 5.5 or from Exchange 5.5 to AD. The ADC supports one-way or two-way replication of both recipient objects, which include mailboxes, public folders, e-mail contacts, and configuration information, such as connectors, protocols, and other server-related information. LDAP is used to replicate changes in object information between directories.

The ADC is used when you are migrating to Exchange 2000 from earlier Exchange versions and need to transform your Exchange 5.5 users into Windows 2000 recipient objects. Windows 2000 Server creates and stores all objects, including recipients, inside the Active Directory database structure and stores the physical mailbox inside a storage group. The ADC is installed in addition to both Windows 2000 Server and Exchange 2000 Server. There are actually two different versions of the ADC: one for Windows 2000 and one for Exchange 2000. The Windows 2000 version of the ADC helps you prepare AD for Exchange 2000 before you actually install Exchange 2000 Server. You cannot deploy an Exchange 2000 server without first populating your AD structure with user objects. Make sure you have user objects in AD for every existing Exchange 5.5 server mailbox to ensure that Exchange 5.5 servers and Exchange 2000 servers coexist peacefully in the same environment.

If you decide to use the Exchange 2000 ADC, you need at least one server in your Exchange Server 5.5 site that runs Service Pack 3 so that you have complete synchronization. You don't have to upgrade all servers in your site to SP3, but we recommend upgrading all ADCs to the Exchange 2000 version so that you can completely replicate all configuration and recipient information.

Although the ADC might seem like an optional tool that helps you synchronize information between directories, it's required in mixed-mode environments. If you no longer maintain Exchange 5.5 mailboxes (or no longer run Exchange 5.5 servers), however, you no longer need the ADC. In general, you need to use the ADC in the following situations:

- When you have user information on an Exchange 5.5 server that you do not want to duplicate in AD and Exchange 2000 Server
- When you need to enable coexistence between Exchange 2000 Server and Exchange Server 5.5
- If you want to increase replication efficiency when modifying objects in AD (AD allows you to modify any object on any server containing a replica of your Windows 2000 site.)

When installing the ADC on a server, you might not want to use the Exchange 5.5 service account because it will not have the appropriate permissions for AD or the global catalog in Windows 2000.

The Site Replication Service

Installing the ADC also makes other services available, such as the Site Replication Service (SRS), which helps you with coexistence and migration strategies when you deploy Exchange 2000 Server. This service allows an Exchange 2000 computer to be placed inside an Exchange 5.5 site so that it emulates an Exchange 5.5 computer to other Exchange 5.5 computers in the site. The SRS helps the ADC translate information between the Exchange 5.5 directory service and the AD service. You could say it's functionally equivalent to the Exchange 5.5 directory service, even though all MAPIs are disabled. Figure 4-1 shows the relationship between the ADC and the SRS.

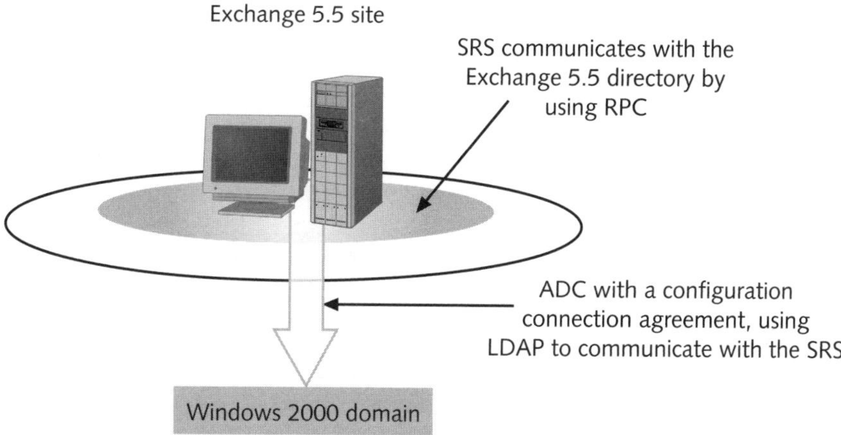

Figure 4-1 The relationship between the ADC and the SRS

It's easy to confuse the purposes of all the components that have been discussed so far, but the following points should help you remember what's important about the ADC and its components:

- The ADC uses LDAP to communicate with both SRS and AD.
- The SRS communicates with the Exchange 5.5 directory service by using an RPC updated style sheet or simple e-mail messages.
- With the SRS, you can view an Exchange 2000 server in the Exchange 5.5 Exchange Administrator program.
- The Exchange 2000 Setup program automatically installs the SRS, which is known as a "helper service." It is activated when you place your first Exchange 2000 server in a site or when you upgrade any directory replication

bridgehead computer. On other Exchange 2000 servers you install, the SRS is present but deactivated.

- The actual file or executable that starts the SRS is Srsmain.exe; however, the SRS also uses a Site Consistency Checker to maintain replication links and the Srs.edb database to store Exchange 5.5 directory information.

Deploying Connection Agreements

What is a connection agreement, and how does it fit into the scheme of the SRS, ADC, and AD? Deploying Exchange 2000 Server means not only installing the relevant Windows 2000 Server services, but also defining the relationships that depend on these services. If you install the ADC on a server running Exchange 2000 Server, you have merely defined a new service in AD without specifying the actual method of replicating data between the services. You have yet to define how recipient changes should be replicated between the SRS and AD. This is where connection agreements come into play.

Connection agreements allow full directory synchronization between AD and your Exchange 5.5 site. This synchronization allows users in your Exchange 2000 organization to see any Exchange 5.5 users in their global address list (GAL). The GAL, usually stored on a GC server, is a compilation of all recipient addresses in Active Directory. The GAL is used by Exchange clients (such as Microsoft Outlook clients) to search for recipients when sending e-mail messages. These agreements are capable of replicating both recipient and public folder data between Exchange Server 5.5 and the global catalog of Windows 2000 Server. Connection agreements also synchronize migrated user accounts from a Windows NT 4.0 domain to associated mailboxes in Active Directory. You can plan on setting up two types of connection agreements using the ADC:

- User connection agreements that replicate recipient objects or data between Exchange 5.5 and Active Directory
- Configuration connection agreements that replicate configuration information between Exchange 5.5 and Active Directory

You can view both types of agreements by using the Active Directory Connector Management tool (Adcadmin.exe) in Exchange 2000 Server. The ADC shows the name and direction of all user connection agreements (see Chapter 6 for a fuller explanation of the Active Directory Connector); it also displays bridgehead servers for all configuration connection agreements. You can set up multiple connection agreements for every occurrence of the ADC if, for example, you want one connection agreement to attach to a unique Exchange 5.5 site. However, you could have multiple connection agreements attached to the same Exchange 5.5 site but configured with different object classes and replication schedules.

If you are planning on deploying the ADC with connection agreements, keep in mind that you can create only user connection agreements, which replicate recipient objects and their associated information. Exchange 2000 Server creates configuration connection agreements that are read-only by default, so you cannot change them in any way.

Also, the SRS is responsible for creating the first default configuration connection agreement, called the Config CA_<*administrative group name*>_<*Exchange 2000 server name*>. For example, a server named Orion containing an administrative group named AG1 has a connection agreement called Config CA_AG1_Orion configured in System Manager. Any agreement to replicate configuration information is actually established between AD and the SRS, not AD and the Exchange 5.5 directory. Setting up and viewing configuration connection agreements means that your Exchange 2000 servers must reside in an Exchange 5.5 network.

Connection agreements usually modify attributes of the Exchange 5.5 directory or the Windows 2000 Server Active Directory. For example, a configuration connection agreement contains the MsExchReplicateNow attribute. If the value of this attribute is True, then the ADC undergoes a replication cycle immediately, which forces a replication of Exchange 5.5 configuration data to the configuration naming context of Active Directory. Another important attribute is MsExchHomeServerName, which contains the server that users normally send their e-mail messages to. A third attribute is legacyExchangeDN, which equates to the distinguished name of an object in the Exchange Server 5.5 directory.

When you set up connection agreements, you can replicate information to or from an Exchange 5.5 site, meaning replication can be defined by one-way or two-way connection agreements. When using two-way connection agreements, a good rule of thumb is to define connection agreements to each Exchange 5.5 site in your organization. If the only result you want is to migrate an Exchange 5.5 directory over to Active Directory, however, then you should define a one-way connection agreement *from* Exchange 5.5 *to* AD, assuming that you never need to write information back to the original Exchange 5.5 directory. There is also less replication traffic in a one-way connection agreement.

Before deploying the ADC, the SRS, and any connection agreements, consider the questions in the following list:

- *On what type of server should I install the ADC?* Microsoft recommends placing the ADC on member servers in your Windows 2000 domain because you don't want to add unnecessary processing loads to domain controllers whose main tasks include user authentication for network logons.
- *What should be the endpoints of my connection agreements?* Whether your connection agreement is configured as one-way or two-way, you should configure one endpoint as a Windows 2000 GC server and the other endpoint as an Exchange 5.5 bridgehead server (especially in large Exchange 5.5 sites). If you are not able to use a GC server, you should deploy ADCs with connection agreements on servers that are physically close to a GC server, preferably in the same Windows 2000 site. (Remember that a site is a range or collection of IP subnets, and one Windows 2000 site can span multiple domains.) Even in a large Windows 2000 multidomain environment, you should ensure that all GC servers exist in the same Windows 2000 site.

- *How am I going to manage recipient objects after they have been replicated?* This question is really asking, "Which management tool will be used to manage objects after they have replicated—Active Directory Users and Computers in Windows 2000 or User Manager for Domains in Windows NT 4.0?" If you want to use AD exclusively to manage these recipient objects, then deploy all connection agreements as one-way agreements and make sure these agreements can write and make modifications directly to the Exchange 5.5 directory. Every time an object is replicated to AD, it can be modified in some way, which could result in decreased network performance and increased network traffic. Changing the time of replication (see Chapter 6 for more details on this task) reduces this negative impact on your network.
- *At what point do I plan to upgrade my Windows NT 4.0 domains?* If you don't follow proper procedures when deploying the ADC with connection agreements, you face the prospect of having duplicate user accounts in AD. (See Chapter 6 for further details on configuring the ADC.) Recall that every object in Exchange 5.5 was associated with a primary Windows NT 4.0 account, defined in the User Manager for Domains tool. If you deploy the ADC before upgrading your Windows NT 4.0 domain to Windows 2000, the ADC creates new recipient objects in AD for the users that existed in the NT 4.0 domain. If you upgrade your domains to Windows 2000, you have to somehow merge these ADC-created objects with Windows 2000 upgraded user accounts. To do that, you use the Active Directory Account Cleanup Wizard, found under Microsoft Exchange in your Start, Programs menu. If you decide to deploy the ADC after upgrading your domains to Windows 2000, there is no need to merge objects in AD with objects from the NT 4.0 domains.

Troubleshooting the Active Directory Connector and Connection Agreements

You can reduce your troubleshooting efforts by following recommended procedures when configuring the ADC or connection agreements. First, make sure that all mailboxes in Exchange 5.5 are associated with only one user account. Exchange 5.5 is not strict about associations between mailboxes and user objects, and it even allows multiple users to own a single mailbox. When replicating objects to AD, the ADC might associate an improper user account with a given mailbox object. Consider what happens when users are associated with resource objects in Exchange 5.5, such as conference rooms, in addition to their personal mailboxes. The ADC does not discriminate between these associations and may end up associating this user object with the conference room resource in AD. Cleaning up these objects in your Exchange 5.5 site helps prevent this type of error.

Next, consider deploying at least two ADC servers in your Exchange 2000 organization and installing them as member servers, not domain controllers. One acts as a primary ADC server and the other becomes your secondary, or back-up, ADC server. This back-up server can be used for fault-tolerance purposes in a disaster and can be brought online if the primary server shuts down for any reason. The focus is more on fault tolerance versus load balancing, even though both roles are important in any messaging environment. Load balancing comes into play when using multiple connection agreements to replicate different attributes and different objects using custom replication schedules. However, these multiple connection agreements are usually configured on one server, which eliminates any chance of fault tolerance. If problems occur with your deployment of the ADC or connection agreements, you can always turn off your connection agreements or shut down your ADC services until the problem has been resolved.

In times of severe distress, you can use the Windows 2000 support tool called LDAP Viewer (LDP.exe) to view and modify data in your Active Directory databases. LDAP Viewer is a graphical tool that's easy to use when you want to view or modify data in the AD database of your Windows 2000 forest. To install LDP.exe, run Setup.exe from the /Support/Tools directory of your Windows 2000 Server CD-ROM. This installs a Support Tools kit, which installs LDP.exe. This tool is placed in the /Program Files/Support Tools directory.

Finally, be careful when deploying the ADC and connection agreements over low-bandwidth WAN links, such as dial-up connections. Many Exchange 5.5 sites cover a wide area of low-bandwidth connections, and many Windows 2000 domains can cover widely dispersed geographic areas, such as connections between remote branch offices. In some cases, the connection between these remote offices consists of low-bandwidth 56-Kbps (kilobits per second) connections that are not permanent. You have to use relevant protocols that apply to these situations; however, some protocols handle low-bandwidth connections better than others. SMTP, for example, handles low-bandwidth connections better than RPC by design, yet the protocol used between a server running the ADC and a server running the Exchange 5.5 directory service is a combination of LDAP *and* RPC, and both these protocols require direct TCP/IP connections between servers.

The Recipient Update Service

The Recipient Update Service (RUS) adds address list information to recipient objects. You can use the RUS to update recipient objects that have been merged or migrated from an Exchange 5.5 site using the ADC with connection agreements. Sometimes you will notice a delay in displaying proper address information for new recipient objects or for upgraded recipient objects from an Exchange 5.5 site. The RUS runs as part of the System Attendant process in Exchange 2000, and it can update all address information in the background according to an update interval you define. This service is in the System Manager snap-in under the Recipients container (see Figure 4-2).

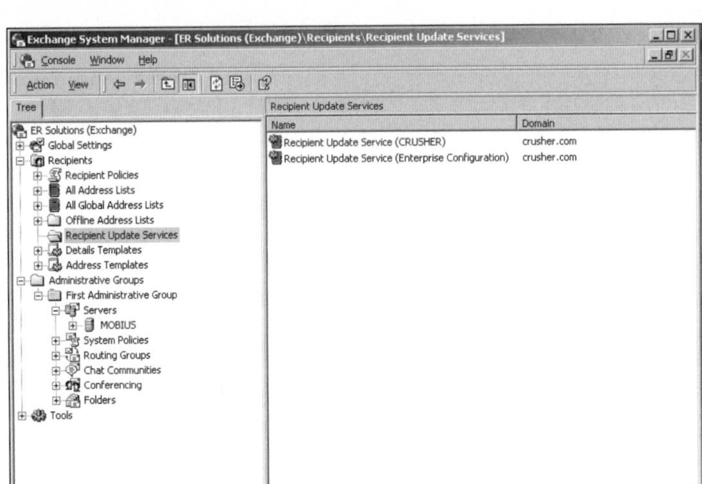

Figure 4-2 Recipient Update Services in System Manager

You may notice two different service objects: one for updating the domain-naming context of Windows 2000 Server and another used to update the Active Directory configuration-naming context. All recipient objects are controlled within the AD domain-naming context. Right-clicking an RUS object allows you to apply new domain settings or adjust existing domain settings. Click All Tasks, Update Now on the shortcut menu to force an immediate update of all address lists within your domains (see Figure 4-3).

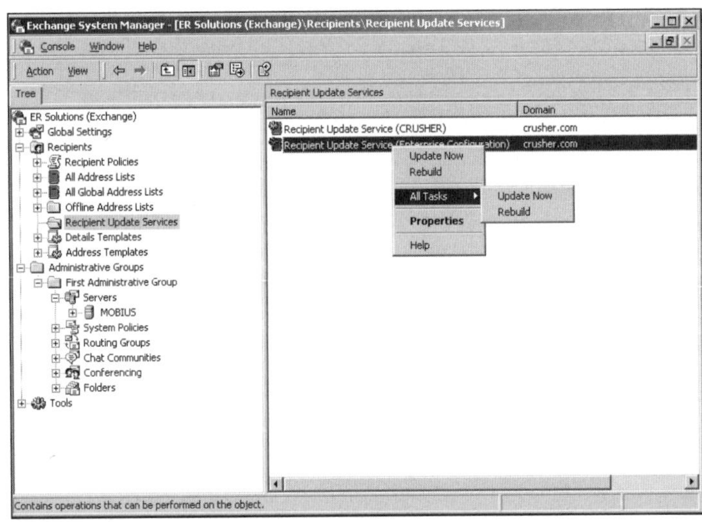

Figure 4-3 Forcing an update on an RUS object

An important rule to keep in mind is that each domain has its own RUS, so deploying multiple Windows 2000 domains requires at least one RUS per domain. However, if you install only one Exchange 2000 server in each domain, you will automatically have a new RUS object in System Manager for that domain.

Some domains in your Windows 2000 forest will *not* contain an Exchange 2000 server, yet you can still run the RUS inside this domain. An RUS object appears automatically in System Manager only in domains that have an Exchange 2000 server. This means that mailbox-enabled recipients cannot exist in a domain where the RUS is not configured because no e-mail addresses are generated.

Deploying Administrative Groups and Routing Groups

As mentioned previously, administrative groups and routing groups are used in Exchange 2000 to define your network structure or layout. The following sections offer deployment tips to help you avoid configuration errors when using these features with some of the elements discussed previously, such as organizational units or connectors.

Administrative Groups

You use administrative groups to simplify managing permissions. After creating an administrative group, you assign objects to it; these objects then inherit the permissions that have been set for the group. You can use only the default Exchange 2000 administrative group, called the First Administrative Group, or you can decide to create additional administrative groups. Additional administrative groups are needed if you want to group servers to manage permissions, so that one group of administrators can manage one group of servers while another group of administrators manages a different group of servers. It is not uncommon to create administrative groups for separate divisions or even separate regions within a company.

Administrative groups are not displayed by default, so before you create any new administrative groups, you have to make the Administrative Groups container visible in System Manager by right-clicking the topmost object in System Manager (the Organization object), clicking Properties on the shortcut menu, and then clicking the Display administrative groups check box on the General tab (see Figure 4-4). Then you must restart System Manager for the change to be visible. When the container becomes available, you can right-click it, point to New, and then click Administrative Group on the shortcut menu to set up additional administrative groups.

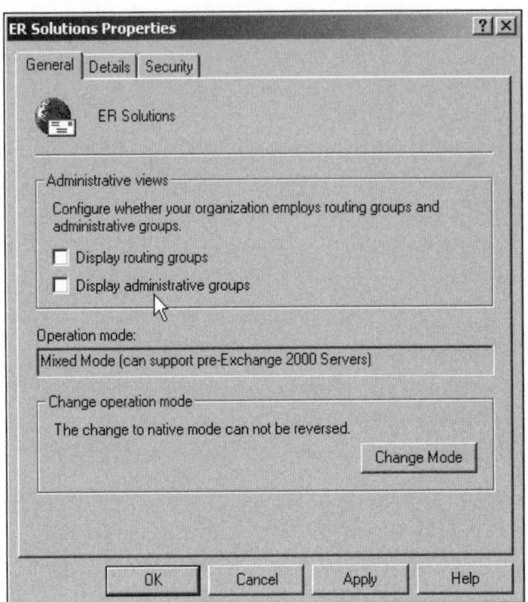

Figure 4-4 Displaying administrative groups in System Manager

Deploying Administrative Groups

Deploying administrative groups after installing Exchange 2000 Server in your production environment means deciding what objects to contain and manage in those administrative groups. For example, you can place system policies, routing groups, servers, or even chat communities inside a particular administrative group, or they can all be placed in your First Administrative Group. Your objective in creating these groups is to manage permissions for objects (such as system policies or routing groups) to increase network security for your company. (For instance, you can set the View Only permission on a system policy object, which prevents this policy from being modified by users.) Even if you grant permissions to objects at a higher level, such as the Organization object level, these permissions eventually propagate down to all administrative groups you create. (For instance, in the previous View Only permission example, this permission set on the system policy object would also appear in the administrative group.)

If you are running a mixed-mode environment, only one administrative group is allowed per site. In native-mode environments, there is no limit to how many administrative groups you can create or configure. However, you shouldn't have an excessive number of administrative groups. Use the fewest groups possible to adequately separate permissions in your organization.

Administrative Groups and Roles

Some objects in System Manager do not have a Security tab in their Properties dialog boxes, so you need to use the Exchange Administration Delegation of Control Wizard. To start it, in the Exchange System Manager snap-in, right-click an administrative group, and choose Delegate Control to assign permissions for these objects. This wizard can specifically assign permission to the Organization object in System Manager or to certain administrative groups in the Administrative Groups container in System Manager. Exchange 2000 allows you to assign one of three different roles to a user or group (or anyone who can log on to your Exchange 2000 Server or Windows 2000 Server domain controller):

- *Exchange View Only Administrator*—This role is for users who need read-only capabilities for configuration information, without being able to modify the configuration settings.
- *Exchange Administrator*—This role is for users who want to fully administer your Exchange 2000 organization, without being able to modify permissions on configuration items or change access controls. They cannot change security settings for any Exchange databases or address lists, but they can create new administrative groups.
- *Exchange Full Administrator*—This role is for users who want to fully administer all system information in your Exchange 2000 organization on a day-to-day basis. These users can also modify permissions on all objects, regulate access controls to your Exchange servers, and manipulate all objects in the AD configuration-naming context.

Remember that permissions assigned to the Organization object can be different from permissions assigned to an administrative group object. Trying to pinpoint a permission-related problem for users can be difficult if they belong to multiple security groups, administrative groups, or routing groups with varying levels of permissions. Permissions sometimes conflict; for example, a user could have permission on an individual basis to access a file, but she might be denied access to this file if the group she belongs to has been assigned Deny permissions for this file. Also, if you assign permissions to the Organization object or administrative group object, you are not necessarily giving users local control of your Exchange 2000 server. In other words, users can't make local Registry changes or stop and start all services unless you make them members of the local administrators group for the machine they want to manage.

Another point about permissions is that one role usually contains the role beneath it. For example, if you grant someone the role of Exchange Administrator at the Organization object level in System Manager (the first object seen in the tree in the System Manager snap-in), that person also has the "lesser" role of Exchange View Only Administrator. However, if you grant this same person the Exchange View Only Administrator role for the topmost object in System Manager (the Organization object), he or she has only the Exchange View Only Administrator role at the administrative group level. In other words, there is no role "lower" than the Exchange View Only Administrator role at the Organization object level. Taking this one step further, if you grant someone the Exchange Full Administrator role for an administrative group, he or she now has both the Exchange Administrator *and* the Exchange View Only Administrator roles because these roles are *included* in the Exchange Full Administrator role.

Keep the following points in mind when using the Exchange Administration Delegation of Control Wizard:

- Exchange Full Administrators have full control of the Organization object in System Manager, and they have full control over all administrative groups.
- Exchange Administrators do not have change permissions on the Organization object and do not have Receive As or Send As permissions on the Organization object or child objects. They do not have change permissions on any administrative groups or connections containers, but they do have read and write access to all Offline Address List containers.
- Exchange View Only Administrators can view the Information Store status on the Organization object and all child objects and can do the same for all administrative group containers or child containers. They also have read-only access to all policy containers (for example, the Recipient Policies container), address list containers (for example, the All Address Lists container), and the Global Settings containers.

The key to deploying administrative groups is to simplify your organizational design. You will learn that the design of your administrative groups does not have to relate in any way to the design of your routing groups. If all servers can fit inside one administrative group, then use that design because that single administrative group can contain multiple routing groups, if necessary. Your deployment of administrative groups should be somewhat final, however, because you can't move servers between different administrative groups after the fact.

Routing Groups

The use of routing groups presents a somewhat different picture from administrative groups. You create routing groups to mirror your physical network topology, but the actual creation of these groups depends on the status of your organizational network layout and whether you are managing a mixed-mode or native-mode Exchange 2000 environment. The following sections outline important points for integrating routing groups and administrative groups.

Integrating Routing Groups and Administrative Groups

- You can place a server in one administrative group and place that same server in a routing group that belongs to a different administrative group.

Remember that administrative groups are only "logical" containers, and they do not describe the actual physical network of your company. So you could place server A in administrative group B, but at the same time, server A could belong to routing group A, which belongs to administrative group C. You are not moving servers by performing these actions; you are simply defining different boundaries for this server: a physical boundary as defined by your routing group, and a logical boundary as defined by your administrative group placement (see Figure 4-5).

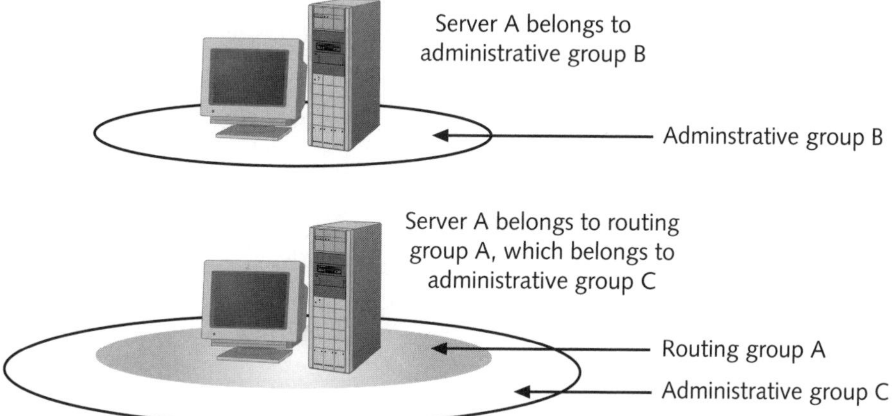

Figure 4-5 Servers belonging to administrative and routing groups simultaneously

- You can create a routing group container inside an administrative group container, and then place multiple routing groups inside the routing group container. You can then assign different servers to different routing groups.
- If your organization does not have any Exchange Server 5.5 computers and you configure a native-mode operation, you can assign a server to a routing group without worrying about which administrative group it belongs to. For example, if a server belongs to an administrative group named AG1 and you place that server in routing group RG1, which belongs to administrative group AG2, that server still belongs to administrative group AG1.

The deployment scenarios you select for your company depend on the administration model that your company follows. Some companies prefer a centralized management approach, whereas other companies prefer a more distributed management approach. In a distributed management model, many separate branch offices are responsible for managing different administrative and routing groups. In that case, your deployment of Exchange 2000 Server depends on how these branch offices are connected. If messages are going to cross semipermanent or low-bandwidth connections, it may be advisable to create separate routing groups for these offices. You need high-bandwidth connectivity within a routing group, but you must also decide how to connect routing groups so that messages can flow without interruption.

Comparing Connectors

Because the basics of messaging have already been discussed in Chapter 1, that information can be incorporated to help you understand the deployment of routing groups. Remember that all servers inside a routing group communicate directly using native SMTP. No connectors are needed within a routing group. However, connectors are needed to connect one routing group to another. You can use the Routing Group Connector (RGC), the SMTP Connector, or the X.400 Connector for this purpose. The RGC is the easiest connector to set up. However, best practices dictate that you configure multiple connectors between two routing groups even if they are of the same type. For instance, you can connect two routing groups using two SMTP Connectors and one RGC. This method is used for fault-tolerance purposes so that if one connector becomes unavailable, all servers within the routing group can check their link state tables and reroute messages using other connectors. The RGC can use SMTP or RPC to transfer messages. If it's connecting two routing groups in Exchange 2000, it uses SMTP; if it's connecting to an Exchange 5.5 server, messages are transferred using RPC. The RGC resembles the Site Connector used in Exchange 5.5. The SMTP Connector is used to connect to other SMTP messaging systems or to connect to the Internet because the RGC is incapable of connecting to external messaging systems. You rarely use SMTP Connectors for the sole purpose of connecting two routing groups, but you could use them when migrating from an Exchange 5.5 site that uses the Internet Mail Connector. X.400 Connectors are used to connect routing groups or to connect your Exchange 2000 system to external X.400 systems. The X.400 Connector does not use SMTP or RPC as transport mechanisms; it uses the Message Transfer Agent (MTA) component for message transfers.

To determine which connector offers the most functionality or which one is the "preferred" connector to use in a given situation, review the following guidelines:

- The RGC works best when you have permanent and reliable network connections between any two different routing groups. The RGC is also the easiest connector to configure.
- The RGC might not operate as well over low-bandwidth or less reliable network connections between different routing groups. If used in a mixed-mode setting with computers running Exchange Server 5.5, an RGC is functionally equivalent to an Exchange 5.5 Site Connector and uses RPC as its primary messaging transport protocol.
- Both the RGC and the SMTP Connector support the use of multiple bridgehead servers in a domain for load-balancing purposes. A bridgehead server is the endpoint for the connector. X.400 Connectors can use only one bridgehead server, so you have to configure multiple X.400 Connectors to achieve any level of load balancing or fault tolerance.

- Use SMTP Connectors if you want to authenticate any of your connections or encrypt all or part of your messaging traffic. SMTP Connectors cannot use any messaging transport mechanism other than SMTP.
- The X.400 Connector uses two major network transport mechanisms for message delivery: the TCP/IP transport or the X.25 transport. TCP/IP is obviously the more widely used network transport stack.
- You can have fewer routing groups in your company by using Exchange 2000 instead of Exchange 5.5 because Exchange 2000 uses SMTP, which handles low-bandwidth connections better than the RPC used in Exchange 5.5.
- If you use the SMTP Connector, your SMTP mail cannot be compressed in any form, which could increase the server load. Also, SMTP mail is not encrypted unless you manually enable Internet Protocol security or the Transport Layer Security protocol (which are advanced features involving extra administration and maintenance).

Routing Groups and Link State

Deploying routing groups requires an understanding of how to maintain link state information between servers in a routing group. Exchange 2000 Server uses a routing engine to make routing calculations (similar to the MTA component of Exchange Server 5.5). The routing engine, in turn, uses link state tables for routing information. Link state information is most efficient when you have multiple routing groups in your company. This information is sent between routing groups using SMTP on port 25. However, it is somewhat different *inside* a routing group because a special computer, known as the routing group master, propagates this information. Every routing group must contain one computer chosen as the routing group master, which maintains link state information for all members of that routing group. To select a routing group master, in System Manager right-click a server inside a Routing Group container, and then click Set as Master on the shortcut menu. Link state data is considered volatile information because it is never saved to the physical disk; it is saved only in physical RAM or server memory. If you happen to restart any server in a routing group, including the routing group master, it must refresh all link state information by receiving that information from other servers in the group.

The choice of connectors in your organization affects the levels of messaging traffic in your network. If your network has less permanent or less reliable connections, you could consider using the SMTP Connector, but there are drawbacks to this connector in environments that transfer large message attachments over extremely slow WAN links (less than 10 Kbps, for instance). In these cases, you could deploy one or more X.400 Connectors to reduce the size of the attachment, or you could use a combination of the SMTP and the X.400 Connectors so that smaller messages are transferred using SMTP and larger messages are transferred using the X.400 protocol. Cost values are used as a basis for selecting from multiple connectors between routing groups. You enter cost information when you configure a connector in System Manager. These costs usually range between 1 and 100, and the connector with the lowest cost value is chosen from the group.

DEPLOYMENT IN MIXED-MODE ENVIRONMENTS AND LEGACY WINDOWS NT 4.0 DOMAINS

Most organizations are considered mixed-mode environments because they run many different versions of Exchange Server. Microsoft has made it convenient to run different versions of Exchange Server within one company by offering management tools and utilities that support both versions. For example, the ADC synchronizes directory information between an Exchange 5.5 server directory and Active Directory in Windows 2000. The following sections offer deployment guidelines for mixed-mode environments.

Deployment Guidelines for Mixed-Mode Environments

Exchange 2000 operates in mixed mode by default because Microsoft expects the majority of companies to continue managing Exchange 5.5 servers, even when introducing an Exchange 2000 server. The presence of an Exchange 2000 server does not eliminate all the functionality of the Exchange 5.5 server; rather, it incorporates and enhances this functionality by introducing new transport mechanisms and new features inherent to the Windows 2000 operating system. Many concepts new to Windows 2000 are also used in the Exchange 5.5 environment. For instance, there is a one-to-one relationship between administrative groups and routing groups in Exchange Server 5.5 because these groups are seen as additional site objects in the Exchange Administrator program. This concept works both ways, however, because an Exchange 5.5 server site that's replicated to AD is seen as an administrative group in the Exchange 2000 System Manager. Mixed-mode operations are not necessarily ideal, however. There are limitations you must deal with if you continue to run your organization in mixed mode. For example, you cannot move a mailbox between servers if they are in different administrative groups. Also, a routing group can consist only of servers that belong to the same administrative group. In other words, routing groups cannot cover multiple administrative groups in mixed mode, even though administrative groups can cover multiple routing groups in mixed mode.

Most people become somewhat frustrated when trying to grasp the relationships between administrative groups and routing groups in mixed-mode Exchange Server environments, especially when they have little experience managing Exchange. Native-mode operations change all this, of course, but as long as you have even one Exchange 5.5 server in your network, these rules apply. In essence, you cannot put servers from different administrative groups into the same routing group.

Migration Issues

Although migration issues are addressed in more detail in Chapter 6, if you are deploying Exchange 2000 in a site consisting of Exchange 5.5 servers running on Windows NT 4.0 machines, there are a few considerations worth mentioning here. If you are installing Exchange 2000 in your existing Exchange 5.5 site consisting of a Windows NT 4.0

domain, you must set up a trust relationship between your NT 4.0 domain and your Windows 2000 domain (most likely a one-way explicit trust relationship). This trust relationship adds Windows NT administrator rights to your Exchange 2000 administrator account. Remember, your Exchange 2000 organization is set to operate in mixed mode by default to enable permanent interoperability with earlier versions of Exchange. In System Manager, the msExchMixedMode attribute for the Organization object is set to a value of True (in other words, specifying that you're running in mixed mode) until you manually convert your organization to native mode.

Managing Resources in Mixed-Mode Environments

Managing resources can also present problems in mixed-mode environments. Many administrators try to use the old Exchange Administrator program to manage Exchange 2000 resources, but you should use the Exchange Server 5.5 Exchange Administrator program to manage Exchange 5.5 resources, and the Exchange 2000 System Manager program to manage Exchange 2000 resources. The reason for this is that Exchange Server 5.5 cannot officially recognize AD, and without the SRS operating on your Exchange 2000 machine, Exchange 2000 cannot recognize the Exchange 5.5 directory database. You should not use Windows 2000 tools to manage mailbox resources in Exchange Server 5.5 because the directory structures in Exchange 5.5 and Windows 2000 are quite different in nature.

Public folders are also an area of concern in mixed-mode environements because Exchange 2000 Server provides item-level security for all public folders, but Exchange Server 5.5 does not offer this protection. If you happen to move or replicate a public folder from Exchange 2000 to an Exchange 5.5 directory, you lose this granular level of protection. If you are using distribution lists in Exchange Server 5.5, they are automatically converted into a special Windows 2000 group called a universal distribution group (UDG), which cannot assign permissions in Windows 2000.

Mixed-mode operations occur primarily because you are moving an Exchange 2000 server into an existing Exchange 5.5 site. There are times, however, when you might want to move an Exchange 5.5 site into an existing mixed-mode Exchange environment. If Organization A consists solely of Exchange 5.5 servers, and Organization B consists of one Exchange 5.5 server and three Exchange 2000 servers, you may want to move one Exchange 5.5 server from Organization A into Organization B. For this to happen, you must make sure that Organization A can contain *only* servers running Exchange 5.5 (not Exchange 5.0 or earlier), and that Organization B has at least one Exchange 5.5 server. All servers in Organization B can be placed into one distinct administrative group, but Organization B cannot be a native-mode organization if this additional Exchange 5.5 server is placed in it.

If the server in Organization A has a connection agreement configured (such as the ADC user connection agreement discussed in "Deploying Connection Agreements," earlier in this chapter), you must remove this connection agreement and place it on another server in Organization A *before* you move the server to Organization B. If you do it after moving the server, you could experience replication problems when controlling this site from Active Directory.

You can visit *http://support.microsoft.com/support/kb/articles/Q196/4/13.asp* to get more details on using the Move Server Wizard.

Deciding whether an upgrade or a migration is best for your company could mean the difference between moving to Windows 2000 and Exchange 2000 in bits and pieces or performing a "clean sweep" installation from scratch. Whichever approach you adopt, you should aim for minimal disruption to end users and a low risk of failure for your network infrastructure. For companies that currently maintain multi-domain Windows NT 4.0 architectures running Exchange Server 5.5, the choices include performing an in-place upgrade to Windows 2000 or migrating to Windows 2000 while managing a coexistence between Exchange 2000 and Exchange 5.5. You must upgrade all Exchange 5.5 servers to Exchange 2000 and simultaneously upgrade your account domains to Windows 2000 when performing an in-place upgrade. Even though this process is relatively straightforward, you have more downtime when attempting to recover your original Exchange Server 5.5 topology should disaster strike. This situation also requires proper installation and configuration of the ADC so that configuration connection agreements are in place.

Using Front-End and Back-End Deployments

A front-end/back-end configuration offers easy scalability to existing Exchange 2000 organizations, meaning you can scale your implementation to accommodate many more users. Deploying Exchange 2000 in this manner allows you to distribute server tasks among different machines. All client requests received by a front-end server are immediately proxied (communicated) to a back-end server for processing. The back-end server is responsible for hosting mailbox stores or public folder stores because these resources are not configured on the front-end server. The front-end server uses LDAP to query Active Directory when trying to locate the relevant back-end server.

The front-end/back-end configuration is useful for a number of reasons, including the following:

- This configuration is recommended for companies who want to give their employees e-mail access over the Internet, especially companies who use Outlook Web Access.
- This configuration is also useful when you want to have a single DNS domain name for all external e-mail users. Normally, users must know the fully qualified domain name of the server that hosts their specific mailbox database; however, using the OWA client with a front-end/back-end configuration means external users can simply type in a common DNS name to access their mail.
- For companies who want to encrypt all communication over public channels such as the Internet, a front-end/back-end design helps increase encryption

efficiency because all external communication can be encrypted or decrypted at the front-end server before being proxied to the back-end server. If the front-end server didn't handle the encryption, the back-end server would have extra overhead caused by the processing needed for encryption and decryption in addition to hosting mailbox or public folder stores. A front-end server can contribute to decreasing this additional processing by performing its own encryption service.

- A front-end server can offer additional layers of security to an internal private network if configured inside a firewall (such as a Cisco PIX firewall or a computer configured with Checkpoint Software's Firewall-1 product). It serves as protection from the Internet because it does not contain any user data, and it can also be configured to accept only authenticated requests from external users.
- A front-end server can be used to refer external clients to proper public folder locations. When external clients make requests for public folder information, they are sometimes referred to a back-end server that does not contain this information. The back-end server notifies the front-end server that received the original request, and the front-end server then refers this client to the back-end server that does have the public folder information. This process happens only with IMAP4 clients who support a feature known as IMAP4 referral. Not all clients support this feature, however.
- The front-end/back-end design is meant for Internet clients who use HTTP, POP3, or IMAP4 to access e-mail in a private network. It was not designed for regular MAPI clients, such as those who use Outlook 2000 or Outlook 97, to access e-mail on Exchange 2000 Server. MAPI is not an Internet protocol, and the front-end/back-end configuration was designed primarily for Internet protocols.

Guidelines for Front-End/Back-End Servers

The whole purpose of a front-end/back-end server configuration is to eliminate the need for users to know which server in their network is hosting their specific mailbox or public folder store. In some companies with many branch offices, however, users are required to log on to a specific server to make user administration more manageable. (This type of management is found in decentralized administrative models, not centralized administrative models.) A front-end/back-end design works best when storage groups are used to hold user mailboxes and users do not expect all the functionality of a MAPI-based client, such as Outlook 2000.

Microsoft recommends that you install the Windows 2000 Network Load Balancing service on all front-end servers before installing Exchange 2000 Server because normal front-end/back-end designs incorporate more front-end servers than back-end servers. The front-end servers act in unison to handle incoming client connections, so it is best to load-balance these connections across all front-end servers. Microsoft also recommends creating separate DNS entries for these front-end servers in the form of host resource records, or "A" records (configured in the DNS Manager snap-in utility found on the Windows 2000 Administrative Tools submenu), so users can access a front-end server by using a simple display name instead of a complicated IP address. It's also a good idea to physically remove the Information Store from a front-end server, even though users are instructed not to access any data in this repository. This configuration is an example of the flexibility demonstrated by Exchange 2000 Server in distributing server tasks among dedicated Exchange 2000 servers. Even moving mailboxes between back-end servers isn't noticeable to your users because all external users continue to access the same bank of front-end servers, which then send their requests to the appropriate Information Store on the back-end server.

Because you can place front-end servers behind a firewall, you need to make sure certain ports are open for clients who access the front-end servers from the Internet. Most clients use HTTP, but they might also use some form of encryption that involves an additional port. These are the main protocols, with the port numbers in parentheses:

- HTTP (80)
- LDAP (389)
- POP3 (110)
- SMTP (25)
- IMAP4 (143)

Chapter Summary

- Your deployment of Exchange 2000 should allow time to test all the features you want to use in your production network. For example, if you are not currently using any real-time collaboration features, such as Instant Messaging, in your production environment, be sure to test those features to determine whether additional server processing is needed.
- Any Exchange 2000 deployment also tests the use of third-party connectors to see which ones are no longer viable in a new production environment using Exchange 2000 Server. An analysis of your current network environment can help determine the appropriate e-mail client to use in your organization.
- Exchange 2000 Server requires more processing power and memory resources than earlier versions of Exchange Server. You need a minimum of an Intel Pentium 166 MHz or faster processor with at least 128 MB of RAM. Plan system resources according to the role your servers play.

- You should deploy Exchange 2000 Server following the MSF specifications; this model helps you achieve your deployment objectives in a methodical manner and ensures that you have considered all contingencies in your deployment plan by outlining a method for fully testing all components before putting them into a production network.
- The developing phase includes validating your design plans, building your Exchange 2000 systems, and completing user pilot tests in a test environment.
- The deploying phase involves migrating users to your new messaging system, handing the control over to the team who will operate and manage Exchange 2000, and formally completing the project and evaluating its success.
- Deploying the ADC is necessary in mixed-mode environments to synchronize and replicate information between the Exchange Server 5.5 directory database and the Active Directory database. You can synchronize *from* the Exchange 5.5 directory or *to* the Exchange 5.5 directory, but you must always prepare for the effect increased replication traffic has on your network. You should always use the Exchange 2000 version of the ADC because of its enhanced functionality.
- The SRS is an ADC component that helps with coexistence and migration strategies when deploying Exchange 2000 Server. It allows an Exchange 2000 machine to emulate an Exchange 5.5 computer to other Exchange 5.5 computers and also translates information between AD and the Exchange 5.5 directory service.
- Deploying the ADC and the SRS means you have to create and configure connection agreements, which allow full directory synchronization between AD and your Exchange 5.5 site, and ensure that all users in your organization maintain one common global address list. You can create only user connection agreements because Exchange 2000 installs and maintains configuration connection agreements automatically.
- Administrative and routing groups help define the logical and physical topology of your organization. Administrative groups simplify managing permissions because you can assign objects to them; these objects then inherit whatever permissions have been set for the group. Routing groups enable servers within the group to communicate with each other using native SMTP. You can place servers in administrative groups and also in routing groups belonging to different administrative groups.
- Connectors are used to connect routing groups; you can use a Routing Group Connector, an SMTP Connector, or an X.400 Connector in your messaging environment. Use the RGC for high-bandwidth connections, the SMTP Connector for encrypted communications, and the X.400 Connector for large message attachments or extremely low-bandwidth connections between servers.
- Exchange 2000 operates in mixed mode by default to enable interoperability with earlier Exchange versions. In mixed mode, there is a one-to-one relationship between administrative groups, routing groups, and sites so that Exchange 5.5 users

see all administrative and routing groups as sites. Remember some of the limitations that mixed-mode environments have; for example, you cannot move servers between administrative groups in mixed mode. If you no longer need Exchange 5.5 or earlier versions, you should use System Manager to switch over to native mode (an irreversible process).

- A front-end/back-end design allows you to scale your organizational needs and increase the number of users who can access your Exchange 2000 servers over the Internet. It is designed to work only with HTTP, POP3, and IMAP4 client access protocols; it does not function with MAPI clients. Advantages of a front-end/back-end design include the use of a single DNS namespace for all external users and encrypted communications at the front-end server.

KEY TERMS

connection agreement — An object that establishes a relationship between an existing Exchange 5.5 site and Active Directory by replicating recipient objects and configuration information between AD and the Exchange 5.5 directory service. You can define multiple connection agreements for each instance of the Active Directory Connector that you configure in Exchange 2000.

full-text indexing — A Windows 2000 service that allows users to perform searches for messages, documents, or attachments. This is done by integrating the query engine component of the Information Store with the Microsoft Search service, which is installed as part of the Exchange 2000 Setup program.

gateway connectors — Connectors used in Exchange 2000 Server to connect to external computer systems, such as IBM mainframes running other operating systems, or to external programs that supply features such as fax or voicemail.

Kerberos version 5 authentication — The client authentication method that uses the Kerberos protocol, a fundamental security protocol in Windows 2000 Server. This mechanism issues tickets containing encrypted information so that clients can access network services; for example, the Kerberos service issues Exchange service tickets to clients who need access to the Exchange 2000 server.

multi-master replication — An Active Directory feature that ensures that any changes to a domain controller or Global Catalog server in a Windows 2000 forest are copied to all other domain controllers in the same domain. These changes include configuration changes made to Exchange 2000 Server.

routing connectors — A component of Exchange 2000 Server that connects two or more routing groups. The two major types of connectors include those that bypass the Message Transfer Agent and use SMTP directly and those that use the Message Transfer Agent and the X.400 protocol directly. The three connectors used in Exchange 2000 are the Routing Group Connector, the SMTP Connector, and the X.400 Connector.

Review Questions

1. SMTP mail cannot be ______________ or ______________ when you use the SMTP Connector to connect routing groups in your organization.

2. Which of the following procedures cannot be successfully tested when you are ready to deploy Exchange 2000 Server?

   a. installing Exchange Server 5.5 on a Windows 2000 computer

   b. configuring Exchange 2000 Server on a Windows NT 4.0 Enterprise computer

   c. installing Exchange Server 5.5 on a Windows NT 4.0 Enterprise computer

   d. configuring Exchange 5.5 Enterprise Server on a Windows NT 4.0 computer

3. You are testing the deployment of Exchange 2000 Server storage groups in a test network and need to validate how many users can exist on each storage group. Which of the following procedures is *not* recommended for your production network?

   a. creating more than five mailbox stores per server

   b. creating more than five storage groups per server

   c. creating more than five databases per storage group

   d. creating more than four public folder stores per server

4. Why should you *not* migrate equipment used in a test network to a production environment, even if the test network produced no significant errors?

   a. You must create a new Exchange organization name to accommodate the new test environment in your production network.

   b. The increased numbers of users on a production network damages system resources on equipment used in the test environment.

   c. Hardware in production environments must always differ from hardware used in test environments.

   d. There is a lot of overhead associated with production networks that cannot be seen in a test network.

5. You manage a production Exchange 2000 network of 1000 users and want to test the functionality of Chat Services on a test network of 100 users. Should you connect your test network to your production network at any time?

   a. Yes, but only if you need to share an Internet connection for testing purposes.

   b. Yes, but only if you are using Instant Messaging services in the production network to complement the Chat Services on your test network.

   c. No, because Chat Services require at least 500 users to establish a chat community.

   d. No, you have not tested the impact that Chat Services would have on 1000 users in your test network.

6. You successfully test the use of Instant Messaging in a test environment and are considering using this service in a production environment. Which one of the following statements is true?
   a. You should immediately connect your production network to the machine that successfully implemented Instant Messaging services in your test network.
   b. You should replace production hardware with the machine that was successfully tested in your test environment.
   c. Your test machine is best used for back-up purposes in your production network.
   d. You should clone the hard drive of your test machine that successfully implemented Instant Messaging and reproduce this drive in your production network.
7. John is managing two Exchange 5.5 servers with a Site Connector configured between them. If he upgrades these servers to Exchange 2000 Server, what will become of the Site Connector?
   a. It is automatically upgraded to an SMTP Connector in Exchange 2000.
   b. It can be upgraded to a Routing Group Connector in Exchange 2000.
   c. It is upgraded to the X.400 Connector by default in Exchange 2000.
   d. It becomes a Site Connector in Exchange 2000 by default.
8. Which one of the following represents a gateway connector in Exchange 2000 Server?
   a. the Exchange 2000 SMTP Connector that communicates with an external SMTP relay host
   b. the Exchange 2000 Routing Group Connector
   c. a third-party fax connector that allows you to send broadcast faxes using Exchange 2000 Server
   d. the Exchange 2000 Server PROFS Connector
9. You want to configure e-mail clients that are capable of directly accessing directory information in a Global Catalog server. Which client should you consider using?
   a. Outlook 2000
   b. Outlook Express
   c. any POP3 mail client
   d. any HTTP mail client using the WebDAV protocol
10. Your staff is using Outlook Web Access and Windows 2000 Professional to retrieve e-mail from your corporate Exchange 2000 Server computer. You also have an Exchange 5.5 server configured with a legacy PROFS Connector. Can a user use OWA to access both types of Exchange servers?
    a. Yes, you can install multiple versions of the OWA client on a single Windows 2000 machine.
    b. No, the OWA version of Exchange Server 5.5 is no longer supported by Microsoft.

c. Yes, any OWA client can access any version of Exchange server using HTTP.

d. No, the OWA in Exchange 2000 Server is not compatible with the OWA in Exchange Server 5.5.

11. Which browser is considered the preferred browser to use with the Outlook Web Access client?

a. Internet Explorer 5.0

b. Netscape Navigator with IE extensions

c. Internet Explorer 4.0 with Service Pack 1

d. Any version of Internet Explorer is preferred over other browsers.

12. Clients who use IE version 5 as part of an OWA configuration can benefit from which of the following features? (Choose all that apply.)

a. context menus

b. Windows Integrated authentication

c. XML viewing of data

d. Kerberos authentication

13. You have three servers configured in one storage group, and two of these servers are configured in one routing group. How do servers communicate with each other within the routing group?

a. They use the DIRSYNC native transport.

b. They use the RPC native transport.

c. They use the SMTP native transport.

d. They use the X.400 transport stack.

14. Sue has created two routing groups named RG1 and RG2. All servers in RG1 belong to an administrative group named AG1. Can she place servers in RG1 into a new administrative group named AG2?

a. Yes, servers within a routing group can belong to multiple administrative groups.

b. Yes, as long as she configures an SMTP Connector between the two routing groups.

c. No, each administrative group can contain only one routing group.

d. No, each routing group can span only one administrative group.

15. How many connectors could you use to connect two different routing groups named RG1 and RG2?

a. Microsoft recommends only one connector be defined to connect multiple routing groups.

b. There is no limit as long as the first connector installed is a Routing Group Connector.

c. There is no defined limit on how many connectors can be used to connect these two routing groups.

d. You can install multiple connectors as long as they are of the same type and cost value.

16. Which of the following statements describes a difference in replication methods used by Exchange 2000 and Exchange 5.5?
    a. Exchange 5.5 supports intersite replication using SMTP or RPC, whereas Exchange 2000 uses only SMTP.
    b. Exchange 2000 supports intersite replication using SMTP or RPC, whereas Exchange 5.5 uses only SMTP.
    c. Both Exchange 5.5 and Exchange 2000 support intersite replication using SMTP or RPC.
    d. Exchange 5.5 uses the globally unique identifier (GUID) for replication purposes, whereas Exchange 2000 Server uses an object's distinguished name for replication purposes.
17. Which Exchange 2000 service helps MAPI clients access information in Active Directory without being referred to a Global Catalog server?
    a. the Web Storage System service
    b. the System Attendant service
    c. the Windows 2000 Proxy Service
    d. the DSProxy service
18. Mike is managing an Exchange 5.5 organization that coexists with Exchange 2000 Server while all his Exchange 5.5 servers are being upgraded to the current version. All domains have been upgraded to Windows 2000 Server domains, but most servers are still running Exchange Server 5.5. What tool will help him replicate object data from Exchange 5.5 to Active Directory now?
    a. the Windows 2000 Active Directory Connector
    b. the Exchange 2000 Active Directory Connector
    c. the Windows 2000 Site Replication Service
    d. the Exchange 2000 Active Replication Connector
19. Janice is in the process of migrating 60 users from an Exchange 5.5 site to a Windows 2000 domain running Exchange 2000 Server. She has successfully configured an Active Directory Connector with a user connection agreement. After the users have been imported into AD, she notices that certain Outlook users cannot see these new objects in their global address lists. What can Janice do to remedy this situation?
    a. She can set up a two-way connection agreement so that address lists are updated automatically in Active Directory.
    b. She can configure the Recipient Update Service to add address list information to recipient objects.
    c. She can configure the Site Replication Service to add address list information to recipient objects.
    d. She can set up a configuration connection agreement to add address list information to recipient objects.

20. Bob is managing a mixed-mode Exchange organization containing five separate Windows 2000 domains and two separate Windows 2000 sites. He wants to use the flexibility of administrative groups to take advantage of permission management. How many administrative groups can Bob create in this scenario?
    a. It's easier to assign permissions if all servers are placed in the First Administrative Group created by default.
    b. He is allowed to create multiple administrative groups as long as they each contain no more than one routing group per site.
    c. He can create only one administrative group per Windows 2000 site in a mixed-mode organization.
    d. He could create multiple administrative groups per Windows 2000 site as long as they did not span more than a single domain.
21. Users who need to fully administer your Exchange 2000 organization but who do not want to modify permissions on configuration items need the ________________ permission assigned to them.
22. If you assign someone permissions for the Organization object in System Manager, you are also giving him or her permission to make local Registry modifications on your computer. True or False?
23. If you have Exchange Full Administrator rights to the Organization object in System Manager, which of the following rights do you *not* have?
    a. the right to modify this object
    b. the right to list the contents of this object
    c. the Receive As right
    d. the right to modify child objects of this object

Hands-on Projects

These projects assume that you have a computer with an Internet connection and Internet Explorer 5.0 or higher as your Web browser. You should have already started the computer and logged on, if necessary.

Project 4-1

At times you will be confronted with errors that apply specifically to deploying the Active Directory Connector, even though you have followed all recommended procedures. This hands-on project sharpens your troubleshooting skills by searching the Microsoft Knowledge Base for solutions to ADC errors you might encounter in actual practice.

To troubleshoot the ADC:

1. Click **Start**, point to **Programs**, and then click **Internet Explorer** (or double-click the icon on your desktop) to open your Web browser. In the Address text box at the top of your browser page, type **http://search.support.microsoft.com/kb/c.asp**, and then press **Enter**.
2. In the My search is about drop-down list, click the list arrow and select **Exchange 2000 Server**.
3. Under the words "I want to search by," for Step 2 on the Web page, make sure the Keyword Search using the radio button is selected, and then click **All Words** in the drop-down list if it's not already selected.
4. Type **ADC Replication** in the My question is text box for Step 3 on the Web page, and then click the **Go** icon.
5. Write down five article numbers that appear on the following page in your browser and keep them on hand for future reference. You should become adept at using the Microsoft Knowledge Base to troubleshoot and fix problems, not only with the ADC, but also with other Exchange 2000 components.
6. Close your Web browser window and any other open windows. If you have a dial-up connection, you can disconnect from the Internet.

Project 4-2

This project shows you how to access information about hardware and software compatibility in Windows 2000 Server. The information on the Microsoft Web site about this compatibility is constantly changing. The URLs given in this project were accurate at the time of writing, but might have changed since the book went to press. You should be aware of alternative sites that can help you find information about compatibility or other issues with Windows 2000 Server. For example, you can visit *http://search.support.microsoft.com/kb/c.asp* and perform general searches on any topic affecting any Microsoft product (including the HCL for Windows 2000 Server).

To verify hardware requirements for Exchange 2000 Server:

1. Click **Start**, point to **Programs**, and then click **Internet Explorer** (or double-click the icon on your desktop) to open your Web browser. In the Address text box, type **http://www.microsoft.com/windows2000/server/howtobuy/upgrading/compat/default.asp**, and then press **Enter**.
2. The Check Hardware and Software Compatibility page opens. Scroll down to the middle of the page until you see the Search for Compatible Hardware and Software section. Click the box in the middle labeled **Hardware Devices** to display a new page called Search for Compatible Hardware Devices.

3. Scroll down to the bottom of this page until you see three text boxes. Type the following information in the order presented (the bold items are the exact name you should type in the text box):

   Company: Type the name **3Com**.
   Model: Type the model number **3c905**.
   Device Type: Click the list arrow and click **Networking**, and then click the **Find** button.

   You will see a page labeled Search for Compatible Hardware Devices; this page now lists all 3Com 3c905 type network adapter cards that are compatible with the Windows 2000 Server operating system (scroll down to the bottom of the page to see a more complete listing of these adapter cards). Figure 4-6 shows the bottom part of this Web page. Notice the icons used at the top of the Web page.

4

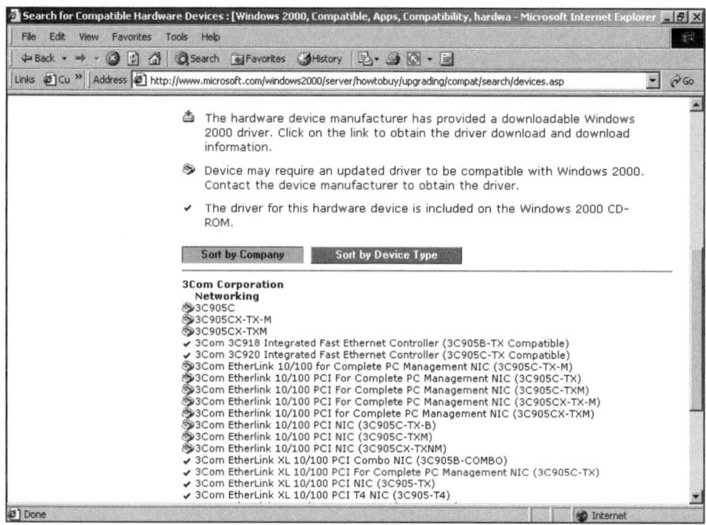

Figure 4-6 Searching for compatible hardware devices

4. Now compare what you found to the HCL on your Windows 2000 Server installation CD-ROM. Place the CD-ROM in the CD-ROM drive and wait for the Auto Run menu to appear. When it does, click the **Browse This CD** option.

If your computer does not support the AutoRun feature when you initially insert the CD-ROM, you can still find the Hcl.txt file on the CD by clicking Start, clicking Run, typing *E:*\Support\Hcl.txt in the Open text box, and then clicking OK (*E:* represents your CD-ROM drive).

5. Double-click the **Support** folder, and then select the **Hcl.txt** file (see Figure 4-7). Notice the date and file size for this particular file. Double-click this file to open it and view its contents, and compare it with the HCL on the Web page you found in Step 3.

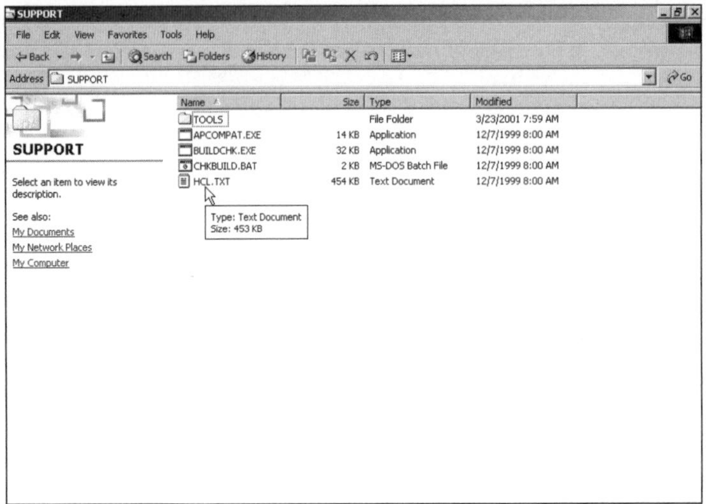

Figure 4-7 Viewing the Support folder

6. Close your Web browser and any other open windows. If you have a dial-up connection, you can disconnect from the Internet.
7. Now compare what you saw on either version of the HCL to your particular hardware. Jot down information that describes various components of your system, as shown in this sample:

Your machine Listed on HCL

CPU ____________________

Hard Disk ____________________

Memory ____________________

Sound Card ____________________

Video Card ____________________

CD-ROM ____________________

DVD-ROM ____________________

Network Card ____________________

Modem ____________________

(Include other components in your system that are not listed above.)

Project 4-3

This project assumes that your Windows 2000 Server environment has already been established. The purpose of this project is to remind you of the integration between Windows 2000 and Exchange 2000 through the use of domain controllers and Global Catalog servers. Domain boundaries define a namespace for Exchange 2000, and each domain contains at least one domain controller computer. Recall that a domain controller holds data related to a domain, but a Global Catalog server contains both domain-related data *and* a copy of attributes from selected Exchange objects (such as mailboxes and public folders). Global Catalog servers help Exchange servers perform fast searches for users so that they have access to resources.

To view the setting that converts a domain controller into a Global Catalog server:

1. To open the AD Sites and Services console, click **Start**, point to **Programs**, point to **Administrative Tools**, and then click **Active Directory Sites and Services**.
2. If necessary, you can maximize this window. You can also adjust the middle column or bar that separates the Contents pane from the Details pane by placing your mouse over it; when your mouse pointer changes to a double-headed arrow, click and drag to move this column to see all objects in either pane.
3. Double-click all containers in the Contents pane to expand them. You should see a Sites folder with three containers underneath it.
4. Double-click the **Default-First-Site-Name**, and then double-click the **Servers** folder so that your *Server* object becomes visible (*Server* represents the actual name of your server). Double-click this object so that you can see two more container objects underneath it—a folder called Exchange Settings and an object called NTDS Settings. Figure 4-8 shows what your screen should look like at this time.

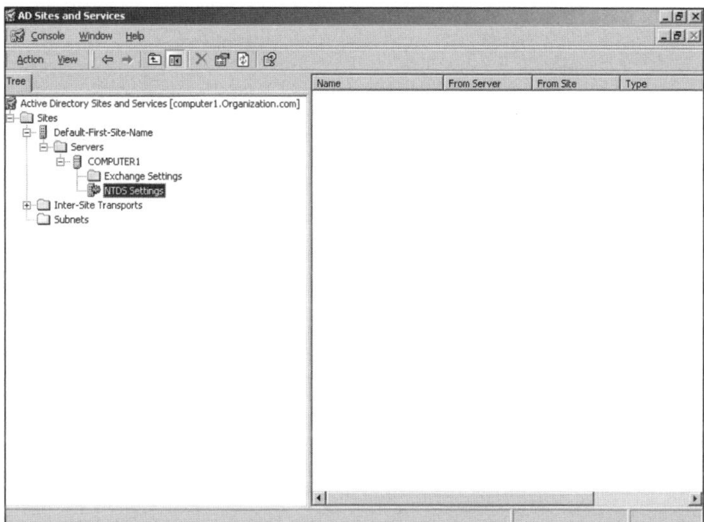

Figure 4-8 The AD Sites and Services console

5. Right-click the **NTDS Settings** container, and then click **Properties** on the shortcut menu. The NTDS Settings Properties dialog box opens and displays the General tab by default. Leave the Description box and Query Policy box empty. If this is the first server installed in your Windows 2000 forest, the Global Catalog check box should be checked by default.

For all subsequent servers installed in your forest, you can enable this check box and include multiple Global Catalog servers for fault tolerance. Microsoft recommends having at least one Global Catalog server in every Windows 2000 site.

6. Click **OK**. Close any open windows or applications.

Project 4-4

Windows 2000 has many tools for viewing and editing object attributes. For example, you might want to tag an attribute for replication to the Global Catalog server for your Outlook Express users so that they can search on this attribute when looking for e-mail messages (for instance, an object's Department attribute may not be replicated, so you have to enable this feature). Or you may simply want to edit an object attribute by using tools such as Active Directory Services Interface Edit (ADSI Edit) or the LDAP Viewer (LDP.exe). Both tools are on the Windows 2000 installation CD-ROM in the \Support\Tools directory, and they help you define and manage custom object attributes and provide important integration between Windows 2000 and Exchange 2000.

Using ADSI Edit or the LDP utility incorrectly to modify the attributes of Active Directory objects could cause serious system problems that require you to reinstall Microsoft Windows 2000 Server and/or Microsoft Exchange 2000 Server. Microsoft does not promise to solve all problems resulting from improper use of these tools, so be extremely cautious when using these utilities.

To modify object information by using the Windows 2000 ADSI Edit tool:

1. To open the Active Directory Users and Computers console, click **Start**, point to **Programs**, point to **Administrative Tools**, and then click **Active Directory Users and Computers**.
2. Expand your Organization object, which is the top object in the Contents pane (underneath the root object labeled Active Directory Users and Computers).

To expand an object, you can either click the + next to a container or icon or double-click the object.

3. Click the **Users** folder underneath the Organization object, and notice the users that appear in the Details pane. Right-click the **Administrator** object, and then click **Properties** on the shortcut menu. The Administrator Properties dialog box opens to display the General tab by default.
4. Notice that only the Display name, Description, and E-mail text boxes are populated on the General tab by default. Type the word **Cleveland** in the Office text box (as shown in Figure 4-9), click **OK**, and then minimize the window for this console.

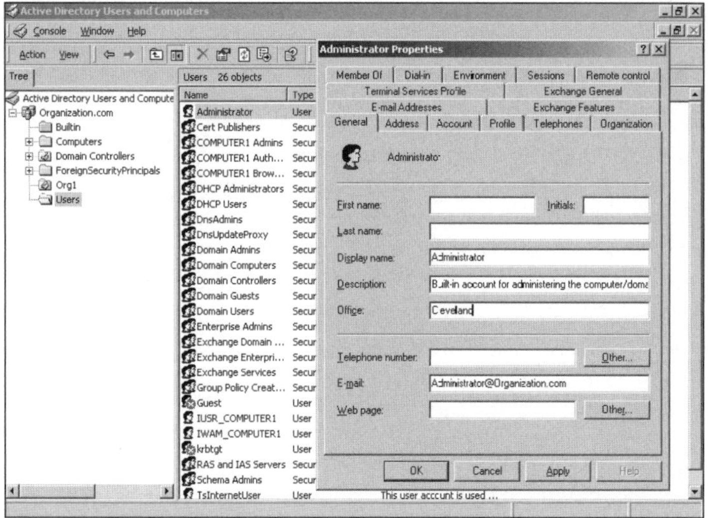

Figure 4-9 Entering object information in the Administrator Properties dialog box

5. Open the Active Directory Services Interface Edit tool (ADSI Edit), while keeping the Active Directory Users and Computers console open but minimized. To open ADSI Edit, you must first install the Windows 2000 Support Tools from the Windows 2000 Installation CD-ROM.

You can install all support tools by running Setup.exe from the \Support\Tools directory on the Windows 2000 CD-ROM. Windows 2000 automatically places all support tools, including ADSI Edit, in the Program Files\Support Tools directory.

6. Place your Windows 2000 CD in your CD-ROM drive. If the Windows 2000 splash screen appears, click **Exit** to close this screen. Click **Start**, click **Run**, type ***E*:\Support\Tools\Setup.exe** (*E* represents your CD-ROM drive), and then click **OK**. The Windows Installer window initially appears, and then the Windows 2000 Support Tools Setup Wizard appears. Click the **Next** button to continue the installation.
7. In the User Information window, type **Administrator** in the User name text box, type your organization name in the Organization text box, and then click the **Next** button.
8. In the Select An Installation Type window, click the **Typical** option, which includes the most commonly used options, and then click the **Next** button.
9. In the Begin Installation window, click the **Next** button to begin installing the Windows 2000 Support Tools on your local machine.

10. The Installation Progress window opens, which shows all modules and files being copied to your local system. When the file copying is finished, the Completing the Windows 2000 Support Tools Setup Wizard window opens. Click the **Finish** button to exit the installation program.
11. You can now find the Support Tools directory on your local hard drive (usually C:\Program Files\Support Tools). Another way of accessing these tools is from the Start menu. To use the ADSI Edit utility from the Start menu, click **Start**, click **Run**, and then type **adsiedit.msc** (any file ending in .msc refers to a Microsoft Management Console utility) in the Open text box. Click **OK** to continue.
12. When the ADSI Edit console opens, maximize the window. In the Contents pane, expand **ADSI Edit**, the topmost object in the hierarchy, if necessary.
13. You can select from three different naming contexts when using ADSI Edit: a domain naming context, a configuration naming context or container, and a schema naming context or container. Expand the **Domain NC** container, and then expand the **DC=Organization** folder directly underneath it.
14. You should now see nine subfolders. Expand **CN=Users**, right-click the first folder underneath called **CN=Administrator**, and then click **Properties** on the shortcut menu. The CN=Administrator Properties dialog box opens to display the Attributes tab by default.
15. The Attributes tab indicates the object's distinguished name in Active Directory and the object class (in this case, Administrator belongs to the user object class). Leave the default setting of Optional in the Select which properties to view text box (your choices are Mandatory, Optional, or Both).
16. Click the **Select a property to view** list arrow, and then click the **physicalDeliveryOfficeName** attribute. In the Attribute Values section, notice the value DirectoryString in the Syntax text box (this value cannot be changed). The Value(s) text box contains the information you entered in Step 4 (when you first typed Cleveland as an Office location for the Administrator account).
17. Edit this value by typing **Brooklyn** in the Edit Attribute text box. Click the **Set** button, which is now enabled (see Figure 4-10), and then click **OK** to close this dialog box.
18. Maximize the Active Directory Users and Computers console. Click the **Users** folder under the Organization object in your domain hierarchy, and then locate the Administrator user object in the Details pane (it should be the first user object at the top of the list). Right-click the **Administrator** object, and then click **Properties** on the shortcut menu. In the General tab, notice that Brooklyn appears in the Office field (because that's the value you entered in Step 17 when using the ADSI Edit tool). Click **OK** to close this dialog box, and then close the Active Directory Users and Computers console.
19. Close any open windows or applications.

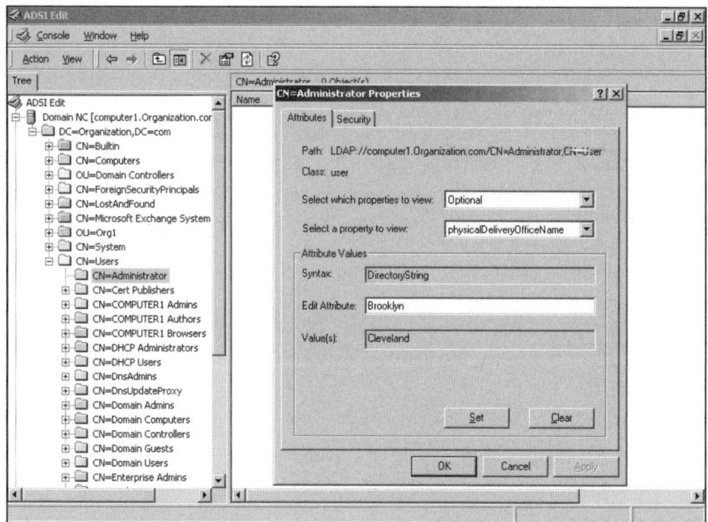

Figure 4-10 Editing an attribute in the CN=Administrator Properties dialog box

Project 4-5

Previous versions of Exchange Server require all directory data to be replicated among all Exchange servers within a site and between sites. Windows 2000 (through Active Directory) and Exchange 5.5 allow a special form of directory replication known as selectable-field replication, which prevents certain attributes from replicating to other sites (in Exchange 5.5) or Global Catalog servers (for Active Directory and Windows 2000 Server).

To select attributes for replication to a Global Catalog server using Windows 2000 Server Support Tools:

1. Install the Windows 2000 Active Directory Schema Manager utility by clicking **Start**, clicking **Run**, and then typing **Regsvr32 schmmgmt.dll** in the Open text box. Click **OK** to register and enable the Schema Manager console (if you see a message box stating "DllRegister Server in schmmgmt.dll succeeded," simply click **OK**).

2. You can now create a custom MMC console containing the Schema Manager tool (it's not in the Administrative Tools section of the Start menu). To create a custom MMC console, click **Start**, click **Run**, type **mmc** in the Open text box, and then click **OK**.

3. When the Console1 - [Console Root] window opens, click **Console** on the menu bar, and then click **Add/Remove Snap-in**. The Add/Remove Snap-in dialog box opens to the Standalone tab, with no snap-ins added by default.

4. Click the **Add** button at the bottom of this dialog box to open the Add Standalone Snap-in dialog box (see Figure 4-11). In the Available Standalone Snap-ins list, click **Active Directory Schema** so that you can view and edit the

Active Directory schema. Click **Add**, and then click **Close** to close the Add Standalone Snap-in dialog box.

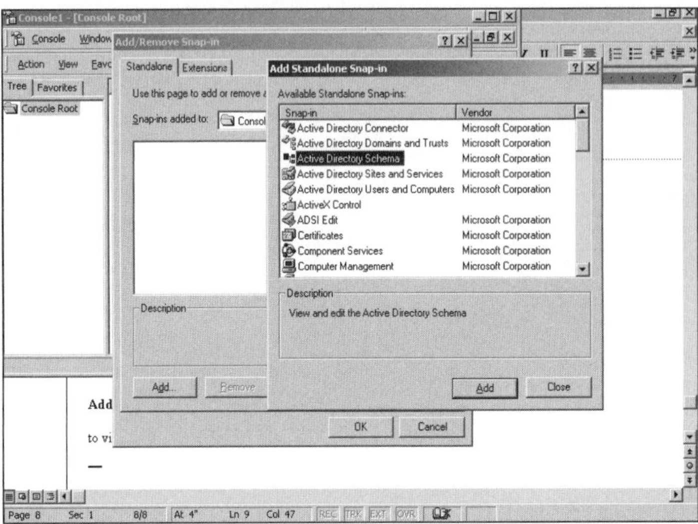

Figure 4-11 Adding the Active Directory Schema snap-in

5. In the Standalone tab of the Add/Remove Snap-in dialog box that you opened in Step 3, you should now see Active Directory Schema listed. Click **OK** to close this dialog box, and return to the Console1 - [Console Root] window.
6. In the Console Root window, expand **Active Directory Schema** to display the two folders underneath it: the Classes folder and the Attributes folder. Click the **Attributes** folder to display a list of attributes in the Details pane.
7. To see whether certain attributes are automatically replicated to a Global Catalog server in Windows 2000, double-click the **displayName** attribute in the Details pane to open the displayName Properties dialog box (as shown in Figure 4-12).

   Notice the check boxes at the bottom of the General tab. The last check box indicates that this item is automatically replicated to a Global Catalog server in a Windows 2000 forest.
8. Click **OK** to close the displayName Properties dialog box, and double-click the **maxPwdAge** attribute in the Details pane of the Console1 - [Console Root] window to open the maxPwdAge Properties dialog box. Notice that the Replicate this attribute to the Global Catalog check box is not enabled. This particular attribute will not be replicated to the Global Catalog server unless you manually enable it at this point (leave this option disabled for now). Click **OK** to close the maxPwdAge Properties dialog box.
9. Click **Console** on the menu bar, and then click **Exit** to close this MMC console. When prompted to save console settings to Console1, click the **No** button.
10. Close any open windows or applications.

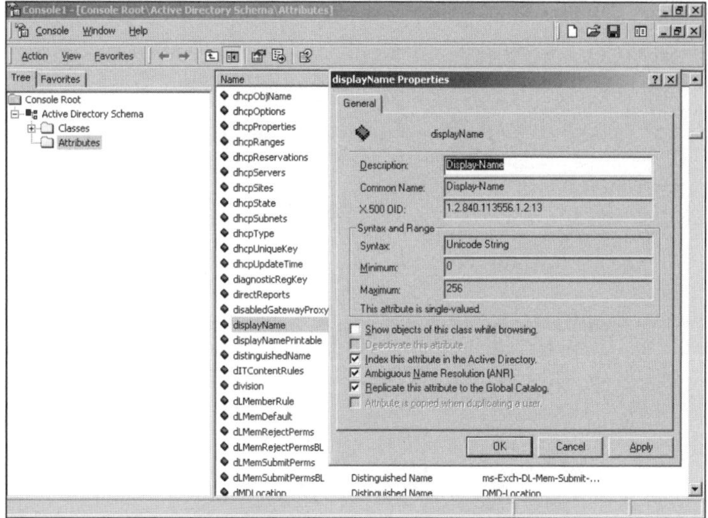

Figure 4-12 The displayName Properties dialog box

Project 4-6

To deploy organizational units in Exchange 2000:

1. Click **Start**, point to **Programs**, point to **Administrative Tools**, and then click **Active Directory Users and Computers**.
2. Right-click your domain object, point to **New**, and then click **Organizational Unit** on the shortcut menu, as shown in Figure 4-13.

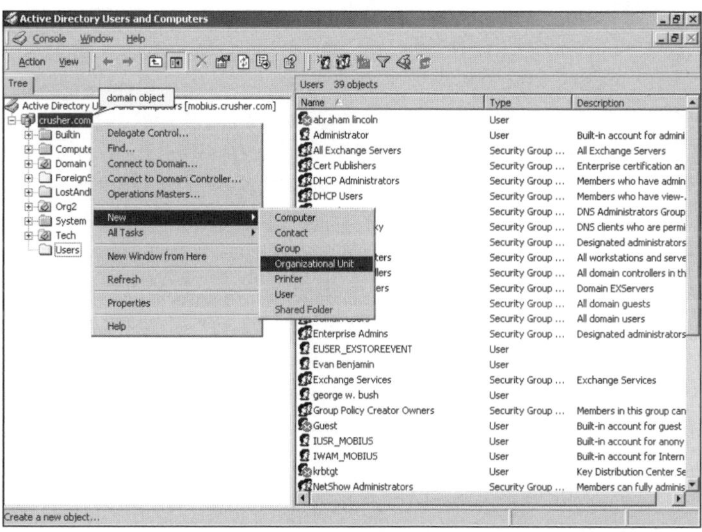

Figure 4-13 Creating a new OU for your domain object

3. In the New Object - Organizational Unit dialog box, type **Org1** in the Name text box (see Figure 4-14), and then click **OK**. Locate your new object in the Contents pane of Active Directory Users and Computers.

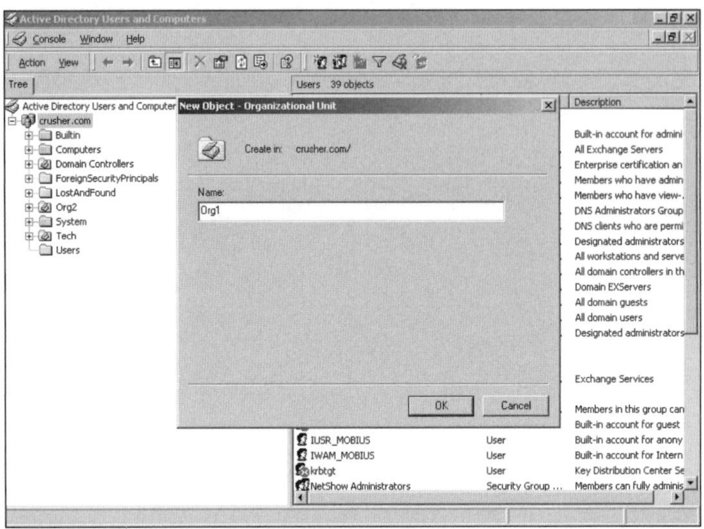

Figure 4-14 Creating a new OU name

4. Repeat Steps 2 and 3 for a second organizational unit object named **Org2**. Notice the placement of Org2 in relation to Org1 in the tree in the Contents pane.

5. Right-click the **Org1** folder in the Contents pane, and then click **Move** on the shortcut menu. When asked to select a container, click the **Org2** folder to select it, and then click **OK**.

6. Verify in Active Directory Users and Computers that Org2 now contains the Org1 object by expanding the Org2 item. You should see Org1 listed as a subcontainer below Org2. To delegate permissions for only the Org1 object, right-click the **Org1** folder, and then click **Delegate Control** on the shortcut menu to start the Delegation of Control Wizard. Click the **Next** button to open the Users or Computers dialog box. (It should be empty, with no users or groups in the list.)

7. Click the **Add** button to open the Select Users, Computers, or Groups dialog box. Click the user or group you want to add from the list, and then click the **Add** button (see Figure 4-15). Click **OK** when you are finished adding users or groups.

8. Click the **Next** button to progress to the Tasks to Delegate window, as shown in Figure 4-16. Click the **Create, delete, and manage user accounts** and **Create, delete and manage groups** check boxes, and then click the **Next** button.

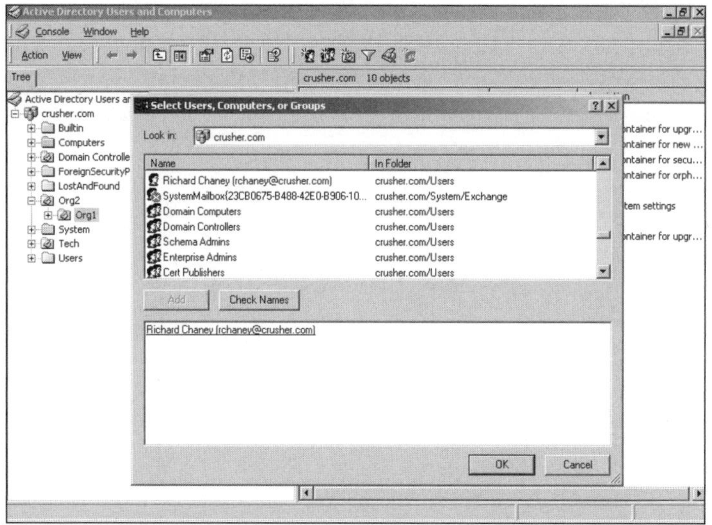

Figure 4-15 Delegating administration to selected users or groups

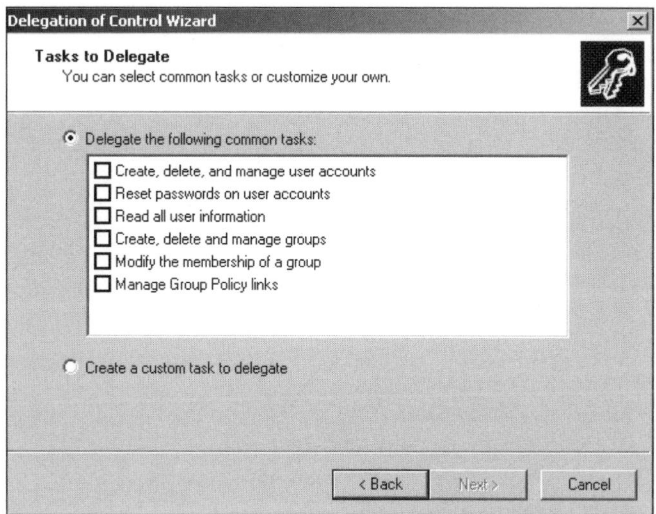

Figure 4-16 Selecting tasks to delegate to users or goups

9. In the Completing the Delegation of Control Wizard window, review the information that's shown. Click the **Finish** button if you are satisfied, or click the **Back** button to change any information.
10. At this point you are ready to place users in your new OUs. To do so, right-click the **Org1** folder, point to **New**, and then click **User** on the shortcut menu (see Figure 4-17). In the New Object - User dialog box that appears, create a user

named Jack French with a logon name of Jfrench. Type **Jack** in the First name text box, type **French** in the Last name text box, type **Jfrench** in the User logon name text box, and make sure your domain name shows in the list box next to the User logon name text box (see Figure 4-18). Click the **Next** button to go to the next dialog box.

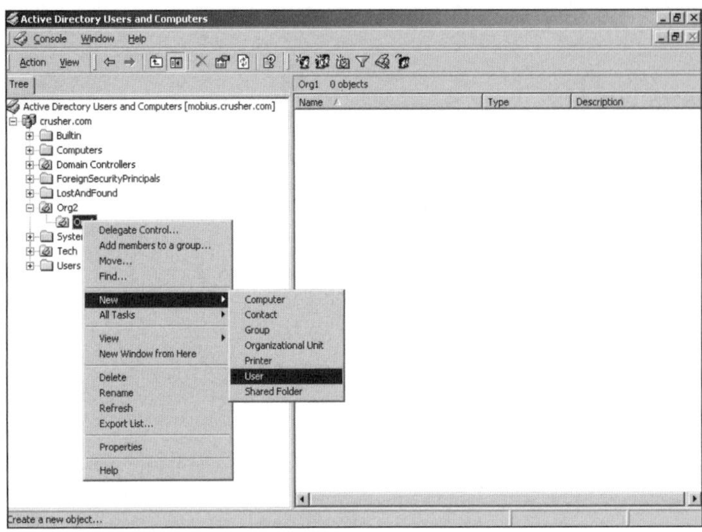

Figure 4-17 Creating a new user in the Org1 object in Active Directory Users and Computers

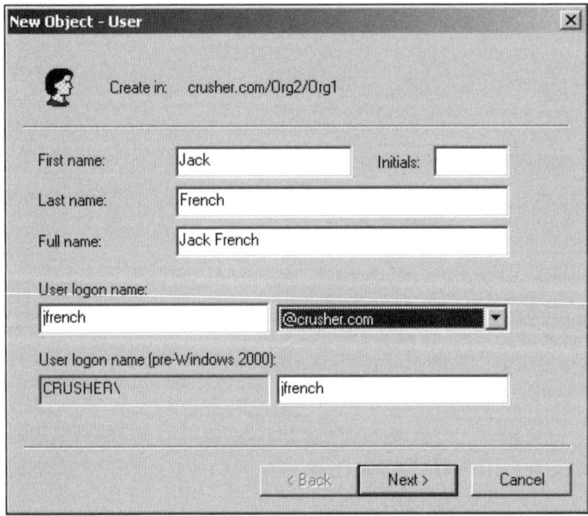

Figure 4-18 Entering new user information in the New Object – User dialog box

11. Type **password** in the Password text box, retype this password in the Confirm password text box, and then click the **Next** button.
12. In the next dialog box, make sure the Create an Exchange mailbox check box is checked (see Figure 4-19), and verify that you are using the correct alias, server location, and mailbox store for this object. Then click the **Next** button.

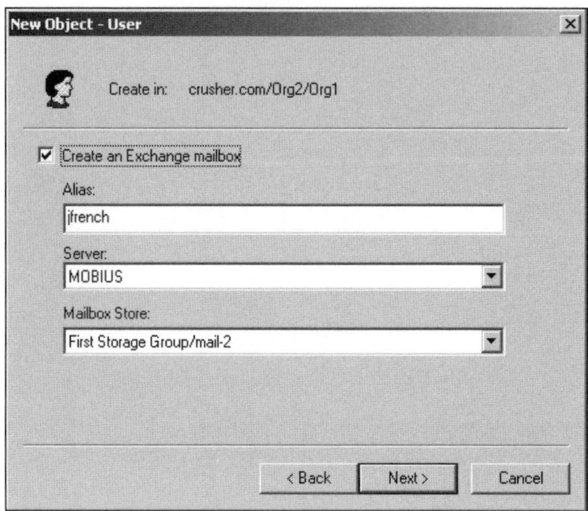

Figure 4-19 Mailbox-enabling a new user and selecting the mailbox store

13. Click the **Finish** button in the last window (see Figure 4-20), and make sure that Jack French appears in the Details pane of the Org1 object in Active Directory Users and Computers (see Figure 4-21).

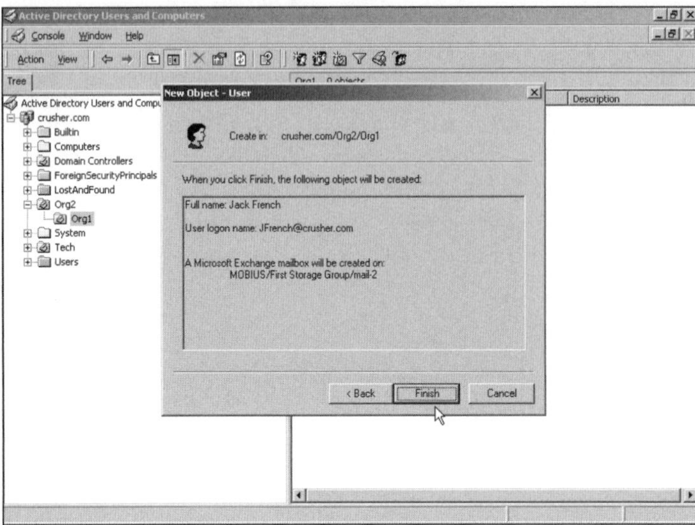

Figure 4-20 Verifying information for a new user

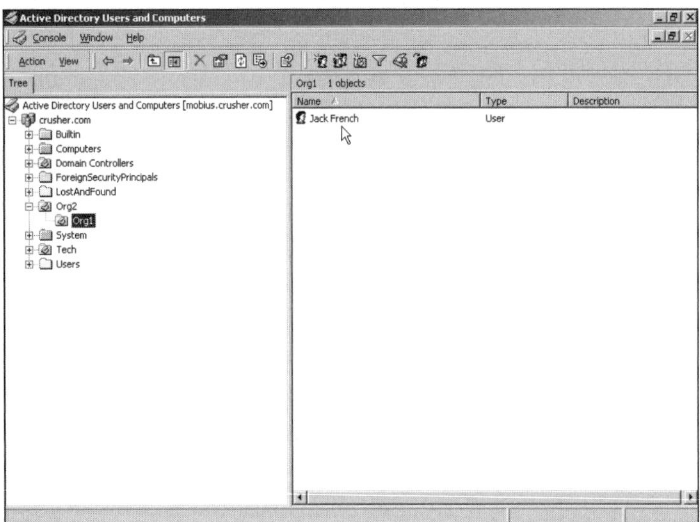

Figure 4-21 Showing the new user in the Org1 object

14. Close any open windows.

CASE PROJECTS

Case 1

You have successfully set up Exchange 2000 to interoperate with an Exchange 5.5 computer using the Active Directory Connector. Your company is using a mixture of Windows 2000 domains and Windows NT 4.0 domains. When one of your Exchange 2000 users tries to send e-mail messages to an NT Server 4.0 recipient, he receives a Non-Delivery Report stating the following: "Your message did not reach some or all of the intended recipients." What do you think could cause an error like this to appear?

Case 2

Your manager has asked you to implement a new messaging network and replace your old messaging system (your organization has been using a messaging system that was originally set up 10 years ago using a small third-party software package). You set up a test network with legacy hardware and decide to test Exchange 2000 Server, but you don't know which components to test or how to best simulate your production environment. How should you proceed so that you can make a fair evaluation of Exchange 2000 Server?

Case 3

Your company has two teams, one responsible for administering the Windows 2000 network and one responsible for administering the Exchange 2000 messaging system. The president of the company promotes you to administer both the network and the messaging system. You believe there's a direct relationship between the two and claim that you must take care of both. Your co-workers have a different opinion and feel that these responsibilities should not be combined. How can you convince them to welcome the integration between the two teams?

Case 4

You manage the network for a global telecommunications firm composed of 10 global offices and 50 branch offices. The firm has 10,000 users, who all use Exchange 2000 for their messaging needs. You have taken over the role of e-mail administrator, and you want to reorganize your company's hierarchy. You want to partition your network into logical groups so that different administrators can manage different groups. What are some of the tools you can use in Exchange 2000 Server to help you achieve these objectives?

Case 5

You are the network administrator for Manhattan University, and you have been asked to set up Internet access to e-mail using Exchange 2000 Server. The faculty normally works out of their homes, and they want access to their inboxes and calendars from remote locations using a standard Internet browser. You have just configured an Internet firewall for extra security because your network has recently been subject to denial of service attacks. How can you accommodate the faculty's needs while still protecting your internal campus network?

CHAPTER

5

INSTALLATION OF EXCHANGE 2000 SERVER IN NEW ENVIRONMENTS

After reading this chapter and completing the exercises, you will be able to:

- Understand Windows 2000 integration to see how Exchange 2000 will integrate with the operating system
- Understand preinstallation steps that can help make your installation faster and easier
- Understand how to install your first Exchange 2000 server to prepare you for your first implementation of Exchange 2000 Server
- Better understand what issues might have to be addressed after the installation is finished, having reviewed postinstallation issues
- Understand how to troubleshoot failed installations to help you quickly pinpoint problems that can arise during an Exchange installation
- Develop an unattended installation that can help save valuable time when performing multiple Exchange 2000 Server installations

In Chapter 4, "Preparing to Deploy Exchange 2000 Server," you learned more about the developing and deploying phases in the Microsoft Solutions Framework. You also learned more information on deploying Exchange 2000, including how to integrate it with Active Directory Connector and how administrative and routing groups function.

In this chapter, you learn how Exchange 2000 integrates with Windows 2000 and the preinstallation steps en route to learning how to install your first and subsequent Exchange 2000 servers. In addition, you learn about issues that may arise after the installation is finished, and how to troubleshoot problems when an installation fails. Finally, you learn how to implement an unattended installation, a time-saving process that could come in very handy if you need to perform multiple installations.

Reviewing Windows 2000 Integration

As you learned in Chapter 4, you need to understand the integration that takes place when installing Exchange 2000 Server on a Windows 2000 Server installation, including how Exchange 2000 integrates into Active Directory and the critical role that AD plays in Exchange 2000. AD is required for Exchange 2000 to operate because it tightly integrates user and group management of Exchange mailbox resources directly into the AD schema and AD forest. No longer does Exchange rely on its own separate dedicated directory; rather, it integrates with the AD structure, offering some very useful benefits. Table 5-1 lists some of the key benefits of AD and Exchange 2000 integration.

Table 5-1 Key Benefits of Active Directory and Exchange 2000 Integration

Benefit	Explanation
Centralized management of users and data	You can manage any users and data from within the AD structure instead of managing users and data over several different locations.
More efficient security management	As a function of the centralized security management, Exchange 2000 now uses AD access control lists and other security features to manage security in Exchange.
Ease of distribution list management	Whenever a group of users is created in Windows 2000, Exchange 2000 can use that group as a distribution list instead of having to generate and manage additional groups and lists, as in Exchange 5.5.
Simpler administration of multiple Exchange 2000 servers in one AD forest	If multiple Exchange 2000 servers are installed within the same AD forest, management can be assigned to any individual or group within each site or to one administrator for all Exchange sites. In addition, it is much easier to synchronize multiple sets of public folders and enable tight integration with Global Catalog servers for a unified global address list.

Windows 2000 Protocols

Exchange 2000 uses two important protocols included with Windows 2000—Simple Mail Transport Protocol (SMTP) and Network News Transport Protocol (NNTP)—to provide basic mail and newsgroup services. SMTP is integral to Exchange 2000 operation and must be present on every server where you install Exchange 2000, but NNTP is required only if you want to provide newsgroup services.

Simple Mail Transport Protocol

SMTP is the backbone of message transfer for Exchange 2000, and Exchange 2000 relies entirely on the SMTP services in Windows 2000 to provide message transport services. SMTP is, simply put, a standardized message transfer protocol used to transfer messages between systems and servers over networks and the Internet. When Exchange 2000 is installed, it takes the existing SMTP services and modifies them from their default configuration. The protocol is expanded to include additional features, such as link status routing, advanced message-queuing functions, and improved message categorization agents. (See Chapter 8, "Configuring Internet Clients in Exchange 2000 Server," for more details on these features.) The basic functionality of SMTP stays the same; it is just improved so that Exchange 2000 can take advantage of newer message routing functionality and features.

Network News Transport Protocol

Exchange 2000 uses NNTP to connect to and provide access to newsgroups. Newsgroups are a collection of message boards where readers can post and retrieve messages and files on a wide variety of topics. NNTP functionality is part of the Internet Information Server (IIS) version 5 services included in Windows 2000 as well as in previous versions of IIS. When Exchange 2000 is installed, it performs no modifications to the protocol and uses NNTP in its native form.

Windows 2000 Services

Windows 2000 servers provide some system services that Exchange 2000 either requires to operate or could benefit from in some way. The single most important service is DNS, which is required for AD, and consequently Exchange 2000, to operate.

Domain Name System

Although not directly related to integration, you learned in Chapter 2, "Planning for Windows 2000," about Active Directory and its dependence on the Domain Name System (DNS) to install or function properly. Therefore, because Exchange 2000 requires AD, Exchange 2000 in turn depends on and utilizes DNS for naming conventions and name resolution services. You should keep this DNS dependence in mind while implementing your first Exchange 2000 installation, as it can weigh heavily on how Exchange 2000 is installed and configured. For instance, you should establish a proper, well-laid-out DNS naming scheme for your domains, systems, and server names so that they are easier to administer and manage.

Exchange 2000 can use any enabled or active DNS that's available and functioning on a Windows 2000 server; however, it benefits from the Microsoft DNS service included in Windows 2000 with its improved management features, fault tolerance, and efficient replication of data between domains.

As you learned in Chapter 2, there are some things to keep in mind when planning your domain naming context:

- Assign workstation and server names that correlate with registered domain names.
- Never use the same domain name twice.

- Create only the number of separate domain trees that you require.
- The first part of the domain name should be the system's NetBIOS (computer) name—for example, server1.xyz.com.

A poorly thought-out domain naming convention for your AD installation can cause quite a few headaches for users and require additional administrative effort to correct or manage on the part of the AD and Exchange administrators. Poor naming can make locating and administering users, data, and other objects much more difficult. For instance, naming an e-mail server in Calgary "Bill's Server" after the server's administrator, Bill, might seem like a good idea at first; however, two years later when Bill has left, will the name really make sense to anyone? A more suitable name for this domain is Calgary-Mail.

Optional Windows 2000 Services

You can install a few optional services included with Windows 2000, such as **Routing and Remote Access Services (RRAS)**. RRAS enables remote users to connect to network servers via a modem or another connection method to access services such as Exchange 2000. Also, if you do not have a constant Internet connection, such as a T1 line, DSL, or ISDN, you might need to set up RRAS to facilitate Exchange 2000 connecting to the Internet to send or retrieve messages, among other networking duties. Although dial-up connections are not used as often as they used to be, the services are available in Windows 2000 through RRAS if needed.

If you want to provide remote e-mail client access, another service you can install is Outlook Web Access (OWA). OWA is a function of both Exchange 2000 and IIS. IIS is necessary to host and provide the Web site that users connect to so that they can access their Exchange mailboxes using a Web browser. OWA can also be used as a message gateway to shuttle messages to an Exchange server that exists behind a firewall.

Thankfully, most services and protocols that a typical Exchange 2000 installation requires can be found in Windows 2000 Server or from the Exchange 2000 installation itself. Having the required services and protocols readily available can make implementing these optional features and services much quicker and easier to plan.

PREINSTALLATION STEPS

As with any large-scale software or hardware implementation, a series of preinstallation steps must be followed to ensure that the installation goes smoothly. Exchange 2000 Server is no exception, so there are a couple of steps that must be accomplished before you can even think about starting the software's full installation.

It would certainly be easy to start the Exchange 2000 installation and allow it to start installing, but you could run into instances in which you have to cancel the installation and start again because you didn't install or configure a setting properly before you started the installation. You can also perform some maintenance steps to ensure that your installation goes smoothly and the software performs to the best of its ability. Take a look at the following list of important preinstallation steps you should go through to ensure a smooth Exchange 2000 installation:

- Gather information for the Exchange 2000 installation.
- Verify that hardware meets minimum requirements.
- Apply patches, security hot fixes, and service packs for Exchange 2000, Windows 2000, and IIS 5.
- Optimize current system settings for performance.
- Verify that appropriate system protocols and services are available.
- Create any special accounts required for installation.

If you followed the MSF properly, you have probably determined or performed many of these steps already and are ready to move on to the installation portion of the process.

Gather Information for the Exchange 2000 Installation

To proceed with the necessary preinstallation steps, you should collect information not only on the hardware configuration of the server you intend to install to, such as processor speed and amount of memory, but also on the server's intended role—for example, determine whether the server will be strictly a mailbox server or whether it will also provide connectors to other e-mail servers. If you did not follow the MSF to gather this information when planning your Exchange 2000 deployment, you need to determine what kind of server hardware you are installing Exchange 2000 on and which features and capabilities you want your Exchange 2000 server to have. For instance, if your one Exchange server will be providing any and all services, connectors, and mailboxes for your entire domain, you should make sure the server has adequate hardware to provide enough processing power and memory for these options, which could be more than the minimum requirements. For more information on what you need to gather before an Exchange 2000 installation, refer to Chapter 3, "Planning an Exchange Server 2000 Design Scenario," and Chapter 4.

Verify That Hardware Meets Necessary Requirements

Before any installation can take place, you must verify whether the server hardware configuration meets the minimum Exchange 2000 Server requirements. The current minimum and recommended hardware configurations for Exchange 2000 Server are shown in Table 5-2. (You can also check out the following URL for more information about minimum requirements for Exchange 2000 Server: *http://www.microsoft.com/exchange/evaluation/sysreq/default.asp.*)

Table 5-2 Minimum and Recommended Hardware Configurations for Exchange 2000 Server

Minimum Requirements	Recommended Configuration
166 MHz Pentium processor	400 MHz Pentium II processor
128 MB RAM	256 MB RAM
500 MB on the drive where you install Exchange 2000; 200 MB on the system drive	Any additional required space for mailboxes, public folders, and other Exchange storage

You should keep in mind that the minimum requirements are just that—the minimum required for Exchange 2000 to operate. With the minimum requirements, Exchange 2000 can function, but you could see problems such as poor performance or the inability to implement more complex configurations, like front-end/back-end server configurations or multiple storage groups. Understanding in advance what role your Exchange 2000 server will take and what additional hardware the configuration requires, if any, can go a long way toward ensuring a trouble-free Exchange 2000 Server installation and configuration.

Apply Patches, Security Hot Fixes, and Service Packs

It is well worth your while during the preinstallation steps to check various sources for the latest software patches, **security hot fixes** (security-specific fixes), and, most important, **service packs** (complete packages of typically hundreds of patches and fixes). Quite a few patches and hot fixes are already available for Windows 2000, including Windows 2000 Service Pack 2, which includes most of the patches and hot fixes available up to its release in mid-May, 2001. At a minimum, you should install the latest available service pack to provide the best possible foundation for your Exchange 2000 installation.

Furthermore, you should check the Microsoft Exchange Web site at *http://www.microsoft.com/exchange/downloads/2000/SP1.asp* for the latest service packs for Exchange 2000 Server. At the time of this writing, Service Pack 1 for Exchange 2000 had just been released. (If you choose to order, versus download, it can take "4–6 weeks" and costs $23.) Just as in the service packs for Windows 2000, the Exchange 2000 service packs contain patches, security hot fixes, and other fixes for problems related to Exchange 2000. Applying these service packs can help fix problems and keep your Exchange 2000 server operating to the best of its ability.

Optimize Current System Settings for Performance

Even if you have a brand-new, fresh installation of Windows 2000 Server, there are at least a few things you can do to optimize the performance of your Windows 2000 installation and hardware configuration before installing Exchange 2000. The following list includes some of the optimizations you can consider performing to enhance your Windows 2000 system:

- If you have the hardware to do so, use one hard drive for the operating system and another hard drive for just the Windows pagefile because Windows operating systems perform better when the pagefile is on a separate hard drive.
- Increase the size of the Windows pagefile so it is at least 50 to 100 MB larger than the amount of installed memory in the server to allow enough space in the pagefile so that Exchange 2000 and Windows can function efficiently. For example, if your server had 256 MB of installed RAM, you would want a pagefile that was at least 306 MB, but preferably 356 MB.
- An optional hard drive configuration is to set up a RAID 5 hard drive array, preferably with a hardware RAID controller, and place the Exchange Information Stores and other critical components on this array to increase data redundancy and, in many cases, disk access performance. Although it is possible to set up a RAID 0 array to achieve similar performance, this configuration lacks any data redundancy, which is typically a concern for most installations and thus should be avoided.
- Run the **Disk Defragmenter** (hard drive optimization program) on any hard drives and partitions on the server. By defragmenting the hard drives and partitions, you can ensure that the file system is properly organized and optimized before installing Exchange 2000. It might not be a bad idea to defragment after the installation as well. Figure 5-1 shows the Windows 2000 Disk Defragmenter analyzing the fragmentation status of a system partition. When a hard drive is fragmented (which can happen during the course of normal operations, especially when software packages are installed or uninstalled often), the bits of information that make up documents, programs, and other software are scattered around the hard drive. When the hard drive needs to access information, it has to look all over the hard drive to find it, which tends to slow down the computer. When you defragment a hard drive, the defragmentation software sorts out all the data on the hard drive and organizes it for the most efficiency. This organization makes the hard drive (and then the system as a whole) perform better.
- Unload or uninstall any applications or services that are not required by Exchange 2000 Server, such as Telnet or IIS (if not using Outlook Web Access).

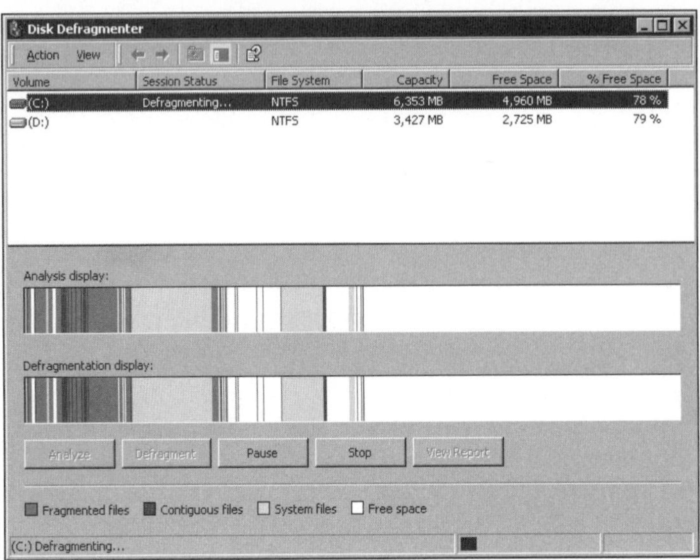

Figure 5-1 Using Disk Defragmenter to optimize hard drive performance

Make sure you perform these optimization steps before installing Exchange 2000 because many of them, including configuring a RAID array, defragmenting, and adjusting other hard drive-related settings, can be difficult or impossible to perform without a substantial amount of time spent backing up and restoring data, which can cause lengthy downtime.

Verify That Appropriate System Protocols and Services Are Available

You are nearly ready to start the installation of Exchange 2000 Server, but you need to check a few other steps and settings to ensure that the Exchange 2000 Server installation will go through with little difficulty. The following list details the additional steps required to prepare for installation of Exchange 2000:

- Ensure that the **NetBIOS name** (name given to the system) of the server is appropriate before installing Exchange 2000. If you realize that the name is inappropriate, it's much easier to rename the server before Exchange 2000 is installed, and it is pretty much impossible after Exchange 2000 has been installed. In most cases, changing the name requires a complete reinstallation of Windows 2000 and Exchange 2000 Server. Figure 5-2 shows the System Properties dialog box where you can change the NetBIOS name before installing Exchange 2000.
- If you plan to install Exchange 2000 in a domain that spans multiple domain trees, ensure that the appropriate trust relationships and security for your configuration are set to allow Exchange 2000 to function across the trees it will service.

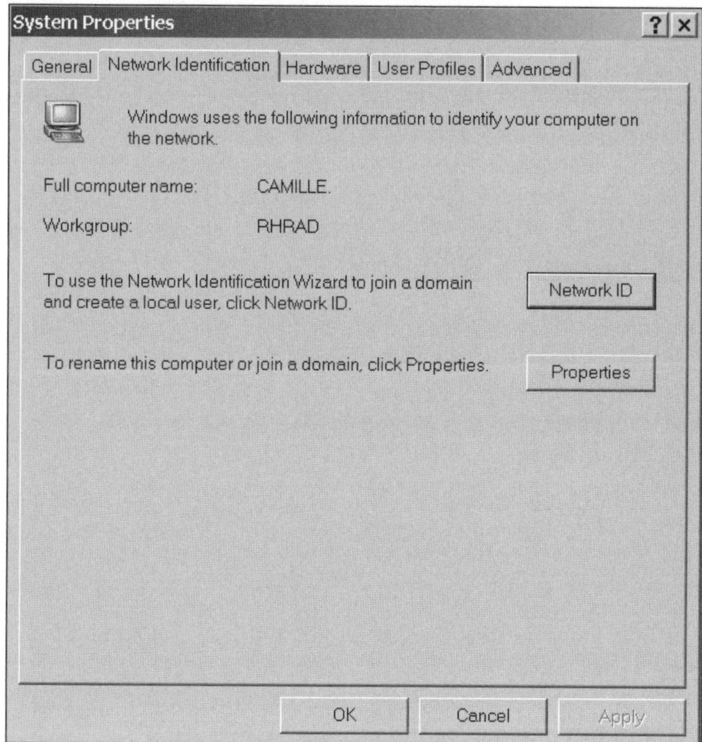

Figure 5-2 Using the System Properties dialog box to set a meaningful name for your server

- TCP/IP must be configured and functioning properly before installing Exchange 2000 because Exchange 2000 relies on SMTP, and SMTP utilizes TCP/IP for transport.
- If you're using NNTP or OWA, then IIS version 5.0 or later must be installed on the server. If you plan to activate NNTP services from the start rather than later, the NNTP Service must be started before installing Exchange 2000. NNTP is typically installed, but disabled by default by Windows 2000.
- If you will be using the advanced security features of Exchange 2000 Server, including encrypted e-mail services, you must have the **Key Management Service (KMS)** installed and configured. The KMS is part of the Microsoft Certificate Services that are included with Windows 2000; it enables keys to be generated for encrypting and decrypting e-mail sent to and from Exchange 2000. You will learn more about the KMS and other security-related features in Chapter 12, "Security and Encryption in Exchange 2000 Server."
- If your plans call for a cluster of Exchange 2000 servers for redundancy, you must take the appropriate steps to set up clustering under Windows 2000 Server, per the steps outlined for that operating system. (For more information

on clustering technologies, you can visit *http://www.microsoft.com/windows2000/technologies/clustering/default.asp*.)

- You can support Microsoft Mail for AppleTalk Networks with Exchange 2000 and provide support for Macintosh users connecting to the Exchange 2000 server. To implement this feature, you must have Windows 2000 Services for Macintosh installed and configured before installing Exchange 2000.

Create Any Special Accounts Required for Installation

Exchange 2000 Server requires that a pair of user accounts be available to facilitate installation and administrative duties and maintenance after the installation is completed. These two accounts—the Exchange Service account and the Exchange Administrator account—can be any current, existing user accounts, but it's better to create dedicated accounts just for these functions.

Creating dedicated accounts for Exchange administration is useful particularly from a security standpoint. It is much better to perform Exchange administration and maintenance from one dedicated Exchange Service account with heightened security than to use your regular administrator account that has rights to everything. If that regular account were compromised, or left logged on or unattended, hackers could potentially infiltrate your systems, servers, and network and create huge problems with your Exchange server. The same advice stands for the dedicated Exchange Administrator account you use to administer user privileges, settings, and other Exchange configuration components. These accounts should have a well-thought-out password that's as secure as possible, and you should lock the Exchange server when you walk away or make sure the Administrator account is logged out when it's not in use.

Create an Exchange Service Account

Many software packages utilize user accounts to interact with the systems and servers to perform their functions and duties. For instance, Veritas BackupExec has a backup service account for interacting with the servers and systems it is backing up or restoring to. Exchange 2000 is no different, and you must create an Exchange Service account before you begin your installation. The reason for this is that every part of Exchange functions as an individual Windows 2000 service, and this account is required for these services to communicate with and authenticate each other. Therefore, the Service account is necessary before any of the services, let alone Exchange 2000, can start.

During the Exchange 2000 installation, the setup software asks which account is the Exchange Service account, and you must specify the user account to use. You will learn how to create and configure the Exchange Service account and the Exchange Administrator account in the "Hands-on Projects" section, later in this chapter.

Create an Exchange Administrator Account

Windows 2000 Server and Exchange 2000 Server are administered with separate administrative user accounts. Just because an administrator has rights to make changes in Windows 2000 doesn't necessarily mean you want that administrator to have similar rights in Exchange 2000. Having separate administrator accounts increases security for both Windows 2000 and Exchange 2000 by allowing you to delegate administrative duties to the people who actually need to do the work, instead of possibly giving rights to a user who doesn't need them. Typically, you should have one main Exchange account for administration; however, if you need to set up other Exchange administrators, you can do that after the Exchange 2000 installation is finished.

The Exchange Administrator account should be included in the following security groups:

- Domain Administrators
- Enterprise Administrators
- Schema Administrators

Optional Preinstallation Steps

After you have completed the preinstallation steps and are ready to proceed to the Exchange 2000 installation, you should do at least two things to help provide a backup of your system settings in case the installation fails.

First, create an emergency repair disk. An emergency repair disk includes settings and configuration information that can help bring the system back to its previous state before the Exchange 2000 installation. To make an emergency repair disk, use the wizard included in the Windows Backup utility.

The second step is to perform a complete backup of the server in its current state before the installation takes place. After the installation of Exchange 2000 is finished, regular backups should be performed, but doing one before Exchange 2000 is installed can make it easier to recover from a failed installation. You will learn more about backing up data and how it works with Exchange 2000 in Chapter 15, "Disaster Recovery in Exchange 2000 Server."

INSTALLATION OF THE FIRST EXCHANGE 2000 SERVER

If you have performed the preinstallation steps outlined previously, then you are ready to install the first Exchange 2000 server on your network. Depending on what point you have reached during the Microsoft Solution Framework process, this initial installation might be the test installation before the testing phase, after which you implement your final Exchange 2000 installation. Regardless, the steps for installation are the same; you will encounter differences only if you have decided to implement additional features beyond the basic Exchange 2000 installation. In this section, you focus on a basic Exchange 2000 Server installation to become familiar with the steps to quickly get an Exchange 2000 server up and running.

It is necessary to be logged on as the account you intend to use for Exchange administration when the time comes to start your installation of Exchange 2000.

By this point in the installation process, you should already have a Windows 2000 server with the following steps completed and infrastructure changes in place:

- Active Directory installed and configured
- Functioning DNS services in place
- Administrator and Service accounts created
- Have run ForestPrep to prepare Active Directory for Exchange 2000 (see "Hands-on Projects" in Chapter 2)

Starting the Installation

To start the installation, you can simply insert the Exchange 2000 Server installation CD-ROM into the server's CD-ROM drive and wait for it to automatically run (if Auto Run is enabled) the setup program. If you are installing from a directory on the server, if the CD-ROM in your server has Auto Run disabled, or if you are installing from a network share, locate the Setup.exe file and double-click it to start the installation. Typically, Setup.exe is under \Setup\386 in the installation CD-ROM or folder.

After you run Setup.exe, you are greeted by the Microsoft Exchange 2000 Installation Wizard, as shown in Figure 5-3.

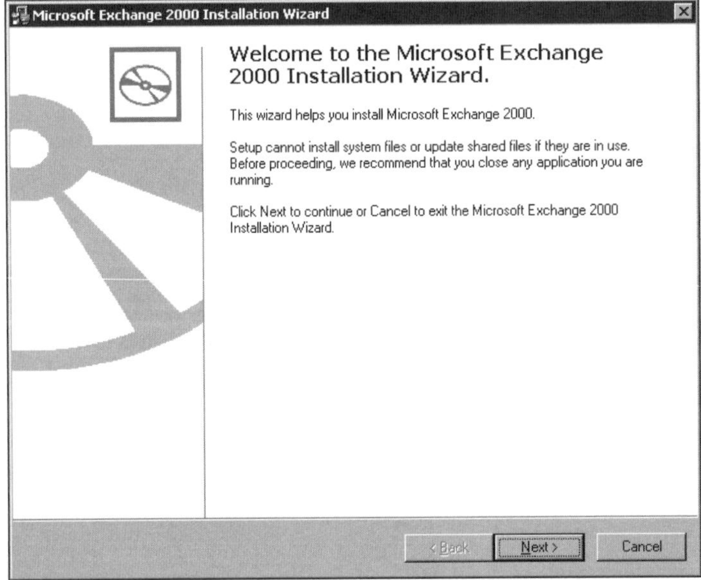

Figure 5-3 The Microsoft Exchange 2000 Installation Wizard

Depending on the additional software or services you have functioning on your server, you might see the Installation Wizard pop up a window requesting that you shut down any unnecessary software. Antivirus software in particular should be disabled or shut down entirely because it can interfere with installing software such as Exchange 2000 that modifies sensitive system files during installation. If you need to shut down any software or services, do so in the application itself, cancel the setup, or press Ctrl+Alt+Del to start Task Manager so that you can click End Process for any open software.

In the first Microsoft Exchange 2000 Installation Wizard window, click Next. The Microsoft Exchange End-User License Agreement window opens. Read through it and make sure you agree with it. If you do, click the I agree radio button, and then click Next. After you have accepted the license agreement, the next window requires you to enter your Exchange 2000 Server CD key. Enter the CD key from the Exchange 2000 Server package you received. The key is usually on an orange label attached to the back of the protective case that the installation CD came in. Enter the key, and then click Next to proceed to the Component Selection window. In the Component Selection window, you see a wide selection of Exchange 2000 Server components that can be installed.

The components are grouped into three installation modes (typical, minimum, and custom). Typical is the default installation mode and includes every available component; minimum mode installs the basic software required for Exchange 2000 to function as a messaging server. Custom mode allows you to pick and choose any features you want to install. In this installation mode, you can also specify the installation directory for Exchange 2000, allowing you to select where you want the software to be installed. For example, you might want to change the installation directory if you want Exchange 2000 to be on a partition or hard drive with more space or better performance than the default location, which is typically C:\Program Files\Exchsrvr. Figure 5-4 shows the Component Selection window.

If your intended installation is for a basic e-mail server with the simplest functionality, use the minimum installation mode, which gives you the simplest installation and the basic functionality you need and takes up the least disk space. However, it's a good idea to install the Microsoft Exchange Messaging and Collaboration Services and Microsoft Exchange System Management Tools in case you decide you want to use them later. If you do not know which services you will end up using, or if you intend to set up some services later for testing or in a production setting, select the typical mode of installation and install every option available. Any unused components can be left in or removed later, if necessary. For a better idea of what the various components can do for you, refer to Table 5-3 for a basic description of each component.

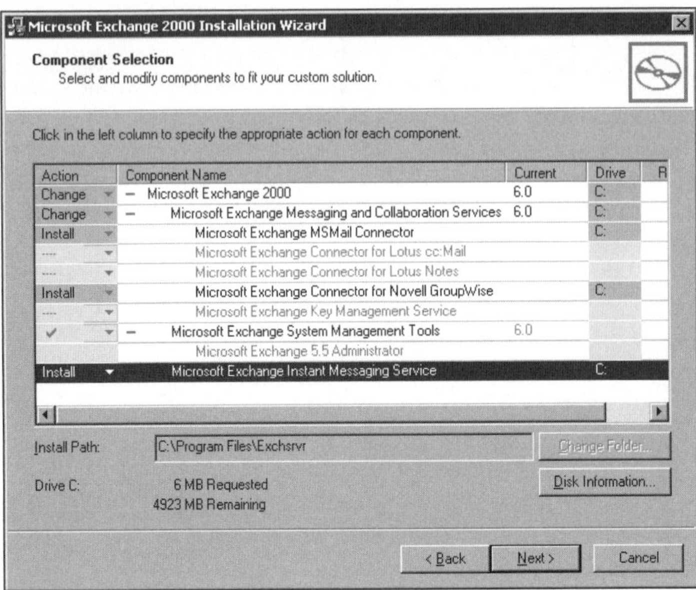

Figure 5-4 The Component Selection window

Table 5-3 Functions of Exchange 2000 Components

Component	Function
Microsoft Exchange 2000	The core software installation package that must be selected for every installation
Microsoft Exchange Messaging and Collaboration Services	The option that installs every optional Exchange messaging and collaboration component available. Any components you don't want installed must be deselected manually. Remember that NNTP must be installed and functioning if you want to install this option.
Microsoft Exchange MSMail Connector	The connector required to support data transfer between Exchange 2000 and Microsoft Mail servers
Microsoft Exchange Connector for Lotus cc:Mail	The connector required to support message and data transfer between Exchange 2000 and Lotus cc:Mail
Microsoft Exchange Connector for Lotus Notes	The connector required to support message and data transfer between Exchange 2000 and Lotus Notes
Microsoft Exchange Connector for Novell GroupWise	The connector required to support message and data transfer between Exchange 2000 and Novell GroupWise

Table 5-3 Functions of Exchange 2000 Components (continued)

Component	Function
Microsoft Exchange Key Management Service	The component that installs the enhanced Exchange 2000 dedicated security enhancements that integrate with Windows 2000 Certificate Services to provide e-mail encryption
Microsoft Exchange System Management Tools	The component to install a new Exchange management utility that improves management of the various Exchange 2000 components. This component can also be installed separately from Exchange 2000 on any Windows 2000 system to facilitate remote Exchange 2000 management.
Exchange Chat Service	The option that adds a user chat feature to Exchange 2000
Microsoft Exchange Instant Messaging Service	The option that adds instant messaging server components to Exchange 2000, allowing users to send instant messages to each other

If you decided not to run ForestPrep before your installation, after you have finished selecting the components you want to install during your Exchange 2000 installation, you must move on to the next step: creating a new Exchange Organization. This Organization is based on the network and plan you developed while following the MSF (if you used it). To ensure that the installation process goes quickly and that your domain has been expanded to support Exchange 2000 properly, Microsoft recommends that you run ForestPrep before the installation.

If you have run ForestPrep successfully before, the window following the Component Selection window is the Component Progress window, shown in Figure 5-5. Otherwise, you see the Exchange Organization Selection window, where you specify the Organization you will create. Remember, this can be done only once and cannot be changed after the installation without rebuilding the entire server! So make sure you use the information gathered in the MSF or take some time to plan what your organizational structure will be called and how it will look.

The Component Progress window shows the progress of the installation as it moves through the various steps, with a progress bar on the bottom. Copying the files and performing the necessary setup and cleanup takes a few minutes; after the copying is finished, you see the wizard's completion window, indicating that the installation was successful. Click the Finish button to complete the Exchange 2000 installation. After the installation is finished, you will notice a new folder under Start, Programs, called Exchange 2000, which contains shortcuts to several key Exchange 2000 tools. Table 5-4 lists these tools and their functions.

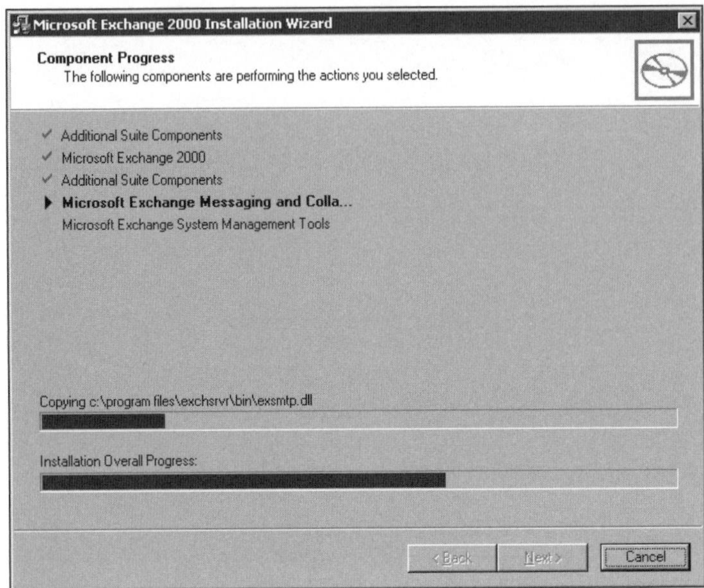

Figure 5-5 The Component Progress window

Table 5-4 Key Tools in Exchange 2000 Server

Component	Function
Active Directory Cleanup Wizard	A wizard used to locate multiple accounts in Active Directory that reference the same user and merge this information into one unified account to reduce the number of objects, thus simplifying management.
Active Directory Users and Computers	A shortcut to the main Active Directory management console, which allows you to manage user and computer settings. Using this tool, you can specify any necessary Exchange settings, including e-mail addresses and more.
Migration Wizard	A wizard that helps you migrate users and their mailboxes from other existing messaging services, such as Lotus Notes, Novell GroupWise, and others.
System Manager	The core management utility for Exchange 2000 Server. You can make changes to almost every facet of Exchange 2000 and configure how it functions, including settings for connectors and more.

Installation of Subsequent Exchange 2000 Servers

If your installation calls for multiple Exchange 2000 servers after you have performed the initial Exchange 2000 setup, then installing additional servers in the domain is not very difficult at all. In fact, it is very much like the first installation, except for a couple of differences you should be aware of:

- The first and most major difference occurs when you start the installation. This time you cannot change the name of the Exchange 2000 Organization you created when you set up the first server or ran ForestPrep during the preinstallation steps. The Exchange Organization Selection window shows the name of the existing Organization, but the information is grayed out, and you cannot modify it.
- There is no need for Exchange 2000 to expand the schema as it did during the first installation or during ForestPrep, if you ran it before installation. This makes the installation proceed much faster than the initial Exchange 2000 installation.

As you can see, any differences between your first installation of Exchange 2000 and subsequent installations only make the installation quicker, with fewer steps than the first installation. After Exchange 2000 has been integrated with Active Directory, any further Exchange 2000 installations integrate with AD as well and thus are easy to administer with the included AD management tools.

If you followed the MSF model to plan your additional Exchange 2000 servers, you should continue to follow it for testing during the developing phase to ensure that any subsequent servers are set up per the deployment plan you laid out during the planning and developing phases of the MSF.

Postinstallation Steps

Now that you have finished the basic installation of your first and subsequent Exchange 2000 servers, you still need to perform some important steps to verify that the installations were finished successfully and that the server is functioning the way it should:

- Restart the computer after the installation. The Exchange 2000 installation copies many files and changes many system settings. To free up system memory used during the installation and to ensure that any files that were replaced or modified during the installation are functioning properly, it's a good idea to reboot.
- After the server has restarted, check the event logs for any information, warnings, or errors that pertain to Exchange 2000. There are six different event logs to view, and it is a good idea to inspect each one of them because different errors in the various server components can affect how your Exchange 2000 server functions. Tend to any errors or warnings that require attention to make sure the Exchange 2000 installation runs the way it should (see "Troubleshooting Failed Installations" later in this chapter).

- As you learned earlier, every component of Exchange 2000 runs as its own individual service. You can view the status of the three main Exchange 2000 services in the Windows 2000 Services window found under Start, Programs, Administrative Tools, Services, as shown in Figure 5-6. Use this window to check the following services (if you installed additional Exchange 2000 components, you might also see services for them, such as Instant Messaging):
  - Microsoft Exchange System Attendant
  - Microsoft Exchange Information Store
  - Microsoft Exchange Routing Engine

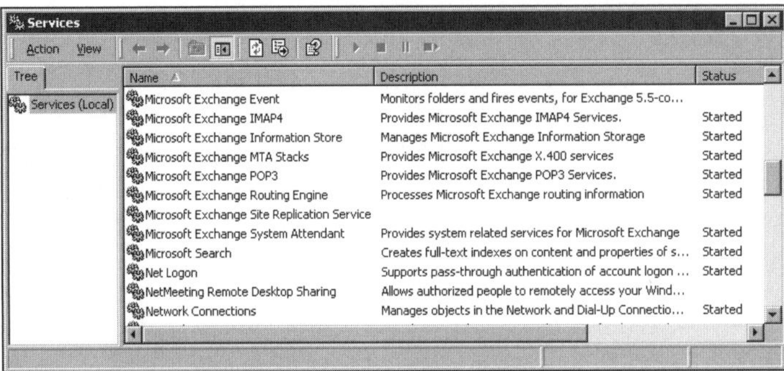

Figure 5-6 Viewing Exchange services in the Windows 2000 Services window

- The most important step is to locate and install any available service packs for Exchange 2000 after the installation is finished and verified as functioning. At the time of this writing, Service Pack 1 for Exchange 2000 Server is just becoming available. As mentioned previously, service packs can sometimes have problems shortly after release, so you might want to wait before installing one to see what the reaction is from IT-related sources, like *Windows 2000* magazine, or consider testing it on a nonproduction test server.
- If time allows, defragment all the server's partitions and hard drives, as you did during the preinstallation steps. Running Disk Defragmenter on the server's hard drives and partitions helps keep it running at peak performance and should be done periodically as part of regular system maintenance.

After you have completed the installation and verified that Exchange 2000 is functioning by performing the postinstallation steps, you are now ready to configure the Exchange 2000 server or install additional Exchange 2000 servers as needed. (You can find more information on configuring Exchange 2000 Server in the later chapters of this book.) Although it's a good idea to investigate what the Exchange 2000 Server components do and what options might need to be set so you can familiarize yourself with Exchange 2000, refrain from changing settings that are unfamiliar to you. Changing unfamiliar settings can cause more problems in the long run, especially if you change a setting and then forget you made the change. That changed setting could make the component or service—or even Exchange 2000—work incorrectly, thus generating more administrative work for you, some of it in the form of troubleshooting.

It is not unusual for operating system service packs to cause problems for existing software on the system. Sometimes, installing a service pack can cause the installation to fail, possibly creating reliability or functionality issues, such as broken network services. Also, the service pack might replace a critical file used for a software package and thus cause that service to fail. It's always best to see how any service pack for Windows 2000 or Exchange 2000 works out after release. Also, make sure to read any included information to see if the service pack has any known issues that would keep you from installing it.

Troubleshooting Failed Installations

Because Exchange 2000 Server has a fairly simple installation process, the odds of having a successful base installation are better than they were in previous versions of Exchange Server. Problems are more likely to happen if AD or DNS have not been set up properly before you attempt to install Exchange 2000. In many cases, the installation fails partway through because the Exchange 2000 installation program cannot communicate with the domain controller to perform a schema update or to make the appropriate changes to the Exchange Service account you created or selected during the preinstallation steps. Thankfully, there are some resources you can access to help with your troubleshooting efforts.

Resources for Troubleshooting

If you are in the middle of the installation and get an error stating that the installation cannot find a specified file, click the Retry button in the error message box at least once; sometimes there are anomalies when copying files to a system, especially if the installation files are located on a network share. If, after a retry or two, the file still cannot be found, it's usually advisable to cancel the installation and try to figure out what's going wrong.

A failed installation can also be the result of a few simple mistakes or problems that can be rectified quickly, allowing you to retry the installation, this time with more success. These are some of the common mistakes and problems:

- You are logged on as a regular user, not as an appropriate administrator or with the Exchange Administrator account.
- The Active Directory structure to which you are installing has applied tightened security measures, and your Administrator account cannot access or modify the schema. Therefore, Exchange 2000 cannot perform the schema update it requires during ForestPrep or the regular Exchange 2000 Server installation process.

- The server hardware or operating system installations are unreliable, and one or the other fails during the installation process. (You can check the event logs to look for any peculiar errors or problems.)
- The Exchange 2000 Server CD-ROM has defects or there was data corruption when copying the data from the network or local hard drive, thereby causing the installation to fail.

Many other issues can arise during the installation that make it fail, but these problems are the most common ones. In most cases, it's easier to troubleshoot failed installations by performing a test installation on a server that is independent of your main network. If you have followed the MSF correctly, you have already done this; however, things can go wrong even with the best planned deployments, so you might have to roll up your sleeves and start trying to figure out what went wrong.

Some other resources are available to help locate the problem and find a solution for it. In addition to the Microsoft tech support phone line, Microsoft Web sites can assist you in finding solutions to your problems when you enter the necessary information about the problem. To use these Web sites more efficiently, check the system event logs for valuable information, such as event IDs or error codes, that can be entered at *www.microsoft.com/technet* to search for Web pages that address those problems.

To get those event IDs and error codes, use the Event Viewer application under Start, Programs, Administrative Tools, Event Viewer. When looking at any event logs, pay particular attention to the entries that look like a yellow yield sign with an exclamation point (warnings) and the ones that look like a red stop sign (errors). Figure 5-7 shows an example of the Event Viewer window.

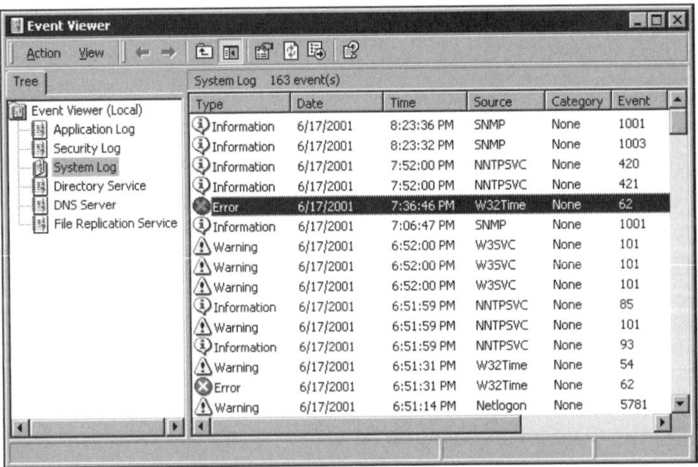

Figure 5-7 Viewing event logs in Windows 2000 Event Viewer

Even though the messages you come across might be only warnings right now, these warnings could become a problem if not taken care of as soon as possible.

Each recorded event in the log has an event ID, a description of the error or event, and sometimes a brief description of how to fix the problem (if any). Be forewarned that these event descriptions or instructions on how to fix the error can be cryptic at the best of times; however, since Windows NT 4.0, Microsoft has improved the descriptions and level of detail to make them more useful. Figure 5-8 shows an example of an Event Properties dialog box.

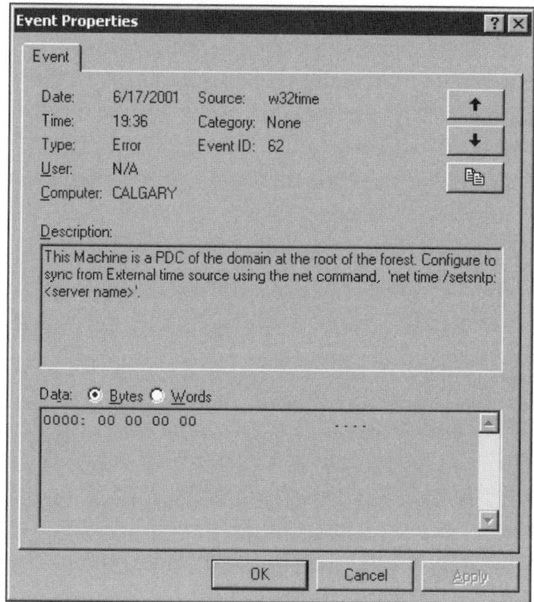

Figure 5-8 The Event Properties dialog box

In addition to the regular Windows 2000 event logs, Exchange 2000 generates an event log during the installation process that tracks what happened during the installation, and if the setup failed, it records the pertinent information in this file. The file, named Exchange Server Setup Progress.log, is created in the root directory on the hard drive. Not all the information in these files is in readable English; some of it is in code or strange abbreviations that are likely useful only to Microsoft programmers or support personnel. The main point to keep in mind with this file is that it records only errors that stop the installation of Exchange 2000. Any minor errors that do not stop the installation are not recorded; for instance, if you mistakenly select a component that requires another component to be selected and a error window pops up informing you of this, that error is not recorded in the log file. If you do decide to try to understand some of the information in this log file, the following short list contains some of the more important abbreviations you may come across in the error information. You can also supply this information to Microsoft technical support if you decide to contact them to help solve the problem.

- 55 = Microsoft Exchange Server 5.5
- PT or Platinum = Microsoft Exchange 2000 Server
- Underdog = Microsoft Exchange 2000 Setup
- Cartman = Microsoft BackOffice Setup

By using the Windows 2000 event logs, you can quickly access information on the problem from the wealth of technical information on Microsoft's various support sites. The information in TechNet or the Knowledge Base tends to be more detailed, with links to related information. Also, Microsoft has placed an Exchange 2000 Server Setup Troubleshooter online that asks basic questions in an effort to lead you through a systematic resolution of your problem. The Exchange 2000 Server Setup Troubleshooter at *http://support.microsoft.com/support/tshoot/exch2ksetup.asp* is a useful tool for troubleshooting basic setup difficulties in Exchange 2000 Server.

When to Perform an Uninstall of Exchange 2000

While troubleshooting failed installations, if you determine that you must uninstall Exchange 2000 Server (if you managed to get a complete installation performed), there are a couple of ways to do it. In some cases, your installation of Exchange 2000 could have installed completely, but have errors that cannot be corrected with regular troubleshooting methods, and it can be easier and far more efficient to remove the software entirely. The quick and easy way to uninstall is with the Add/Remove Programs utility under Start, Settings, Control Panel. In the Add/Remove Programs utility, you can select Exchange 2000 from the list of installed software and click Change/Remove. Exchange 2000 Server Setup appears and asks you what components you want to remove. You can select every component (by clicking the Action list arrow and selecting Remove) to remove the application entirely; the Component Selection window, shown in Figure 5-9, can also be useful if you want to install additional components left out during the initial Exchange 2000 installation.

Keep in mind that before removing the Exchange 2000 installation, you must delete any users who have mailboxes on the system, including the Exchange Administrator account you created during the installation. After you have deleted the users and removed the software, you should move through the preinstallation steps again to ensure that everything is in place before attempting the reinstallation. You should also take care of the problem that caused you to remove Exchange 2000 in the first place.

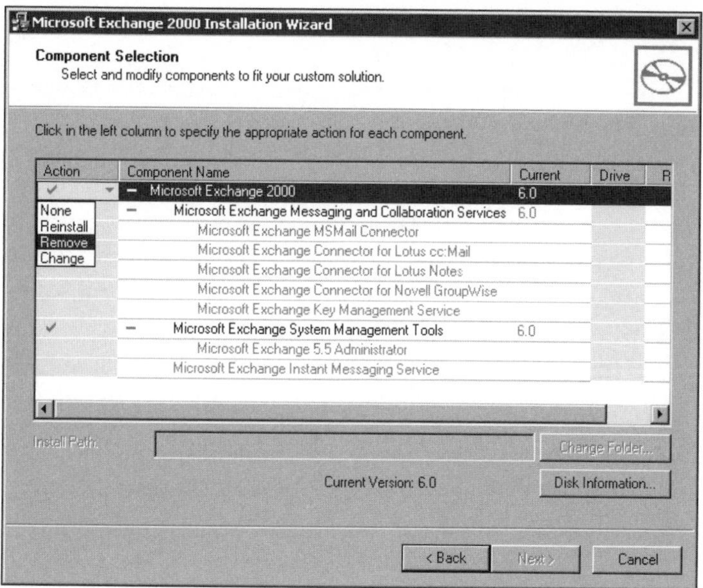

Figure 5-9 Using the Component Selection window to remove components

Even though you can uninstall Exchange 2000 Server components from the server, keep in mind that the schema changes to AD will not be modified, changed, or removed at all and will remain after the uninstallation. It is advisable to run ForestPrep again before reinstalling Exchange 2000 Server to ensure that the schema changes are intact and that the schema update wasn't the issue in the first place. Also, you need to reboot after the schema update to make sure the changes worked the way they should. The schema updates can usually be confirmed by looking for errors in the event logs, as explained earlier.

These examples of issues that can arise are perfect examples of why it's a good idea to perform a test installation of Exchange 2000 before deploying it on a production server. If the installation goes poorly, substantial downtime could occur, and in most environments, that is not acceptable. The issues are not limited to Exchange 2000 alone; first-time deployments of AD can be troublesome as well, and this can often be the root cause of your Exchange 2000 problems. Even if you have the most bulletproof plan for deployment, it is likely you will have an issue or two with AD the first time you try to implement it. The MSF can definitely be a great aid during the planning and developing phases, but even if you decide not to use it, a test installation before deployment is definitely recommended.

Performing an Unattended Installation

In some situations, you might want to install Exchange 2000 on servers without having to watch over the entire installation or click Next repeatedly to finish the installation. With Exchange 2000, you can perform an unattended installation that frees you up for other tasks by minimizing how much time you must spend performing additional installations. To do that, start the Exchange installation as you normally would, but run the installation from the command prompt instead of using the CD's AutoRun feature. You need to add the /createunattend *filename*.ini option to the executable file; *filename*.ini is the name of the output file that contains the unattended installation information. For instance, your command line would look something like this:

```
d:\setup\i386\setup.exe /createunattend custominstall.ini
```

This command launches a regular Exchange installation, but it records the settings you select during the installation in the custominstall.ini file, which can be used for future installations. Note that you cannot modify this .ini file manually to adjust the configuration and settings in it.

The only downside to the unattended installation function is that you cannot automate most of the installation process, so you will have to perform some of the preinstallation and postinstallation steps and configuration manually. The following list outlines the components and procedures supported and not supported by an unattended installation:

- **Supported Exchange Components**
  - Microsoft Exchange 2000 Messaging and Collaboration Services
  - Microsoft Exchange 2000 System Management tools
- **Supported Procedures**
  - Mixed- or native-mode Exchange 2000 Server installations (when not upgrading from Exchange 5.5)
  - Subsequent Exchange 2000 Server installations into a mixed-mode Exchange 5.5 environment, as long as it's not the first Exchange 2000 server installed in that Exchange 5.5 environment
- **Unsupported Exchange Components**
  - Microsoft Exchange 2000 Instant Messaging
  - Microsoft Exchange 2000 Chat Services
- **Unsupported Procedures**
  - ForestPrep
  - DomainPrep
  - Upgrading Exchange 5.5 servers to Exchange 2000
  - Uninstalling Exchange 2000 Server

- Exchange 2000 Cluster Node installation and configuration
- Add/Change mode to alter installed components
- Initial Exchange 2000 Server installation into an existing Exchange 5.5 organization

After you have an unattended installation .ini file generated, you can use it to perform an installation identical to the one you just used to create the .ini file. To do this, run Exchange 2000 Setup with the /unattendfile *filename*.ini option after the setup executable file, as in this example:


```
d:\setup\i386\setup.exe /unattendfile custominstall.ini
```

This command launches an Exchange 2000 installation using the settings and steps contained in custominstall.ini.

As you can see, this method is useful for performing simple, standard installations that could be rather repetitive. Even though you have to do a lot of the pre- and postinstallation steps, not having to manually set components, options, or settings and click the Next button several times can certainly take a load off. Unattended installations can also be useful when you need to have another administrator install Exchange 2000 on a remote server from over the network and you don't want him or her to make any changes or you want to limit the possibility of the administrator making any errors. By simply giving the administrator the command line that includes the /unattendfile string with the appropriate .ini file, you can ensure a proper installation without having to worry about the administrator making a mistake.

It is certainly possible to create more than one .ini file to customize different installations. If you require a component or setting on one or two servers, but not the rest, you can create an unattended installation file for just those servers and simply change the .ini file specified during the setup.

CHAPTER SUMMARY

- Understanding how Exchange 2000 Server integrates with Windows 2000 Server helps you gain perspective on what's required to perform a proper, fully functioning Exchange 2000 installation. The SMTP and NNTP protocols as well as the Active Directory and DNS services are all necessary for Exchange 2000 to function properly.
- Several preinstallation steps should be followed before every Exchange 2000 Server installation, including performance-enhancing procedures, required configuration changes, software updates, and verification of essential protocols and services.
- Installing Exchange 2000 Server and subsequent servers is fairly straightforward, but several key steps and services must be in place before the installation will succeed, including the preinstallation steps, Active Directory, and DNS services. You should also have an effective plan for the naming and structure of your Exchange 2000 organization.

- Make sure you go through these postinstallation steps after your installation is completed: restart the server, check event logs for any warnings or errors, check system services, and install any service packs (after checking that they are stable) available for Exchange 2000 Server.
- If you need to troubleshoot a failed installation, a wealth of information is stored in the system event logs and a log file that Exchange 2000 generates during the installation that records any errors that caused the installation to fail. You can use the information in these logs to search for solutions on Microsoft technical support Web sites, such as TechNet or the Knowledge Base.
- Unattended installations can be performed with Exchange 2000, but not all services and components can be installed or implemented. Generating an unattended installation template is quick, easy, and repeatable, and requires no additional utilities. Unattended installations are useful when the same installation must be performed for several servers or when you want to standardize an installation process for another administrator who's performing a remote installation.

KEY TERMS

Disk Defragmenter — A system utility that analyzes a hard drive or partition and then defragments it. When the defragmentation software defragments a hard drive or partition, it rearranges the various bits of data on the hard drive into the proper order to optimize data retrieval.

Key Management Service (KMS) — A set of services integrated with Microsoft Certificate Services, which is included with Windows 2000. KMS provides message and data security by generating keys for encrypting and decrypting e-mail sent to and from Exchange 2000.

NetBIOS name — The system name given to a system or server for easier identification over a network. Make sure you apply an appropriate name when setting up Active Directory because the name will stay; if it's hard to understand or doesn't mean anything (for instance, K37T110 or ASDFJGL), it could become difficult to efficiently manage naming on the domain.

Routing and Remote Access Services (RRAS) — The services that allow remote users to connect to servers via a modem or another connection method, such as ISDN, to provide networking connections over the Internet or phone lines.

security hot fix — A software patch for operating systems and other software that focuses entirely on security-specific issues.

service pack — A collection of patches, hot fixes, and other preexisting service packs that can perform wholesale system patching. To save time, service packs are used instead of installing each individual hot fix or patch because often hundreds of these patches are included in a service pack.

Review Questions

1. Which of the following functions are a benefit of Exchange 2000 integration with Active Directory? (Choose all that apply.)
   a. centralized user and data management
   b. security management
   c. distribution list management
   d. easier Exchange 2000 Server deployment

2. Which of the following protocols are integral to Exchange 2000 and its basic functionality? (Choose all that apply.)
   a. SMTP
   b. TCP/IP
   c. LDAP
   d. NNTP
3. When you install Exchange 2000 Server, what happens to the SMTP Service during installation?
   a. The installation deletes the protocol.
   b. The installation renames the protocol.
   c. The installation integrates the protocol with NNTP.
   d. The installation modifies the protocol to add extra functionality.
4. It is necessary to disable NNTP services before installing Exchange 2000. True or False?
5. During the course of the installation of Exchange 2000 Server, the ________________ service undergoes a complete modification to provide the functionality Exchange 2000 needs.
6. Which of the following services are necessary to install Exchange 2000 and have it function properly? (Choose all that apply.)
   a. Active Directory
   b. Domain Name System
   c. Routing and Remote Access Service
   d. Network News Transport Protocol
7. Installing and using RRAS can provide what useful functionality for Exchange 2000 Server? (Choose all that apply.)
   a. enables remote connections by users via a modem
   b. provides core connectivity between Active Directory, DNS, and Exchange 2000
   c. allows Exchange 2000 to connect to the Internet when a persistent connection is not available
   d. allows other mail systems to connect via a modem to deliver mail to the Exchange 2000 server

8. What is(are) the main benefit(s) of performing preinstallation steps before installing Exchange 2000 Server? (Choose all that apply.)
   a. ensures that the installation is successful
   b. complies with the Microsoft Solutions Framework plan
   c. ensures a smoother installation process
   d. makes the installation quicker
9. Before installing any operating system or even Exchange 2000 Server, it's important to verify that the ________________ meets minimum requirements for both the operating system and Exchange 2000.
10. Even if you follow the Microsoft Solutions Framework, you still need to gather much of the information required for your Exchange 2000 installation. True or False?
11. What is the minimum processor requirement for Exchange 2000 Server?
    a. 200 MHz Pentium II
    b. 400 MHz Pentium II
    c. 166 MHz Pentium
    d. 500 MHz Pentium III
12. Which of the following items are typically included in a service pack for operating systems or software? (Choose all that apply.)
    a. security hot fixes
    b. previous service packs
    c. debugging updates
    d. software patches
13. To improve the performance of your server before installing Exchange 2000 Server, what is the range of additional space you should have, beyond your installed system RAM, for your server's pagefile?
    a. 30 MB to 50 MB
    b. 50 MB to 100 MB
    c. 100 MB to 200 MB
    d. 5 MB to 10 MB
14. Defragmenting helps improve the performance of which of the following system components and software?
    a. Active Directory
    b. DNS
    c. hard drive
    d. processor

15. It is important to set an appropriate ______________ name on the server before installing Active Directory or Exchange 2000.
16. The Key Management Service is used to provide ______________ for Exchange 2000 Server.
17. Microsoft Exchange 2000 can provide support for Macintosh users connecting to Exchange. True or False?
18. Two accounts that should be created before installing Exchange 2000 are ______________ and ______________.

19. Which Exchange 2000 installation mode installs all available components by default?
    a. full
    b. typical
    c. custom
    d. minimum
20. What is the first thing you should do following a successful Exchange 2000 installation?
    a. Defragment the hard drives and partitions.
    b. Check the event logs for failed installations.
    c. Increase the size of the pagefile.
    d. Reboot the server.
21. After you have installed Exchange 2000, you can use the ______________ window to modify which Exchange 2000 components you want installed after the installation has finished.
22. When a service pack for Exchange 2000 becomes available, it's a good idea to install it as soon as possible. True or False?
23. Which of the following situations could cause a failure of an Exchange 2000 Server installation? (Choose all that apply.)
    a. if you are logged on as a regular user account
    b. if you have unreliable server hardware
    c. if Network News Transport Protocol is disabled
    d. if the installation CD-ROM has defects
24. Where on your system can you find information on system errors or other related issues when troubleshooting your Exchange 2000 installation?
    a. Active Directory Services
    b. Event Viewer
    c. Exchange 2000 Management console
    d. Microsoft TechNet

25. There are two command-line options for creating and using .ini files for an unattended Exchange 2000 installation. The command-line option used to create the .ini file is ________________, and the one used to perform the unattended installation using the .ini file is ________________.

HANDS-ON PROJECTS

Project 5-1

As you learned during the section "Preinstallation Steps," there are two accounts that you should create: one to facilitate Exchange administration and one for Exchange to use as a service account. Creating these accounts is quick and easy, and certainly a good idea. This project requires a system with Windows 2000 Server installed and a functioning installation of Active Directory. This project assumes that you will proceed to Project 5-2 after finishing this project.

To create special accounts used for Exchange 2000 installations:

1. Log on to your Windows 2000 Server with an account that has the administrative rights to create users under Active Directory (typically Administrator).
2. To open the Active Directory Users and Computers console, click **Start**, point to **Programs**, point to **Administrative Tools**, and then click **Active Directory Users and Computers**.
3. In the pane on the left, you will see a list of folders, including Computers and Users. Click the **Users** folder to view a list of all the accounts in the domain, as shown in Figure 5-10.

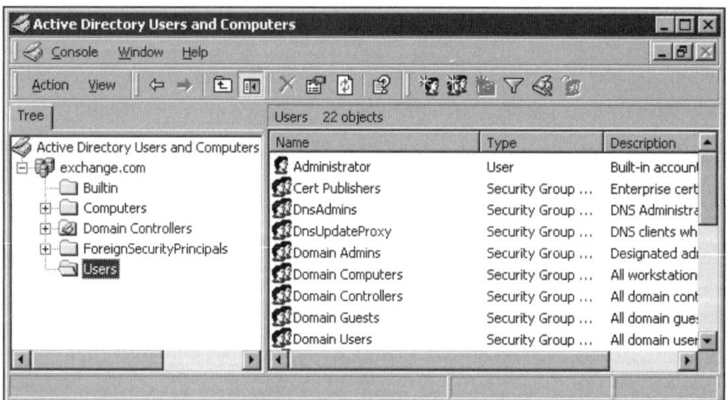

Figure 5-10 The Active Directory Users and Computers console

4. Right-click in an open area of the Details pane, point to **New**, and then click **User** on the shortcut menu. The New Object - User dialog box opens, where you specify pertinent user information, including the account name. Enter the following information for the first user account you create, the Exchange Administrator account:
   - First name: **Exchange**
   - Initials: Leave blank
   - Last name: **Admin**
   - Full name: **Exchange Admin**
   - User logon name: **exadmin**
5. For these special accounts, it isn't necessary to enter the first name/last name information; however, it does make the account creation more complete and perhaps helps keep absent-minded administrators from accidentally trying to delete the account. After you have entered this information, the window should look similar to Figure 5-11. Click the **Next** button to proceed to the next dialog box.

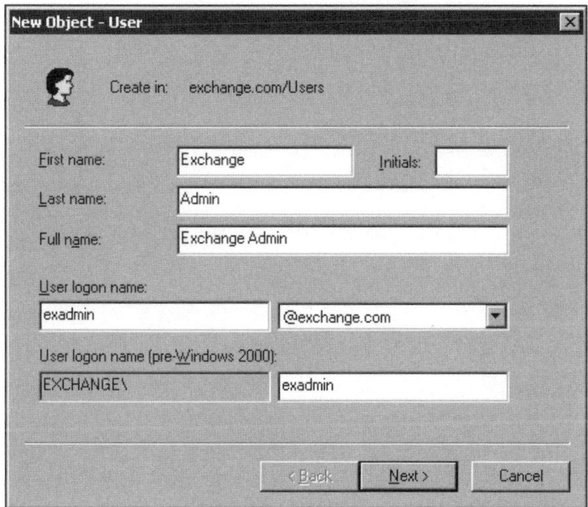

Figure 5-11 Creating the Exchange Administrator account in the New Object - User dialog box

6. Next you must supply a password for this account. For the sake of this project, enter **test** in the Password text box, and enter it again in the Confirm password text box.

7. Of the four options in this window, click to select the **User cannot change password** check box and the **Password never expires** check box (see Figure 5-12). After making these changes, click the **Next** button. If a window appears asking whether you want to create an Exchange mailbox for the user, click the check box to either select or deselect that option, and then click the **Next** button. A summary appears that describes the account that will be created; if everything looks correct, click the **Finish** button to create that user. (You should continue creating the accounts in Project 5-2.)

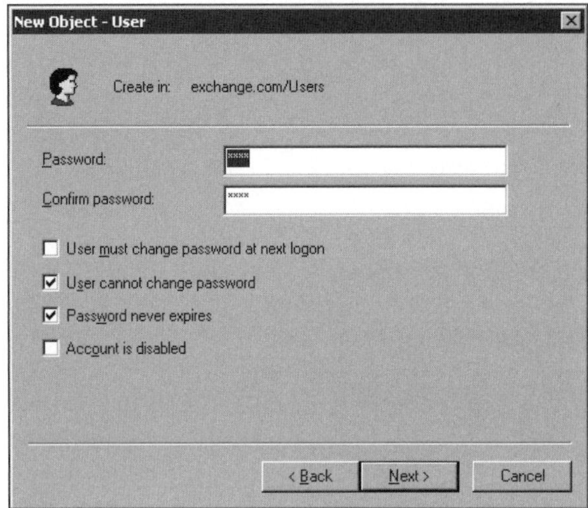

Figure 5-12 Setting password options in the New User - Object dialog box

Project 5-2

This project assumes that you have completed Project 5-1 and are continuing through this project to finish setting up the accounts.

To create special accounts used for Exchange 2000 installations:

1. Repeat Steps 2–7 from Project 5-1 for the Exchange Service account. For the user information, enter the following:
   - First name—**Exchange**
   - Initials—Leave blank
   - Last name—**Service**
   - Full name—**Exchange Service**
   - User logon name—**exservice**
   - Password—**test**
   - Click the same two password check boxes as in Step 7 of Project 5-1.

2. After you have created the two accounts, you are returned to the Active Directory Users and Computers console; you're now ready to assign the appropriate group membership to the accounts so that they can have access to the services and rights they require. To do this, right-click the **exadmin** account you created in Project 5-1, and then click **Properties** on the shortcut menu to open the exadmin Properties dialog box. Click the **Member Of** tab to assign group memberships.
3. Click the **Add** button to open the Select Groups window. In the top half of this window are the groups you can add this account to, and in the bottom window is a listing of the accounts you have added this user to. After using Ctrl+click to select the following three groups, click the **Add** button to add the user to these groups: **Domain Admins**, **Enterprise Admins**, and **Schema Admins**. After you have finished adding the user to these three groups, click the **OK** button to return to the Member Of tab. Your screen should look similar to Figure 5-13.

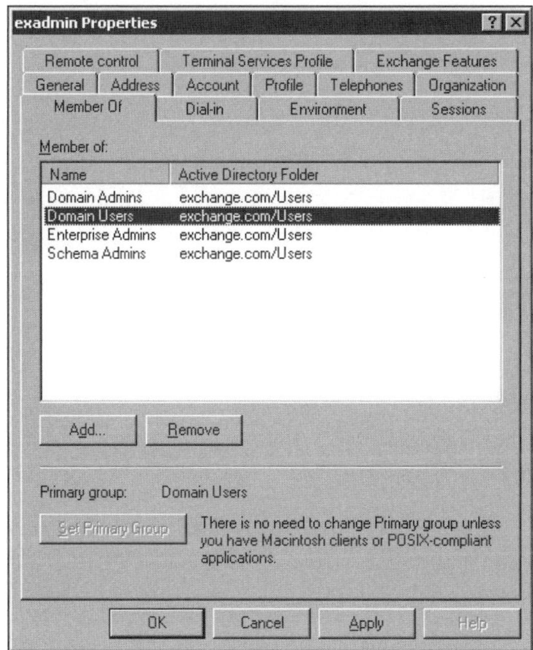

Figure 5-13 Assigning group memberships in the exadmin Properties dialog box

4. After you have finished setting the rights for this user, click the **Apply** button to save the settings. You can then close this window, or you can click the General tab and continue to enter information in the Description text box. This can be useful for supplying extra information, such as the account's full name and a description of what the account is used for, to help minimize administrative errors and help organize the Active Directory Users folder a bit better, but it's totally optional.

5. There's no need to perform Steps 2–4 for the exservice account because the Exchange 2000 Server installation makes the necessary setting changes to this account.
6. After finishing the previous steps, close any open windows.

Project 5-3

This project shows you how to ensure that the NNTP and SMTP services are installed and running before your Exchange 2000 Server installation. Both protocols are required for the Exchange 2000 installation; moreover, SMTP will be modified during the installation, as you learned in the "Windows 2000 Protocols" section. This project requires one system running Windows 2000 Server, and it should have IIS installed and functioning. However, you don't need AD, DNS, and Exchange 2000 installed for this project.

To enable NNTP and SMTP services:

1. Log on to your Windows 2000 server with an account that has administrative privileges on the system.
2. To open the Windows 2000 Services console to determine whether the two protocols are installed or active on the system, click **Start**, point to **Programs**, point to **Administrative Tools**, and then click **Services**.
3. Scroll down the list and locate the Network News Transport Protocol service and the Simple Mail Transport Protocol service. Both services should be present, both should have their Status set to Automatic, and both should be started. (If NNTP is not present, see Step 5.) If you see any entry that is neither started nor stopped, then the service is most likely disabled or set to manual. For reference, the two services should look like Figure 5-14. (NNTP is disabled in Figure 5-14, although it might not be on your system.)
4. If the status is set to Manual or Disabled for either service, double-click it (in this example, you would double-click **NNTP**) to open the Properties dialog box for that service (see Figure 5-15). In the middle of this window is the Startup type list box. Click the list arrow, and then click **Automatic** in the list of available choices. If the Service status field says Stopped, click the **Start** button just below it. The service should start (if it was stopped) in a few seconds. Perform this step for the other service if necessary.

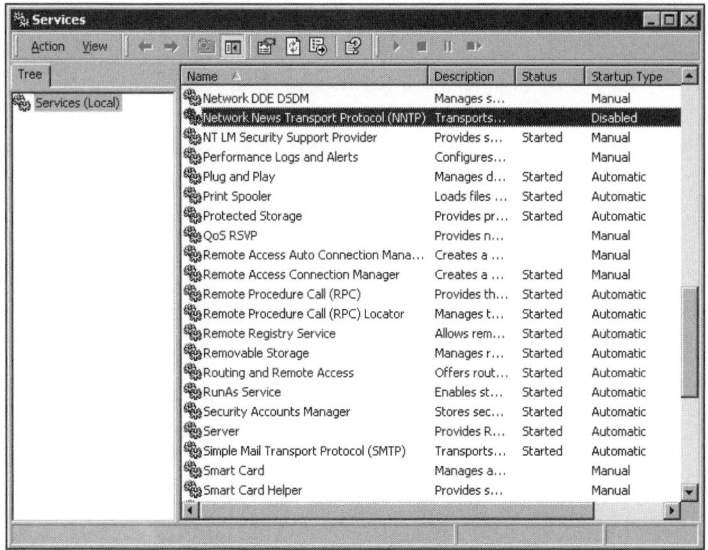

Figure 5-14 Checking the status of NNTP and SMTP Services in the Windows 2000 Services console

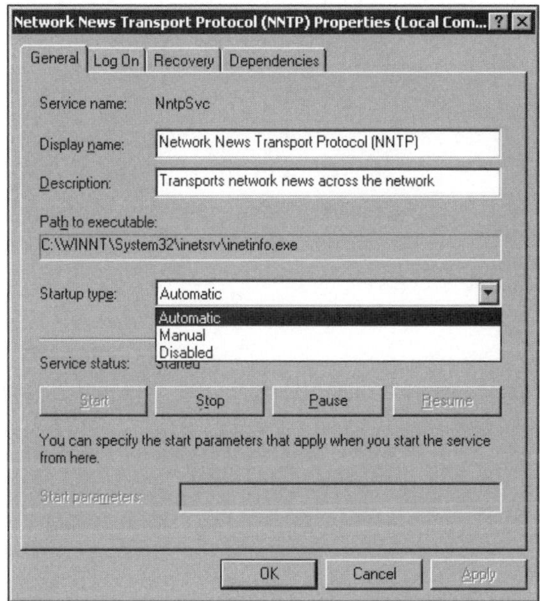

Figure 5-15 The Properties dialog box for the NNTP Service

5. Both of these services are typically installed by default when you install Windows 2000 Server; however, both can be missed if you choose not to install IIS. If this is the case, and the two services are simply not installed, then you must install them. Open the Add/Remove Programs utility by clicking **Start**, pointing to **Settings**, and clicking **Control Panel**. Double-click **Add/Remove Programs**.
6. Click the **Add/Remove Windows Components** button on the left side of the window and wait a few seconds until the operating system has had a chance to determine which software is installed on the system. Scroll down the list and click **Internet Information Services (IIS)** to select it, and then click the **Details** button to open the Internet Information Services (IIS) dialog box, where you can select components. Find the NNTP Service and the SMTP Service and make sure there's a check mark in the box to the left of each selection, as shown in Figure 5-16. If you do not have any other IIS components installed, the system prompts you to install other required IIS software. Click **OK** to add it to the software to be installed.

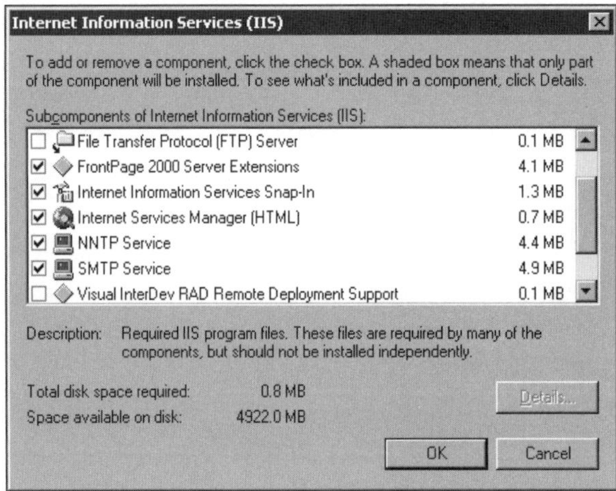

Figure 5-16 Using the Windows 2000 Add/Remove Programs utility to install components

7. After you have made sure the necessary services will be installed, click the **OK** button; the system then prompts you for the Windows 2000 Server source files. Either insert the Windows 2000 Server CD-ROM, or click the **Browse** button to locate the source files if they are on a hard drive or a network share. After you have located the source files and clicked **OK**, the file copying starts. After the files have been copied, you might be required to restart for the changes to take effect. If prompted to restart, close any open windows or applications and restart the system. Once the system has been restarted and you have logged on again, perform Steps 2–4 to ensure that the two services are started and have their Status set to Automatic.
8. Close any open windows or applications.

Project 5-4

After you have completed all the necessary planning and preinstallation steps, you are ready to install your first Exchange 2000 server. This project walks you step by step through a first-time Exchange installation, the same process you learned in the previous projects. It is assumed for this project that you have a system with Windows 2000 Server installed and that all the required preinstallation steps have been performed, including making sure you have a functioning DNS and AD, running ForestPrep, and creating the user accounts (which you did in Project 5-1 and 5-2). This project also assumes a domain name of exchange.com; however, your name can be different, so substitute as necessary. Also, you need the installation media on a CD-ROM, a hard drive, or a network share.

To install the first Exchange server:

1. Insert or locate the appropriate installation media. Click **Start**, and then click **Run**. In the command box, type ***X*:\setup\i386\setup.exe**, and then press **Enter**. Replace *X* with the appropriate drive letter, or make any changes necessary to point the command line to the location of your files. The Microsoft Exchange 2000 Installation Wizard opens. Click the **Next** button to continue.
2. The End-User License Agreement window opens. Click the **I agree** radio button, and then click the **Next** button to proceed to the next window.
3. In this window, you enter the CD Key for the installation. If you are using an evaluation copy, the CD Key is already present; otherwise, enter the information, and then click the **Next** button. The Component Selection window opens.
4. The default installation Action should be set to Typical. If it's not, change it to that, and then click the **Next** button, leaving the Install Path as its default: C:\Program Files\Exchsrvr.

If you haven't previously installed Exchange 2000 or run ForestPrep, the next windows allow you to specify the Exchange organization you want to install. First, you have to indicate whether you are creating a new Exchange organization or joining an existing Exchange 5.5 organization. Because you are creating a new organization, click the Create a new Exchange Organization radio button, and then click the Next button.

The Exchange Organization window allows you to name the organization. For the sake of this installation, type Exchange in the Organization name text box. Remember, when the time comes to do a production installation, you cannot change the name of the organization, so make sure it's the right one the first time! Click the Next button after you have entered the name of the organization.

5. If you are running a full version of Exchange 2000 (not the evaluation version), you see the Exchange 2000 Server Licensing Agreement window that asks you to agree to a per seat license, which means every user connecting to Exchange 2000 has a software license to do so. Click the **I agree** radio button, and click the **Next** button. The Component Summary window opens.

6. In the Component Summary window, you see a summary of the choices you made during the previous steps. If everything looks fine, click the **Next** button to proceed with the file transfer. If not, click the **Back** button to go back and make the appropriate changes.
7. The file copying process can take some time, especially if you are copying across a network. Observe the progress screen to monitor how the installation is going. Do not be surprised if the install process takes 30 minutes or more to finish copying files and changing system settings!
8. When the installation is completed, you should see a message stating that the installation was successful. Click the **Finish** button to exit the Microsoft Exchange 2000 Installation Wizard, and restart the system.
9. After the system has rebooted, if there are no errors about a failed service when the logon screen comes up, the installation was successful. Log on normally and check the Event Viewer logs to see if there are any alerts you should be aware of.
10. Close any open windows and shut down your computer.

Project 5-5

This project lets you go through the steps of installing a second server into an existing Exchange 2000 organization. As you learned earlier in this chapter in "Installation of Subsequent Exchange Servers," installing an additional server is typically quick and easy, so this project repeats many of the steps you performed during the first installation. This project requires a second system identical to the one used in Project 5-4, as well as the original system with the initial Exchange installation from Project 5-4. These two machines should obviously be members of the same Active Directory forest and should be connected on the same network hub or switch. In addition, this project assumes that any necessary preinstallation steps and configuration have been performed for the second system used in this project.

To install a second server:

1. Power on and allow both systems to start normally. Log on as exadmin from Project 5-1. Insert the installation CD-ROM or find the setup files on your system. Click **Start**, and then click **Run**. In the command box, type ***X*:\setup\i386\setup.exe**, and then press **Enter**. (You should replace *X* with the appropriate drive letter or make any changes necessary to point the command line to the location of your files.) The Microsoft Exchange 2000 Installation Wizard opens. Click the **Next** button.
2. The End-User License Agreement window appears. Click the **I agree** radio button, and then click **Next** to proceed to the next window to enter the CD key for the installation. If you are using an evaluation copy, the CD key is already present; if not, enter the information, and then click the **Next** button.

3. The Component Selection window appears. The default installation Action should be set to Typical. If it's not, change it to Typical, and then click the **Next** button, leaving the Install Path as its default: C:\Program Files\Exchsrvr.
4. In the next window, you will notice a difference; you cannot change the information in the Organization name box. The name of the organization you installed in the first installation (in Project 5-4) is listed here, but is grayed out. Click the **Next** button.
5. If you are running a full version of Exchange 2000 (not the evaluation version), the Server Licensing Agreement window opens, asking you to agree to a per seat license, which means that every user connecting to Exchange 2000 has a software license to do so. Click the **I agree** radio button, and then click the **Next** button. The Component Summary window opens.
6. In the Component Summary window, you see a summary of the choices you made during the previous steps. If everything looks fine, click the **Next** button to proceed with the file transfer, or click the **Back** button to go back and make the appropriate changes.
7. The file copying can take some time, and if you are copying across a network, it could take even longer (30 minutes or more). Observe the progress screen to monitor the installation.
8. When the installation is finished, you should see a message stating that the installation was successful. Click the **Finish** button to exit the Microsoft Exchange 2000 Installation Wizard. Restart the server.
9. After the system has rebooted, if there are no errors about a failed service when the logon screen comes up, then the installation likely went fine. Log on normally and check the Event Viewer logs to see if there are any alerts you should be aware of.
10. Close any open windows or applications.

Project 5-6

This project leads you through opening the system event logs and viewing a couple of events to see the information in them. As you learned in the section "Troubleshooting Failed Installations," the information in the event logs can be useful when troubleshooting failed installations or even monitoring functioning installations to determine how they are running. This lab requires one system, preferably with Windows 2000 Server installed. Exchange 2000 should be installed, but it's not necessary. Having Exchange 2000 installed simply adds more events with Exchange-related information that could be of interest.

To check system event logs:

1. Log on to your Windows 2000 Server with an account that has administrative rights, or at least rights to view event logs. To open the Event Viewer, click **Start**, point to **Programs**, point to **Administrative Tools**, and then click **Event Viewer**.

2. You should see the list of event log categories in the left side of the Event Viewer window (Application Log, Security Log, System Log, Directory Service, DNS Server, and File Replication Service). The two logs you will focus on in this project are the Application Log and the System Log. Start by clicking the **Application Log**.
3. In the Application Log, you find events posted by the applications on your system. Events typically involve an application failing to start or relate to how the application runs; for instance, if the Windows SMTP Service fails to start, an event will be logged here. Take the time to view some events here, especially those with an error symbol (a red stop sign) next to them. Open three or four errors of different types and record the event ID information as well as any error IDs that might be listed in an event's Properties dialog box. When you have finished looking at this log, click the **System Log** in the left side of the Event Viewer window.
4. The System Log typically contains events that pertain to the actual operating system and is where the bulk of the crucial errors reside. Usually, if a service or component of Windows 2000 is not functioning properly, it's listed in the System Log. As you did in Step 3, take some time to view any errors or informational events listed here. Record the event ID and any error IDs you find during your reading.
5. If time allows, you can take the event and error IDs you recorded in Steps 3 and 4, and use them to perform searches on the Microsoft TechNet Web site. If your system has Internet access, open the Web browser, enter the address **www.microsoft.com/technet**, and then press **Enter**. In the upper-left corner of this Web page is a box where you enter a subject for searching TechNet. Enter an event or error ID in this search box, and then click the **Go** button to the right of this box. Spend some time reading through any results of your searches. You might want to broaden your search by looking for information in the Knowledge Base articles if you are not having any luck finding what you want in TechNet. The Knowledge Base is at *http://search.support.microsoft.com/kb/c.asp*.
6. Close any open windows or applications.

CASE PROJECTS

Case Projects Background

The company you work for, Widgets Inc., is implementing Exchange 2000 across both of its networks. Currently, there are two separate divisions with two separate networks, which for security and financial purposes must remain apart. The first network is for the Engineering Department. Engineering has a preexisting Exchange 5.5 deployment that is already part of its Windows 2000 Active Directory mixed domain, with an NT 4.0 server hosting the Exchange 2000 system. Because of the data's sensitivity and the minimal amount of downtime Engineering can tolerate, they cannot take down the current

Exchange 5.5 installation until the new Exchange 2000 server is verified as running and stable. The second network is for the Sales Department. This department is rather new, and up until now has been using e-mail services from your Internet service provider. It has a fresh Windows 2000 AD configuration in place with no preexisting Exchange 2000 installs.

Case 1

Widgets Inc. wants you to install an Exchange 2000 server on the Engineering network, but as described in the Case Projects Background, you cannot remove the existing Exchange 5.5 installation before installing Exchange 2000. What steps do you have to take during your Exchange 2000 installation to ensure that the Exchange 2000 server continues to participate in the preexisting Exchange 5.5 installation?

Case 2

Widgets Inc. wants you to install an Exchange 2000 server on the Sales Department's network with the information described in the Case Projects Background. What steps do you have to take to implement a new Exchange 2000 deployment for the Sales Department?

Case 3

Widgets Inc. has decided, now that both Exchange 2000 deployments are completed and the old Exchange 5.5 server has been removed and sold, that they do not want the additional overhead of running both Exchange 2000 servers in separate networks. They also want to implement redundancy to make sure the Engineering Department has constant uptime for its e-mail and collaboration services. What can be done, using the two servers you have available, to fulfill the request? Can the one Exchange implementation provide services for both separate networks? If not, what will have to be done?

Case 4

Widgets Inc. requires that you install a couple of Exchange 2000 servers for its sister company, Gidgets Inc., which has now been migrated into your AD forest. The administrator for Gidgets Inc. is not experienced at installing Active Directory, and you want the installation to go smoothly. What can you do to make sure the installation goes smoothly without your having to be there? What basic steps should you have the other administrator follow?

CHAPTER

6

UPGRADING OR MIGRATING FROM EXCHANGE 5.5 TO EXCHANGE 2000

After reading this chapter and completing the exercises, you will be able to:

- Describe how a migration to Windows 2000 Server affects a migration to Exchange 2000 Server and gain insight into the integration between Windows 2000 and Exchange 2000
- Upgrade an existing Exchange 5.5 server to Exchange 2000 Server using a variety of upgrade methods and be able to select which upgrade method is the most appropriate for your organization
- Manage coexistence between Exchange Server 5.5 and Exchange 2000 Server in a mixed-mode environment so that existing Exchange Server users can benefit from the advanced features of Exchange 2000 Server
- Install, configure, and implement the Active Directory Connector in a mixed-mode Exchange Server environment so that you can easily migrate information from Exchange 5.5 to Active Directory and Exchange 2000
- Troubleshoot issues related to upgrading or migrating Exchange Server 5.5 to Exchange 2000 Server and optimize message flows between these two versions of Exchange Server found in most organizations

The previous chapter concentrated on installing Exchange 2000 Server in a new messaging environment. Although installing Exchange 2000 is a relatively straightforward process on new hardware, different issues arise when installing Exchange 2000 on servers already running Exchange Server 5.5 or earlier versions. Many companies already manage networks that consist entirely of Exchange 5.5 servers organized into site boundaries. Their new challenge includes upgrading or migrating these legacy servers to the current incarnation of Exchange—Exchange 2000 Server. Several factors must be addressed when considering a task of this magnitude, even though Microsoft offers many useful tools to aid in the migration process. One of the most important goals in the migration process is moving existing mailboxes onto new server hardware that's running a new version of Exchange, with the least amount of errors. This chapter shows you the best practices, which can help you achieve this goal.

Understanding How Migration to Windows 2000 Server Affects Exchange 2000 Migration

You should never assume that migrating to new operating systems or messaging systems is a simple process. Many companies spend countless dollars and personnel hours trying to migrate or upgrade existing infrastructures to new environments without considering potential problems. You should never assume that an upgrade or migration to a newer version of hardware or software automatically leads to dramatic gains in performance or scalability. The immediate gains might be dramatic and beneficial, but the long-term results are more telling. Given enough time, many administrators notice problems in their networks that could have been prevented had they spent more time planning a strong deployment strategy for the upgrade or migration.

Upgrading Versus Migrating

This chapter discusses upgrading and migrating earlier forms of Windows and Exchange Server. "Upgrading" and "migrating" are two separate and distinct terms, even though they are often used interchangeably. A pure upgrade, for example, involves installing Exchange 2000 on an existing Exchange 5.5 server so that all Exchange 5.5 components become Exchange 2000 components. No trace of Exchange 5.5 is left, and the only management tool provided is the Exchange System Manager Microsoft Management Console (MMC) used by Exchange 2000. In contrast, a migration strategy implies a coexistence phase between Exchange 5.5 and Exchange 2000, during which two management tools are supplied: the Exchange Administrator interface used by Exchange Server 5.5, and the System Manager MMC provided by Exchange 2000 Server. A coexistence phase, which results in a mixed-mode Exchange Server environment, has no time limit, so Exchange 5.5 mailboxes can be migrated or moved to the Exchange 2000 server at any time. When all mailboxes have been migrated to a server running Exchange 2000 and there is no need for Exchange 5.5, the organization is said to be running in native mode. Because these terms have different meanings depending on the context, you will have to decide what's best for your organization. Table 6-1 shows how Exchange Server integrates with the Windows operating system to produce a native-mode or mixed-mode organization.

As you can see in Table 6-1, your current or future infrastructure depends on the operating system that runs Exchange Server (either Windows NT 4.0 or Windows 2000), and it also depends on the domain structure you have chosen for your organization (that is, whether you are managing a Windows NT 4.0 domain or a Windows 2000 domain). The combination of operating system and domain structure helps you determine what type of organization you run. The terms "mixed mode" and "native mode" apply to both Windows 2000 Server and Exchange 2000 Server, but not in the same manner (see also Chapter 2, "Planning for Windows 2000," for more information on mixed- and native-mode operations in Windows 2000).

Table 6-1 Mixed and Native Modes for Windows 2000 and Exchange 2000

Domain or Site	Windows NT 4.0 PDC or BDC Running Exchange 5.5	Windows NT 4.0 Member Server OR Windows 2000 Domain Controller (Both Running Exchange 5.5)	Windows 2000 Domain Controller OR Windows 2000 Member Server/Standalone Computer (Both Running Exchange 2000)	Windows 2000 Member Server or Standalone Computer Running Exchange 5.5
Windows 2000 Domain	Mixed-mode Windows 2000 domain	Native-mode Windows 2000 domain	Native-mode Windows 2000 domain	Native-mode Windows 2000 domain
Windows NT 4.0 Domain	Normal Windows NT 4.0 domain	Normal Windows NT 4.0 domain	Normal Windows NT 4.0 domain	Normal Windows NT 4.0 domain
Exchange 5.5 Site	Normal Exchange 5.5 site	Normal Exchange 5.5 site	Mixed-mode Exchange environment	Normal Exchange 5.5 site
Exchange 2000 Organization	Mixed-mode Exchange environment	Mixed-mode Exchange environment	Native-mode Exchange environment	Mixed-mode Exchange environment

6

Examining Mixed- and Native-Mode Operations in Windows 2000 and Exchange 2000

You will understand Table 6-1 better if you are aware of the different systems that can run Exchange 2000 Server. For example, you can never install Exchange 2000 on a Windows NT 4.0 computer (whether it's a PDC or a BDC) because Exchange 2000 Server requires Windows 2000 Server for the underlying operating system. This is why Table 6-1 shows a column for "Windows NT 4.0 PDC or BDC Running Exchange 5.5." If your current environment consists of a Windows 2000 domain that includes Windows NT 4.0 PDCs or BDCs, your organization is said to be running a mixed-mode Windows 2000 domain, as shown in the row labeled "Windows 2000 Domain" in Table 6-1. If you manage a Windows 2000 domain that contains Windows NT 4.0 member servers or workstations, you are not running a mixed-mode Windows 2000 domain. The same is true if you manage Windows NT 4.0 domains that include Windows 2000 Server or Windows 2000 Professional machines. A true mixed-mode environment is seen from the reference point of a Windows 2000 domain containing Windows NT 4.0 domain controllers.

If you manage only Windows 2000 domains, you are said to be in native-mode operation, even if you decide to incorporate Windows NT 4.0 member servers or workstations in these domains. However, you might want a mixed-mode Windows domain so that you can use older applications and services. Some applications designed for Windows NT 4.0 cannot be ported (migrated) over to the Windows 2000 operating system. Therefore, some companies are forced to use a combination of Windows NT 4.0 servers and Windows 2000 servers in their network design.

The row labeled "Windows NT 4.0 Domain" in Table 6-1 contains entries called "Normal Windows NT 4.0 domain" because Windows NT 4.0 did not use the terms "mixed mode" or "native mode" to describe these domains. Therefore, even if you introduce a Windows 2000 system into a Windows NT 4.0 domain, the domain structure does not change and you are managing a "regular" Windows NT 4.0 domain. Finally, notice that the next to last row in Table 6-1 has entries called "Normal Exchange 5.5 site," even if Exchange 5.5 is running on a Windows 2000 domain controller. A mixed-mode Exchange Server organization is created when you introduce Exchange 2000 into the Exchange 5.5 site (notice that Exchange 2000 can run on a Windows 2000 domain controller, member server, or standalone computer).

Some administrators use the terms "member server" and "standalone computer" interchangeably, but in reality, a member server belongs to a Windows 2000 domain, whereas a standalone computer does not belong to a domain. (Although, it could belong to a workgroup of computers or just "stand by itself" and not belong to any group.)

The final item of interest in Table 6-1 concerns the last two rows of the table. You might have noticed that all entries in the last row of Table 6-1 reverse the entries directly above them. For example, managing a Windows NT 4.0 PDC or BDC running Exchange 5.5 is considered normal for any Exchange 5.5 site. However, introducing the same Windows NT 4.0 PDC or BDC running Exchange 5.5 into an Exchange 2000 organization suddenly changes the organization into a mixed-mode Exchange 2000 environment (because you are now dealing with two types of domain controllers: a Windows NT 4.0 domain controller running Exchange 5.5 and a Windows 2000 domain controller running Exchange 2000).

What can be concluded by looking at Table 6-1? Does this table provide some sort of "magic formula" that helps you decide on the optimal organizational mode to manage at all times? Hardly. Just be aware that many companies are currently managing mixed-mode environments consisting of Windows NT 4.0 PDCs running Exchange 5.5 computers that will be running for some time to come. If Exchange 2000 is eventually introduced into these organizations, there's a strong chance these companies will undergo some type of coexistence between Exchange 5.5 and Exchange 2000 before migrating their entire network designs completely to Exchange 2000. Therefore, it's important to know how to maintain a healthy balance between these different versions of Exchange Server.

Upgrading to Windows 2000 Server

Your deployment of Windows 2000 Server has a direct impact on your deployment of Exchange 2000 Server. You must decide whether you will continue running Exchange 5.5 on a Windows NT 4.0 platform or a Windows 2000 platform. A decision to move to Windows 2000 involves planning for an AD implementation strategy, which includes choosing the number of forests, domains, and other AD objects that have to be created (see Chapter 2 for more details on an AD implementation strategy). If you plan to deploy Exchange 2000, then you have no choice but to install and configure Windows 2000 because Exchange 2000 will not function on a Windows NT 4.0 server. Even though Exchange 2000 can run only on a Windows 2000 computer, you can still have Windows NT 4.0 servers in your network. Exchange is dependent on Windows, but Windows is not dependent on Exchange. That is, you have to upgrade your Windows NT 4.0 machines to Windows 2000 machines before even considering an upgrade from Exchange 5.5 to Exchange 2000. However, you don't have to upgrade Exchange 5.5 servers to Exchange 2000 before upgrading your Windows NT 4.0 computers.

When upgrading your Windows NT 4.0 network, you can upgrade your entire network infrastructure; you can upgrade just one Windows NT 4.0 domain containing an Exchange 5.5 server, and join this domain to another Windows 2000 forest; or you can upgrade one Windows NT 4.0 server to Windows 2000 Server, and then move this server to a separate Windows 2000 domain in a separate Windows 2000 forest. There are many combinations you can consider, but you should choose the option that meets all organizational objectives while minimizing downtime for users. You might also face restrictions that prevent you from completing one of these upgrade options. For instance, you could plan to upgrade all Windows NT 4.0 servers to Windows 2000 servers, but the hardware used to support Windows NT 4.0 might not be on the current Windows 2000 Hardware Compatibility List (the HCL; found on *http://www.microsoft.com/hwtest/hcl*). For example, many companies used servers configured with an Alpha-based processor instead of an Intel CPU and discovered they could not upgrade to Windows 2000 because Microsoft stopped supporting this type of processor with the introduction of Windows 2000.

A Sample Upgrade Scenario

The Bronx University, a not-for-profit organization, is running Windows NT 4.0 domains containing multiple Exchange 5.5 servers. The administrator, Camille, wants to upgrade one of her domains to a Windows 2000 domain and join this new domain to a new Windows 2000 forest she has configured, named Bronx. This new domain will be added to the Bronx forest as a root domain in that forest. The existing Exchange 5.5 servers all reside in a single site named Site1, and they all reside in an existing Windows NT 4.0 domain named Domain1. After the upgrade, all servers will belong to a new Active Directory domain called AD1 in the Bronx forest. Knowing the configuration of each Windows NT computer in your existing domain helps determine the upgrade order for these Exchange 5.5 servers. Camille has configured some Exchange 5.5 servers as BDCs and others as PDCs.

Microsoft recommends that Exchange Server 5.5 be installed on member servers of a Windows NT 4.0 domain, not domain controllers, because domain controllers are responsible for user logon authentication services, which require more server resources and administration. Integrating Exchange Server with domain authentication functions can impair server performance and place unnecessary loads on the server's CPU.

The Role of Active Directory Naming Contexts in Upgrading

When Camille upgrades the domain containing her Exchange 5.5 servers, she first upgrades her PDCs to Windows 2000 Server from Windows NT 4.0 Server. Doing this promotes the PDC to a regular Windows 2000 domain controller, which she can join to the Bronx forest.

Remember that Windows 2000 does not label domain controllers as primary or back-up; rather, all such machines share the generic label of "domain controller" and become peers to one another (so that one domain controller replicates domain information to all other domain controllers within the same forest structure).

The newly promoted domain controller (the former PDC) is now added to the AD database in the Bronx forest and holds a copy, or replica, of three types of naming contexts, or partitions in AD (see Chapter 2 for information on the types of naming contexts in Windows 2000): the schema naming context, the configuration naming context, and the domain naming context. As explained in Chapter 2, AD uses these naming contexts to define boundaries for holding certain types of information and for replicating this information throughout the forest. All domains share one common configuration and schema naming context, and each domain contains a unique domain naming context.

The naming contexts not only help organize your Windows 2000 domains, but also affect information in Exchange 2000. When you install your first Exchange 2000 server in a Windows 2000 forest, the AD schema is automatically extended with new Exchange-specific attributes. All such attributes start with the label ms-Exch-attribute, for instance, ms-Exch-DisableUDGConversion. Always remember that AD stores a large portion of Exchange 2000 data, such as recipient objects or the global address list, in the configuration naming context.

The Role of Global Catalogs in Upgrading

Although the former PDC has become a Windows 2000 domain controller, it has not risen to the ranks of a Global Catalog server in AD.

A GC server is a special type of domain controller that supports AD queries from users throughout an entire Windows 2000 forest. By default, only the first domain controller you install in a Windows 2000 forest is classified immediately as a GC server. However, you can always add more GC servers if, for example, you are planning a fault-tolerant configuration in case one GC server becomes unavailable.

All GC servers contain a read-write copy of the domain naming context for the domain in which they are located, but they can also contain read-write replicas of the configuration naming and schema naming contexts shared by all domain controllers in the forest. GC servers play an important role in the Windows 2000 AD; for instance, all native-mode

Windows 2000 domains access a GC server when processing user authentication requests. In fact, if a domain controller is unable to contact a GC server to process logon requests in a native-mode domain, that logon request is immediately rejected.

GC servers are important to Exchange 2000 because Exchange distributes all search requests among available GC servers, and it tries to use the GC server in the domain that contains the user account performing the AD search. Users who need address information when using an e-mail client such as Outlook 2000 can query a GC server for this type of information. GC servers act as central repositories for users to access information about AD.

Completing the Upgrade Scenario

After the PDC has been upgraded, Camille can then upgrade all the BDCs. Not all BDCs have to be configured as domain controllers in Windows 2000; some can become member servers or even standalone servers (standalone servers do *not* belong to any domain, but member servers do). When Camille has finished upgrading a BDC, she runs the Active Directory Installation Wizard, which joins a domain controller to a Windows 2000 domain, but it can also be used to demote a server to a **member server** even after it has joined a domain. A member server is preferred to a domain controller because it will not be responsible for user authentications in the domain and because it can be moved freely between administrative groups after Exchange 2000 is fully deployed.

Camille must decide how many domain controllers she wants to include in the new Windows 2000 domain, and how many of these domain controllers to configure as GC servers. Many organizations run Exchange 5.5 servers on Windows NT 4.0 PDCs and BDCs; however, they might not want to run Exchange 5.5 or Exchange 2000 Server on Windows 2000 domain controllers after an upgrade. In this case, these companies decide to install new Windows 2000 systems operating as domain controllers, and the former Exchange 5.5 servers run on machines configured as Windows 2000 member servers. The upgrade process for companies wanting to install new server hardware and create new domain controllers in existing Windows 2000 domains (while running Exchange 2000 on member servers) includes the following steps:

1. Install a Windows NT 4.0 machine into your existing NT domain as a BDC; this machine will become a new Windows 2000 domain controller.

2. Promote this new server to a PDC in your existing NT domain (the previous NT 4.0 PDC will be demoted to an NT 4.0 BDC in the same domain).

3. Upgrade the new PDC to Windows 2000 and run the Active Directory Installation Wizard so that this new PDC (which has become a Windows 2000 domain controller) can join a new AD forest (you will select the option to create a new Windows 2000 forest if there's no existing Windows 2000 forest).

4. Upgrade all existing Exchange 5.5 servers to Windows 2000, and then run the Active Directory Installation Wizard to demote these servers to member servers so that they do not become domain controllers in the new Windows 2000 forest.

If you decide to migrate Exchange 5.5 servers to Windows 2000 and run them as domain controllers, Microsoft recommends upgrading all PDCs before upgrading any BDCs. It does not matter which BDC is upgraded first.

Incorporating Multiple Windows 2000 Forests Remember that AD (a Windows 2000 component) plays a strategic role in defining the boundaries for your Exchange 2000 organization. Exchange 2000 is usually deployed in one AD forest. However, what happens if you deploy Exchange 2000 in environments with multiple Windows 2000 forests? You cannot deploy a single Exchange 2000 organization in such an environment, so you're forced to create separate Exchange 2000 organizations for each forest. Directory information in both forests must be replicated separately, using external and explicit one-way trust relationships configured between root domains in each forest. Another synchronization tool used to synchronize information between separate forests is the Active Directory Connector (ADC). The problems with creating multiple and separate Exchange 2000 organizations in multiple forests include the following:

- Recipients in one forest are not able to log on directly to the other forests. They lose the status of security principal in all forests. (A **security principal** is any user who can log on to a domain and authenticate himself or herself in AD.) Recipients who are not security principals have to be treated as mail-enabled contacts in AD.
- You lose access to public folders in other forests as well as other users' calendar information.
- You lose access to the conferencing and instant messaging features of Exchange 2000 in other forests.

If you are trying to consolidate two or more Exchange 5.5 organizations, you can use the Exchange 5.5 Move Server Wizard. Microsoft recommends merging or combining organizations before upgrading to Exchange 2000, because currently there's no method for merging two or more Exchange 2000 organizations. Also, there is no way to migrate or move Exchange private or public data stores between multiple Exchange 2000 organizations, even though you can migrate user accounts, and even Windows servers, between multiple forests or organizations.

You can use the Move Server Wizard to move Exchange 5.5 servers into a Windows 2000 forest running an Exchange 2000 organization, but the server being moved must be in a site containing only Exchange 5.5 servers; also, one Exchange 5.5 server must already be running in the destination Windows 2000 forest.

UPGRADING EXCHANGE SERVER 5.5 TO EXCHANGE 2000 SERVER

Migration of Exchange 5.5 to Exchange 2000 was covered in Chapter 3, "Planning an Exchange 2000 Server Design Scenario." Recall from that chapter that you can use one of three Microsoft-recommended procedures when upgrading an Exchange 5.5 server to Exchange 2000 (depending on existing server configurations and expected results). These three methods are outlined in the following list:

- *In-place upgrade*—Upgrade your Exchange 5.5 server and all its databases on one single computer (see the section "An In-Place Upgrade Scenario: A Closer Look" later in this chapter for a more detailed explanation of this method). The only disadvantage to this method is that you must physically take your server offline while performing the upgrade, thereby interrupting service for your users for an indefinite amount of time. Also, if you are running versions of Exchange Server prior to version 5.5, you must upgrade to Exchange 5.5 before upgrading to Exchange 2000 Server.
- *Move mailbox upgrade*—Install a new Exchange 2000 server into an existing Exchange 5.5 site and move mailboxes by using the Active Directory Users and Computers snap-in (see the "Hands-on Projects" section for a step-by-step look at this method). Single-instance message storage is preserved after you move the mailboxes to the new server. (This feature, found in both Exchange 5.5 and Exchange 2000, helps save disk space by storing only one copy of a message on the hard drive and providing pointers to this copy for users who need to access the message.) One disadvantage of this method is that you cannot move any Key Management Services servers configured in your Exchange 5.5 site, and older connectors cannot be moved. If you have KMS or older connectors on your Exchange 5.5 server, then opt for an in-place upgrade.
- *Leapfrog upgrade*—Also called the "swing" method, it's equivalent to moving mailboxes to a new Exchange 2000 server with some modifications. You add a new Exchange 2000 server to an Exchange 5.5 site, and then move all mailboxes from one Exchange 5.5 computer. That Exchange 5.5 computer is formatted clean and Exchange 2000 Server is installed in its place. Then another Exchange 5.5 server is selected to move mailboxes to and placed on this newly formatted Exchange 2000 server. You continue this process until all Exchange 5.5 mailboxes have been moved to Exchange 2000 servers.

Your choice of an upgrade method depends on your plan for using existing hardware. For example, if you plan to use new hardware, it is easiest to use the move mailbox method to move mailboxes between servers, rather than perform an in-place upgrade on existing Exchange 5.5 servers. Use the in-place upgrade method if your existing hardware is already adequately configured and you aren't able to buy newer, more expensive server hardware. The leapfrog method, similar to the move mailbox method, is appropriate if you have the necessary hardware to temporarily host all mailboxes and public folders, without keeping them there permanently. Use the guidelines in Table 6-2 to determine which method is best for your situation.

Table 6-2 Advantages and Disadvantages of Each Upgrade Method

Upgrade Method	Advantages	Disadvantages
In-place Upgrade	No need to purchase hardware, so it's is the most economical option.	Interruption of service while server is being upgraded and hard to recover information in case of disaster; could also cause loss of information stored in mailboxes if upgrade fails.
Move Mailbox Upgrade	Easy to recover information, if necessary; the only method you can use if you want to replace your existing servers with new hardware. Minimizes interruptions to users.	New hardware expense, and it could take a long time to move thousands of mailboxes in a large organization.
Leapfrog Upgrade	Minimizes interruptions to users and might be your only choice for certain server configurations. Also, it ensures that each server is working properly before moving forward.	Needs extra hardware to implement properly. It can also be a lengthy procedure, with complex steps that need to be planned in advance.

The goal of any migration or upgrade is to minimize the impact these processes have on your end users. Migrations and upgrades should be relatively low risk and provide fall-back strategies to recover your original infrastructure, if necessary. You have to decide which migration or upgrade strategy is best for you. Given a multiple-domain Windows NT 4.0 environment, for example, you could upgrade these domains to Windows 2000 and then restructure them later if necessary, you could migrate to Windows 2000 and then integrate an Exchange 2000 server with your existing Exchange 5.5 sites, or you could simply purchase new Windows 2000 servers to migrate all Exchange 5.5 mailboxes over to Exchange 2000. Of course, all these approaches share similar features, but every approach also has its own set of pitfalls that should be avoided.

When deciding to upgrade any Exchange 5.5 site to Exchange 2000, first make sure that Exchange 5.5 Service Pack 3 is deployed in your site before you upgrade (you could also run SP4 for Exchange 5.5, but SP3 is the stated minimum according to Microsoft). Running SP3 or later ensures that your Exchange servers can be upgraded to Windows 2000. It also ensures that the Windows 2000 AD service can connect to your Exchange 5.5 SP3 server to synchronize directory information.

If you run a single-server Exchange 5.5 site, that server must run SP3 to be upgraded, although Microsoft recommends running the latest service pack for Exchange, which at the time of this writing is Service Pack 4. SP4 contains additional files that allow a smoother and faster transition to Exchange 2000. If you manage a multisite Exchange 5.5 organization, there must be *at least one* Exchange 5.5 server in each site running SP3. The AD service performs two-way directory synchronization with this server.

Next, pay attention to your existing domain structure and server roles. Servers configured for one role in Exchange 5.5 might function differently in Exchange 2000. For instance, any Exchange 5.5 servers installed on a BDC can be placed into a new Windows 2000 domain as a member server. Next, consider what happens if users still need access to legacy mailboxes in the Exchange 5.5 site after an upgrade. When upgrading a Windows NT 4.0 domain to a Windows 2000 domain, users should still be able to access their Exchange 5.5 mailboxes because they should be using the same security identifier (SID) used in the Windows NT 4.0 domain. Problems can occur with user accounts, however, because the upgrade creates a new and duplicate Windows 2000 account for all mailboxes that were migrated earlier. The ADC must be used to merge these duplicate accounts and associate the Exchange 5.5 mailboxes with their Windows 2000 AD counterparts. This procedure is covered in the section "Using the Active Directory Connector in a Mixed-Mode Environment" later in this chapter. First, you need to examine the steps to prepare your environment for Windows 2000.

Preparing the Windows 2000 Forest and Domain Structure

Before you upgrade your first Exchange 5.5 server, you have to plan for and prepare a Windows 2000 forest structure so that Exchange 2000 has the proper OS to support it. For instance, if you plan to perform an in-place upgrade on a server already running Exchange 5.5 server, then you must upgrade the OS to Windows 2000 Server before you can upgrade the messaging system to Exchange 2000 Server. This means you must also prepare your Windows 2000 domains and Windows 2000 schema.

It is assumed that you have already upgraded your operating system to Windows 2000 Server, as the scope of this book does not include discussing an OS upgrade. For information on upgrading the operating system, consult the Microsoft Web site at *www.microsoft.com/windows2000/server/howtobuy/upgrading/*.

Preparing a Windows 2000 forest involves preparing the forest schema, and preparing the forest consists of running the Setup program for Exchange 2000 using the ForestPrep option from a command line. You use this command-line switch only one time regardless of how many domains you want in your AD. You also specify that you are running an upgrade during the ForestPrep setup program. Preparing domains involves running the same setup program with the DomainPrep switch. These two processes can be run independently of the actual upgrade. The ForestPrep option simply prepares the

Windows 2000 schema, and the DomainPrep option helps set appropriate rights and permissions. After preparing for your Windows 2000 forest and domain, you can then consider how to populate the Active Directory database in Windows 2000 (see the section "Populating Active Directory Using the Active Directory Connector" later in this chapter).

An upgrade scenario is presented next to reinforce and illustrate some of the concepts discussed previously, including upgrading the operating system to Windows 2000 and populating AD with user accounts that can be mapped to Exchange 5.5 mailboxes. Upgrading the operating system can be performed in one of two ways: by upgrading an existing Exchange 5.5 resource domain containing an Exchange 5.5 SP3 server to Windows 2000 and connecting that domain to an existing forest, or by upgrading your existing Exchange 5.5 servers and moving them to a new Windows 2000 domain. Once either action has been performed, you are then ready to upgrade or migrate existing Exchange 5.5 mailboxes to Exchange 2000.

An In-Place Upgrade Scenario: A Closer Look

The in-place upgrade is a sequence of planned steps that you should follow to minimize errors. Remember that this method is used when you do not want to purchase new server hardware and is also the most economical of the upgrade methods.

The in-place upgrade method is given more coverage than the other upgrade methods mentioned in Table 6-2 simply because it's the easiest and most economical of the three upgrade methods.

The major steps of this process are preparing your Exchange 5.5 organization, preparing your AD services, and upgrading your Exchange 5.5 server. Here is a more detailed description of these steps:

1. Install Windows 2000 SP1 on all domain controllers or GC servers in your organization because Exchange 2000 Setup checks only for SP1 on those machines on which it has been installed. It cannot physically check all domain controllers to see if they are running the latest service pack or hot fix. Many administrators underestimate the problems that can occur in the absence of these service packs (readily downloadable from *www.microsoft.com/exchange/downloads/2000/SP1.asp*), such as getting nondelivery reports or services not starting.

Currently, Microsoft recommends installing the latest Windows 2000 Service Pack, SP2, for all Exchange 2000 servers, ADCs, and GC servers or domain controllers. This service pack includes the latest updates and patches needed to correct problems that have existed since Exchange 2000 Server was first introduced.

2. Make sure that at least one domain in your forest is running in native mode so that any Exchange 5.5 distribution lists can be mapped to a Windows 2000

universal distribution group (UDG) or Windows 2000 **universal security group (USG)**. The ADC can be used to replicate distribution lists directly into this native-mode Windows 2000 domain. By default, the ADC can create only a UDG; however, the Exchange 2000 Store.exe is capable of converting a UDG to a USG if needed (for example, to set permissions on public folder access). You can change one mixed-mode domain to a native-mode domain in Windows 2000 (an irreversible process), or you can create a new native-mode domain solely for the purpose of containing USGs (known as a transition domain). Verify that you are running SP3 or higher on your Exchange 5.5 servers because in-place upgrades do not work unless you use SP3 or higher. Finally, if Exchange 5.5 is installed on a domain controller (a PDC or BDC in Windows NT 4.0), you have to change the LDAP port used by that Exchange 5.5 server because AD causes contention by "grabbing" the same port number—port 389—for LDAP communications. Therefore, Exchange 5.5 cannot use port 389 to communicate with the ADC. Microsoft recommends changing the Exchange 5.5 LDAP port number to 390, using the Exchange 5.5 Administrator program, but only if port 390 is not being used by other applications or services on your network.

3. Check for valid organizational and site display names, and set permissions so that your server can be upgraded without errors. You need to check these display names because you cannot use invalid characters when migrating or upgrading to Exchange 2000. Every object in Exchange 5.5 actually contains two different names: an internal or directory name, which forms an object's distinguished name, and an external or display name, which forms the user-friendly name seen in the Exchange 5.5 Administrator interface. (See Chapter 8, "Configuring Internet Clients in Exchange 2000 Server," for information on distinguished names.) Internal names cannot be changed after they are created; external names can be changed at any time. Certain characters used for external names in Exchange 5.5 are no longer supported in Exchange 2000, so you might have to rename Exchange 5.5 objects to remove any characters not supported in Exchange 2000 (such as the parenthesis).

Exchange 2000 allows the following characters: uppercase A–Z, lowercase a–z, 0–9, the hyphen, and the space.

Not changing incorrect display (external) names could cause problems with the Exchange 2000 Server Setup program when using ForestPrep. Don't worry about the directory (internal) names because AD simply stores them for future reference, even if they contain invalid characters.

4. Run the utilities MTACheck or Knowledge Consistency Checker (KCC) to verify that you're progressing as planned or to troubleshoot upgrade errors. These tools can help resolve server problems caused by corruption or failure.

MTACheck is used to check the MTA component database files on the Exchange 5.5 server for corruption. This tool can also be used to remove directory replication messages, link monitor messages, or corrupted messages from your message queue. MTACheck should not be treated as a pure maintenance tool; rather, you should treat it as a repair tool used only to repair corrupted MTA database files.

Before running MTACheck on your Exchange 5.5 servers, stop the MTA service using the Control Panel and back up all data in your \Exchsrvr\Mtadata directory. Then open the \Exchsrvr\Bin directory on the same server and run MTACheck.exe.

You should also run the KCC on your Exchange 5.5 servers using the Exchange Administrator program. The KCC helps determine directory integrity in Exchange 5.5 sites and is designed to check servers' directory databases for consistency every three hours. It ensures that the directory information about the servers or sites on your network actually exists on your network. The KCC can make changes to a site's directory so that it matches your network's current state. Every Exchange server computer in the site will contact another Exchange server in the site to compare information and verify their knowledge of other Exchange server computers in that site.

5. Remove any unused access control list (ACL) entries on Exchange 5.5 objects before you install your very first Exchange 2000 server. This step applies mostly to access control permissions on Exchange 5.5 public folders. How do unused entries appear in the first place? Objects such as a mailbox have permissions to a public folder, but that object (mailbox, user, and so forth) has been deleted. In this case, the access control properties are not deleted, even though the user object that had permissions to the folder was deleted. Because the goal is to upgrade to Exchange 2000 Server, this "deleted user but not deleted ACL entry" issue creates problems when the public folder hierarchy tries to replicate to Exchange 2000. Because the ACL entries are never converted, these public folders might not be accessible to some Exchange 2000 users.

You can use another Exchange 5.5 utility, the DS/IS Consistency Adjuster, to remove any unused ACL entries. For more information, please visit *http://support.microsoft.com/support/kb/articles/Q156/7/05.asp*. Although this site mentions only Exchange 4.0, the information can be applied to Exchange 5.5.

6. Verify that you have adequate disk space and perform an online backup. The upgrade to Exchange 2000 requires approximately 30% of the total size of your message store databases—including the Priv1.edb and Pub1.edb files on the same hard drive partition containing your transaction log files. You should always perform an online backup of your Exchange 5.5 directory and

Information Store before finally attempting the upgrade to Exchange 2000. You want to be able to roll back to your current condition if serious mistakes occur during the upgrade.

When all six steps have been addressed, you have essentially prepared your Exchange 5.5 environment, but you still need to prepare your Windows 2000 AD environment, as explained in the following section.

Preparing Your Windows 2000 Environment

1. *Install the Windows 2000 Support Tools*—You are going to use several useful tools, such as Nltest, on the Windows 2000 CD-ROM, so you might as well install the complete \Support\Tools\Setup.exe program in your C:\Program Files\Support\Tools directory (created by default when you install the Support Tools on your local hard drive). The Nltest.exe utility can be used to troubleshoot some setup failures. For instance, when you first install Exchange 2000, the Setup program checks AD to make sure it's configured correctly. Setup queries AD using the Directory Service Locator to verify that your local server is in a valid AD site. Some people inadvertently change the name of the default first site without placing correct IP address information in these sites. You can run Nltest from the command line with various switches to test whether AD and DNS services are properly configured in your environment.

6

2. *Create an instance of the ADC service and then create ADC connection agreements*—The ADC is used to replicate directory information between the Exchange 5.5 directory and the Windows 2000 AD using LDAP, which works well over both high-speed and low-speed network connections. The ADC can migrate accounts to Windows 2000 from Exchange 5.5 server, but it relies on connection agreements to do this. These agreements are objects that define replication schedules, the direction of replication, and the objects to be replicated. (Refer to the section "Using the Active Directory Connector in a Mixed-Mode Environment" for further details on the ADC.) At a minimum, you need to create one-way or two-way connection agreements, and you must verify that all user connection agreements are fully replicated before upgrading any Exchange 5.5 servers (or you will have problems accessing the Exchange 2000 public folder hierarchy).

3. *Prepare your Windows forest using the Setup/ForestPrep command*—People with Schema Administrator rights and Enterprise Administrator rights already have full permissions to the AD database. However, these schema administrators need to prepare for an Exchange 2000 upgrade, so they must run the Exchange 2000 Setup program using the ForestPrep option. This is the syntax to run it from a command line:

   ```
   <CD-ROM drive>:\setup\i386\setup /forestprep
   ```

   The ForestPrep utility creates an Exchange Organization object in AD and extends the AD schema with Exchange 2000 schema extensions. It also sets permissions for the first Exchange Administrator who will maintain your

Exchange organization. Running the ForestPrep option gives you a choice of creating a new Exchange 2000 Organization or joining an existing Exchange 5.5 Organization. If you're joining an existing Exchange 5.5 Organization, you must know the Service account configured in Exchange 5.5. After selecting the first Exchange Administrator account, you can log on with this account to upgrade your Exchange 5.5 server. The important part of this step is to send all schema changes created by ForestPrep to all domain controllers in your organization. If you have several domain controllers, this process could consume a lot of time.

You can use a number of Windows 2000 Support Tools to check the status of AD replication, such as the Active Directory Replication Monitor (ReplMon), which checks the overall status of replication in your organization, and LDP.exe, which checks specific domain controllers to see if any Exchange 2000 schema extensions have been replicated to it.

4. *Prepare each domain with the DomainPrep command*—Using the DomainPrep switch with the Setup program prepares your AD domain for Exchange 2000 users. The syntax is similar to the ForestPrep command:

   ```
   <CD-ROM drive>:\setup\i386\setup /domainprep
   ```

   This utility changes your domain controller security policies so that all Exchange servers can manage the auditing logs on these servers. Only users with Domain Administrator rights can use this tool, and it must be run in every domain that will host an Exchange 2000 server. DomainPrep creates special group objects that provide the basis for permission assignments in Exchange 2000. The first group created is the Exchange Domain Servers global security group (in the Users container in Exchange System Manager). This group is placed inside another specially created group, Exchange Enterprise Servers (a local security group in the Users container). Membership in these groups is necessary because many Exchange 2000 services need to run under the security context of a local server, and these groups help define permissions for user objects in your domains. The Exchange Enterprise Servers group is given permissions to the domain naming and configuration naming contexts in your Windows 2000 forest. As in Step 3, you must wait for all domain changes to replicate to all domain controllers, and you can use Windows Support Tools such as ReplMon or LDP.exe to verify replication in an entire domain or to a specific domain controller. You must verify that the domain controller security policy has been fully replicated within your domain. If it has not, the Exchange databases on your servers cannot connect.

5. *Final preinstallation tasks*—These tasks include verifying that SMTP and NNTP are installed on the Exchange 5.5 server because Exchange 2000 extends both these protocols when you upgrade Exchange 5.5. Also, you must disable all antivirus software running on the Exchange 5.5 server before the upgrade starts. Because the antivirus software incorrectly thinks the system is

under attack, it could cause certain services to stop or prevent Setup from finishing. Finally, it's best to disable and remove all server monitors or link monitors running on Exchange 5.5, because Exchange 2000 normally stops all Exchange 5.5 services during the upgrade and might trigger an unwanted alert by the Exchange 5.5 monitors, which then try to restart services that have been disabled.

The preceding steps have been enumerated to show you that an upgrade (no matter which form it takes) needs complete attention to detail to be successful. Problems can still occur, but are relatively easy to troubleshoot if you have taken the necessary precautions. Remember that an in-place upgrade does not happen all at once; the required time varies depending on the components selected and the hardware used. It takes time to modify the database schema and copy new files to the server. After the upgrade is completed, all user and mailbox information is migrated into AD and Exchange 2000, and you are able to log on to a mailbox and send mail to other users.

MANAGING COEXISTENCE IN A MIXED-MODE ENVIRONMENT

A mixed-mode Exchange environment contains both Exchange 2000 servers and Exchange 5.5 servers. It does not matter if an Exchange 2000 server is added to an existing Exchange 5.5 site, or if an Exchange 5.5 member server is added to a Windows 2000 domain containing other Exchange 2000 servers. Either setup results in a mixed-mode operation. A native-mode operation precludes any Exchange 5.5 servers from communicating with any Exchange 2000 servers. You might think this is an ideal upgrade situation; however, Exchange 5.5 servers might be needed for legacy purposes, such as maintaining connectors that do not work with Exchange 2000 Server (for example, the PROFS or SNADS connectors used with mainframes in Exchange 5.5). When you upgrade an existing Exchange 5.5 computer to Exchange 2000 in a site with multiple Exchange 5.5 servers, you must remain in a coexistence phase until the last Exchange 5.5 server has been upgraded. In this case, any user on an Exchange 5.5 server has to be represented as a mailbox-enabled object in AD before you can actually start deploying Exchange 2000. The only way you can synchronize information, such as recipient objects, between an Exchange 5.5 directory and AD is with the ADC, which is usually deployed along with the migration of your Windows NT 4.0 domains to Windows 2000 domains. Because it's so important, Microsoft recommends that you install the ADC before running the Exchange 2000 Setup program with the ForestPrep switch. The recommended course of action is as follows:

1. Install and configure the ADC so that schema changes can be made and replicated to all domain controllers in your new forest. Changes to the configuration naming context are also replicated to all domain controllers in your forest.
2. Run ForestPrep to perform even more schema updates, which are replicated to all domain controllers in your forest.

3. Run DomainPrep to make changes to the local domain naming context. These changes are then replicated to all domain controllers in your local domains.
4. Run the Exchange 2000 Setup program to upgrade an existing Exchange 5.5 server or to add a new Exchange 2000 server to an already existing Exchange 5.5 site.

This last step creates an object in AD known as a configuration connection agreement (see the section "A Review of the Active Directory Connector" later in this chapter). This object helps write information about your Exchange 5.5 sites to the configuration naming context in AD. The information can then be replicated to all domain controllers in the Windows 2000 forest. Replication traffic increases when Exchange 5.5 coexists with Exchange 2000 because both configuration information and user object information are being replicated between AD and Exchange 5.5.

There is a difference between configuration information and "user object" information. Configuration information is replicated using a configuration connection agreement, and user object information is replicated using a user connection agreement. You can create user connection agreements with the ADC, but only Exchange 2000 automatically creates a configuration connection agreement. (See the next section "Using the Active Directory Connector in a Mixed-Mode Environment.")

You must plan for a higher volume of directory changes that are replicated in either direction after you introduce Exchange 2000 into your Exchange 5.5 sites. Remember that you are not just planning for Exchange 2000 Server, but also for Windows 2000 Server.

Using the Active Directory Connector in a Mixed-Mode Environment

Probably no other component is as important to an upgrade or a migration of Exchange 5.5 as the ADC and its related component, the SRS. The ADC comes into play only when you are considering a coexistence strategy between Exchange 5.5 and Exchange 2000. If you plan to remove and decommission all Exchange 5.5 servers in your enterprise, you have no need for the ADC or its components. Many companies today favor coexistence because a pure migration consumes more resources in the form of hardware and personnel hours.

A Review of the Active Directory Connector

The ADC is absolutely essential for coexistence between Exchange 5.5 and Exchange 2000 or for upgrading Exchange 5.5 to Exchange 2000 (see Chapter 4, "Preparing to Deploy Exchange 2000 Server," for a first look at this subject). Recall that the ADC replicates and synchronizes information between two very different directory structures, the Exchange 5.5 directory and the Windows 2000 AD. You cannot upgrade Exchange 5.5 to Exchange 2000 directly because Exchange 2000 has no way of accessing configuration or recipient data in the Exchange 5.5 directory database. Therefore, you use the ADC to perform one of two types of replication between Exchange 5.5 and Exchange 2000: one-way or two-way, depending on whether you are upgrading to or coexisting with Exchange 2000 Server. In either case, LDAP is used to replicate the actual information between the two directories.

You can install the ADC on a domain controller or a member server, but Microsoft recommends using a member server because of the potential drain on system resources that occurs on domain controllers. Microsoft actually offers two different versions of the ADC: one for Windows 2000 and one for Exchange 2000 Server. You should use the Exchange 2000 ADC on the Exchange 2000 installation CD-ROM because it has more features and enhances the Windows 2000 version of the ADC.

The ADC uses connection agreements to replicate directory and configuration information between Exchange 5.5 and AD. There are two types of connection agreements (CAs); however, only one of them can actually be created by an administrator to replicate directory or recipient information. A **user connection agreement** replicates recipient objects and the data they contain between Exchange 5.5 and AD. To see the name used to identify the CA and check the direction of its replication, you can view the user CA in the Active Directory Connector Management snap-in (see Figure 6-1).

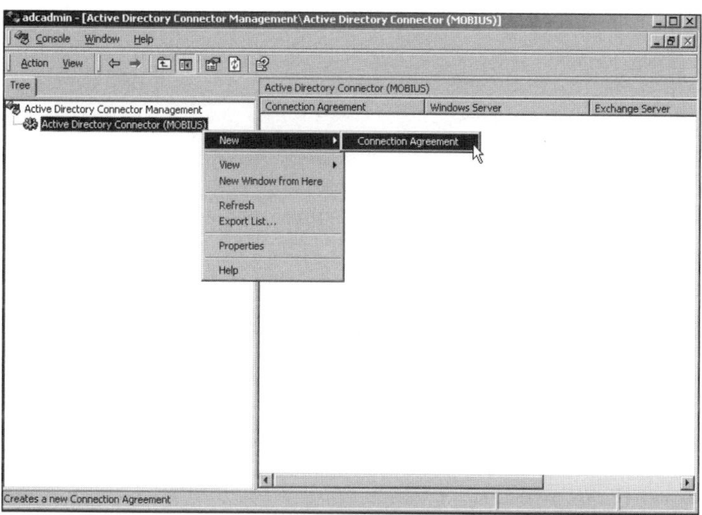

Figure 6-1 Creating a new connection agreement

A **configuration connection agreement** replicates Exchange-specific configuration information between the two directories and helps Exchange 2000 coexist with earlier versions of Exchange Server and Windows 2000. Each type of CA has unique features, but regardless of which CA is being used, you should track information such as replication schedules or the types of objects being replicated. You can install only one instance of the ADC on any computer running Windows 2000 Server (including your Exchange 2000 server), but you can define multiple connection agreements per ADC, if you choose. Each specific CA can be designed to perform specific replication or synchronization tasks, such as replicating only new mail-enabled objects to AD on a daily basis after midnight. You can even create a primary connection agreement, which creates new objects in either directory. All other CAs then merely replicate information to either directory.

Exchange 2000 has a feature called auto-generated connection agreements, used to automatically generate a configuration CA between Exchange 5.5 and AD when you install Exchange 2000 into an existing Exchange 5.5 site. You don't see these auto-generated connection agreements in the ADC console, however, until you manually create at least one two-way connection agreement between Exchange 5.5 and AD.

A successful implementation of the ADC means that all Exchange 5.5 sites are shown in AD as administrative groups, and all Exchange 2000 servers are represented as Exchange 5.5 sites. The configuration CA, which makes this representation possible, replicates Exchange-specific configuration information between AD and the Exchange SRS. Every time you install an Exchange 2000 server into an existing Exchange 5.5 site, the SRS is used to replicate intrasite directory information using RPC. If you are using an Exchange 5.5 bridgehead server for replication and you upgrade it to Exchange 2000 Server, the SRS provides directory replication services via e-mail to other Exchange 5.5 sites still coexisting with Exchange 2000.

All servers configured with an ADC communicate with an Exchange 5.5 bridgehead server using TCP port 389, or port 379 if using the SRS. However, if you deploy Exchange 5.5 on a Windows 2000 domain controller, you have to configure your CA for a different port number because AD always initiates service calls before Exchange and locks port 389 for its own use. Recall that Microsoft recommends choosing another port number for LDAP in the Exchange 5.5 Administrator program (for example, port 390) so that the Exchange 5.5 directory can initiate its own LDAP communications without causing any conflicts with AD. Connection agreements do not need an LDAP port number configuration for AD because communication with AD always takes place on TCP port 3268, a port reserved for GC servers.

Even though the ADC uses LDAP for most communications, it can use RPC communication in some cases. For example, you might create a user object in Active Directory Users and Computers, but the user's mailbox is on an Exchange 5.5 server. When directory replication occurs, the ADC creates a new instance of the mailbox object in AD and communicates with other Exchange components to generate a new proxy e-mail address for this newly created mailbox object. However, the service that generates these e-mail addresses relies on RPC communication, not LDAP.

Populating Active Directory Using the Active Directory Connector

You learned previously how you can synchronize the actions of the ADC with a Windows NT 4.0 domain upgrade; now you'll see how to populate AD with user accounts. When you populate AD with user objects from earlier versions of Exchange, those user objects do not include any Exchange-specific attributes. However, after installing Exchange 2000 into this mixed-mode environment, the user objects do include Exchange-specific attributes. The ADC is used to populate AD with mailbox, distribution list, or public folder information from an Exchange 5.5 directory. On the other hand, the ADC populates Exchange 5.5 directories with user and group information directly from AD. Therefore, we can state the following rule: *Before you can synchronize two directories, you must populate user information from your existing directory (most likely the Exchange 5.5 directory) into Active Directory*. AD is fully populated when user information from the Windows NT 4.0 account database, called the Security Accounts Manager (SAM) database, is combined with Exchange-specific directory information in AD.

The Strategies for Populating Active Directory

You have to concentrate on two major stages here: getting user information from the Windows NT 4.0 SAM database and getting user information from the Exchange 5.5 directory service database. Strategies for populating AD usually involve one or more of the following activities:

- Performing an in-place domain upgrade and then installing the ADC, which creates disabled user accounts in Windows 2000.
- Installing the ADC first, and then upgrading your existing domains and using the Active Directory Cleanup Wizard to merge any duplicate accounts that might exist in Windows 2000.
- Installing the ADC first, and then cloning your user accounts to Windows 2000 by using the Active Directory Migration Tool (ADMT).
- Using the ADMT with the SIDHistory user attribute, and then configuring an ADC. The SIDHistory attribute maintains information about a user's unique security identifier (SID) in a domain and preserves the SID after migrating this object to another domain.
- Using the ADMT without the SIDHistory user attribute, re-creating any ACLs for users if necessary, and then configuring the ADC.

Depending on the objectives you want to achieve, you have a choice of five strategies for populating AD, listed in Table 6-3. For example, if you want to preserve existing user information, including objects' SIDs, you can upgrade your existing Windows NT 4.0 user accounts by upgrading your Windows NT PDC to a Windows 2000 domain controller. This upgrade preserves existing user information, including SIDs. If this process is not possible, you can use the ADMT to clone user account information in AD, meaning you create a native-mode Windows 2000 domain account that mirrors properties from a Windows NT 4.0 account. In this case, the new user account in AD has an entirely different SID than the account it was copied from; however, the original account's SID is copied to an attribute of the new account (the SIDHistory attribute). This process allows the new user account to access any resources available to the original user account as long as trust relationships exist between the Windows NT 4.0 domains and the new Windows 2000 domains.

After receiving user information from a Windows NT 4.0 database, you can get user information from the Exchange 5.5 database using the ADC with CAs. The ADC synchronizes any AD objects sharing the same SID with objects in the Exchange 5.5 directory database. So if the ADC finds a user in the Exchange 5.5 directory who does not have a matching SID in AD, the ADC creates a disabled user account in AD and stores the original Exchange 5.5 SID in the SIDHistory attribute of the new user account. Table 6-3 shows five strategies for fully populating AD, which you can do before or after you implement the ADC.

Table 6-3 Strategies for Populating Active Directory

Strategy	Steps	Additional Steps Needed
One	Upgrade your Windows NT 4.0 domain, and implement the ADC.	No additional steps needed.
Two	Use the ADMT to create new Windows 2000 accounts, and then implement the ADC to synchronize the Exchange 5.5 directory with the new Windows 2000 accounts.	No additional steps needed.
Three	Implement the ADC to synchronize the Exchange 5.5 mailboxes with Windows 2000 accounts, and then upgrade your NT 4.0 domain to a Windows 2000 domain.	Use the Active Directory Account Cleanup Wizard to merge any duplicate accounts.
Four	Implement the ADC to synchronize the Exchange 5.5 mailboxes with Windows 2000 accounts, and then use the ADMT to create new Windows 2000 accounts.	Use the Active Directory Account Cleanup Wizard to merge any duplicate accounts.
Five	Implement the ADC to synchronize the Exchange 5.5 mailboxes with Windows 2000 accounts, and then enable all accounts that have been created, using the ADC.	Run the ADMT to match NT 4.0 accounts with accounts created by the ADC.

Notice that the first two strategies in Table 6-3 begin by populating AD with Windows NT user account information, and then running the ADC with CAs to add information stored in the Exchange 5.5 directory service to user objects stored in AD. The second strategy allows your organization to implement Exchange 2000 before upgrading your Windows NT domain structure. You can install Exchange 2000 after deploying the ADC. The rest of the strategies start by implementing the ADC and creating disabled Windows 2000 users. They illustrate how you can deploy Exchange 2000 after implementing the ADC. Exchange 2000 requires AD, but neither Windows 2000 nor AD need to be fully deployed before you install Exchange 2000. Exchange requires only a small base directory, so you do not have to upgrade your entire Windows NT 4.0 infrastructure before upgrading to Exchange 2000.

The Active Directory Account Cleanup Wizard (ADClean.exe) can search your Windows 2000 forest for duplicate Windows NT accounts. You can review or modify the duplicate accounts and merge them into one destination user account. If you merge duplicate accounts, all group membership or distribution list membership is preserved, and access to any existing network resources is not affected. Duplicate accounts occur because a Windows 2000 forest could contain several Windows NT 4.0 accounts for the same person or group, especially if you're using a variety of tools or strategies to populate AD with account information. In the five strategies in Table 6-3, new accounts can be created when you perform in-place domain upgrades to Windows 2000 or when you use the ADMT. Every separate account that's created contains different information, depending on the application used to create it.

To avoid creating duplicate accounts in your organization, you should upgrade all your Windows NT 4.0 PDCs to Windows 2000 domain controllers before you configure any user CAs with the ADC.

The Site Replication Service and Coexistence

Remember the relationship between the ADC and the SRS when managing coexistence or migration strategies with Exchange 2000 and Exchange 5.5. An instance of the SRS must be configured for one of three different server setups: on the first Exchange 2000 server installed in an Exchange 5.5 site, on the first server in a site you want to upgrade, or on a directory replication bridgehead server in an Exchange 5.5 site. The SRS participates in directory replication the same as any other Exchange 5.5 server and enables all Exchange 2000 servers to resemble Exchange 5.5 servers. Keep the following points in mind when working with the SRS:

- The SRS runs only in a mixed-mode administrative group. It is a required service because the ADC is not capable of emulating an Exchange 5.5 server.
- The SRS can perform other functions, such as detecting directory replication topology changes or making sure you have properly configured the ADC.
- The SRS uses the same configuration CAs created when you first install Exchange 2000 Server. Configuration CAs replicate Exchange-specific configuration information between AD and the SRS.

- The SRS, which contains the same Dir.edb file used on every Exchange 5.5 server for the directory database, is actually displayed in the Exchange 5.5 Administrator program as the Exchange 5.5 directory service.
- The SRS informs all Exchange 5.5 servers about your entire Exchange 2000 configuration. It is the link to the Exchange 5.5 directory structure, whereas the ADC is the link to AD.

TROUBLESHOOTING EXCHANGE UPGRADING AND MIGRATING ISSUES

No installation or upgrade is error-free, so administrators of Exchange systems should expect to face unknown error codes or problems of some type. If you expect problems, you're better equipped to handle them when they do appear. The good news for many administrators is that for every Exchange 2000 problem, there's ultimately a solution. When working with Exchange 5.5 and Exchange 2000, errors can happen during the installation, setup, or upgrade. For example, the ForestPrep option used during setup might not work because the user account that applied this switch did not have appropriate permissions (the account must belong to the Schema Admins, Enterprise Admins, and the Local Administrator account on the server running ForestPrep). Errors are common, too, when upgrading from Exchange 5.5 to Exchange 2000 Server. Simple activities, such as configuring the ADC, can set into motion hidden issues or problems that have a snowball effect down the road. You might not notice problems or errors until you install or configure related components in Exchange 2000 Server. The goal in troubleshooting problems is to develop a proactive mentality so that you can effectively find solutions to problems that prevent users from enjoying an optimal messaging environment.

Troubleshooting Setup Issues

Many problems revolve around incomplete setup routines or the use of the ForestPrep and DomainPrep installation switches. When you get an error message, you should first check the permissions assigned to the user or group trying to implement these tools. As stated previously, the account running ForestPrep must belong to the Schema Admins, Enterprise Admins, and Local Administrator accounts. The account running DomainPrep, however, can belong only to Domain Admins or the Local Administrator account. If permissions or rights are not the problem, but you are still having trouble installing or upgrading Exchange 2000 Server in your mixed-mode environment, it is always best to simply reinstall Exchange 2000. You should verify, however, that basic network problems are not standing in the way of finishing the installation—for example, a badly configured network adapter that prevents you from accessing the network share containing Exchange 2000 Setup. If you decide to reinstall Exchange 2000, you must first turn off or disable all Exchange 2000 services by using the Services applet in Control Panel.

Other problems can happen when you try to join a computer running Exchange 2000 Server to an existing Exchange 5.5 server site. You might see the following message:

```
Setup was unable to bind to the Exchange Server
```

This error message occurs because the account you're using to start Exchange 2000 Setup does not have correct permissions for the destination Exchange 5.5 server directory. You need to give this account Administrator permission at the Site and Configuration levels of your Exchange 5.5 server to solve this problem. Some installation errors are caused by only one file that Exchange 2000 is trying to copy to the hard drive. For instance, you could install Exchange 2000 and see the following error message:

```
Setup failed while configuring registry entries for
Exchange System Management Snap-ins (error 0xC103798A: An
internal component has failed.)
```


This error can be attributed to a single file on your system, Exchmem.dll. Exchange 5.5 has one version of this file, and Exchange 2000 is trying to copy a newer version of it during setup. To resolve this error, simply rename the existing Exchmem.dll, (for example, Exchmemold.dll) and then run the Exchange 2000 Setup program.

Some setup issues can be traced to protocol conflicts. For example, if you attempt to join an Exchange 2000 computer to an existing Exchange 5.5 site with many servers, you could see the following error message:

```
Idispatch not found for (Microsoft Exchange conferencing
mmc snap-in)
```

To solve this problem, use the Exchange Server Administrator program in Exchange 5.5 and modify settings for LDAP in the Protocols container (under Organization, Site, Configuration on the menu bar).

The Setup program could also fail while you are trying to join an Exchange 5.5 server site on a Windows 2000 domain controller. Suppose that you run Exchange 2000 Setup on a member server in a Windows 2000 Server domain, and setup fails after the Windows 2000 domain controller has been upgraded from Windows NT 4.0 while still running Exchange Server 5.5! In cases like that, setup fails when you try to join an existing Exchange 5.5 server site because both Exchange Server 5.5 and the domain controller are trying to access TCP port 389 for LDAP communications. You should change the LDAP port number for Exchange Server 5.5 even before you upgrade your Windows NT 4.0 domain to Windows 2000.

You must make sure to restart your Exchange Server Directory Service in Exchange Server 5.5 when changing port numbers; otherwise, your system could become unstable.

Sometimes you upgrade an Exchange 5.5 server to Exchange 2000 only to find that Exchange 2000 tries restarting services that do not exist, or in worst-case scenarios, Exchange 2000 attempts to restart the server. If this happens, it could mean your

Exchange 5.5 servers have been configured to monitor the server you're trying to upgrade to Exchange 2000 Server, and they are looking for services that no longer exist in Exchange 2000. Your best bet is to remove any configuration in your Exchange 5.5 site that causes server monitors to monitor the servers being upgraded to Exchange 2000. You can always place your Exchange 5.5 servers in maintenance mode until you have upgraded your intended server to Exchange 2000. If you upgrade an Exchange 5.5 server that has server monitors already configured and do not remove them after upgrading to Exchange 2000, then no notifications are configured and the server cannot monitor other servers. As a general rule, Exchange 5.5 servers should be configured to monitor only other Exchange 5.5 servers, and Exchange 2000 servers should be configured to monitor only other Exchange 2000 servers.

Troubleshooting Active Directory Connector Issues

The previous problems have all dealt with setup and installation. Assuming that the setup process is completed and error-free, you could still face problems with AD and the ADC. If you are unable to modify AD, for example, the object being modified probably has read-only permissions assigned to it. Some objects in AD actually reference objects in another Windows 2000 site, so you might need permission to this other site to modify them. Another ADC issue relates to the management tools in Exchange 2000 and Windows 2000. You might find that the Exchange 2000 options or extensions are not available in the Active Directory Users and Computers snap-in in Windows 2000 Server, for example. Suppose you are trying to add a new Exchange 2000 mailbox using the Active Directory Users and Computers tool but are unable to do so after numerous attempts. A possible reason is that you're trying to make administrative changes to your organization but the Exchange Management tools are not properly installed. You might have installed Exchange 2000 on a member server but used Active Directory Users and Computers on a domain controller, so you can't see any Exchange 2000 extensions. There are two solutions you can pursue: You can use Active Directory Users and Computers directly from the Exchange 2000 member server, or you can install the Exchange System Manager snap-in on the domain controller. In any case, your goal is to consolidate the operation of both tools on one machine.

You will find that ADC replication is an annoying but easily treatable problem. If you realize that the ADC is not updating your AD schema, make sure you are logged on as a user in the Administrator group with Enterprise Administrator rights. After running Setup with the ForestPrep option, you might discover that the schema extensions are not being replicated to all domain controllers in your forest. You can use tools such as LDP.exe to manually check a specific domain controller to see whether any Exchange 2000 schema extensions have been replicated to it. LDP.exe is a Windows 2000 Support Tool in the \Support\Tools directory on the installation CD-ROM; for instructions on finding this tool, see Chapter 4, "Preparing to Deploy Exchange 2000 Server." If you receive an "object not found" error, the schema extensions have not been replicated to this domain controller. For more information on the LDP.exe utility, please visit *http://support.microsoft.com/support/kb/articles/Q252/3/35.asp.*

Network and DNS Issues Affecting Active Directory

If schema extensions have not been replicated after some time, you can manually initiate AD replication by using the Active Directory Sites and Services MMC snap-in or the ReplMon tool in the Windows 2000 Support Tools. Both methods support remote administration, so you can use these tools from any Windows 2000 computer. When installing or configuring AD, you might encounter problems with your current DNS configuration or network configuration that could cause a loss of AD functionality. This loss further complicates problems when you try to replicate objects from an Exchange 5.5 directory into AD using CAs. You might want to check your current DNS configuration to see if all necessary host records ("A" records) and server records (SRV records) are in place. You must pay attention to specific network components to ensure that AD is working as it should on your network. For instance, File and Printer Sharing must be enabled on your Windows 2000 domain controllers; otherwise, you get error messages when attempting to join this domain. All non-Windows 2000 clients (Windows 95, Windows 98, Windows NT) that want to participate in your Windows 2000 domain must be able to use NetBIOS name resolution. When upgrading Windows NT 4.0 servers, you have to make sure DNS is installed on AD domain controllers so that DNS records are registered for that domain.

A final issue involves client access problems at the end of your upgrade. Remember that the upgrade could take a while to finish because it takes time to modify the database schema as files are being copied to the server. Microsoft has estimated that the average time for this part of the Setup program is around 9 GB per hour. All database entries are upgraded in the background so that the overall upgrade can be completed as quickly as possible. However, if users try to access their mailboxes soon after this part of the upgrade, the Store.exe process tries to upgrade their individual mailboxes on demand. As more and more users demand an upgraded database store, Exchange 2000 is forced to slow down. Therefore, it's advisable to upgrade your Exchange 5.5 server when most of your users are not present or do not need to access their mailboxes immediately after the upgrade is done. There are many more AD issues you could wrestle with, so make sure you plan your AD deployment thoroughly and get enough information on common problems and their recommended solutions before you perform an upgrade. The Microsoft Knowledge Base is invaluable in this area.

Chapter Summary

- Decide if your organization will run in mixed mode or native mode. Only native-mode Windows 2000 domains offer the full Windows 2000 feature sets, including protocol enhancements and complete AD functionality.
- Exchange 2000 Server operates in mixed mode by default, meaning it can interoperate fully with Exchange Server 5.5. Native mode precludes all interoperability with Exchange 5.5 or earlier versions.
- You can deploy Exchange Server 5.5 on a Windows 2000 domain controller or member server, but you cannot deploy Exchange 2000 Server on a Windows NT 4.0 domain controller or member server.

- Three naming contexts are found in Active Directory: a schema naming context, a domain naming context, and a configuration naming context.
- All Exchange 2000 servers should have access to a GC server in your forest to support AD queries by users. Only the first domain controller you install in a Windows 2000 forest is classified immediately as a GC server, but you can always add more GC servers for fault tolerance. All GC servers contain copies of the domain naming context for the domain in which they're located and copies of the configuration and schema naming contexts shared by all domain controllers in the forest.
- You can deploy Exchange 2000 in organizations using multiple Windows 2000 forests; however, you have to create separate Exchange 2000 organizations for each forest, and directory information in both forests must be replicated separately using external one-way trust relationships between root domains in each forest.
- There are three distinct upgrade methods you can use to upgrade your Exchange 5.5 servers: an in-place upgrade, a move mailbox upgrade, or a leapfrog upgrade.
- Upgrading Exchange 5.5 means preparing your Windows 2000 forest and domain structure using the Setup tools ForestPrep and DomainPrep. The first tool prepares the Windows 2000 schema, and the second tool sets appropriate rights and permissions. AD has to be populated with user accounts by configuring the ADC with a connection agreement.
- Performing an in-place upgrade means installing the Windows 2000 Service Pack 1 on all domain controllers, making sure at least one domain is running in native mode, checking for valid organizational and site display names, removing any unused ACL entries on existing Exchange 5.5 objects, and performing an online backup.
- There are two versions of the ADC: a Windows 2000 version and an Exchange 2000 version. You should always deploy the Exchange 2000 ADC for full functionality. The ADC creates a configuration CA by default that can't be removed, but you can create additional user CAs to replicate recipient information between the Exchange 5.5 directory and AD.
- The ADC uses LDAP to communicate directly with AD and the SRS, which communicates with the Exchange 5.5 directory service using RPC or e-mail messages.
- The ADC is capable of creating disabled Windows 2000 users if you populate AD before deploying Exchange 2000 Server. You can use the Active Directory Account Cleanup Wizard to search your Windows 2000 forest for duplicate Windows NT accounts and merge them. To avoid creating these duplicate accounts, upgrade all Windows NT PDCs to domain controllers before configuring CAs with the ADC.
- It's easy to troubleshoot problems with upgrading or migration if you know what area is affected. For example, most installation or setup errors during an upgrade can be attributed to an incorrect permissions assignment to the account performing the upgrade. The Microsoft Windows Support Tools can greatly assist you in finding the solutions to these problems.

KEY TERMS

configuration connection agreement — A read-only connection agreement that transfers two-way configuration information. This CA cannot be changed but you can view configuration information using the Active Directory Connector Management tool that's installed when you first configure the ADC. This CA replicates configuration information specific to Exchange 2000 between the Exchange 5.5 directory and AD.

member server — A Windows 2000 computer that has joined a Windows 2000 domain, but does not handle any authentication or logon validation for users wanting to access the domain. A member server can be changed to a domain controller at any time by using the Active Directory Installation Wizard or Dcpromo.exe.

security principal — A user object in Windows 2000 and AD that is capable of logging on to a domain. Some mail-enabled objects, such as contacts, are not considered security principals in AD, but most mailbox-enabled users and groups are.

universal distribution group (UDG) — A type of group in Windows 2000 used for nonsecurity purposes, such as sending e-mail messages to a group of users simultaneously.

universal security group (USG) — A type of group created in Windows 2000 Server that's used to assign network permissions to group members. This group can be mail-enabled via an SMTP proxy address, which allows the group to function as a distribution list. Security groups are also used to assign permissions to public folders in Exchange 2000.

user connection agreements — An object you create in Exchange System Manager that's used with the ADC to replicate recipient objects and their properties between the Exchange 5.5 directory and AD. The Active Directory Connector Management console displays these CAs, showing their names and the direction of replication.

REVIEW QUESTIONS

1. When you install Windows 2000 Server into a Windows NT 4.0 domain, you are said to be operating in a(n) ________________ environment.
2. How can you install Exchange 2000 Server on a Windows NT 4.0 PDC?
   a. You can install Exchange 2000 and select the Mixed Mode option in the Component Selection window.
   b. This configuration is not possible because Windows 2000 Server is needed.
   c. You can only install Exchange 2000 Server using Windows 2000 Advanced Server.
   d. You have to demote the PDC to a member server before installing Exchange 2000 Server.

3. You have enabled your Windows 2000 domain controller to be the Global Catalog server for your domain and have configured Exchange 5.5 on this computer. Service Pack 1 for Windows 2000 has just been installed. Which service pack should you install on this machine so that Exchange 5.5 will be ready for AD when you are ready to upgrade to Exchange 2000?
   a. Service Pack 1 for Windows 2000 only
   b. Service Pack 2 for Windows 2000 and Service Pack 4 for Exchange 5.5
   c. Service Pack 3 or later for Exchange 5.5 and Service Pack 1 for Windows 2000
   d. Service Pack 1 for Exchange 2000
4. Which of the following statements is considered a true statement?
   a. You always have to upgrade your Windows domains before upgrading your Exchange servers to Exchange 2000.
   b. You must always upgrade Exchange servers before upgrading your Windows domains.
   c. You have to upgrade to Exchange 2000 Server before taking advantage of secure dynamic DNS updates.
   d. You should continue using the Exchange 5.5 Administration program after upgrading an Exchange 5.5 computer to Exchange 2000.
5. Reji wants to manage a mixed-mode Exchange server environment and she wants to use a combination of Windows 2000 computers. Which of the following computers can run Exchange Server 5.5? (Choose all that apply.)
   a. a Windows 2000 PDC
   b. a Windows 2000 member server
   c. a Windows 2000 BDC that is promoted to a PDC
   d. a Windows NT 4.0 PDC
6. Which of the following naming contexts contain data that is replicated to every domain controller in the AD forest? (Choose all that apply.)
   a. configuration naming context
   b. schema naming context
   c. replication naming context
   d. domain naming context
7. The ________________ naming context defines the classes and attributes of objects that exist in AD.
8. A universal security group known as Enterprise Admins has Full Control permissions to the configuration naming context of Active Directory. True or False?

9. Mike has just installed two domain controllers in a new Windows 2000 forest consisting of three different sites. The first site contains an Exchange 2000 server that hosts 500 mailbox-enabled users. Which of the following statements about GC servers in this new forest is true?
   a. Both domain controllers automatically become GC servers in the forest.
   b. Mike has to configure one GC server for every unique site in his forest.
   c. By default, the first domain controller Mike installed has become a GC server in the forest.
   d. Mike has to select which domain controller should become the GC server after installing them into his new forest.

10. Which of the following naming contexts is found on a GC server?
    a. only a read-write replica of the domain naming context
    b. a read-write replica of the domain naming context and the schema naming context
    c. only a read-only replica of the configuration naming context
    d. read-write replicas of all naming contexts
11. Mary is logging on to her Windows 2000 native-mode domain, named Westchester. Her domain controller, named Rye, has not been configured as a GC server. Mary complains that her logon requests are continually denied. What could cause this problem?
    a. Her domain controller is unable to contact a GC server anywhere in that Windows 2000 forest.
    b. There has to be a GC server configured in the same domain as her domain controller, Rye.
    c. Her domain controller must be configured as a GC server.
    d. There is no backup domain controller in her Westchester domain.
12. What are two functions of the Active Directory Installation Wizard?
    a. to promote a member server to a domain controller
    b. to demote a domain controller to a member server
    c. to join a Windows 2000 domain controller to a Windows NT 4.0 domain
    d. to demote a Windows 2000 domain controller to a Windows NT 4.0 BDC
13. Conrad wants to run Exchange Server 5.5 on a machine configured as a Windows 2000 member server and install a new Windows 2000 domain controller into his existing Windows NT environment. What is the first step that Conrad must take?
    a. install a new Windows 2000 domain controller that becomes a PDC in his existing NT domain
    b. install a new Windows 2000 domain controller that acts as a member server in his existing NT domain
    c. install a new Windows 2000 domain controller into his existing NT domain that acts as a BDC
    d. install a new Windows NT 4.0 domain controller into his existing NT domain that acts as a PDC

14. Gabriella is managing an Exchange Server 5.5 computer named Bronx that runs on Windows NT 4.0 Server. She wants to upgrade this machine to a Windows 2000 machine in a domain named Manhattan. However, she also wants to be able to move this machine to another domain, named Queens, with the least amount of administrative effort. How should she plan her upgrade?
    a. She should upgrade her NT 4.0 server to a Windows 2000 primary domain controller because they are easy to move within a forest.
    b. She should upgrade her NT 4.0 server to a Windows 2000 domain controller because they are easy to move within a forest.
    c. She should place her NT 4.0 server into an existing Windows 2000 domain and not upgrade it to Windows 2000 Server.
    d. She should upgrade her NT 4.0 server to a Windows 2000 member server and join the Manhattan domain.
15. Fahmida is managing a global bank and wants to deploy two Windows 2000 forests for her Exchange 5.5 organization, one forest for North American operations and one for South American operations. Can she keep her organization name of Money World after she upgrades to Exchange 2000?
    a. Yes, her original organization name will be migrated to Exchange 2000 after an upgrade.
    b. No, she must adopt a new organization name and use this new name for both forests in Windows 2000.
    c. No, it is not possible to deploy a single organization with multiple Windows 2000 forests.
    d. Yes, as long as she merges the two forests sometime after the upgrade.
16. How do you replicate directory information in two different Windows 2000 forests containing multiple Exchange 2000 servers?
17. When deploying multiple Exchange 2000 forests, a recipient in one forest cannot log on to another forest because recipients are not considered to be ________________ in all forests.
18. When configuring multiple Windows 2000 forests for an organization, a user in one forest has access to public folders in all other forests. True or False?
19. Monica is managing two different Exchange 5.5 organizations and wants to upgrade these organizations to Exchange 2000 Server organizations. How can she best manage the upgrade process?
    a. by merging the two organizations after she upgrades to Exchange 2000 Server
    b. by merging the two organizations before she upgrades to Exchange 2000 Server
    c. by allowing users to log on to both organizations simultaneously after the upgrade to Exchange 2000 Server has been completed
    d. by upgrading each organization separately to Exchange 2000 Server and then replicating their directories using the ReplMon tool

20. Single-instance message storage is preserved when you perform a move mailbox upgrade. True or False?

21. Which upgrade method is appropriate if you are using temporary hardware to host all mailbox stores and public folder stores, but not on a permanent basis?

    a. the across-the-wire upgrade

    b. the leapfrog upgrade

    c. the in-place upgrade

    d. the move mailbox upgrade

22. You are managing an Exchange 5.5 organization consisting of five separate sites. All sites are connected using a site connector. What must be true if you want to upgrade each site to Exchange 2000 Server?

    a. All Exchange 5.5 servers must be placed into a common administrative group before upgrading each site to Exchange 2000.

    b. The site connectors must be removed before upgrading each site to Exchange 2000.

    c. At least one Exchange 5.5 server in each site must be running Service Pack 3 or later.

    d. Every Exchange 5.5 server in each site must run Service Pack 3 or later.

23. What happens to an Exchange 5.5 distribution list that is replicated into a native-mode Windows 2000 domain?

    a. It will be converted into a universal distribution group.

    b. It will be converted into a universal security group.

    c. It will be converted into a domain local distribution group.

    d. It will be converted into a global distribution group.

24. The ForestPrep utility can be used to create a(n) ______________ in AD and to extend the AD schema with Exchange 2000 schema extensions.

HANDS-ON PROJECTS

It's not always easy to remember whether you are operating in mixed mode or native mode for your Windows 2000 domains or your Exchange 2000 organization because Windows and Exchange use these terms differently. The next two projects assume that you are running Exchange 2000 Server on a Windows 2000 Server or Advanced Server machine, and that you are logged on as an Administrator.

Project 6-1

To determine the status of your Windows 2000 domains and change to native mode:

1. Click **Start**, point to **Programs**, point to **Administrative Tools**, and then click **Active Directory Users and Computers**.
2. Click to select your domain object in the console tree, click **Action** on the menu bar, and then click **Properties**.
3. Locate the Domain operation mode section in the General tab of the Properties dialog box. You will see this text: "Mixed mode (supports both Windows 2000 and pre-Windows 2000 domain controllers)."
4. Read the Domain mode warning on the bottom of the screen. Click the **Change Mode** button to see the message box in Figure 6-2.

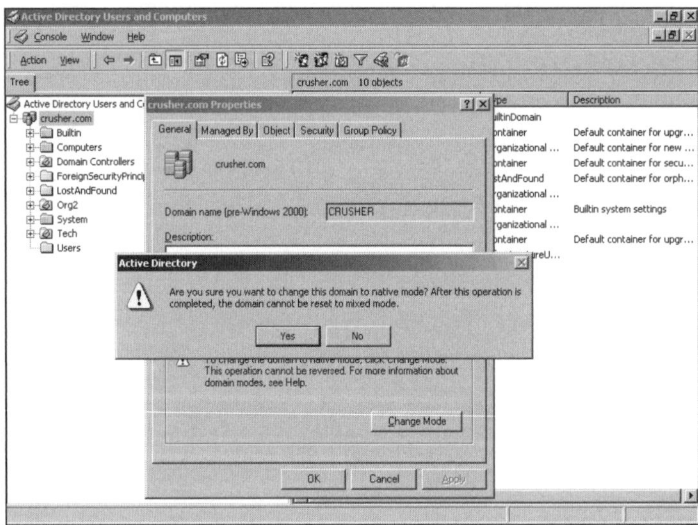

Figure 6-2 Changing Windows 2000 to native mode

5. Click **Yes**, knowing that this change to native mode cannot be reversed. Notice that the text in the Operation mode section changes to state that the domain is now in native mode. Click **OK** to close the Properties dialog box.

6. A message box appears, stating that this operation is successful and that it could take at least 15 minutes for this information to replicate to all domain controllers. Click **OK**.

Project 6-2

To enable native-mode operations for your Exchange 2000 organization:

1. Select **Start**, point to **Programs**, point to **Microsoft Exchange**, and then click **System Manager**.
2. Right-click your Organization node, and then click **Properties** on the shortcut menu.
3. In the General tab, note the text in the Operation mode box. The default text is "Mixed Mode (can support pre-Exchange 2000 Servers)."
4. To change the operation mode from mixed to native, click the **Change Mode** button. You will see the message box shown in Figure 6-3. Click **Yes**. After you have changed to native mode, remember you cannot change back to mixed mode! Click **OK** to close the Properties dialog box.

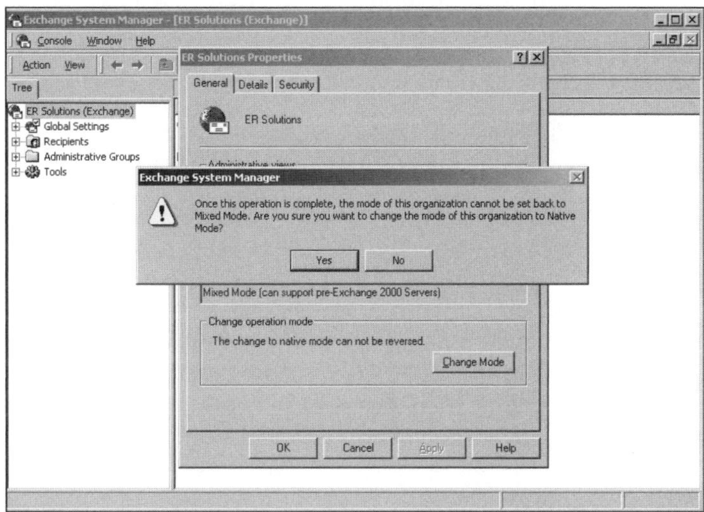

Figure 6-3 Changing Exchange 2000 to native mode

Project 6-3

This project assumes that you are logged on as a member of the Schema Administrators, the Enterprise Administrators, and the Domain Administrators groups. This project also assumes that you are logged on to a GC server and that you are installing the ADC in every domain in your organization.

To install the Active Directory Connector:

1. Insert the Exchange 2000 Server CD into your CD-ROM drive. Browse to the \ADC\i386 directory and double-click the **Setup.exe** file. The Microsoft Active Directory Connector Setup Wizard displays the Welcome message. Click the **Next** button to proceed.
2. In the Component Selection window, click the **Microsoft Active Directory Connector Service component** and **Microsoft Active Directory Connector Management components** check boxes, and then click the **Next** button.
3. In the Install Location window, either accept the default folder location of C:\Program Files\MSADC, or click the **Browse** button to select another folder location for the ADC, and then click the **Next** button.
4. In the Service Account window, enter the account name that you want the ADC to use in the Account name text box. The default account is your logon account or services account for all Exchange 5.5 services. Enter a password in the Account password text box, and then click the **Next** button.
5. Wait until the next window, showing the progress bar, is finished. You should see the installer process 10 files of AD schema updates. This process takes some time to complete, but it will run faster if you install the ADC on a GC server that's also configured with the operations master role of Schema Master. When you see the Completing the Active Directory Connector Setup Wizard window, click the **Finish** button.

Project 6-4

Now it is time to configure the ADC that was just installed. For small environments with one Exchange 2000 server and less than 500 mailbox-enabled objects, you create a single recipient or user connection agreement that populates AD with Exchange 5.5 directory information. This CA can be configured for two-way replication if you want, but it's not essential. In larger Exchange environments, you might need more ADC configuration agreements for your additional Exchange 5.5 sites. Multiple CAs are needed for multiple Exchange 5.5 sites because each site is responsible for directory information only in that site and cannot change information in other sites' directories.

To configure the ADC for a relatively small environment:

1. Click **Start**, point to **Programs**, point to **Microsoft Exchange**, and then click **Active Directory Connector**. The Active Directory Connector Management console appears.
2. Right-click the Active Directory Connector for your server, point to **New**, and then click **Connection Agreement** on the shortcut menu. This creates a recipient CA that allows the ADC to transfer recipient information between AD and Exchange 5.5.
3. In the General tab, type **First CA** in the Name text box, and then click the radio button next to the type of CA you want in the Replication direction area. The default is From Exchange to Windows, but you can also select Two-way or From

Windows to Exchange, as shown in Figure 6-4. Leave the default settings and click the **Connections** tab.

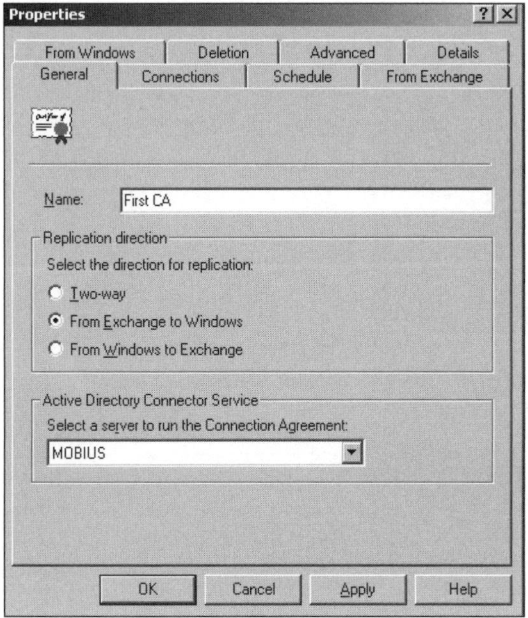

Figure 6-4 Selecting the name and replication direction

4. In the Connections tab shown in Figure 6-5, specify an account that has read-write access to all items in the Exchange 5.5 directory that will be replicated or modified. You can select the Exchange 5.5 service account or another account with equivalent permissions. Enter the computer that will be upgraded in the Server text box, click to select an authentication method for users in the Authentication text box, and then click the **Modify** button to select an account that will connect to this machine (select the Local Administrator account here). Type a password for this Administrator account, and then click **OK**.

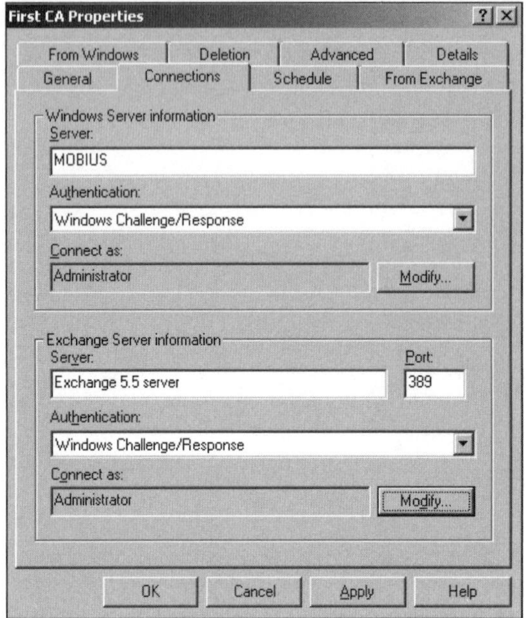

Figure 6-5 Specifying server information in the Connections tab

5. In the same Connections tab, type relevant information under the Exchange Server information section: the name of your Exchange 5.5 server in the Server text box and a port number to be used for LDAP in the Port text box (select a port number other than port 389). Select an authentication method, enter a relevant account in the Connect as text box, and then click the **Schedule** tab.
6. In the Schedule tab, choose the timing for your replications. Notice that replication occurs early in the day by default, but click the **Always** radio button in this case. Also click the **Replicate the entire directory the next time the agreement is run** check box near the bottom of the dialog box to force a replication (see Figure 6-6).
7. Click the **From Exchange** tab, and then configure which Exchange recipient containers will be replicated into AD. Click the **Add** button to display the Choose a container dialog box, click the **Recipients** container, and then click **OK**. You can design it so that a subcontainer replicates even though its parent root container does not.
8. In the Default destination area, click the **Modify** button, and then select a container in AD that will serve as the destination folder for the replication process. Click the **Users** container, and then click **OK**. In the Objects list box, click the check boxes for the objects that you want replicated. In this case, click the **Mailboxes**, **Custom recipients**, and **Distribution lists** check boxes (see Figure 6-7).

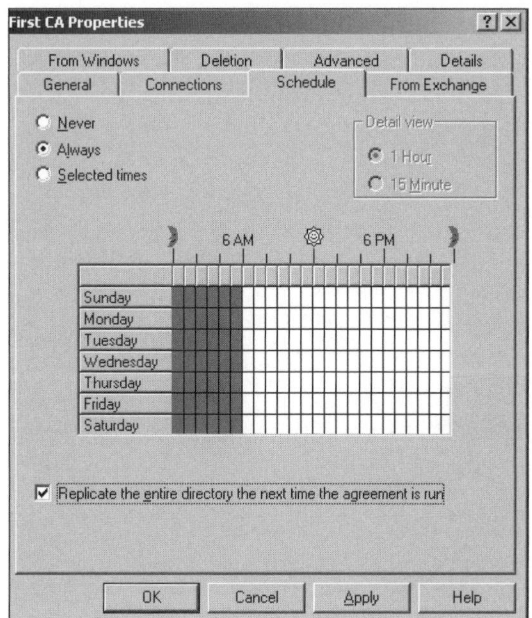

Figure 6-6 Setting the replication schedule

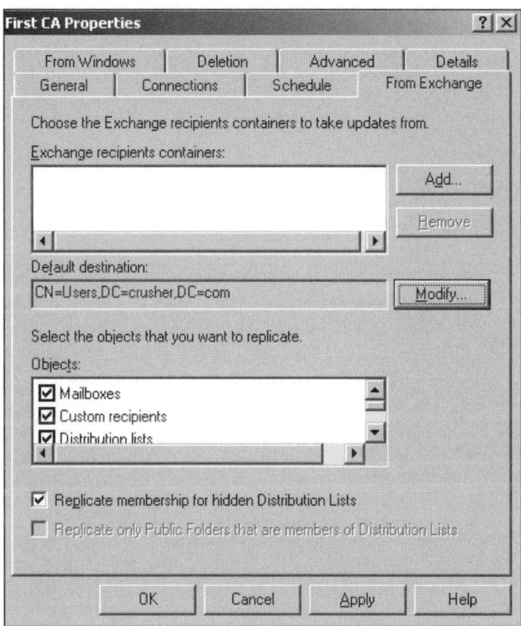

Figure 6-7 Choosing an Exchange recipient container for ADC replication

6

9. If you configured a two-way replication in the General tab, then you must repeat Steps 7-8 in the From Windows tab. If not, proceed to Step 10.
10. Click the **Deletion** tab. This is where you determine whether you want ADC to automatically delete entries in one directory if it detects deletions in the other directory. For instance, if you delete objects in Exchange 5.5, the corresponding Windows 2000 account can also be deleted. If you do not want this type of connection agreement, then configure the ADC to write deleted objects to a file that deletes these objects for you later. Figure 6-8 shows only the bottom half of this tab as active because you configured one-way replication in the General tab. Keep all the default settings, and then click the **Advanced** tab.

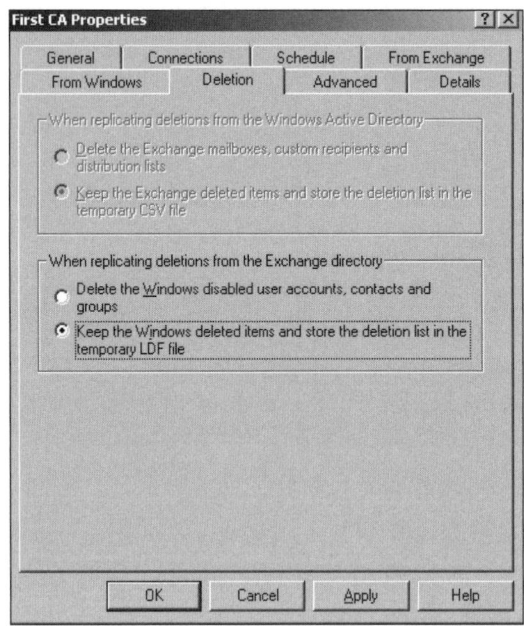

Figure 6-8 Determining replication deletions

11. The Advanced tab (see Figure 6-9) allows you to designate whether a CA is primary. A primary CA not only replicates information, but also creates new objects if necessary. A nonprimary CA only replicates information about objects.

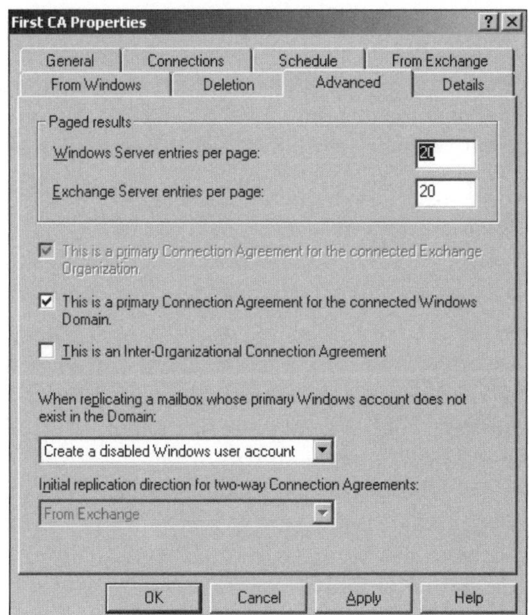

Figure 6-9 Specifying primary CAs

Be careful about arbitrarily creating new primary connection agreements, because each primary CA creates a new AD account for every new Exchange account you add, resulting in duplicate accounts within AD.

In the lower half of this tab, you can specify what type of object to create in AD whenever an Exchange mailbox is created. The default setting of Create a disabled Windows user account is best used in a mixed-mode Exchange environment so that a Windows NT 4.0 account can access its Exchange 2000 mailbox. Leave all default settings in this case, click **Apply**, and then click **OK** (do not select the option to Create a Windows contact unless you want to connect two separate Exchange 5.5 organizations).

12. You might see a message box about the replication of distribution lists. Simply read it, and then click **OK**. It's telling you that the ADC tries to create universal groups in Windows 2000 when replicating an Exchange 5.5 distribution list (DL) to AD. Universal groups are accessible to everyone in your organization; however, the CA cannot create universal groups in a mixed-mode domain (and you might not be able to replicate your DLs). If your Exchange 2000 users use DLs, consider creating a native-mode Windows 2000 domain to host these DLs.

The This is an Inter-Organizational Connection Agreement check box in the Advanced tab should be selected only if you want to replicate object information between multiple Windows 2000 forests—in which case you need to create multiple Exchange 2000 organizations. You must also configure external and explicit trust relationships between multiple forests for replication to be successful.

Project 6-5

The move mailbox upgrade requires an existing Exchange 2000 server, which must be in the same site as servers that host mailboxes you want to upgrade. In Exchange 5.5, the Exchange Administrator program was used to move mailboxes. Now you must use a computer on which you have installed Exchange 2000 management tools, such as System Manager. You will also use the Windows 2000 Active Directory Users and Computers MMC snap-in to move mailboxes between Exchange 5.5 and Exchange 2000. Make sure you back up your Exchange 5.5 server before moving mailboxes or public folders and verify that the users being moved have actual Windows 2000 accounts in AD. If they don't, then set up an ADC so that you can populate accounts from Exchange 5.5 into AD.

To move mailboxes to Exchange 2000 Server:

1. Install one Exchange 2000 server into an existing Exchange 5.5 site.
2. Start the Active Directory Users and Computers tool. To do this, click **Start**, point to **Programs**, point to **Administrative Tools**, and then click **Active Directory Users and Computers**.
3. Click a user object in the Contents pane, right-click the user object when it appears in the Details pane of this console, and then click **Exchange Tasks** on the shortcut menu.
4. In the Welcome to the Exchange Task Wizard window, click the **Next** button.
5. In the Available Tasks window, click the **Move Mailbox** option to select it, and then click the **Next** button (see Figure 6-10).
6. In the Move Mailbox window, verify that the Current Mailbox Store text box points to your Exchange 5.5 computer and that the Server text box displays your Windows 2000 server name. Under Mailbox Store, click the storage group and mailbox store that you want to move the user to, and then click the **Next** button (see Figure 6-11).

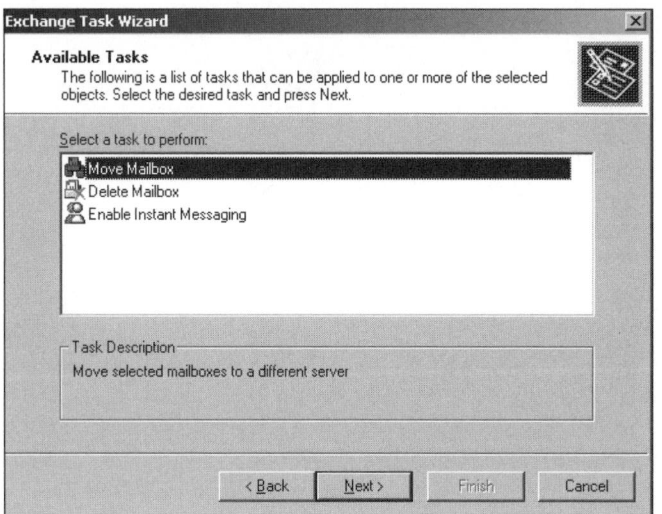

Figure 6-10 Selecting a task to perform

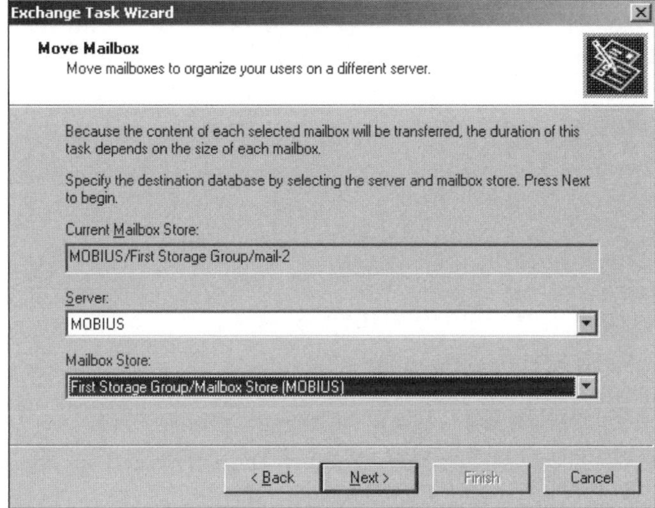

Figure 6-11 Selecting the mailbox store

7. The Task In Progress window shows the progress and overall status of the mailbox that is being moved, as shown in Figure 6-12.

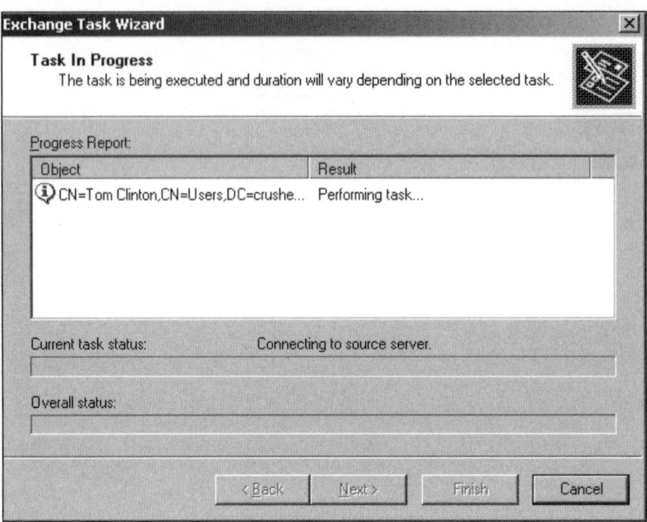

Figure 6-12 Checking the status of the moved mailbox

8. Verify the information in the Completing the Exchange Task Wizard window, and then click the **Finish** button to close the Exchange Task Wizard. Repeat Steps 3–8 for each mailbox you want to move, or highlight several mailboxes at once and move them together.

Project 6-6

To view administrative groups in System Manager:

1. To start System Manager, click **Start**, point to **Programs**, point to **Microsoft Exchange**, and then click **System Manager**.
2. Locate your Organization object in the upper-left corner of the Contents pane. Right-click your Organization object, and then click **Properties** on the shortcut menu. You should see the <*Organization name*> Properties dialog box.
3. Click the **Display routing groups** and **Display administrative groups** check boxes, and then click **OK** to enable the features.
4. The Administrative Groups container where you can create new administrative groups for permission management is now visible. In this container is the First Administrative Group container. To create new administrative groups in the future, simply right-click the **Administrative Groups** container, point to **New**, and then click **Administrative Group** on the shortcut menu, as shown in Figure 6-13.

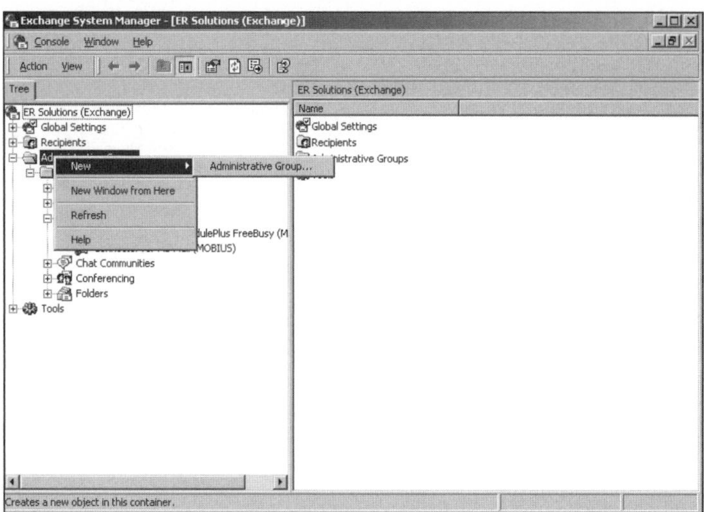

Figure 6-13 Creating new adminstrative groups in System Manager

5. Close any open windows.

Project 6-7

This exercise assumes that you have configured the display of routing groups in System Manager as described in Project 6-6.

To deploy routing groups with administrative groups:

1. To start System Manager, click **Start**, point to **Programs**, point to **Microsoft Exchange**, and then click **System Manager**.
2. Expand your **Administrative Groups** container (you can expand the containers by double-clicking them or by clicking the + sign to the left of each item), and then expand the **First Administrative Group** container. Expand the **Routing Groups** container, and notice the First Routing Group container; this container appears by default when you enable the display of routing groups in System Manager.
3. To create new routing groups, simply right-click the **Routing Groups** container, point to **New**, and then click **Routing Group** on the shortcut menu. In the General tab, type a descriptive name for your group in the Name text box, and then click **OK**.
4. Every Exchange routing group has one server designated as the routing group master, which propagates link state information to all routing group members. To enable a server to become the routing group master, expand the **Routing Groups** container, and then expand the routing group containing the server you want to configure (usually it is the First Routing Group, but it can be any routing group you create).

5. Click the **Members** folder appearing under the First Routing Group container, and then right-click your server in the Details pane. Finally, click **Set as Master** on the shortcut menu, as shown in Figure 6-14.
6. Close any open windows.

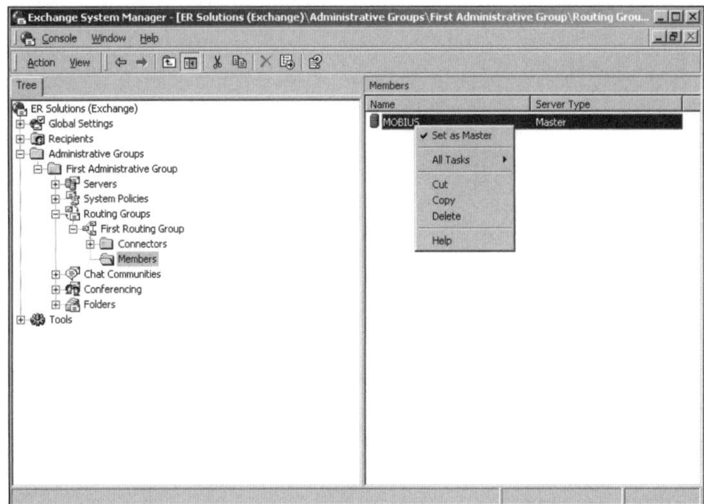

Figure 6-14 Choosing a routing group master in System Manager

CASE PROJECTS

Case 1

Paola is about to upgrade her Exchange 5.5 organization to Exchange 2000. She has three sites that use Exchange 5.5 servers, and she wants to migrate all users to the new AD structure of Windows 2000. She knows that a lot of configuration is involved with the ADC and the SRS. She is working within a limited timeframe and needs to complete the full upgrade in three days. What are some actions she can take to reduce the amount of ADC configuration needed in this situation?

Case 2

Jared has been concerned about the existing server hardware at the hospital where he works. He has been under pressure to upgrade his legacy Exchange 5.5 servers because they have slowed down due to an increase in client access. His manager has given him a budget to upgrade existing hardware, but Jared feels that his Exchange servers can all be upgraded to Exchange 2000 without purchasing or configuring new hardware. What criteria can Jared use to help make the best decision for his hospital about the planned upgrade to Exchange 2000? What upgrade methods are available to him at this time?

Case 3

Joel is the network administrator for Car World. He has been getting many Event Viewer messages about AD. His network team has met and decided that Joel has not correctly configured certain network components, which is affecting the performance and functionality of the AD service on his entire network. The team agrees that these errors can be placed into three distinct categories: DNS configuration errors, network configuration problems, and errors arising from the upgrade of his Windows NT 4.0 domains to Windows 2000 domains. To remedy some of these problems, Joel performs the following actions:

1. He disables File and Printer Sharing on his Windows 2000 domain controllers.
2. He disables NetBIOS over TCP/IP for all clients in his network.
3. He continues to run his DNS server on a Windows NT 4.0 computer.

Has Joel helped the situation or has he made it worse? Why?

Case 4

Jamie is about to upgrade her Exchange 5.5 server to Exchange 2000 and Windows 2000. She is confused about whether she needs Exchange 2000 Server and considers running Exchange 5.5 on a Windows 2000 machine. Her company maintains connections to an IBM mainframe on which important financial records are kept. She has also been maintaining a third-party fax connector on her Exchange 5.5 machine and wonders if it will work in Exchange 2000. She consults her VP of information technology for advice on whether she should add her Exchange 5.5 server to an existing Windows 2000 administrative group or whether she should convert her entire organization so that it runs only Exchange 2000. What advice should the VP give her in this situation?

CHAPTER

7

CONFIGURING MAPI CLIENTS IN EXCHANGE 2000 SERVER

After reading this chapter and completing the exercises, you will be able to:

- Understand client software configuration and the various types of clients available for use with Exchange 2000 Server, to make the best choices for your organization
- Install Outlook 2000, a common choice for client software to communicate with Exchange 2000 Server
- Configure Outlook 2000, including local and remote access, to choose the best configuration for your users
- Understand messaging profiles in relation to Exchange 2000 Server and Outlook 2000, and see how they can be used to customize the configuration of Exchange user accounts
- Troubleshoot common Outlook 2000 issues, which can help you detect and rectify many problems that can happen while using Outlook 2000

In Chapter 6, "Upgrading or Migrating from Exchange 5.5 to Exchange 2000," you learned about upgrading an existing Exchange Server 5.5 organization to Exchange 2000 Server, including mixed-mode versus native-mode operation and how they work with both Windows 2000 Server and Exchange 2000 Server. You also learned about using the various upgrade methods and options, using the Active Directory Connector, and migrating/moving existing mailboxes over from Exchange 5.5 to Exchange 2000.

In this chapter, you learn about configuring various clients that can be used with Exchange 2000 and look at the different types of client software packages, including Outlook 98 and 2000. You also learn the steps for installing and configuring Outlook 2000, including configuring Outlook 2000 for both local network and remote network access and configuring messaging profiles for use with Outlook 2000. Finally, you take a look at troubleshooting common problems that arise with Outlook 2000, including security, recovery of lost data, and other permissions issues. There's certainly more to using Exchange 2000 Server than just installing and configuring the server end of things. After you have a server installed and set up the way you require, you need clients to connect to the server to actually make the whole endeavor worthwhile. You can choose from a wide variety of e-mail client software packages from both Microsoft and third-party vendors to connect to Exchange 2000. Each client software package and setup is different, but they all typically use the same configuration and settings. As you will see, you can entirely customize which e-mail client you want the client to run, even taking into account specific user needs and the operating system being used.

REVIEWING DIFFERENT TYPES OF CLIENTS

Most recent Windows operating system installations include a basic e-mail and newsgroup reader client software package called Outlook Express (which is discussed in more detail in the "Outlook Express" section later in this chapter). Simple clients like this can offer the e-mail connectivity a user needs. However, more full-featured client software packages, such as Outlook 98 or Outlook 2000, can provide not only e-mail connectivity, but also more robust contact management, calendar, and task list features, among others. Your choice of client software to use with your Exchange 2000 deployment varies greatly, based on what your users use Exchange 2000 for and what features you have enabled.

If users simply need to get e-mail messages, Outlook Express is more than adequate; however, if they need some of the collaboration features in Exchange 2000, including access to public folders, it is much more beneficial to use Outlook 98 or Outlook 2000 and profit from its support of these features. Table 7-1 outlines some of today's popular clients along with standard features they support. The following sections describe the Outlook clients and a few of the other e-mail client packages in more detail.

Table 7-1 Popular Client Software Packages

Client	Manufacturer	Supported Exchange Features	Supported Platforms
Outlook 2000/2002	Microsoft	E-mail, public folders, calendar, contacts, tasks, scheduling, deleted item recovery	Windows 9x, 2000, XP
Outlook 97/98	Microsoft	E-mail, public folders, calendar, contacts, tasks, scheduling, deleted item recovery	Windows 9x, 2000, XP
Outlook Express	Microsoft	E-mail	Windows 3.1, 9x, 2000, XP, Mac OS 7.x or higher
Outlook Web Access	Microsoft	E-mail, public folders, calendar, contacts, tasks	Any platform with a Web browser and Internet access
Outlook for Macintosh	Microsoft	E-mail; other features vary version to version	Mac OS 8.6 or higher
Eudora 5.x	Qualcomm	E-mail	Windows 3.1, 9x, 2000, XP, Mac OS 7.x or higher
Any e-mail client software with support for POP3 or IMAP4 protocols	Various	E-mail	Any platform with Internet access

The supported features of the Outlook client software packages depend on the type of client installation you performed and the supported features you configured with Exchange 2000. For instance, Outlook Web Access does not have access to all the functionality of a regular Outlook client installation unless Exchange 2000 has been configured to support access to the feature for OWA clients. For instance, if the administrator has decided not to allow public folder access for OWA clients because of security concerns, users can't access public folders unless they are logged on with a properly configured Outlook client, such as Outlook 2000.

Thankfully, a vast selection of e-mail clients is available for a multitude of different platforms; even UNIX/Linux operating systems can take advantage of e-mail through Exchange 2000 by utilizing an e-mail client that supports POP3 or IMAP4. Macintosh operating systems have a version of Outlook that provides more functionality with every new release. Macintosh Outlook 2001 is currently in **beta testing** (a period in a software's development and testing phase in which typical users can test for functionality and bugs in the software), but it offers an experience similar to what Windows users have with Outlook 98 or Outlook 2000.

Even given the wide variety of other e-mail clients you can use to access Exchange 2000 services, to truly benefit from Exchange 2000 you must install Outlook 98 or Outlook 2000/2002.

Messaging Application Programming Interface and E-Mail Clients

Messaging Application Programming Interface (MAPI) is a core messaging and e-mail component of Windows operating systems that follows the industry standard for writing messages and e-mail. With MAPI, Exchange 2000 and a wide variety of other e-mail and messaging servers can transfer mail between each other in a standard format that can be read and handled by any server. A multitude of applications can have MAPI support integrated.

MAPI can be used by any software application by including a particular software call to the appropriate MAPI DLL file in the software application, and passing the messaging or e-mail information to that DLL in the supported structure. This makes it easy to include e-mail and messaging features in various types of software, not just e-mail clients. Advanced MAPI features and functionality, such as sending and receiving e-mail within a game, can be integrated into software, but doing so requires adding programming in the software.

MAPI support has been built into every Windows operating system since Windows 9x, including Windows NT 4.0 and Windows 2000. Therefore, any e-mail or messaging software application that sends MAPI information in the supported standard can use the MAPI support built into the operating system to send and receive messages and e-mail. MAPI support eliminates the need for software programmers to write and implement their own message transfer interface. Because Microsoft has included an industry-accepted implementation of MAPI in Windows operating systems, it can guarantee that there are no inconsistencies in the ways that different e-mail and messaging products support message transfer and handling.

Outlook 2000

Microsoft Outlook is the flagship client communication and collaboration software product in the Microsoft fleet of software. Outlook 2000 is part of the popular Office 2000 software suite or can be purchased on its own. It makes an excellent standalone e-mail client with calendars, task lists, and contact lists that can be used independently of Exchange 2000. Match Outlook 2000 with Exchange 2000, however, and you can tap into the wide range of collaboration features that make Exchange 2000 Server an attractive product for organizations.

Although Outlook 2002 was recently made available on its own and as part of the Microsoft Office XP software suite, this section focuses on Outlook 2000, which will likely still be the dominant installed client for the next year or longer, given the already large installed base of Office 2000. Outlook 2002 provides much the same overall experience as Outlook 2000 and does not introduce any new Exchange-specific functionality. For all intents and purposes, Outlook 2000 and 2002 are the same core product; the only major benefit to Outlook 2002 is a slightly improved interface that makes it easier to configure Outlook options and administer multiple e-mail accounts. It also features improved task management with Group Scheduling and a Suggest New Time function. For more information on Outlook 2002 and its new features, go to *http://www.microsoft.com/office/outlook/evaluation/guide.htm* or reference Appendix D, "Outlook 2002, Outlook Express 6, and Exchange 2000 Server," in this book.

Outlook combines the same core functionality that was originally introduced with the Microsoft Mail client software and Microsoft Schedule+. Microsoft Outlook, as we know it first appeared as a full-featured client to go with the new (at the time) Microsoft Exchange 5.0 Server. Microsoft foresaw the wide acceptance and demand for e-mail and collaboration software and created Outlook as a way to integrate the e-mail functionality of Microsoft Mail and the scheduling and task-management features of Schedule+. Presently, Outlook 2000 is the most current Outlook client, with the largest installed base. In terms of user interface and core components, Outlook 2000 does not look much different from previous versions. See Figure 7-1 for a basic Outlook 2000 client screen.

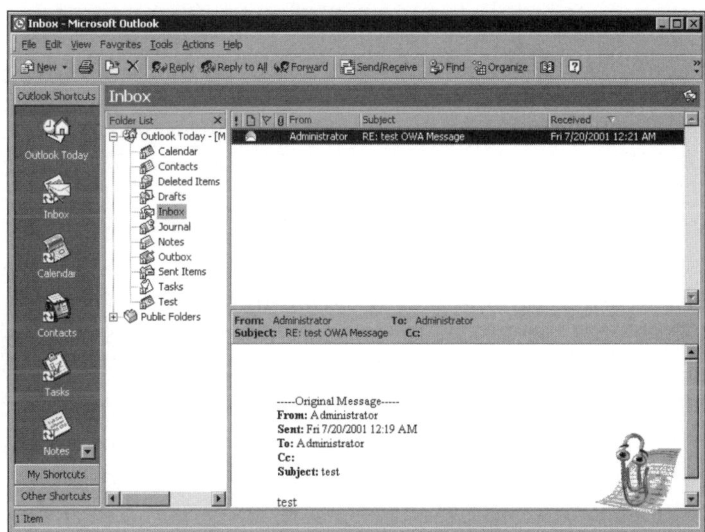

Figure 7-1 The basic Outlook 2000 user interface

As mentioned previously, there's more to Outlook than being an e-mail client and a utility to access Exchange 2000 functionality; it also has a good selection of helpful time-management tools, including:

- *Calendar*—A necessary utility for almost every business, worker, or home office worker. Using the calendar, you can insert dates and appointments as visual reminders of your schedule. You can also have actual reminder messages pop up at a particular time (even a year in advance if you so choose) to remind you of the event. Recurring events, such as weekly meetings, can also be inserted into the calendar, and when combined with Exchange 2000, you can have other users send meeting requests to you. If you accept these requests, they are inserted directly into your calendar.
- *Contacts*—A multifeatured contact management system that contains a wide array of information about a contact and gives you the ability to sort contacts into groups. Although not as robust as many full-fledged contact management applications, it typically serves the needs of most users.
- *Notes*—An electronic version of the sticky note that allows you to quickly type simple reminders and drag them onto your desktop for easier viewing.
- *Tasks*—An extension of the calendar, used for configuring tasks to allow you to follow a train of events. For instance, if you have four steps in a project, you can enter each step as a separate task; as you finish each task, put a check mark next to it, indicating the task is completed and showing what tasks remain, much like a to-do list. Other users can also send you tasks, and after you accept them, they are entered in your tasks list. If needed, you can assign deadlines for each task and have a reminder pop up just before the deadline.
- *Journals*—A useful feature for salespeople or other workers who need to track their activity with a particular contact or their progress with a project. If journaling is enabled, you track every phone call, fax, or e-mail in Outlook Journal and match it to a particular contact, giving you a detailed "paper trail" for that contact or project. You can even generate reports showing the progress that has been made to date, using the information in the journals.

Many of these listed features were included when the original Outlook was released, but have been fine-tuned over the various releases. Lest you think that, like Outlook 2002, Outlook 2000 is a simple version update to go with the updated version of Office, you should be aware that some features have been added to Outlook 2000 that could be worthwhile for your implementation. The following list outlines some of the more important features added in this version of Outlook:

- Single-step publishing of a personal or team calendar to a Web page
- Activity tracking for contacts, so you can monitor e-mail, scheduled appointments, and tasks assigned to the contact

- An improved, easier-to-use Mail Merge feature that can merge specific fields of information in your Outlook contacts into e-mail, fax, or printed documents
- Support for a wide variety of protocols and services, including POP3, SMTP, IMAP4, LDAP, NNTP, and S/MIME
- Ability to create a shortcut to any file, Web page, or folder contained in Outlook
- Full Outlook Today functionality (originally introduced in Outlook 98 with less functionality) as a centralized point to give you an overview of new e-mail, tasks, or calendar events scheduled for today's date

The default page that users see when they run Outlook 2000 for the first time is Outlook Today. Outlook Today outlines the pertinent information a user might want immediate access to when opening Outlook. In its default configuration, Outlook Today can be a useful feature if users must quickly keep track of several different aspects of their day, such as scheduled events, new e-mail, tasks, and so on (see Figure 7-2).

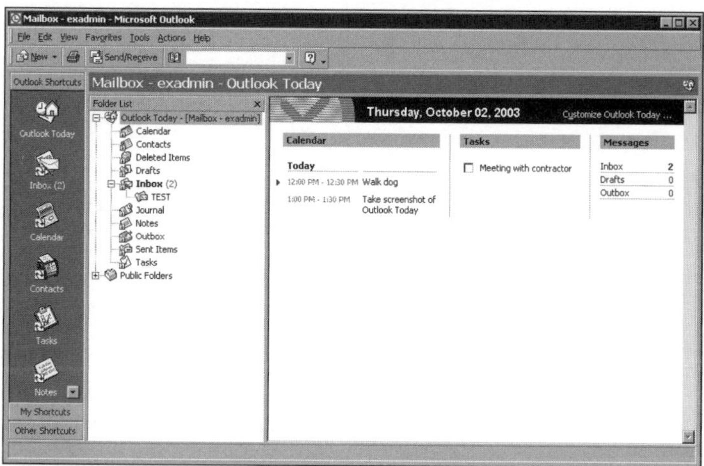

Figure 7-2 The Outlook Today introductory screen

Many users opt to simply disable Outlook Today without giving it the chance to show its mettle. Many users and administrators don't realize that Outlook Today can be customized for the user, including personalizing its appearance. You will learn how to change some of the basic settings in Outlook Today in the "Hands-on-Projects" section later in this chapter.

In addition, Outlook Today can be customized with a new feature called a **digital dashboard**, which is simply the high-tech HTML Web page you see with Outlook Today. Companies dedicated to the development of customized digital dashboards have created a wide selection for you to choose from; in addition, as an administrator, you can develop your own, using the free digital dashboard starter kit included in Exchange 2000 Server. The starter kit allows you to customize your own digital dashboard for your organization or workplace, offering a one-glance access to all the information a user needs, instead of having to search for it in several places. In fact, there are ways to integrate a digital desktop into **Active Desktop** (the feature that enables Windows desktop backgrounds to display HTML information and pages) and supply links directly to Outlook 2000 information, such as messages and calendars, meaning that users rarely, if ever, have to open the Outlook client itself.

To learn more about digital dashboards and how to start creating your own with Outlook 2000, visit this Web site: *http://www.microsoft.com/TechNet/tcevents/itevents/fall/tnq20011/html/default.htm*. In addition, a free version of the digital dashboard Resource Kit is available at this Web page: *http://msdn.microsoft.com/downloads/default.asp?URL=/code/sample.asp?url=/MSDN-FILES/027/001/584/msdncompositedoc.xml.*

Digital dashboards can constitute a large investment of time and require knowledge of special HTML languages. Don't expect to be able to institute a full digital dashboard out of the gate; you will probably have to spend some time researching, planning, and tweaking your digital dashboard installation before it's ready for deployment. However, if you do manage to design and build a digital dashboard, your users will gain a helpful time-management tool to make Outlook 2000 even more useful.

As you can see, Outlook 2000 has many features and options, and its basic installation and setup is fairly easy. You will learn how to install Outlook 2000 and configure various settings, accounts, and other features in the "Hands-on Projects" section later in this chapter.

Outlook 97/98

Because Outlook 2000 is the dominant e-mail client platform used with Exchange 2000, not as much needs to be said about Outlook 98, other than it can be used with Exchange 2000 for every major Exchange 2000 feature and function available. If your company or organization uses Outlook 98, you should experience no difficulties integrating it with Exchange 2000 and giving users the functionality they need. As you learned earlier, Outlook Today was originally introduced in Outlook 98, although it lacks the polish of the version integrated into Outlook 2000.

Outlook 97 is another Outlook sibling in circulation, and you may come across this version in your travels. However, it's wise to upgrade systems with Outlook 97 to Outlook 98 or Outlook 2000 as soon as possible. Outlook 97 has had some stability and performance problems; hence, Outlook 98 was released on its own (not as part of a major Microsoft Office release) as a free upgrade to Outlook 97 a few years ago. If you have Outlook 97 users who are having problems with it not responding to user input or if the software is simply crashing, an upgrade is necessary to rectify the situation.

Outlook Express

The free version of Microsoft Outlook Express 5.x is included in every current Windows operating system since Windows 98se. Outlook Express on its own is a useful and easy-to-use Internet e-mail client, but it also allows users to access Internet newsgroups, which are rather handy because of the large gathering of information that's available. If you plan to implement newsgroup features in Exchange 2000 Server, you can use Outlook Express to access them. The Outlook Express interface, shown in Figure 7-3, is clean and easy to use.

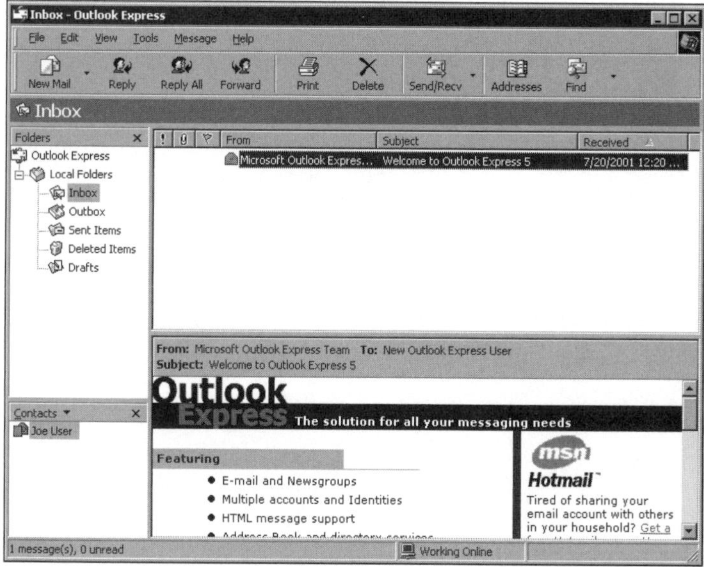

Figure 7-3 The main Outlook Express user interface

Outlook Express also includes a feature similar to Outlook Today: an introductory start screen that gives you quick access to the various Outlook Express features, namely e-mail, newsgroups, and contacts (see Figure 7-4). The following discussion outlines these features of Outlook Express.

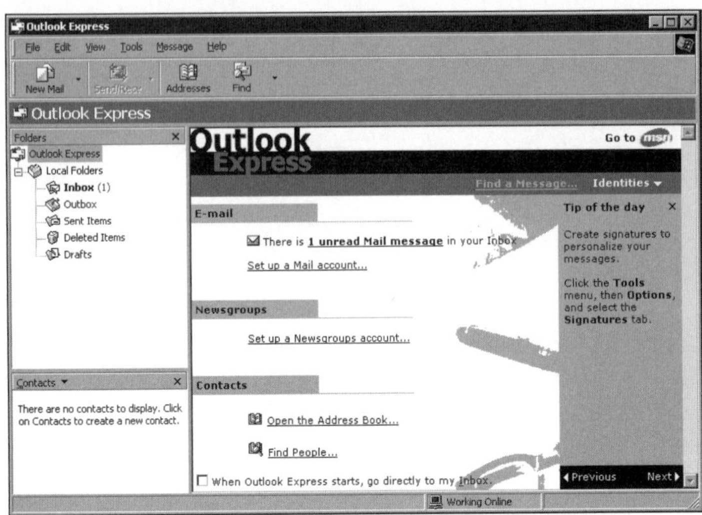

Figure 7-4 The Outlook Express introductory screen

E-mail messaging is the backbone of Outlook Express, which performs this basic function very well. Outlook Express can allow you to configure multiple e-mail accounts with different servers and configurations. It includes support for POP3, IMAP4, and SMTP. Even though you can utilize Outlook Express to communicate and send/retrieve e-mail using Exchange 2000, it's not a supported Exchange 2000 client software package; only Outlook 9x, 2000, 2002, and OWA are. Outlook Express behaves the same with Exchange as any other regular Internet e-mail client software does, in that it connects to Exchange 2000 servers by using IMAP4 or SMTP, but it does not include any of the calendar, public folder, or collaboration features that Exchange 2000 supports.

With Outlook Express, you can also create multiple profiles (a great feature if it's being used at home with other family members) and set up some custom e-mail rules for sorting or discarding e-mail. For instance, if you are getting an abundance of junk e-mail from a particular Web site or person, you can create a custom rule that deletes this e-mail as soon as it arrives in your inbox. The rules editor, shown in Figure 7-5, is a very pared-down version of the rules editor in Outlook 98 or 2000.

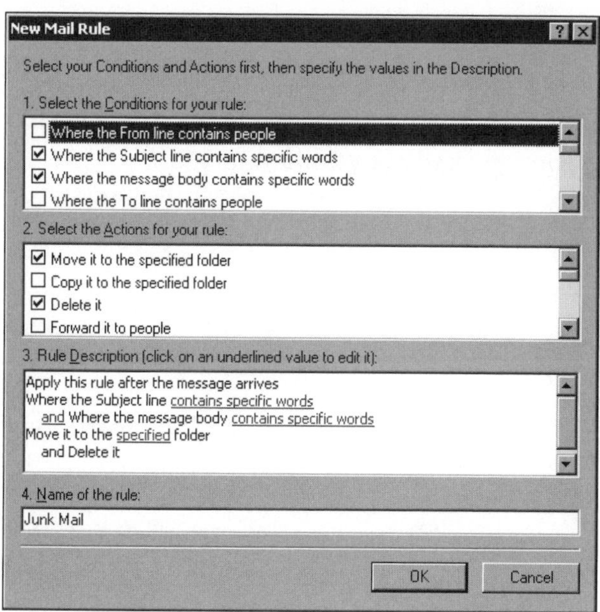

Figure 7-5 The Outlook Express rules editor

As a basic newsgroup reader, Outlook Express is quite useful. You can create connections to multiple newsgroup servers, both public and private (if you have the appropriate access to that site), and browse newsgroup content as quickly and easily as reading an e-mail (see Figure 7-6).

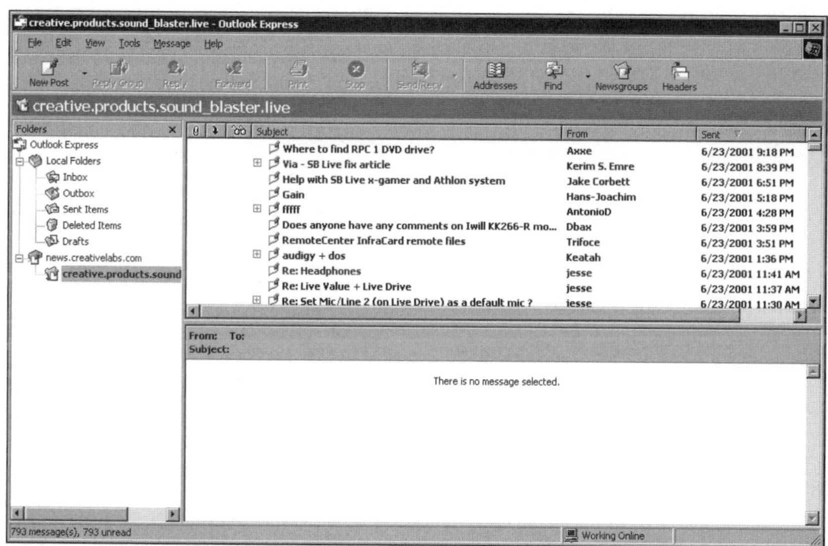

Figure 7-6 The main interface of the Outlook Express newsgroup reader

Outlook Express provides support for NNTP, which is required for connectivity to newsgroup servers of any type, including Exchange 2000 Server if support for newsgroups has been added while configuring Exchange 2000. When Outlook Express connects to an Exchange 2000 newsgroup server, it does so to the Exchange 2000 public folders that provide the basic newsgroup functionality and structure for Exchange 2000. Any information in the public folders, beyond notes, that has been created by an Outlook client, such as Outlook 98 or Outlook 2000, is not accessible to Outlook Express. This includes calendar information, journal entries, tasks, or contacts, which does limit its usefulness for Exchange 2000 newsgroups. Regardless of this, if your intention is to use notes as a simple newsgroup message system or if you have other Outlook Express users accessing and posting messages to the Exchange 2000 newsgroups, Outlook Express works rather well because it can read any message posted by another Outlook Express client to an Exchange 2000 newsgroup server.

This limited access to public folder content in Outlook Express extends to any other third-party Internet newsgroup reader and is caused mainly by NNTP's limited functionality.

The final service that Outlook Express provides is contact and directory services. Outlook Express has a contact manager that allows you to enter basic address, phone, and e-mail information for the contact and shares this contact list with any other software that accesses the Windows Address Book, namely Microsoft Instant Messenger. In addition to having this contact functionality, you can also connect to third-party directory service lookup servers to perform lookups on users and their e-mail addresses, using LDAP. This feature is useful if you're trying to locate the address for a particular person; using a directory service lookup server to look up the person's name gives you basic information on the contact that can help narrow down your search. If you need to use Outlook Express to perform a directory service lookup, you do not do so directly to an Exchange server; rather, the request is routed to a Windows 2000 Active Directory server using LDAP to fulfill the lookup request.

Outlook Express is a quick and easy client software package for basic e-mail and newsgroup functionality. On its own, it provides good Internet mail connectivity, but is not as practical for a Exchange 2000 client solution as Outlook 2000. However, Outlook Express can be useful when users are accessing e-mail from home but you do not have an OWA server configured on the network or the users do not own a copy of Outlook 98 or 2000. You will learn more about Outlook Express configuration in the "Hands-on Projects" section.

Outlook Web Access

For the past couple of years, OWA has been a popular client for use with Exchange Server, especially for remote access users. OWA services on an Exchange server can enable users with the appropriate rights to connect to an OWA Web page that allows them to log on and validate their accounts against the Exchange server. After the user has logged on, the OWA client looks very similar to the Outlook 98 or Outlook 2000 client software, with selections for Inbox, Calendar, Contacts, and Public Folders (see Figure 7-7).

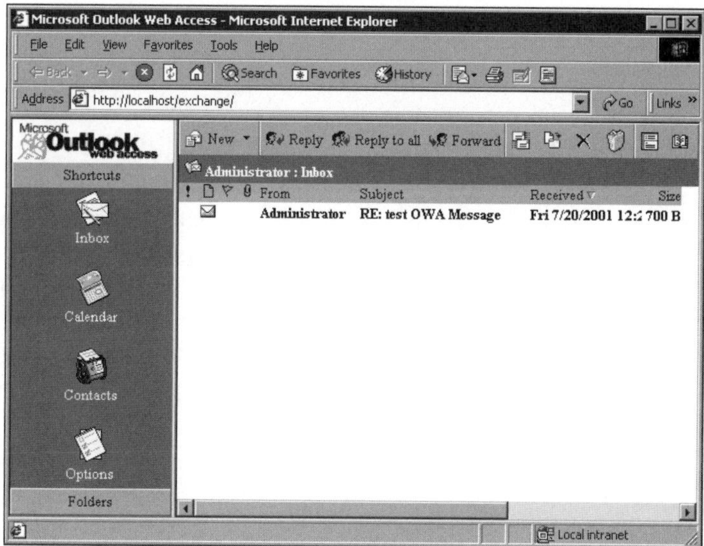

Figure 7-7 The OWA main interface Web page

These features are more pared down that what you find in the full Outlook clients; for instance, the calendar function allows you to view and enter data into your calendar, but not much else. The reason for cutting back on these features is that the OWA client is not intended to replace the full Outlook client functionality. However, as far as features go, OWA is by far the best of the smaller "free" e-mail clients that can be used with Exchange 2000.

As mentioned previously, OWA has a few limitations in its connectivity with Exchange 2000. The following list outlines some of the major features that are not supported in an OWA client connection to Exchange 2000:

- Cannot access your personal address books (stored on local PC)
- Cannot spell-check when composing e-mail messages
- Cannot apply message flags to e-mail in your Inbox
- Cannot use Inbox message-sorting rules
- Cannot drag and drop from one folder or window to another
- Cannot perform message searches

- Cannot view or manage task lists
- Cannot export data to external software, files, or devices
- Cannot access Outlook forms or templates
- Cannot access any .pst files (personal folders; stored on local PC)

For most users, these limitations will not hamper their ability to use OWA or access the critical information they need, such as contacts, e-mail, or scheduled calendar dates. OWA is by far the best method for remote users, especially those using an alternative operating system such as Linux, to access their e-mail and information in a consistent and easy-to-use software package from virtually anywhere they have Internet access.

Depending on e-mail use and calendar functions, some organizations may want their users to utilize OWA as their main and only client access to Exchange 2000. For instance, if the company has a large pool of Linux workstations that engineers use for specialized software packages, and it's not practical to have a separate PC with Windows installed, the organization could enable OWA. The engineers in this group could then use OWA without the need for a third-party e-mail client that cannot access some of the more advanced features of Outlook and Exchange 2000, such as calendars and public folders. The numerous potential uses and applications for OWA provide flexibility that certainly makes it an attractive client application for users connecting to Exchange 2000.

Older 16-Bit Clients

As mentioned in the section on Outlook 2000, Outlook is the end result of two older **16-bit clients** (older software originally designed for 16-bit operating systems, for instance, Windows 3.1) having their basic functionality combined into one application. These two 16-bit clients are Microsoft Mail (Exchange Client) and Schedule+. The following list outlines the core functionality of each application:

- Microsoft Mail (Exchange Client)
  - E-mail
  - Personal calendar
  - Task lists
- Schedule+
  - Contact management
  - Scheduling
  - Personal calendar

Both the Exchange Client and Schedule+ were originally 16-bit applications, but over the years have been upgraded to 32-bit applications to support use in Windows 9x and higher and in Macintosh operating systems. Both software packages are still supported by Exchange 2000, but there have been no more functionality updates.

If your organization has been using Exchange for a long time, some installations or remnants of one of these software packages probably still exist. By now, most organizations have upgraded to Outlook 98 or Outlook 2000 to take advantage of the collaboration features or the ease of having all the features and functions in one simple program, rather than spread across two. Although the Exchange Client and Schedule+ provide much of the functionality that Outlook 2000 does, a few important features are not supported at all by either client, such as:

- Journaling
- Notes
- Task assignments
- Access to calendars in public folders

If you come across users who are still using Schedule+ for contacts or scheduling events in their calendars, you will be happy to know you can export the data from Schedule+ and import it into Outlook 2000 without a hitch and with all the data intact. If you do still have users on the Exchange Client or Schedule+, Microsoft recommends upgrading their client software at your earliest convenience so that they can take advantage of the more advanced time-management and collaboration features available with Exchange 2000, such as public folders or the ability to assign tasks to other users.

Selecting Your Client Software

As you learned previously in the "Outlook Express" section, a wide variety of third-party e-mail clients can be used to connect to Exchange 2000 to retrieve e-mail. The one downfall is, of course, that you cannot access any of the features Exchange 2000 has to offer. This connectivity to Exchange 2000 does make client software, such as Outlook in its various forms, useful for users with non-Windows operating systems or, in the case of OWA, for remote access users.

Selecting the appropriate client for your application entirely depends on which operating system is being used, whether you require remote access for users, and what functionality you want your remote users to have access to. By far, Outlook 2000 is the premier client software that allows you to take advantage of all the special functionality Exchange 2000 has to offer. However, because of the cost or time involved in moving users over to different operating systems or client software, it might not be practical to install Outlook 2000 if you have a large installed base of other operating systems, such as Linux, or widespread installations of Exchange Client with Schedule+.

The flexibility of Exchange 2000 means you can gain good functionality with a wide variety of different client software packages; which one you choose depends on your situation and goals.

INSTALLATION OF OUTLOOK 2000

Installation of Outlook 2000 is a fairly easy process; in fact, it may already be installed on a PC that has Microsoft Office 2000 installed. As you learned previously in the "Outlook 2000" section, Outlook 2000 is available as part of the various Microsoft Office 2000 software suites and also in its own software package. A copy of Outlook 2000 is also included with Exchange 2000 Server when you purchase it, but only one license is included, so you must purchase additional licenses for the systems you plan to use it on.

Although installing Outlook 2000 is an easy affair, configuring it after the fact can be a different matter, but you will learn about configuration in the "Configuring Outlook 2000" section later in this chapter. As an administrator, you should be aware of a variety of installation choices, including the ability to use custom installation files to install Outlook 2000 with a set configuration, similar to the unattended installation you learned about in Chapter 5, "Installation of Exchange 2000 Server in New Environments."

Later in this chapter in the Hands-on Projects section, you will learn how to install Outlook 2000 in a step-by-step fashion; for now, you'll learn about the various options and settings that best prepare you to roll out Outlook 2000 to your PCs.

Most applications now have an easy-to-use setup installation wizard. Outlook 2000 is no different, and starting the Outlook 2000 installation process is as simple as inserting the installation CD in your CD-ROM drive and letting the installation program run. However, you should be aware of the software's minimum requirements before attempting an Outlook 2000/2002 installation on any PC:

- A PC with a Pentium 133 MHz or faster processor
- 32 MB of RAM installed (if using Windows 2000, 64 MB of RAM is required)
- At least 135 MB of hard drive space on the drive where Outlook 2000 is installed, plus an additional 115 MB of hard drive space on the drive where the operating system is installed to make room for swap files and additional support software and drivers
- Windows 98 or later OS (Windows NT 4.0 must have SP6a installed)

Note that the amount of hard drive space required can change depending on the operating system you're using. For more details on hardware requirements, visit *http://www.microsoft.com/office/previous/outlook/2000Tour/SysReqs.htm*. Outlook 2002 requirements are slightly higher; for more information, check out *http://www.microsoft.com/office/outlook/evaluation/sysreq.htm*.

After you have assessed the current requirements and are ready to proceed with the installation, insert the Outlook 2000 installation CD-ROM or start the setup from the hard drive or network share where the software resides. Next, you're greeted with the new Windows Installer application that was implemented with Office 2000 products (including Outlook 2000). With the Windows Installer, an administrator has an even wider array of options and methods to customize the installation of Microsoft software. For every single component of the Outlook 2000 installation package, an administrator can select the installation method that component performs during installation. These are the main selections that can be made for each component:

- *Install component to run from hard drive*—The typical option for component installation (called "Run from My Computer" in the dialog box); most administrators select this option for nearly every component.
- *Install component to run from CD*—A useful option when users are accessing the component only rarely or if minimal hard drive space is available (called "Run from CD" in the dialog box). This option is not recommended unless absolutely necessary, however, because the CD must be in the drive to run the software, and because of the typical system slowness you experience when accessing the software from the CD-ROM drive.
- *Install component to run from network (from a shared installation)*—A useful option for installations in which users access the software from a terminal workstation or a system with minimal available hard drive space.
- *Install component on first use*—A rather handy option that installs the component only when the user actually tries to access it (called "Installed on First Use" in the dialog box). If the user never tries to use the component, there's no need to install the component; if the user does install it, however, you might need to help the user complete the installation with the appropriate installation media or location.
- *Do not install component*—An option (called "Not Available" in the dialog box) that allows the component to be manually installed later by using the Add/Remove utility in the Control Panel.

The Windows Installer is easy to use and allows you to quickly set the various options, as shown in Figure 7-8.

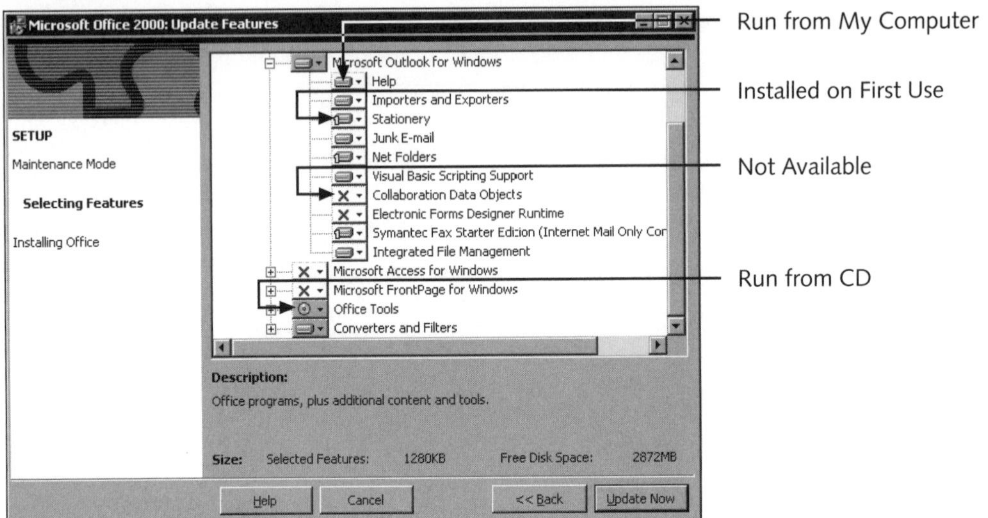

Figure 7-8 The Microsoft Windows Installer interface

After you have applied the component settings and are satisfied with your installation settings, Windows Installer takes over and copies the software to your system and applies the components you selected to the installation. After the file copying and system configuration have taken place, start Outlook 2000. In the Outlook Startup Wizard, click the Next button twice. You then choose from three different e-mail configuration options for this Outlook 2000 installation. These configuration options, described in the following list, dictate which features the user has access to and how Outlook 2000 functions:

The components you selected during the initial installation do not have any effect on the available configuration options during this part of the installation.

- *Internet Only*—Allows Outlook 2000 to function solely as an Internet e-mail client. It also enables the user to take advantage of the calendars, contacts, and other basic features, but Outlook 2000 cannot interact with advanced Exchange 2000 services, such as public folders. This installation method is useful for someone working from home who uses Outlook 2000 for personal e-mail, but wants the option to retrieve mail from work as well.
- *Corporate or Workgroup*—Allows Outlook 2000 to be utilized with an Exchange 2000 server and take advantage of all the installation's components. This installation also enables you to create other e-mail accounts that use Internet connections, such as POP3 or IMAP4. This configuration option should be the type of installation used for networks with Exchange 2000.
- *No E-mail*—Allows Outlook 2000 to act as a standalone contact-management software package with access only to the calendar, contacts, tasks, and scheduler functions. There is no support for Exchange features or any kind of Internet e-mail connectivity.

To continue the installation, select the configuration you want Outlook 2000 to use by clicking the radio button to the left of the option, as shown in Figure 7-9, and then click the Next button to proceed with the installation.

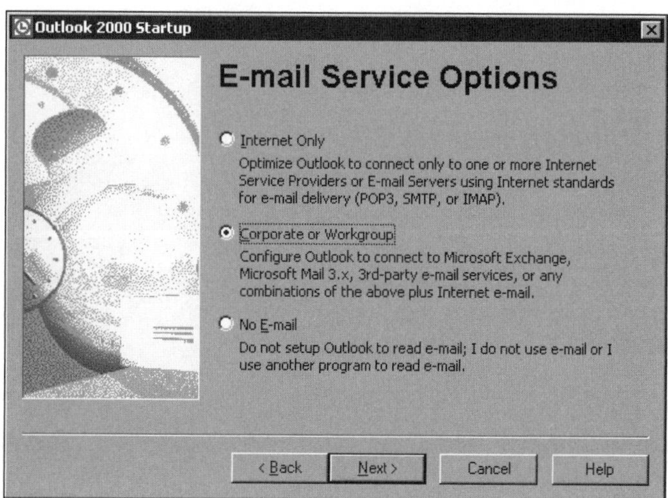

Figure 7-9 The E-mail Service Options window in Outlook 2000 Startup

Next, you enter the account information for the user. If the system is operating in Internet Only mode, you must enter the name, e-mail address, server information, and optionally a user name and password. You can enter only one e-mail account during the initial installation phase; however, you can enter any additional e-mail accounts you require after you have set up and started Outlook 2000. If you selected the Corporate or Workgroup option, you need to select the information service (Microsoft Exchange Server), and then click the Next button. Next, you must specify the user name and Exchange 2000 Server address or the resolved domain name of the Exchange 2000 Server. After you have entered the appropriate account information, click the Next button to specify whether you will travel with this computer (more on offline use later in this chapter). Leave it at the default option (No), and click Next to finish the installation.

It is important to have the correct user name and server information when entering the account information for the Corporate or Workgroup option because if either the account or the server name (or both) is wrong, you cannot finish the installation properly, and you are forced to cancel it. You must enter the information before you can start to use Outlook 2000; if you haven't, the first time you attempt to start Outlook 2000, a dialog box opens asking you to enter the information.

As you can see, basic Outlook 2000 installation is fairly straightforward; however, a few different types of installations (although a little more involved as far as necessary steps) can be quite useful, especially when you need to perform multiple installations. Often, the most tedious task for administrators or IT staff is the repetitive installation of software on new systems or the upgrading of software on existing systems. Outlook 2000 offers a few time-saving features that can help beleaguered administrators and IT staff recover some of the lost time spent installing software such as Outlook 2000; these time-saving features are command-line switches, setup information files, and the Office Custom Installation Wizard.

Command-Line Switches

Command-line switches are certainly not new to installation software; they have offered ways to customize how installations proceed for a long time. For most installations, command-line switches are not needed, but they definitely become necessary when you want to use two of the other installation features: setup information files and the Office Custom Installation Wizard. There are some additional switches that may or may not be handy for your particular needs; Table 7-2 outlines the switches and their uses.

Table 7-2 Command-Line Switches and Their Functions

Command Line Switch	Function
/a *<.msi file>*	Generates an administrative installation point for future client installations using an .msi file
/f [Option] *<.msi file>*	Starts Outlook in installation repair mode; options and an .msi file can be specified
/g *<Language ID>*	Allows you to specify the language for the installation; English is the default
/I *<.msi file>*	Specifies the .msi file to be used for the installation (not to be used with the /a switch)
/j [Option] *<.msi file>*	Generates an icon that can be used to install a feature not available during the initial installation configuration for the .msi file
/l [Option] *<LogFile>*	Specifies the log file used to log the installation
/x *<.msi file>*	Uninstalls a current Outlook 2000 installation
/q [Option]	Allows you to specify the level of onscreen information displayed during the installation
/wait	Instructs the installation to wait until the installation is finished before exiting the install
/settings	Specifies the path and settings file for automated installations, including the location of the .ini file generated during the setup information file process

Remember that the command-line switches are case sensitive, so make sure you match the capitalization in the table when using these switches. To get a more detailed list of command-line switches and some of their associated options, type the following at the command prompt for the folder where the Outlook 2000 setup files are located: setup.exe /?.

Setup Information File

By default, if a file called Setup.ini is in the same folder as the Setup.exe file for Outlook 2000 when you start Outlook 2000 Setup, Setup uses the information stored in this Setup.ini file for the installation. As you learned in the section "Command-Line Switches," you can specify the .ini file you want to use by starting Setup.exe with any of the switches listed in Table 7-2. You might want to use other .ini files to specify different configuration settings or to make it easier to enter long command-line switches without worrying about spelling mistakes. In addition, you can force specific options to be set even if the user or another installer is using the regular, interactive installation in which they can usually modify the settings and options during setup and installation.

Editing the .ini file is easy and can be done using any standard text editor, including Microsoft Word, Microsoft Notepad, or Microsoft WordPad. Every line in the .ini file is a different setting or part of the installation process that can be modified. An example of an Outlook 2000 .ini file can be seen in Figure 7-10. Note that in the Setup.ini file, semicolons (;) can be used to comment out lines that will be ignored by the installer. In the default Setup.ini file, there's more detailed information on each option and what it does; this information can be deleted in your custom Setup.ini file for the sake of organization or to make the file easier to read.

7

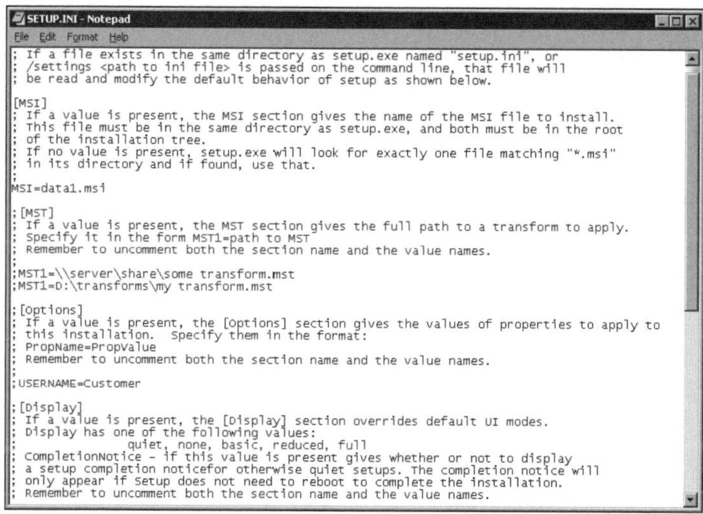


```
; If a file exists in the same directory as setup.exe named "setup.ini", or
; /settings <path to ini file> is passed on the command line, that file will
; be read and modify the default behavior of setup as shown below.

[MSI]
; If a value is present, the MSI section gives the name of the MSI file to install.
; This file must be in the same directory as setup.exe, and both must be in the root
; of the installation tree.
; If no value is present, setup.exe will look for exactly one file matching "*.msi"
; in its directory and if found, use that.
;
MSI=data1.msi

;[MST]
; If a value is present, the MST section gives the full path to a transform to apply.
; Specify it in the form MST1=path to MST
; Remember to uncomment both the section name and the value names.
;
;MST1=\\server\share\some transform.mst
;MST1=D:\transforms\my transform.mst

;[Options]
; If a value is present, the [Options] section gives the values of properties to apply to
; this installation.  Specify them in the format:
; PropName=PropValue
; Remember to uncomment both the section name and the value names.
;
;USERNAME=Customer

;[Display]
; If a value is present, the [Display] section overrides default UI modes.
; Display has one of the following values:
;                quiet, none, basic, reduced, full
; CompletionNotice - if this value is present gives whether or not to display
; a setup completion noticefor otherwise quiet setups. The completion notice will
; only appear if Setup does not need to reboot to complete the installation.
; Remember to uncomment both the section name and the value names.
```

Figure 7-10 A sample Outlook 2000 Setup.ini file

If you do decide to use Microsoft Word, Microsoft WordPad, or Notepad to edit the .ini file, make sure that when you save changes to the file, you save it as a text file with the .ini extension, with no other extensions on the end. Often these programs attempt to change the file format or add their file extension (.doc) to the end of the file, which the Outlook 2000 installer cannot understand.

Office Custom Installation Wizard

The Office Custom Installation Wizard can be used to generate custom installations of not only Microsoft Office 2000, but also any component of Microsoft Office 2000, including Outlook 2000. The Office Custom Installation Wizard is a powerful installation configuration utility that allows you to adjust and set almost every single aspect of the installation process. The following list outlines some of the installation settings you can set with the wizard:

- Client installation path
- Certain options to be hidden during setup
- Alternative network servers to install from if the main installation point is not available
- Component installation options
- Additional software to be installed after Outlook has finished, including non-Microsoft software, such as Adobe Acrobat
- Custom Windows Registry settings
- Specific Outlook 2000 desktop shortcuts to be created, including the icon used for the shortcut
- Default options, such as changing the default folder view in Outlook

The Office Custom Installation Wizard is a separate software utility, not part of the standard Office 2000 or Outlook 2000 package. You can get the wizard only from the Microsoft Office 2000 Resource Kit or the Office 2000 Resource Kit Web site under the "Office Resource Kit core tool set" heading at *http://www.microsoft.com/office/ork/2000/appndx/toolbox.htm*.

There is a fourth option available for creating custom installations; however, it is outside the scope of this book. **Systems Management Server (SMS)** is a specialized Microsoft application that enables large-scale deployment of software and configuration over networks. SMS requires additional knowledge and ability to properly implement it, and should only be considered if you have a medium to large network (more than 500 users).

Configuring Outlook 2000

After you have successfully installed Outlook 2000, set the appropriate configuration options, and included the default information that the installation program requests (user name, server, and so on), you are finally ready to enter Outlook 2000 and start making modifications to its configuration. Almost every feature in Outlook 2000 has one or more options that can be set. Among the more important options are the account configuration settings and the settings that control how Outlook 2000 handles e-mail and other important tasks. The majority of these settings can be altered or set under Options on the Tools menu and in the Control Panel Mail configuration menu.

In the Options menu, you set what Outlook 2000 looks like and how it functions; in the Mail configuration menu, you configure mailboxes, accounts, offline folders, and the back-end information Outlook 2000 needs to supply the data users require. Creating an offline folder can be especially useful if you use Outlook 2000 on a laptop computer that's used away from the office or when you're connected to the network for only a short time.

By using an offline folder, you can connect to the network and Exchange Server and download any new mail, tasks, messages, and information and take them with you. While disconnected, you can work with the data, reply to messages, and create new messages, and then after reconnecting to the network and the Exchange 2000 server, you can go online and send any data or messages and download any new information. If you do not use an offline folder configuration in this type of environment, you lose access to the data stored in your Inbox, public folders, and so on as soon as you disconnect from the network and Exchange 2000 Server.

Using Outlook 2000 offline is very similar to using it online. You can view any folders or calendars you would normally see online; however, if you haven't synchronized these folders, you cannot see any of the information contained in them. If you have synchronized these folders, then using Outlook is just like being directly connected to the Exchange 2000 server, except that you cannot retrieve new information or send out any messages until you have connected to the server again. Any messages you have created or replied to are held in the Outlook 2000 Outbox. To configure Outlook 2000 to synchronize data in your mailboxes and public folders so that you can retain information offline and then transfer the data back when you are online again is a fairly simple task. By default, the main folders are synchronized once the offline folders are configured; however, if you have created subfolders under the main folders (Inbox, Deleted Items, Calendars, Sent Items, Outbox, Journal, Tasks, Notes, and Contacts), then you must manually specify that those folders be synchronized.

Synchronizing folders in Outlook 2000 is a concern only if you are using Outlook 2000 with Exchange 2000. When Outlook 2000 has been configured with the Internet Only option for e-mail (to an Exchange 2000 server or another type of e-mail server) or the No E-mail option, Outlook retains all information in the various folders locally on the hard drive. Because of this, setting up Outlook 2000 to transfer data when not connected is not an issue.

The basic steps for adjusting the offline folder settings are as follows:

1. Open Outlook 2000.
2. Select the folder you want to make available offline (for instance, Inbox).
3. Click **Tools** on the menu bar at the top of the screen, point to **Synchronize**, and then click **Offline Folder Settings** on the shortcut menu.

4. If offline access has not been configured, Outlook asks if you want to configure an offline folder so that you can enable offline access to the folder. Click **Yes** to open the Offline Folder File Settings dialog box. Select where you want the offline file to reside (the default location is usually fine), and then click **OK**. Outlook informs you that it cannot find the .pst file you specified and asks if you want it created; click **Yes**.
5. The Offline Folder Settings dialog box opens; select which folders you want to enable for offline synchronization, as shown in Figure 7-11. In this dialog box, you can also change how and what Outlook synchronizes by using the Settings and Download Options buttons.
6. After you have finished setting the options you want, click **OK**, and the folders are ready to go and enabled for offline synchronization. To synchronize them, click **Tools** on the menu bar, point to **Synchronize**, and then click This Folder, to synchronize the folder you have selected, or All Folders, to synchronize every folder you have set up for offline use.

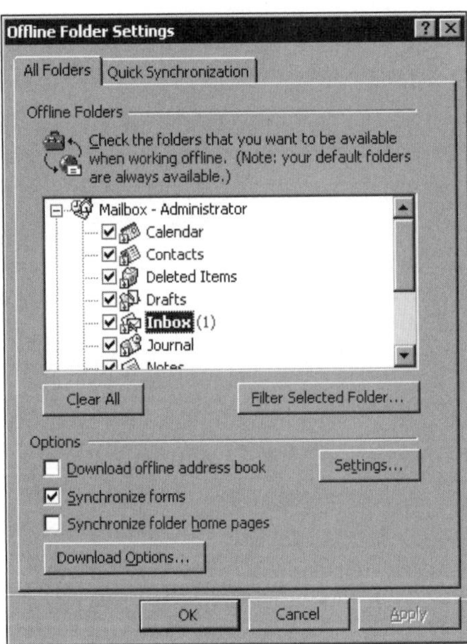

Figure 7-11 The Offline Folder Settings dialog box

After you have specified folders for offline synchronization, you will notice a small white-and-blue icon in the lower-left corner of the folder icon. Folders can also be set to automatically synchronize instead of forcing users to synchronize manually, which can be handy, especially if a substantial amount of data needs to be synchronized or if the user is forgetful.

There are many configuration options in Outlook 2000 that pertain to its appearance or even how it sorts messages (using the Organize feature to sort messages based on rules). If you want more information on these options, use Microsoft Outlook Help by pressing the F1 key to bring up the Help menu.

Remote Access Using Outlook 2000

While you're online and connected to an Exchange 2000 server, Outlook 2000 operates straightforwardly; configuring Outlook 2000 to function offline is slightly different, but not difficult. When using Outlook 2000 offline from Exchange 2000 (meaning not directly connected to the Exchange 2000 server on the network), you can configure offline synchronization with the Exchange 2000 server.

To do that, first connect to the Exchange network and configure folders for offline synchronization as you did earlier in "Configuring Outlook 2000"; however, you must have a network connection established that allows you to connect to the Exchange server via a virtual private network (VPN) or dial-up connection. With these types of connections, you have support for all the Exchange 2000 functionality via a direct remote connection; however, if you do use a dial-up connection, synchronizing data between the client and Exchange 2000 server can be rather slow.

Outlook 2000, like Outlook Express, can be configured as an Internet e-mail only client and be set up to retrieve mail from Exchange 2000 through SMTP or IMAP4, but then you lose some functionality of Exchange 2000 and Outlook 2000. This option can be useful for users who don't need access to the additional features or who are using Outlook mainly for e-mail access when they are at remote locations. The Internet Email Properties dialog box, shown in Figure 7-12, is used to configure these options for remote users.

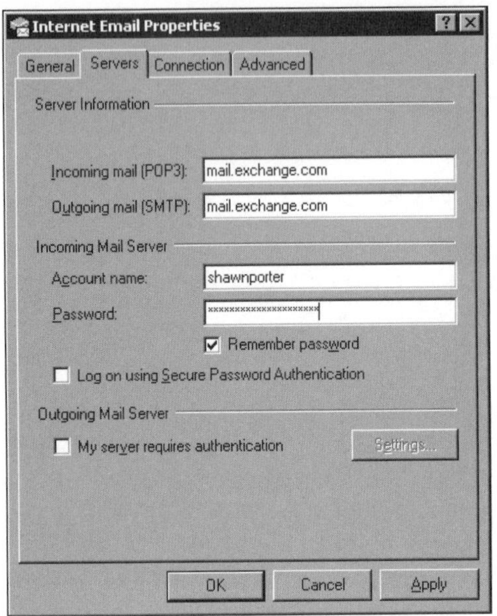

Figure 7-12 The Internet Email Properties dialog box

CONFIGURING MESSAGING PROFILES

Outlook 2000 can have multiple users configured to use the services in Outlook 2000; to do that, you set up multiple user profiles in Outlook 2000. The profiles you make are stored client side, not managed by Exchange 2000. Profiles are especially useful for offline use because you can create a separate logon account for each user, thus keeping configurations, settings, and preferences in individual profiles.

After you have two or more profiles created and have configured Outlook to show the profile selection dialog box at startup, a profile selection dialog box opens when you start Outlook 2000 and asks which profile you want to use for that session. If you select a user's profile that you do not have the rights to access, Outlook 2000 informs you that you do not have the rights to view information in that profile and asks if you want to open the default system profile, which opens the information within My Computer in the main Outlook 2000 window. When using multiple profiles with Exchange 2000, each profile being used on the server must have an account on the Exchange 2000 server and have a properly configured mailbox. The profile configuration data is still held on the client system, but the e-mail, calendar, and other data is, as usual, retained on the Exchange 2000 server.

Configuring multiple message profiles is quick and easy. When you first launch Outlook 2000 and enter the necessary configuration information, you are essentially creating a profile for yourself (or the user); after Outlook has this configuration information, you can go about creating more profiles. The following list is a basic outline of how to configure an additional profile:

The options in this list are available only if you have selected the Corporate or Workgroup option during the initial Outlook 2000 setup.

1. Ensure that Outlook 2000 is closed, and then open the mail configuration window. (Click **Start**, point to **Settings**, click **Control Panel**, and double-click **Mail**.)
2. In the initial window, click the **Show Profiles** button to open the profile setup dialog box shown in Figure 7-13.

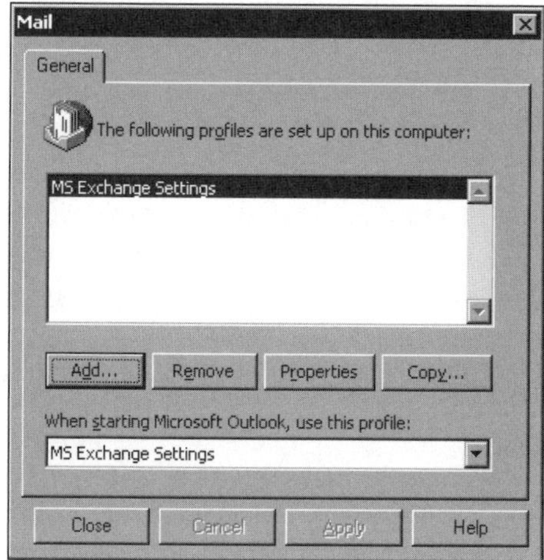

Figure 7-13 The Mail dialog box used for configuring Outlook 2000 accounts and settings

3. Click the **Add** button, and the Microsoft Outlook Setup Wizard opens, as it did for your initial Outlook 2000 configuration and installation. Select the type of account you want to create (Microsoft Exchange Server or Internet e-mail), and click the **Next** button to proceed.
4. On the following screens, enter the appropriate server, user, and other pertinent information to create an additional profile. Click **Close** in the mail configuration window, and then open Outlook 2000. By default, Outlook opens the default profile that was configured. If you attempt to open the other profile but do not have rights to that user's account, you cannot open Outlook.
5. To configure Outlook 2000 to prompt for a profile at startup, open Outlook and click **Tools**, **Options** on the menu bar. In the Options dialog box, select the **Mail Services** tab, and then under the Startup settings section, click the **Prompt** for a profile to be used radio button. The next time you start Outlook, the Choose Profile window, as shown in Figure 7-14, appears.

Figure 7-14 Selecting a profile to use in Outlook 2000

Configuring Outlook 2000 to request which Outlook profile should be used is far more useful under Windows 95, 98, or Me when it is being used with an Internet e-mail configuration with multiple users because those operating systems do not have the type of security model that Windows NT and Windows 2000 do. Under Windows 9x and 98/ Me operating systems, there's no requirement to log on; therefore, allowing users to select which profile they want to use is a good idea security-wise because it forces users to authenticate themselves before they can log on to a particular mailbox.

With Windows NT or Windows 2000, on the other hand, you cannot open Outlook with a profile that's not associated with your logon account unless you specify that the other profile can have access to your mailbox data, a setting that must be configured in the target profile itself. When you grant permission to other users to access all or individual components of your mailbox, they can open your mailbox or the selected components as though they were you. To set permissions for a particular folder, simply right-click the folder, select Properties on the shortcut menu, click the Permissions tab, and then set the appropriate permissions; an example of the Permissions tab can be seen in Figure 7-15.

An administrator can also set these permissions for multiple users to access a particular mailbox. These permissions are set on the Exchange Advanced Configuration tab for the mailbox in question without the administrator having to bother the users involved; the next time the users log on to Outlook 2000, the changes are in effect. Assigning permissions to other users' mailboxes can be quite useful. For instance, administrative assistants who must maintain their bosses' e-mail, calendar, or task information when the boss is out of the office can access the information they need without the boss having to give out sensitive password information or the assistant having to use the boss's system—a great timesaver!

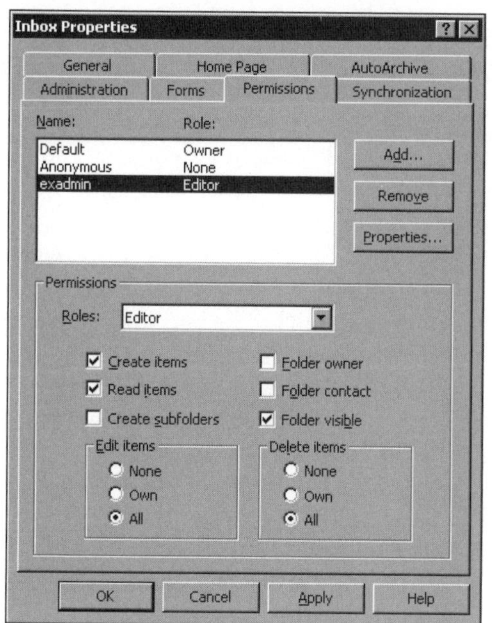

Figure 7-15 The Inbox Properties dialog box

Forcing Outlook 2000 to request a profile can also be useful with Windows NT or Windows 2000; for instance, a user could check mail with a separate Internet e-mail configured account, with personal configuration and data, but have the profile configured for offline use, whereas his or her "regular" Exchange profile is not. This concept can also be applied to a shared laptop that has profiles configured for each user who uses the laptop to access e-mail; each user can have his or her own settings and information to use while on the road.

There are many different methods and options for configuring Outlook 2000 profiles, certainly more than what can be covered in this chapter. For more information and setup tips on profiles, refer to the Microsoft Outlook Help by pressing the F1 key.

TROUBLESHOOTING COMMON OUTLOOK 2000 PROBLEMS

As with any other software product on the market, a time will come when you must troubleshoot an Outlook 2000 installation. Problems can vary from simple user issues to problems synchronizing folders to users accidentally deleting e-mail. Some other likely troubleshooting candidates are security issues related to permissions and connectivity with both Exchange and Internet e-mail services. Some of the problems that arise have been covered in the previous sections on "Configuring Outlook 2000" and "Configuring Messaging Profiles"; the next three sections outline some of the more common troubleshooting issues in Outlook 2000, including recovery of deleted items, permissions-related issues, and synchronizing offline data.

Recovery of Deleted Items

A common problem among users is inadvertently deleting one or more e-mail messages and emptying the Deleted Items folder while cleaning out their Inbox or Sent Items folder. In most other applications, such as Windows operating systems, after you have emptied the Deleted Items folder (Recycle Bin), the information is, for all intents and purposes, gone. However, Exchange 2000 Server enables you to recover deleted items even if they have been emptied from the Deleted Items folder. To locate and restore the deleted items, follow these steps:

1. First, make sure Outlook 2000 is open. Select the **Deleted Items** folder from the Folder List.
2. Click **Tools**, **Recover Deleted Items** on the menu bar. You might have to expand the menu by clicking the small down arrow at the bottom of the menu to reveal infrequently used commands. The Recover Deleted Items From dialog box opens, as shown in Figure 7-16.

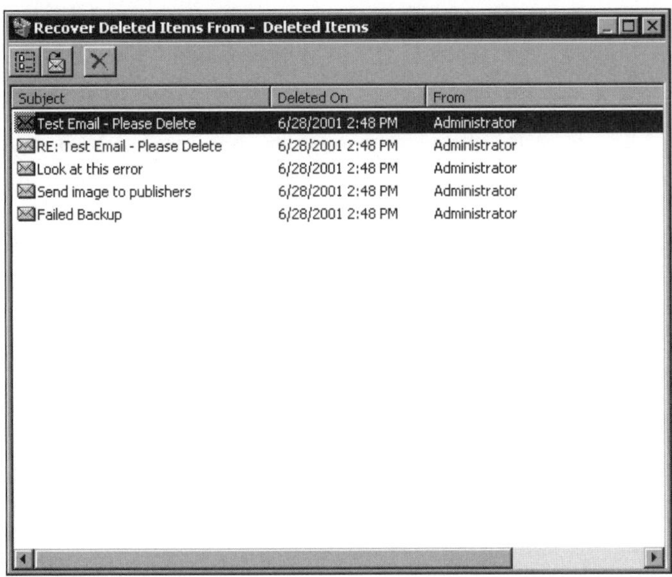

Figure 7-16 The Recover Deleted Items From dialog box

3. As you can see in Figure 7-16, messages have been deleted but are still retained. To restore a message (or folder, task, and so on), simply select the ones you want to restore, and then click the **Recover Selected Items** button (the little yellow envelope icon). The messages are then restored to the Deleted Items folder in Outlook 2000, and you can move the messages to the appropriate folder.

By default, Exchange 2000 allows deleted items to be retained for 0 days, which means that as soon as a user deletes the item, it's gone. It's up to the administrator to set the retention time for deleted items; typically, 14 days is enough. You use System Manager to configure this setting for each mailbox store managed in the domain. If the administrator has set message retention to a particular number of days, the deleted items are purged from the system after the specified day and cannot be recovered unless you restore the information from a known good backup with the data intact.

Recovery of messages and items deleted accidentally by users does not have to be a crisis and can be easily managed if the appropriate feature is enabled in the mailbox store on the Exchange 2000 server. If this feature is not enabled or if the time for retaining items and messages held by Exchange has lapsed, your only choice is to restore the information from backup.

Permissions-Related Issues

Most permissions-related issues that you or users come across are the direct result of users simply not having the appropriate rights within their own user accounts. As you learned previously, when a user tries to access another user's mailbox or profile, he or she is likely not allowed access to it; however, this can be resolved by having the mailbox owner delegate rights to the other user or by having the administrator set up the permission in the Active Directory Users and Computers console. Many other potential permissions-related issues exist, but most solutions for them simply require the administrator to adjust the rights according to what the user needs access to.

It's a good idea to confirm or confer with the user in question or the manager of the department to make sure that the user should have rights to the information he or she is requesting. Instead of simply giving users rights as soon as they request them, it might be wiser to ask questions first and fix problems later so that you do not give a user access to inappropriate information and get yourself in trouble.

Almost every function of Outlook 2000, especially the public folders, has enabled a security method in the form of rights or permissions to data or folders. Customizable security for items, folders, and data in Exchange 2000 is implemented so that different departments can have their own security settings for their data and make sure only the appropriate users are accessing the data. For instance, the Management Committee probably doesn't want bonus structure information posted to the public folders to be available to everyone; they want it to be available only to the Management Committee group and the Payroll Department group. Managing permissions for folders and mailboxes can be a time-consuming ordeal, but if your organization has guidelines and rules about how this issue should be handled, that will go a long way toward ensuring that you don't waste time—and do keep your sanity.

Problems Synchronizing Data

Even if the entire synchronization configuration has been performed properly and you have synchronized data correctly in the past, occasionally synchronization fails to work properly. This can happen when you're reconnecting to Exchange 2000 Server and, even more so, when you are performing the synchronization over a slower connection such as a dial-up modem.

If you encounter a problem with synchronizing data and folders in Outlook 2000 with one of your users, you are not going to be left in the dark. Whenever synchronization fails, it leaves a synchronization error log file in the Deleted Items folder. This log file gives the time of the failure, the successful synchronization information, and any error information related to the synchronization process. This information can assist in troubleshooting the actual cause of the problem. Not every log file includes useful information, but the error information is a step in the right direction. An example of a synchronization log is shown in Figure 7-17.

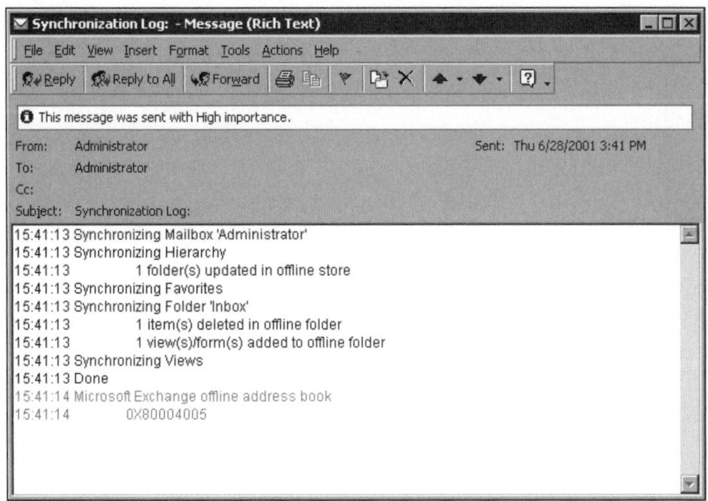

Figure 7-17 A sample synchronization error log message

Even if synchronization fails, it could have been a minor interruption that caused the failure, so first simply try to perform the synchronization again by selecting the folder in question, clicking Tools on the menu bar, and choosing the appropriate action from the Synchronization menu. If this method fails again, it might be the result of a bigger problem, and you should check the error logs in Outlook for more information and then check the connection to the Exchange server, whether it's a dial-up connection or a connection through the network. If all else fails, try deleting the offline folder, re-creating the profile from scratch, and trying again; quite often this method can rectify a wide variety of problems in Outlook 2000.

During synchronization, if Outlook determines that your connection is too slow, it automatically stops the synchronization process so as not to slow down Outlook 2000 or make it become entirely unresponsive to user input.

CHAPTER SUMMARY

- Exchange 2000 supports a wide variety of different client software packages, although not every software package can take advantage of the multitude of features Exchange 2000 offers. The different versions of Outlook (98, 2000, XP) represent the best client software when you want to use the advanced collaboration features of Exchange 2000, but other useful client software exists that fills gaps the various Outlook versions cannot fill.

- Client software like Outlook Express provides essential services such as e-mail access to Exchange 2000, with the addition of a useful newsgroup reader and basic access to Exchange 2000 public folders. Client software such as OWA gives you access to many Outlook-supported features—public folders, contacts, tasks, and so on—from any PC with a current Web browser and Internet access, requiring no additional software or configuration.
- Exchange 2000 still supports client access from 16-bit clients, such as the Exchange Client and Schedule+. Although both of these clients are supported, development and improvement to them have stopped, so you should upgrade to Outlook 2000 to get more advanced features.
- Exchange 2000 supports a wide variety of third-party clients as long as they support SMTP or IMAP4. Although these clients are limited to sending and receiving e-mail, they do help provide access for platforms that do not support Outlook or Outlook Express client software.
- The standardized MAPI architecture supported by the Windows operating systems makes it much easier for any application, e-mail or otherwise, to provide e-mail and messaging support. Programmers can include MAPI support in a wide range of applications, client access programs, personal information managers, and more.
- Installing Outlook 2000 is quick and easy. You have a wide range of options for customizing your Outlook 2000 installation and many ways to implement customized installations that require minimal to no user intervention. The ability to develop preconfigured installation packages with the Office Custom Installation Wizard can be a boon to administrators who have to install Outlook on several systems.
- Outlook 2000 configuration has many features, options, and settings that can be applied, which makes it customizable to suit your user's needs and requirements. Outlook 2000 can be configured to access information both locally on the network from the Exchange 2000 server and offline through the Exchange 2000 server and a VPN or dial-up connection.
- Messaging profiles can be handy when you have multiple users on one PC or when you have different accounts for different e-mail services that you want to keep separate from each other. The user must have the appropriate permissions to connect to another user's mailbox or profile.
- Common troubleshooting issues that happen while using Outlook 2000 are typically related to accidental deletions, permissions-related problems, and data synchronization problems. Setting the appropriate permissions or using the Recover Deleted Items utility can quickly and easily correct most of these problems. Synchronization issues can be harder to sort out, but are often caused by slow connections to the Exchange 2000 server.

Key Terms

16-bit clients — Older client software packages that have been created for 16-bit operating systems, such as Windows 3.1 or Windows 3.11 for Workgroups. Windows NT and Windows 2000 are both 32-bit operating systems that support 16-bit applications for backward-compatibility. Although 16-bit clients function on 32-bit operating systems, they tend to not perform as well as 32-bit clients.

Active Desktop — A useful feature that enables the Windows desktop to display HTML information and pages, including JPEG images as background files and active content such as the digital dashboard.

beta testing — A phase in software development and testing during which users test for functionality and bugs in the software and provide feedback to the software publisher to help resolve user issues and bugs in the software.

digital dashboard — A high-tech HTML document that allows you to include active content from various sources, such as other Web pages, Outlook, and similar Microsoft Office applications. An example of a digital dashboard is the Outlook Today interface.

Messaging Application Programming Interface (MAPI) — A core messaging and e-mail component of Windows operating systems that follows the industry standard for writing messages and e-mail.

Systems Management Server (SMS) — A specialized Microsoft application that enables large-scale deployment of software and configuration over networks.

Review Questions

1. If you use third-party client software packages, you typically do not have access to Exchange 2000 services such as ________________.
2. Which of the following e-mail client software packages support complete functionality with Exchange 2000? (Choose all that apply.)
   a. Outlook Express
   b. Outlook 98
   c. Outlook 2000/2002
   d. Outlook Web Access
3. Which of the following clients support access to Exchange 2000 e-mail through the Internet? (Choose all that apply.)
   a. Outlook 2000
   b. Outlook Web Access
   c. Outlook Express
   d. Eudora 5.x

4. Which operating systems can use Outlook Web Access to connect to an Exchange 2000 server? (Choose all that apply.)
   a. Windows
   b. UNIX
   c. Macintosh
   d. DOS
5. If your users needed the following list of features—calendars, public folders, and task lists—which software package would you recommend to support these features?
6. The two programs that provided the core functionality in Outlook 2000 were ________________ and ________________.
7. From the following list, what improvements does Outlook XP (2002) offer over Outlook 2000? (Choose all that apply.)
   a. single-step publishing of team calendars to a Web page
   b. support for POP3
   c. use of Outlook contacts to perform mail merges
   d. introduction of Outlook Today
8. Outlook Today supports the ability to customize the content displayed when a user accesses the page. True or False?
9. What type of programming language is used to create and provide content to a digital dashboard such as Outlook Today?
   a. Active Desktop
   b. C++
   c. HTML
   d. Pascal
10. Outlook Today can be integrated into ________________ to supply links directly to Outlook 2000/2002 information.
11. Why is it a good idea to upgrade Outlook 97 to Outlook 98 or higher? (Choose all that apply.)
   a. Outlook 98, 2000, and XP all include new features and improvements to existing features.
   b. Outlook 97 has known bugs and issues related to stability and performance.
   c. Outlook 97 is outdated and does not support most Exchange 2000 Server features.
   d. Outlook 97 is a 16-bit client software package that doesn't run well on Windows NT or Windows 2000 operating systems.

12. Which feature does Outlook Express have that sets it apart from other third-party Internet e-mail client software packages?
    a. faster downloads of e-mail messages
    b. direct access to Exchange 2000 inboxes
    c. ability to connect to Exchange 2000 using IMAP4
    d. use of the newsgroup reader to access the Exchange 2000 public folders
13. In the following list of statements, which one is true about Outlook Web Access?
    a. OWA requires configuration on the remote client system.
    b. OWA supports a wider range of features than Outlook 2000 does.
    c. OWA provides only basic e-mail messaging functionality.
    d. OWA supports text-based Web browsers.

14. Which of the following software packages are examples of 16-bit clients? (Choose all that apply.)
    a. Exchange Client
    b. Outlook Express
    c. Schedule+
    d. Eudora
15. MAPI provides an industry-supported method for incorporating e-mail and messaging features in various software packages. True or False?
16. Which of the following Outlook configuration types does not support calendars, scheduling, and tasks?
    a. Internet Only
    b. Corporate or Workgroup
    c. No E-mail
    d. none of the above
17. What information is required when setting up an account for Internet e-mail access in Outlook 2000? (Choose all that apply.)
    a. user name
    b. password
    c. server address
    d. e-mail address
18. Which Setup.exe command-line switch should you use to start an installation of Outlook 2000 using a custom Setup.ini file?
    a. /x
    b. /I
    c. /settings
    d. /a

19. The software package you can use to edit your custom Setup.ini file is ________________.
20. The Office Custom Installation Wizard allows you to install additional non-Microsoft software after the Outlook 2000 installation is completed. True or False?
21. If you wanted to allow users to work with information in the folders on the Exchange 2000 server while offline, which feature would you configure?
22. Which of the following connection types allows you to connect to your Exchange 2000 server using Outlook 2000 while away from the office? (Choose all that apply.)
    a. network connection
    b. VPN
    c. dial-up
    d. OWA
23. If an assistant needed access to her boss's mailbox, what would you, as the mail administrator, have to do to give her access to the boss's Exchange 2000 mailbox?
24. Which of the following are common troubleshooting issues when using Outlook 2000 with an Exchange 2000 mailbox? (Choose all that apply.)
    a. Users accidentally delete messages.
    b. Folder synchronization fails because of a slow connection.
    c. You cannot create an Internet e-mail connection.
    d. The user does not have proper permissions to access an item or folder in public folders.
25. Where does Outlook 2000 place an error log when synchronization fails on a folder?
    a. Inbox
    b. Sent Items folder
    c. Deleted Items folder
    d. Synchronized Items folder

Hands-on Projects

Project 7-1

Configuring Outlook Express is fairly straightforward, but it's good to know the ins and outs of creating an Internet e-mail access account in Outlook Express. With Outlook Express, you can install multiple Internet e-mail accounts and newsgroup accounts. In this project, you will also learn how to configure a basic Outlook Express e-mail rule that can come in handy to delete unwanted junk mail and to sort messages from certain people or messages with a particular subject into a custom folder.

To configure Outlook Express for Internet e-mail access:

1. If necessary, log on to your system. After the system has finished booting to the desktop, connect to the Internet (if you're automatically connected to the Internet by the network, ignore this step).
2. Locate and start Outlook Express by clicking **Start**, pointing to **Programs**, and then clicking **Outlook Express**.
3. Click **Tools** on the menu bar, and then click **Accounts** to open the Internet Accounts dialog box.
4. In the Internet Accounts dialog box, you can configure the different e-mail or newsgroup accounts you need. The All tab (as shown in Figure 7-18) lists every available connection, the Mail tab lists e-mail connections, the News tab lists newsgroup connections, and the Directory Service tab contains name lookup directory servers. Click the **Mail** tab.

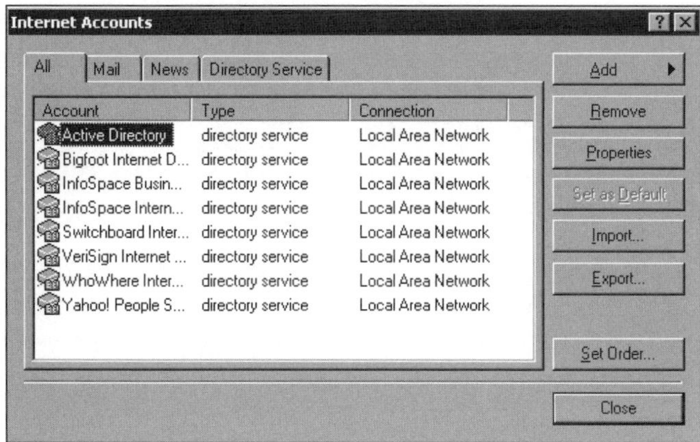

Figure 7-18 The Internet Accounts dialog box for Outlook Express

5. Click the **Add** button on the right side of the window, and then click **Mail** to open the Internet Connection Wizard. In the first window, you should enter your full name in the Display name box, and then click the **Next** button.
6. Enter your Internet e-mail address. If you already have an address provided by your instructor or your own personal account, enter the information in the e-mail address box in the format <*myname*>@<*emailprovider*>.com. If you do not have an account created yet, you can click the **I'd like to sign up for a new account from: Hotmail** option at the bottom of this window and follow the steps. If you have already entered your e-mail address information, click the **Next** button.
7. Enter the necessary information about the server, including its type and address. If the e-mail service you are using is Hotmail or a similar HTTP-type e-mail provider, make sure the My incoming mail server is a drop-down box that says HTTP. If the service you are using is a regular ISP or Exchange 2000 Server, select POP3

or IMAP (whichever the server supports, usually POP3), and proceed to Step 8. If you have selected HTTP service, click the appropriate type in the My HTTP mail service provider is drop-down list. By default, Hotmail and MSN should be in the drop-down list; Outlook Express is already configured for both of them. If it's another provider, click **Other**, and in the Incoming mail text box, enter the address that corresponds to the HTTP e-mail provider's logon screen.

8. If you selected POP3 or IMAP4, you will have to enter the address information in the Incoming mail and Outgoing mail text boxes that appear when you select either of the server types. The server information is typically entered in the format mail.<*myserver*>.com. Each server can have its own address or both might be the same; find the information for your service before making any entries in this window. After entering the information, click the **Next** button.
9. Enter the appropriate logon information, including user name and password. Enter the appropriate account name in the Account name text box and optionally enter your password in the Password text box. Notice the check box underneath the Password field that you can toggle to have Outlook Express remember your e-mail password. Either select or deselect this check box, and click the **Next** button. The last window indicates that creating the account was successful; click **Finish** to complete the Internet Connection Wizard.
10. Click **Close** in the Internet Accounts window to bring you back to the main Outlook Express window. Try composing an e-mail and sending it to a lab partner and vice versa. The mail should come through (give it a minute or two); if not, click the **Send/Receive** button on the Standard toolbar in Outlook Express to force the transfer of messages to the server. If you do not get any messages from your lab partner or if your lab partner does not receive yours, check your respective settings, including server information, logon account, and password, and try again.
11. After you have successfully sent e-mail back and forth with your lab partner, close any open applications or windows.

Project 7-2

If you have a network with Exchange 2000 installed, there will undoubtedly come a time when you have to install Outlook 2000. The fundamental Outlook 2000 installation for use with Exchange 2000 is quick and easy, as long as you know what you want to install. In most cases, you should install every component available, especially for the first installation when you're testing functionality to see what the different features do. This lab assumes that you have access to a functioning Exchange 2000 mailbox, including the user name and server information for that mailbox. Exchange 2000 Server must be active and connected to the same domain and network as the system.

To install Outlook 2000:

1. If necessary, log on to your system. After the system has finished loading to the desktop, insert the Microsoft Office 2000 installation CD into the CD-ROM drive or open the folder where the installation files reside on your network or hard drive.
2. The installation should automatically start; if not, double-click **My Computer**, and then double-click the CD-ROM drive to start Setup. (If the installation wizard doesn't automatically start, double-click Setup.exe.) When the Microsoft Office 2000 Setup Wizard opens, click the **Next** button, enter the requisite user information, and then click the **Next** button again. In this window, accept the license agreement, and then click the **Next** button again.
3. In the Ready to Install window, click the **Customize** button; in the Installation Location window, click the **Next** button to accept the default installation path, bringing you to the Selecting Features window. Click the small hard drive icon with the down arrow for each option, and then click **Not Available** for each one except Microsoft Outlook for Windows. For the Microsoft Outlook for Windows option, click **Run all from My Computer**. After you have finished selecting the appropriate options, click the **Install Now** button in the lower-right corner of this window to start the copying and setup of Outlook 2000.
4. Copying should take a minute or two. After it's finished, a small window pops up explaining that Microsoft Office 2000 Setup was successful. Click **OK** to finish the installation.
5. If you are running Windows 9x, Windows NT, or Windows Me, you are asked to restart; if you are running Windows 2000 or XP, restarting isn't necessary. If you have to restart, do so, and when you're finished, leave the system at the desktop for Project 7-3.

If you are installing Outlook 2000 from the Outlook 2000 installation media, the installation methods are nearly identical, except that you do not have to set the other Office 2000 components to Not Available.

Project 7-3

When you first start Outlook 2000, you are prompted for information used to create your initial profile. Creating your second profile is very similar to creating the first one. Outlook 2000 profiles can be useful for storing individual configurations and data when you have multiple users accessing Outlook 2000 from the same computer, or if you have a user who accesses multiple mailboxes on behalf of others. Understanding how profiles are created can make administering this useful feature much easier in the long run. This lab assumes that you have access to two functioning Exchange 2000 mailboxes with the user name and server information for each mailbox. Exchange 2000 Server must be active and connected to the same domain and network as the system.

To configure a first and second profile in Outlook 2000:

1. Start with the system you configured in Project 7-2 that should still be powered on and booted to the desktop with a fresh installation of Outlook 2000. Double-click the **Microsoft Outlook** icon on the desktop to start the Outlook 2000 Startup Wizard. In the Welcome window, click the **Next** button to proceed with the configuration.
2. The E-mail Upgrade Options window opens, if Outlook Express is on the system. In the middle of this window you will see a box with the choices Outlook Express and None of the above (see Figure 7-19). Selecting Outlook Express allows you to migrate the configuration information in Outlook Express (if any) into Outlook 2000. Because you do not want to do this, click **None of the above**, and then click the **Next** button.

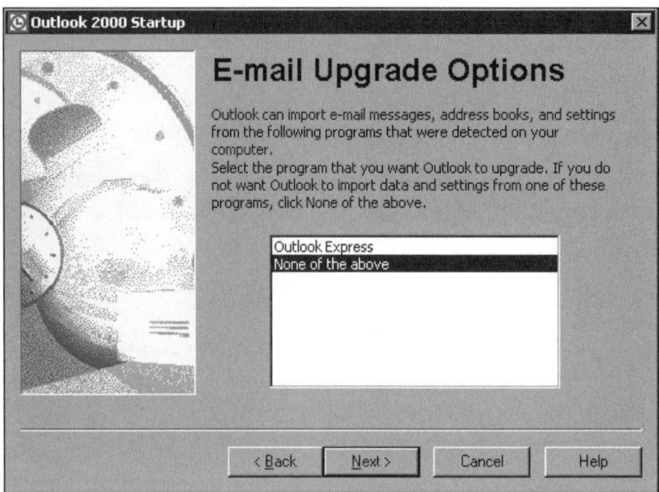

Figure 7-19 The E-mail Upgrade Options window in the Outlook 2000 Startup Wizard

3. The E-mail Service Options window appears, where you can select how Outlook 2000 will be configured. Your choices are Internet Only, Corporate or Workgroup, or No E-mail. Click the **Corporate or Workgroup** radio button, and then click the **Next** button to proceed to the Microsoft Outlook Setup Wizard.
4. In the Microsoft Outlook Setup Wizard, you can choose to configure either Microsoft Exchange Server or Internet E-mail. Click to select the **Microsoft Exchange Server** check box, and then click the **Next** button to proceed to the next window, where you enter the name of the Exchange server and the name of the mailbox you are connecting to. Enter this information (supplied by your instructor), and then click the **Next** button.

5. The next window asks if you travel with this computer. If you wanted to preconfigure the system to have all the various folders, Inbox, tasks, and so on set as offline folders that can be synchronized, you would click Yes to have Outlook configure this setting automatically. For this project, however, you do not want this option, so click the **No** radio button, and then click the **Next** button to proceed.
6. The final window outlines what was configured and tells you the installation was successful. Click **OK** and allow Outlook to finish setting up. When Outlook 2000 has finished loading, close the program and return to the desktop.
7. To add another profile, click **Start**, point to **Settings**, click **Control Panel**, and double-click **Mail**. You will see the settings for the default profile you just configured. To add a profile, click the **Show Profiles** button to open the Profile Manager dialog box. In this dialog box, you should see the default profile, probably called MS Exchange Settings. Click the **Add** button to start the Microsoft Outlook Setup Wizard again. Follow Steps 1–6 again, and enter the information (supplied by your instructor) for the second Exchange mailbox; when prompted to name the profile, enter **New Profile**.
8. Remember you can configure Outlook 2000 to ask which profile you want to use when it opens. To do this, follow the steps in the "Configuring Messaging Profiles" section earlier in this chapter. This is an optional step, to be performed if time allows.
9. Close all open windows and applications and return to the desktop. Leave the system at the desktop for Project 7-4.

Project 7-4

Configuring a profile in Outlook 2000 can be rather handy, especially when you have a user with one Exchange account with its own information and another account through a third-party ISP, and the user needs to keep this data separate. Configuring a profile for Internet e-mail can also be useful if this is the only type of e-mail service you have available. There is a wide array of possible reasons for having an Internet e-mail profile on its own or in addition to Exchange 2000, so knowing how to implement these types of connections is very useful.

To configure a profile for Internet e-mail in Outlook 2000:

1. Start with the system you configured in Project 7-3, which should still be powered on and booted to the desktop with an installation of Outlook 2000 and the two profiles. Click **Start**, point to **Settings**, click **Control Panel**, and double-click **Mail**. When the mail configuration window opens, you will see the settings for the profiles you just configured. Click the **Show Profiles** button.
2. In the Profile Configuration dialog box, you should see the profiles you created in Project 7-3. Click the **Add** button to start the Microsoft Outlook Setup Wizard.
3. In the Microsoft Outlook Setup Wizard, you can select the Microsoft Exchange Server or Internet E-mail option to configure. Click to select the **Internet E-mail**

check box, and then click the **Next** button to proceed to the next window, where you enter the name of the profile. Enter any name you like, such as "Internet Connection," and then click the **Next** button to continue.

4. Click the **Setup Mail Account** button in the center of the window to open the Mail Account Properties window. In the General tab, enter a name for the account in the top text box. Enter the other information in this tab, including the e-mail address for the account, based on what your instructor has provided.
5. Click the **Servers** tab, and enter the information your instructor supplies in the Incoming mail and Outgoing mail text boxes as well as the account name and password information for the logon account. Click the **Connection** tab and choose the type of network connection you'll use to connect to the Internet e-mail account: LAN, phone line, or manual connectivity. Your instructor should provide you with this information. Click the radio button next to the option you want, and then click **OK** to return to the Setup Mail Account window. Click the **Next** button.
6. The Personal Folders Selection window opens. The default location is fine unless you have a particular need to put it in a different location. Click the **Next** button to proceed to the Wizard Completion window, which outlines what was completed successfully. Click the **Finish** button to complete the wizard.
7. Close any open windows. As an optional step, start Outlook 2000 (preferably with Outlook 2000 requesting which profile to use). Using the new profile you just created, connect to the Internet e-mail account and test sending and receiving messages with a lab partner. If you haven't set up Outlook 2000 to request a profile when it starts, follow the steps outlined in the section "Configuring Messaging Profiles" earlier in this chapter.
8. Close any open windows or applications to return to the desktop, and leave the system running for Project 7-5.

Project 7-5

Outlook Today is a useful feature included with Outlook 2000 that can help users gauge their activities at a glance. Many users and administrators quickly disable Outlook Today before giving it a chance to shine. Most people don't realize that you can modify the information in Outlook Today to better customize your user experience. Understanding how the fundamental information can be changed can help make Outlook Today more useful for you and other users.

To modify Outlook Today settings in Outlook 2000:

1. Start with the system you configured in Project 7-4, which should still be powered on and loaded to the desktop with an installation of Outlook 2000 and the two profiles. When you are at the desktop, double-click the **Microsoft Outlook** icon on the desktop.
2. Locate and click **Outlook Today** (if it isn't already open) in the Folder List on the left side of the screen. Outlook Today is displayed on the right side of the window. Click the **Customize Outlook Today** button in the upper-right side of

the Outlook Today window. The Customize Outlook Today window opens and shows all the options you can change, as you can see in Figure 7-20.

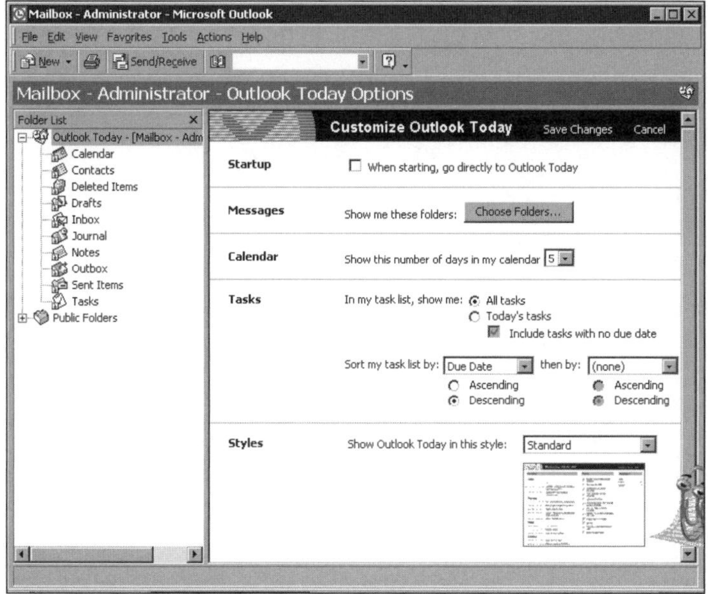

Figure 7-20 Outlook Today custom configuration options

3. Try modifying the different settings in the Startup, Messages, Calendars, and Tasks sections of Outlook Today.
4. In the Styles section of Outlook Today, click the list arrow to the right of the Styles drop-down list to display the five preset styles you can set for Outlook Today. Click the **Winter** style in the drop-down list, and then click the **Save Changes** button in the upper-right corner of the Customize Outlook Today window to ensure that the changes you made were saved.
5. After clicking the Save Changes button, you are returned to the main Outlook Today display, which should now reflect the changes you made. Try changing different settings to see what the changes look like in Outlook Today until you find a setting you like.
6. Close all open windows and applications.

Project 7-6

Beyond providing access to e-mail servers through a variety of protocols, such as POP3, SMTP, and IMAP4, Outlook Express can be configured to connect users to newsgroup servers. Newsgroups are a useful feature in that several users can connect to a newsgroup server and exchange messages and files, much like reading e-mail from their own servers. Newsgroups can be organized into subjects that allow readers and posters to customize their newsgroup according to specific needs or topics that interest them. Outlook Express, with its newsgroup functionality, enables users to connect to Exchange 2000 public folders that have been published and made accessible as newsgroup servers, although some of the more advanced public folder functionality, such as calendars, does not work in Outlook Express when accessed through newsgroups. By understanding how Outlook Express is configured to connect to a newsgroup server, you can better understand how the process works, for future installations. This lab requires a standard system with Outlook Express installed and access to the Internet.

To configure Outlook Express to connect to a newsgroup server:

1. If necessary, log on to your system.
2. Start Outlook Express by clicking **Start**, pointing to **Programs**, and then clicking **Outlook Express**. Outlook Express might be in a different directory, such as Internet Explorer, but by default this is the location for the shortcut. If you already have Outlook or another e-mail program installed and configured, Outlook Express might ask if you want to make Outlook Express your default e-mail software package. Click **No** to clear the message.
3. Click **Tools** on the menu bar, and then click **Accounts**. The Internet Accounts dialog box opens, and you will see four different tabs (All, News, Mail, and Directory Service).
4. Click the **News** tab to show currently installed news servers; there should be none listed. Click the **Add** button. In the list that appears, click **News** to start the Internet Connection Wizard.
5. The first window of the Internet Connection Wizard asks you to enter your display name. In the text box, enter your first and last name. After entering that information, click the **Next** button to proceed to the Internet News E-mail Address window, where you specify the e-mail address you want to associate with posts you make to the newsgroup server. Enter any e-mail address you like for this project, but typically you should enter an address at which you want to receive messages. Click the **Next** button to proceed.
6. The Internet News Server Name window opens, where you specify which Internet newsgroup server you want to connect to. You can specify a newsgroup server that you have created on your Exchange server or one of the free newsgroup servers available on the Internet. For this lab, enter **ccnews.thu.edu.tw** in the News (NNTP) server text box. If you were specifying a newsgroup server that required an authenticated logon for security purposes, you would click the My news server requires me to log on check box. After you have entered the server address, click the **Next** button to proceed to the final window.
7. The final window notifies you that you have successfully created this new server connection. Click the **Finish** button to complete your installation, and then close the Internet Accounts dialog box.
8. After you have closed the Internet Accounts dialog box, Outlook Express offers to log on to the newsgroup server you just defined to download a list of newsgroups

that the server hosts. Click **Yes**, and after a few seconds, you should see a list of newsgroups that the server hosts, signifying that the server was successfully set up. Spend some time trying out the various newsgroups to get a feel for how the client works.

9. After you have finished Step 8, close any open windows or applications.

Sometimes the newsgroup servers that allow public access change from time to time. For an updated list of active public newsgroup servers, go to *http://www.elfgrin.com/mine/nntpserv.html*.

CASE PROJECTS

Case Projects Background

The company you work for, Mabel Fuels, has a medium-sized network of approximately 500 computers all connected to a Windows 2000 Active Directory domain called mabelfuels.com. On this network, they have just migrated from Exchange 5.5 to Exchange 2000 and removed all traces of the old network. The clients on the network vary, depending on the department. Each department (Sales, Engineering, and Marketing) used to have its own IT Department that operated independently. The company also has a pool of approximately 20 laptops of varying configurations for use by employees in the field. All Exchange 2000 servers, including mailboxes, are backed up after the company closes for the day at 6:00 p.m. Currently, four other IT staff personnel work under you, the IT manager.

Case 1

The Sales Department has expressed interest in accessing and using the company's public folder resources. Half of the department uses Outlook Express and the other half uses the Exchange Client. The Sales Department wants to use the public folders to post product schedules, messages, and data that pertain to the department. What is the best plan of action to give the users the access they need?

Case 2

After seeing the great success and productivity enhancements the Sales Department has experienced, the president of Mabel Fuels wants the entire company upgraded and moved over to Outlook 2000. The upgrade will be done a department at a time so as not to cause more downtime than necessary. What is the best way to implement these changes for the number of systems in the company and still have other IT personnel perform the installations without selecting the wrong information? At the same time, you want to deploy a specialized fuel measurement software package. Is there an easy way to do this while deploying Outlook 2000?

Case 3

During the previous upgrade to Outlook 2000, some IT personnel found that they couldn't properly complete installations after trying several times. After doing some research, they realized that many of the systems have older equipment. From the following list of systems, which systems must be upgraded to properly install Outlook 2000 and which ones should be adequate? Also, if the president of the company decides that the cost of upgrading the equipment is too high, what is the best option to provide a consistent interface that supports as many Exchange 2000 features as possible?

- Five Compaq Deskpro 2000 desktops with Pentium 133 MHz processors, 24 MB of RAM, and 300 MB free hard drive space, using Windows 95
- Seven IBM Aptiva towers with Pentium 166 MHz processors, 64 MB of RAM, and 900 MB free hard drive space, using Windows 2000 Professional
- Two generic IBM-cCompatible desktops with Pentium 166 MHz processors, 32 MB of RAM, and approximately 50 MB free hard drive space, using Windows 95
- One Dell desktop with a Pentium II 300 MHz processor, 48 MB of RAM, and 2 GB free hard drive space, using Windows 2000 Professional
- Three generic IBM-compatible desktops with Pentium III 550 MHz processors, 128 MB of RAM, and 4 GB free hard drive space, using Windows 98

Case 4

The president of the company recently reached the 500-MB limit that had been set on his Exchange 2000 mailbox. He was notified by an IT staff member that deleting his messages would help bring his overall mailbox size down to a usable level so that he could freely send and receive e-mail again. Taking the IT staff member's advice, the president deleted all the messages in his inbox, including messages he hadn't read that had been in the mailbox since lunch time the day before. Unfortunately, you haven't had time to change any default message management features in Exchange 2000 Server yet. What can be done to retrieve the items the president lost? Also, what can be done to help make fixing this problem easier the next time it happens?

CHAPTER

8

CONFIGURING INTERNET CLIENTS IN EXCHANGE 2000 SERVER

After reading this chapter and completing the exercises, you will be able to:

- Understand the basics of various Internet protocols and how they work with and are supported by Exchange 2000 Server
- Explain the Internet Information Server process, including how the Web Storage System and the Exchange Interprocess Communication layer work, and how these technologies relate to Exchange 2000 Server
- Understand when it is necessary to implement Outlook Web Access in an Exchange 2000 Server environment
- Understand how to install, configure, and implement an Outlook Web Access installation on your network

In Chapter 7, "Configuring MAPI Clients in Exchange 2000 Server," you learned about the clients that can be used to connect users to Exchange 2000 and the features that each provide. You also took a look at the different types of Microsoft client software packages, including Outlook 98 and 2000, and learned how to install and configure Outlook 2000. Finally, you learned about troubleshooting common problems that can happen with Outlook 2000, including security, recovery of lost data, and other permissions issues.

In this chapter, you will learn about the various Internet protocols and how they work with and are supported by Exchange 2000 Server. Understanding how these protocols function and what they can do for your installation can be quite useful when you implement their related services. After this, you will learn about the Internet Information Server (IIS) process and how the Web Storage System works with Exchange 2000. You will learn more about Outlook Web Access and how to install, configure, and secure OWA on your Exchange 2000 deployment. And finally, you will learn how OWA works with front-end and back-end environments, useful knowledge if you plan on widespread OWA use in your organization. Previous chapters mentioned many of these protocols; however, in this chapter, you will learn more about the nuts and bolts of what makes these protocols actually work.

OVERVIEW OF INTERNET PROTOCOLS

Exchange 2000 Server uses a wide variety of industry-standard protocols to provide the services and features that users need. Each protocol provides a particular function for Exchange 2000, and some protocols go hand in hand with other protocols to fulfill requirements of certain services. These are some of the most common protocols:

- SMTP
- POP3
- IMAP4
- LDAP
- HTTP with WebDAV
- NNTP

Each of these protocols gives you functionality of some type for Exchange 2000. For instance, SMTP, POP3, and IMAP4 are protocols for transmitting messages or e-mail. LDAP is used for directory services. HTTP is used for Outlook Web Access (covered later in this chapter in the section "Hypertext Transfer Protocol with Web Distributed Authoring and Versioning Extensions"). NNTP, as you learned in Chapter 7, is used to provide newsgroup functionality for Exchange-enabled clients, such as Outlook 2000 or Outlook Express.

An overview of these protocols follows. By understanding what each protocol does for you and Exchange 2000 Server and how it functions, you can get a better idea of what protocols you need and how they interact with outside services, such as external e-mail systems or newsgroup services. A better understanding of these protocols and services helps facilitate the setup, configuration, and troubleshooting of your Exchange 2000 services.

Virtual Protocol Servers

Exchange 2000 Server provides the ability to create **virtual protocol servers**, which allow a single Exchange 2000 server to act as many different servers all at once. For instance, on a single Exchange 2000 server, you can have many different SMTP, NNTP, IMAP4, and other virtual servers, all with their own configurations, addresses, and information. This setup can be quite useful for servers that must support a wide variety of customers, such as those of an Internet service provider or those in a shared office space environment where many small companies rent network services from a single service provider.

The virtual server concept can also be applied to large organizations that want to have separate mail configurations or services for each department or even different branch offices, but want them all supported by the same Exchange 2000 server. For example, you could have a separate SMTP server for the calgary.exchange.com domain and branch office, and another SMTP server for the vernon.exchange.com domain and branch office, thus enabling you to implement the settings and configuration each site requires—and all from the same Exchange 2000 server, which could be located in Toronto.

In Exchange 2000, virtual servers are created by using the Exchange System Manager console and are relatively easy to install for most of the protocols that Exchange 2000 supports (listed in the "Overview of Internet Protocols" section). To set up a virtual server, you need a separate IP address for each type of virtual server (for example, a separate IP address for each SMTP virtual server), although the same IP address can be used for different protocols. Table 8-1 helps explain the correlation of IP addresses to virtual protocol servers.

Table 8-1 A Sample IP Configuration with Virtual Protocol Servers

IP Address	Virtual Server
192.168.1.1	SMTP Virtual Server 1
192.168.1.2	SMTP Virtual Server 2
192.168.1.1	POP3 Virtual Server 1
192.168.1.2	POP3 Virtual Server 2
192.168.1.1	NNTP Virtual Server 1

Virtual servers of different types—including SMTP, NNTP, IMAP4, POP3, HTTP, and X.400—are created by default when you first install Exchange 2000 Server. You can start adding more as soon as you have finished installing Exchange 2000 Server for the first time, should you need to run multiple virtual servers for the different domains your Exchange 2000 server services. In the following sections, you will learn more about the various Internet protocols that can have virtual servers created for them in Exchange 2000 Server. Also, you will learn how to configure default virtual protocol servers later in this chapter in the "Hands-on Projects" section. (In Chapter 10, "Connector and Routing Management in Exchange 2000 Server," you will learn how to create a new SMTP virtual server.)

Simple Mail Transport Protocol

In Chapter 5, "Installation of Exchange 2000 Server in New Environments," you learned how SMTP works with Windows 2000 and Exchange 2000; in this chapter, you will receive additional background information on how the protocol actually works and how e-mail software, such as Exchange 2000 Server, functions with SMTP.

As you know, SMTP is the default protocol that Exchange 2000 uses to communicate with other servers and clients. Other protocols, such as POP3, IMAP4, and **HTTP with WebDAV** (the protocol that Outlook Web Access uses to communicate with the OWA services on an Exchange 2000 server), can also be used to access e-mail functionality in Exchange 2000 Server, but SMTP is the preferred protocol because of its flexibility and better overall performance. The other protocols are included to facilitate communications with other servers and client software packages that may not have SMTP functionality or services available.

As strange as it might sound, SMTP is loosely related to FTP services. Before the availability of current e-mail standards, users communicating with each other would simply transfer text files to each other using FTP. The main problems with this method was that you had no way of knowing exactly who sent the message or where the reply should be sent, and this method of copying text files here and there was rather cumbersome. Eventually, SMTP was fleshed out in the Request for Comment document RFC 561, and further refinements were made to the protocol, until the current standard was "finalized" in RFC 822. Now, instead of a simple text file, any message sent contains the following standard and optional information fields in its **message header** (the part of the document containing pertinent message information, such as sender and recipient):

Required Information

- Creation time
- Source address
- Destination address

Optional Information

- Received status
- Message subject
- Reply-to address
- Return path

When you send an e-mail message, every e-mail server that handles the file on its route makes sure the required information has been included. Each server then adds its own information in the message header, allowing you to see the path the message took on its way to you.

In many cases, e-mails traveling from the sender to the recipient do not go in a straight line, especially over the Internet. Servers using standardized protocols, such as SMTP, handle these messages and relay them to the appropriate destinations. When a server relays the message, it tags an address onto the message, much as labels for different locations are added to a trunk as it travels around the world. Reviewing information in the message header is useful when troubleshooting messages that failed to be delivered or took a long time to get to their intended recipient. You will learn more about troubleshooting different types of connections and connectors in Chapter 10.

SMTP Transport

SMTP, by its very nature, is an open protocol because it enables connections and message relaying by almost any other SMTP service. The SMTP service does not need a set message transfer path to perform its relaying; all the SMTP service does is reference the next closest mail server, based on Mail Exchange (MX) records in the server's DNS service, and pass the message on to that server.

Every server follows a standard model when transporting a message via SMTP. The following list outlines the steps in a simplified fashion. SMTP cannot process multiple commands sent simultaneously for the same message, so the entire command process is much like two people talking on walkie-talkies.

1. A user creates a message and sends it to the sending server, SMTP Server 1.
2. SMTP Server 1 creates a two-way communication with the receiving server, SMTP Server 2.
3. SMTP Server 1 creates the necessary commands to send the message and transfers them to SMTP Server 2.
4. SMTP Server 2 receives the commands and then sends the appropriate response commands back to SMTP Server 1.

This list is a simplified version of how the message transport process takes place. Actually, the SMTP servers send each other several commands during the final two steps to transfer the message. Table 8-2 lists the common SMTP commands and the basics of what each command does when sent.

Table 8-2 SMTP Commands and Functions

SMTP Command	Function
HELO	Initiates the connection between the sending and receiving SMTP servers by sending each server's identity information to the other.
MAIL	Starts the transfer of mail with the original server listed first; additional servers are added, with the last server to relay the message listed at the top of the message header. This listing is used to provide information for undeliverable messages.
RCPT	Identifies one of the message recipients; multiple recipients are listed one after the other, each with its own RCPT command. Listing recipients in this way means that no single recipient can cause delivery failure for the other recipients.
DATA	Tells the receiving SMTP service that the message is ready to send.
RSET	Resets the message transfer; any information that was received will be discarded.
VRFY	Requests verification from the receiving SMTP service that the e-mail address is valid.
EXPN	Requests confirmation of the mailing list and the members of that list.
HELP	Requests help for a command.
NOOP	Asks the receiving SMTP service for an OK response.
TURN	Forces a reversal of the status of the sending and receiving SMTP services (the sender becomes receiver and vice versa).
QUIT	The sending SMTP service sends a connection termination request. When received, the receiving SMTP service responds with an OK and terminates the connection.

SMTP Commands and Character Sets

Standard SMTP commands and messages are created with 7-bit character sets; an extra bit is added for parity to include a level of redundancy and to make the SMTP commands comply with the TCP standard of an 8-bit character set. This configuration works fine for communication in English because all characters in the English language, including capitalization and standard punctuation, fit within the 128 possible characters that 7-bit character sets support. When dealing with external e-mail systems that use languages other than English or when expanded character sets are required, a full 8-bit character set is used to allow for 256 total characters, and the parity bit is not used. Unfortunately, standard SMTP supports only 7 bits, so for messages using the expanded 8-bit character set to be able to function properly, extra data is added to the command or message and then packed up and sent to the receiving SMTP service. When the packaged message or command arrives at the destination, it is unpacked and handled accordingly.

Exchange 2000 Server and SMTP

SMTP is the focal point of the Exchange 2000 Server messaging services. In Chapter 5, you learned how the SMTP services included with IIS 5 are modified during the installation of Exchange 2000 Server to add functionality that Exchange 2000 uses for communication with other Exchange 2000 servers. This additional command set is referred to as Extended SMTP (ESMTP) commands and includes the following functionality changes:

- An advanced message queuing engine
- Enhanced message categorization
- Support for link status information
- The new Installable File System (IFS) driver used with Exchange 2000 public folders

As you learned earlier, with Exchange 2000 you can create multiple SMTP virtual servers. The SMTP services provided by default allow only one SMTP server, but by using virtual servers, you can have as many servers as you like—each configured differently, and you should be able to start, stop, or pause each server without affecting any other SMTP server. In most Exchange 2000 configurations, additional virtual SMTP servers are not required because the core SMTP server provides all the necessary messaging functionality.

Virtual SMTP servers can be useful, though, if you are supporting multiple domains from one Exchange 2000 server and you want a different mail configuration for each domain; in this case, a virtual server for each domain makes it easier to set up separate mail configurations. Every virtual server requires its own IP address and port number. The default SMTP virtual server created when Exchange 2000 Server is installed automatically monitors port 25 for every IP address assigned to the virtual server.

As you can see, there's certainly more to SMTP than can be discussed in the confines of this chapter. However, understanding its basic functionality and how it works with Exchange 2000 makes SMTP easier to configure, manage, and troubleshoot when you implement your Exchange 2000 installation.

Post Office Protocol 3

As you learned in Chapter 1, "An Overview of Microsoft Exchange 2000 Server," POP3 was developed to help client systems that do not have the continuous network connection that SMTP requires to retrieve and manage messages on the server. POP3 is predominantly used with clients that connect over a network such as the Internet via a dial-up connection or a high-speed service. POP3 connections are designed to connect to servers and download the messages that are waiting for them, unlike Exchange 2000 Server, which allows you to manipulate messages on the server all you want (deleting, forwarding, replying, and so forth). Unless you have set your POP3 client to do otherwise, the server then deletes any messages you have downloaded from the server to your client software. POP3 is intended for retrieving messages from an e-mail server, not for sending messages to the server. When the e-mail client sends messages, it uses the standard SMTP service on the system to transfer the messages to an SMTP server, such as Exchange 2000.

When the POP3 service connects to an e-mail server, it uses certain commands while communicating with the server. The POP3 commands are very similar to the SMTP commands, but there are a few differences, as shown in Table 8-3.

Table 8-3 POP3 Commands and Functions

POP3 Command	Function
USER	Sends the user name for the mailbox being connected to
PASS	Sends the password for the mailbox being connected to
STAT	Asks the server for information about the messages and the size of those messages being stored on the server
LIST	Requests the list of all messages, including the information found by using the STAT command
RETR	Requests that the server send the messages specified by the client
DELE	Requests that the server delete the messages specified by the client
NOOP	Keeps the connection open between the client and server (essentially a keep-alive command)
RSET	Causes the server to undo any message deletions
QUIT	Forces deletion of messages selected for deletion during the session, and then ends communication between the client and server

When supporting POP3 functionality in Exchange 2000 Server, the only requirement is to have a virtual server configured with support for POP3. Each POP3 virtual server can be configured with its own IP address or can be set to monitor any IP addresses for which the server is configured. Configuration of these virtual servers is quite simple and very similar to configuring the other protocols covered in this chapter.

All in all, POP3 provides convenient, quick access to e-mail for users without a constant network connection to the Exchange 2000 server. Although it isn't intended to be a full-featured e-mail transport protocol, it does work well hand in hand with SMTP to provide remote users with e-mail connectivity to Exchange 2000 or any other POP3-enabled e-mail server.

Internet Messaging Access Protocol Version 4

As you just learned, by default POP3 deletes messages that have been downloaded from the server. This action can be turned off with a configuration change in the client software, but doing so could be a nuisance for users who need to access their e-mail from many different systems, client software packages, or locations that might be outside the network. Enter IMAP4, designed to provide a wide array of user-configurable options, including the ability to dictate what messages are stored on the server, the sharing of your and other users' mailboxes, and the ability to modify and manage e-mail held on the server from the client software. As you can see, IMAP4 is a far more robust protocol than POP3 because it has more management and configuration options for users to take advantage of.

Administering IMAP4 in Exchange is, like POP3 administration, relatively easy. After you create a new IMAP4 virtual server, you can specify a few options for the protocol, including whether you want IMAP4 to allow the client software to view the contents of the public folders or whether you want Exchange 2000 Server to optimize the way it estimates file sizes to the client software.

When users issue commands to an IMAP4 server, the server can be in one of four different states. Although several different commands can be issued to an IMAP4 server, only certain ones work when the server is in a specific state. For instance, you cannot send a Create or Delete command when the server is in the initial connection state because you haven't even been logged on yet. The four different states for an IMAP4 server are:

- *Waiting for connection/welcome message for a new connection*—The server is either waiting for a new connection or has received a new connection and is passing the connection to the authentication state.
- *No authentication*—The server has received the new connection, but has not authenticated it yet or authentication has failed.
- *Connection authenticated*—The server has authenticated the connection, so activity during the connection can now take place.
- *Selected state*—This state is basically a loop that returns the state to the connection authenticated state after a Close command has been issued or the Select or Examine commands have failed.
- *Waiting for connection*—Although not a state on its own, after receiving a Logout command, the server reverts to a waiting for connection state.

Just as POP3 and SMTP do, IMAP4 has a list of commands that are issued to the server. As mentioned, only some of these commands can be issued when the server is in a specific state. Thankfully, you do not have to know when to send these commands because your IMAP4-enabled client software package takes care of that for you. IMAP4 has quite a few more commands than POP3 does because the protocol is capable of much more functionality than POP3; these commands are described in Table 8-4.

Table 8-4 IMAP4 Commands and Functions

IMAP4 Command	Function
CAPABILITY	Sends a query to the server to determine what capabilities the server has
AUTHENTICATE	Sends the type of authentication mechanism used for this connection
LOGIN	Sends the appropriate logon and password information for the user
SELECT	Tells the server which mailbox the user wants to access
EXAMINE	Same as the SELECT command, but the mailbox is opened in read-only mode
CREATE	Issues a create mailbox command to the server
DELETE	Issues a delete mailbox command to the server
RENAME	Issues a rename mailbox command to the server
SUBSCRIBE	Requests that the server add the specified mailbox to the user's list of active mailboxes
UNSUBSCRIBE	Requests that the server remove the specified mailbox from the user's list of active mailboxes
LIST	Sends a query to the server requesting a list of a range of mailboxes
LSUB	Sends a query to the server requesting a list of mailboxes to which the user has subscribed
STATUS	Sends a query to the server requesting the status of a specified mailbox
APPEND	Requests that the server add a particular message to a specified mailbox
CLOSE	Requests that the server close a specified mailbox and force any deletions selected by the user
EXPUNGE	Requests that the server force any deletions selected by the user
SEARCH	Sends a search request to the server for a specified mailbox based on the user's search criteria
FETCH	Sends a request to the server to retrieve specific selections from the main body of a particular message
STORE	Causes the server to save the changes made to a message in a specified mailbox
COPY	Sends a copy command to the server to move a specified message from one mailbox to another
NOOP	As in POP3 and SMTP, this is a keep-alive command intended to keep the connection active
LOGOUT	Sends a disconnection request to the server, logging off the currently connected user

The commands in Table 8-4 are listed in more or less the order they could be issued to the server, although this is by no means a definitive guideline for when to use the commands.

Like POP3, IMAP4 can provide quick and easy access to a user's e-mail on Exchange 2000 or another IMAP4-enabled e-mail server. However, IMAP4 has a much larger feature set and offers a wider variety of user management and usage features, as outlined in the IMAP4 commands. You will learn how to configure an IMAP4 virtual server later in this chapter in the "Hands-on Projects" section.

Lightweight Directory Access Protocol

Earlier implementations of LDAP (first designed for X.500 Directory Services) required much more overhead and configuration to provide the same functionality as the current LDAP. As you learned in Chapter 5, LDAP provides a protocol for clients to request information on various network objects, such as users, printers, and applications, from a collection of information called the **Directory Information Tree (DIT)** that is held on the directory server. The DIT is a selection of information about objects stored in the directory; each object in the database has various attributes, such as a name or address. In addition to these other objects, any LDAP servers that are providing access for the same DIT must also have entries in the DIT.

Every directory has its own schema; like the schema for Active Directory, the schema for these directories dictates the guidelines for the directory's structure and contents. When an object is created, it is given a particular attribute called the ObjectClass. The ObjectClass attribute specifies the mandatory attributes for objects and any additional attributes for the objects, based on the schema guidelines. The DIT also registers and automatically maintains four other attributes for each object:

- *CreatorsName*—Contains the name used to create the entry
- *CreateTimestamp*—Contains the time the entry was created
- *modifiersName*—Contains the name used to last modify the entry
- *modifyTimestamp*—Contains the time the entry was last modified

The design of each LDAP Directory Information Tree is the same as an AD tree, with the root being the directory and the "branches" of the tree extending from the root to represent different layers of information (domain, network, server, group, and so on), until the branch gets to the end where the lowest possible object—the user—resides. Each object in the directory is recognized by a unique entry called the **distinguished name (DN)**. The DN is built by taking the information in the Directory Information Tree leading to the object in hierarchical order, starting from the topmost entry in the directory (typically country) and going down, in order, to the name of the object (typically a user account). A basic DN entry for a user in a company looks something like this:

```
cn=Shawn Porter, o=LANW, c=US
```

In this DN entry, "cn" represents the common name that identifies the object, "o" represents the organization that is next up in the hierarchy from the common name, and "c" represents the country (next up in the hierarchy again) where the organization is located. You can add a wide variety of attributes to a DN, which can get rather long if the directory gets more complex. Additional attributes are associated with the various object classes. For instance, the Shawn Porter DN could have 50 different attributes, including e-mail, fax, telephone, title, manager, address, and so on, but typically only the main hierarchical entries are recorded in the DN. Thankfully, the DN's length is of little concern to users because they do not have to enter the string of information; rather, they simply enter their search information, and the LDAP server wades through the DIT until the appropriate information is found and displayed.

You can also apply a level of security to information in the DIT by using access control lists (ACLs), much like the method for securing an object in AD. Access control can be applied to a branch on the directory tree, a particular entry in the directory, a specific attribute, or even to users as individuals or as a member of a group. The actual user the object is related to can also be given rights to modify the information in the object. Granting this type of access right is usually done to take some administrative load off the administrator in charge of the DIT, especially if the user is changing information fairly often.

LDAP communications are sent packaged within an LDAP message over TCP/IP, which contains the message ID (to organize the messages coming in) and the command itself (or the response to the command if the server is filling the client's command request). Some of the more common commands sent as part of an LDAP message are listed next; most are fairly self-explanatory:

- SearchRequest
- SearchResultEntry
- SearchResultDone
- SearchResultReference
- ModifyRequest
- ModifyResponse
- Add Request
- AddResponse
- DelRequest
- DelResponse
- ModifyDNRequest
- ModifyDNResponse
- CompareRequest
- CompareResponse
- AbandonRequest

There are more commands that can be passed, but unless you are programming software to use LDAP services, you will likely never have to issue a command because the client software performs the requests on your behalf. Knowing the commands could come in handy, however, if you ever need to troubleshoot a problem-prone LDAP server installation or client application, and you are checking the inner workings of the software or configuration.

As with implementing an effective AD solution, implementing an LDAP server can be a lot of work; if you are having difficulties, articles that outline LDAP troubleshooting steps can be found at Microsoft TechNet: *http://www.microsoft.com/technet/*. Perform a search for

LDAP troubleshooting to find the most up-to-date articles available. LDAP can be a complex subject, and there's certainly more to the protocol than what can be covered in this book's scope. For more detailed information on the inner workings of LDAP, take a look at *http://www.microsoft.com/windows2000/techinfo/howitworks/activedirectory/ldap.asp*.

Hypertext Transfer Protocol with Web Distributed Authoring and Versioning Extensions

Hypertext Transfer Protocol (HTTP) with Web Distributed Authoring and Versioning (WebDAV) extensions is standard HTTP, with WebDAV protocol extensions that enable users to collaboratively edit and manage files on remote Web servers. The long-winded explanation aside, WebDAV is simply a special HTTP feature that allows a remote file system to be viewed and modified through a Web site. WebDAV can be useful in, for example, a company intranet (an internal company site designed to be accessed through a Web browser) where users can post files and share them with co-workers; before WebDAV functionality was available, intranets were largely static, and updating was typically done only by the intranet administrators.

8

By using IIS 5 services on Windows 2000, you can set up a WebDAV-enabled folder on your Web site so that users can manipulate and share documents quickly and easily. Some of the other abilities available to users are the following:

- *Create and modify documents and folders*—Users can create, move, delete, and edit any document or folder that they have rights to in the WebDAV directory structure.
- *Edit a document's properties information*—Users with the rights to a particular file can edit the document's properties, including the author, document notes, and other information.
- *Enable locking of documents*—Any number of users can view the document simultaneously, but only one user at a time can modify it.
- *Perform searches of the WebDAV directory structure*—Users can perform advanced searches for documents in the WebDAV directory structure. Searches can be extremely specific, such as looking for documents written on a certain date by one particular user.

WebDAV comes into play with Exchange 2000 Server in its support by Outlook Web Access. In Exchange 2000, a new feature called the **Web Store** (which you've been introduced to in previous chapters as the "Web Storage System") enables OWA users to connect to the WebDAV-enabled directories configured with the IIS 5 services and access them as any other user would access files in the public folders. You will learn more about the Web Store and Exchange 2000 later in this chapter in the section "The IIS Process."

The Web Store is not limited to Outlook Web Access; users can access the Web Store with many different methods, including through public folders using Outlook 2000, through a directory shortcut or share using Windows Explorer, or through an Office 2000 application (much as you would with Windows Explorer). This ease of access makes the Web Store an attractive feature for almost any company that wants to give users the ability to collaborate on documents quickly and easily.

Network News Transport Protocol

Network News Transport Protocol (NNTP) is used to provide access to newsgroup servers. The information on the newsgroup servers is usually not a typical news service, as some might expect; newsgroups tend to act as message bulletin boards where users can post messages, files, and information for other users to read, download, access, and collaborate on ideas.

NNTP is an evolutionary development over the older method of sharing news and information and collaborating with other users: the **list server**. A list server is, in essence, the same as a newsgroup server, except that instead of the user connecting to a server with a client software package, the user receives the information from an e-mail server that sends out the information at preset intervals. With this particular method, managing user lists can be difficult unless you implement a third-party NNTP management utility. Also, list servers can use a lot of network bandwidth to send all the messages passed back and forth on the list server to every member of the service. Despite these drawbacks, list servers are still quite common; they maintain their popularity by bringing the information directly to your mailbox instead of requiring that you go look for it.

NNTP really shines in its reduced administrative effort, lower hardware and software requirements, and overall lower network bandwidth consumption. These benefits are made possible by storing all the posts and information on a central server. Instead of the server sending information to each and every user when it is posted, users connect to the NNTP Service and select the messages they want to read; in most cases, this method cuts back dramatically on wasted bandwidth. In addition, the NNTP Service runs in the background on one server and can accept connections from any system on the network or even over the Internet.

Another benefit of NNTP newsgroup servers is that the user has the opportunity to subscribe to various groups on the newsgroup servers, which are typically sorted by subject or general topic. Sorting newsgroups helps users subscribe to just the information they want, which also lessens the network bandwidth being used. When users subscribe to several newsgroups, they can request a listing of new messages for each subscribed channel or for all channels, if they want. New messages are then listed (the number displayed at one time is typically a software option that can be configured based on the users' needs), and users can select individual messages or groups of messages to download to the client system.

Many new software packages that support newsgroup reading, such as Outlook Express 5, allow you to view the message as soon as you click it instead of having to wait until the message has been transferred to your client system. Although the message data is actually still being transferred, it's much like reading an e-mail message. Previously, you had to select the messages you wanted and then download them before they were available on your client system for reading, replying to, and so on.

When clients and servers communicate with each other, they use NNTP, which in turn uses TCP/IP over port 119 by default. Many of the NNTP commands are very similar to SMTP commands. Commands are limited to a maximum string of 512 characters, including punctuation and spaces, thus allowing fairly lengthy command strings. When the server and client receive responses back and forth from each other based on the commands that were sent, each response starts with a three-digit number that represents the status of the command that was sent. The following list describes common response codes that could be received from the server; this list is by no means complete, but it represents the different types of responses a user or the client software would probably see:

- Code 100—A message containing help information
- Code 200—Server is ready; new posts are allowed
- Code 201—Server is ready; new posts are not allowed
- Code 215—List of newsgroups follows
- Code 235—Message transferred successfully
- Code 400—NNTP services disconnected (server timeout, connection drop, and so on)
- Code 411—Newsgroup does not exist on this server
- Code 500—Server does not recognize the command that was sent
- Code 501—Command was issued improperly; check the command string used
- Code 502—Invalid permissions to access the server, newsgroup, or message
- Code 503—Program error; command has failed to execute

NNTP does not rely on client software alone. Users could access the information on a newsgroup server by connecting with a Telnet program and issuing the text commands manually. With the widespread availability of free newsgroup client software packages, however, this method usually isn't necessary. You might use Telnet to connect to your NNTP newsgroup server if you are trying to troubleshoot why you can't retrieve or post messages or to investigate a host of other issues. Table 8-5 lists the common commands for NNTP.

Table 8-5 NNTP Commands and Functions

NNTP Command	Function
HELP	Provides a list of NNTP commands for the newsgroup servers.
MODE READER	Informs the server that the connection is for reading messages, not sending messages in from another server.
LIST	Generates a full list of the newsgroups on the server (can take upward of 15 minutes in some cases).
GROUP A.B	Establishes the current group that you want and lists the number of messages.
ARTICLE 123	Displays the specified message represented by the (123) attribute, which is usually the message number.
IHAVE	Informs the server that you have a message to send to the server. The server then responds by requesting that the message be sent or informing you that the message is not wanted.
POST	Sends the server the message that you offered when you issued the IHAVE command.

The Exchange 2000 newsgroup functionality can be used for many other purposes besides user access to Internet newsgroup feeds. You can also create your own newsgroups for use within the company or even create newsgroups to support a client base. For instance, Creative Labs, a multimedia hardware company, has a dedicated newsgroup server with the sole purpose of giving users a support forum to help other users.

There's a lot you can do with newsgroup servers. Their basic design makes them fairly easy to understand, but if you decide to create and manage your own newsgroup server, you could face a lot of configuration and organizational issues, especially if the server gets large enough to encompass your entire organization. If managed correctly, however, the server's benefits can far outweigh the time and effort spent putting it in place.

Introduction to Internet Information Server

The Internet Information Server (IIS) version 5 that is included with Windows 2000 Server works hand in hand with Exchange 2000 Server to provide a variety of services. These services include two important features for Exchange 2000: Outlook Web Access and the Web Storage System.

IIS 5, as you learned in Chapter 5, is installed by default during the Windows 2000 Server installation with a default Web site and FTP site installed, ready for you to install additional virtual Web servers and to set up and configure OWA for Exchange 2000 Server.

IIS 5 might be deselected during the Windows 2000 installation process. Therefore, you should make sure IIS 5 is installed before performing any Exchange 2000 installations.

IIS is certainly not new to the Windows world. IIS version 4 provided much of the functionality of the current version, but IIS 5 does have some improvements over the old design, such as:

- *Improved reliability and performance*—A new method of running Web services separately from other applications makes both performance and reliability better than in IIS 4. Among these improvements is the much-touted IIS Reliable Restart. With this feature, if IIS goes down, an administrator can quickly restart IIS 5 services with a few short clicks instead of reloading the server, not always a feasible option.
- *Improved management*—Better wizards and an easy-to-use interface (thanks to Windows 2000 consoles) makes IIS 5 management easier than before.
- *Improved security*—Although the jury is still out on this one, many security fixes for IIS 4 have been incorporated into IIS 5, thus making it more secure. In addition, new security task wizards make it easier to quickly implement effective security for related IIS information and settings.
- *Improved application environment*—Association with Windows 2000 Server Active Directory, improved memory handling, and better handling of errors and program failures (all made possible through the IIS 5 association with Windows 2000 Server) make IIS 5 run better and promote additional development by third-party software programmers.

With these improvements and the improved OWA services that you will learn about shortly, you can see that IIS 5 is a generational improvement over the IIS 4 services. These improvements, in many cases, owe much to the benefits Windows 2000 Server brings with it, including stability and high performance.

Next, you will take a quick look at the Web Storage System included with IIS 5; to round out the chapter, you'll delve into Outlook Web Access, including how it is installed and configured, and how security is implemented with this useful Exchange 2000 service, brought about thanks to IIS 5.

The Web Storage System

The Web Storage System essentially provides a single holding point for many different types of information. The Web Store typically includes the design and general feature set of a regular Windows file system as well as a collaboration server, and all this functionality is accessible over a Web page from a single address. The overall design of the Web Store is much like the Exchange 2000 Information Store, so it offers a great deal of flexibility in its configuration.

This flexibility was included so that Exchange 2000 administrators could give their users a wide array of features that Microsoft refers to as knowledge management features. Some of the features the Web Store can provide, such as being able to build and run applications from a Web Store–enabled server and to access files, documents, contacts, and HTML files from a Web browser, not only increase functionality for remote users, but also give local users a constant interface that can be as simple or complex in design as you like. The Web Store can be accessed in a wide variety of ways. Outlook Web Access, Office 2000, Outlook 2000, and Windows Explorer can all be used to access documents and folders published to the Web Store.

The Exchange 2000 Web Storage System is a rather in-depth topic. For more information, take a look at the various design and planning documents available at *http://www.microsoft.com/technet* or at *http://www.microsoft.com/exchange*.

The Exchange Interprocess Communication Layer

The Exchange Interprocess Communication (ExIPC) layer is a message-queuing layer built between IIS and the Exchange 2000 Web Store to facilitate fast data exchanges between the two interfaces, thus ensuring the best possible performance when requests and information are being sent between the two components. For instance, when a client sends a retrieve mail command to an Exchange 2000 server through something like OWA, the ExIPC DLL is put into effect as a go-between for Web Store–IIS server communication. The complex functionality of the Web Store and ExIPC layer are covered in more detail in Chapter 10.

Outlook Web Access

Outlook Web Access, a very handy feature of Exchange 2000, provides much of the functionality of a regular client software package, such as Outlook 2000, including access to e-mail, contacts, and public folders. For users on non-Windows operating systems such as UNIX, OWA is also the most common method of client access, and is often the only way for those users to access Exchange 2000 features other than POP3 or IMAP4 e-mail, making OWA even more useful than as just a simple remote access Web client for Exchange 2000.

Depending on your needs and requirements, a fair amount of effort can go into creating an effective OWA configuration; however, Microsoft has made it relatively easy to get a simple OWA server up and running in little time. The additional features, security, redundancy, and scalability are what take extra time and effort to implement. OWA is certainly not a new feature to Exchange 2000, but the version included with Exchange 2000 Server features a host of improvements and additional functionality over the previous version included with Exchange Server 5.5. The following list includes some of these improvements and additional features:

- Support for public folders that have Contacts and Calendar objects
- Support for embedded media in e-mail messages
- Support for Internet Explorer 5.0 or higher
- Support for embedded ActiveX objects

As you learned in Chapter 7, OWA is not able to support all the features that a typical fully supported Exchange 2000 client, such as Outlook 2000, can. The unsupported features include the following:

- No offline message reading because the Web browser must be logged on and connected to the Exchange server to read messages
- Limited viewing options for calendars, tasks, and similar functions
- No synchronization of offline folders

The rest of this chapter focuses on OWA installation and initial configuration and security considerations that you should think about when planning your installation.

Installing Outlook Web Access

OWA is installed and administered through IIS, which provides the core functionality for Exchange 2000 Server and OWA. To install and enable OWA in your Exchange 2000 installation, you must have a Web site for your users to connect to that's installed and configured within IIS. Even if you plan to use OWA only as your internal client and no users from the Internet will access OWA, you still need to have the Web site installed and configured before installing OWA.

Once you have the site, you can start configuring and administering the required IIS options. The term "installing" OWA could be a bit misleading because technically Exchange 2000 Server installs OWA to your IIS server during the Exchange 2000 installation; however, you need to "install" and configure the various IIS settings to get OWA active and functioning. When you open the Internet Information Services console, you are greeted by a window that looks similar to Figure 8-1.

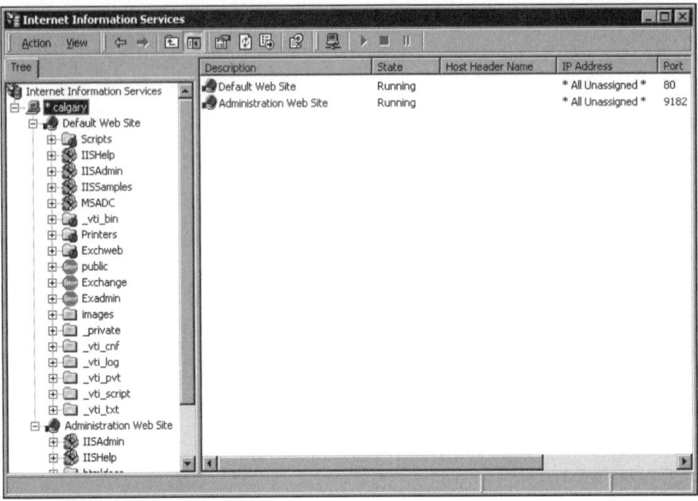

Figure 8-1 The Internet Information Services main window

In the pane on the left, the various servers installed to this server are listed; on the right, you'll see the information that's displayed when you click on a server or subfolder under a server. When you expand the items under your main server, you should see the following four entries that have been created by Exchange 2000 during installation:

- *public*—By default, points toward the public folder/newsgroups folder
- *Exchange*—By default, points toward the Exchange 2000 mailbox folder (Mbx)
- *Exchweb*—Stores the graphics that the user sees when connecting to and using OWA
- *Exadmin*—By default, points toward the root directory of the Exchange administration tool to manage public folders

If these four folders have red stop signs instead of a regular folder icon next to the name, as shown in Figure 8-1, try opening the folder's Properties dialog box by right-clicking the folder and clicking Properties. Next, click the Browse button next to the Local Path text box. Then simply click OK in the Browse for Folder window that opens, click Apply in the Properties dialog box, and then click OK. This should reset the IIS to the proper default directory. During the initial installation of Exchange 2000, although the directory is correct, sometimes it doesn't register properly in IIS.

Although the default installation paths should be correct and the default settings should allow basic OWA functionality, you can set up additional security measures and other configuration options, which you will learn about in the following sections,

"Configuring Outlook Web Access" and "Security and Outlook Web Access." To test basic OWA functionality, open a Web browser, type *http://localhost/exchange/* in the Web browser's Address bar, and then press Enter. If everything is working, you should be greeted with the introductory OWA screen, which looks similar to Figure 8-2. If not, you will likely find a variety of error pages displayed in your Web browser. If the page does not load, you might want to confirm that the directories outlined previously point to the appropriate folder, and make sure you did not click in error when you were confirming the directory choice.

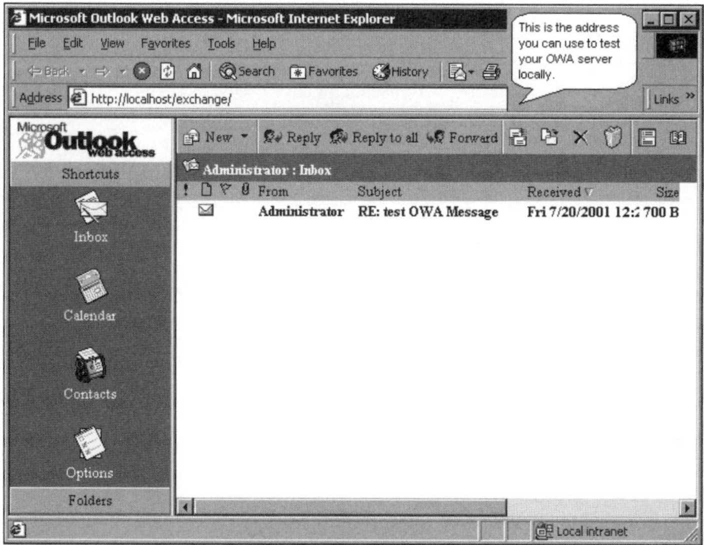

Figure 8-2 The main OWA window

The next few figures are for those of you who have not seen OWA before, and show some of the more important screens in OWA. Note the striking similarity that the most up-to-date version of OWA with IIS 5 and Exchange 2000 has to Outlook 2000.

Figure 8-3 shows the main OWA Calendar view with a sample entry.

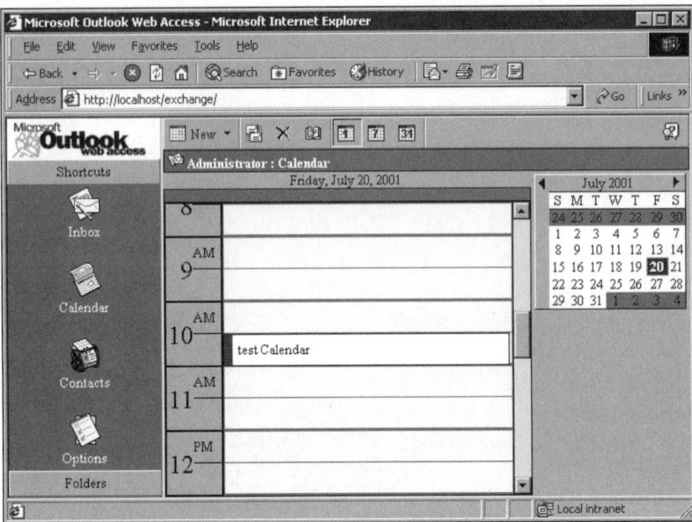

Figure 8-3 The main OWA Calendar view

Figure 8-4 shows the OWA Contacts view with a sample entry.

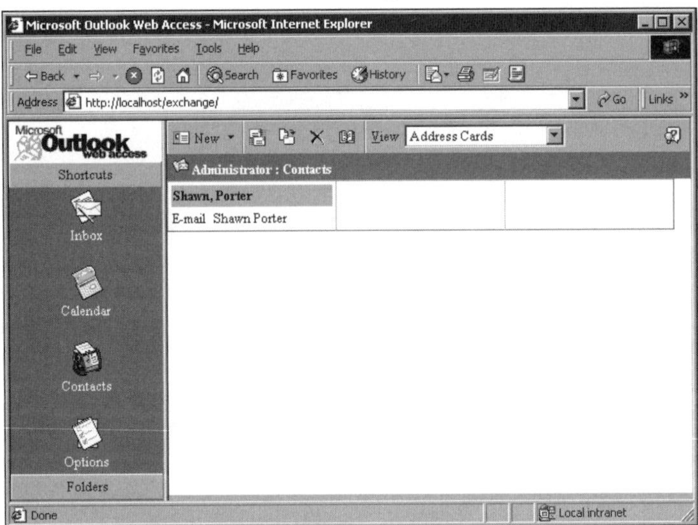

Figure 8-4 The main OWA Contacts view

Figure 8-5 shows OWA set to the Folders view, which allows easier access to other folders such as Deleted Items, Sent Items, or Outbox, much like the Outlook 2000 Folder list.

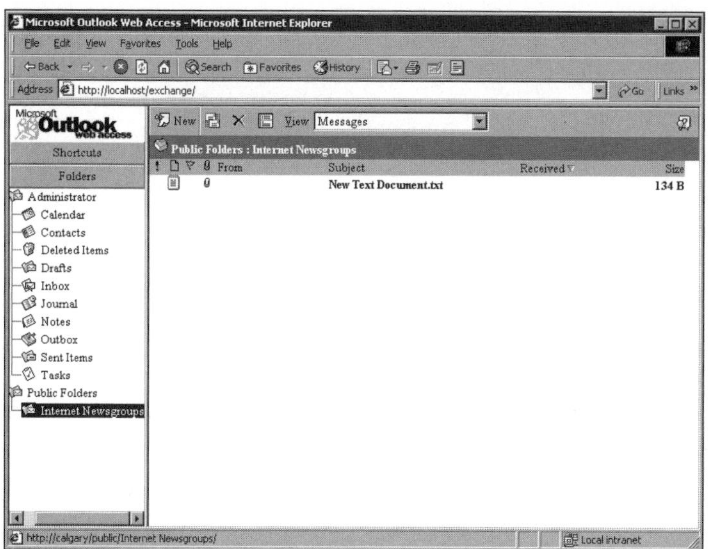

Figure 8-5 OWA with the Folders view enabled

And finally, Figure 8-6 shows the OWA Options window. As you can see, there are a wide variety of configuration options that can be set for users to customize their OWA experience.

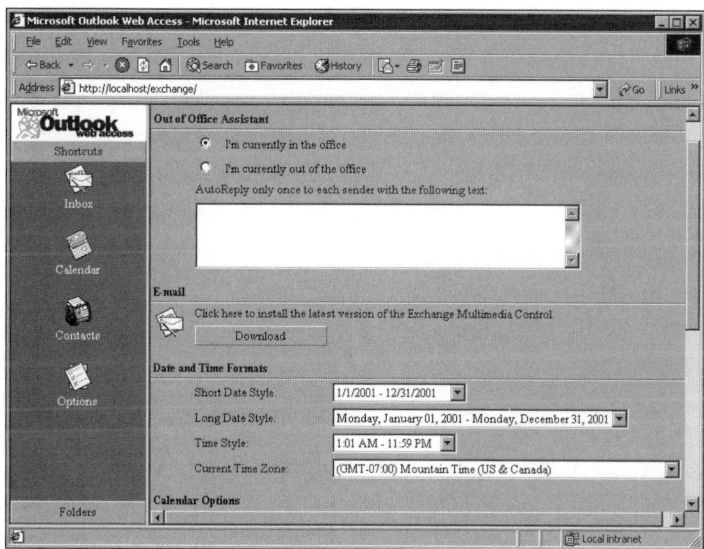

Figure 8-6 Part of the OWA Options window

No further steps are required to get the basic OWA installation up and running. By default, Exchange 2000 Server performs much of the duties during its initial installation.

However, you might have to install and configure your own OWA installation if you need multiple OWA servers running on your network. You will learn about installing a new OWA server in the "Hands-on Projects" section later in this chapter. You should spend some time reviewing the available options when configuring the sections related to OWA within IIS.

Configuring Outlook Web Access

As mentioned, there isn't much to installing OWA; in fact, Exchange 2000 Server takes most of the fun out of it. Configuring OWA can be a different story, however. Depending on your particular needs for OWA, you might need to set several different configuration options, including those for the ever-important securing of OWA, explained in the next section, "Security and Outlook Web Access." This section outlines the most pertinent configuration options that Exchange administrators need to be aware of.

Nearly all OWA configuration is performed through the Internet Information Services console in Windows 2000. IIS contains all the necessary configuration information for creating additional mailboxes, public folders, storage groups, and the like for use with OWA (if you want specific or additional items for OWA users), which is handled by Exchange 2000. Otherwise, everything else is done through IIS. If you view the properties of the four entries (public, Exchange, Exadmin, Exchweb) mentioned previously in "Installing Outlook Web Access," you will see the array of options that can be set. The Exchange Properties dialog box (for the Exchange entry) shown in Figure 8-7 looks the same as the Properties dialog box for the other three folders. Following are the most important options in the various tabs:

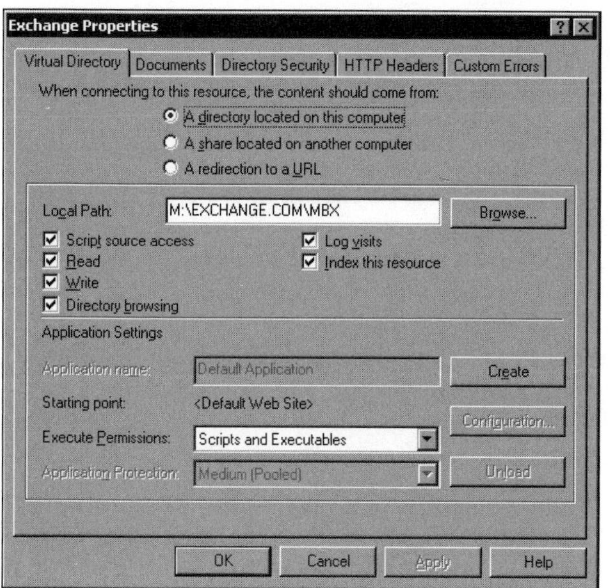

Figure 8-7 The Exchange Properties dialog box in IIS 5

The options established by Exchange 2000 when these four entries are installed are usually fine. Especially for the Exchange entry, you should not change the default settings, or you could prevent OWA from functioning properly.

Virtual Directory

- *Location of the information for that entry*—For the Exchange entry, the Local Path field should point toward the mailboxes that will be supported by that OWA server. For users accessing information in the Local Path directory, the following rights can be set:
  - Script source access: Allows scripts to run in this directory
  - Read: Allows users to read the contents of the directory
  - Write: Allows information updates to be written to the directory
  - Directory browsing: Allows users to browse the contents of the directory and others underneath it
  - Log visits: Enables logging activity of visitors to the page; enabling this setting is highly recommended in most cases
  - Index this resource: Allows indexing of this directory; this option typically improves access and searching performance

- *Application Settings*—These settings can be adjusted to change how IIS implements the feature. For the Exchange entry, Scripts and Executables should be selected in the Execute Permissions drop-down list.

Documents

- This tab allows you to change which default Web pages or Active Server Pages are presented to users connecting to that particular service, as shown in Figure 8-8. The default sites are fine in almost every case, but if you have custom pages you want to use, you can change them here.

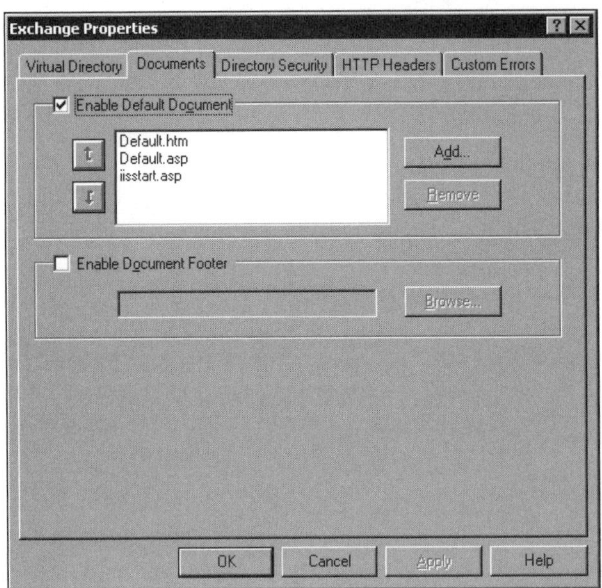

Figure 8-8 The Documents tab in the Exchange Properties dialog box

Directory Security

- This tab has three sections that allow you to set even tighter security controls than the default:
  - *Anonymous access and authentication control*—Allows you to specify whether you allow anonymous access and what type of authentication methods you want. For OWA, the Anonymous access and Integrated Windows authentication check boxes should be selected. To change or confirm these settings, click the Edit button in this section to open the dialog box shown in Figure 8-9.

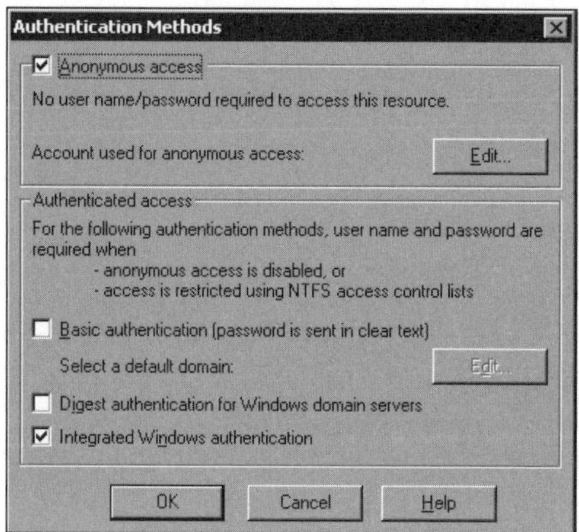

Figure 8-9 The OWA Authentication Methods dialog box

- *IP address and domain name restrictions*—Allows you to granularly specify which systems or domains can or cannot access the OWA service, based on IP address or domain name. By default, this setting allows any system to connect to the service.
- *Secure communications*—Allows you to specify the types of secure communications you want. You must have secure certificate services installed and functioning before configuring these settings.

HTTP Headers

- This tab allows you to set the information you provide to a user's Web browser about when the content on your site expires and thus should be refreshed (not an issue with OWA). It also allows you to configure what types of content rating you want (adult, general, and so on). This tab is usually not used for OWA services and can most likely be skipped.

Custom Errors

- This tab allows you to edit the error message text that users see if they encounter an error. The typically cryptic information might not suffice, so you have the option of specifying your own error messages that can be entered into a file for IIS to reference when that particular error comes up. This option allows you to give your users more detailed or user-friendly messages, possibly including an e-mail address or a phone number for users to contact the help desk.

In most cases, you can leave all this information at its default settings and be just fine. You should look at your security settings, however, and ensure that they are adequate for your needs, which will vary from site to site. For instance, security might not have to be tight if OWA is being used internally, not accessed over the Internet.

Security and Outlook Web Access

Securing OWA is much like securing any other Web site. As you learned in the "Configuring Outlook Web Access" section, you can set a variety of security features, including specifying your authentication method, using secure certificates, and limiting access based on IP addresses or domain names. Among your better options for securing OWA besides using secure certificates (which are discussed in Chapter 12, "Security and Encryption in Exchange 2000 Server") are setting the type of authentication methods you want and securing IIS itself. Securing IIS is essential to protect not only OWA, but also your other IIS services and your server in general. You will learn more about Exchange 2000 security in Chapter 12, but if you want additional reading on securing IIS and other Microsoft products, take a look at this site: *http://www.microsoft.com/technet/security*.

IIS can use several different methods, listed in Table 8-6, to authenticate users to your site.

Table 8-6 IIS Authentication Methods

Method	Upside	Downside
Anonymous	Works with any client software and is the easiest way to allow access to public folders that do not require security.	Does not really provide security. Anonymous users are limited to what the IUSER_*Computername* account has access to. This account is likely to be secured if you have secured Windows 2000 Server properly.
Basic	Works with most client software and can be used to easily pass authentication through firewalls.	Sends password as clear text, which could be intercepted by a hacker. The Secure Socket Layer (SSL) protocol can be used to encrypt the information.
Digest	Sends password in a hashed (jumbled) format which is supported by most current Web browsers. This method works through firewalls as well and provides more protection than Basic authentication.	This authentication method cannot be used with Exchange 2000 front-end servers, so the password is held unencrypted on the Windows 2000 domain controller, which decreases the level of security this option provides.
Certificate	Remains a very popular and fairly secure method supported by most common e-mail clients and Web browsers.	Requires additional administrative time to configure, implement, and maintain certificates and the certificate service on your server and client systems.

Table 8-6 IIS Authentication Methods (continued)

Method	Upside	Downside
Integrated Windows (Kerberos)	Sends users' passwords in an encrypted format; this method is the most secure one available in IIS.	Works only through a front-end server if the client is using Internet Explorer 5.0 or higher on a Windows 2000 operating system. This method is currently supported only by Internet Explorer 2.0 and higher.

As mentioned, securing your IIS server in general can help provide much of the security you need for OWA. You should keep up on the wide variety of IIS fixes and patches that are constantly being released to make sure your IIS and OWA servers stay as secure as possible.

Another security step you could take is to place your OWA server behind a firewall to limit access to OWA. Keep in mind, though, that even if you decide to put OWA behind a firewall, you should still ensure that your Windows 2000 Server and IIS servers are patched with the most up-to-date security fixes, and any unnecessary software and services should be disabled or removed entirely.

8

Outlook Web Access in Front-End and Back-End Environments

As you learned in Chapter 3, "Planning an Exchange 2000 Server Design Scenario," you can configure Exchange 2000 Server to use front-end and back-end server configurations, which can be used to accomplish a few key benefits for your OWA service, such as:

- Enabling support of additional users when use of your OWA services starts exceeding your OWA server's capacity (this depends on hardware and other processing the server is performing). By adding more back-end servers (the servers that process information and store mailboxes), you can help spread out the workload and increase the load your OWA configuration can support.
- Allowing additional front-end servers to be used to give several different back-end servers a common namespace (for example, Calgary.com). These front-end servers can also take over the processing of certificate authentication and provide additional security because there is another server between the Internet and the back-end servers, where all the processing and storage of sensitive data take place for requests sent through the OWA server.

A basic front-end/back-end configuration is shown in Figure 8-10.

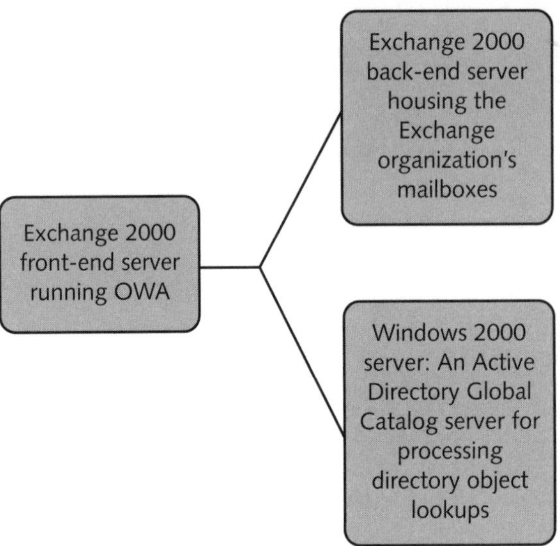

Figure 8-10 A basic front-end/back-end configuration

With front-end and back-end servers, information being passed with Basic authentication methods usually takes place as shown in these steps:

- A user connects to the front-end server (OWA) and is prompted for his or her user name and password.
- The user enters the appropriate user name and password, and the front-end server processes the authentication information.

Remember that the password information sent via Basic authentication is unencrypted and therefore vulnerable to interception by a third party (hacker).

- After the user is authenticated, the user is given access to his or her mailbox information being held on the back-end server.

For Basic authentication to work on the front-end server, the appropriate user and password information must be stored on the front-end server; however, this could be a vulnerable spot if the server is not secured properly—sensitive user account information can be exposed if the server is hacked. If you want a higher level of security, you must move toward using encryption, such as the Kerberos method. However, front-end servers cannot handle this type of authentication; only the back-end servers can process this method. With this type of authentication, you are also limited to using only Internet Explorer 5.0 and Windows 2000, but if you know that all your users are going to be using those two pieces of software, Kerberos security is definitely recommended to provide a more secure environment.

Although a detailed explanation of front-end/back-end configurations and advanced security configurations for OWA is outside the scope of this chapter, basic guidelines can be summarized as follows:

- Front-end servers typically provide the authentication for users connecting through OWA.
- Front-end servers ensure an additional level of security by placing another server between the outside world and your servers.
- Front-end servers provide a unified OWA existence for multiple back-end servers that use different namespaces.
- Back-end servers perform all the processing and house the mailboxes and public folder information.
- Back-end servers provide load-balancing to help distribute the processing of requests by front-end servers that get heavy use.

For further discussion and additional technical information on the OWA topics covered in this chapter, check out the Microsoft TechNet Web site at *www.microsoft.com/technet*. You can also find a sample chapter of the *Exchange 2000 Server Resource Kit* that deals specifically with OWA at *http://www.microsoft.com/technet/treeview/default.asp?url=/TechNet/prodtechnol/exchange/reskit/ex00res/deploygd/part5/c25owa.asp*.

Chapter Summary

- Exchange 2000 supports a variety of protocols that allow Exchange 2000 to communicate with a wide range of e-mail services and server products.
- Virtual protocol servers allow a single Exchange 2000 server to be configured as multiple servers, each with its own configuration information. Virtual servers are useful for supporting multiple organizations or departments that need their own special configurations, addresses, and security settings.
- IIS 5 provides support for various Exchange 2000 services, including the Web Store and OWA. The Internet Services Manager console is where you create, configure, and manage your OWA servers.
- Every protocol that Exchange 2000 supports has a variety of commands used to pass information to and from the server. During troubleshooting (especially newsgroup servers), these commands can help diagnose problems and find the source of errors.
- Exchange uses SMTP as the primary protocol for its message transfer between other Exchange servers. When Exchange 2000 is installed, it expands the SMTP command set and provides a few new features that Exchange 2000 uses, such as an advanced message queuing engine, enhanced message categorization, link status information, and the Installable File System used with Exchange 2000 public folders.

- POP3 is widely used for clients to connect and download e-mail over the Internet. However, sending mail back to a server is a task usually reserved for SMTP. SMTP typically requires a continuous network connection to manage and retrieve messages, but POP3 can issue sets of commands to be fulfilled when needed, making POP3 much more useful for clients on the Internet without a constant connection.
- IMAP4 enables message retrieval as the other protocols do, but expands on the abilities of POP3 by offering a wider array of user management features, such as specifying which messages are downloaded from the server and when they're downloaded. With IMAP4, you can also modify e-mail and messages while they are on the server instead of having to download messages from the server before you can access and work with them.
- LDAP is, as the name suggests, a protocol for directory access. LDAP servers are mainly used to report information on network objects (users, printers, files) to users. LDAP servers are commonly used on the Internet for performing name and address lookups, but this concept can be easily applied to company networks, especially those with many employees or several network objects that users need to sort through.
- NNTP can be used for a variety of services in Exchange 2000, such as providing Internet newsgroup services, hosting an internal newsgroup that can be used as message board, or even creating a newsgroup used solely to support your clients.
- IIS 5 is included with Windows 2000 by default. IIS 5 provides many different services for Exchange 2000 features, such as virtual servers and OWA. IIS 5 is relatively easy to learn, but effectively using and securing IIS 5 can be a daunting task.
- IIS 5, with new security features, also has new features intended to improve the overall setup, configuration, and maintenance experience for administrators. However, you must deal with an array of IIS 5 security issues, especially if you plan to run any kind of HTTP service connected to the Internet, such as OWA.
- HTTP, supported by Exchange 2000 through IIS 5, primarily provides support for OWA, a useful client package for connecting to Exchange mailboxes using any current Web browser, without requiring additional client software or configuration on the user's part. OWA is the closest client to Outlook 2000 in terms of features and functionality; in fact, the newest version of OWA included with Exchange 2000 and IIS 5 looks almost identical to the full Outlook 2000 client software package.
- It's fairly easy to install OWA and configure a basic setup for it. By default, when Exchange 2000 is installed, it creates a fully functioning OWA configuration. You might want to configure your own settings for the default site in the Internet Information Services console. Advanced OWA configurations can require more work, but configurations such as front-end and back-end servers can provide additional security and load-balancing if your OWA services get heavy use and traffic. Update your IIS security patches and configuration not only to protect your OWA server, but also your server and network as a whole.

Key Terms

Directory Information Tree (DIT) — A selection of information on various objects held in the directory. Each object in the database has attributes, such as a name or an address, and the DIT retains this information. To search this data, users use directory access servers connected with LDAP.

distinguished name (DN) — The unique name given to each object in the directory. The DN is built by taking the information in the Directory Information Tree leading up to the object in hierarchical order, starting from the topmost entry in the directory and moving down in order to the name of the object.

HTTP with WebDAV — The protocol that Outlook Web Access uses to communicate with the back-end services on an Exchange 2000 server.

list server — A service that enables users subscribing or posting to a mail list to receive, at preset intervals, the information that the e-mail server sends out.

message header — The part of the document that contains the pertinent message information, such as senders, recipients, and their addresses.

virtual protocol server — A server created and managed through the Exchange System Manager console that can allow a single Exchange 2000 server to simultaneously have many different servers, each with its own unique configuration.

Web Store — An Exchange service that allows users of OWA to connect to WebDAV-enabled directories configured with IIS 5 services and access these directories as any other user accesses files in the public folders.

Review Questions

1. In the following list, which protocol is used to support directory information searches?
   a. POP3
   b. IMAP4
   c. LDAP
   d. HTTP with WebDAV
2. A virtual protocol server can allow Exchange 2000 Server to use one Exchange 2000 server to support ________________.
3. Which type of virtual protocol server is not created by default when Exchange 2000 Server is first installed?
   a. NNTP
   b. POP3
   c. SMTP
   d. LDAP

4. Exchange 2000 virtual protocol servers are created, configured, and maintained with ________________.
5. Which of the following is required information that needs to be sent with an SMTP message in the message header? (Choose all that apply.)
   a. received status
   b. creation time
   c. return path
   d. source address
6. Information stored in the ________________ can help administrators track down problems with messages not being delivered or taking a long time to arrive.
7. Which of the following commands tells an SMTP server to reverse the status of the sender and receiver SMTP services (sender becomes recipient)?
   a. NOOP
   b. HELO
   c. TURN
   d. EXPN
8. E-mail systems that use languages other than English typically use an expanded full 8-bit character set to send messages because ________________.
9. When Exchange 2000 Server is installed, it expands the default SMTP functionality to include some new features that Exchange 2000 uses. Which of the following are new features built into this expanded set of SMTP services? (Choose all that apply.)
   a. support for the Installable File System (IFS)
   b. support for advanced message delivery performance
   c. support for link status information
   d. support for advanced message queuing
10. Your network's users must connect over slow, undedicated network connections. Which protocol should you use to provide the best e-mail connectivity for these users?
11. IMAP4 is considered a better overall protocol than POP3, which it's based on, because it can enable users to perform ________________, which POP3 does not allow.
12. An IMAP4 server can be in four different functional states, including "Waiting for authentication" and "No authentication." What are the other two states?
13. IMAP4 has a long list of commands, some of which can be issued only when the server is in a particular state. What command would you send if you wanted to query the server for a list of mailboxes to which the user has subscribed?
    a. LSUB
    b. STATUS
    c. SEARCH
    d. FETCH

14. Which of the following items contains information that an LDAP server uses to answer a user's query?
    a. Active Directory
    b. global address catalog
    c. domain forest tree
    d. Directory Information Tree
15. The unique entry that contains address information on an object, which LDAP references when responding to requests, is called a(n) ________________.
16. Which of the following features apply to a WebDAV-enabled folder on your Web site?
    a. allows fast searching of documents in the WebDAV-enabled folder
    b. enables the editing of a document's properties for a file stored in the WebDAV-enabled folder
    c. gives as many users as needed the ability to simultaneously edit the same document in the WebDAV-enabled folder
    d. enables the creation and modification of documents in the WebDAV-enabled folder
17. NNTP and newsgroup servers are considered an evolutionary development over a previous method of news distribution, the ________________.
18. Which of the following is a service that IIS 5 does not provide?
    a. firewall
    b. newsgroups
    c. OWA
    d. FTP
19. The design and basic functionality of the Web Storage System (Web Store) is very similar to that of the ________________.
20. The Exchange Interprocess Communications (ExIPC) layer is a message-queuing layer between two Exchange 2000 components: IIS 5 and ________________.
    a. Exchange 2000 Information Store
    b. Exchange 2000 Web Store
    c. Exchange 2000 storage groups
    d. Exchange 2000 back-end servers
21. Outlook Web Access (OWA) is the only client software package that UNIX users can use with Exchange 2000 Server to retrieve their e-mail messages. True or False?

22. Which of the following is not an entry created by Exchange 2000 for its default installation of OWA into IIS 5?
    a. public
    b. Exadmin
    c. Exchange
    d. Exmail
23. To configure OWA, you use several tabs in the Properties dialog box that contain options you can set. Which tab allows you to change the default Web page that is displayed to users when they connect to that site?
    a. Directory Security
    b. Virtual Directory
    c. Documents
    d. HTTP Headers
24. Of the available authentication options for use with OWA, the ______________ option is the most secure option, and the ______________ option is the least secure.
25. Which of the following are benefits of implementing a front-end/back-end server configuration with OWA? (Choose all that apply.)
    a. redundancy for Exchange 2000
    b. load-balancing for users connecting to the front-end servers
    c. common namespace for multiple servers
    d. security for back-end servers

Hands-on Projects

Project 8-1

Installing new virtual servers for Exchange 2000 Server using IIS 5 is relatively easy, but knowing how to create a new virtual server can prove quite helpful when your Exchange 2000 Server installations start growing in size and capability. This project shows you how to use IIS 5 and the Exchange System Manager console to create a new IMAP4 virtual server.

To create a new IMAP4 virtual server:

1. Log on to your Windows 2000 Server using an account with administrative privileges.
2. To open the Exchange System Manager console, click **Start**, point to **Programs**, point to **Microsoft Exchange**, and then click **System Manager**. The Exchange

System Manager console (see Figure 8-11) is where you perform nearly every administrative duty for Exchange 2000 Server.

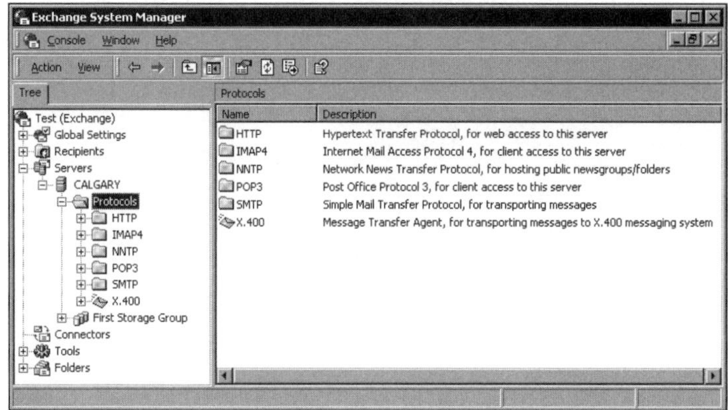

Figure 8-11 The Exchange System Manager console

3. Expand the **Servers** container in the Contents pane, expand your default Exchange server, and then expand the **Protocols** container to see the list of supported protocols for which you can create or manage virtual protocol servers. (If you have the display of administrative groups enabled, you might have to double-click the Administrative Groups folder, and then the First Administrative Group folder before you see the Servers folder.) Your window should now look similar to Figure 8-11. Click the **IMAP4** folder to display the folder's contents in the Details pane, where you should see the default IMAP4 virtual protocol server.
4. To install the new IMAP4 virtual server, right-click an empty area in the Details pane, point to **New**, and then click **IMAP4 Virtual Server** on the shortcut menu. The New IMAP4 Virtual Server Wizard opens, as shown in Figure 8-12.
5. In the Name text box, type a descriptive name for this virtual server. For the purpose of this project, type **Test IMAP4 Virtual Server**, and then click the **Next** button to move to the Select IP Address window.

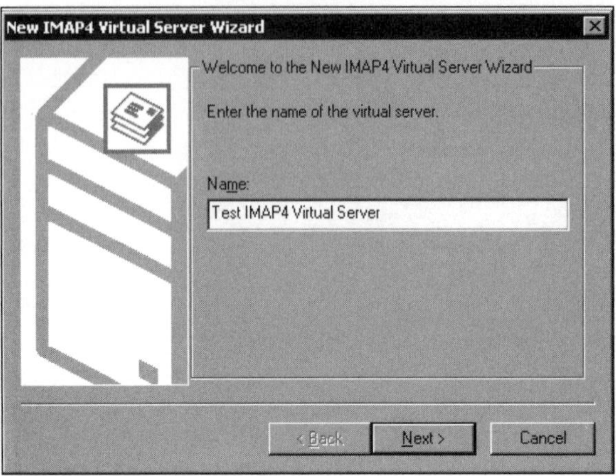

Figure 8-12 Selecting a server name in the New IMAP4 Virtual Server Wizard

6. In the drop-down list, you must select which IP address you want this virtual server to use, as shown in Figure 8-13. The default selection is configured to (All Unassigned), but you cannot use this selection because every virtual server must have its own address. Typically, you select the IP address you have already chosen for this connection, but for this project, select the IP address for the server. This selection will vary based on your server's configuration; for this project, however, the IP that's selected is not important as long as it isn't the (All Unassigned) option. Click the IP address, and then click the **Finish** button to complete the wizard.

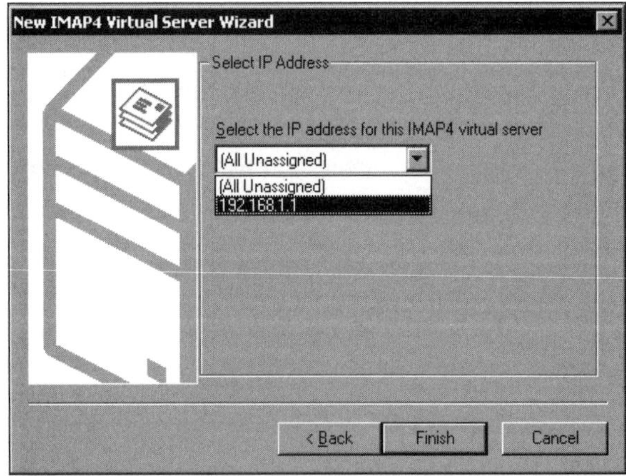

Figure 8-13 Selecting an IP address in the New IMAP4 Virtual Server Wizard

7. In the Details pane of Exchange System Manager, the new IMAP4 server, Test IMAP4 Virtual Server, should be listed. Close any open windows or applications.

Project 8-2

Configuring an IMAP4 virtual server is nearly as easy as installing one, although there are a few different options you can set after the IMAP4 virtual server has been installed, which is useful knowledge if you need to configure any default or additional IMAP4 servers in your Exchange 2000 installation. This project assumes you have completed Project 8-1.

To configure an IMAP4 virtual server:

1. If necessary, log on to your Windows 2000 Server using an account with administrative privileges.
2. To open the Exchange System Manager console, click **Start**, point to **Programs**, point to **Microsoft Exchange**, and then click **System Manager**.
3. Expand the **Servers** container in the Contents pane, expand your default Exchange server, expand the **Protocols** container, and then click the **IMAP4** folder. You should see the default IMAP4 virtual protocol server and the server you created in Project 8-1.
4. Right-click the virtual protocol server you created in Project 8-1, and then click **Properties** on the shortcut menu. The Properties dialog box for this virtual protocol server opens and should look similar to Figure 8-14.

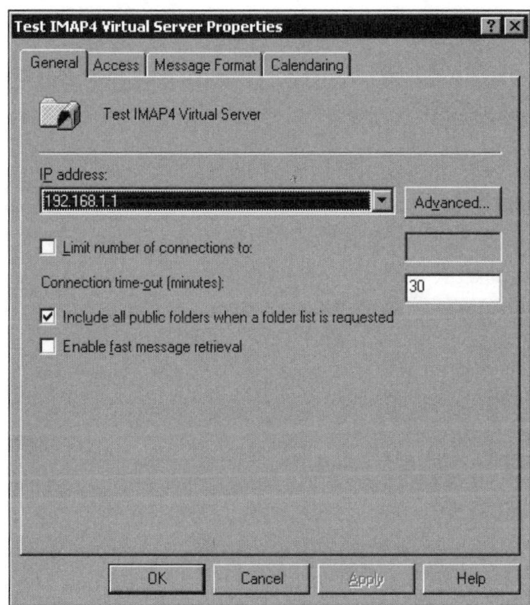

Figure 8-14 The Properties dialog box for the IMAP4 virtual server

5. In the General tab, the main options to pay attention to are the IP address drop-down list (where you can change the IP address this virtual server uses) and the

Limit number of connections to check box. Click the **Limit the number of connections to** check box to enable this option, and in the text box to the right, type **30** for the number of connections you want.

6. Make sure the Include all public folders when a folder list is requested check box is selected. Enabling this option is necessary if you want your IMAP4 users to view all the public folders they have access to using this server. However, it should be enabled by default.
7. Click the **Access** tab, where you set security for this virtual server. The three sections in this tab (Access control, Secure communication, and Connection control) have options for modifying security settings.
8. Click the **Message Format** tab, as shown in Figure 8-15. This is where you set the type of message encoding you want to use for this virtual server. By default, the format should be set to Provide message body as HTML. You might want to change this option if several of your users have older browsers that do not support HTTP e-mail messages (most current client software packages do, though); if this is the case with your client, click the **Provide message body as plain text** radio button.

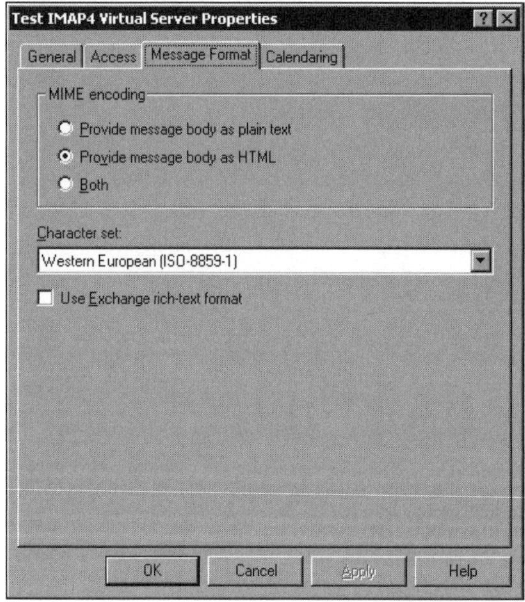

Figure 8-15 Selecting a message format for the IMAP4 virtual server in the Properties dialog box

9. Click the **Calendaring** tab. This tab allows you to set options for OWA and its calendaring feature. For example, you can specify which server users are directed to when they receive an e-mail notifying them of a meeting request. The default options in this tab are typically fine for most configurations. Click the **Apply**

button at the bottom of the dialog box to save the settings you changed, and then click the **OK** button. If you are continuing to Project 8-3, you can leave the system at its current state. Otherwise, close any open windows or applications.

You have finished configuring your IMAP4 virtual protocol server. As you can see, there is not an overabundance of options to worry about here, but some, especially the security options, are important for ensuring that you have the appropriate level of security.

Project 8-3

As in Project 8-2, understanding how to configure a virtual server is quite useful. In many cases (especially smaller installations), the default SMTP virtual server configured in Exchange 2000 Server during the first install is more than adequate. However, understanding the various options you can change as well as understanding how to configure a SMTP virtual server is useful when you must deviate from the default installation. Although configuring an SMTP virtual server is very similar to configuring an IMAP4 server, there are some SMTP-specific configuration options of which you should be aware.

To configure the default SMTP virtual server:

1. If necessary, log on to your Windows 2000 server using an account with administrative privileges. If you are continuing from Project 8-2, you can skip this step and the next one.
2. To open the Exchange System Manager console, click **Start**, point to **Programs**, point to **Microsoft Exchange**, and then click **System Manager**.
3. Expand the **Servers** container, expand your default Exchange server, and then expand the **Protocols** container. Click the **SMTP** folder to display its contents in the Details pane.
4. Right-click the **Default SMTP Virtual Server** entry, and then click **Properties** on the shortcut menu to open the Default SMTP Virtual Server Properties dialog box (which looks similar to the Properties dialog box you saw in Project 8-2). In the General tab, you can set the virtual server's IP address and specify whether you want to enable logging for this server. In most cases, you will want logging enabled, so click to select the **Enable logging** check box.
5. Click the **Access** tab. This is where you configure security settings for this virtual server; review the options to see which ones you might need to configure for your production Exchange 2000 server.
6. Click the **Messages** tab, where you can set the messaging limits for this virtual server. The options include limits on message size and the number of messages your virtual server will handle per connection (see Figure 8-16).

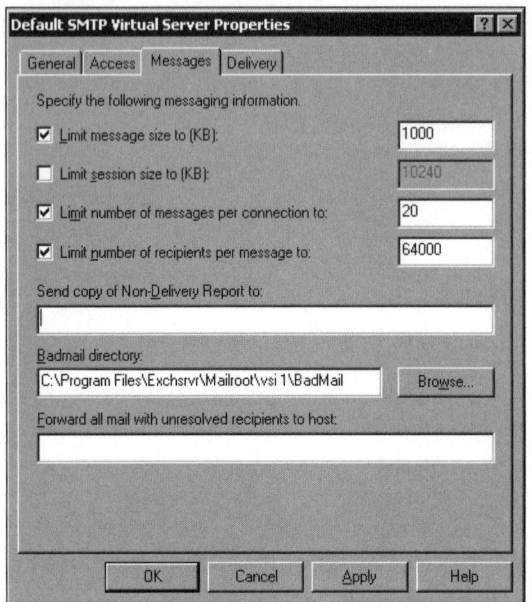

Figure 8-16 Reviewing messaging limits for the default SMTP virtual server

You can also specify the directory for storing undeliverable messages in the Badmail directory text box. For this project, however, leave this entry at its default. To limit the size of e-mail attachments, click to select the **Limit message size to (KB)** check box, and in the text box to the right, type **1000** (which is 1000 KB, or 1 MB).

7. Click the **Delivery** tab, shown in Figure 8-17, which allows you to set how this virtual server handles the delivery of e-mail messages to external servers.

If your environment requires that messages be sent as quickly as possible, you might want to set these retry options lower to expedite sending messages. A good rule of thumb here is to leave at least the third retry attempt a bit longer to give the destination time to rectify the problem before it tries sending for the last time.

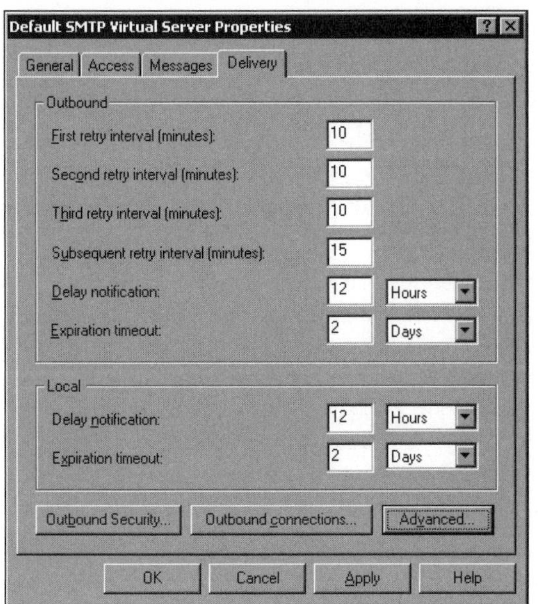

Figure 8-17 Setting retry options for the default SMTP virtual server

In this tab, you can also set how often this virtual server attempts to retry sending messages that were not sent because of network problems or because the external e-mail server was busy. Set the three separate retry values to the following: in the First retry interval (minutes) text box, enter **5**; in the Second retry interval (minutes) text box, enter **5**; and in the Third retry interval (minutes) text box, enter **15**. These settings are by no means the ultimate rule to follow; you will likely need to adjust these settings to match your circumstances, but these entries are typically adequate.

8. The Delivery tab also has three buttons at the bottom that allow you to adjust outbound security, outbound connections, and advanced delivery options for the virtual server. Click each of these buttons and take note of the available options. After you have finished looking through the different options, click the **Apply** button, and then close any open windows or applications.

Project 8-4

The Internet Information Services console is where you manage IIS 5 settings, including your Outlook Web Access server(s). Exchange 2000 includes a default OWA installation in IIS 5 that uses the default Web site included with IIS 5. This project shows you some of the important settings for the default Web site in IIS 5 in case you have to reconfigure the default sites or create new ones of your own to get the configurations you need.

To view configuration settings for the default IIS Web site using the Internet Information Services Console:

1. If necessary, log on to the Windows 2000 server using an account with administrative privileges.
2. To open the Internet Information Services console, click **Start**, point to **Programs**, point to **Administrative Tools**, and then click **Internet Services Manager**.
3. In the Contents pane of the Internet Information Services console is a list of the currently installed sites on the server, which should include the Default Web Site and the Administration Web Site. Typically, for security reasons, disabling the Administration Web Site is recommended. To do so, right-click the **Administration Web Site** container, and then click **Stop** on the shortcut menu. This stops the Administration Web Site from running and helps limit potential intrusions through that site. Unless you have a very good reason to use it, it should remain disabled at all times.
4. After you have stopped the site, right-click the **Default Web Site** container, and then click **Properties** on the shortcut menu. The Default Web Site Properties dialog box opens, as shown in Figure 8-18.

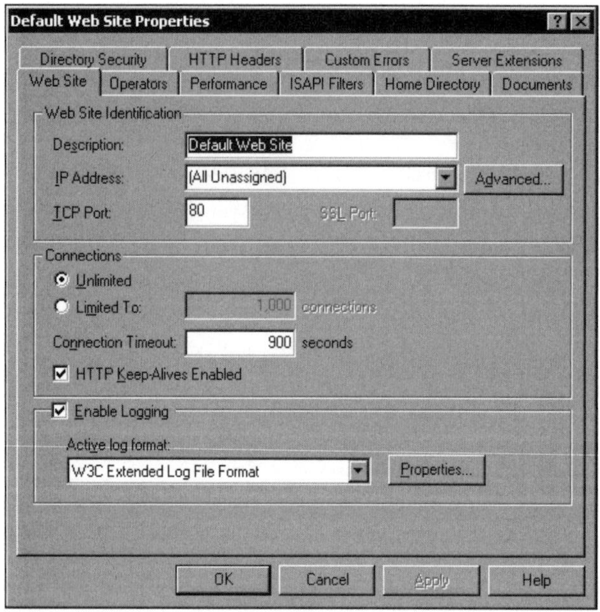

Figure 8-18 The Default Web Site Properties dialog box

5. This dialog box has 10 tabs, each containing options that can be set or configured to match your needs. Take some time to review the major settings and options in each tab.
6. List the 10 tabs in the Default Web Site Properties dialog box on a piece of paper. Under each tab, list one major option or selection, and then write down your opinion of what the option or selection does or what benefit it brings to the Web site configuration.
7. If you are performing Project 8-5, close the Default Web Site Properties dialog box, and leave your system at the Internet Information Services console. Otherwise, close any open windows or applications.

Project 8-5

You might need to install additional OWA servers if you want load-balancing because of excessive use or if you have a separate domain, company, or similar entity that is configured differently from the main OWA server you already have. This project shows you the basic steps for installing a new OWA server in addition to the default OWA server in IIS 5, so that in the future you can create and configure additional OWA servers as needed.

To install a second Outlook Web Access server:

1. If necessary, log on to your Windows 2000 server using an account with administrative privileges. If you are continuing from Project 8-4, you can skip Steps 1–2.
2. To open the Internet Information Services console, click **Start**, point to **Programs**, point to **Administrative Tools**, and then click **Internet Services Manager**.
3. To create your second OWA server, you should first stop your existing Web site. To do so, right-click the **Default Web Site**, and then click **Stop** on the shortcut menu. Stopping this site ensures that nothing interferes with your new OWA server. When you have a production server and are using the default Web site as an OWA server, however, it's not necessary to stop the existing one.
4. After stopping the default Web site, minimize the Internet Information Services console, and then open the Exchange System Manager console by clicking **Start**, pointing to **Programs**, pointing to **Microsoft Exchange**, and then clicking **System Manager**.
5. In the Exchange System Manager console, double-click the **Servers** container to expand its contents, double-click your default Exchange server, and then double-click the **Protocols** container to expand the list of protocols that Exchange supports. Right-click the **HTTP** folder, point to **New**, and then click **HTTP Virtual Server** on the shortcut menu. A new Properties dialog box opens, as shown in Figure 8-19.

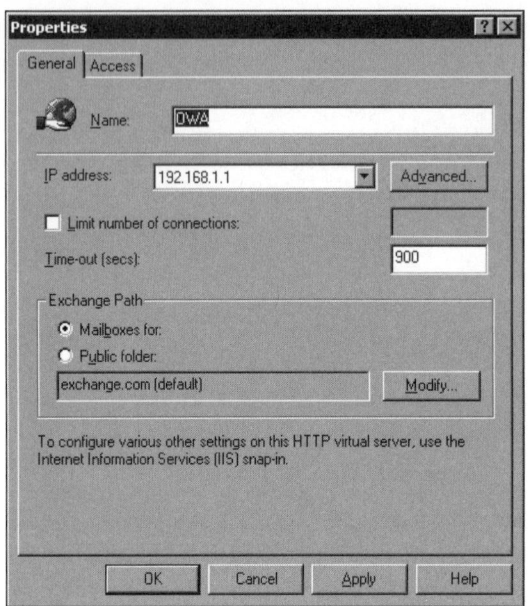

Figure 8-19 The Properties dialog box for creating a new OWA server

6. In this Properties dialog box, enter a unique name (for this project, use **OWA**) in the Name text box. Each OWA server requires its own IP address; in the IP address drop-down list, select the local IP address for the server. The rest of the settings are fine at their default, but you can set a limit on the number of connections here if you like. (You might see a message box warning you that the virtual server won't start if the combination of IP addresses, port, and host name matches that of any Internet server Web site. If so, make sure you selected the server's local IP address.)
7. Click the **Access** tab. In the Access Control section, you can change the settings if you need to grant rights different from the default setting, although for most situations the default settings you see in Figure 8-20 are fine. After you have set the appropriate rights, click the **Apply** button, and then click the **OK** button to return to the Exchange System Manager console.

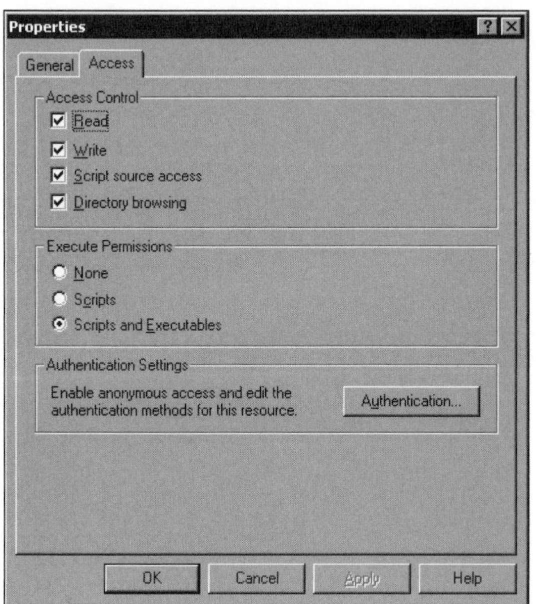

Figure 8-20 Configuring access settings for the new OWA server

8. Under the HTTP folder, you should now see the new OWA HTTP virtual server you created. If you maximize the Internet Information Services console, you will notice a new Web site called OWA in your list of sites. You can now restart the default Web site by right-clicking the entry, and then clicking **Start** on the shortcut menu.
9. Switch back to the Exchange System Manager, right-click the new OWA server you just created, and then click **Browse** on the shortcut menu. A new Internet Explorer window opens and should load your new OWA server. If the account you are logged on as does not have an Exchange mailbox configured, you might need to log on with a user account that does have an Exchange mailbox. After you have finished experimenting with OWA, close the browser window.
10. If you want to adjust the configuration settings for your new OWA server, you can do so through the Internet Services console, as you learned in the "Configuring Outlook Web Access" section earlier in this chapter. Spend some time looking through the various configuration options. After you have finished doing this and you have confirmed that your new OWA server is functioning, you can close any open windows or applications.

CASE PROJECTS

Case Projects Background

Snappers.com is a new IT company that is developing high-tech multimedia widgets for the North American market. The company is flush with capital and is establishing a new network from the ground up, including its e-mail infrastructure. Because Snappers.com will be designing, building, and selling a new product, it has Engineering, Sales, and Marketing Departments that all require e-mail access and collaboration. Snappers.com expects to expand rapidly in the coming months as its product comes closer to launch time, but right now the most important task is to have the network and infrastructure in place as quickly as possible.

Case 1

You have been contracted by Snappers.com to perform a new Exchange 2000 deployment for the new network. Snappers.com has a wide variety of users with different client access needs, so it needs an array of varying connection methods. The Engineering Department uses UNIX as its operating system, the Marketing Department is located entirely on the local network, and the Sales Department is typically out of the office, unlike the Engineering Department. However, Sales personnel need access to e-mail only through their laptops, using a Windows operating system. Which different protocols should you implement and what client software would you recommend for each department? Also, which protocol will be the primary one used with each client software package?

Case 2

After using your initial configuration for a year or so, Snappers.com is ready to make some changes. Snappers.com has been expanding rapidly and, based on very positive user feedback from the Engineering Department about OWA, has decided to use Outlook Web Access as its primary client for every user on the network. You determine that this will overburden the default OWA configuration, which up to now has seen light use. Snappers.com wants you to recommend a plan to alleviate the potential burden on OWA and ensure that users have consistent access to their e-mail in case of failure. Also, the company wants to make sure it retains a standard Web site address so that users have only one address to go to when they want to access OWA. Is this possible with the changes you suggest? What plan do you come up with to alleviate the burden on OWA?

Case 3

Two years have passed since the first Exchange 2000 server was put in place, and Snappers.com is planning to release its first new product: the Widget Wheel. Because of this project's cutting-edge nature, Snappers.com expects to have a heavy amount of end-user support. Snappers.com wants suggestions on what it can do to improve the overall customer support with the equipment it has right now. It realizes that additional e-mail addresses will be created, but what are some other options you can offer? Suggest two ways Snappers.com can improve its customer support situation with the existing hardware.

Case 4

Snappers.com has had an overnight success with its new Widget Wheel product. The product is such a success that it has attracted the attention of hackers to the Web site. Because Snappers.com employees all use Outlook Web Access (some through the Internet while in the field), they have been seeing consistent attacks against their Web servers. These attacks have included unauthorized attempts to use the passwords belonging to one of the Sales Department's employees to access the OWA server. Thankfully, none of the attacks has been successful to date. What would you recommend to Snappers.com, as a possible fix for the potential password capturing that appears to be happening right now? Keep in mind that default authentication methods are currently in place.

CHAPTER

9

EXCHANGE 2000 SERVER MANAGEMENT

After reading this chapter and completing the exercises, you will be able to:

- Understand the design of the Exchange 2000 System Manager MMC snap-in and how to effectively use it for server configuration
- Create and configure a system policy to simplify the administration of servers, mailbox stores, and public folder stores
- Efficiently use the Windows 2000 snap-ins and utilities, including Computer Management, the Performance console, Event Viewer, and Task Manager, to manage various Exchange 2000 processes
- Efficiently manage Exchange 2000 Server resources, such as storage groups and Information Store databases, to accommodate increasing levels of messaging traffic within your organization
- Create and configure resources for recipients, such as recipient policies, address lists, and full-text indexing, to simplify administration of all mail-enabled and mailbox-enabled recipient objects

This chapter focuses on managing an Exchange 2000 server. The words "managing" and "administering" are sometimes thought to have the same meaning (and most Microsoft exams use these terms interchangeably, along with the term "implementing"). Some people use the phrase "managing an Exchange server" for monitoring or optimizing the server, and other people use the term "managing" or "administering" when they mean configuring and installing Exchange 2000 components. To lift this veil of confusion, this chapter will adopt a simple yet practical definition of "management" that encompasses all these objectives. Managing an Exchange 2000 server means knowing how to use the tools provided by Exchange 2000 and Windows 2000 so that the Exchange 2000 components—for example, storage groups, messaging databases, and administrative groups—can all function at optimal levels to provide an efficient and reliable messaging structure for your organization. The concepts in this chapter prepare you for troubleshooting more advanced problems that occur in Exchange 2000 (see Chapter 14, "Maintaining and Monitoring Exchange 2000 Server," for details on troubleshooting Exchange Server).

USING EXCHANGE 2000 SERVER TOOLS FOR SERVER MANAGEMENT

As you know, Exchange 2000 is fully integrated with Windows 2000, and with the link AD supplies between Exchange 2000 and Windows 2000, you might wonder whether you can simultaneously manage Windows 2000 and Exchange 2000 with the same set of tools. Even though Microsoft has designed many utilities, such as Task Manager, to manage and/or monitor multiple programs or processes, major applications such as Exchange 2000 have their own built-in management interfaces. For Exchange 2000, you use System Manager to manage its components.

Exchange 5.5 also uses Exchange Administrator to manage its components. However, this program has no bearing on managing its related operating system, Windows NT 4.0 Server.

The System Manager Console and Its Components

The System Manager console enables centralized administration for many settings, including message formats, recipient configuration, system policies, administrative groups, address lists, protocols, and connectors. You can use this general-purpose console to make fine-tuned modifications to Exchange Server that result in a stable, functional, and efficient messaging environment. Administrators know that these configurations can take a lot of time, but the time invested in learning the intricacies of System Manager offers a multitude of administrative rewards, such as less downtime for users, faster problem solving, and optimal message flows in your organization.

Although System Manager is used to centrally manage your organization's Exchange servers, it can also be installed locally on any Windows 2000 Professional or Server computer to remotely manage your Exchange 2000 servers. As shown in Figure 9-1, the System Manager console displays four main nodes (also referred to as folder structures or container items), each containing its own set of subfolders and other configuration containers. All four folders are housed underneath a central Organization object, which forms the root of your messaging environment and the starting point for your configuration.

The four main folders in System Manager are Global Settings, Recipients, Administrative Groups (or Routing Groups), and Tools. The following list explains what you'll find in these folders (the subfolders are described in more detail in Table 9-1):

- *Global Settings*—Settings that apply to all the servers or recipients in your organization. Examples of global settings include Internet Message Formats, Message Delivery, and Instant Messaging.
- *Recipients*—Any objects that can receive e-mail, including users, groups, or contact objects. The Recipients container is used primarily for recipient management through the establishment of recipient policies.

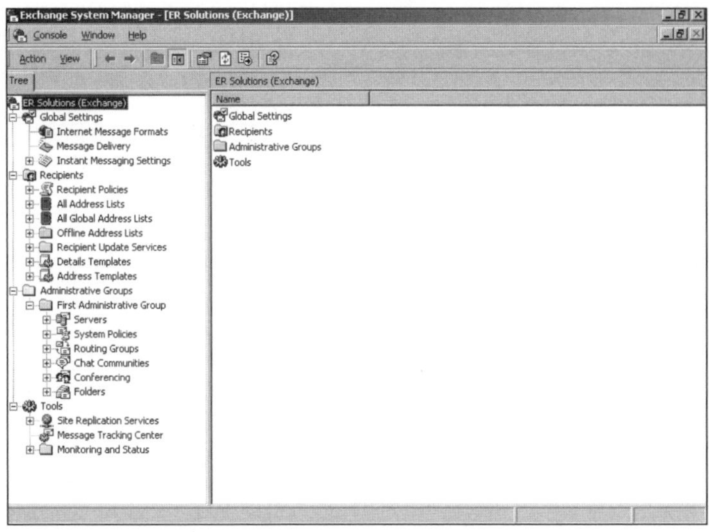

Figure 9-1 The System Manager console

- *Administrative Groups (or Routing Groups)*—Groups used to organize objects, such as users and groups, into containers so that multiple administrators can centrally manage them. Each administrative group can contain other objects, such as routing groups, system policies, and server objects. (Routing groups are covered in more detail in Chapter 10, "Connector and Routing Management in Exchange 2000 Server.")
- *Tools*—A set of tools that help monitor the status of your Exchange 2000 server.

Table 9-1 describes the subfolders within the four main System Manager components.

Table 9-1 System Manager Folders in Exchange 2000

Folder Name	Subfolder Name	Description
Global Settings	Internet Message Formats	Defines acceptable message formats, including message encoding, character sets, and multipurpose Internet mail extensions (MIME) mappings.
	Message Delivery	Defines how and when messages are delivered, including quotas for mail delivery and message filters.
	Instant Messaging	Defines your firewall topology if instant messaging is being deployed with firewalls in your organization.

Table 9-1 System Manager Folders in Exchange 2000 (continued)

Folder Name	Subfolder Name	Description
Recipients	Recipient Policies	Defines the manner in which proxy e-mail addresses (such as new SMTP or X.400 addresses) are created for your users.
	All Global Address Lists Offline Address Lists	Simplifies the search for users and resources across your organization (for example, the GAL is a default address list found in Exchange 2000 Server).
	Recipient Update Services	Updates existing e-mail addresses or address lists in AD; new addresses are replicated immediately throughout the organization. Two update service objects are displayed for the AD domain naming context and the AD configuration naming context.
	Details Templates Address Templates	Defines the appearance of information in the Exchange 2000 address book and can be used to address messages to mailboxes that are *not* located in the GAL or a personal address book.
Administrative Groups	Servers	Defines the collection of Exchange 2000 servers in the administrative group.
	System Policies	Controls settings for Exchange 2000 servers and Information Stores via policies for servers, mailbox stores, and public folder stores.
	Routing Groups	Defines how messages are routed through your organization.
	Chat Communities	Manages the Exchange 2000 Chat service and consists of a set of channels, bans, and user classes assigned to a server running the Chat service.
	Conferencing	Manages virtual meetings or online conferences if you install the additional components of the Conference Management Service, the Data Conference Provider, and the Video Conference Provider.
	Folders	Creates and manages separate public folder trees, also known as public folder hierarchies, so that you can design flexible workflow solutions for your organization.

Table 9-1 System Manager Folders in Exchange 2000 (continued)

Folder Name	Subfolder Name	Description
Tools	Site Replication Services	Configures a directory service that provides directory interoperability between Exchange 2000 Server and Exchange Server 5.5 in mixed-mode environments.
	Message Tracking Center	Enables message tracking for your organization, to locate messages in message queues, or verify that certain messages have been successfully delivered to users.
	Monitoring and Status	Contains two user interfaces used to monitor and manage the overall health of your Exchange 2000 servers: the Notifications interface to set up e-mail or script notifications if your server reaches certain threshold levels, and a Status interface that displays the current status of your Exchange servers or connectors.

As Table 9-1 illustrates, the System Manager console is not a tool to be taken lightly. It takes a lot of administrative effort to properly configure all the necessary Exchange properties for any organization, and no two organizations have exactly the same needs. Although all the elements in the System Manager console are relevant in some way for any Exchange 2000 organization, certain elements or components get more attention simply because they are more widely deployed and contribute more toward reducing administrative burdens for most Exchange 2000 organizations. An example of such a component is system policies.

Configuring Servers Using System Policies

System policies are used to apply settings to servers simultaneously. Policies usually take effect on common server-side objects, such as mailbox stores and public folder stores, and they can be applied to an entire Exchange 2000 server or to individual databases. You initially choose the settings that you want incorporated into a policy, and then associate this policy with objects from a common object class (for example, servers belong to one object class, and users belong to a separate object class). System policies increase administrative efficiency because any configuration change requires editing only one policy object and applying this change only once in System Manager. These are the three types of system policies in Exchange 2000:

- *Server policies*—Enable configuration of logging, message tracking, or log file maintenance on several servers simultaneously. The policy can be applied to servers in one or more administrative groups.

- *Mailbox store policies*—Apply settings such as mailbox limits and maintenance intervals for public folder stores to several mailbox stores simultaneously. You can even define deleted items or deleted mailbox retention periods for all servers in your organization by using one mailbox store system policy.
- *Public folder store policies*—Apply maintenance settings, replication intervals, and storage limits to multiple public folder stores simultaneously.

You can incorporate system policies into your administrative group structure by creating a system policy in one administrative group, and then applying this policy to servers in other administrative groups in your organization. This allows different administrators to control different settings, using policies defined for all administrative groups. System policies benefit all types of organizations, especially those supporting many Exchange 2000 servers, because one policy can be associated with any number of servers, even if they belong to separate administrative groups. Before you can create a system policy, however, at least one Administrative Group container in System Manager must have a System Policies container (see the "Hands-on Projects," later in this chapter, for a project on creating and configuring a mailbox store system policy in Exchange 2000).

A System Policies container does not exist by default in System Manager; you have to manually create it before configuring any system policy, whether it's for servers, mailbox stores, or public folder stores. Each administrative group can contain only one System Policies container.

When you initially create a system policy, you are asked to select property pages for the policy. These property pages are used to select configuration settings that you want applied to all servers in your administrative groups. For server system policies, you can select only a General property page; system policies for mailbox stores, however, can have up to four property pages. The following sections preview some configuration details for each type of system policy you can create in System Manager and show how to configure a sample server system policy to demonstrate the simplicity of system policies in general.

Configuring System Policies for Servers

To create a new server system policy in System Manager, first you need to create a System Policies container in your Administrative Groups folder. (Detailed instructions on these steps are given in the "Hands-on Projects" section.) Next, create a new server policy. You are then prompted to select a property page in the New Policy dialog box, shown in Figure 9-2. As mentioned, you have only one choice for server policies: General. Next, you use the Server Policy Properties dialog box to configure settings, such as entering a descriptive name for the policy. Figure 9-3 shows the main configuration settings—on the General (Policy) tab—you can select for every server policy you create. These settings can be applied en masse to any number of Exchange 2000 servers within the administrative group you are currently working, or they can be copied to servers in other administrative groups in your organization.

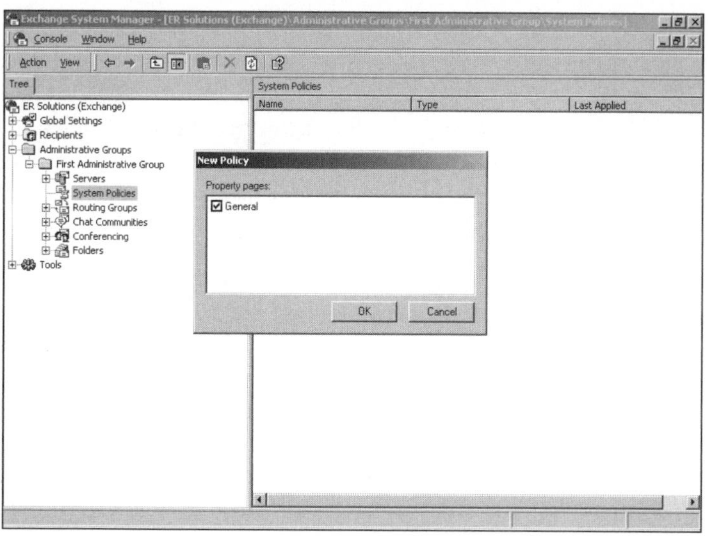

Figure 9-2 Selecting a property page for the new server system policy

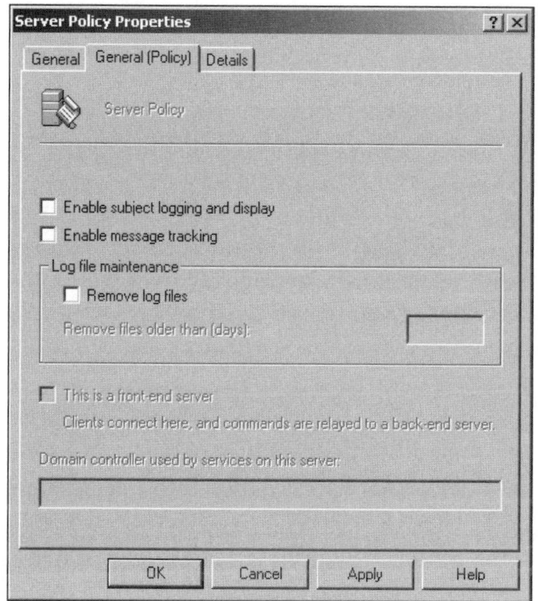

Figure 9-3 The General (Policy) tab of the new Server Policy Properties dialog box

A common configuration task is enabling message tracking for a group of servers within an administrative group by clicking the Enable message tracking check box in the General (Policy) tab. Many administrators enable message tracking in Exchange 2000 because they want to follow messages as they make their way through an organization, in case troubleshooting is needed at a particular point in the message flow. For example, if users complain that their messages are not being received in a timely manner, you can use message tracking to see where these messages might be (or if they are stuck in a queue, for instance). If message tracking is enabled through a system policy, all messages flowing through a server located within an administrative group are added to a tracking log. Message tracking is disabled by default, so server policies make it easier to apply this feature to multiple servers simultaneously. (Message tracking is covered in more depth in Chapter 14.)

Configuring System Policies for Mailbox Stores

Mailbox store system policies are used mostly to set maintenance cycles and define storage limits for all mailbox stores on a server. You can use up to four property pages to configure mailbox store policies; these property pages are described in the following list. Refer to "Managing Exchange 2000 Recipients," later in this chapter, for more information on some of the features described in this list.

- *General*—Used to select a default public folder store and offline address lists, to configure secure/multipurpose Internet mail extensions (S/MIME) support for your users, and to specify whether you want to show plain-text e-mail messages in a fixed-size font (so that all messages are displayed consistently and do not require extra processing or rendering for different size fonts).
- *Database*—Used to select a maintenance interval for online defragmentation of Exchange server databases.
- *Limits*—Used to configure storage limits for your users. If users exceed your defined threshold levels, you have the following options in this tab: Issue a warning at (KB), Prohibit send at (KB), or Prohibit send and receive at (KB). You can also configure deletion retention settings for messages and mailboxes. Selecting a long retention time for messages or mailboxes is not advised, however, because system resources can become overtaxed.
- *Full-Text Indexing*—Used to define special time periods, known as intervals, for the Windows 2000 Server Indexing service. With this service, you can search for items in mailboxes or public folders by using the Microsoft Web Storage System, which provides access to Exchange resources using HTTP.

Each mailbox store policy you configure can contain different property pages. For example, one policy might have only a General page, and another policy has both General and Database pages. You can add or remove property pages, and you can add or remove mailbox store policies for your administrative groups. The downside to this flexibility is that you could unintentionally create two separate policies with conflicting settings that apply to the same mailbox store. For example, you might wind up with one policy that prohibits sending messages if users have exceeded a storage limit, and a second policy that doesn't. If such a conflict occurs, System Manager displays a warning message advising you to remove the mailbox store from any conflicting policies before applying the current policy's settings.

Configuring System Policies for Public Folder Stores

Configuration settings for public folder stores are roughly equivalent to those for mailbox stores; you can configure settings for maintenance cycles, storage limits, and retention periods. However, items specific to public folders appear in the form of public folder replication intervals and public folder replication limits. Public folder store policies have the same property pages as mailbox store policies, with the exception of a new page: Replication. The Replication tab defines intervals during which new or changed items are replicated, or copied, to another instance of the same public folder on other servers. Details on public folder system policies are covered in Chapter 13, "Public Folders and Exchange 2000 Server."

Using Windows 2000 Tools for Exchange Server Management

Exchange 2000 uses the System Manager interface to manage common objects. However, Windows 2000 provides additional tools and utilities that help manage Exchange 2000 services or files. Because Exchange 2000 is architecturally integrated with Windows 2000 through the AD database, any utility used to manage AD is also used (directly or indirectly) to manage Exchange 2000. Exchange 2000 not only takes advantage of the network architecture of Windows 2000, but it also makes use of the Windows 2000 security features. The following sections describe these additional tools.

Windows 2000 tools are discussed here in the context of managing Exchange 2000 Server, not Windows 2000 Server. Each tool provides some level of integration with Exchange 2000, and you should always look for this integration when examining the tools in the following sections.

Active Directory Users and Computers

The Active Directory Users and Computers console is a Microsoft Management Console (MMC) snap-in. MMCs, which developers and administrators use as a framework for managing Windows 2000 and Exchange 2000 Server, are multiple-document interface (MDI) applications. These applications define a user interface in which users can work with more than one document simultaneously.

Therefore, the MMC is basically a "skeleton" that Exchange 2000 developers use to create snap-ins. MMCs provide the look for administrative utilities, but snap-ins supply the content. The Active Directory Users and Computers snap-in, shown in Figure 9-4, provides the content for managing user accounts and their associated mailboxes. It replaces the User Manager for Domains utility—found in all Windows NT 4.0 domain controllers—used to manage Exchange Server 5.5 user accounts.

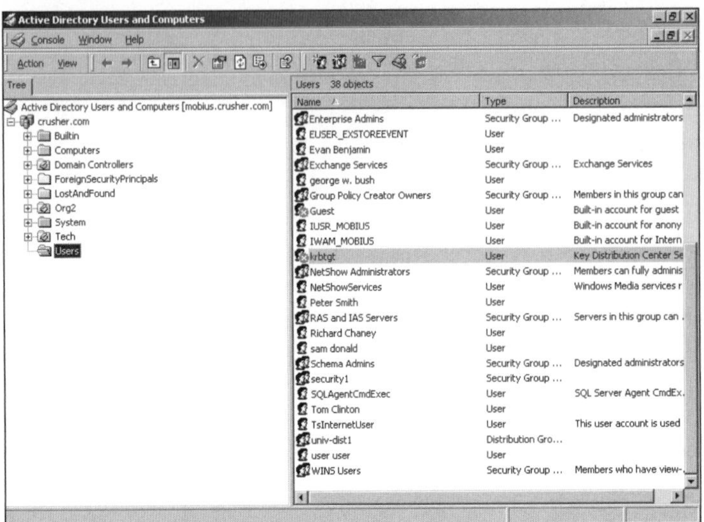

Figure 9-4 The Active Directory Users and Computers console

Active Directory Users and Computers is used to create potential recipient objects such as users, groups, or contacts; however, it does not formally create a mailbox object because a physical mailbox object is actually stored in the Information Store component of Exchange. On the other hand, you can use Active Directory Users and Computers to mail-enable or mailbox-enable a recipient object that you have just created by adding e-mail or other Exchange-specific information to these objects (see the "Managing Exchange 2000 Recipients" section later in this chapter for details on mail-enabling or mailbox-enabling these recipient objects).

Computer Management

The Computer Management utility, or snap-in, is a collection of other snap-ins used to manage both Windows 2000 and Exchange 2000 services and applications. It gives you one centralized, consolidated tool for managing local or remote computers. The benefits offered by this tool include the ability to perform the following tasks using the Computer Management snap-ins:

- Monitor system events, such as application errors
- Create and manage shared folders
- Start or stop critical system services on the fly and manage server applications and services, including the DHCP and DNS services

Most of the containers visible in this snap-in can be opened in separate or custom MMC snap-ins. Computer Management has three main containers: System Tools, Storage, and Services and Applications. You can expand each of these containers to display additional subcontainers for further configuration. Each container directly or indirectly affects the management of Exchange 2000. Figure 9-5 shows the containers in the Computer Management snap-in.

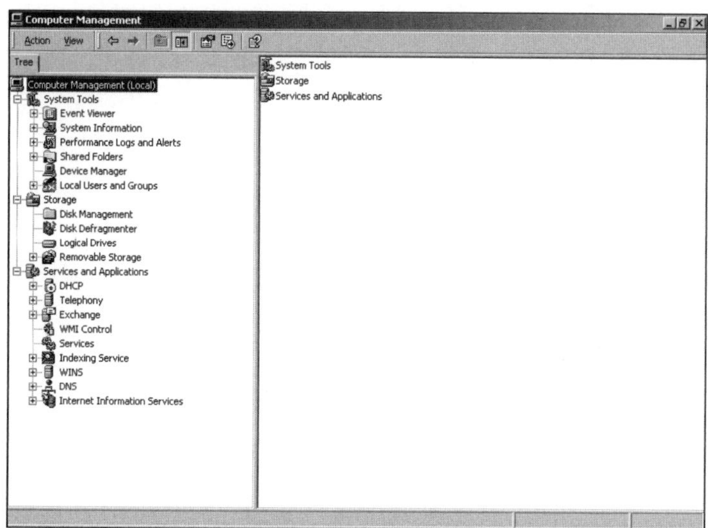

Figure 9-5 The containers in the Computer Management console

Not all subcontainers are used to the same degree when managing Exchange 2000. For example, the Shared Folders subcontainer in System Tools does not contribute much to managing Exchange 2000 services or mailbox stores, although it is useful for making shared information, such as a contact list or spreadsheet, available over your network. On the other hand, the Event Viewer subcontainer in System Tools is invaluable for detecting and troubleshooting services and files directly related to Exchange 2000 (see the upcoming section "Event Viewer"). The subcontainers of most interest to Exchange 2000 administrators include the following:

- *System Tools\Event Viewer*—Used to view various logs, such as the system log, to detect which drivers or services are acting as bottlenecks to Exchange 2000.
- *System Tools\Performance Logs and Alerts*—Used to define counter logs to measure performance for Exchange 2000 components, such as memory, physical disk, or network resources (TCP/IP parameters, bytes transferred, and so on). You can even configure Exchange 2000 to alert you when critical services have stopped (see the upcoming section "Performance Console," later in this chapter).
- *System Tools\Local Users and Groups*—Used to create users and groups that are configured to receive e-mail; however, this tool is found only on servers acting as member servers, not domain controllers (domain controllers use Active Directory Users and Computers).

- *Services and Applications\DHCP*—Used when you are running DHCP services and Exchange 2000 services on one server and you need to configure the range of IP addresses that Exchange clients should get when they connect to your network. However, running multiple-processor or memory-intensive services on one computer is not a Microsoft-recommended procedure because server performance will be overtaxed.
- *Services and Applications\Exchange*—Used to create new storage groups, mailbox stores, or public folder stores. You can also define access controls for most protocol virtual servers (such as an SMTP virtual server for clients to connect to your Exchange 2000 computer remotely through the Internet) or start and stop these virtual servers.
- *Services and Applications\Services*—Used to display a list of all configured services. Each service displays columns indicating a description of the service, its current status (Started, Stopped, or Paused), its startup type (Automatic, Manual, or Disabled), and how the service has logged on to the system (LocalSystem, Administrator, and so on). You should check this utility first if you are noticing problems with external message routing or local message delivery, to see whether a relevant service has been disabled or paused for some reason.
- *Services and Applications\Indexing Service*—Used to index, or catalog, documents on hard disks. You can search for documents by using the Start, Search feature or a standard Web browser. This service creates a catalog containing properties for a group of file system directories.
- *Services and Applications\Internet Information Services*—Used to configure settings for HTTP virtual servers that define access control levels for users retrieving their mail remotely over the Internet. All configuration changes are made in another subcontainer, the Default Web Site, which is displayed if you expand IIS.

Registry Editor

The Registry Editor is an advanced tool used by system administrators to change settings in the Windows 2000 Registry. The **Registry** is a database containing information used by Windows 2000 and Exchange 2000 during normal server operations, such as user profiles or programs and services currently running. It is a hierarchical structure composed of hives, keys, and value entries. To open the Registry Editor, click Start, Run, and then type regedit or regedt32 in the Open box. Both Regedit.exe and Regedt32.exe open the same Registry database in Windows 2000; however, Regedt32.exe opens each Registry key in a separate window and allows you to configure permissions on these keys to prevent users from being able to make unwanted or accidental deletions. Opening the Registry with the command regedit does not give you the same functionality and protection as Regedt32.

Each hive in the Registry is represented by a folder icon and contains subfolders known as keys. Keys can contain other keys (subkeys) and values you can manually enter or alter. The values contain the actual information stored in the Registry and can exist in one of three forms: a string value, a binary value, or a DWORD value. The following list shows the form that most Registry values take when they are stored in the central database of the underlying operating system. (Windows 2000 stores the actual Registry database in the <*systemroot*>\System32\Config directory on your system's local hard disk.)

The visible values or keys differ, depending on whether you use Regedit or Regedt32. For example, when using Regedit, you cannot view MULTI_SZ or EXPAND_SZ values or keys, but you can view these items with Regedt32. This is why Regedt32 is preferred to Regedit when working with the Windows 2000 Registry database.

- REG_BINARY—Stores Registry values as raw binary data and applies mostly to hardware component information for Exchange 2000 and Windows 2000.
- REG_DWORD—Usually reserved for Boolean (true/false) values and applies mostly to device drivers and services used by Exchange 2000 and Windows 2000.
- REG_SZ—Represents a standard string value (that is, human-readable text).
- REG_MULTI_SZ—Represents Registry values that contain lists or multiple values.
- REG_EXPAND_SZ—Applies to strings of text containing a variable (such as <*systemroot*>) that is replaced by an actual value when called by an application. For example, the value <*systemroot*> is replaced by the actual location of the directory containing the Windows 2000 system files.

You can use the Registry Editor to configure Exchange 2000–specific information, such as changing the default replication time for the ADC or limiting logons for a specific service. (See the "Hands-on Projects" section to see how the Registry can be used to limit logons to the Information Store service.) The Registry Editor can also be used to delete duplicate entries or to delete entries for programs and applications that you want removed from the system, although Microsoft recommends uninstalling programs and applications by using the Add/Remove Programs applet in the Control Panel. If you have difficulty removing an application from your system because of a missing dynamic link library (DLL) file (it might have been accidentally removed from your system), using the Registry to remove or delete programs is a viable option, but this procedure is best reserved for advanced system administrators.

You should not, under any circumstance, edit your Registry unless it is absolutely necessary. Windows 2000 will, under normal conditions, make its own modifications to the Registry. If you edit the Registry improperly (by adding an incorrect value or unknown key, for instance), your system could stop functioning. When editing the Registry, be prepared to restore the Registry if necessary. Microsoft recommends backing up and saving all Registry information by selecting the Export Registry File option from the Registry menu.

Performance Console

The Performance console, new to Windows 2000 Server, is used to monitor the state and health of your Windows 2000 and Exchange 2000 servers. This console is actually a combination of two utilities: a System Monitor utility for displaying performance data in real time, and a Performance utility for actually monitoring the performance counters for Windows 2000 objects (hard disk, processor, network, memory, and so on) and Exchange 2000 objects (Information Store, MTA stack, storage groups, and so on). Windows 2000 does not care if these objects represent physical or logical entities; what matters is that each object has performance counters or metrics that can be monitored regularly. If you are monitoring the Information Store object, for example, you select the MSExchangeIS performance object in the Performance utility. Many counters are associated with this object, including Connection Count (the number of client processes connected to your Information Store) and Maximum Users (the maximum number of concurrent users since you started your Exchange 2000 server).

You can access the Performance utility by using the Computer Management snap-in or the standalone Performance snap-in (from the Administrative Tools menu). You use this tool to monitor performance counters on both local and remote Exchange servers, and then summarize the data collected in a chart or report view. This console is also used to generate alerts when system activity exceeds predetermined threshold levels. Alerts can take the form of system messages being written to an event log or a special application being opened to analyze the situation. The Performance console is covered in more depth in Chapter 14.

Event Viewer

The Event Viewer, like the Performance console, is available as a standalone MMC snap-in or as part of the Computer Management snap-in. This tool allows you to view many system events, such as application errors or errors related to the Windows 2000 Directory Service. All system events are recorded in event log files. Although there are actually six different event logs, not all logs are used at the same time. In Event Viewer, you'll see the following containers for event logs:

- *Application Log*—Contains events logged by applications or programs.
- *Security Log*—Records security events, such as valid logon attempts or resource usage events (creating or deleting a file, for example). Security

logging is disabled by default in Windows 2000, but you can configure a group policy that enables this feature. Only those with Administrator permissions have full access to the security logs in Event Viewer.

Administrators can even configure an audit policy in the Registry so that the Exchange 2000 system stops functioning if the security log in Event Viewer becomes full. The system notifies you with a message box when any log in Event Viewer becomes full. By default, each log can grow to a maximum of 512 KB before you are prompted to overwrite it with new entries or clear it to make room for new entries. This setting can be increased or decreased in 64-KB increments.

- *System Log*—Contains events logged by Windows 2000 or Exchange 2000 system components, such as drivers or services. Windows 2000 will most likely determine in advance which events are logged by system components—the events that occur behind the scenes, not as a result of applications you install. Because of the many components that are constantly running in the background when Exchange 2000 and Windows 2000 are operational, the system log fills up faster than other logs, so you must regularly archive or delete outdated system logs. Failure to do so can cause high levels of instability or affect functionality in your system.
- *Directory Service*—Contains events related to Active Directory configuration, such as online defragmentation or directory service corruption.
- *DNS Server*—Contains events related to zone files and resource records that could affect normal operations for Exchange 2000 (for instance, an Exchange 2000 client queries the DNS server for an SRV resource record that does not exist in the DNS database).
- *File Replication Service*—Contains events associated with directory replication throughout a Windows 2000 forest. The FRS copies files on multiple Windows 2000 servers simultaneously and replicates the Windows 2000 system volume known as Sysvol on all domain controllers. (The Sysvol folder contains system data as well as data used in system policies and logon scripts.) The FRS starts automatically by default on any domain controller and can be started manually on any member server in your Windows 2000 domain.

9

Task Manager

You can access Task Manager with more than one method: right-click an empty area of the taskbar and click Task Manager, press Ctrl+Shift+Esc, or press Ctrl+Alt+Del and click Task Manager from the shortcut menu. (See the "Hands-on Projects" section for a demonstration of working with this tool.) Task Manager can be used for monitoring and troubleshooting purposes, and it provides information about running applications, system processes, and memory usage. Use Task Manager to view the status of running programs or to end programs that have stopped responding to system requests. It can also assess activity of running processes by using a variety of parameters, such as Process ID or CPU time, and display common performance measures for processes, including the total number of threads and processes running on your system and the total physical and kernel memory available to your system.

MANAGING EXCHANGE 2000 SERVER RESOURCES

By now, you should have gained an appreciation for all the management resources that Windows 2000 Server and Exchange 2000 Server offer. You know how system resources can be managed and what tools can be utilized for this purpose. However, the concept of management also includes what is being managed and when certain items should be managed. This section reviews the Exchange 2000 components that function best when they are micromanaged on a regular basis: administrative groups, storage groups, and Information Store databases, such as mailbox stores and public folder stores. These resources need to be managed and monitored for growth so that your current levels of messaging traffic always stay within your control.

Managing Administrative Groups

An Exchange 2000 Server organization is not meant to be managed on a global scale as one unit. Administrative groups, discussed in Chapter 4, "Preparing to Deploy Exchange 2000 Server," make it possible to manage servers on a consolidated basis. An administrative group is one form of server grouping that represents a logical group of servers banded together administratively, not physically. When you configure an administrative group, you are most concerned with permission management, which is controlled with the Exchange Administration Delegation Wizard.

Managing administrative groups involves some important decisions: which user or group should have control of the administrative group, how many administrative groups should exist in the organization, and which administrative group a server should belong to. If your organization is running in mixed mode, Exchange 2000 handles administrative groups in the same manner that Exchange Server 5.5 handles sites. In other words, Exchange 2000 Server uses the site concept to define an administrative group. In any mixed-mode environment, you lose the ability to move mailboxes from servers in one administrative group to servers in a different administrative group. Converting your organization to native-mode operation removes these two limitations.

You do not always have to integrate your administrative group design with your routing group design. In other words, there is not always a one-to-one correlation between the number of administrative groups and the number of routing groups. The key to administrative group design is simplification—designing the fewest administrative groups possible for your organization. In many cases, multiple administrative groups help companies segregate divisions or branch offices into separate administrative units; however, this setup does not indicate a need to deploy multiple routing groups simultaneously.

Servers can be administered in multiple administrative groups while belonging to one routing group, however. Consider using multiple routing groups only when needed—for example, if you have branch offices that are geographically dispersed or your company has unstable WAN links that could affect the transfer of messages across your organization.

Administration Models

The decision of who should manage an administrative group depends on the administration model your organization uses. Most management scenarios involving Exchange 2000 Server revolve around the following three administration models:

- *Centralized model*—All Exchange servers, and hence all administrative groups, are managed from one centralized location (usually the company's headquarters). This model is most successful if your company has multiple branch offices connected to headquarters via permanent or high-bandwidth network connections. Because administrative groups usually contain routing groups, it's best to keep all mailbox servers in the central location in one routing group hub for this management model. You should strive to place all Exchange 2000 servers into one administrative group (even if you use administration models other than the centralized model) because it is easier to manage one administrative group that can contain several routing groups.
- *Distributed model*—All administrative groups (and routing groups) are managed directly by the branch offices they correspond to. If you have branch offices that are managed independently, this model serves you best. You can create one administrative group per branch office (even though you should still create the fewest administrative groups possible, for the sake of simplicity). The decision to place servers in corresponding administrative groups is extremely important because you cannot move servers between administrative groups.
- *Hybrid model*—All administrative and routing groups can be managed from both centralized and distributed locations, combining the advantages of centralized and distributed administration. This approach works best if your branch offices are connected to your central office with high-bandwidth network connections. The hybrid model also affords you a variety of routing group options; for example, you can assign a central hub routing group to a main headquarters office and other routing groups to your branch offices.

Adding and Removing Servers from Administrative Groups

Keep in mind that, by default, servers are not organized into administrative groups in Exchange 2000. The Exchange Server designers knew that organizations with few Exchange 2000 servers would not need to create administrative groups (although large organizations do need them). If you install Exchange 2000 into your organization, and then display administrative groups in System Manager, the Exchange 2000 server automatically joins the default First Administrative Group. The only way to add a server to a new administrative group is to manually display administrative groups in System Manager.

A rather strange event occurs if you attempt to clear the option to display administrative groups after you have defined administrative groups in System Manager. All your servers are placed in the Servers container in System Manager, and you no longer benefit from a hierarchical grouping of servers. If you try again to display administrative groups at this time, your Exchange 2000 servers will automatically join the default First Administrative Group, and your previous configurations will not return.

New administrative groups become empty containers under the Administrative Groups folder in System Manager. To create a new administrative group, simply right-click the Administrative Groups folder, point to New, and then click Administrative Group. The only required element for a new administrative group is a name, which can contain from 1 to 64 characters. You can always rename an administrative group if you need to, but you can never move a server to another administrative group without reinstalling that server directly into the other administrative group. If you need to remove a server from an existing administrative group, you use the Exchange 2000 Setup program. The Remove option appears in the Component Selection window of the installation wizard. Alternatively, you can right-click your server object in System Manager, point to All Tasks, and then click Remove Server. However, only servers that are truly unavailable (for example, servers that have shut down or been physically separated from all network connections) can be removed using this technique.

Managing Storage Groups

Storage groups are used to define boundary limits for all mailbox and public stores in Exchange 2000 Server. Remember that the Exchange 2000 System Manager utility shows a default storage group named First Storage Group (under *Organization object*\\Administrative Groups\\First Administrative Group\\Servers\\<*your server object*>\\First Storage Group). By default, the First Storage Group gives you access to one mailbox store and one public folder store; however, you can add storage groups if your computer runs the Enterprise version of Exchange 2000.

In the Exchange 2000 Enterprise edition, each server can handle a maximum of four separate storage groups, and each storage group can consist of up to five mailbox stores or public folder stores (or a combination of the two, as long as the total number of stores does not exceed five per storage group). Hence, each Exchange 2000 server is capable of managing up to 20 different messaging stores.

If you configure multiple databases in one storage group, they all share one common set of transaction log files. Each database in the storage group contains one .stm file representing the Internet message stream format, and one .edb file representing the Messaging Application Programming Interface (MAPI) message format. Becoming familiar with the makeup of storage groups helps you properly configure them in the property pages for the storage group. Right-clicking a storage group in System Manager displays the storage group's Properties dialog box, as shown in Figure 9-6.

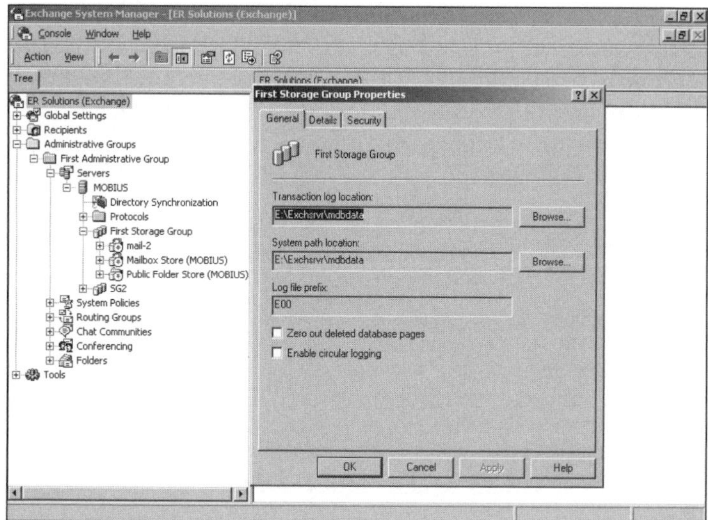

Figure 9-6 The Properties dialog box for a storage group in System Manager

The properties of a storage group include the following:

- *Transaction log location*—Selects the local directory path where all database transaction log files are located (the default path is <*systemroot*>\Exchsrvr\mdbdata).
- *System path location*—Displays the location of temporary files existing during an online backup; usually, it is the same path as the transaction log location.
- *Log file prefix*—Is the name of the active transaction log, for example, "E00." A prefix of E00 results in a transaction log filename of E00.log. Any new storage groups will have this prefix incremented by one (for instance, E01, E02, and so forth).
- *Zero out deleted database pages*—Increases the security of Exchange 2000 by removing any deleted entries from all database files. Exchange 2000 increases the size of its databases by creating new data pages and writing information to them. By zeroing out deleted database pages, Exchange 2000 can reuse a previously created page of information. (If Exchange removed these pages, instead of "zeroing them out," it would have to continually create new data pages.) This activity results in slight performance improvements for the Exchange server.

By design, you cannot "zero out" deleted database pages at the mailbox store or public folder store level, only at the storage group level. This is because information is managed according to storage group configurations, not by individual mailbox or public folder configurations.

- *Enable circular logging*—Reuses existing log files for new transactions. Transaction log files are overwritten after their data has been committed to the database. This option might not always be desirable, because overwriting old transactions means that after server shutdowns or other disasters, you can recover Exchange Server only up to the point of your last full backup. Recovering transactions made after the backup is not possible with circular logging. As with zeroing out deleted database pages, enabling circular logging is a task performed at the storage group level; each storage group can have a different criterion for logging.

In some cases, the database files in a storage group are accidentally deleted or somehow disappear. If this happens, you will see the following error message when you attempt to start the Information Store:

```
Event type: Error
Event Source: ESE98
Event Category: Logging/Recovery
Event ID: 454
Description: Information Store (976) Database
recovery/restore failed with unexpected error – 1216
```

The Extensible Storage Engine (ESE) tries to bring all databases in a storage group to a homogeneous state during a recovery or restore and keeps track of all database files for the storage group. The missing database files can be restored from tape backups while the remaining databases in the storage group are installed.

Managing Growth of Message Stores and Messaging Traffic

Although the concepts of Information Stores, storage groups, and data stores are related, they are not identical. Managing Information Stores essentially includes managing storage groups, data stores (mailbox stores and public folder stores), and databases. Databases are associated with data stores, which are, in turn, associated with storage groups. You can effectively manage these resources by using properly configured system policies, or you can manage these resources individually. Many files associated with storage groups and databases, such as the Res1.log file, provide a measure of control for Exchange 2000 because they help Exchange Server continue writing transactions to disk even when your disk drive is running low on space. The configuration of files and databases in your servers, as explained in the following section, can prepare your organization for growth and optimal performance. If these files and databases are configured properly, it's easy to scale your organization in the future while maintaining optimal message flow for your users. When planning for future growth, or even when managing current messaging levels, you need to consider several server issues for your organization: configuring the placement of Exchange server databases and storage groups, developing strategies for managing increased messaging traffic, and configuring virtual memory use on your servers for high usage loads.

Configuring Data Files

The placement of databases and storage groups in Exchange 2000 has a direct bearing on server performance and message flow architecture. For example, database files for all mailbox stores and public folder stores should not always be put on the same physical hard drive partition as the transaction log files. Any decision on the number or placement of these files should be based on the overall size of your organization. Relatively small organizations (consisting of one to two Exchange servers hosting up to 250 users, for example) might not have the same performance requirements or storage group requirements as large organizations (those with more than 10 Exchange 2000 servers and hosting at least 10,000 users, for instance). Small organizations can survive using just one storage group for all mailbox and public folder stores, and they can place all data files and transaction log files on the same physical drive (even though Microsoft recommends placing transaction log files on separate physical drives for performance reasons, regardless of the organization's size). Large organizations tend to use multiple storage groups and organize their data by placing storage groups on separate drives. Even the databases within these storage groups occupy separate drives or drive partitions. In any case, these large organizations should always place transaction log files and system files on different physical drives and implement RAID technology to protect these drives in case of failure.

Many organizations implement RAID 1 or RAID 5 technology to protect their data from disaster. Both technologies are available in software and hardware forms, and they are fault-tolerant mechanisms for protecting data. A hardware RAID implementation is usually preferred to a software RAID implementation because hardware solutions are faster and more reliable than their software counterparts (using dedicated hardware for RAID implementations is usually preferred to incorporating RAID features within a software framework). However, hardware implementations can be cost prohibitive for many organizations, so a software RAID package could be the only available alternative if data protection and recovery are important.

Using multiple storage groups or databases also aids the recovery process for Exchange 2000 because each storage group or database can be backed up or restored individually without affecting the operation of other running storage groups or databases.

Strategies for Managing Messaging Growth

Organizations with rapid growth in their user population often look for ways to control connections to their Exchange server, usually with bandwidth allocation software, such as Checkpoint Software's Floodgate-1 product. However, simple methods are available that achieve the same goal without purchasing expensive third-party software.

One simple method is limiting the number of people who have permission to log on to the Information Store in Exchange 2000 by editing a Registry key in Windows 2000. After stopping the Information Store service, open the Registry Editor using Regedt32 and add a value called Logon Only As (using the data type REG_MULTI_SZ). This value is added to the following Registry path:

```
HKEY_LOCAL_MACHINE\SYSTEM\CurrentControlSet\Services\
MSExchaneIS\ParametersSystem
```

This Registry value allows you to specify the names of users who can access the Information Store. If modifying the Registry is frowned on in your organization, consider the safer alternative of distributing mailbox resources across multiple servers to balance the load. This action effectively limits the number of logons to one Exchange 2000 server by distributing connections throughout your organization.

There's no such thing as too many warnings about editing the Windows 2000 Registry without first backing it up. Changes to the Registry should *never* be made unless they are absolutely necessary. You should export the Registry in its entirety to a safe, known location before attempting changes or deletions.

Public folders might not benefit from this distribution in the same manner as mailbox stores because public folders normally reside on one server; they also replicate to other servers in the organization and should not be distributed among servers in the same fashion as mailbox stores. Configuring dedicated mailbox servers and public folder servers helps reduce the workload performed by one server and contributes to an increase in server performance and efficiency. If dedicated servers are not possible (because of budget constraints or other reasons), the most workable option for managing increased levels of messaging traffic is configuring multiple Information Stores and multiple storage groups in one Exchange 2000 server.

Large numbers of mailboxes should not compete for the attention of one mailbox store in one storage group. By using multiple Information Stores or databases, you can realize performance gains for your servers, as long as transaction log files are placed on separate physical drives. The downside of using multiple databases is that you lose the single-instance storage feature of Exchange 2000. Recall that the single-instance storage feature in both Exchange 5.5 and Exchange 2000 preserves disk space and makes the use of distribution lists more efficient in Exchange 2000 Server.

Configuring Virtual Memory for High User Loads

When using Exchange 2000 Server or Exchange 2000 Enterprise Server on a Windows 2000 Server computer, you could have scalability issues to deal with. Even though Exchange 2000 runs on any version of Windows 2000 Server, Microsoft recommends running all versions of Exchange 2000 on a computer running Windows 2000 Advanced Server because the Advanced Server operating system has a larger memory support system than Windows 2000 Server does.

Windows 2000 Advanced Server reserves approximately 2 GB of virtual address space for the kernel (the regular version of Windows 2000 Server reserves less than 1 GB of virtual address space). Advanced Server also enables the Exchange 2000 Information

Store process to use 2 GB of virtual address space (this address space is reserved at system startup and gradually increases as memory is used during normal system operations). If the Information Store depletes the available amount of virtual address space because of growing databases and message storage, all memory reservations and allocations will fail, and you will have to restart the Store.exe service.

Many factors affect the available virtual address space for the Information Store, including the amount allocated at startup, the number of storage groups on your Exchange 2000 server, and the overall size of your Information Store database caches. Because the number of connections to your server has a direct effect on virtual memory, you should control or reduce the total user connections by reducing the number of mailboxes in your storage groups (or distributing your mailbox resources to other dedicated mailbox servers in your organization). You can also increase the physical RAM on your Exchange 2000 server to help alleviate virtual memory problems because the amount of virtual memory is proportional to the amount of physical RAM in your server. Virtual memory is often manually adjusted by system administrators to increase performance of their Exchange 2000 servers, and it should be approximately twice the level of physical RAM in your server.

Administrative efforts to manage virtual memory for Exchange 2000 become more involved for servers running Windows 2000 Advanced Server and containing over 1 GB of physical RAM. In such cases, Microsoft recommends modifying the Boot.ini file so that 3 GB of virtual memory is available for user-mode programs. You can find more information on this feature by visiting *http://support.microsoft.com/support/kb/articles/Q266/0/96.asp*. You should also apply the latest service pack for Exchange (SP1, as of this writing) because it enhances allocation of virtual memory in Exchange 2000.

MANAGING EXCHANGE 2000 RECIPIENTS

Recipient management in Exchange 2000 means managing user accounts, mailboxes, public folders (if mail-enabled), and contacts. User accounts are the only objects in AD that can have mailboxes associated with them. Recall that all "users" are objects that are either mail-enabled or mailbox enabled; in Exchange 2000, a user or group can be both mail-enabled and mailbox-enabled, but contacts are usually only mail-enabled and public folders are mail-enabled by default when you install Exchange 2000. Management duties for recipients usually involve some combination of the following activities:

- Using the Active Directory Users and Computers snap-in to create mail-enabled or mailbox-enabled objects
- Modifying users' aliases or display names (if changing their Microsoft Mail, SMTP, or X.400 address)

- Modifying or deleting e-mail addresses for user accounts (if you have updated a user's display name or alias, new default e-mail addresses are created, but old addresses remain in the system)
- Enabling special features for user accounts (such as voicemail or instant messaging)
- Configuring delivery restrictions on individual mailboxes, such as outgoing message size and message restrictions (such as specifying that only messages from certain users or contacts are accepted for delivery)
- Moving mailboxes to new servers or storage groups in your organization (for load-balancing purposes or to preserve hard disk space on your servers)

Managing Exchange 2000 Using Recipient Policies

Recipient policies are used to manage objects created in Exchange 2000, such as users, groups, or contacts. These policies usually describe a setting applied to a set of recipients; this setting is produced by an LDAP condition or filter. For example, a policy can be used to automatically generate e-mail addresses for all mail-enabled users and contacts throughout your organization (see the "Hands-on Projects" section for an example of configuring a recipient policy). All recipient policies use a feature known as background-apply to carry out any configuration changes you have made. The process of implementing a recipient policy includes the following steps:

1. Create the actual recipient policy by using the Recipients container in the System Manager snap-in.
2. Define all settings that you want the policy to implement.
3. Associate this policy with one or more objects (including users, OUs, or servers).
4. Schedule the policy to be applied by using the RUS or the Address List Service (which are System Attendant components in Exchange 2000).

The central point of recipient policies is that they allow you to define system settings across your AD organization. Once you implement a policy, you can change configurations or settings at any time with one operation. When Exchange 2000 is initially installed, recipient policies are used to generate e-mail addresses for various address types, including MS Mail, Lotus Notes, SMTP, and X.400 systems. Rules for e-mail address generation have changed since Exchange 5.5, in which separate addressing rules are required for each site. Another important change is that Exchange 5.5 does not allow multiple SMTP and X.400 addresses, but Exchange 2000 does. Exchange 2000 creates a default recipient policy that applies to all mail-enabled objects in your organization. You can modify this default policy to update your default e-mail-addressing scheme, or enable a new e-mail-addressing scheme that generates and displays secondary addresses.

Recipient Policy Priority

Your organization could conceivably have multiple recipient policies in effect; however, only one such policy can be applied to any particular object. Exchange 2000 checks the priority of all recipient policies and applies a higher-priority policy before it applies a lower-priority policy. The default recipient policy is always set to the lowest priority in your organization, which means it is applied only if no other recipient policy is available for users, groups, or contacts in your organization. All recipient policies are applied according to the update interval in the RUS, and this update interval defaults to Always Run; therefore, new recipient policies are applied as soon as they are created. You might want to try other settings, however, because frequent updates and modifications of e-mail addresses could degrade server performance over time. Other valid settings include Run every hour, Run every 2 hours, Run every 4 hours, Never run, and Use custom schedule. You should choose the most appropriate setting for your organization, taking into account the number of users and servers being managed and your overall network topology.

Exchange 2000 assigns priorities to recipient policies based on their position in the Recipient Policies list in System Manager. Remember that the default recipient policy always has the lowest priority, and this condition can never be modified. However, you can always change priorities of other recipient policies you create by right-clicking the appropriate policy in System Manager, pointing to All Tasks, and clicking either Move Up (for higher priority) or Move Down (for lower priority). Normally, changes to recipient polices are applied within a reasonable amount of time (depending on your network configuration and the total number of servers or users being managed in your organization). In some rare situations, however, these changes might not appear at all (even after this reasonable amount of time has expired). If that happens, you can rebuild the default recipient policy to generate default e-mail addresses for your organization by right-clicking the appropriate RUS in System Manager and then clicking Rebuild.

Rebuilding your default recipient e-mail address generation rules may take longer than anticipated. Some nervous system administrators cancel this routine by stopping all Recipient Update Services or shutting down their Exchange servers before the process has had time to finish. This action is not recommended because the RUS must then be rebuilt from scratch again, and it could take even longer for the process to finish. Patience is the key to rebuilding the RUS correctly!

Managing Address Lists

Address lists are an Exchange 2000 recipient management component; you manage them in the Recipients folder in the System Manager snap-in. Similar to recipient policies, they are created by using filter rules that search AD and find users, groups, or contacts matching particular criteria. The Exchange 2000 address lists started out as address book views in Exchange Server 5.0. These address book views allowed the system administrator to display views based on certain groupings to Outlook clients. All Outlook clients (regardless of the version being used) can view sites and containers when querying server-based address lists. Exchange 2000 has incorporated many of the features in the Exchange 5.x address book views, but it uses a somewhat different method to specify how these lists appear.

Users sometimes experience problems with the address book views in Exchange 5.5 because the rules for creating these views are not flexible enough for large organizations. Exchange 2000 has tried to remedy this problem by using LDAP filter rules to create containers for your address lists. For example, if you want to create a special address list for all temporary contractors who work in the New York Finance Department of Books, Inc., you can create one container by using the LDAP search filter syntax with the following rule:

```
(&(mail=*) (&(department=Finance) (l=NewYork)
( Extension-Attribute-3=Contractor)))
```

The Exchange 2000 address lists are not compiled in AD and have no direct association with the Windows 2000 directory service (even though address book views in Exchange 5.5 are stored in the server's directory service database).

The RUS is responsible for populating the address list. It actually populates the showInAddressBook attribute for each AD object. Every mail-enabled object in AD contains this attribute, including users, groups, and public folders. The RUS adds address list information to recipients; it does not add recipient objects to address lists. So every time you add a new user or group to AD, the RUS intercepts this object and determines which address list this object is a member of. The address lists are then added to the showInAddressBook attribute of this object.

Six default address lists are configured in Exchange 2000: Global Address, All Users, All Groups, All Contacts, Public Folders, and All Conferencing resources. Each list represents a view of the GAL specifically designed for users, groups, contacts, public folders, and conferencing objects, respectively. These default lists show mail-enabled objects, not mailbox-enabled objects. You can create other address lists, but if you are upgrading to Exchange 2000 from Exchange Server 5.5, only these default address lists are created. Any custom address book views that existed in your Exchange 5.5 organization will not transfer successfully in the upgrade process (in a mixed-mode environment, not every Exchange 2000 address list can be represented in the Exchange 5.5 directory).

Managing Full-Text Indexing in Exchange 2000

The final component of your recipient management duties is full-text indexing. Many advanced server products, including Web servers such as Microsoft IIS 5 and mail servers such as Exchange 2000 Server, incorporate this feature. Indexing is a good feature to offer your users so that they can search for specific messages in their mailbox stores and specific postings in their public folder stores. This capability was not developed to its highest potential in Exchange 5.5 because users had to search every item in their mailboxes to locate a specific item. System administrators can take advantage of content indexing in Exchange 2000 so that users can efficiently utilize the Find feature in their

Outlook clients to search for items against an index, instead of individual items in the Information Store.

The Indexing Process in Exchange 2000

Actually, two types of indexing occur in Exchange 2000: standard indexing and full-text indexing. Standard indexing, performed by the Exchange server storage engine, is used to search common fields found in most e-mail messages (such as the Subject or To field). Standard indexing can also be used to search the Subject field for public folders. The only limitation of standard indexing is that Exchange 2000 does not search through message attachments. Full-text indexing works around this limitation by building an index of all text in mailboxes and public folder stores before users attempt to search them. Full-text indexing works with all data hosted on an Exchange server, but does not index data in personal folder stores (.pst files on a user's local hard drive).

The Microsoft Search service (Mssearch.exe) plays an important role in maintaining full-text indexes for Exchange 2000. Even though the Search service is configured for automatic startup, full-text indexing is not configured for automatic startup in Exchange 2000. You establish this feature for each mailbox store or public folder store that appears in System Manager. This flexibility means that some message stores can be configured for standard indexing, and others can be configured for full-text indexing.

Although full-text indexing is a wonderful user benefit, it is resource intensive in terms of CPU performance, memory requirements, and hard drive requirements. A new index can consume approximately one-fifth the total size of your Exchange 2000 messaging database (for example, a 2-GB database requires an index of approximately 400 MB).

When you first configure full-text indexing using System Manager (see the "Hands-on Projects" section for an example of how to do this), Exchange 2000 inspects each folder in the mailbox or public folder store you are configuring. Every document in this store is aggregated into a single master index. Once the master index is completed, all subsequent user queries are issued against this master index. There is constant communication between the Information Store service and the Search service when new messages or public folder postings are added to a store. The Search service indexes new files and updates the master index, but this process is not always immediate because full-text indexing is sometimes configured to run on a scheduled basis. Large organizations managing thousands of users who frequently access e-mail or public folder content do not want performance degradations resulting from too-frequent updates to the master index.

The full-text indexing feature allows users to use the Advanced Find feature in Outlook 2000 to locate messages stored in the Exchange 2000 Web Storage System. However, only certain types of messages or attachments can be searched for, including:

- MIME messages with an .eml extension
- Internet documents with an .html, .htm, or .asp extension

- Microsoft files containing .xls, .ppt, or .doc extensions (Excel, PowerPoint, and Word documents, respectively)
- Messages or attachments containing .txt extensions (text files)

Files containing other extensions are listed centrally in a gather file, which is created during indexing and placed in the directory path \Exchsrvr\ExchangeServer_<*servername*>\GatherLogs. In this directory, you will find files with a .gthr extension, which contain lists of documents or messages that could not be successfully indexed. Also, be aware that only certain clients can take advantage of full-text indexing, such as MAPI clients, IMAP4 clients, and some custom clients that use the WebDAV protocol to access messaging content or public folder data.

Full-Text Indexing: Best Practice Recommendations

Managing full-text indexing not only entails creating indexes for users, but also includes configuring an index priority to determine the level of resource usage for the server that hosts the master index. You configure priorities on a server-by-server basis, selecting from one of four possible priority levels:

- *Minimum*—Sets the index priority to its lowest level and has the least impact on system resources. (CPU and memory are the two most important resources used by indexes.) This level requires the longest time to index files.
- *Low*—Has a minimal impact on system resources, and indexes are built at a satisfactory rate. This setting is the default priority level.
- *High*—Has a more noticeable impact on system resources than the Low setting (although a direct measurement of this setting cannot be determined).
- *Maximum*—Forces indexes to be built in the quickest time possible for the system being used.

Managing full-text indexing also involves monitoring indexing statistics to ensure that the Search service is functioning correctly. The following is a more complete list of best practice recommendations (as prescribed by Microsoft) for full-text indexing:

- Configure your Exchange 2000 server for optimal performance by adding enough physical memory. Microsoft does not recommend using full-text indexing if your server has less than 512 MB of RAM.
- Maintain and monitor all hard disk configurations when using full-text indexing in your organization. The Search service usually requires that your index or catalog be located on a physical disk drive containing 15% free disk space at all times. Microsoft also highly recommends some type of RAID configuration that enhances both performance and fault-tolerance (such as a RAID-0+1 configuration).
- Each full-text index contains four primary files or file types that are crucial to this feature's success: one catalog (the main index file for full-text indexing—you can have only one catalog per Information Store); one property store (a

database containing properties of the catalog's indexed items—there is only one property store per server); temporary files to hold temporary information used by the Search service; and gather files, which contain log information for the indexing service (there's only one set of gather logs for every catalog you create). Catalog files, the property store, and all temporary files should be placed on a RAID array for better performance. The gather files can stay in their default location.

- You must run a full population (or "crawl," as it is sometimes called) after creating your full-text index to populate it with data. The population process can run in the background and be performed anytime if you set the index priority setting to low. All normal user activities are ranked higher in priority than this population process so that client access to your Exchange server is not disrupted.
- Use the tools in the Performance console to monitor full-text indexing, especially counters for disk usage. You want to ensure that you have ample disk space for your catalogs, property stores, temporary files, and gather logs. If your system is running out of disk space, the catalog can become corrupted (and other system problems can occur as well). Monitor these two counters in particular: Physical Disk: Current Disk Queue Length (should not exceed two items per spindle in your disk system) and Physical Disk: Avg. Disk sec./read (the time it takes per disk read, typically 10 milliseconds).

Chapter Summary

- Many tools are available to configure and manage Exchange 2000 Server. The primary console used is System Manager. Familiarizing yourself with each of the main containers in System Manager can simplify your administrative burdens.
- Viewing administrative groups or routing groups in System Manager is not enabled by default when you install Exchange 2000 Server, so you must enable that option manually.
- System policies are collections of configuration items applied to one or more Exchange servers within an administrative group; policy settings configured within one administrative group can be copied to servers in a separate administrative group.
- You configure server policies, mailbox store policies, and public folder store policies in System Manager. The number of property pages differs for each type of policy: Server policies use one property page (General), mailbox store policies use up to four property pages (General, Database, Limits, and Full-Text Indexing), and public folder store policies use five property pages (General, Database, Limits, Full-Text Indexing, and Replication).
- You can use many Windows 2000 utilities to manage Exchange 2000. For example, the Active Directory Users and Computers snap-in is used to create recipient

objects. Other Windows 2000 management tools include Computer Management, Registry Editor, Performance console (which includes System Monitor and the Performance Logs and Alerts snap-ins), Event Viewer, and Task Manager.

- You should set up an administrative group hierarchy based on the administration model adopted by your organization. Most organizations use a centralized administration, distributed administration, or hybrid administration model.
- Storage groups define boundary limits for all mailbox and public folder stores in Exchange 2000. Managing storage groups involves configuring properties such as the location for transaction log files, a system path location, and a log file prefix. It also involves enabling circular logging.
- Managing recipients in Exchange 2000 consists of creating user accounts, enabling special features for users (such as voicemail or instant messaging), and configuring delivery restrictions on mailboxes. Applying recipient policies to a group of recipients eases the management burden.
- Address lists and full-text indexing are features in Exchange 2000 that make it easier for users to perform searches and directory queries when locating other objects. Exchange 2000 contains six default address lists—one for users, groups, contacts, public folders, conferencing objects, and the default GAL. Full-text indexing allows users to use the Find feature in their Outlook clients to search for items against a master index, instead of individual items in the Information Store service.

Key Terms

recipient policy — An Exchange 2000 Server feature that controls the generation of e-mail addresses. It is similar to the site addressing concept found in Exchange Server 5.5. Recipient policies allow administrators to assign more than one SMTP address to a user so that external addresses can be maintained for users in an organization.

Registry — A database repository in Windows 2000 that contains most of the information relating to the hardware and software configuration of a Windows 2000 computer. Adding new keys or values to it can sometimes cause problems; therefore, you need to back up the entire database structure and export it to remote storage locations before you make any changes.

system policy — An Exchange 2000 Server feature that allows administrators to apply configuration settings to a collection of server objects at the same time. There are three types of system policies: for server objects, for mailbox store objects, and for public folder store objects.

Review Questions

1. Administrative groups are disabled by default in System Manager when you first install Exchange 2000 Server Enterprise Edition. True or False?

2. You can enable message tracking for a new server policy you are configuring by using the ________________ tab of the server policy's Properties dialog box.
3. You have just configured a mailbox store system policy in the First Administrative Group container. You want to add three mailbox stores to this new policy. Which property page is used to specify the default public store used for this policy?
   a. Database
   b. Limits
   c. General
   d. Full-Text Indexing
4. Full-Text Indexing is a property page unique to public folder stores. True or False?
5. If two server system policies are applied to an Exchange 2000 server named Orion, which policy takes precedence?
   a. the first server policy
   b. the second server policy
   c. both server policies
   d. neither server policy
6. Before you can configure any settings for a system policy, you must enter a ________________ for this policy.
7. Which configuration component in System Manager is used to define message-encoding formats for e-mail messages?
   a. Global Settings
   b. Recipients
   c. Administrative Groups
   d. Tools
8. Which of the following computers can remotely manage an Exchange 2000 Server computer? (Choose all that apply.)
   a. a machine running Windows 2000 Professional
   b. a machine running Windows NT 4.0 Workstation
   c. a machine running Windows 2000 Advanced Server
   d. a machine running Windows 98 Second Edition
9. A custom recipient that has been converted into a contact in Exchange 2000 can send and receive messages because it has a mailbox associated with it. True or False?
10. Servers within a routing group communicate with each other by using which protocol?

11. Which of the following statements about administrative groups is true?
    a. In a native-mode environment, Exchange 2000 handles administrative groups in the same manner that Exchange 5.5 handles sites.
    b. In a mixed-mode environment, Exchange 2000 handles administrative groups in the same manner that Exchange 5.5 handles domains.
    c. In a mixed-mode environment, Exchange 2000 handles administrative groups in the same manner that Exchange 5.5 handles sites.
    d. In a native-mode environment, Exchange 2000 puts administrative groups and routing groups in one central site.
12. If server A is placed into administrative group A, and server B is placed into administrative group B, server A and server B can belong to the same routing group if the organization is running Exchange 2000 in mixed mode. True or False?
13. The Recipient Policies container in System Manager performs which of the following?
    a. defines the manner in which proxy e-mail addresses are created for users
    b. controls settings for Exchange 2000 servers and Information Stores via mailbox, folder, or server policies
    c. defines acceptable message formats, including message encoding and character sets
    d. updates address lists in AD and creates two objects in System Manager: one for the AD configuration naming context and one for the AD domain naming context
14. The ______________ updates existing e-mail addresses or address lists in AD.
15. The Internet Message Formats container in System Manager performs which of the following?
    a. defines the manner in which proxy e-mail addresses are created for users
    b. controls settings for Exchange 2000 servers and Information Stores via mailbox, folder, or server policies
    c. defines acceptable message formats, including message encoding and character sets
    d. updates address lists in AD and creates two objects in System Manager: one for the AD configuration naming context and one for the AD domain naming context
16. A transaction log policy is an example of which of the following types of policies?
    a. system policy
    b. server policy
    c. system and server policies
    d. A transaction log policy does not exist.
17. Before creating a system policy, you must create a ______________ ______________ ______________ in System Manager.

18. The Windows 2000 Indexing service provides access to mailboxes and public folders using SMTP. True or False?
19. Which of the following statements describes the principal function of a Microsoft Management Console (MMC)?
    a. It represents a single-document interface (SDI) application that defines a user interface where users can work with one document at a time.
    b. It represents a multiple-document interface (MDI) application that defines a user interface where users can work with multiple documents simultaneously.
    c. It provides the content to manage user accounts and their associated mailboxes.
    d. It creates potential recipient objects, such as users, groups, or contacts.
20. Which Windows 2000 service is responsible for replicating the Sysvol volume to all domain controllers in a Windows 2000 forest?
    a. DNS
    b. ADC
    c. FRS
    d. SRS
21. A file known as ________________ is reserved for every storage group and acts as buffer memory for transactions when a physical disk becomes full.
22. All default address lists configured in Exchange 2000 Server display only ________________ objects.
23. Which of the following statements correctly describes one limitation of performing standard full-text indexing in Exchange 2000?
    a. You cannot search for items in the Subject field of an e-mail message.
    b. You cannot search through e-mail message attachments.
    c. You can search for items only in mailbox stores, not in public folders.
    d. You cannot search for data in personal folder stores (.pst files).

HANDS-ON PROJECTS

Project 9-1

This project helps you create a new System Policies container in an administrative group, and then create a mailbox store policy so that all servers associated with this policy retain deleted messages for a period of 14 days.

To create a new System Policies container and configure a new mailbox store policy in System Manager:

1. Click **Start**, point to **Programs**, point to **Microsoft Exchange**, and then click **System Manager**.

2. Expand your Organization object, and then expand the **Administrative Groups** container. You should see a folder labeled First Administrative Group in the Administrative Groups container.

If the administrative groups aren't displayed, right-click your Organization object, click Properties, and then click the Display administrative groups check box to enable it.

3. Right-click the **First Administrative Group**, point to **New**, and then click **System Policy Container** on the shortcut menu.
4. Right-click the **System Policy** container, point to **New**, and then click **Mailbox store policy** on the shortcut menu. When the New Policy dialog box (shown in Figure 9-7) opens, click the **General**, **Database**, and **Limits** check boxes to create those property pages, and then click **OK**.

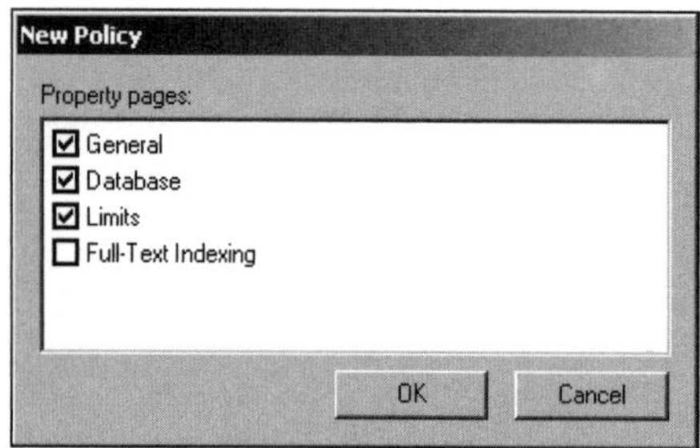

Figure 9-7 Selecting property pages for a mailbox store policy

5. Type a name for your new policy in the General tab, and then click the **General (Policy)** tab. Click the **Browse** button to select your default public folder store.
6. Click the **Database (Policy)** tab, and then click the **Maintenance interval** list arrow to view the available options. Leave the default setting of Run daily from 11:00 p.m. to 3:00 a.m., and then click the **Limits (Policy)** tab.
7. In the Limits (Policy) tab, click the **Issue warning at (KB)** check box in the Storage limits section, and type **20000** in the text box to the right to configure a 20 MB storage limit for user mail (see Figure 9-8). Also, type **7** in the Keep deleted items for (days) text box in the Deletion settings section. All other settings should be left at their defaults.
8. Click **Apply**, and then click **OK** to close the policy property pages. Your new policy now appears underneath the System Policy container you created in Step 3.
9. Right-click your new policy, and click **Add Mailbox Store**. The Select the items to place under the control of this policy dialog box (shown in Figure 9-9) opens; click the mailbox store listed in the Name section that you want to add, and then click the **Add** button.

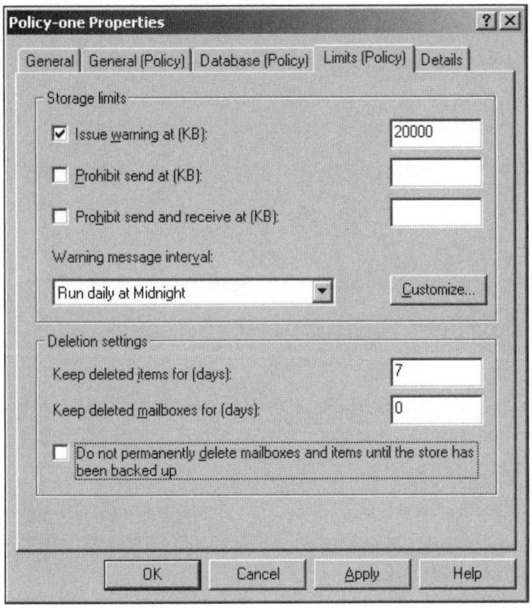

Figure 9-8 Configuring message settings in the Limits (Policy) tab

When configuring settings in the Limits (Policy) tab, you do not want to keep deleted items or mailboxes for too many days; otherwise, your server will become overburdened with deleted items or deleted mailboxes, potentially filling up valuable hard drive space.

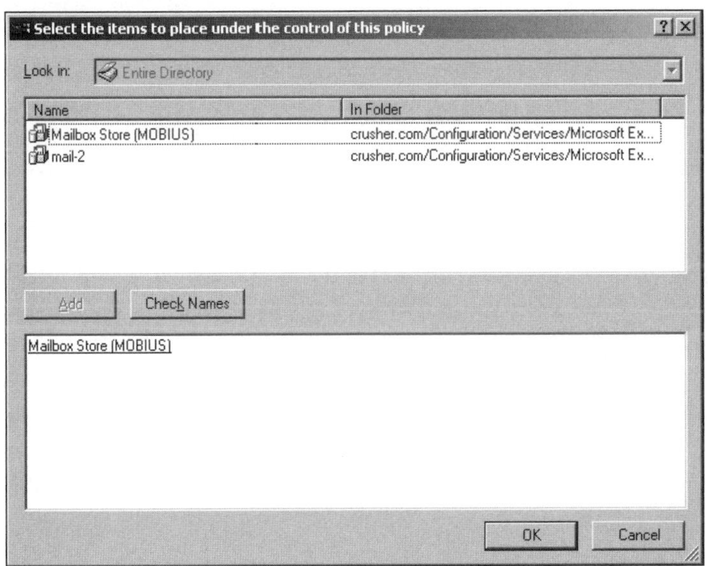

Figure 9-9 Selecting a mailbox store for the new mailbox policy

10. Click **OK** to return to the System Manager console.
11. When you see the Exchange System Manager message box asking "Are you sure you want to add the item(s) to this policy?", click the **Yes** button. Your mailbox policy is now configured for use and you can add mailbox stores at any time.
12. Close any open windows or applications.

Project 9-2

To create a new storage group and a new mailbox store within the storage group:

1. Click **Start**, point to **Programs**, point to **Microsoft Exchange**, and then click **System Manager**.
2. Expand your Organization object, and then expand the **Administrative Groups** object. You should see a folder labeled First Administrative Group in the Administrative Groups container.
3. Expand the **First Administrative Group** container, and then expand the **Servers** container directly underneath it. Right-click your ***<server_name>*** object, point to **New**, and then click **Storage Group**.
4. In the Properties dialog box that opens, type a name for your new storage group (for example, Group-2), and then click the **Enable circular logging** check box. Notice the information in the Transaction log location and the System path location text boxes; both are set by default to <*systemroot*>\Exchsrvr\<*name of storage group*>, but you can change these locations if you want.
5. Click **OK** to close the Properties dialog box. If you see the message "With the circular logging option enabled databases in this storage group can only be restored to the time of the last backup. Additionally, incremental or differential backups will no longer be allowed. Are you sure you want to continue?", click the **Yes** button.
6. Now you are ready to add a mailbox store to this newly created storage group. Right-click your new storage group (found under the First Storage Group container in System Manager), point to **New**, and then click **Mailbox Store**. The Properties dialog box opens to the General tab by default, as Figure 9-10 shows. Type a name for this new mailbox store (for example, Executive-Mail).
7. Click the **Database** tab, and notice the default names given to the Exchange database and the Exchange streaming database files. Then click the **Limits** tab, and enter **14** in the Keep deleted mailboxes for (days) text box (the default is 30 days). Click **OK**.
8. The Executive Mail message box appears with this message: "The new store was created successfully. Do you want to mount it now?" Click the **Yes** button. The new mailbox store will now be added within the new storage group you created in Steps 1–5. Click **OK**.
9. Close any open windows or applications.

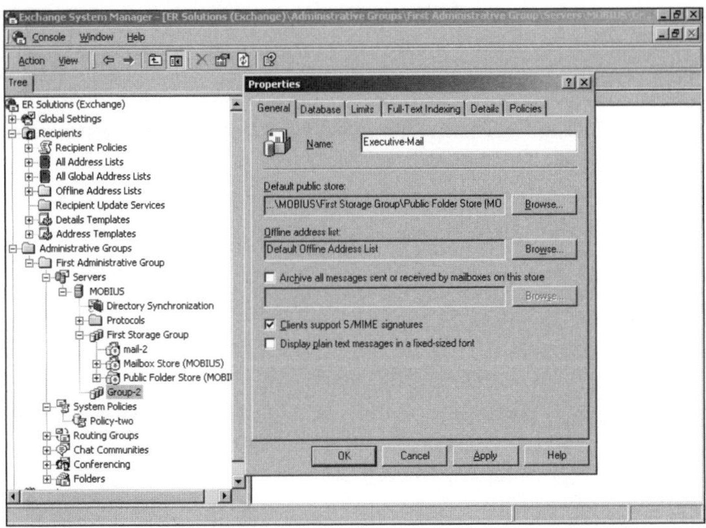

Figure 9-10 Configuring a new mailbox store within the new storage group

Project 9-3

In this project, you view and modify data in the Windows 2000 Registry. In general, however, the Registry should never be modified unless absolutely necessary in your environment (for example, to delete values entered accidentally or to add a new key/value combination to optimize your server's performance). You should always back up your Registry and save the file to a remote location before using the Registry Editor!

In certain situations, you can use the Windows 2000 Registry Editor to change configuration settings for Exchange 2000 Server. For instance, you can edit the Registry to limit the number of users who are allowed to log on to the Information Store service on a particular server if you need to perform server maintenance.

To view and modify Exchange 2000 data in the Windows 2000 Registry:

1. Stop the Information Store service on your Exchange 2000 computer by opening the Services menu. Click **Start**, point to **Programs**, point to **Administrative Tools**, and then click **Services**. The Services dialog box opens.
2. Scroll to and click the **Microsoft Exchange Information Store** service. Click **Action** on the menu bar, and then click **Stop** to stop this service. If a message box appears informing you that other services will stop when the Information Store stops, click the **Yes** button. Close the Services dialog box.

3. Click **Start**, click **Run**, type **regedt32** in the Open text box, and then press **Enter** to open the Registry Editor. Locate the window for HKEY_LOCAL_MACHINE on Local Machine, and then navigate to the following key inside this window:

```
HKEY_LOCAL_MACHINE\SYSTEM\CurrentControlSet\Services\
MsExchangeIS\ParametersSystem
```

4. Click the **ParametersSystem** folder, click **Edit** on the menu bar, and then click **Add Value** to open the Add Value dialog box (see Figure 9-11). Type **Logon Only As** in the Value Name text box, and then click **REG_MULTI_SZ** in the Data Type drop-down box. Click **OK** to view the Data box.

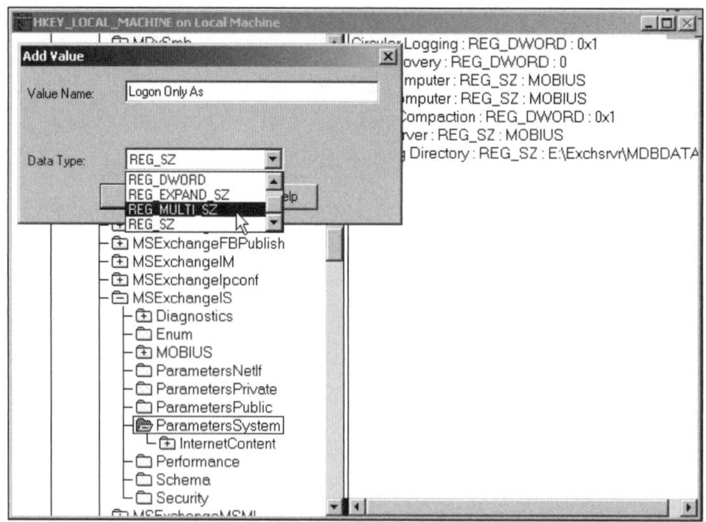

Figure 9-11 Adding a new Registry value to limit logons to the Information Store service

5. In the Data box (Multi-String Editor), type the names of all users you want to allow to log on to the Information Store on separate lines in the box, and then click **OK**. Your entries will use the users' distinguished names, as shown in this example:

```
/o=ERSolutions/ou=Sales/cn=recipients/cn=Bsmith
```

In this format, "o" is the Organization object in System Manager, "ou" is your organizational unit object, and "cn" is the common name of your users. The "cn=recipients" item is the Recipients container where all users are normally located.

6. When you finish typing the names, close the Registry Editor by clicking **Registry** on the menu bar, and then clicking **Exit**. Finally, restart the Information Store service and any other services that might have been stopped by using the Services menu (refer back to Steps 1 and 2).

7. Close any open windows or applications.

Project 9-4

To view and configure the system log in Event Viewer:

1. Click **Start**, point to **Programs**, point to **Administrative Tools**, and then click **Event Viewer**.
2. In Event Viewer, right-click the **System Log** container, and then click **Properties** on the shortcut menu. The System Log Properties dialog box opens (see Figure 9-12).

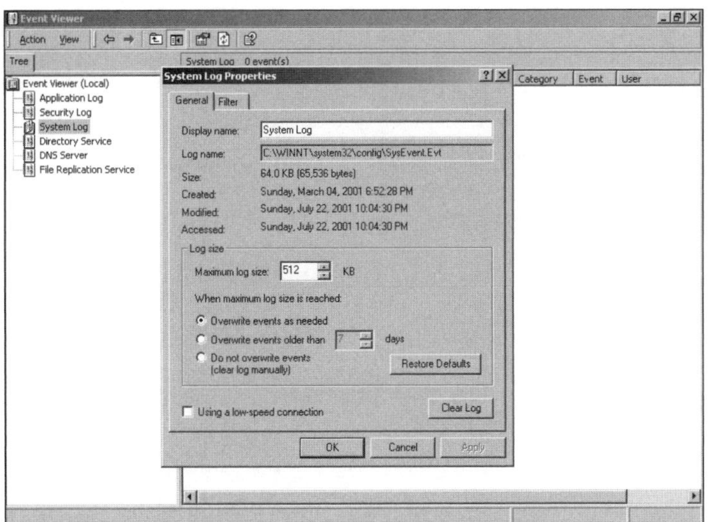

Figure 9-12 Increasing the maximum log size in the System Log Properties dialog box

3. In the General tab, enter **576 KB** in the Maximum log size text box.

When changing settings for log size, keep in mind that Windows 2000 allows increments of only 64 KB to better control the growth of these log files.

4. Click the **Filter** tab, shown in Figure 9-13, to see options for the type of information you want displayed in the system log. Uncheck all the check boxes at the top except for the Warning and Error check boxes. Notice also that you can filter by event source (for example, displaying information only for particular events, such as the Netlogon service) and category (those categories associated with the event source you select). Finally, note that you can display information within a given date range by selecting the option Events On in the From and To list boxes. By default, the system log shows From First Event and To Last Event. When you're finished selecting options, click **OK**.

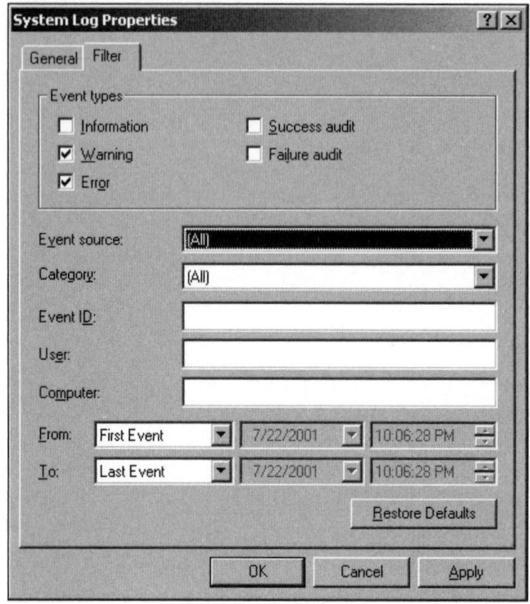

Figure 9-13 The Filter tab of the System Log Properties dialog box

5. Close any open windows or applications.

Project 9-5

To view process and application information using Task Manager:

1. Open the Task Manager utility by clicking **Start**, clicking **Run**, typing **Taskmgr** in the Open text box, and then pressing **Enter**. The Windows Task Manager opens to the Applications tab.
2. Click the **Processes** tab to view all currently running processes. To end a process, right-click the process, and then click End Process. To set the priority of a process, right-click the process, and then point to Set Priority. You can choose from among six different priorities, including Realtime, High, AboveNormal, Normal, BelowNormal, and Low.

It is best to leave the default priority setting of Normal for most processes. Choose High or AboveNormal only in rare circumstances when you want to give certain CPU-intensive applications more priority (such as database applications or firewall applications). Choosing Realtime is not recommended because the system reserves this priority setting for highly critical situations, such as kernel mode operations (for example, actions performed by the Input/Output Manager or Security component of the Windows 2000 kernel).

3. Click the **Performance** tab to view statistics on CPU usage and memory usage. Administrators often consult this tab if certain applications or processes appear to "hang" the system, causing other applications or processes to abort or become suspended. If you notice the CPU usage section indicating 100% CPU use, you could click the Processes tab and change the priority of the offending application or end this process altogether.
4. Close any open windows or applications.

Project 9-6

You can create a full-text index for a mailbox store or a public folder store; if you create an index for a mailbox store, this index is applied against all text found in a message body and any associated message attachments. Any data in a personal folder store (or .pst file) on a local computer hard drive is not included in a full-text index.

To configure full-text indexing for mailbox stores in Exchange 2000:

1. Click **Start**, point to **Programs**, point to **Microsoft Exchange**, and then click **System Manager**. Expand your Organization object, and then expand the **Administrative Groups** folder.
2. Expand the **First Administrative Group** container, and then expand the **Servers** container underneath it.
3. Expand your ***server*** object (replace ***server*** with the actual name of your server), and then expand the **First Storage Group** underneath it.
4. Right-click the mailbox store you want to index, and then click **Create Full-Text Index** on the shortcut menu.
5. Enter a folder location for the index files when prompted to do so—Exchange will create a folder location if the location you entered does not exist.
6. Click **OK**. The new index will be created and will be approximately 20% of the size of your mailbox store.

You will have to manually update or rebuild your full-text indexes because Exchange 2000 does not do this automatically. An updated index contains changes to the mailbox store, but a rebuild re-creates the index for the mailbox store. To update or rebuild an index, right-click the mailbox store that you just configured for full-text indexing, and then click **Start Incremental Population** (if you want to *update* your existing index) or **Start Full Population** (if you want to *rebuild* your existing index). Confirm either action by clicking the **Yes** button in the message box that appears.

7. Close any open windows or applications.

Project 9-7

This project requires you to perform two separate tasks. First, you will use the Windows 2000 Active Directory Users and Computers snap-in to create a mailbox-enabled user and associate this new user to a mailbox store in System Manager. Then you will use System Manager to create a recipient policy that applies to this new mailbox-enabled user.

To create a new mailbox-enabled user and apply a new recipient policy to that user:

Creating a New Mailbox-Enabled User

1. Click **Start**, point to **Programs**, point to **Administrative Tools**, and then click **Active Directory Users and Computers**.
2. Expand your ***domain*** object (replace ***domain*** with the actual name of your domain) at the top of the console root.
3. Right-click the **Users** container, point to **New**, and then click **User** on the shortcut menu.
4. When the New Object - User dialog box (shown in Figure 9-14) opens, type the following information: **Samuel** in the First name text box, **Jones** in the Last name text box, and **Sjones@*your_domain.com*** in the User logon name text box (replace ***your_domain.com*** with the name of your domain).

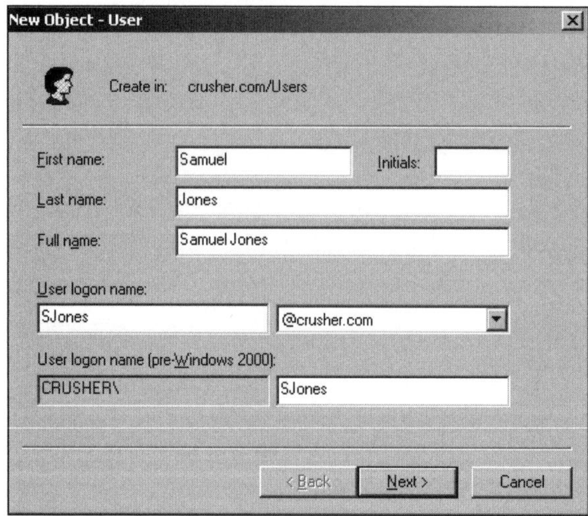

Figure 9-14 The New Object - User dialog box in Active Directory Users and Computers

5. Click the **Next** button. Type **password** in the Password text box, type **password** again in the Confirm password text box to confirm the password, and then click the **Next** button.

6. In the next dialog box that opens, click to select the **Create an Exchange mailbox** check box. Leave all other settings intact, including the Alias, the Server, and the Mailbox Store, and then click the **Next** button.
7. Review all information in the final dialog box that opens, and then click the **Finish** button. A new user object called Samuel Jones appears in the Users folder in the Details pane of Active Directory Users and Computers.

Creating and Applying a New Recipient Policy

8. To open the System Manager console, click **Start**, point to **Programs**, point to **Microsoft Exchange**, and then click **System Manager**.
9. Expand the **Recipients** container underneath the Organization object. Right-click the **Recipient Policies** container, point to **New**, and then click **Recipient Policy** on the shortcut menu. The New Policy dialog box opens. Click the **E-mail Addresses** check box to select this property page.
10. In the General tab of the Properties dialog box that opens, type **Policy-One** in the Name text box, and then click the **Modify** button at the bottom of this tab. The Find Exchange Recipients dialog box opens, as shown in Figure 9-15. In the General tab, click to deselect all the check boxes except Users with Exchange mailbox, and then click the **Find Now** button.

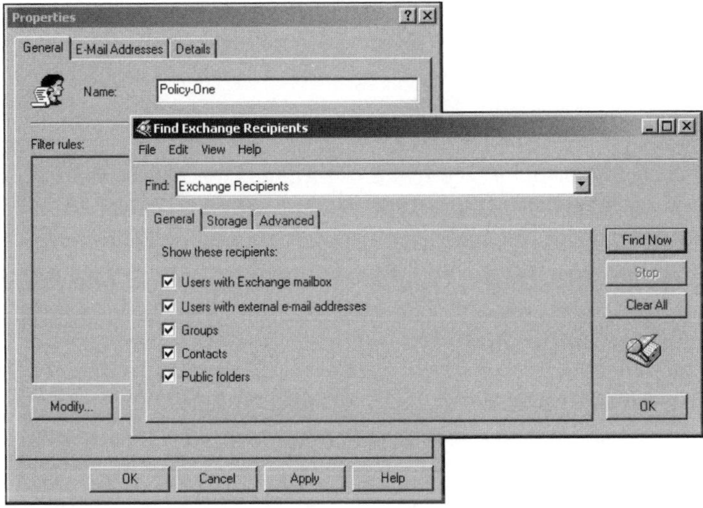

Figure 9-15 The Find Exchange Recipients dialog box

11. Double-click **Samuel Jones** in the list of users that appears. If you see an Exchange System Manager message box asking you to "Apply this policy now," click **OK**. The Find Exchange Recipients dialog box automatically closes, and you see the Properties dialog box again. In the General tab, you will see a new entry in the Filter rules section, as shown in Figure 9-16.

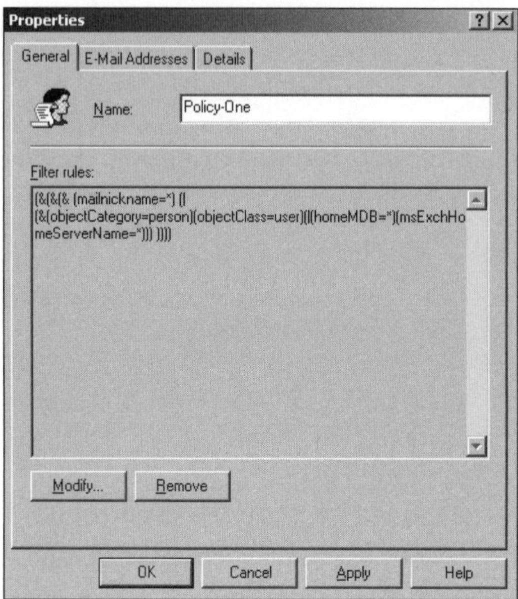

Figure 9-16 The new policy filter in the Properties dialog box

12. Click **OK** to create the new recipient policy. You can return to this policy at any time to change the default e-mail addresses that will be generated.

To modify this policy in System Manager, simply right-click this policy under the Recipients container, and then click Properties. Click the E-Mail Addresses tab, where you can modify the current SMTP address, or click the New button to enter a new SMTP addressing scheme for your organization. The policy will be applied to all members affected by the policy. The RUS applies all new recipient policies.

13. Close any open windows or applications.

CASE PROJECTS

Case 1

Phillip manages a LAN for a small university computer center. His daily tasks include backing up five Windows 2000 servers and managing three Exchange 2000 servers to support 1000 students. He has experience managing Exchange Server 5.5 with the Exchange Administrator management tool and has frequently commented to his staff that he wishes there was a good management tool for Exchange 2000 that's functionally equivalent to the Exchange Administrator tool for Exchange 5.5. He has instructed his staff to shop for a third-party utility that will help manage his growing network. What Exchange tools or third-party utilities would you recommend to Phillip for managing his Exchange 2000 server?

Case 2

Gina is managing a packaging company, APS, Inc., headquartered in New York. The company has three branch offices in St. Louis, Atlanta, and Dallas. Gina wants to select an appropriate administration model for her company so that she can properly configure her four Exchange 2000 servers. She is used to managing everything herself, but recent events have taken her away from daily system administration. Gina is considering hiring dedicated Exchange 2000 administrators and delegating control of certain resources to them, but she is torn between micromanaging her Exchange 2000 servers for optimum performance or devoting more time to growing her company. All branch offices have high-speed T-1 connections to New York. What factors will help Gina decide which administration model to use in this scenario?

Case 3

9

Tarek and Camille manage the IT Department for a large hospital in Genoa, Italy. The organization consists of 10,000 doctors, nurses, and administrative personnel. Tarek, the network manager, has installed and configured 24 Exchange 2000 servers. He has hired Camille, the e-mail administrator, to manage these servers and distribute users to each server. Camille has configured each server to contain three storage groups and each storage group to contain three mailbox stores and two public folder stores. She has also organized users into separate administrative groups for management purposes and assigned these groups the permissions they need to access resources. Camille now wants to configure storage group limits and maintenance schedules on an organization-wide basis. Her users are constantly deleting items that should not be deleted, so she wants to configure a retention period of five days so that users can retrieve these deleted items using their Outlook 2000 client. How can Camille configure these items with the least amount of administrative effort or overhead?

Case 4

You are the network administrator for a law firm that employs 5000 attorneys. The company has clients in 20 countries, including the United States. You manage five separate Exchange 2000 computers, two Windows 2000 domain controllers, and one Web server running Microsoft IIS 5. You are concerned about increasing levels of network traffic caused by the number of connections to your Exchange servers as well as the traffic generated by clients who need to access Exchange 2000 remotely from home. Users also complain that they are unable to perform searches on text contained in message attachments. You are considering options that would help optimize e-mail messaging for all users in your company. What are some of the actions you can take that would help you achieve your objectives?

CHAPTER

10

CONNECTOR AND ROUTING MANAGEMENT IN EXCHANGE 2000 SERVER

After reading this chapter and completing the exercises, you will be able to:

- Optimize messaging traffic between servers in your organization by placing routing group barriers, thus helping you balance the technical, economic, and business needs of your organization
- Manage connectivity between Exchange 2000 servers in your organization as well as with other messaging systems outside your organization, ensuring timely delivery and transparent sharing of business information
- Quickly identify, troubleshoot, and resolve message routing and delivery problems that can occur in your Exchange organization and with external messaging systems, allowing you to correct many delivery problems before they have a chance to affect users
- Use Non-Delivery Reports to quickly identify and locate the source of problems users have when sending mail
- Understand how Exchange 2000 uses the link state algorithm to route messages between Exchange 2000 servers and external messaging systems, enabling you to predict and control how messaging traffic will affect network resources

At its core, any messaging system is primarily concerned with intelligently routing messages from one user to another. For users on the same Exchange server and storage group, the server effectively accepts the message from the sender, stores it, and places a pointer to it in the recipient's mailbox. However, for recipients hosted outside the local Exchange organization, the server must identify the most efficient route to get the package to its final destination. This requires taking into account any failed routing paths, possible message format conversion, and delivery status monitoring.

In this chapter, you learn the architecture in Exchange 2000 Server that provides the highly scalable, reliable, and easily administered message routing functionality. You learn about the "intelligent" side of Exchange Server that enforces message compliance with corporate standards, converts messages between formats when necessary, and guarantees reliable message delivery. You also learn about the "functional" side of Exchange Server that carries out the communication with other mail servers and updates the link state table with availability information on remote servers.

A thorough understanding of how Exchange Server routes messages from sender to recipient gives you a solid foundation on which to build and manage routing groups, monitor message routing, and troubleshoot messaging connectivity. In Exchange 2000 Server, this routing functionality comes from its totally revamped internal transport architecture. In the organization, it comes through the use of routing groups, similar to Exchange 5.5 sites, with connections between them. External connectors provide messaging and directory synchronization with external messaging systems.

EXCHANGE 2000 CONNECTIVITY OVERVIEW

Exchange 2000 relies on **connectors** to perform handshaking and message transfer with other Exchange 2000 servers in the Exchange organization. In addition, connectors act as gateways to other messaging systems, allowing Exchange to interact directly with external messaging systems as though they were part of the Exchange organization. Connectors can be configured to synchronize directory information between messaging systems, adding users from each messaging platform to the address lists of the other platform. They also enable message transfer, provide access to public folders, and extend the functionality of Exchange 2000.

By default, native connectors for SMTP (and its hybrid cousin, the Routing Group Connector) and X.400 (TCP and X.25) are installed during the Exchange Server setup. Native connectors are also available and can be installed during the Exchange Server setup for Lotus Notes, cc: Mail, and Novell GroupWise. As in earlier versions of Exchange, third parties can use the **Exchange Development Kit (EDK)** to create value-added connectors for such features as integrated fax messaging, COLD Imaging (paperless document management), workflow management tools, and Integrated Messaging Services (voicemail via e-mail).

Simple Mail Transport Protocol Virtual Servers

On the opposite side of an Exchange 2000 connector is either an external messaging system or another Exchange 2000 server. And if you're connecting to Exchange, you're connecting to an SMTP virtual server. Because SMTP is the default protocol for messaging traffic in an Exchange 2000 organization, SMTP virtual servers also send messages on behalf of the Exchange server. When Exchange is installed, a Default SMTP Virtual Server is created and bound to all IP addresses on a server. However, as with Web sites in IIS, you can have multiple SMTP virtual servers on a single computer, each assigned a unique IP address and configured independently of the others. For instance, you can create one public SMTP virtual server for sending and receiving messages over the Internet, which accepts only messages destined for your company, and a second private SMTP virtual server for internal message transfer, which allows relay but is available only to employees.

Configuring SMTP virtual servers is discussed in Chapter 8, "Configuring Internet Clients in Exchange 2000 Server," but once configured, how are SMTP virtual servers used by Exchange and managed by administrators? Each SMTP virtual server has two subcontainers. The first, Current Sessions, is an administrative tool supplying status information on current inbound sessions to this SMTP virtual server. If necessary, sessions can be forcibly terminated from this view by right-clicking the session and selecting Terminate. The second container, Queues, is a monitoring, management, and troubleshooting tool of the message delivery process for this SMTP virtual server. From here, you can view the status of the SMTP virtual server's outbound queues, freeze or unfreeze all or some of the messages in a queue to control message delivery, and filter for messages based on sender, recipient, size, or delivery status. Messages in a queue are sent in first-in-first-out order. To expedite delivery of one or more messages, you must freeze all messages in the queue, unfreeze the messages to be expedited, wait for those expedited messages to be delivered, and then unfreeze all other messages. 10

Modern users have come to expect e-mails to be delivered instantaneously, and sometimes react almost with shock if they receive a nondelivery report two to four days after they sent the message. Although you should allow a sufficient retry period to overcome transient errors, some administrators customarily send delay notifications after only 30 minutes and nondelivery reports in as little as 4–24 hours.

Restricting Unsolicited Broadcast E-Mail (UBE)

Senders of unsolicited broadcast e-mails (UBEs) are notorious for using unprotected SMTP servers to relay their unwelcome get-rich-quick schemes and X-rated invitations to their hapless victims. In addition to consuming processing and bandwidth resources, allowing your server to be used in such a manner quickly gets your company on an Internet blacklist, which could prevent you from sending valid e-mails to outside contacts. For any SMTP virtual server available to the Internet, ensure that message relay restrictions are in place!

The good news is that Exchange 2000 Server restricts relay by default unless the client is successfully authenticated first. Relay restriction settings can be viewed or modified by clicking the Relay button in the Access tab of the SMTP virtual server, as shown in Figure 10-1.

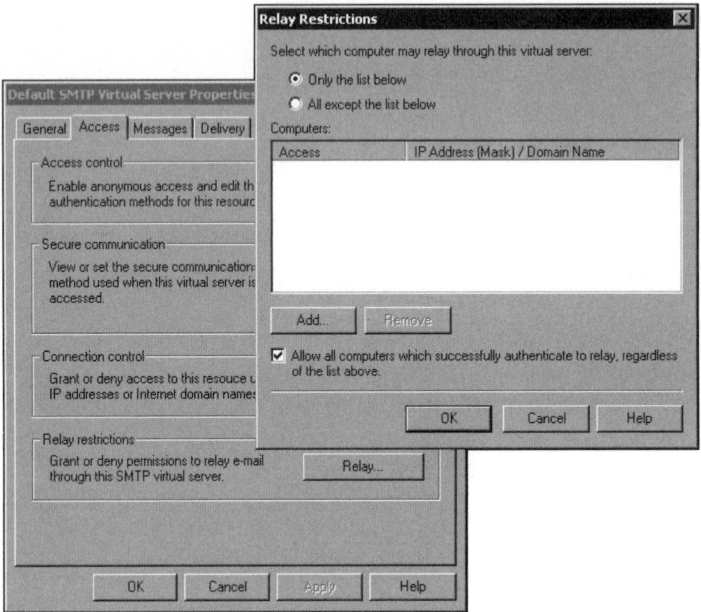

Figure 10-1 Restricting message relay

Message Filtering

Message filtering refers to the capability of Exchange 2000 to stop troublemakers from sending unwanted e-mails to internal users. Out of the box, Exchange 2000 can be configured to filter based on two criteria. The first, discussed in the previous section, rejects communication with specific remote SMTP servers. The second criterion filters on senders. First, the administrator compiles a list of known senders of spam (or other unwanted messages) and adds them to a list of restricted addresses defined for the Exchange organization (this is a global setting). Second, the filter is bound to any IP addresses used by the SMTP virtual server that should apply the filter; binding only public IP addresses to the filtering rule prevents excessive processing overhead on the Exchange server.

To configure a global list of unwanted senders, open the Global Settings root container in Exchange System Manager. Right-click Message Delivery, and then click Properties. In the Filtering tab, add full or partial e-mail addresses of senders that should be rejected. If you want to keep a record of all filtered messages, enable the Archive filtered messages option. Because many spammers send messages with no From address defined, it's also a good idea to enable the Filter messages with blank sender option. If you don't want remote senders to know their message is being blocked, enable the Accept messages without notifying sender of filtering option. After configuring the list of unwanted senders, filtering must be bound to each IP address of each SMTP virtual server that should apply the filter. In the General tab of the SMTP Virtual Server Properties dialog box, click the Advanced button to edit the properties of each IP address to apply the filter.

As is usual for feature sets considered "extended functionality" by the Microsoft development team, the message-filtering functionality in Exchange works, but leaves room for third-party improvement. UBE senders have adapted to filtering by using pseudo-random e-mail addresses at large ISPs to send their spam, so unless you are willing to stop all inbound mail from AOL or Hotmail, you'll need a much more powerful approach—such as one that message transport events can support, discussed in "Event Handling and Event Sinks," later in this chapter. (Transport events are the type of technology that makes a real tech-head's heart flutter.)

MESSAGE ROUTING CONCEPTS

Within a routing group, messages are always delivered directly from the sender's server to the recipient's server, in what is called an intrinsic full-mesh routing topology. This design, which is easy to administer, is most efficient in high-speed environments. When connecting offices with slow (less than 128 KB) or unreliable WAN links, arrange well-connected servers together in routing groups, with one or more servers in each routing group designated as a bridgehead server. Messages between routing groups are then funneled through the bridgeheads on either side of the Routing Group Connector (RGC), and finally to the recipient's server. Therefore, the downside of creating routing groups is a slightly increased administrative burden and an extra step for message delivery, but the upside is protecting precious WAN bandwidth by configuring the RGCs.

Because high-speed, permanent connections are assumed to exist between routing groups, the administrator is given a good deal of flexibility in configuring the way routing groups manage messaging traffic. One of the intrinsic benefits of using RGCs is the way they handle broadcast messages to a number of Exchange servers in a single remote routing group. Instead of sending the message to each remote server directly, the message is sent only once, to the remote bridgehead server, where it is routed to its final destination. RGCs can be further configured to hold messages for delivery during off-peak hours, place caps on the size of messages allowed over the connection, or restrict low-priority system messages.

Technical Overview of Message Routing

Suppose you have six Exchange servers: A, B, C, D, E, and F. Servers A, B, and C are in the West Town office, and Servers D, E, and F are in the East Town office. The offices are connected by a 64-KB frame relay WAN link, as shown in Figure 10-2. The corresponding logical routing group structure is illustrated in Figure 10-3.

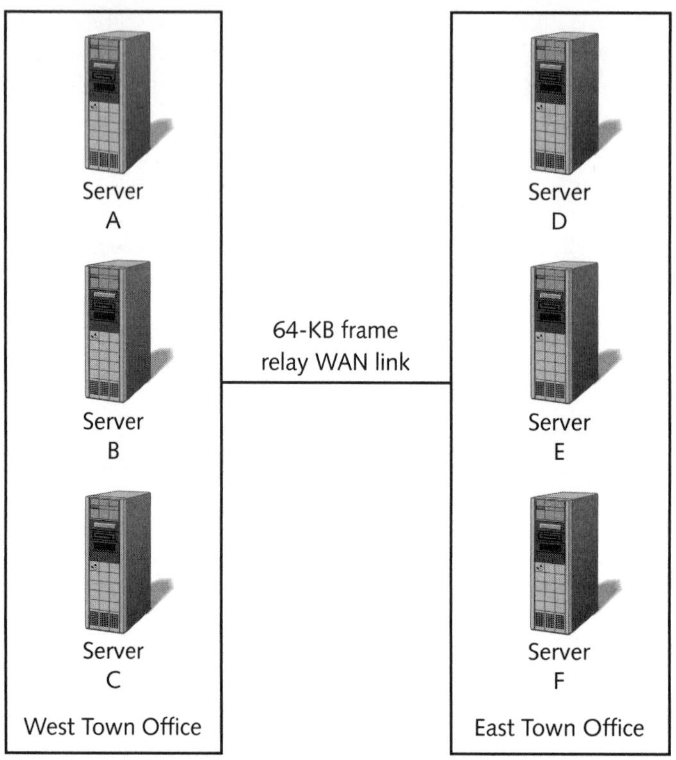

Figure 10-2 Physical WAN links between two offices

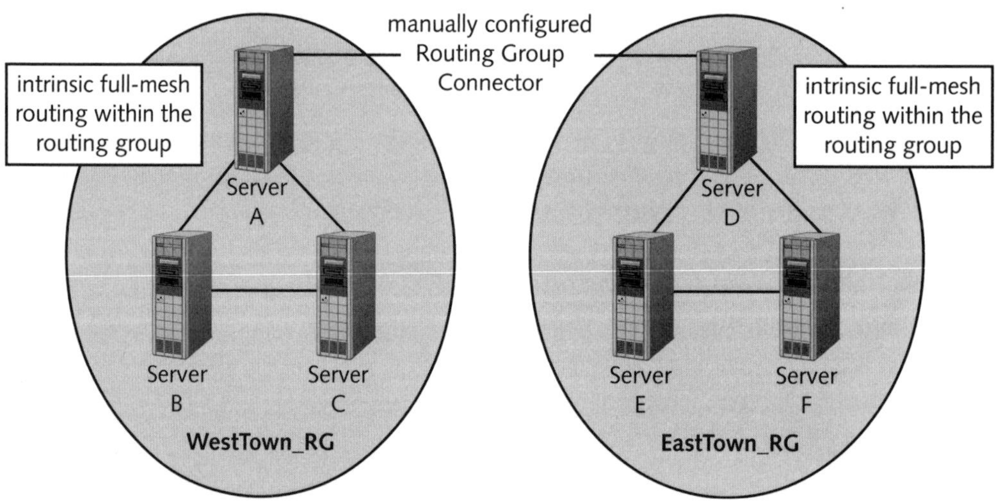

Figure 10-3 Message routing topology within and between routing groups

Suppose that a user on Server B sends a broadcast message to recipients homed on all six servers. Delivery takes place in three steps, as shown in Figure 10-4.

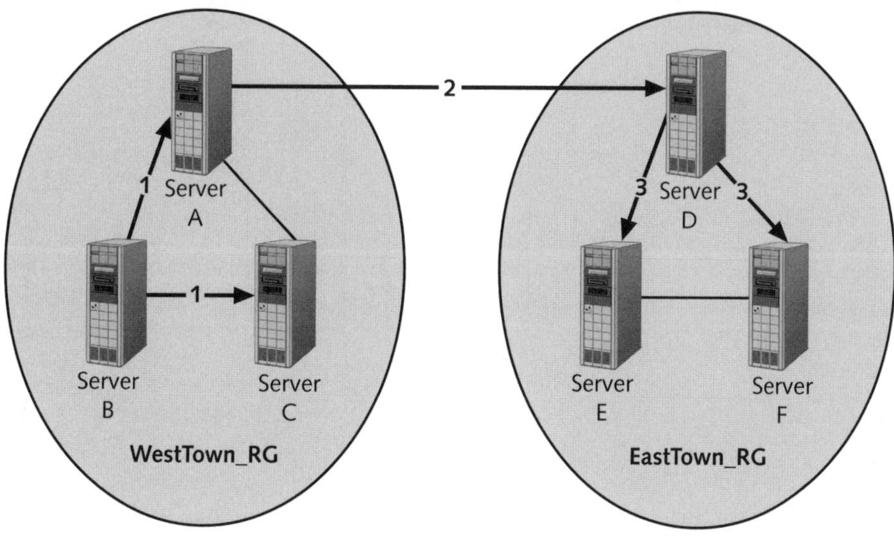

Figure 10-4 The three steps of message delivery between routing groups

1. Server B delivers the message directly to servers in WestTown_RG, but uses its bridgehead, Server A, to route the message outside the realm of its local routing group.
2. Server A routes the message to the remote bridgehead in EastTown_RG, Server D.
3. Server D distributes the message to Servers E and F.

Table 10-1 describes the functional differences in how messages are routed within and between routing groups. In short, within a routing group, the speed of message transport is of primary importance. Between routing groups, however, more effort is made to conserve WAN bandwidth and handle link failures.

Table 10-1 Message Routing in Routing Groups

Category	Message Routing Within Routing Groups	Message Routing Between Routing Groups
Network Connectivity Assumptions	A full-mesh, permanent, high-speed routing topology is always assumed.	Connectivity between routing groups must be manually configured.
Message Routing	The sender's server delivers the message directly to the recipient's server.	The sender's server delivers the message to a local bridgehead server for further routing.

Table 10-1 Message Routing in Routing Groups (continued)

Category	Message Routing Within Routing Groups	Message Routing Between Routing Groups
Message Delivery Scheduling	Message delivery is processed immediately for all messages and all users.	Messages are delivered immediately by default, but delivery can be scheduled for all messages or based on message size, type, or sender.
Route Failure Handling	If the sender's server cannot contact the recipient's server, the message is held at the source until the recipient's server is available or the message times out.	Bridgehead servers attempt to reroute the message until all possible paths have been exhausted; if a bridgehead server determines that no more routes are available, the message is held for delivery until the recipient's server is available or the message times out.
Public Folder Referrals (if requested public folder is not available on client's server)	The client is referred to a random server within the routing group.	If no public folder replica exists in the client's routing group, the client is redirected to the routing group with the lowest cost that allows public folder referrals.

EXCHANGE 2000 TRANSPORT ARCHITECTURE

As an administrator, you will generally approach message routing from the functional side, giving consideration primarily to the flow of traffic from one server to another in your enterprise. However, it's helpful to understand the process in Exchange 2000 Server that empowers that routing functionality. That process is the **Exchange 2000 Transport Architecture**, which describes how messages are routed and stored in an Exchange server and is the underpinning of all message flow. A sound understanding of the Transport Architecture gives you a foundation for intelligently designing, monitoring, and troubleshooting routing groups and connectors used in your Exchange organization and with external messaging systems. The Transport Architecture has radically changed from previous versions, in which a monolithic **Message Transfer Agent (MTA)** was responsible for all traffic into and out of the Exchange Store. Although the Exchange 5.5 MTA still exists in Exchange 2000, it is used only for X.400-based connectors and as an access point for external messaging connectors.

With Exchange 2000, the task of routing messages within a server has been divided into many individual components, grouped into three primary categories. Components responsible for storing and retrieving messages from the physical databases are located in the Information Store service. Most of the components involved in routing messages between the local system and other servers are now managed by the **advanced queuing engine (AQE)** as part of the SMTP Service in IIS. Finally, the components for providing connectivity to clients and servers are split between IIS, which supports standards-based connectors and protocols, and Exchange, which supports proprietary ones. Although separating message routing and standards-based connectivity from the Information Store makes Exchange 2000 much more extensible and reliable than Exchange 5.5, it also creates a requirement for a very high-speed Interprocess Communication facility to glue IIS tightly on top of Exchange. This facility is the Exchange Interprocess Communication (ExIPC) layer (fittingly dubbed "the Epoxy layer").

This separation of message routing and standards-based connectivity from storage and access is the empowering technology behind front-end/back-end server configurations. Slightly more subtle, the proprietary nature of protocols such as MAPI prevents their being managed by IIS, and hence prevents their use of front-end servers.

Although these advances add significantly to the power of Exchange 2000 in the eyes of the administrator, one advance in the Transport Architecture enjoys the distinct favor of most users—the Web Storage System (WSS). The WSS isn't a specific service or function, but an abstraction layer within the Information Store process (Store.exe). It acts as governor and single point of contact for all protocols and internal APIs that can access the private and public stores. As such, the WSS provides the same access to data in the stores to all clients, whether they are connecting through MAPI, POP3, IMAP, CDO, or Windows Explorer (via the Installable File System). More details on the WSS as it applies to client access are in Chapter 8.

10

Figure 10-5 illustrates the Transport Architecture in Exchange 2000 as a whole. Although the administration and functionality of each connector is discussed in "Using Exchange 2000 Connectors" later in this chapter, message transport in Exchange 2000 is reviewed in the following sections. Refer to Figure 10-5 as each component of the Transport Architecture is discussed in more detail. You'll recognize many of these components from previous chapters, but these sections focus on their functions as they relate to message transfer.

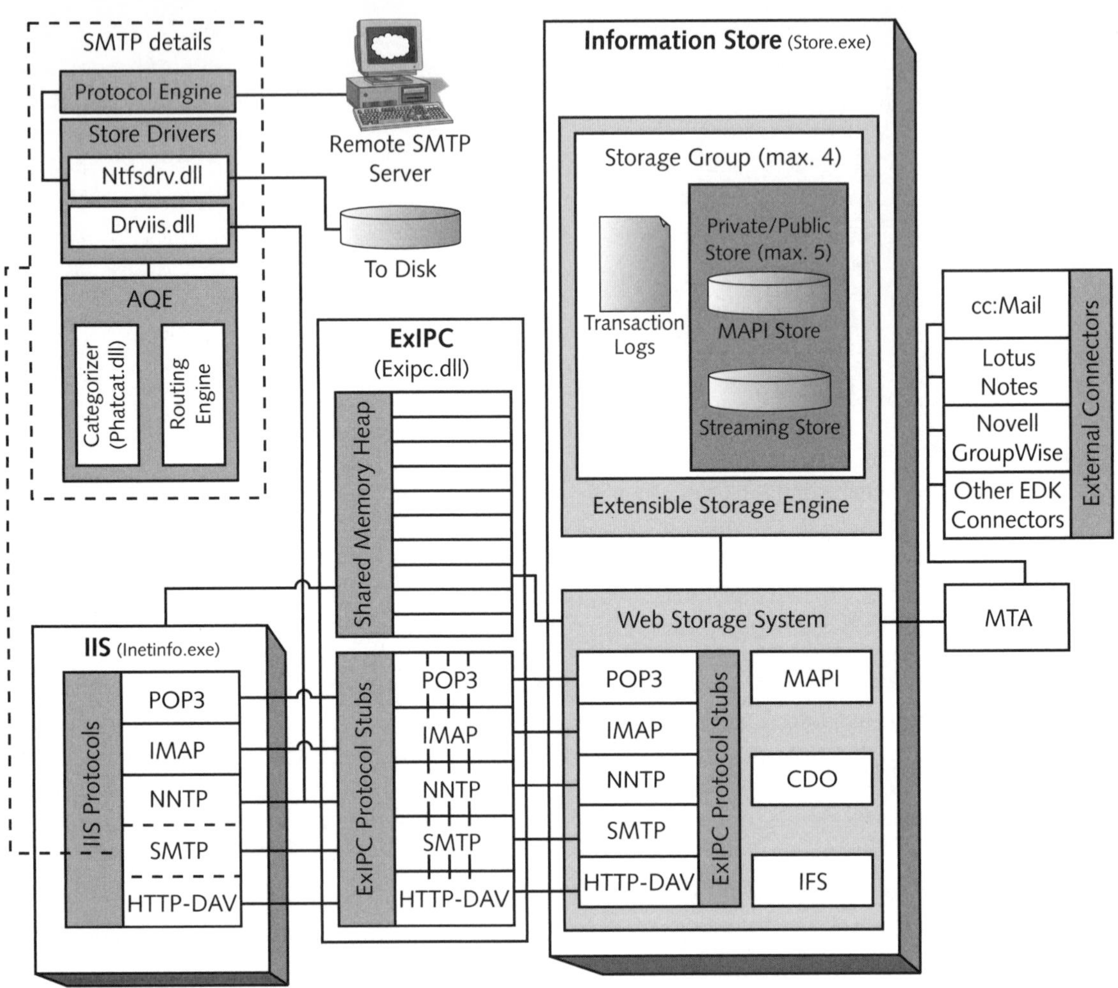

Figure 10-5 Components in the Exchange 2000 Transport Architecture

Message Storage and Retrieval

As Figure 10-5 shows, the primary function of the Information Store is to hold the components for storing and retrieving messages on the physical private and public store databases and to provide a uniform method of accessing that data through the WSS.

As you'll recall from Chapter 1, "An Overview of Microsoft Exchange 2000 Server," the **Extensible Storage Engine (ESE)** maintains up to four storage groups. Each storage group maintains only a single set of transaction logs, but can contain up to five private or public stores sharing those logs. The private and public stores, in turn, each contain a native MAPI Store, used primarily for Outlook clients, and a Streaming Store for other clients. Potentially, then, you could have up to 4 storage groups, 4 sets of transaction logs, and a total of 20 private and public stores. In addition to its operational duties (placing and retrieving messages from the physical database files), the ESE is also responsible for the background duties of managing those files. It uses transaction logs as a functional "to-do list" for completing unfinished work in case of system failure and as a historical record of all changes made to the physical databases since the last full or differential backup, allowing a lossless restore of the database in case of corruption. The ESE is also responsible for periodically defragmenting the database files and performing some basic checks on database consistency.

The only component that communicates directly with the ESE is the WSS. As discussed previously, the WSS governs all access to and from the Information Store. It authenticates user requests and directs them to the ESE, the AQE, or another connector through the MTA.

Message Routing

One of the most impressive improvements to Exchange 2000 from previous versions, at least in administrators' eyes, is in its routing architecture, which is now primarily part of the SMTP Service in IIS. This extended SMTP Service is composed of three functional groups, shown in Figure 10-5.

SMTP's first function is the **protocol engine**, which acts as a courier for the AQE. It initiates and accepts SMTP sessions over TCP port 25 and transfers messages with other SMTP servers. Although it might seem that the protocol engine plays only a small part, it is the most configurable aspect of the Exchange 2000 Transport Architecture. Responsible for all communication with remote SMTP servers, the protocol engine manages the SMTP virtual servers created in Exchange System Manager, customizing its activity based on the options set in the SMTP virtual server properties.

The next aspect of the SMTP Service is the **store drivers**, which provide transaction logging and message transport or storage for all messages the AQE sends or receives. The store drivers are the most visible aspect of the Exchange 2000 Transport Architecture. The first store driver, Ntfsdrv.dll, uses the local disk (\ExchSrvr\MailRoot) to manage the message queue between the protocol engine and AQE. Each SMTP virtual server has its own queue and can be viewed in Exchange System Manager (\Servers*ServerName*\Protocols\SMTP*SMTP Virtual Server*\Queues). The second store driver, Drviis.dll, is the IIS interface driver that provides connectivity with the Web Storage System through ExIPC. This queue is also displayed in the SMTP virtual server queues, but communication between IIS and Exchange is extremely fast, so if any messages are sticking in this queue long enough to be viewed, there's a serious problem.

The AQE receives messages for transport through the store drivers from the Web Storage System or the protocol engine. The WSS may be sending system messages to other Exchange servers or acting on behalf of a MAPI client or a proprietary connector. The protocol engine delivers messages received from a remote SMTP server. When the AQE receives a message, it places it in the **pre-categorization queue** (viewed in Exchange

System Manager as the "Messages awaiting directory lookup" queue of the SMTP virtual server) and fires a series of events referred to collectively as the **Categorizer (PhatCat.dll)**, which does the following:

1. Expands distribution groups, if the server is configured to do so
2. Resolves sender and all recipient addresses
3. Determines the recipient's home (local server name or external domain name)
4. Detects and removes loops in distribution groups and duplications in the recipient list (as can happen if a recipient is named explicitly and is also part of a distribution group named as a recipient)
5. Marks each recipient as "Gateway" (meaning that the message must be routed outbound through the SMTP Connector) or "Local" (which sends the message to the WSS to be delivered to the local ESE or routed through a connector governed by the WSS)

The AQE then places the message in the **pre-routing queue** (the "Messages waiting to be routed" queue) and passes each destination domain to the **routing engine**, which responds with next-hop information for that destination. Next, the AQE places the categorized message in a per-destination-domain queue, creating queues if necessary. The next-hop information from the routing engine is listed in the properties of each per-destination-domain queue. After the message has thus been categorized, the AQE sends it to the store drivers for delivery. If the message is destined for a remote server through the SMTP interface (one or more recipients marked as "Gateway"), it is sent to Ntfsdrv.dll, stored in the file-based queue, and transmitted to the remote SMTP server by the SMTP protocol engine.

If one or more recipients are marked as "Local," the AQE uses Drviis.dll to place the message body in the ExIPC shared memory heap, and the recipient list is delivered to the Web Storage System through the SMTP **protocol stub** (the protocol-specific connection between IIS and Exchange) along with a pointer to the message body. The WSS then sends the message to the ESE for local recipients and/or to an appropriate proprietary connector for further routing. To view the AQE queues, open the Servers*ServerName*\Protocols\SMTP\Default SMTP Virtual Server\Queues path in Exchange System Manager.

- The pre-categorizer queue is "Messages awaiting directory lookup."
- The pre-routing queue is "Messages waiting to be routed."
- The "*OrganizationName* (Local delivery)" queue is for messages waiting to be delivered to the Web Storage System. "(Local delivery)" indicates that the Categorizer labeled these messages "Local," meaning they need to be sent to the Web Storage System to be stored in the ESE, or passed on to an external messaging connector.

- All other queues are per-destination-domain queues (perhaps better named "per-address-space queues"). External domain names, fully qualified domain names (FQDNs) of Exchange servers in the enterprise, and local connectors are listed here. Next-hop information from the routing engine is listed in the Properties dialog box of each per-destination-domain queue.

Event Handling and Event Sinks

During the early beta development of Microsoft Commercial Internet System v. 2.0, the standard programming model, CDONTS, would not scale to the level of functionality needed to host the thousands of users often found on customer systems. In response, Microsoft developed a powerful programming model that relies on **event sinks**, or triggers, that could scale to literally millions of users. To the great pleasure of Exchange administrators everywhere, this functionality is added to IIS after Exchange is installed and has been extended to support the Web Storage System in Exchange 2000 Server.

This event model is similar to the programming model commonly used in Windows. For example, the Start button is an object in the Windows environment that has events sinks registered with it. When you click the Start button, an event occurs and a Start button event sink associated with the MouseDown (*left*) event displays the Start menu. Similarly, right-clicking the Start button causes the event sink associated with the MouseDown (*right*) event to display a different context-sensitive menu. By using this event-driven programming model, objects can respond immediately when called, but don't use system resources when they're not needed.

Literally thousands of built-in event sinks are used to process and route messages through the Exchange 2000 Transport Architecture, yet those event sinks consume system resources *only* when they are needed to perform their function. With any Component Object Model (COM)-compatible scripting language, you can add or modify the functionality of Exchange 2000 to completely suit your needs. There are three categories of Exchange 2000 event sinks: storage events (managed by the WSS), transport events, and protocol events (managed by IIS). In the following three sections, you will learn the benefits of some of the more commonly used events in Exchange 2000. Detailed instructions on creating and registering events is beyond the scope of this book, but can be found at *http://msdn.microsoft.com* by performing a search on any storage or transport event name.

Storage Events

Storage events, managed by the WSS, operate on messages in the Information Store. For events that should process messages as they are moved in or out of the Information Store, either synchronous or asynchronous events can be used, according to the event criticality. Synchronous events, triggered *before* messages are submitted to the Information Store, ensure that critical processing (such as virus scanning) is completed before a user has access to the message. However, because synchronous events must be completed before a message can be submitted to the Information Store, it is important that they do not create unnecessary delays in message delivery. For less critical events, asynchronous events, triggered *after* the message has been delivered to the local Information Store, are more appropriate. System events fire on a fixed schedule or at system startup and shutdown. Table 10-2 shows the Web Storage System event names and their categories.

Table 10-2 Exchange 2000 Web Storage System Events

Asynchronous Events (triggered after message submission)	Synchronous Events (triggered before message submission)	System Events
OnSave	OnSyncSave	OnTimer
OnDelete	OnSyncDelete	MDBOnStartUp
		MDBOnShutDown

Transport Events

When Exchange 2000 is installed, the IIS process is augmented to support transport events, which are used to process messages as they are sent into or out of the messaging server. As discussed in the "Exchange 2000 Transport Architecture" section, most of the components for message transport are now housed in IIS; this includes transport events. Transport events can be used for gateway virus protection (detect and clean viruses en route) or to take custom actions based on message properties (for example, sender, recipient, message size, inappropriate language). Some of the most common transport events are listed in Table 10-3.

Table 10-3 Exchange 2000 Augmented IIS Transport Events

Transport Event Name	Description
OnMessageSubmission	Processes all messages upon receipt by the AQE before placing them in the pre-categorization queue; used for virus protection and can be used to restrict message delivery from specific senders or to add recipients to message
OnMessagePostCategorize	Fires after the Categorizer has resolved all recipients; used to create special recipient-based rules

Protocol Events

Protocol events are used to modify or extend the functionality of the protocol engine. InBound protocol events extend the protocol engine's feature set during inbound SMTP sessions (such as adding recognition of new SMTP commands). OutBound protocol events extend the protocol engine's feature set during outbound SMTP sessions.

Planning Routing Groups

Although Exchange handles message traffic within routing groups, configuring and troubleshooting message traffic *between* routing groups does entail administrative overhead, so it is best to keep the number of routing groups in your organization to a minimum. A permanent, high-speed network topology *is* assumed to exist between servers within a routing group, but the servers need not necessarily be on the same LAN segment. As long as the WAN link between two servers is reliable and there's sufficient bandwidth between them to support direct communications, the servers can be consolidated into a single routing group. As for how much bandwidth is enough, it really depends on your situation. Generally, 128 KB of available bandwidth is suggested as a minimum, but that guideline is based on average messaging traffic between servers in the average company. For heavy messaging traffic between servers, you might need more. In the real world, if messaging traffic is very low between servers, you may be able to bring that floor as low as 64 KB, but do so with caution.

Remember to account for existing WAN traffic when making bandwidth recommendations. A 192-KB frame-relay link that averages 50% utilization could become overtaxed if Exchange servers on both sides of the link are placed in the same routing group.

Although geography is only a secondary concern when defining routing group boundaries, routing groups generally should not cover vast geographical areas or extend beyond continental boundaries. In these situations, network traffic generally travels through multiple backbone carriers and has numerous hops, resulting in increased latency. True, SMTP in Exchange 2000 is much more forgiving of network latency than is the X.400 RPC protocol used by Exchange 5.5, but it's nonetheless a consideration for routing group placement. Further, traffic across seas must be routed through satellite or through cable laid on the ocean floor, creating even more hops and possible points-of-failure. As a result, communication across extended distances tends to be problem prone—a cardinal sign of a routing group barrier.

As shown in Figure 10-6, optimum boundary placements often create regional routing groups, such as East Coast, Gulf Coast, or South West. Watch out, though, for sites that have slow (less than 128 KB), unreliable, or saturated links—sure indicators of routing group barriers!

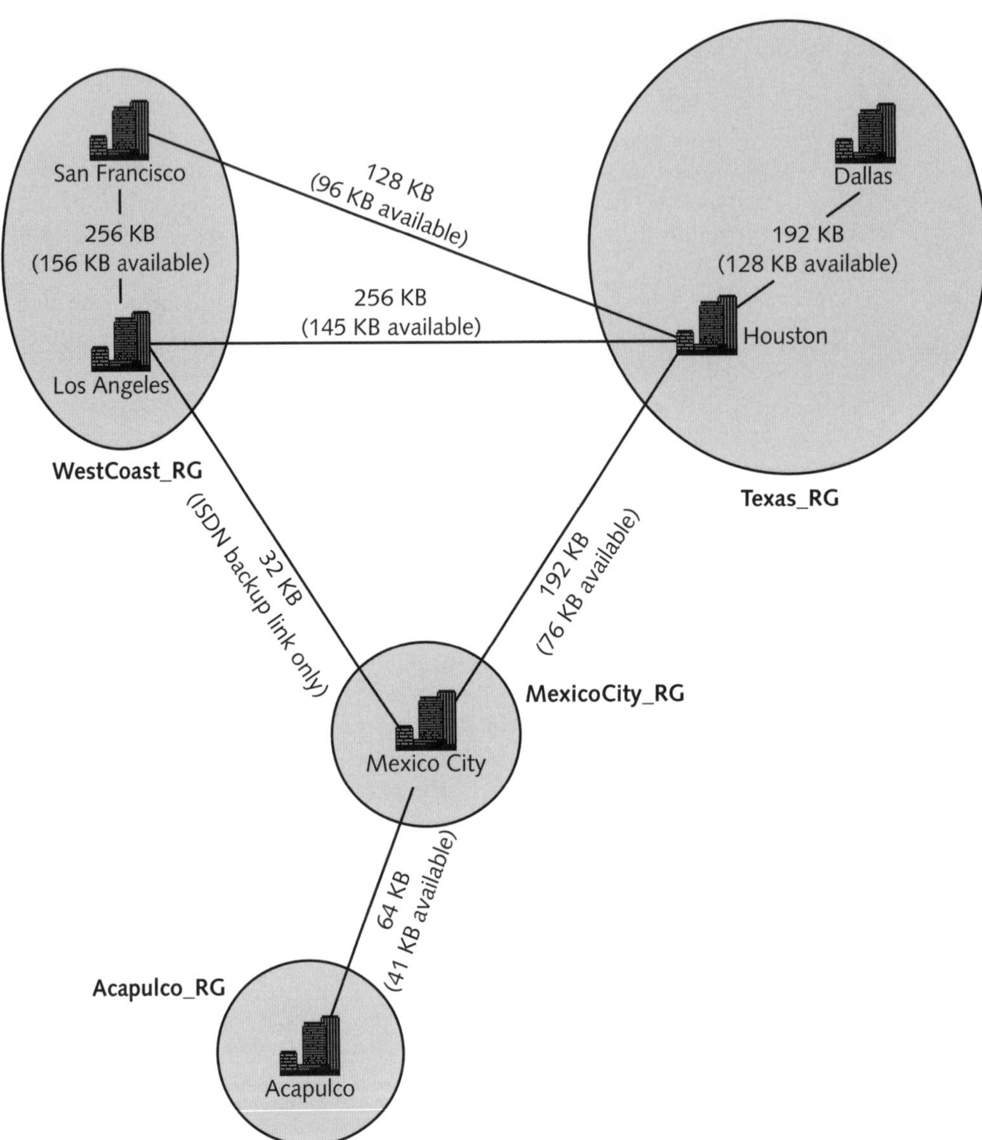

Figure 10-6 Geographical placement of routing groups

At times, it's best to have a routing group that covers only a single office or campus. Suppose, for example, that Server A in West Town is sending a broadcast message to Servers B–F in West Town. If all servers are in the same routing group, the message is sent five times over the slow WAN link, wasting bandwidth and delaying delivery of the message. By consolidating servers in East Town, as in Figure 10-7, the message is sent only once over the WAN link and distributed to the rest of the servers over a high-speed LAN.

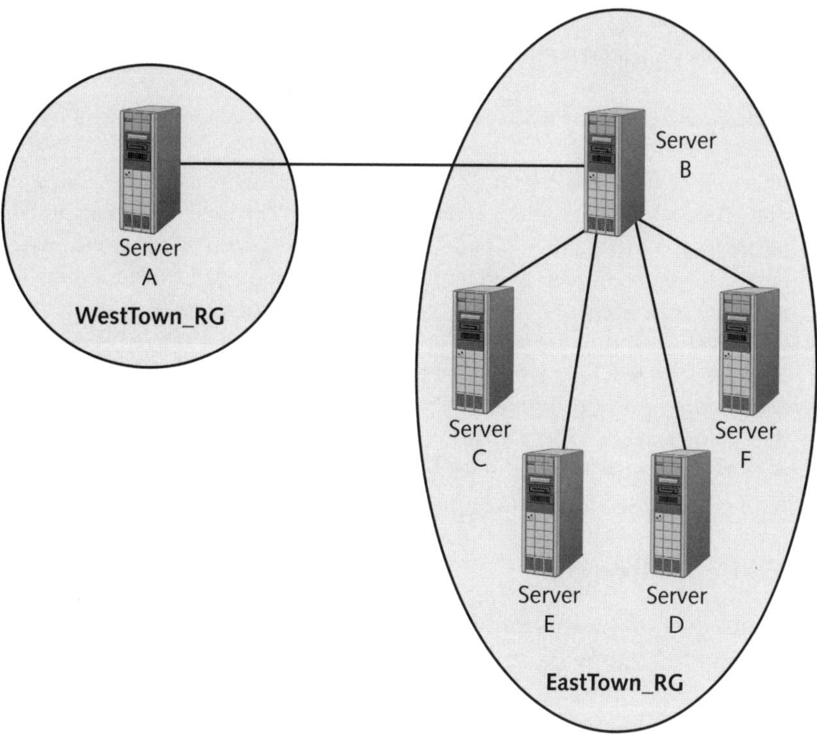

Figure 10-7 Broadcast messages between routing groups are sent once to each routing group

In most medium or large organizations, the network infrastructure administrator provides redundant frame links or ISDN backup links between offices large enough to warrant a local Exchange server (after all, Exchange isn't the only service that suffers if the link between your main offices goes down). Therefore, a single RGC between routing groups on opposite sides of such links is often enough. However, you should generally have multiple bridgehead servers configured in each routing group because if one bridgehead server fails, messages can still be routed through the remaining ones.

Administering Routing Groups in Administrative Groups

In Exchange 5.5, message routing is configured during setup by defining site boundaries, which cannot be changed after they are set. In Exchange 2000, such rigid restrictions for defining boundaries have been mostly removed, although during the Exchange 2000 Server installation, the server must be assigned to an administrative group that cannot be changed later. After Exchange 2000 is first installed, the Exchange server is placed in the First Routing Group in its home administrative group; however, routing groups can be created and deleted, and Exchange servers moved between them at will, within the server's home administrative group. Although connectors can be created between routing groups in separate administrative groups, Exchange 2000 servers cannot be part of a routing group in a remote administrative group. Hence, routing groups cannot span administrative groups.

At one level, this restriction makes sense. After all, administrative groups act as barriers to prevent remote administrators from changing the configuration of the local administrative group—and there's the potential for grave consequences if differences in configuration settings for administrative groups are not taken into account. However, in most organizations, at least one or two high-level administrators have full rights to every administrative group in the organization; accounting for subtle changes that occur as a result of their actions is one of their responsibilities. Therefore, many administrators hope that these restrictions on administrative groups will be lifted in the future. For now, however, the inherent rigidity in the administrative group structure is a compelling reason to use these groups only when truly necessary.

Creating Routing Groups

After designating routing group boundaries for your organization, you can begin creating the routing groups, populating them with Exchange servers, and then explicitly connecting them to ensure message flow. If the Routing Groups container is not visible in System Manager, click Display routing groups in the Properties dialog box for the Organization container.

When Exchange 2000 Server is first installed in an organization, all servers are placed in the First Routing Group of their home administrative group. To create another routing group, right-click the Routing Groups container, point to New, click Routing Group, and then enter a descriptive name for the routing group. In the Details tab, note the date, your name, and a brief note on the tasks performed. (Good note-taking makes future administration much easier.) Then click OK, and the new routing group appears under the Routing Groups container. After creating routing groups, you can rename or delete them as necessary.

When routing groups are created, they have two subcontainers. The first is Connectors (covered in "Using Exchange 2000 Connectors"), where the logical links that provide message transport between routing groups and with external organizations are created. The second container is Members, which lists all Exchange 2000 servers in the routing group. To move servers between routing groups, drag and drop the server from the Members container in the source routing group to the Members container in the destination routing group.

Connecting Routing Groups

You can connect your routing groups in several ways. Generally, the **routing group topology** (the logical arrangement of server connections in an organization) roughly follows the physical WAN topology because a logical connection between groups without a physical connection between those groups' bridgeheads serves little purpose. However, routing group topology can differ somewhat from the physical WAN topology for the sake of additional control of bandwidth utilization, bridgehead redundancy, or simplified administration. The most basic routing group designs are the hub-and-spoke topology, the linear (or ring) topology, and the full-mesh topology. Not surprisingly, the basic routing group topologies are patterned after LAN wiring topologies.

Technically, Routing Group Connectors (RGCs) are unidirectional, with traffic flowing only one direction. However, when creating an RGC in one routing group, Exchange automatically creates a matching connector in the remote routing group. As a result, most administrators, as well as this chapter, treat RGCs as bidirectional. Do keep in mind, though, the unidirectional nature of RGCs when modifying existing connectors or troubleshooting messaging traffic—because there are actually two connectors involved, one going in each direction. Both must be configured and monitored individually after creating them.

As its name indicates, a hub-and-spoke topology has a central routing group, with the other connected routing groups radiating out from the center, like spokes on a wheel. This design has the benefit of keeping administration and troubleshooting simple and straightforward and keeping the number of connections to a minimum. In addition, messages never need to be routed through more than three routing groups (for example, spoke 1 to the hub to spoke 2). The problem with the hub-and-spoke topology is that it creates a single point-of-failure; if the bridgehead servers at the hub become unavailable because of a system failure or a WAN link failure, message routing ceases for the entire organization. The hub-and-spoke routing group topology is similar to the star topology in physical LAN wiring.

The next basic routing group topologies are the linear and ring topologies, which map to the bus and ring LAN architectures, respectively. In both topologies, each routing group is connected to the next in a series. With the limited number of RGCs needed, this design is simple to set up, but it's seldom used in large production environments because of its inherent problems. First, message traffic can be crippled with just a single link failure. If a link in the middle of the linear topology fails, messaging on either side of the failure continues, but no messages can be sent between servers on opposite sides of the failed link. The second problem is that messages might have to make numerous hops between routing groups before finally reaching their destination, thus creating excessive network traffic and unnecessary delays in message delivery.

By connecting the remote ends of the linear topology (in Figure 10-8, for example, connecting RG7 to RG1), you create a logical ring. In doing so, you create a secondary path for messages to travel in case of a single link failure. This design removes the single point-of-failure inherent in the linear topology, but transport efficiency is still an issue because messages might still have to be routed between many routing groups on the way to their destination.

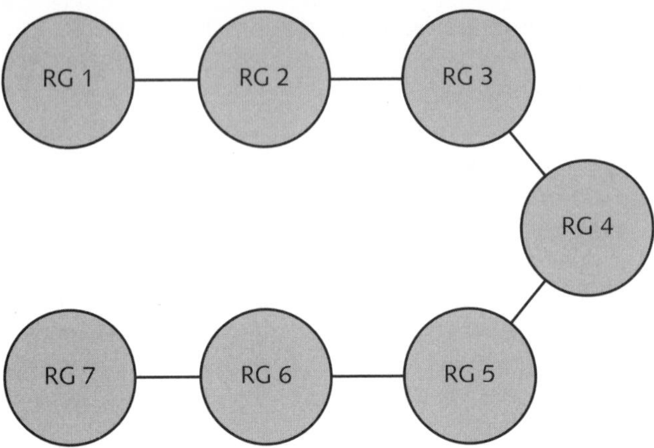

Figure 10-8 Linear topology

The final basic routing group topology is the full-mesh topology, shown in Figure 10-9. In this design, each routing group is connected logically to every other routing group, which offers two benefits. First, there's no single point-of-failure. Unless all links to a site go down, traffic continues to flow to that site; no single-site failure can disrupt traffic between other sites. Second, messages are routed directly from the sender's site to the recipient's, keeping routing traffic to a minimum. The problem with this approach is that because every routing group must be connected to every other routing group, the number of connectors that must be administered grows exponentially as the number of routing groups increases. For instance, a company with only three routing groups requires only 3 RGCs, but a company with 7 routing groups requires 21 RGCs. Therefore, the full-mesh topology is rarely used except in the smallest of operations.

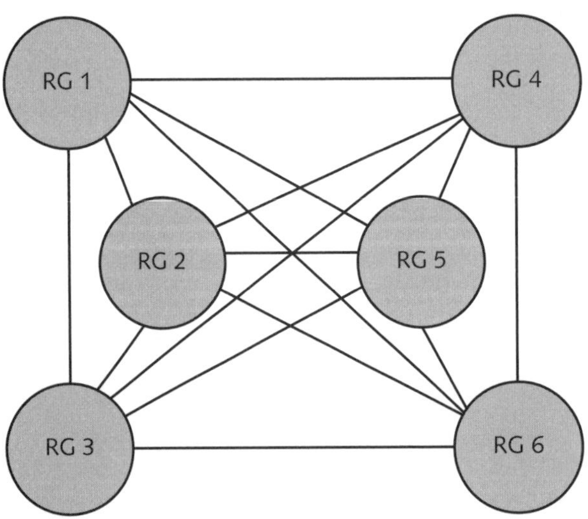

Figure 10-9 Full-mesh topology

Although these routing group topologies cover the basic configuration options, in reality you generally construct a mix, or hybrid, of two topologies. A hybrid hub-and-spoke topology (shown in Figure 10-10) has two hubs, with all spokes connected to both hubs. This design removes any single point-of-failure and keeps message hops down—unfortunately, it also doubles the number of logical and physical connections between routing groups. A hub-ring hybrid topology, shown in Figure 10-11, is another approach to removing the single point-of-failure at the hub. In some situations, you might choose the partial-mesh topology, illustrated in Figure 10-12. This design helps balance the traffic load running through any single site, but must be built with care to prevent any single points-of-failure while keeping the number of necessary connectors under control. In the end, it's up to you as the administrator or consultant to identify the best approach for a given situation.

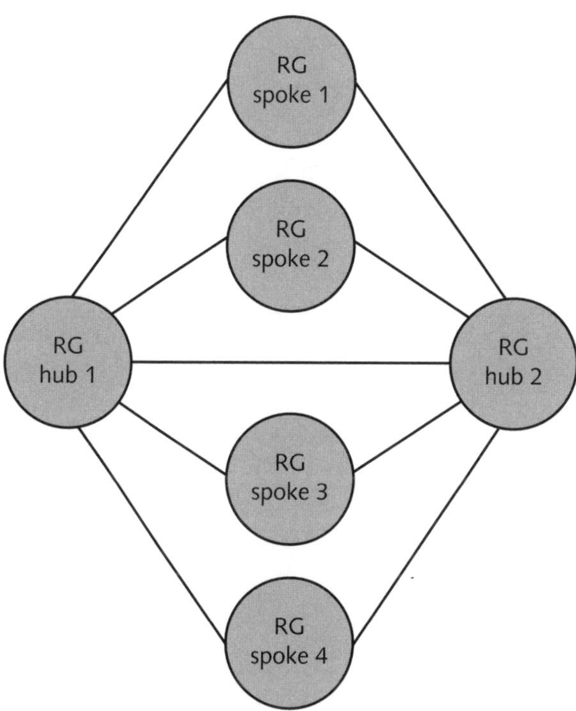

Figure 10-10 Hybrid hub-and-spoke topology

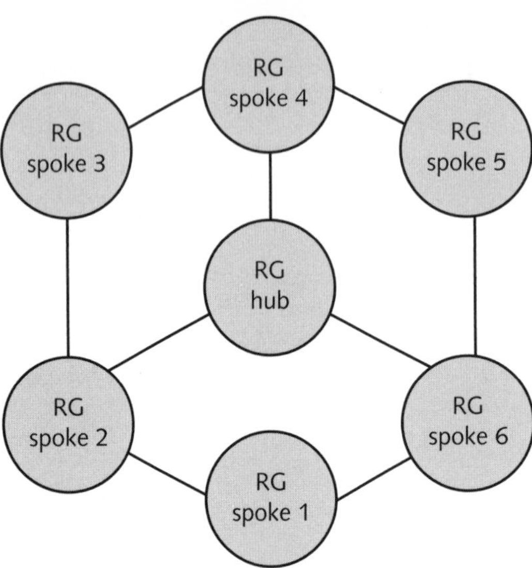

Figure 10-11 Hybrid hub-ring topology

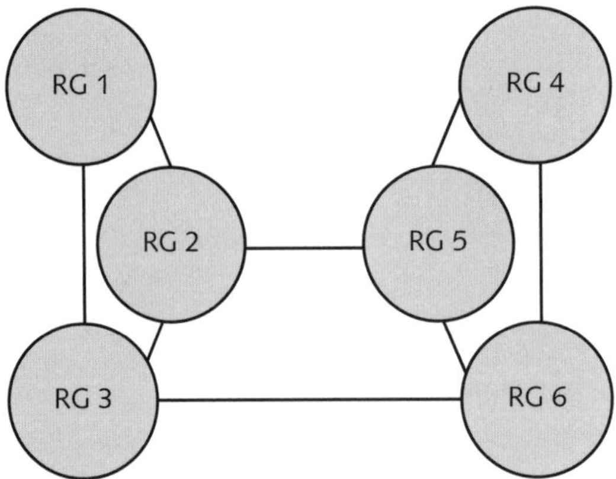

Figure 10-12 Partial-mesh topology

USING EXCHANGE 2000 CONNECTORS

By default, Exchange 2000 installs the Routing Group, SMTP, and X.400 connectors during installation. However, connectors for Lotus Notes and cc:Mail, Novell GroupWise, and MS Mail (and Schedule+) are available during the Exchange 2000 installation. If needed, these connectors can be added later by rerunning Exchange 2000 Setup. (See Chapter 5, "Installation of Exchange 2000 Server in New Environments," for more information on installing Exchange 2000.)

Although standards-based connectors (Routing Group, SMTP, and X.400) provide built-in redundancy by using multiple local and remote bridgehead servers, proprietary connectors are intrinsically tied to a specific server, so you must manually configure transport redundancy by creating multiple connectors with separate local and remote bridgehead servers. Even with the RGC and the SMTP Connector, multiple connectors can be configured for administrative purposes. For instance, you might want to restrict the size of messages allowed to pass through a connection for all users except executives. In this case, you can create one RGC that restricts message size and a second that does not restrict message size but accepts messages only from executives.

Although connectors for external systems can be installed on multiple servers in a routing group, each connecting to a separate bridgehead or platform, only one instance of each connector can exist on a server. Functionality, message flow, and configuration of these connectors on the Exchange side are discussed in the following sections. These connectors also require configuration on the external system, however, which is outside the scope of this book.

When configuring a new type of connector for the first time, especially if you need directory synchronization between messaging platforms, you must create proxy addresses for the users in your organization who should appear in the address list of the external messaging system. This is done with recipient policies (explained in detail in Chapter 9, "Exhange 2000 Server Management").

The Routing Group Connector

As with Exchange 5.5 Site Connectors, RGCs are used only to connect servers in one routing group to those in another routing group in Exchange 2000 organizations (but Exchange 5.5 servers can be included when running in mixed mode). RGCs, the easiest connectors to set up, provide automatic load-balancing and redundancy for routing messages from point A to point B in the organization. If WAN bandwidth is overtaxed during peak hours, you can schedule the connector to hold all outbound message traffic (or only oversized messages) until non-peak hours. Of course, some employees, such as executives, don't want to wait for their messages to be delivered, so you might need to create a special (nonscheduled) RGC for these users.

Keep the following cautions in mind when using schedules:

- Because outbound messages are queued on the bridgehead server until the schedule permits transmission, if the schedule does not allow enough time to send all queued messages for the RGC, the queue continues to grow until the messages time out and NDRs are returned to the senders.
- If a schedule is set for an RGC, the connector is considered available at all times for routing purposes. If both a scheduled RGC and an unscheduled RGC can be used to deliver a message, assign a higher cost to the scheduled connector to ensure that qualifying messages are sent immediately instead of being queued (costs are discussed in "Managing Link State Information").

Scheduling connectors can be a great way to alleviate stress on an overburdened WAN link, but can easily create some unexpected problems with message transport if the implications are not fully understood!

RGCs are unique in that they're the only connectors that use different protocols based on the remote system they're talking to. Because the RGC can be used only in Exchange 2000 organizations, and the default protocol for Exchange 2000 is SMTP, RGCs usually communicate over SMTP. However, if the Exchange 2000 server is part of an Exchange organization that was upgraded from Exchange 5.5, and there are still Exchange 5.5 servers in the organization, the RGC uses RPC over X.400 when communicating with remote Exchange 5.5 bridgehead servers.

The RGC utilizes bridgehead servers on both sides of the connector to enable message transport. Although remote bridgehead servers must be manually configured, by default all servers in the local routing group act as bridgeheads, which ensures that no single-server failure can disrupt message transport. If message traffic between routing groups is heavy, however, it's more efficient to assign just two or three dedicated bridgehead servers in the local routing group to perform this function. To do that, open the Properties dialog box for the RGC, and in the General tab, click the These servers can send mail over this connector radio button. Click the Add button to open the Add Bridgehead Server dialog box, and select the bridgehead servers in the list (see Figure 10-13).

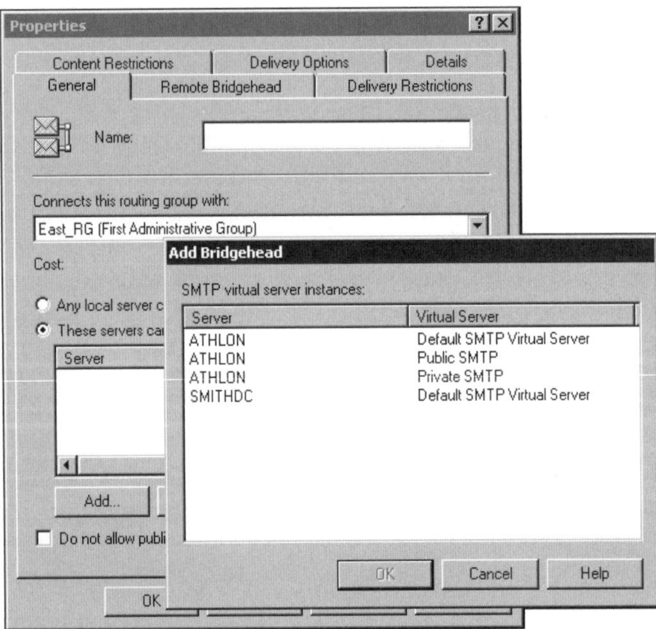

Figure 10-13 Assigning local bridgehead servers to handle message transport

The SMTP Connector

Because the RGC is based on SMTP, it is not surprising that the SMTP Connector functions much like the RGC. As with the RGC, the SMTP Connector can be used to connect routing groups in the same organization (it lists remote bridgeheads as smart hosts); to restrict messages based on priority, type, or size; and to provide scheduling functionality. SMTP Connectors can also be used to connect with an Exchange 5.5 bridgehead server via the Internet Mail Service.

The primary purpose of the SMTP Connector, however, is to connect with SMTP servers outside the organization. As a result, there are some significant differences in configuring SMTP Connectors. First, a single SMTP Connector can manage a connection with multiple external SMTP **address spaces**. In addition to scheduling delivery, SMTP Connectors can queue messages until a remote SMTP server requests them with the ETRN/TURN command.

Exchange 2000 online help incorrectly states that an SMTP Connector can have only one smart host per connector. Although the SMTP Connector uses secondary smart hosts only if the first is unavailable, multiple smart hosts can be configured for redundancy (separated by a comma or semicolon). This typographical error was corrected in Exchange 2000 Service Pack 1, but SP1 is not required to use multiple smart hosts.

The X.400 Connector

The X.400 Connector is primarily used to connect Exchange to an external X.400 messaging system. Although it can also be used to connect Exchange 2000 routing groups, configuration is complex, and the SMTP Connector is more efficient (and hence faster) for all but the largest messages. When connecting routing groups, therefore, reserve the X.400 Connector as a secondary connector, if possible, to deliver only oversized e-mails over very slow links (less than 16 KB). Of course, the X.400 Connector is the only one to support X.25 and that may be the overriding consideration for its use.

Because the X.400 Connector can operate over one of two dissimilar network protocols (IP or X.25), a software layer called an X.400 transport stack must be configured on the Exchange server before an X.400 Connector can be configured. The X.400 transport stack essentially defines how communication takes place between X.400 systems. To create an X.400 transport stack, open the \Servers*ServerName*\Protocols container in System Manager. Right-click X.400, point to New, and then click TCP/IP X.400 Service Transport Stack, or point to New, and then click X.25 X.400 Service Transport Stack. Supply a descriptive name for this transport.

Optionally, specify the T, S, and P selectors (functionally, they uniquely identify Exchange traffic for this transport stack against any other X.400 communication that may be taking place between the same servers—technically, they define the Transport, Session, and Presentation service access points, respectively). For the X.25 X.400 transport stack, you can also enter the X.121 address of the remote bridgehead server (the X.25 equivalent of a phone number), X.25 service provider options (charge reversals, and so forth), and the physical I/O port of the X.25 adapter. After an X.400 transport stack is in place, you can configure an X.400 Connector to use it.

The Lotus Notes Connector

The Lotus Notes Connector links the Exchange 2000 organization to a Lotus Notes organization. It provides bidirectional messaging, directory synchronization, public folder synchronization, and calendaring and meeting request functionality between Exchange and Lotus Notes servers. Lotus Notes users are added to the Windows 2000 AD as contacts, mail-enabled users, or disabled Windows accounts, and Windows 2000 mailbox-enabled users are added to the Lotus Notes Address Book.

The Lotus Notes Connector uses a single bridgehead server on both ends of the connector and requires that a Lotus Notes client version 4.6 or higher be installed locally on the Exchange 2000 bridgehead server. When the Notes client is installed, a Notes.ini configuration file is placed on the server; the default location is <*Systemroot*>\Notes.ini. A Notes router mailbox (usually called mail.box) is used to route messages from the Exchange organization to the Notes organization; Notes mail destined for the Exchange organization is placed in a connector mailbox in the Notes Mail Router database associated with the Windows 2000 domain (usually called exchange.box). The Exchange 2000 Lotus Notes Connector polls the mailbox (by default, every 15 seconds) for mail.

The Lotus cc:Mail Connector

The Lotus cc:Mail Connector links Exchange 2000 to DB8 (Post Office Database Version 8)-type Lotus Notes post offices running on Novell NetWare Server version 3.1x or 4.x. Lotus cc:Mail users are added to the Windows 2000 AD as contacts or mail-enabled users, and Windows 2000 users, groups, and contacts are added to the cc:Mail Directory. cc:Mail is a file-based messaging platform, so no cc:Mail messaging client is needed on the Exchange server running the connector. The Lotus cc:Mail Connector must, however, be able to access the path to the cc:Mail post office files (\CCDATA), which requires that Gateway Services for NetWare be installed on the Exchange server.

Four aspects of the cc:Mail Connector must be configured for replication to take place between Exchange and cc:Mail. The first is the cc:Mail Connector Service, which transfers messages and directory synchronization information between the WSS and the folder on the Exchange server used as the cc:Mail Connector Queue. The cc:Mail Connector Service also periodically calls the Lotus cc:Mail Import and Export programs (Import.exe and Export.exe). The Lotus cc:Mail Import program retrieves the message from the cc:Mail Connector Queue and delivers it to the cc:Mail post office. The cc:Mail Export program, conversely, retrieves pending messages from the cc:Mail post office and delivers them to the local cc:Mail Connector Queue folder, and the cc:Mail Connector Service delivers the data to the MTA.

The Novell GroupWise Connector

The Novell GroupWise Connector provides two-way messaging, directory synchronization, and meeting request functionality between Exchange 2000 and Novell GroupWise servers. Exchange 2000 messages, tasks, and meeting requests are exchanged with GroupWise users; GroupWise messages, appointments, notes, phone messages, and tasks can be sent to Exchange users. Users in the Windows 2000 AD can be added to the GroupWise directory; GroupWise users can likewise be added to the Windows 2000 AD as contacts, mail-enabled users, or disabled user accounts. Full calendaring functionality requires the Calendar Connector, which is available only in Exchange 5.5; mixed-mode operation is, therefore, required. Because GroupWise runs on the NetWare platform, Gateway Services for NetWare must be installed on the bridgehead Exchange server.

Exchanging messages with GroupWise is separated into two functions, each with a service dedicated to it. Between these two services, a series of file-based queues in the \ExchSrvr\ConnData\GWRouter folder are used for message categorization and transfer. The following two paragraphs describe the process used to route messages between Exchange 2000 Server and Novell GroupWise, and Table 10-4 lists the queues used in message transfer.

To transfer messages from Exchange to GroupWise, the Microsoft Exchange Connector for Novell GroupWise service (LME_GWise) communicates directly with the Exchange MTA, polling the MTS_OUT queue for messages to route to GroupWise. Messages there are processed and placed in a series of Exchange-to-GroupWise queues. Directory synchronization and free/busy messages are placed in the ToGWise folder. E-mails are divided into message body and attachments, with the body delivered to the MEx2GW folder and attachments to the MEx2GWa folder. If archiving is enabled, Microsoft Exchange Connector for Novell GroupWise places the messages in the Archive folder, too. The Microsoft Exchange Router for Novell GroupWise (MSExchangeGWRtr) then polls the Exchange-to-GroupWise queues and delivers them to the API_IN and ATT_IN folders of the GroupWise 4.1 API gateway on the NetWare server.

In the reverse process, the Microsoft Exchange Router for Novell GroupWise service polls the API_OUT GroupWise 4.1 gateway for messages to be delivered to Exchange, and places them (and their associated attachments in the ATT_OUT folder) in the appropriate GroupWise-to-Exchange queues on the local Exchange server. Directory synchronization and free/busy messages are placed in the DirSync folder. Message bodies are delivered to the GW2MEx folder, and attachments to the GW2MExA folder. If Microsoft Exchange Router for Novell GroupWise receives a message it cannot parse from the GroupWise API, it places the message in the BadFiles folder. Microsoft Exchange Connector for Novell GroupWise then processes messages in the GroupWise-to-Exchange queues and delivers them to the MTS_IN queue of the Exchange 2000 MTA. If archiving is enabled, Microsoft Exchange Connector for Novell GroupWise places the messages in the Archive folder as well.

Table 10-4 Novell GroupWise Connector Queues

Queue Category	Queue Name	Description
Exchange 2000 MTA Queues	MTS_IN	Exchange 2000 MTA queue for transferring messages from the GroupWise Connector to Exchange
	MTS_OUT	Exchange 2000 MTA queue for transferring messages from Exchange to the GroupWise Connector
GroupWise Connector Transport Queues (folders on the Exchange 2000 bridgehead server, in ExchSrvr\ConnData\GWRouter)	MEx2GW	E-mail messages (minus attachments) pending delivery to GroupWise
	MEx2GWa	Attachments to e-mail messages delivered to MEx2GW
	ToGWise	Exchange directory synchronization and free/busy information pending delivery to GroupWise
	DirSync	GroupWise directory synchronization and free/busy information pending delivery to Exchange
GroupWise Connector Troubleshooting Queues	BadFiles	Microsoft Exchange Router for Novell GroupWise places GroupWise messages that could not be delivered to Exchange recipients here
	Archive	If archiving is enabled for troubleshooting purposes, Microsoft Exchange Connector for Novell GroupWise copies all messages here for further analysis
Novell GroupWise 4.1 API Gateway Queues (folders on the GroupWise server, in *ServerName**VolumeName**GatewayAPIPath*)	API-IN	Directory synchronization and e-mail messages to be delivered to GroupWise
	ATT-IN	E-mail attachments for e-mail messages in API-IN
	API-OUT	Directory synchronization and e-mail messages to be delivered to Exchange
	ATT-OUT	E-mail attachments for e-mail messages in API-OUT

The MS Mail and Schedule+ Free/Busy Connectors

The MS Mail and Schedule+ Connectors provide messaging, directory synchronization, scheduling, and meeting request functionality between Exchange 2000 and MS Mail 3.x post offices over LAN, X.25, or modem transport media. However, because covering all the variables for every possible configuration would require more space than can be dedicated to one connector in this chapter, we will focus only on connecting to MS Mail servers on a LAN. Other configurations are similar, and you can find information on the differences in the Exchange System Manager online help.

The MS Mail messaging platform is based on a collection of loosely coupled post offices, generally configured in a hub-and-spoke topology. Full functionality between Exchange and MS Mail requires configuring three separate services in System Manager; message transfer is configured with the MS Mail Connector, directory replication is provided by configuring a DirSync Requestor or DirSync Server, and free/busy information for scheduling is configured through the MS Schedule+ Free/Busy Connector.

Configuring the MS Mail Connector

The MS Mail Connector has three components for message transfer. The MS Mail Connector Interchange transfers messages between the Exchange 2000 MTA and the local MS Mail Connector post office, and performs any necessary formatting conversion. The MS Mail Connector post office acts as a virtual MS Mail post office for remote MS Mail servers to deliver messages to, and holds messages pending delivery to remote MS Mail servers. MS Mail Connector MTAs (not to be confused with the Exchange 2000 MTA) transfer messages between the MS Mail Connector post office and remote MS Mail servers.

Configuring Directory Replication with MS Mail

Directory replication in the MS Mail organization is provided by designating a master server to own the global MS Mail directory, with all other servers contributing their portion of the address namespace to that master server. The server that owns the global directory is called the DirSync Server; contributors are called DirSync Requestors. Although there are a few advantages to using Exchange as a DirSync Server, it usually acts as a requestor simply because the benefits are too minor to warrant reconfiguring all other post offices in the MS Mail organization to point to the Exchange server as their DirSync Server.

Directory synchronization takes place in three steps. Each step takes place at predefined time points, referred to as T1, T2, and T3, as described in Table 10-5.

Table 10-5 Description of the MS Mail DirSync Schedule

DirSync Time	Description
T1	DirSync Requestors send local directory updates to DirSync Server. Default time is midnight.
T2	DirSync Server processes directory updates and returns a composite list of all directory updates to DirSync Requestors. If Exchange is acting as a DirSync Server, updates are processed on receipt.
T3	DirSync Requestors update the local directory with new information. If Exchange is acting as a DirSync Requestor, updates are processed on receipt.

Configuring the Schedule+ Free/Busy Connector

After the MS Mail Connector is connected to one or more MS Mail post offices, and directory replication is functioning between Exchange and MS Mail, free/busy information can be shared between the systems. This information is necessary for scheduling meetings with other users and for allocating resources. Scheduling functionality is provided via an AdminSch account (*Network*/*Postoffice*/AdminSch) dedicated to every post office in the MS Mail organization, including the virtual post office created by the MS Mail

Connector. Remote MS Mail post offices send scheduling information to the AdminSch account of the MS Mail Connector virtual post office, which the Schedule+ Free/Busy Connector monitors and imports into Exchange. Scheduling information is made available from Exchange to MS Mail by using a distribution list containing the AdminSch aliases for every post office in the MS Mail organization.

Legacy Exchange 5.5 Connectors

In Exchange 2000, support for SNADS and IBM OfficeVision/VM (PROFS) has been removed. In addition, third-party gateways installed in the Exchange 5.5 organization might not have an equivalent connector in Exchange 2000. In these cases, one or more Exchange 5.5 servers should be kept in the Exchange organization until you find Exchange 2000–equivalent connectors or stop using the external system.

If you need connectivity to an external messaging server that does not have an Exchange 2000 connector, and Exchange 2000 has already been changed to native mode, use a messaging gateway between the Exchange 2000 organization and the external messaging system. The easiest gateway to use for this purpose is Exchange 5.5, but most messaging platforms work by following the same principles. For example, suppose you want to provide connectivity to a PROFS messaging system, and the Exchange 2000 organization has already been converted to native mode. First, configure an Exchange 5.5 server to act as the gateway:

1. Create a connector between Exchange 5.5 and PROFS.
2. Create custom recipients for all PROFS users in the Exchange 5.5 directory by using directory synchronization.
3. Create internal SMTP addresses (for example, *AccountName*@PROFS.Gtwy) for all imported PROFS accounts by exporting the Exchange 5.5 directory to an Excel spreadsheet, adding SMTP addresses, and importing the list back to Exchange 5.5.
4. Create an SMTP Connector to an SMTP virtual server in the Exchange 2000 organization, with an address space consisting *only* of the Exchange 2000 address space (mycompany.com, for instance).
5. Test and confirm messaging connectivity with both PROFS and Exchange 2000.

Next, configure Exchange 2000 to connect to the Exchange 5.5 server:

1. Create an SMTP Connector to the Exchange 5.5 server, and assign it the address space that coincides with the SMTP addresses created in Step 3 of the Exchange 5.5 configuration (in this example, *AccountName*@PROFS.Gtwy).
2. Configure an ADC to synchronize the Exchange 5.5 directory with a container in the Active Directory namespace.
3. Test messaging connectivity with the Exchange 5.5 organization and the PROFS organization.

What happens is this: Exchange 5.5 downloads the display names and PROFS addresses for all users in the PROFS messaging system. Because the PROFS accounts don't have any SMTP addresses associated with them, SMTP addresses are manually added to the accounts so that Exchange has a recognizable address space to use in routing. The ADC creates contacts in the Windows 2000 AD namespace, which allows them to be displayed in the Exchange 2000 GAL. When an Exchange client sends a message to an account homed in the PROFS messaging system, Exchange 2000 associates the *AccountName*@PROFS.Gtwy address with the Exchange 5.5 connector and routes the message to Exchange 5.5. Because the account in Exchange 5.5 is a custom recipient, there is no local storage for the account. Because the only address Exchange 5.5 recognizes as routable is the PROFS address, Exchange 5.5 delivers the message to the PROFS server.

Managing Link State Information

When creating connectors between routing groups and external messaging systems, a cost between 1 and 100 is assigned to each connector. These **connector costs** are simply administrator-assigned values that indicate the preferred route for messaging traffic, usually based on WAN link speeds (lower costs indicate preferred connections). Exchange uses these costs to create a link state table, which lists every address space defined in the organization and its associated cost. (The address space can be the X.500 address of the destination routing group or the address space assigned to a connector to an external messaging system.) When traffic is routed through an Exchange organization, the path with the lowest total cost is used. Therefore, if RG_A is connected to RG_B with a cost of 10, and RG_B is connected to RG_C with a cost of 5, RG_A associates RG_C's cost as 10 + 5 = 15.

The link state table is held only in memory. The Exchange 2000 Resource Kit companion CD provides WinRoute.exe (as shown in Figure 10-14), which connects to an Exchange 2000 server and downloads its link state table for viewing.

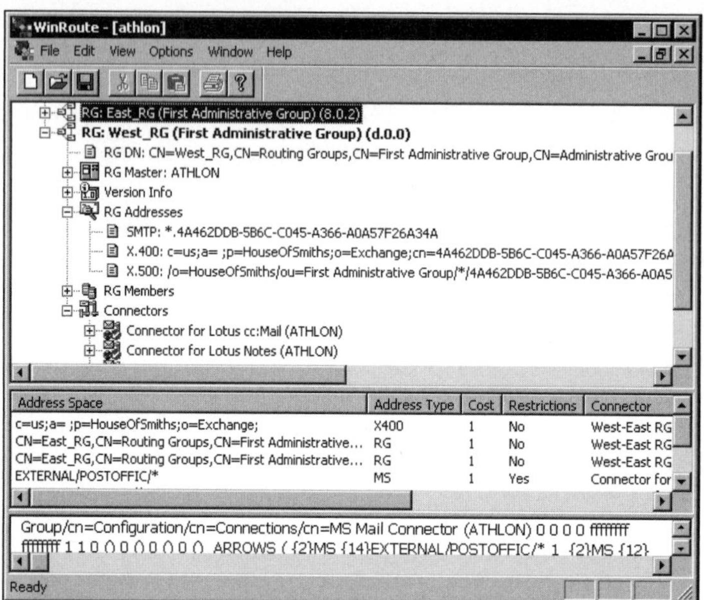

Figure 10-14 Viewing link state information in WinRoute

Because the link state table is the same for all servers in a routing group, one server, the **routing group master**, is responsible for creating, maintaining, and distributing the authoritative link state table for its routing group. If a bridgehead server learns about a connector failure, it notifies the local routing group master, which updates the link state table and notifies all local bridgeheads of the change. In this way, link state updates spread through the organization almost immediately. To further clarify this process, let's watch the link state table in action as a message delivery is attempted from the Oakland_RG routing group in Figure 10-15, and a failure occurs.

1. Routing group master Oakland_RGM builds a link state table that is the binary equivalent of Figure 10-15 and shares that table with Oakland_BH1. Oakland_BH1 then updates its local copy of the link state table.

2. A user in Oakland_RG sends a message to a user in Savannah_RG, and the message is delivered to Oakland_BH1 for routing.

3. Oakland_BH1 looks at its local copy of the link state table, which indicates that the best next-hop for endpoint Savannah_RG is Oak-NY RGC, with a total cost of 3 (2 + 1).

4. Oakland_BH1 opens an SMTP connection to NY_BH1 and transfers the message for further routing.

5. NY_BH1 looks at its local copy of the link state table, which indicates that the best next-hop for endpoint Savannah_RG is NY-Sav RGC, with a cost of 1.

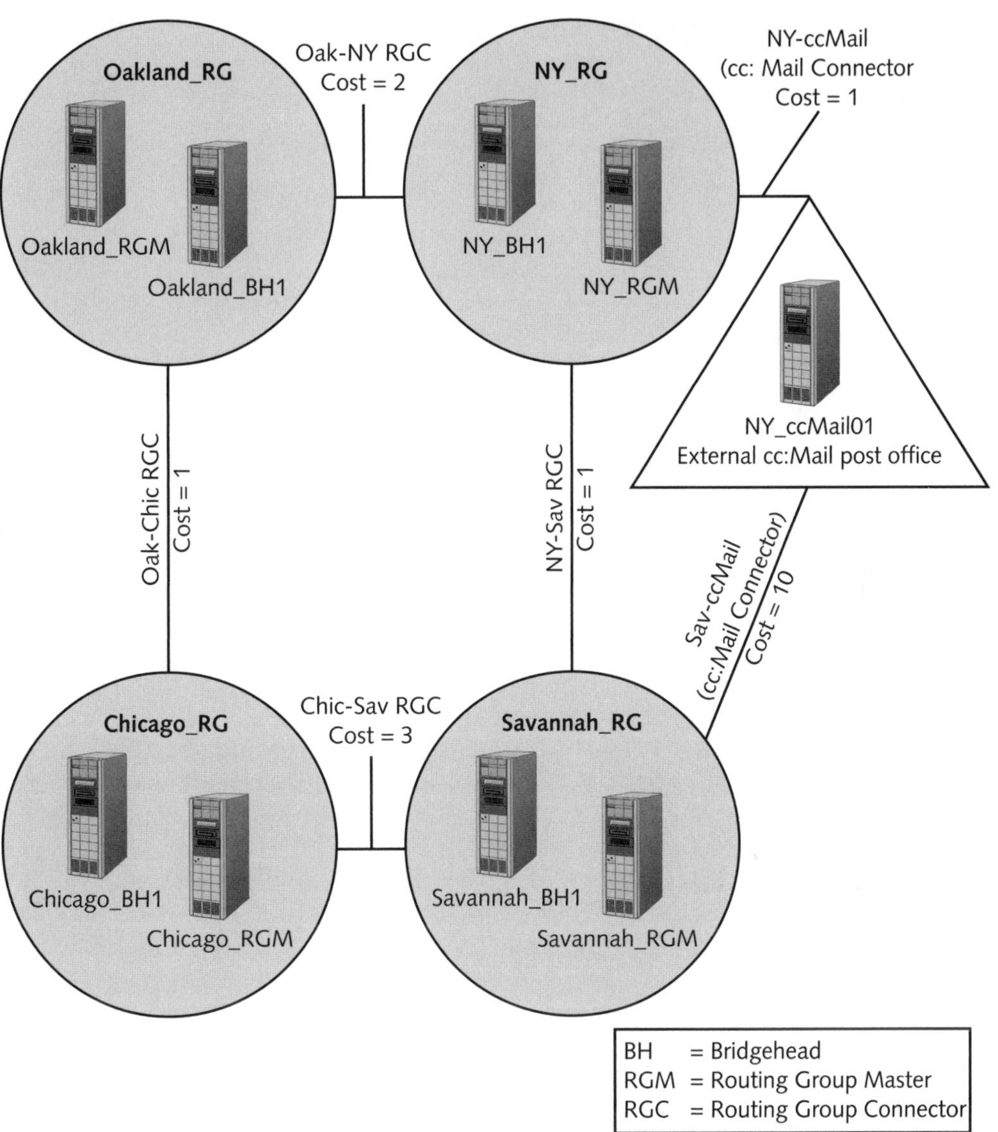

Figure 10-15 Link state tables in action

6. NY_BH1 attempts to open a connection to Savannah_BH1, but gets no response. At this point, NY-Sav RGC is placed in a error-retry state, which is not broadcast to other systems. After making three attempts to talk to Savannah_BH1 at 60-second intervals, NY-Sav RGC is placed in a DOWN state.
7. NY_BH1 sends a "NY-Sav RGC connector is DOWN" link state update to NY_RGM, which updates its link state table and delivers it to NY_BH1. NY_BH1 identifies that the best route to Savannah_RG is now through Oak-NY RGC, with a total cost of 6 (2 + 1 + 3).

8. To make sure no other servers attempt to use NY-Sav RGC to route messages, NY_BH1 sends a link state update message and then the user's message to Oakland_BH1. From this point, NY_BH1 attempts to open a session with Savannah_BH1 every 60 seconds until it succeeds. As soon as the attempt succeeds, the NY-Sav RGC connector is placed in an UP state, and "NY-Sav RGC connector is UP" status update messages are replicated throughout the enterprise.
9. Oakland_BH1 immediately notifies Oakland_RGM of the connector failure, and Oakland_RGM responds with an updated link state table.
10. Oakland_BH1 references its local link state table and routes a link state update message, and then the user's message to Chicago_BH1, and the same link state update process occurs before further routing.
11. Chicago_BH1 attempts to open a connection to Savannah_BH1, but gets no response. Chic-Sav RGC is placed in an error-retry state for three minutes, after which it is flagged as DOWN.
12. Chicago_BH1 sends a "Chic-Sav RGC connector is DOWN" link state update to Chicago_RGM, which updates its link state table and delivers it to Chicago_BH1.
13. A link state update message is replicated throughout the organization in the same manner as before. Because there are no other available routes to Savannah_RG, the user's message remains at Chicago_BH1, which attempts to open a session with Savannah_BH1 at 60-second intervals.
14. One of three things will happen with the user's message from here.
    - Chicago_BH1 will succeed in communicating with Savannah_BH1 and deliver the message.
    - Chicago_BH1 will receive a status update message indicating that NY-Sav RGC is available and reroute the message there.
    - The message will time out before Savannah_BH1 comes back online, and an NDR will be generated for the message.

Delivering messages to external messaging systems is performed in the same way. Continuing with the previous example, assume that an Exchange user in Oakland_RG attempts to send a message to a cc:Mail user in the NY_ccMail01 post office, and NY_ccMail01 is unavailable. Oakland_BH1 routes the message through NY_BH1. NY_BH1 attempts to route the message through the NY-ccMail connector, but receives no response. The message is then rerouted through Savannah, where it sits in the queue until the message is either delivered or returned with an NDR.

Troubleshooting Messaging Connectivity

Properly configured, message routing in Exchange 2000 is robust and resilient. As with all systems, however, hardware failures, configuration oversights, and other issues periodically create situations that require administrative attention. Troubleshooting message failures in Exchange 2000 requires identifying the nature and location of the failure, and then rectifying it or notifying the correct individual.

Using Delivery Status Notifications to Pinpoint Problems

Generally, an administrator first hears of a routing problem when users complain about receiving a **Delivery Status Notification (DSN)**. Usually these notifications come in the form of a **Non-Delivery Report (NDR)** for a message, but DSNs include warning messages that delivery has been delayed, meaning the first attempt at delivery failed, and Exchange will try again before giving up and returning an NDR. A quick review of the DSN is usually enough to identify the nature of the problem. A DSN is sent to users for the following reasons:

- Repeated attempts at sending the message have been made, probably because the destination host could not be contacted, and Exchange will try again (delay notification only).
- The message timed out while the system was attempting delivery (NDR).
- No address space defined in the organization matches recipient address (NDR).
- The system was unable to resolve or contact the remote host (NDR).
- The external messaging host returned an error during delivery (NDR).

Here is an example of a DSN (delay) message:

```
From:      System Administrator
To:        Kevan Smith
Subject:   Delivery Status Notification (Delay)

This is an automatically generated Delivery Status
Notification.
THIS IS A WARNING MESSAGE ONLY.
YOU DO NOT NEED TO RESEND YOUR MESSAGE.
Delivery to the following recipients has been delayed.
    test@serverUnavailable.com
```

DSN (delay) messages usually occur when a user attempts to send a message to an external domain, and either an Internet routing issue or a remote host failure prevents communication. Delay messages also occur when routing messages in an Exchange organization if there is a connector failure (usually because of a WAN link failure). If the DSN can be replicated by sending a test message to the user, follow the troubleshooting steps in the next section, "Resolving Routing Problems."

When a permanent (irrecoverable) error occurs while delivering a message, the response is an NDR. The NDR is a useful tool in troubleshooting messaging problems because it lists the following information:

- Date/time stamp for when the message was sent
- Date/time stamp for when the error was generated
- The recipient(s) who did not receive the message
- A description of the error, often with the error code
- The server that generated the NDR

A sample NDR follows:

```
From:        System Administrator
To:          Kevan Smith
Subject:     Undeliverable: This is a sample NDR sending to
an invalid domain name

Your message did not reach some or all of the intended
recipients.
Subject:     This is a sample NDR sending to an invalid
domain name
Sent:        8/2/2002 11:57 PM
The following recipient(s) could not be reached:
    test@invalidnetwork.com on 8/2/2002 11:57 PM
    The e-mail system was unable to deliver the message,
but did not report a specific reason. Check the address
and try again. If it still fails, contact your system
administrator.
    <MX1.InternalDomain.com #5.0.0>
```

The most interesting lines of an Exchange 2000 NDR are the last three: the name of the failed recipient, a description of the error, and the FQDN of the Exchange server that experienced the problem. Usually, the error description is clear enough for you to immediately recognize the problem. The most common problem is a user mistyping the recipient or domain name. If Exchange is unable to resolve the domain name, the message description in the previous example is generated. If the problem occurs during the SMTP session (for example, incorrect recipient name, protocol error), the error code and description received by the remote host are delivered to the sender.

Sometimes NDR messages indicate problems of a more serious nature, as when errors occur during delivery to Exchange 2000 routing groups or connectors to external messaging systems within the organization. At this point, the real troubleshooting begins—this is when Exchange administrators or consultants really earn their keep.

Resolving Routing Problems

For the purpose of troubleshooting, message routing falls into one of three categories:

- Message routing within a single Exchange server (when both sender and recipient are on the same Exchange server)
- Message routing within a routing group
- Message routing over a connector (to another routing group or an external messaging system)

Troubleshooting Routing Problems Within an Exchange Server

Although problems with message transport within a single server are rare, especially in the absence of client connectivity issues, they can happen. In these cases, when users cannot send messages to other users on the same server, troubleshooting is fairly straightforward. In the Exchange 2000 Transport Architecture, relatively few factors are involved in delivering a message within an Exchange server. Here are a few steps to take when troubleshooting message routing within a single Exchange server:

- Confirm that all Exchange services are running.
- Check the event log for errors.
- In System Manager, under the Default SMTP Virtual Server container of the troubled server, check the Messages awaiting directory lookup queue (the pre-categorization queue that AQE uses for messages awaiting processing by the Categorizer). Messages in this queue indicate that Exchange is unable to contact a GC server through the Directory Services/Active Directory (DS/AD) Access API. The DS/AD Access API is also used to validate users when opening Outlook, so this error usually coincides with client connectivity problems. However, because the DS/AD Access API caches AD lookup information for up to 10 minutes, most existing clients won't have an immediate problem, and some e-mail might still be getting processed. Don't let this fool you; if messages are stuck in this queue, there's a problem. Make sure a GC server is available. If it is, restart the Exchange services (or the server).
- Under the Default SMTP virtual server of the troubled server, check the Messages waiting to be routed queue (the pre-routing queue that AQE uses for messages awaiting processing by the routing engine). If there are messages in this queue, it indicates a problem with the link state table on the local server. This could occur if an Exchange server (or services) is restarted, and the routing group master is unavailable. Reassign the routing group master to force a rebuild of the link state table.

Troubleshooting Routing Problems Within a Routing Group

Message routing between servers in a routing group is only slightly more complex than routing within a server. Indeed, the only difference is that the AQE sends the message to the protocol engine (which initiates an SMTP session with the destination server), rather than to the WSS. The protocol engine initiates an SMTP session over port 25 with an SMTP virtual server of the remote Exchange 2000 server and transfers the message from the per-destination-domain queue to the destination server. If you're having routing problems within a routing group, these are some items to look for:

1. Confirm the source of the problem:
   - Can you deliver messages to other users on the remote server?
   - Can you deliver messages to users on other remote servers?
   - Can users on other servers deliver messages to users on the suspect server?
   - Check the connection status between the source and destination servers.
2. In System Manager, under the Default SMTP Virtual Server of the sender's home server, check the queue that carries the FQDN of the destination server (*DestinationServerName.Win2KDNSname*.com). Right-click the queue and click Properties. The number of messages in the queue is listed, as well as a few other facts. The two most important fields are Status (likely Retry) and an unlabeled text box below it, which states the last error that occurred. Although the exact text of the message varies, these are the most common *types* of errors:
   - *Unable to resolve remote host*—Either the DNS records for the remote Exchange server have been incorrectly modified, or the sending server has the wrong DNS servers configured.
   - *Unable to contact remote host*—It could be a routing issue or problem with the remote SMTP virtual server. If you can ping the destination from the source server, and the error message is not explicit enough, emulate an SMTP session with the remote host as explained in "Advanced SMTP Troubleshooting Steps" later in this chapter.
   - *The remote server returned an error*—This is most likely a problem with the remote SMTP virtual server. If the error message is not explicit enough, emulate an SMTP session with the remote host (see "Advanced SMTP Troubleshooting Steps").

Troubleshooting Routing Problems over Exchange Connectors

Taking the troubleshooting scenario one step further, when messages must be routed through multiple routing groups, they might pass over a number of Exchange servers (through RGCs) before possibly being sent through an external messaging connector. The primary tools and steps for troubleshooting are presented individually; however, when the message routing isn't direct from the sender's server to the recipient's, you need to locate the problem before you can fix it. For this, two tools are available. The first is the NDR message (covered earlier in this section); the last line indicates the server that generated the NDR. The other tool is in the Tools container in Exchange System Manager—the Message Tracking Center.

The Exchange 2000 Message Tracking Center

Much improved over the tracking tools in Exchange 5.5, the **Message Tracking Center** (shown in Figure 10-16) can be used to follow a message from the moment it enters the Exchange organization to the point at which it reaches its final destination (whether it's an Exchange server or a connector leading out of the organization). Used as a troubleshooting tool, it discloses exactly where a message failed. The Message Tracking Center does this by analyzing the Tracking.log files on each server, for each connector on that server. This, of course, requires that Exchange be configured to create these tracking log files. If you're going to turn on tracking, however, you should do so for all servers in the organization, a procedure that lends itself to a system policy.

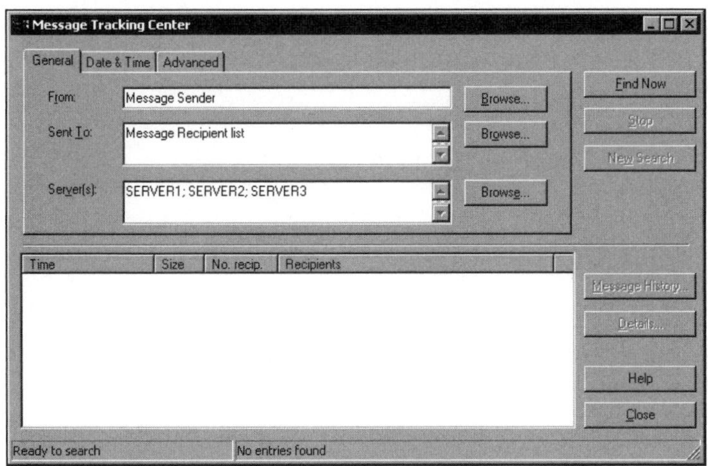

Figure 10-16 The Exchange 2000 Message Tracking Center

After the message-tracking policy is applied to the Exchange servers in the organization, new messages passing in and out of the servers can be monitored in the Message Tracking Center. Use the detailed information in the Message history to identify the source of the problem. Then use the troubleshooting steps outlined in the two preceding sections for the intraserver and intra–routing-group transport issues.

The Exchange 2000 Message Tracking Center is equally adept at tracking messages through Exchange 5.5 servers, even if they're not in the Exchange 2000 organization. If the Exchange 5.5 server does not appear in the list of Exchange servers, enter the computer name in the Server(s) list in the Message Tracking Center.

Advanced SMTP Troubleshooting Steps Sometimes it is the actual connection to an external messaging system that fails. For the most part, troubleshooting can be done in Exchange System Manager, although external tools occasionally come in handy. Suppose, for instance, that you're troubleshooting a connection problem with an

Exchange server in your organization (or with an external SMTP server). If the error message listed in the SMTP virtual server is vague, it might be helpful to walk through a manual SMTP session with the remote server. SMTP is a simple, command-based protocol that operates by default on TCP port 25. To troubleshoot it requires an understanding of just a few of the available commands: HELO, MAIL FROM, RCPT TO, DATA, RSET, and QUIT (a detailed explanation of SMTP commands is in Chapter 8, Table 8-1).

The remote SMTP server does not echo keystrokes, so it's helpful to turn on Local Echo in the Telnet client. In Windows 2000, the default Telnet client is DOS-based and must be configured outside any active session. To do this, start Telnet (type "telnet" from the command line), then type "set local_echo". Type "quit" to exit Telnet or "open" to initiate a Telnet session with a remote server (example: "open *myserver* 25" to initiate an SMTP session with *myserver*).

After you enter each command line, the remote server responds with a status code indicating success or failure. Fully explained in RFC 821, the primary codes to look for are 200-level codes (success) and 500-level codes (failure). Exchange 2000 also provides enhanced status codes, as explained in RFC 1893 (both RFCs can be downloaded from *http://www.faqs.org/rfcs/rfc821.html* and *http://www.faqs.org/rfcs/rfc1893.html*). Briefly, however, the enhanced status codes follow a three-digit dotted-decimal format, as in "x.y.z." The first value is a generic success/failure indicator, and the meaning becomes more specific as you move farther to the right in the code. Similar to the standard status codes, 2.y.z-level codes indicate success, and 5.y.z codes indicate permanent failure. The following example shows a successful SMTP session, initiated from the command line (bold formatting indicates text you type):

```
Telnet athlon.HouseOfSmiths.org 25
220 athlon.HouseOfSmiths.org Microsoft ESMTP MAIL Service,
version: 5.0.2195.2966 ready at Mon, 16 Jul 2002 20:55:08 -
0700
HELO mail1.mydomain.com
250 athlon.HouseOfSmiths.org Hello [192.168.1.3]
MAIL FROM: John.Doe@MyDomain.com
250 2.1.0 John.Doe@MyDomain.com....Sender OK
RCPT TO: kevan@houseofsmiths.org
250 2.1.5 kevan@houseofsmiths.org
DATA
354 Start mail input; end with <CRLF>.<CRLF>
This text will appear in the body of the message as text.
.
250 2.6.0 <ATHLONe45RtbH5pRmfg00000001@athlon.HouseOfSmiths.org>
Queued mail for delivery
QUIT
221 Closing connection
```

Advanced GroupWise Connector Troubleshooting Steps The GroupWise Connector uses a number of folder queues when messages are routed between Exchange and GroupWise. If necessary, you can temporarily enable archiving for all messages passing through the connector by making a Registry modification. To enable archiving for the Exchange 2000 GroupWise Connector, follow these steps:

1. Start the Windows Registry Editor (RegEdt32.exe).
2. Locate the HKey_Local_Machine\System\CurrentControlSet\Services\LME-GWISE\Parameters Registry key.
3. Add a new DWORD value called Archive, with a value of 1.
4. Restart the Microsoft Exchange Router for Novell GroupWise service.

These steps create a \Program Files\ExchSrvr\ConnData\GwRouter folder, and all messages that pass through the connector are copied to this folder.

Leaving archiving enabled indefinitely fills the hard drive with archived messages, which could cause a system or service failure. You should disable archiving after finishing the troubleshooting session.

Chapter Summary

- Routing groups are used to consolidate servers in one or more LAN segments with high-bandwidth connections. Within a routing group, an intrinsic full-mesh topology exists. Routing groups are generally connected by using RGCs, although SMTP and X.400 connectors can also be used. Connectors for external messaging systems run in tandem with Exchange and usually enable messaging, directory replication, and schedule sharing.
- You can create multiple connectors between routing groups or with external messaging systems to provide fault tolerance and/or multiple paths for messages to take, based on the sender. As a result, different delivery rules can be enforced for different users.
- The Exchange 2000 Transport Architecture provides a robust, extensible messaging framework. By using event sinks, Exchange functionality can be extended indefinitely, providing virus protection, workflow tools, collaboration applications, and any other procedural functionality needed in your organization.
- The Exchange 2000 routing model relies on link state tables, ensuring that messages are sent over the most efficient path. Link state updates reflecting connector failures are replicated throughout the organization almost immediately, ensuring a loop-free routing environment.
- The primary tools for troubleshooting messaging connectivity are Delivery Status Notifications (DSNs), SMTP virtual server queues, and the Exchange 2000 Message Tracking Center. WinRoute can also be used to answer questions about a server's link state table.

KEY TERMS

address space — A filter identifying a set of recipients that can be routed through a connector. You can build an address space with any level of granularity, identifying single recipients, groups of recipients, or all recipients of a specific address type (SMTP, X.400, cc:Mail, and so on).

advanced queuing engine (AQE) — A primary component in the extended SMTP Service of IIS, involved in the Exchange 2000 Transport Architecture. Governs the internal processing and categorization of messages, identifies next-hop information, and calls custom event sinks.

Categorizer (Phatcat.dll) — A series of event sinks, called by the AQE, that perform AD lookups to resolve message recipients to their associated SMTP addresses. Removes redundant recipients and enforces transport-level quotas.

connector — Any routine or service that provides message, scheduling, and/or directory synchronization between Exchange 2000 routing groups or between an Exchange 2000 organization and an external messaging system. Although third-party connectors can be developed, Exchange 2000 Server provides native connectors for SMTP, routing groups, Lotus Notes and cc:Mail, and Novell GroupWise.

connector cost — An administrator-assigned value between 1 and 100 that identifies the relative preference for a connector (lowest cost preferred). When routing messages, Exchange uses the path with the lowest total cost to transport messages.

Delivery Status Notification (DSN) — An automatically generated e-mail notifying a user of a message delivery problem. DSNs generally refer to a delay message, although NDR notifications also fall into this category. A DSN (delay) message indicates that the initial attempt at sending a message failed, and Exchange will continue trying.

event sink — An indicator of the registered process called at a predefined point in processing a message. The three categories of event sinks are storage events, transport events, and protocol events.

Exchange 2000 Transport Architecture — A functional description of the logic in Exchange 2000 and IIS that routes the messages within a single Exchange server.

Exchange Development Kit (EDK) — A set of development tools from Microsoft that enables programmatic connectivity to the Exchange organization through the MTA. The EDK is used primarily for developing connectors to external messaging systems.

Extensible Storage Engine (ESE) — A component that manages the physical databases necessary for storing and retrieving messages.

Message Tracking Center — A tracking and troubleshooting tool that tracks messages in an Exchange organization from their point of entry to their point of departure.

Message Transfer Agent (MTA) — An agent that provides X.400-based connectivity with remote X.400 servers and communicates directly with EDK-based connectors.

Non-Delivery Report (NDR) — A type of Delivery Status Notification, indicating that a permanent error has occurred while attempting to deliver a message.

pre-categorization queue — A queue that temporarily holds messages awaiting processing by the Categorizer. In System Manager, it is the Messages awaiting directory lookup queue of an SMTP virtual server.

pre-routing queue — A queue that temporarily holds categorized messages awaiting next-hop information from the routing engine. In System Manager, it is the Messages waiting to be routed queue of an SMTP virtual server.

protocol engine — A component of SMTP that directly connects to remote SMTP servers to send and receive messages.

protocol stub — A protocol-specific interface between IIS and Exchange. Protocol-specific commands and requests are sent between IIS and Exchange through their respective protocol stubs, related data (such as an e-mail message body) is placed in a shared memory heap, and a reference to it is placed in the protocol stub.

routing engine — A component that manages and uses link state information to identify next-hop information for message routing on behalf of the AQE.

routing group master (RGM) — The server in a routing group assigned the task of maintaining that routing group's link state table. Initially, it is the first server added to a routing group, but this can be changed in System Manager.

routing group topology — The design that indicates the architecture used to logically connect routing groups. The basic routing group topologies are hub-and-spoke, linear, ring, and full-mesh. Generally, the topology is a hybrid of the basic routing group topologies.

store drivers (Ntfsdrv.dll, Drviis.dll) — Ntfsdrv.dll uses the local file system to temporarily hold outgoing messages pending delivery by the protocol engine and incoming messages pending processing by the AQE. Drviis.dll is the IIS method of accessing the Information Store via ExIPC.

Review Questions

1. Name at least four commonly used routing group topologies.
2. What is the default message size limit for an SMTP virtual server?
   a. 2048 KB
   b. 4096 KB
   c. 10,240 KB
   d. none of the above
3. You are the Exchange administrator for an international organization. Users in the PNW_US routing group have complained about receiving NDRs for messages sent to users in the China routing group. You suspect the link state table on one

of the local bridgehead servers might be corrupted. Which of the following actions confirms your suspicion?

a. In System Manager, drill down to \Routing Groups\PNW_US\Members. Right-click the routing group master, and then click Link State Table.

b. In System Manager, drill down to \Routing Groups\PNW_US\Members. Right-click the bridgehead server, and then click Link State Table.

c. Using Notepad, open \ExchSrvr\MTAData\LinkState.dat from the bridgehead server.

d. Run WinRoute.exe., and then download the link state table from the bridgehead server.

4. Which Exchange 2000 component is responsible for matching recipient names to their e-mail addresses?

a. advanced queuing engine (AQE)

b. Categorizer

c. routing engine

d. Web Storage System (WSS)

5. You are the Exchange administrator for your company. To comply with government regulations, you must keep a copy of all e-mail messages sent to or received by your users. Which of the following actions should you take? (Choose all that apply.)

a. Create an archive folder on the hard drive, and secure it with NTFS permissions.

b. Enable message archiving for the SMTP virtual server.

c. Under Global Settings\Message Delivery in System Manager, create an "*" filter (match all messages), and then click Archive filtered messages.

d. Create an OnMessageSubmission transport event sink, and register it with IIS.

e. In the Windows Registry, open \\HKLM\System\CurrentControlSet\Services\SMTPSVC\Parameters. Create a new ArchiveDir string value. In the Value data field, enter the path to the archive folder.

f. Restart the Exchange services.

g. Restart the IIS services.

6. You are the Exchange administrator for your company. Recently, a user's laptop was stolen, and all company e-mail addresses were taken from the offline address book and distributed to spammers. As a result, your users are now receiving a lot of UBEs. The CIO has directed you to immediately stop incoming UBEs from both known and unknown senders before they reach users' mailboxes. You must perform this task with a minimum of administrative, server, and user impact. Which of the following steps produces the best results? (Choose all that apply.)

a. Use a system policy to assign new SMTP e-mail addresses to all users, disable their existing e-mail addresses, and direct them to notify external contacts of their new addresses.

b. Under Global Settings\Message Delivery in System Manager, create a filter for keywords that identify UBEs.

c. Under Global Settings\Message Delivery in System Manager, create a filter for known UBE senders.

d. Create an OnMessageSubmission transport event sink to filter for keywords that identify UBEs, and register the event sink with IIS.

e. Bind filtering to the IP address associated with the public SMTP virtual server.

f. Create an OnSyncSave storage event sink to filter for keywords that identify UBEs, and register the event sink with Exchange.

7. All members of a routing group must be able to contact the routing group master. True or False?

8. All members of a routing group must be part of the same ______________.

9. To move an Exchange 2000 server from Routing Group A to Routing Group B, which of the following procedures should you use?

   a. Drag and drop the server from the Members container of Routing Group A to the Members container of Routing Group B.

   b. Right-click the server in the Members container of Routing Group A. Click Move. In the Move dialog box, select Routing Group B, and then click OK.

   c. Servers cannot be moved between routing groups.

10. To move an Exchange 2000 server from Administrative Group A to Administrative Group B, which of the following procedures should you use?

   a. Drag and drop the server from the Members container of Administrative Group A to the Members container of Administrative Group B.

   b. Right-click the server in the Members container of Administrative Group A. Click Move. In the Move dialog box, select Administrative Group B, and then click OK.

   c. Servers cannot be moved between administrative groups.

11. To designate Server1 as the routing group master for Routing Group A, which of the following procedures should you use?

   a. Right-click Routing Group A from the Routing Groups container, and then click Properties. In the Routing group master drop-down list, select Server1.

   b. Right-click the server in the Members container of Routing Group A, and then click Set as Master.

   c. Routing group master servers are managed internally by Exchange and cannot be manually specified.

12. You are an Exchange administrator designing the routing group boundaries for a new Exchange 2000 organization for your company, and are evaluating the bandwidth needs between the Seattle, WA and Portland, OR offices, each of which will have Exchange 2000 servers. You expect average messaging traffic between the

servers and have identified the current average bandwidth utilization between the offices as 64 KB. What is the minimum suggested bandwidth required to place both servers in the same routing group?

a. 96 KB

b. 128 KB

c. 160 KB

d. 192 KB

e. 256 KB

13. Which of the following actions creates cc:Mail addresses for all users in the company?

    a. In the Recipients container in Exchange System Manager, create a new recipient policy.

    b. In Active Directory Users and Computers, assign a GPO to the Users container.

    c. In the System Policies container in Exchange System Manager, create a new recipient policy and assign it to the appropriate mailbox stores.

    d. In the System Policies container in Exchange System Manager, create a new mailbox store policy and assign it to the appropriate mailbox stores.

14. You are the Exchange administrator for your company. Users are reporting problems sending messages. One of them, Jeffrey Giles, has sent you a copy of an NDR he received after attempting to send to Emily Harrison. An excerpt of it reads as follows:

```
The following recipient(s) could not be reached:
Emily Harrison on 8/1/2002 11:57 AM
            Could not deliver the message in the time limit
 specified. Please retry or contact your administrator.
            <WestMail01.Coast2CoastAccounting.com #4.4.7>
```

    Jeffrey is homed on WestMail01 in the West routing group, and Emily is homed on EastMail01 in the East routing group. The West-East RGC connects the routing groups. Where is the first place to look in System Manager when troubleshooting the problem?

    a. On WestMail01, right-click the West-East RGC queue in the Default SMTP Virtual Server container, and then click Enumerate 100 Messages.

    b. On WestMail01, right-click the West-East RGC queue in the Default SMTP Virtual Server container, and then click Properties.

    c. On EastMail01, right-click the West-East RGC queue in the Default SMTP Virtual Server container, and then click Enumerate 100 Messages.

    d. On EastMail01, right-click the West-East RGC queue in the Default SMTP Virtual Server container, and then click Properties.

15. You are the Exchange administrator for your company. Lately, you have had sporadic problems with message and directory synchronization with a Novell GroupWise messaging system used by the Oakland office. You want to enable archiving for the GroupWise Connector on the Exchange 2000 bridgehead server for troubleshooting purposes. What do you do?
    a. In the Windows 2000 Registry, add a new DWORD value to HKey_Local_Machine\System\CurrentControlSet\Services\LME-GWISE\Parameters. Name the value Archive, and set it equal to 1.
    b. In System Manager, open the Properties dialog box for the GroupWise Connector. In the GroupWise connection section of the General tab, click the Archive messages to check box, and then enter the path to the archive folder.
    c. In the \ExchSrvr\ConnData\GWRouter\MTS_IN and MTS_OUT folders in Windows Explorer, remove the Delete permissions to the System account.
    d. In Windows Explorer, create an Archive folder in ExchSrvr\ConnData\GWRouter.
16. Describe what the Exchange Development Kit is used for.
17. To connect an Exchange 2000 organization to a SNADS organization, you should install and configure a SNADS Connector on an Exchange 2000 server. True or False?
18. When identifying the best route for a message, Exchange 2000 uses the connector that provides which of the following?
    a. lowest next-hop cost
    b. lowest total cost
    c. highest next-hop cost
    d. highest total cost
19. When a Routing Group Connector communicates with an Exchange 5.5 bridgehead server in a remote routing group, which protocol can it use?
    a. CDO
    b. WebDAV
    c. X.400 over RPC
    d. X.400 over X.25
    e. SMTP
20. In the NDR example in Question 14, explain which lines are the most important and why.

HANDS-ON PROJECTS

The following projects exercise the skills you have learned in this chapter for Exchange 2000 routing group management. When working on these projects, replace *YourServer* with the name of your computer. This project assumes that your computer has two IP addresses assigned (referred to as *PrivateIP* and *PublicIP*), that the Organization properties are set so that Display routing groups is checked and Display administrative groups is not checked, that you have a mailbox-enabled user account whose mailbox is homed on your server (referred to as *User1*), and that Outlook 2000 is installed on your server and configured with your Outlook profile.

Project 10-1

In this project, you will create and configure two SMTP virtual servers on *YourServer* named Public SMTP Virtual Server and Private SMTP Virtual Server. In the real world, this is often done if you need a single physical SMTP server available on multiple subnets. In this case, we're assuming that one SMTP virtual server is available to the Internet, and another is available to internal clients only. To prevent this Exchange server from being used by spammers, Public SMTP Virtual Server will restrict relaying. To enable POP3 and IMAP users to send messages through this server, Private SMTP Virtual Server will allow relaying but require user authentication.

To create SMTP virtual servers:

1. Log on to your Windows 2000 server using an account with Domain and Exchange administrator privileges. To open the Exchange System Manager console, click **Start**, point to **Programs**, point to **Microsoft Exchange**, and then click **System Manager**.
2. To open the SMTP container for your server, expand **Servers**, expand ***YourServer***, expand **Protocols**, and then expand **SMTP**.
3. To disable the Default SMTP Virtual Server, right-click the **Default SMTP Virtual Server** object, and then click **Stop** on the shortcut menu. A red circle with a white "x" should appear over the Default SMTP Virtual Server object.
4. To create a new SMTP virtual server named Public SMTP Virtual Server, right-click the **SMTP** container, point to **New**, and then click **SMTP Virtual Server**.
5. In the New SMTP Virtual Server Wizard, type **Public SMTP Virtual Server** in the Name text box, and then click the **Next** button. In the Select the IP address for this SMTP virtual server list box, click the first IP address (this will be your *PublicIP*). Click the **Finish** button to return to System Manager.

6. To create a new SMTP virtual server named Private SMTP Virtual Server, repeat Steps 4–5, with the following substitutions: Type **Private SMTP Virtual Server** in the Name text box, and click the second IP address (this will be your *PrivateIP*) in the Select the IP address for this SMTP virtual server list box.
7. Back in System Manager, right-click **Public SMTP Virtual Server**, and then click **Properties** on the shortcut menu to open the server's Properties dialog box. In the General tab, click the **Enable logging** check box, and make sure the selection in the Active log format list box is W3C Extended Log File Format. (It should already be enabled because this system will be available to the Internet.)
8. Click the **Access** tab, and then click the **Authentication** button. Make sure the **Anonymous access** check box is selected, and then click **OK** to return to the Properties dialog box.
9. In the Access tab, click the **Relay** button to open the Relay Restrictions dialog box. Make sure that the Only the list below radio button is selected and that the Computer list box is empty. Click the **Allow all computers which successfully authenticate to relay, regardless of the list above** check box to deselect it. Click **OK** to close the Relay Restrictions dialog box, and then click **OK** to close the Properties dialog box.
10. Back in System Manager, right-click **Private SMTP Virtual Server**, and then click **Properties** on the shortcut menu to open the server's Properties dialog box. Click the **Access** tab, click the **Authentication** button, click the **Anonymous access** check box to deselect it, and then click **OK**.
11. In the Access tab of the server's Properties dialog box, click the **Relay** button. In the Relay Restrictions dialog box, click the **All except the list below** radio button, and make sure the Computers list box is empty. Click **OK** to close the Relay Restrictions dialog box, and click **OK** to close the Properties dialog box.
12. Close System Manager. Click **Start**, click **Run**, and then type **cmd** in the Open text box. Click **OK** to open a DOS command-prompt window.
13. In the command-prompt window, type **telnet *PublicIP* 25** to emulate an SMTP session with the Public SMTP Virtual Server. You should receive a response from your server. Then enter the following commands and note the responses:
    - Type **helo**. You should receive a Hello response in return.
    - Type **mail from: me@me.com**. You should receive a Sender OK response.
    - Type **rcpt to: *User1***. Note the response (*remember to replace User1 with the complete e-mail address assigned to your account*).
    - Type **rcpt to: Somebody@Microsoft.com**. Note the response.
    - Type **quit**.

14. In the command-prompt window, type **telnet *PrivateIP* 25** to emulate an SMTP session with the Private SMTP Virtual Server. You should receive a response from your server. Then enter the following commands and note the responses:
    - Type **helo**. You should receive a Hello response in return.
    - Type **mail from: me@me.com**. You should receive a Sender OK response.
    - Type **rcpt to: *User1***. Note and compare with the response from the Public SMTP Virtual Server.
    - Type **rcpt to: Somebody@Microsoft.com**. Note the response and compare it to the response from the Public SMTP Virtual Server.
    - Type **quit**.
15. Close all open windows and applications.

Project 10-2

This project assumes that you have completed Project 10-1.

To configure filters on incoming messages:

1. Log on to your Windows 2000 Server using an account with Domain and Exchange administrator privileges. To open the Exchange System Manager console, click **Start**, point to **Programs**, point to **Microsoft Exchange**, and then click **System Manager**.
2. To create filters for *spammer1@mymail.com*, **@spam.com*, and *annoy*@me.com*, expand the **Global Settings** container. Right-click the **Message Delivery** container, and then click **Properties** on the shortcut menu.
3. In the Message Delivery Properties dialog box, click the **Filtering** tab, and then click the **Add** button. In the Sender text box, type **spammer1@mymail.com**, and then click **OK**. Repeat this process for ***@spam.com** and **annoy*@me.com**. Click the **Archive filtered messages** radio button, and then click **OK** to return to System Manager.
4. To apply the global filtering rules to the IP address assigned to the Public SMTP Virtual Server, expand the following containers: **Servers**, ***YourServer***, **Protocols**, and **SMTP**. Right-click **Public SMTP Virtual Server**, and then click **Properties** on the shortcut menu to open the server's Properties dialog box.
5. In the General tab, click the **Advanced** button. In the Advanced dialog box, make sure ***PublicIP*** is selected, and then click the **Edit** button. In the Identification dialog box, click the **Apply Filter** check box.
6. Close all dialog boxes. Click **Start**, click **Run**, and then type **cmd** in the Open text box. Click **OK** to open a DOS command-prompt window.

7. In the command-prompt window, you will emulate an SMTP session with the Public SMTP Virtual Server and attempt to send a message from each of the following addresses: *spammer1@mymail.com, spammer2@mymail.com, user1@spam.com, littleoldme@spam.com, listento@me.com, annoying@me.com.* Type **Telnet *PublicIP* 25**. You should receive a response from your server. Perform the following steps for each of the listed addresses:
   - Type **helo**. You should receive a Hello response.
   - Type **Mail From: spammer1@mymail.com**. Note the server's response.
   - If the connection to the host has not been lost, type **quit** to return to the command prompt. If the connection has been lost, start a new Telnet session.
8. After you have tested all the addresses, close the command-prompt window, and return to System Manager. If you closed it previously, refer to Step 1 to reopen it.
9. To delete the Public and Private SMTP Virtual Servers created in Project 10-1, and reenable the Default SMTP Virtual Server, expand the following containers: **Servers**, ***YourServer***, **Protocols**, and **SMTP**. Right-click **Public SMTP Virtual Server**, and then click **Delete** on the shortcut menu. In the SMTP Configuration dialog box, click the **Yes** button. Repeat for the Private SMTP Virtual Server. Next, right-click **Default SMTP Virtual Server**, and then click **Start** on the shortcut menu.
10. Close any open windows or applications.

Project 10-3

In this project, you will create, connect, and modify two routing groups, their members, and their connections. This project requires two Exchange 2000 Server computers and should be completed with a partner (finish each step before beginning the next one). Each step indicates whether it should be performed only by Partner 1, only by Partner 2, or by both. Partner 1 and Partner 2's servers are referred to as *Server1* and *Server2*, respectively.

To create and connect routing groups:

1. *Both Partners*—Log on to your Windows 2000 Server using an account with Domain and Exchange administrator privileges. To open the Exchange System Manager console, click **Start**, point to **Programs**, point to **Microsoft Exchange**, and then click **System Manager**.
2. *Both Partners*—Note and explain the purpose of each queue listed for the Default SMTP Virtual Server of both computers. To do this, expand the following containers in System Manager: **Servers**, ***Server1***, **Protocols**, **SMTP**, **Default SMTP Virtual Server**, and **Queues**. Repeat for *Server2*.

3. *Partner 1*—Using Outlook 2000, send an e-mail message to Partner 2, and then view the SMTP queues for both servers. To view the SMTP queues, right-click **Queues** for the *Server1* Default SMTP Virtual Server, and then click **Refresh** on the shortcut menu. Note any changes and explain why they occurred. Repeat this procedure for *Server2*.
4. *Partner 2*—After Partner 1 is finished with Step 3, repeat the same procedure, sending a message to Partner 1.
5. *Both Partners*—To create a new routing group named *YourServer*_RG and place your server in the newly created routing group, right-click the **Routing Groups** container, point to **New**, and then click **Routing Group** on the shortcut menu. In the Properties dialog box, enter your server name followed by **_RG**, and then click **OK**. Expand the ***YourServer*_RG** container. Click the **Members** container of the First Routing Group. Drag and drop your server from the Members container of the First Routing Group to the Members container of the *YourServer*_RG.
6. *Both Partners*—Repeat Steps 3–4. Did your partner receive the message? Why or why not?
7. *Partner 1*—To create a new *Server1-Server2*-RGC Routing Group Connector between your server's Default SMTP Virtual Server and that of your partner, right-click the **Connectors** container of your routing group, point to **New**, and then click **Routing Group Connector** on the shortcut menu. In the General tab, type **Server1-Server2-RGC** in the Name text box, and then click **Server2_RGC**. Click the **Remote Bridgehead** tab, and then click the **Add** button. Click the **SMTP virtual server instances** list arrow, click **Server2 Default SMTP Virtual Server**, and then click **OK**. After reviewing the possible settings in the Delivery Restrictions, Content Restrictions, Delivery Options, and Details tabs, click **OK**.
8. *Both Partners*—Note any changes to your server's SMTP Virtual Server queue and explain.
9. *Both Partners*—Send an e-mail to your partner. Did your partner receive it? Why or why not?
10. *Both Partners*—Drag and drop to return your server to the First Routing Group. What happens and why? Delete the **Server1-Server2-RGC** from your routing group, and repeat.
11. *Both Partners*—View the queues for the SMTP Virtual Server on both *Server1* and *Server2*. Note any changes and explain why they occurred.
12. *Both Partners*—Close any open windows or applications.

Project 10-4

In this project, you will configure an SMTP Connector to connect to the Internet via a smart host.

This project requires a DNS entry for "smarthost" to be added to the DNS domain used in the lab environment. It *must* be an inactive IP address within the local subnet for this project to be completed successfully (that is, pings to "smarthost" must time out). This is necessary so that messages pending delivery to "smarthost" will remain in the queue for students to view. Your instructor will have configured this setting for you before you begin this project.

To configure SMTP Connectors:

1. Log on to your Windows 2000 server using an account with Domain and Exchange administrator privileges. To open the Exchange System Manager console, click **Start**, point to **Programs**, point to **Microsoft Exchange**, and then click **System Manager**.
2. Expand the following containers: **Routing Groups** and then **First Routing Group**. Right-click the **Connectors** container, point to **New**, and then click **SMTP Connector** on the shortcut menu.
3. In the Name text box, type ***YourServer*.test SMTP Connector**. Click the **Forward all mail through this connector to the following smart hosts** radio button, and type **smarthost** in the text box. Click the **Add** button. In the Add Bridgehead dialog box, click ***YourServer* Default SMTP Virtual Server**, and then click **OK**.
4. Click the **Address Space** tab, and then click the **Add** button. In the Add Address Space dialog box, make sure SMTP is selected, and then click **OK**. In the Internet Address Space Properties dialog box, type ***@*YourServer*.test** in the E-mail domain text box, and then click **OK**. Review the other available options in the Connected Routing Groups, Delivery Restrictions, Content Restrictions, Delivery Options, Advanced, and Details tabs. Then click **OK** to return to System Manager.
5. Open Outlook 2000, and send a message to **TestUser@*YourServer*.test**.
6. In System Manager, expand the following containers: **Servers**, ***YourServer***, **Protocols**, **SMTP**, **Default SMTP Virtual Server**, and **Queues**. Right-click **Queues**, and then click **Refresh** on the shortcut menu. Note any changes to the queues.
7. Right-click ***YourServer*.test SMTP Connector (SMTP Connector – Remote delivery)**, and then click **Properties** on the shortcut menu. In the Properties dialog box, note the following items that can assist you in troubleshooting this connector: Total number of messages, Total message size (KB), Time of submission of oldest message, Status, and the unlabeled text box at the bottom.

8. To delete the YourServer.test SMTP Connector, expand the following containers, if necessary: **Routing Groups**, **First Routing Group**, and **Connectors**. Right-click ***YourServer*.test SMTP Connector**, and then click **Delete** on the shortcut menu. In the message box that opens, click **Yes**.
9. Close any open windows or applications.

Project 10-5

Providing connectivity between Exchange 2000 and an external messaging system requires configuration in both Exchange 2000 and the external messaging system. In this project, you will install the Lotus Notes Connector on your system so that you can configure connectivity with an external messaging system. This project assumes that you will continue to Project 10-6 and configure Exchange to support a connection with a Lotus Notes server named NotesPO1, part of the NotesDom Lotus Notes domain. Notes messages destined for DownLvlNotesDom will also be routed through NotesPO1.

To install the Lotus Notes Connector:

1. Insert the Microsoft Exchange 2000 Server CD-ROM in your server's CD drive (if the Microsoft Exchange 2000 Server Installation Wizard does not appear automatically, manually start the wizard by running Launch.exe from your CD drive). Click to begin Exchange Server Setup.
2. Click the **Next** button. In the Component Selection window, click the **Microsoft Exchange 2000** list arrow, and then click **Change**. Repeat this procedure for **Microsoft Exchange Messaging** and **Collaboration Services**.
3. Click the **Microsoft Exchange Connector for Lotus Notes** list arrow, click **Install**, and then click **Next**. In the Component Summary window, click the **Next** button, and then click the **Finish** button. If you see a message box stating "The system already contains a file that is newer than the one being installed," click the **No to all** button. If you are prompted to Reinstall the Exchange 2000 Service Pack, do so at this time.
4. Click **Start**, point to **Programs**, point to **Administrative Tools**, and then click **Active Directory Users and Computers**. In the Active Directory Users and Computers console, right-click the domain name, point to **New**, and then click **Organizational Unit**. In the New Object - Organizational Unit dialog box, type **Notes Contacts** in the Name text box, and then click **OK**. Click **Console** on the menu bar, and then click **Exit** to close the Active Directory Users and Computers console.
5. Leave your system at the desktop to continue to the next project.

Project 10-6

In this project, you will configure Exchange to support a connection with a Lotus Notes server named NotesPO1, part of the NotesDom Lotus Notes domain. Notes messages destined for DownLvlNotesDom will also be routed through NotesPO1. In System Manager, you'll modify the Default Policy recipient policy to create Lotus Notes addresses for all users, and accept the default address generation key. (Generally, you would need to install the Lotus Notes client before continuing, but for the purposes of this project we'll "pretend.")

To configure connectivity with an external messaging system:

1. Click **Start**, point to **Programs**, point to **Microsoft Exchange**, and then click **System Manager**. Expand the following containers: **Routing Groups**, **First Routing Group**, and **Connectors**. Right-click the **Connector for Lotus Notes (*YourServer*)**, and then click **Properties** on the shortcut menu to open the Properties dialog box.
2. In the General tab, type **NotesPOs** in the Notes Server text box. Note the contents of the Notes.ini file location and the Connector mailbox text boxes.
3. Click the **Address Space** tab, and then click the **Add** button. In the Add Address Space dialog box, make sure Notes is selected, and then click **OK**. In the Lotus Notes Address Space Properties dialog box, type * in the User Name text box, type **NotesDom** in the Domain text box, and then click **OK**.
4. Click the **Import Containers** tab, and then click the **Notes Contacts** container you created in Step 4 of Project 10-5. To do this, click the **Modify** button. In the Choose a container dialog box, click the + next to the domain name. Click **Notes Contacts**, and then click **OK**. Click **Yes** in the message box that opens.
5. Click the **Export Containers** tab, and then click the **Add** button. In the Choose a container dialog box, click the + next to the domain name. Click **Users**, and then click **OK**. If necessary, click **Yes** in the message box that opens.
6. Click the **DirSync Options** tab, click the **Exchange-Notes directory update schedule** list arrow, and then click to select **Run daily at 11:00 PM** in the list.
7. Click the **Advanced** tab. To configure the Connector for Lotus Notes (*YourServer*) to route messages destined for DownLvlNotesDom through this connector, and to schedule database maintenance for midnight, click the **Add** button. Type **DownLvlNotesDom** in the Domain text box, and then click **OK**. Click the **Notes database maintenance schedule** list arrow, and then click to select **Run daily at Midnight** in the list. Click **OK** to close the dialog box.
8. Close any open windows or applications.

CASE PROJECTS

Case 1

XYZ Enterprises has four offices, as shown in Figure 10-17. The WAN links between offices are labeled with total bandwidth and the percentage of bandwidth used for non-messaging purposes.

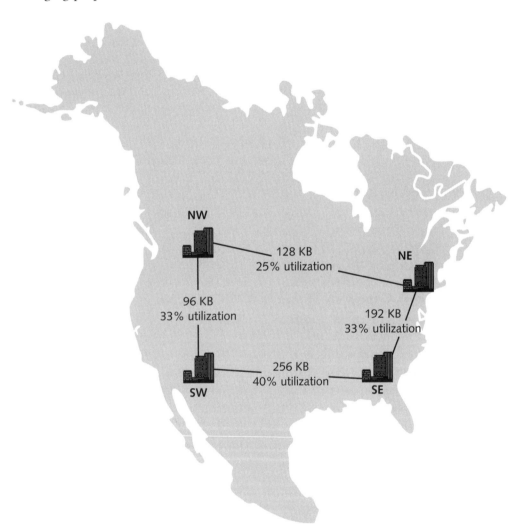

Figure 10-17 The WAN topology for XYZ Enterprises

Each office has one Exchange 2000 server, each in its own routing group. The routing groups have been connected in a ring topology, following the physical WAN structure, and each connector has a cost of 1. Users in NW and SW have complained that message delivery is often slow to SE. Modify the costs assigned to each connector to optimize the mail transfer.

Case 2

International Transport has 12 servers in 6 offices in the United States and Mexico. The current WAN infrastructure is displayed in Figure 10-18. Each frame relay link is marked with total bandwidth and the average percentage used for nonmessaging purposes.

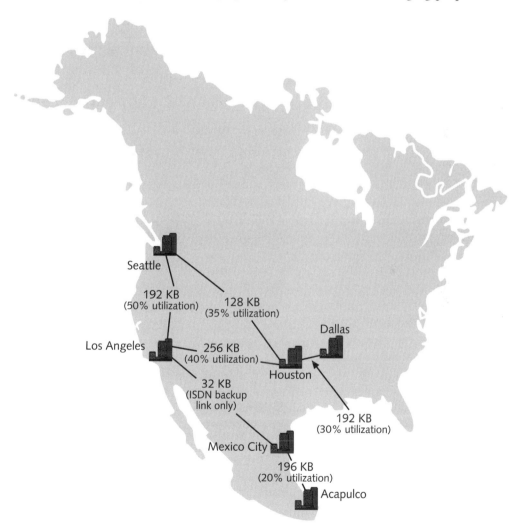

Figure 10-18 The WAN topology for International Transport

You have been asked to create and populate routing groups and their connectors. Diagram your results.

Case 3

ABC Enterprises, with a primary hub in Denver, recently experienced a total halt to all messaging traffic when a network backbone problem at its ISP caused the Denver office to drop off the WAN. A network and messaging infrastructure redesign is now taking place to ensure that no single site failure can prevent messaging flow between any other offices. After collecting some information from users, you note the following facts about messaging trends for this company:

- About 40% of the total messaging volume between offices originates in Denver. About half of that is from Denver to New York; the rest is split equally.
- About 20% of the total messaging volume between offices originates in New York. About half of that is from New York to Denver; the rest is split equally.
- Most of Portland's outbound traffic is to Phoenix.
- About half of New Orleans's outbound traffic is to St. Louis.

There are currently six WAN links, as shown in Figure 10-19.

Management is willing to consider moving any existing WAN links (move the Denver-NY link to St. Louis-NY, for instance) and adding up to three more 32-KB WAN links between offices to bring the total number of links to 10. You've convinced management to make the physical WAN topology and the routing group topology identical, so you have been asked to present your preferred topology to them for review. Make sure there are no single points-of-failure in the messaging pathway. Optimize both the WAN links and the costs of the Routing Group Connectors that will use them to take into account the messaging patterns of the corporate users. Draw lines between the offices that should have direct frame relay links. Label each link with its bandwidth and associated connector cost.

Case 4

You are an Exchange consultant working to upgrade XYZ Inc. to Exchange 2000. The current infrastructure consists of one Windows 2000 domain, with three Exchange 5.5 servers in a single site. Servers A and B are mailbox servers, and Server C has an Internet Mail Connector for Internet e-mail and an active IBM PROFS Connector, with directory synchronization enabled. XYZ Inc. management has asked you for an upgrade plan that conforms to the following requirements:

- Minimize expense
- Minimize impact on users
- Maximize message transport efficiency
- Enable management of all Exchange servers from a single administrative console
- Maintain existing connectivity with the Internet and the IBM PROFS messaging system
- Maintain directory synchronization with the PROFS organization

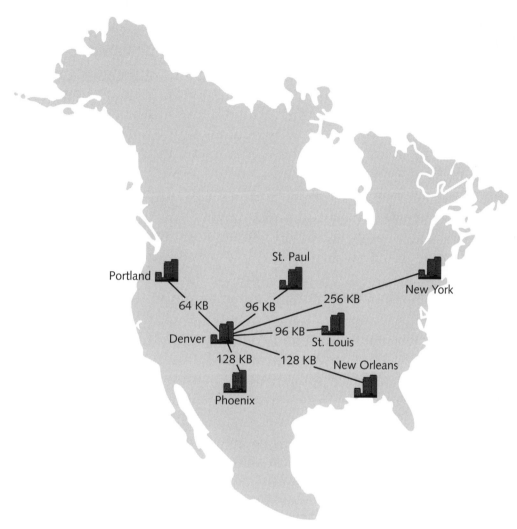

Figure 10-19 The WAN topology for ABC Enterprises

Explain what your upgrade plan would be for XYZ Inc. and how you would take management's requests into account when planning the upgrade.

Case 5

You are the Exchange administrator for your company. Julie Henrite, an employee from the West routing group, reports that a time-sensitive document she e-mailed to Greg O'Donnell, in the East routing group, has not been delivered. In analyzing the Default SMTP Virtual Server at the bridgehead server for West, you realize that the queue is backed up because of unusually high message volume. You need to expedite the delivery of Julie's e-mail. What should you do?

CHAPTER

11

CONFIGURING REAL-TIME COLLABORATION IN EXCHANGE 2000 SERVER

After reading this chapter and completing the exercises, you will be able to:

- Understand how Instant Messaging in Exchange 2000 works, including the protocols used to implement it, as well as how to install, configure, and troubleshoot Instant Messaging services
- Understand how Chat services are integrated into Exchange 2000, including how to install, configure, and troubleshoot Chat services in your Exchange 2000 organization
- Understand how Conferencing Server architecture is designed, including the configuration of Data Conferencing and Video Conferencing
- Monitor and manage Exchange 2000 collaboration features and services, as well as incorporate your organization's future needs for collaboration services

In Chapter 10, "Connector and Routing Management in Exchange 2000 Server," you learned about managing connectors and routing in Exchange 2000 and how to evaluate the economic, business, and technical factors that dictate the placement and configuration of routing groups. In addition, you learned about creating connectors, such as the X.400 or SMTP Connector, to manage connectivity with e-mail servers other than Exchange 2000. You also learned how to monitor and troubleshoot problems with these connectors and routing groups, giving you a solid foundation for effectively managing these services. Finally, you learned how to monitor your link state information for connections between your Exchange 2000 server and other e-mail servers.

In this chapter, you learn about user collaboration features that Exchange 2000 Server provides for your organization, including Instant Messaging, Chat, and Data/Video Conferencing. You learn how each of these features works and how to install and configure the required services to implement them. In addition, you learn about the Exchange Conferencing Server, which enables data and video conferencing, a definite advantage in this day and age. Last, you learn how to monitor and manage the collaboration services you have implemented, including a preview of where user collaboration services and features are headed in the coming years.

INTRODUCTION TO REAL-TIME COLLABORATION IN EXCHANGE 2000

Exchange 2000 Server has several different collaboration services and features your users can take advantage of. The demand for effective collaboration products and features is growing at a brisk pace, as users and companies alike realize the benefits of being able to collaborate quickly and effectively with other users, whether they are on another floor in the same building or on the other side of the planet. Exchange 2000 has integrated several new features that previously required individual software, which increased setup and configuration time because each system had to be configured for several individual services. With Exchange 2000, you can implement the collaboration features you want and manage them all in Exchange 2000. Keep in mind that the appropriate software still needs to be installed, but with the centralized configuration and management that's now available for many of these features, you can limit the possibility of configuration errors and user errors when implementing these services.

Among the collaboration features included in Exchange 2000 are Instant Messaging, Chat, and Data/Video Conferencing. Instant Messaging allows you to send text messages and files instantaneously to another user in a simple chat-like format. If you have used ICQ or AOL Instant Messenger (AIM), for example, you are probably already familiar with this type of collaboration service. Although Instant Messaging is a basic form of collaboration, it does allow quick questions and other information (for example, URLs) to be communicated without picking up a phone or sending an e-mail message. The Exchange 2000 Chat feature allows users to connect to a server to converse using the Microsoft Chat client; if you have seen this product in action, you understand how it differs from the AOL or ICQ products. By default, Microsoft Chat uses a comic book–like format as its main interface, whereas AIM and ICQ use a simple window with text entries for the conversation. In Microsoft Chat, each person in the chat has a character, or avatar. These avatars appear onscreen with their dialogue displayed in text bubbles above their heads. An example is shown in Figure 11-1.

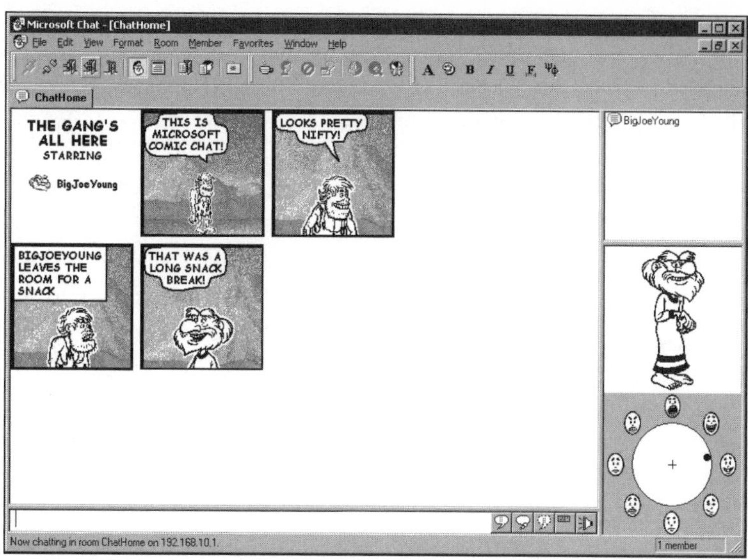

Figure 11-1 The Microsoft Chat client in Comic Strip view

The final collaboration services are Data and Video Conferencing. Again drawing on its diverse selection of software, Microsoft has integrated the same technology that drives its popular NetMeeting software to provide these advanced collaboration features. With Data Conferencing, several users can access a single document and work together to make changes and add notes to the document in real time. In addition, Video Conferencing enables users to chat face to face, using video and audio, which adds a personal touch to your conversations that IM doesn't offer. Many other uses for these collaboration technologies are discussed in detail later in this chapter.

A Detailed Look at Instant Messaging

Instant Messaging (IM) allows for instantaneous communication between users and offers the ability to transfer files quickly and directly. In many cases, an instantaneous messaging system offers far more benefits than a tried-and-true method like e-mail. For instance, assume that you and a co-worker are working on two different documents as part of one project. If you have a quick question for your co-worker, you can send him or her an instant message without having to open your e-mail software, create a new message, and type in the text and address information. Instead, you simply double-click your co-worker's name in your IM software (which runs on your taskbar next to the system clock), and then type the note. Almost instantly, your co-worker receives the message and can reply just as quickly, making IM an efficient and easy-to-use messaging method.

Many organizations do not support the use of collaboration features, such as IM or even Chat, because of the possibility of abuse by users of the service. This abuse could not only lead to loss of productivity, but also bring up issues of liability if these services were used to perform illegal acts.

Other than being a quick way to exchange messages, IM offers these benefits:

- Allows you to leave messages for users who have stepped away from their desks. This way, you can be sure they will see the messages when they return to their computers, instead of hoping they check their voicemail or e-mail.
- Lets you have a convenient message window on the screen alongside another document you have open. This feature is especially useful if you need to review what's in the document while responding to what is being said in the IM window. You can do this easily because IM windows are typically small and easy to tuck into a corner of your desktop. You can also easily cut and paste information and links to and from the IM client and your other applications.
- Saves on long-distance phone costs when users need to communicate with branch offices in other locations, for example. Although e-mail can handle some of these long-distance communication needs, the benefits of IM often make it more attractive than e-mail.
- Enables you to know whether users are at their desks before you attempt to communicate with them. Default settings in the IM client allow the display of away messages (typically after five minutes of inactivity) when users have stepped away from their desks or are not using their computers. If users are present and/or using their computer, their icons appear as online and available. Users can also manually set their status; for example, when they leave for lunch, they can set the IM to show that they are out of the office. This solution is far better than using e-mail or the telephone, especially for critical messages, because with those methods, you have no real way to know whether users are there to receive your message or call.

As you can see, the Instant Messaging functionality offers quite a few benefits to your Exchange organization, helping workers communicate in a timely and effective manner, especially if they are physically separated from their co-workers. Now that you have seen the benefits of Instant Messaging, take a look at how it works.

Protocols Used for Instant Messaging

Microsoft implemented Instant Messaging with the **rendezvous protocol (RVP)**, which is an extension of the WebDAV protocol that Outlook Web Access uses. Using RVP enables IM to offer advanced features and functionality, such as the ability to work through secure servers and networks with installed firewalls and proxy servers.

By using RVP, organizations can create multiple IM servers that are independent of each other, which can be useful because independent IM servers are not required to communicate directly with each other to maintain user lists. Thankfully, if you have users who need to use IM to communicate with users on other physical networks, you can use an Internet connection to connect to those other servers. The benefit of this design is that your AD domain structure and information do not need to be replicated to every domain, network, and site you need to communicate with, thus providing additional flexibility and ease of deployment for IM.

IM issues instant messages and detects when users are connected, online, or out of the office by using RVP to implement a feature called a watcher, which monitors and keeps track of the currently connected users. This feature allows users to know when other IM clients are online and available so that they can send an instant message to these clients, even if they aren't in the same domain or network. Without this information, you have nothing more than a basic e-mail client. In addition to the watcher, IM configurations have a home server that maintains the lists of users connected to and using the server and provides updates on these users' connection status to other users requesting the information (the people who have you in their IM address list). When messages are sent, they come to the sending user's home server first, and then the message is sent to the appropriate recipient, whether on the same server or another server.

When you add a user to your IM address list, you are essentially subscribing for information on that user so that the server will know where the message should go. This gives you the user's return address and connects you to the watcher or home server that doles out the user's connection status for your client. Remember that the user's requests for information are DNS record lookups, so the IM server must have SRV records in its DNS server to provide the necessary IM support.

When the client has connected to a home server and sends the request for information, such as user connection status, the home server fills the request right away if the user account is on the same home server; if the user account is not on the same home server, it forwards the request to the appropriate home server using HTTP over port 80, by default. (This port can be changed, if necessary.) This method allows RVP and IM to work well over networks with firewalls and proxies because these security mechanisms typically allow data and requests to flow unfettered through HTTP port 80—the same protocol and port that regular Internet browsers use to communicate.

The relatively minimal impact on network resources is a key benefit of RVP and what makes Instant Messaging so popular and a wise choice to implement. The low resource impact means you don't have to worry about a glut of messages taking up precious network bandwidth that's needed for other services, such as file transfers or Web servers. Keep in mind that even with this minimal network usage, if enough users and messages flow through the network between servers and the Internet, it can cause network performance degradation, just as any other type of transmission can. If IM's usage is high enough to cause a network slowdown (unlikely except in very large IM implementations), you might want to make the same type of changes you would for any other network performance problem, such as increasing network line speed, providing a dedicated server and/or network switch, or upgrading your connection to the Internet if the issue is Internet bandwidth consumption.

Like any other protocol or service, such as POP3 or SMTP, Instant Messaging has commands that are used with the service. Although it's unlikely you will ever have to use the commands unless you are developing custom software that uses IM functionality, if you ever do need to use them, the basic commands include:

- *Notify*—Used to update server-to-server status information on subscribed users and to send messages between users.
- *Propfind*—Used when users log on to update the properties and status information for users in their address lists.
- *Proppatch*—Usually issued when a user has changed his or her connection status, from online to busy, for example. This command updates the properties and status information for other users who have this user in their address lists.
- *Subscribe*—Sent by a user to another user's home server to request connection status information and to update this information if it changes.
- *Unsubscribe*—Used similarly to the subscribe command, except it asks the home server to stop the subscription.

Given the convenience, added benefits, and minimal performance impact on networks, it's no wonder that Microsoft IM has become an increasingly popular product on the Internet as well as a new Exchange 2000 feature. Lest you think that IM is the only product of this type, you have some widely used third-party instant messaging packages to choose from, but each has its own benefits and downsides, as you will learn in the next section.

Comparing Microsoft Instant Messaging with Third-Party Instant Messaging Products

In the past couple of years, a veritable explosion of different instant messaging products has occurred, and both the general public and organizations have been quick to adopt these useful services. There are always a few competitors in the same market, and instant messaging is no exception to this rule. In fact, literally dozens of different products are available, but currently there are three to four major players in the battle for instant messaging dominance. As with any other software package, incompatibilities between the competing products might not allow interoperability; therefore, depending on which instant messaging software your friends, business partners, and branch offices use, you might need to run more than one product. You should evaluate the benefits and disadvantages of the available instant messaging products to choose the one that works best for your organization.

With the ever-changing landscape of IM software, it is difficult to conclude which software is the best, however. If you go by sheer number of users, ICQ wins hands down. As one of the earliest entries in the field, ICQ has a huge user base; because of this popularity, AOL bought out ICQ, even though AOL has its own competing product, AOL Instant Messenger. Because AIM already had a large user base, AOL was not willing to stop supporting either product, so ICQ and AIM maintain their own user bases and continue to be available separately. Even though the same company owns them, currently neither one supports messaging to the other. ICQ has one option not offered by AIM and MSN, which is the ability to open a simple chat window where both users can communicate in real time and see each other's messages as they are typed, instead of seeing messages entered only after they are finished.

Another popular product is Yahoo! Messenger, which has gained a large following because of its support and availability from the world's most famous search portal, *www.yahoo.com*. Like the AOL products and Microsoft IM, Yahoo! Messenger does not support communication with any of the other software packages.

Which product offers the best usability is a matter of personal choice that cannot be easily summed up. Some people like the multitude of options and extra "fluff" features included in ICQ and Yahoo! Messenger, but others prefer the clean and simple interface of MSN Messenger, as shown in Figure 11-2.

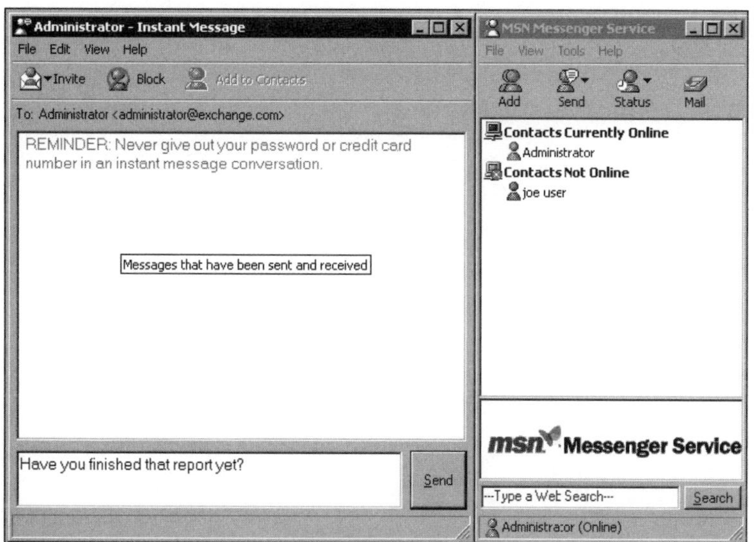

Figure 11-2 The MSN Messenger user interface and chat window

Another issue to consider is that IM products do not use any type of encryption to secure the data and messages being transmitted. Products such as ICQ that have been around for a long time are subject to a whole host of attacks from hackers, such as the ever-popular hijacking of accounts. There are different ways to prevent these situations, but it's important to consider security factors when choosing your IM product.

ICQ uses a numbering system for its user accounts; when users sign up, they are given a number indicating where they are in the total count of ICQ users. As membership numbers have crept into the several millions, it has created a demand for the shorter numbers that long-standing users have. One reason for the demand is the desire to be considered "in," as one of the early users of ICQ, and another is that these shorter numbers are simply easier to remember and hand out.

Another important consideration is the management of users and service configuration. Every major product requires users to connect to a central bank of servers that handle authentication, user creation, and configuration information. Until Exchange 2000 was released, there wasn't an easy, centralized way for an organization to implement instant messaging with its e-mail services and then tie these services together with user accounts. With Exchange 2000, a network administrator can have one user account with e-mail, IM, and regular Windows network access and configuration all managed from one central point—a definite advantage for administrators. The decision on which IM product you use ultimately comes down to which one best meets your organization's needs; however, the benefits of centralized management and integration with Exchange 2000 makes Microsoft IM an attractive choice.

Installing the Instant Messaging Service

IM is installed as one of the default options when you install Exchange 2000 Server. If you selected the Typical installation, IM was installed by default; if you selected Custom or Minimal in the Component Selection window, however, IM might not have been installed to your server unless you selected it manually. To rectify this, simply go to the Add/Remove Programs utility in the Control Panel, select the Exchange 2000 entry, and then click the Change/Remove button next to this entry to open the Exchange 2000 Installation Wizard, which allows you to add (or remove) components for your Exchange 2000 installation. Remember that you will need the Exchange 2000 Installation CD-ROM to copy the required files.

If you have already installed any Exchange 2000 service packs before adding IM or Chat services to your installation of Exchange 2000, you will be required to reinstall the service pack after installing IM and Chat services.

Before you dive in and set users up with Instant Messaging access, some issues require your attention:

- Microsoft recommends at least one IM home server for every 10,000 concurrent users and the addition of one IM router for every 50,000 concurrent users. However, if your organization's network crosses state or national boundaries, you can increase the number of routers and home servers to maintain performance. In addition, the servers hosting the IM home or routing servers for this many concurrent users should be using at least a dual processor–enabled Pentium II or higher 400-MHz server with a minimum 256 MB of RAM to sustain the user base.

- Determine the number of users taking advantage of the IM service to see whether additional IM servers need to be configured. Depending on the population of each of your Exchange 2000 servers, you might want to install additional IM routing servers on other Windows 2000 servers to improve access for your users.
- If you have a large Exchange organization that spreads over widely dispersed geographic areas, you will likely have slow network connections between sites. If this is the case, Microsoft recommends that your IM configuration closely mimic your SMTP server implementation to give your users the best possible service.
- To provide for more localized management of your IM installation, for every IM server you have installed, you can create a dedicated administrative group with an Exchange administrator.

Developing and deploying large-scale IM implementations requires a lot of planning to make sure they work properly and perform as they should. If you are implementing the IM service only for your local domain, there is less to be concerned about; however, if you are installing IM for your enterprise domain or over widely dispersed geographic areas, there are many more installation considerations. For more information on large-scale planning for IM, perform a search on *http://www.microsoft.com/exchange* for the *Exchange 2000 Server Resource Kit* or Instant Messaging.

IM can be installed without Exchange 2000, as its own component, so it is possible to install an IM server in domains or servers that don't have Exchange 2000 installed. You can even use IM in an organization that has Exchange 5.5 installed without having to upgrade to Exchange 2000. The only requirements for installing IM are that you install it to a version of Windows 2000 Server and that you have AD enabled (which is how it's managed) and IIS 5 installed. If you are using IM with an Exchange 5.5 server, you must have the ADC installed and functioning properly. More information on IM and the ADC can be found on TechNet at *www.microsoft.com/technet*.

After you have considered all the installation issues, you are ready to start configuring your IM service and putting it to use. From a user standpoint, the actual IM client software and the necessary settings on the Exchange 2000 server are all that's required. You will learn how to install the IM service in the "Hands-on Projects" section later in this chapter.

Determining Instant Messaging Naming and Addressing

As with any other type of messaging, be it e-mail or newsgroups, you need two addresses for the flow of messages to work properly: one for the sender and one for the receiver. IM is no exception; however, IM handles addresses a little differently than a standard e-mail system does. Although the user address can be in an e-mail format (for instance, *frankdodger@im.exchange.com*), the address pointing to his or her presence on a server is in a URL format, such as *http://im.exchange.com/instmsg/aliases/frankdodger.* Addresses are handled in this manner because IM is essentially a pared-down Web browser that just "browses" Instant Messaging users. Think of the users you add to your user list as "favorites" so that the concept of how addressing works makes more sense.

More information on naming and preparing DNS for IM duty is covered in the "Selecting Domain Names for Instant Messaging" section, later in this chapter.

Configuring and Managing the Instant Messaging Service

There are three main parts to IM. First is the home server, the main server where your users are managed. Second is a routing server, which, as the name suggests, routes messages between different home servers and their respective users. Third is the actual client software, where the clients maintain their user lists and send and receive instant messages.

It is possible for a home server to act as a routing server. Microsoft recommends that for every two home servers you have installed, you should install a routing server (or a home server acting as a routing server) to support the installation.

In small Exchange 2000 installations with few users actually using IM to send and receive messages, installing a routing server is rarely required unless your servers are far apart geographically, thus dictating routing across different networks. When the time comes to configure and manage your IM implementation, the user account for performing these duties must be a member of both the Domain Admins group (for the domain that hosts the server) and the Exchange Admins group to have the necessary permissions for advanced management duties, such as handling how IM works with firewalls and proxy servers and configuring the IM home and routing servers.

After installing IM and specifying an appropriate user account for configuration and management duties, it's time to install your first IM home server. Open System Manager, and expand the Protocols folder (under the server where you're creating the home server). Right-click the Instant Messenger (RVP) entry, point to New, and then click Instant Messaging Virtual Server to start the New Instant Messaging Virtual Server Wizard. Using this wizard is covered in the "Hands-on Projects" section.

Selecting Domain Names for Instant Messaging

Even if you do not plan to use your IM service across the Internet, you should insert DNS information for your IM server in your domain's DNS records. When naming your IM servers, both home and routing servers, Microsoft recommends that you use the DNS domain name "im" for your Instant Messaging servers. For instance, your home server domain name could be im.calgary.exchange.com, and your routing server could be im.south.calgary.exchange.com. This format maintains a standard naming convention for your network and matches other IM servers on the Internet.

For your IM server to function properly, you need to configure one specific record in DNS. You must create an _rvp SRV resource record, which allows IM users to have the same address for IM and Exchange e-mail and facilitates logons for IM on your local network. You will learn how to create the appropriate DNS record in the "Hands-on Projects" section later in this chapter.

More information and configuration is required to implement DNS for your IM servers, but these topics are beyond the scope of this book. For more information, reference the TechNet Web site at *http://www.microsoft.com/technet* and perform a search for "instant messaging DNS," or look up the TechNet article ID 266643.

Using Instant Messaging with Firewalls

As you learned in "Protocols Used for Instant Messaging," IM works through HTTP port 80 by default. This is a benefit to those networks that have a firewall installed because nearly every single firewall has HTTP port 80 open so that users can properly access Web pages with their Web browsers. Therefore, in nearly every network configuration, there should be little worry about having to configure the firewall to allow instant messages to pass through.

If you need to configure IM to pass through a firewall or a proxy server, you can use the Instant Messaging Settings dialog box to specify the IP addresses that are allowed to pass IM information out through the firewall or proxy server. You will learn about configuring your IM servers in the "Hands-on Projects" section.

Troubleshooting Instant Messaging Problems

As with any computer-related component, undoubtedly the time will come when you must troubleshoot problems with your IM server. One of the most prominent problems is addressing difficulties with users logging on to your IM server. According to Microsoft, the following list explains the three main causes of users failing to log on to your IM servers:

- If you have a proxy server enabled on your network and Internet Explorer is configured to use it, you must set up an excluded address for any home and routing servers you use in the proxy settings for Internet Explorer. This allows authentication requests to pass through the proxy server to the Web site that supports IM.
- If you have a routing server on your network, you must ensure that there is an appropriate SRV record in the DNS server entries for that routing server, and the client software should be configured to log on to the proper DNS domain, where the routing server resides.

- Make sure that the client has a proper IP address on the same network as the server, and ensure that DNS services are running. To verify this, ping the host name (not IP address) of the home and/or routing servers and make sure you get the full host name and IP address back—such as, im.calgary.exchange.com.

In addition, Microsoft provides some tips about more catches that can cause you problems:

- You must allow enough time for replication to take place or force a replication of AD objects and information when you create a new IM virtual server. The domain needs time for the new connection information to spread throughout it; unless the information is replicated, you will probably not be able to connect or log on to your IM server.
- If you have deleted an existing, active IM virtual server and then created a new one, you will have to enable all users who had access to the previous virtual server to have access to the new virtual server before any connections or logons can take place.
- All IM clients must have a password of some type to log on to IM. Blank passwords are not accepted by the IM service.
- If everything has been working correctly, but users complain about a sudden loss of connectivity to the IM service, first check the Web server associated with the IM server. If this server has failed or was stopped for one reason or another, the IM service will not function properly because IM relies on the associated Web server to provide connectivity.

If troubleshooting manually is not getting you very far, you can check the IIS 5 logs to see what errors may be occurring as a result of your problems logging on or using the IM service. If you do not have the Web site performing event logging, enable that feature and then try to connect again so that it can catch the error message about your failure to connect. After you have enabled logging for a few connection attempts, read the log files. The IIS logs are usually in the C:\winnt\system32\logfiles directory unless you have manually set them to be written to another directory. Errors recorded for IM will be displayed as though the user were having a problem connecting to a Web site. You can use the error messages in these log files as a reference when searching for articles on the error code at the Microsoft TechNet site or other sites to find more information on what the error actually relates to.

A commonly seen error message is error 404, which indicates that the IM client failed to contact the DNS server to find the appropriate address for the IM server. If you see this message, you should check whether all the appropriate information has been replicated throughout the domain or double-check your configuration in DNS for the record you created for this server to make sure everything has been entered properly.

Microsoft has supplied the information you need to troubleshoot problems, although you usually have to search for it on the Microsoft Web site. Once you have it, though, you can then identify the problem by using resources such as TechNet or the Knowledge Base.

A Detailed Look at Chat Services

Although e-mail has long provided a solid method of communication and collaboration, it has often lacked the dynamic nature of a conversation, which is why telephones are still used as a primary communication method in most organizations. However, with the advent of improved collaboration options, such as IM and **Internet Relay Chat (IRC)**—a medium where many people can get together in a "room" with other users and chat with text messages in real time—real-time collaboration has taken giant leaps beyond the telephone. As you learned, IM provides a reliable platform for users to get together and exchange text messages and includes some fringe benefits, such as knowing when users are in the office; Exchange 2000 Chat services are very similar, except that they allow more users to chat at the same time in one place. In fact, Exchange 2000 Chat services allow you to have up to 20,000 users all chatting in the same place!

The Chat services in Exchange 2000 use IRCX, an extended version of the IRC protocol, which Microsoft developed to provide increased functionality and additional management commands to help administer your Chat server. When users connect to a Chat server with a client, they connect over TCP port 6667 by default; that setting is typically fine for most installations, but you can adjust it to meet your requirements.

Chat Services Nomenclature

There are various components of Chat services that you should be familiar with before installing and configuring a service:

- *Channels*—Like TV channels, specific areas dedicated for a particular topic or for general use. Two different types of channels can be found on a server: a registered channel and a dynamic channel. The difference is that a registered channel is created by the administrator and is permanent, and a dynamic channel is created by a user and can disappear if not occupied or if the administrator deletes it.
- *Sysop*—A user with the responsibility of monitoring and managing dynamic and registered channels for appropriate usage of the actual Chat client software while connected to the server.
- *Channel operator*—A user who has created a dynamic channel. Similar to a sysop, this user has administrative control over the channel he or she created and can bestow operator status on other users. Channel operators do not have control over any other Exchange Chat service administration (unless permission is granted to them).

The following sections introduce additional terminology you should learn when administering the Exchange 2000 Chat service.

Installing Chat Services

Installing Chat services is exactly like installing IM. If you do not install it during the initial Exchange 2000 installation, follow the steps outlined previously in "Installing the Instant Messaging Service." After you have installed the necessary Exchange components for Chat services, all that is required is creating your first **chat community**; similar to a virtual protocol server, the chat community enables the maintenance and management of different chat channels. You can have several different chat communities, but for most organizations, one community is probably enough.

To create your first chat community, in System Manager, expand the familiar Protocols folder, right-click the IRCX folder, and click Properties on the shortcut menu to open the IRCX Properties dialog box (shown in Figure 11-3).

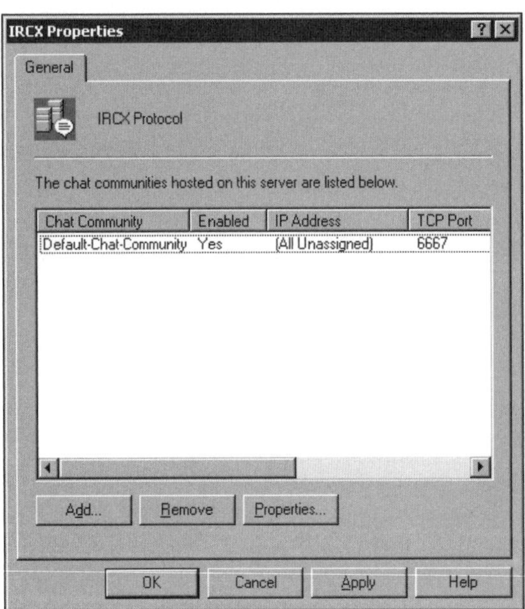

Figure 11-3 The IRCX Properties dialog box for creating a chat community

Your first community, by default, is the Default-Chat-Community, which should be in the Chat Community text box. This is the only community you can create initially (although you can rename it later, if you like). Unlike virtual protocol servers, you do not have to specify a unique IP address for each Chat server hosted on your Exchange server; however, you can select a different one if you want to help separate the Chat services from other Exchange 2000 services. You will learn more about creating chat communities in the "Hands-on Projects" section.

There are some additional configuration options for your Chat server, including adding registered channels, setting connection limits, and specifying the information that users see when they connect to your server. Configuring these options is a straightforward affair, as you will learn in the next section.

Configuring Chat Services

There are several options you can set for your Chat services in Exchange 2000. Among them are options for setting how many users can connect to your servers, specifying the authentication method they will use when they do, and determining the information they can or cannot see when they log on. The following sections outline some of the more pertinent settings you should be aware of when configuring the basic necessities of your Exchange 2000 Chat services and configuring your Chat client software for use with your server.

Creating a New Chat Channel

Each chat community must have at least one channel, which is the main channel for users to converse in. You can even dedicate this channel for helping users who are unfamiliar with using the service, for communicating product information to sales representatives, or for whatever purpose you like. You can create as many channels as you need by using basically the same procedure you used for the first one. Users can also create their own dynamic channels as they see fit, or you can create temporary channels on an as-needed basis for special chat events (for instance, the president of the company addressing shareholders or the public relations manager holding a press conference).

It's easy to create a new channel. After you have your first chat community in place, open the Exchange System Manager console, double-click the Chat Communities folder to show the Default-Chat-Community you first created, and then double-click that entry to show the three folders underneath: Channels, Bans, and Classes. Click the Channels folder, right-click in the Details pane, point to New, and then click Channel on the shortcut menu to open the New Properties dialog box. You will see several tabs with different options, but make sure you are on the General tab to start the process. First, enter a name for this channel, keeping the following guidelines in mind:

- Names must be between 1 and 200 characters with no spaces.
- For regular IRC channels, at the beginning of the name, you must enter a # or an & to signify that it is a regular IRC channel (for example, #helpchannel).
- For IRCX channels (which can be read only by users of IRC clients that support IRCX, such as Microsoft Chat 2.5 or higher), you must enter a % symbol before the name, followed by a # or & to signify an IRCX channel that can be seen only by IRCX clients (for example, %#helpchannel).
- The name should be descriptive enough so that users can determine at a quick glance whether it is the channel they are looking for.

In the Name text box, enter the channel name, using these guidelines. In the Topic text box, enter a name that describes the subject matter or purpose of this channel; once again, make sure you select a descriptive, useful name. The final thing you need to do in this tab is to enable the option for creating the channel when the service starts. This option re-creates the channel every time the Chat service is started, thus making it a "permanent" channel. If you want to create a temporary channel, leave this option unchecked. After configuring the options in this tab, your window should look similar to Figure 11-4.

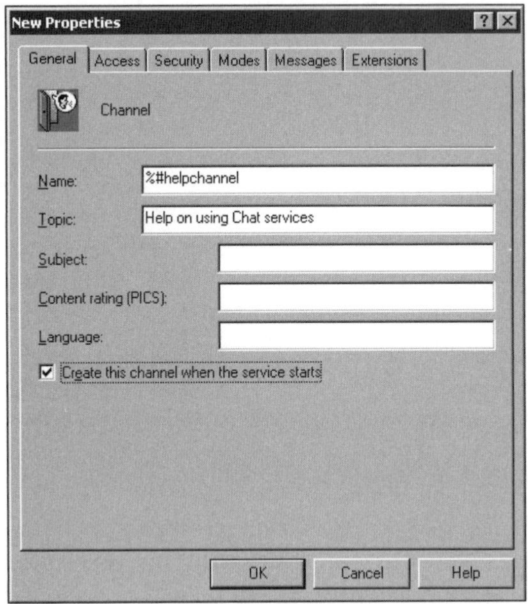

Figure 11-4 Configuring a new channel in the New Properties dialog box

In the Topic text box, you do not have to follow the same naming guidelines used for the Name text box, other than making the name descriptive. You can also use spaces in this topic description.

In the Access tab, you can specify whether the channel appears to users as accessible, set passwords for the channel, and limit the number of users who can join this channel. In addition to these options, you can also specify whether you will allow access to anyone who wants to connect to the server or will restrict access to just those users who were invited or have been authenticated by the server. For instance, you can use the Chat server to host chats for users connecting from the Internet. This option is useful if you have employees who travel or work from home who want to use this service, or if you host discussions with customers in a weekly Q&A forum, for example. To enable this option, click the Visibility to users list arrow and make sure the Public option is selected so that all users can use this channel. (It's the default option, so it should already be selected.) You can then click OK to create this channel, or select the other tabs to set the options outlined in the following list:

- *Security*—Allows you to specify which users in your AD domain can connect to the channel; the default option is Everyone.
- *Modes*—Allows you to set various channel options, such as indicating which users can post messages to the channel and determining the rights that sysops and channel operators should have in the channel.
- *Messages*—Allows you to set a welcome and good-bye message for users connecting to the channel. This message can give details on conduct while in the channel (if any) or any other special message you want your users to see. For instance, you might want to post the times IT staff members inhabit the channel to provide support for users of the Chat services.
- *Extensions*—Allows you to specify whether you want a profanity filter (to filter out bad language) or whether you want to enable Channel Transcription, which allows you to log the conversations in that channel. This option, described in more detail in the following section, can be useful for keeping records of business meetings, catching illicit activities or conversations, or even supplying chat logs to users who couldn't attend a particular chat so that they can read the details of the event (quite common in computer gaming circles).

None of these options needs to be set for your channel to function, but as you can see, some options can be quite useful. For more detailed information or assistance on any of the options in these tabs, simply click the Help button.

Enabling Transcription for a Chat Channel

Enabling transcription for all or selected channels can be very useful. Inevitably, you will get complaints about something that went on in the channel, or someone will want to know what was said so that the information isn't lost for all time; the best way to make sure you can handle these situations is to enable transcription for the channel.

Enabling transcription for any or all channels on your Chat service can cause a noticeable performance degradation on heavily used Chat servers because the server is recording every line entered in the channel. This requires CPU cycles and hard drive activity to perform, which can affect your server's performance in general. In addition, transcription can take up a lot of hard drive space, so you should monitor and manage the transcription logs to make sure disk usage doesn't get out of hand.

To enable transcription, you must first add the transcription extension "TScript" to the IRCX server. To do that, click the Extensions button in the Properties dialog box for the chat community, as shown in Figure 11-5.

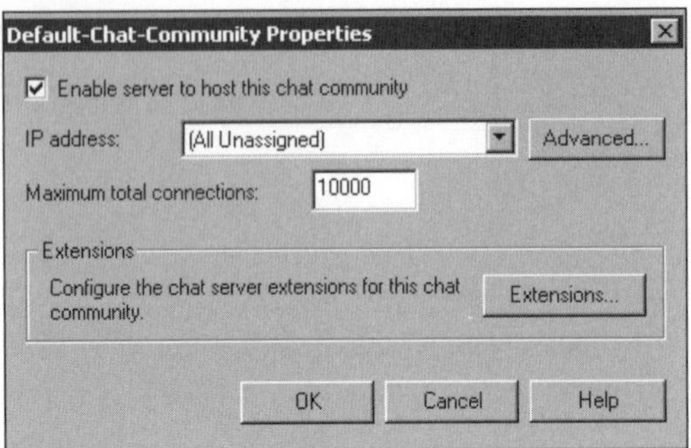

Figure 11-5 Configuring transcription extensions

Figure 11-6 shows the Extensions dialog box, where you add extensions to this IRCX server.

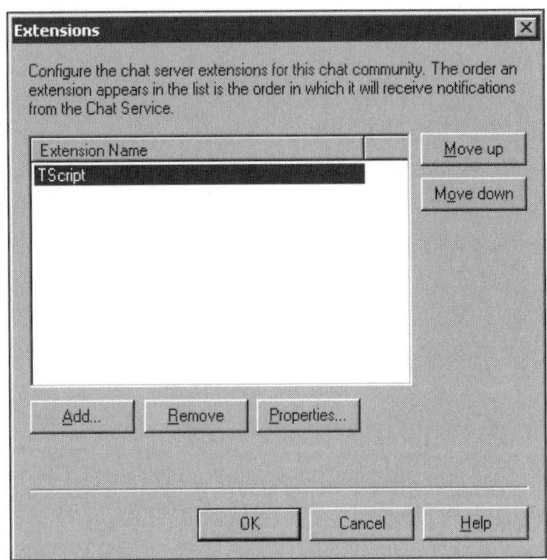

Figure 11-6 The Extensions dialog box for enabling channel transcription

For more information on the exact steps to add extensions, click the Help button in the Extensions tab of the channel's Properties dialog box to reference the Exchange Help system. If the transcription extension has been installed, all you need to do is install the extension for the Chat channel and enable it. To do so, return to the Properties dialog box for the channel where you want transcription enabled (refer to the "Creating a New Chat Channel" section if you need a reminder). Click the Extensions tab, click the TScript entry in the Extensions text box, and then click the Properties button to open the properties for this script. There is only one option in this window; click the Transcribe this channel check box to enable it, and then click OK. You have now enabled transcription; any files transcribed from the channels will be automatically saved to a folder named after the channel (one of the reasons you can't have special characters in the channel name). The transcription file is a simple text file that can be opened in Notepad or WordPad.

Because you might want to transcribe only certain conversations or events in the channel, Microsoft provides a command that can be used in the command line to start and stop transcription in the channel. The syntax looks like this:

```
Extmsg tscript start name=channelname
```

For the *channelname* in the command line, substitute the name of the channel you want to transcribe. To stop transcription for this channel, simply substitute "stop" for "start" in the command line. Using this command line could prove more useful than setting options in the Properties dialog box, especially if transcribing chats is only an occasional requirement for your Chat services.

Configuring the Chat Client Software

As with any of the virtual protocol servers or the IM server, you must have a client software package configured for use with your Chat services. The most likely candidate for use with your IRCX-enabled channels is Microsoft Chat. (Exchange 2000 requires Chat 2.1 or higher.) If you are using only standard IRC channels without support for the Microsoft extensions, any commonly available IRC client does the trick. In this section, you will focus on the current version of Microsoft Chat; at the time of this writing, it's version 2.5. Microsoft Chat (or Comic Chat, as it is sometimes referred to) is not included on the Exchange 2000 installation CD-ROM, and it's rather cumbersome to find on the Microsoft Web site; however, you can download it as a freeware product from any number of software download sites, such as *www.tucows.com*. Simply enter a search for Microsoft Chat or Comic Chat, and you should see the most current version available for download.

11

After you have the chat software downloaded, installation is like that for any other Windows software product: Double-click the icon for the file you downloaded, follow the onscreen prompts, and select all the defaults until the installation process is finished. To open the program, click Start, Programs, Microsoft Chat. The Chat Connection window has two tabs. The Connect tab is where you set options for the server you will use to chat with, and the Personal Info tab is where you set user information, including name, nickname, e-mail address, and other useful information, as shown in Figure 11-7.

In the Connect tab, enter the IP address specified for your Chat server in the Server text box. If you like, you can also set the client to automatically open a particular channel upon connection by clicking the Go to chat room radio button, as shown in Figure 11-8, or you can have the client show the available channels it can connect to.

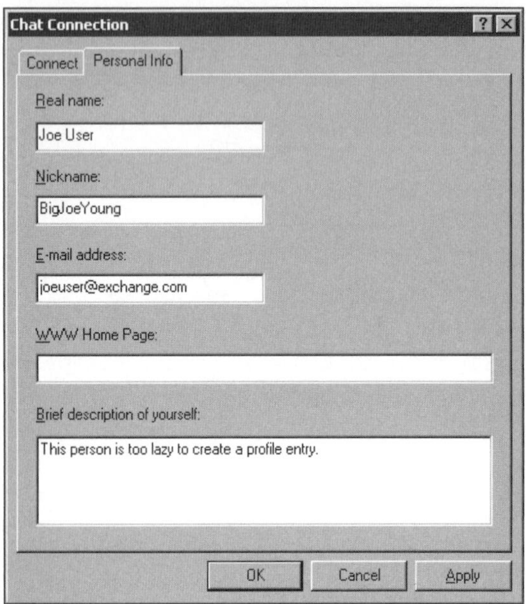

Figure 11-7 The Personal Info tab in the Chat Connection window

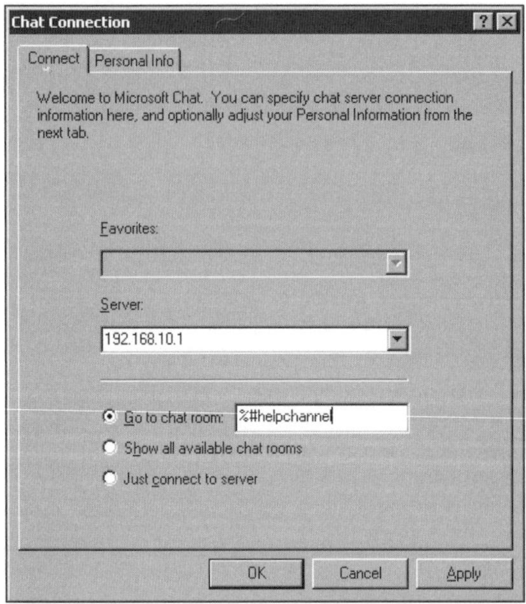

Figure 11-8 The Connect tab in the Chat Connection window

If you have a DNS entry installed for this server and DNS is enabled in the IRCX properties, you can enter a domain name for this server, although an IP address works just as well.

After setting these options, you are ready to start using your Chat client by clicking OK in the Connect tab to connect to the server. The default view is the standard Plain Text view that looks like any typical IRC chat program. To change this mode to the Comic Strip view, click View on the menu bar and then click Comic Strip. Figure 11-9 shows an example of the Comic Strip view and some of the options for backgrounds, avatars (the character you appear as in the comic strip), and text to indicate thoughts, actions, or speech.

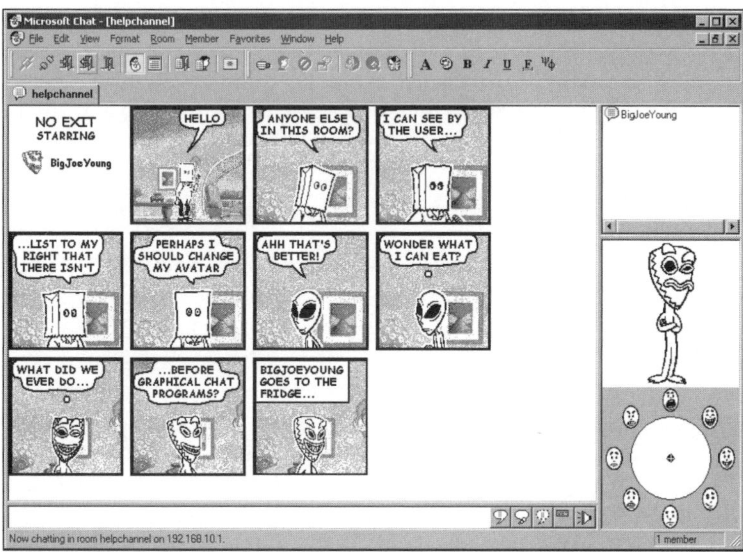

Figure 11-9 Comic Strip view in Microsoft Chat 2.5

Figure 11-10 shows the same conversation in Plain Text view.

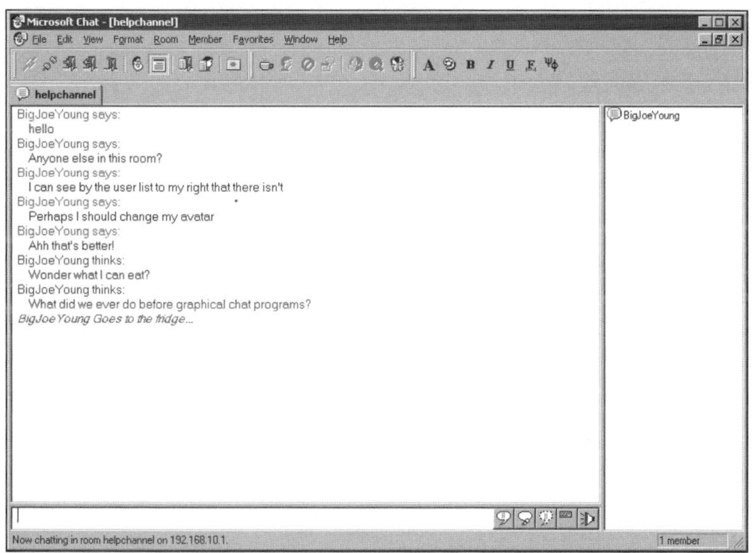

Figure 11-10 The same Microsoft Chat conversation shown in the default Plain Text view

Users can customize many features and options in this client. As you can see, the Microsoft Chat client software can be useful and entertaining at the same time (a rarity these days, it seems).

Troubleshooting Chat Services

Unlike IM, you don't need to be aware of many potential issues for troubleshooting Chat services. The IRCX server in Exchange is either started or stopped. If it's stopped, users cannot connect to or use the service at all. To verify whether it has been stopped because of failure or for another reason, right-click the IRCX folder in System Manager and see if Stop is grayed out in the shortcut menu. If it is, click the Start button to restart the server. Viewing the Windows event logs sometimes provides information on why the Chat services stopped; you can then look up any additional information about the error on Microsoft TechNet.

One particular concern for Chat services is attack from outside users (if the service is available from the Internet). Table 11-1 outlines a multitude of different attacks that can be leveled against an IRC (Chat) server.

Table 11-1 Attacks on Chat Servers

Attack	Cause	Prevention
Flood Attacks	Attacker sends a deluge of information to the server, including logon requests, fake pings, and random erroneous data. Very similar to a denial-of-service attack on a Web server.	Ensure that the Windows 2000 server is completely patched with the latest service packs and hot fixes. For attacks that flood a channel or server with messages, you can set a message delay. The server pauses before accepting the next message from the same user so that a series of messages can't be sent faster than the server can handle them.
Clone Attacks	Attacker initiates many connections to the Chat server from the same IP address. After being connected with these accounts, the attacker sends messages from the same system, potentially causing a flood attack. At a minimum, if the attacker logs on enough, he or she can hit the server's logon limit, thus preventing new users from logging on.	Limit the number of simultaneous connections from one IP address. This option applies only to regular Chat service users, not sysop or administrative accounts.

Table 11-1 Attacks on Chat Servers (continued)

Attack	Cause	Prevention
Client Attacks	If attackers know the IP address of another user connected to the Chat service, they can launch a flood attack directly at the client system, potentially crashing the client software or even the computer.	Enable the IP/DNS masking feature in the Chat service to defend against this type of attack. With this feature enabled, attackers cannot see the entire IP address or DNS information for other users. Sysops and administrators can still see this information, however.

Other problems can crop up with the Chat service on your Exchange 2000 server; however, most of the time, problems are simply a case of users not being able to log on or attacks from the outside world. Do not be surprised if you end up needing a full-time Chat administrator to handle the sysop, administration, and configuration duties on your Chat server. You will probably need one if the service is accessed by a lot of people, and even more so if the service is connected to the Internet and allows any user to log on (which may or may not be a wise choice). In fact, if you do decide to implement Internet connectivity, you might want to consider setting up a dedicated IP address and chat community just for that purpose, leaving your internal Chat service separate.

A Detailed Look at the Exchange 2000 Conferencing Server

The Exchange 2000 Conferencing Server is a completely separate component of Exchange 2000. In fact, there is no way to install it during a regular Exchange 2000 installation. The Exchange 2000 Conferencing Server must be installed with its own installation program; it can even be installed to a server without Exchange 2000 previously installed, as long as there is one Exchange 2000 server somewhere on the domain. As mentioned previously, the Conferencing Server offers both Data and Video (with audio) Conferencing and collaboration using a standard client, NetMeeting. In addition to these two collaboration tools, the Conferencing Server can incorporate advanced Exchange 2000 scheduling abilities through Outlook 2000 to integrate scheduling of meetings and other events on the Conferencing server. This feature helps tie all the related Microsoft products together and enables easier, more efficient meeting and event management.

Each feature of the Conferencing Server has benefits that make it useful for collaboration. These are the more notable benefits of the Data Conferencing features:

- *Application sharing*—This feature allows users to connect to a program and work on the same document while others watch, comment, or pitch in. For instance, the Accounting Department gets together and works on the yearly budget spreadsheet in Excel to make sure they are all on the same page, as each employee adds his or her own information.

- *Chat*—This feature is similar to Instant Messaging, in that it's a simple, clean, text-only interface that enables users to make comments while collaborating on documents.
- *Whiteboard*—This feature allows users to draw diagrams, organizational charts, and such on a virtual whiteboard, much as they would in a boardroom. Everyone looking at the whiteboard sees all the information as it is entered. For instance, the Sales Department could post a picture of a product and ask people in the Engineering Department to enter comments about various features right on the picture for all to see.
- *File transfers*—This feature allows all users to have the same documents that everyone else is viewing or using. You can also send other files that are not in use, much as you would in e-mail. For instance, you could send files that you know other users will need to reference later in the collaboration session after you have finished working on the current document.

The Video Conferencing feature also has benefits that make it a useful addition to the Exchange 2000 Conferencing Server. Besides being able to use this feature like a videophone to communicate face to face with another user, you can use it to make presentations to several people at once. The next best thing to actually being there, a possible application could be watching your presentation on a system with a projector or large TV so that everyone can see it and discuss the presentation with you.

This technology is continually changing, and although the Conferencing Server features represent some of the best Microsoft has to offer, there can be some limitations, especially for slower network connections. Possible problems include poor video and audio quality or sudden drops in the video and audio output that cut off part of the communication or make it difficult to see or hear. With each new revision of NetMeeting and improvements to Web cams and Internet connections, these problems are becoming less of an issue, making this feature of the Conferencing Server much more useful.

The last major feature, scheduling, is handled by the Conference Management Service. With this service, you can organize and effectively plan meetings and keep track of conferences that use the Exchange 2000 Conferencing Server. Outlook 2000/2002 users can simply click a scheduled meeting to bring them right to the appropriate meeting point for the collaboration or conference. Both users and administrators can schedule meetings with the Conferencing Server by using Outlook 2000/2002, which makes using this feature quick and easy.

Installing the Exchange 2000 Conferencing Server

The Exchange 2000 Conferencing Server is a separate installable product that must be purchased at extra cost in addition to Exchange 2000 Server. It gives administrators the freedom to install just the Conferencing Server where needed without the additional configuration tasks of installing more Exchange 2000 servers.

Installing the Conferencing Server is much like installing Microsoft Office or any other Microsoft software. You certainly don't need nearly the amount of preparation or number of steps required for installing Exchange 2000 Server, which is why the decision to keep the product separate, with its own installation process, is beneficial for administrators and users alike. To install the Conferencing Server, follow these steps.

1. After starting the setup for the Conferencing Server from the Installation CD-ROM, you are greeted with the Installation Wizard's Welcome window.
2. Click the Next button to proceed to the License Agreement window, click the I agree radio button, and then click the Next button.
3. In the CD-KEY window, enter the appropriate key for your product in the CD-KEY text box. Click Next to continue to the Setup Type window.
4. The Complete option installs all the Conferencing Server features and is probably the option you want to select; if you want to customize the installation or if you like to see exactly what you're installing, click the Custom radio button and then click the Next button. The next window is the Custom Setup window, as shown in Figure 11-11. As you can see, it looks very similar to most Microsoft programs, especially the installation for Microsoft Office 2000.

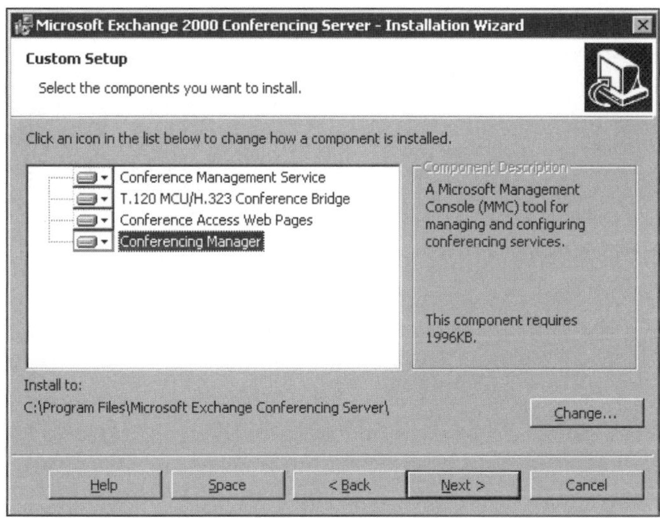

Figure 11-11 The Custom Setup window for Exchange 2000 Conferencing Server

5. After confirming your installation choices, click the Next button to proceed to the Administrative Group window, where you select which administrative group will manage this installation. If you have only one administrative group enabled, you use the default option; if you have another administrative group you want to install to, click the list arrow and select the group you want.

6. Click the Next button to continue to the Ready to Install the Program window, where the installation gives you one last chance to go back and change options before installing the software. Click the Install button to get the ball rolling.
7. In the progress window, you can watch the installation progress until it's finished. When you see the Installation Wizard Complete window, click the Finish button to complete the installation.

The configuration, usage, and architecture of the Conferencing Server is outside the realm of this book and could very well constitute a book of its own. For more information on Conferencing Server, visit Microsoft TechNet and perform a search for Exchange 2000 Conferencing Server Datasheet. You can also check the information at this site: *http://www.microsoft.com/Exchange/techinfo/conferencing/default.asp*.

The Future of Collaboration

Exchange 2000 has raised the bar on the collaboration features and options that users can take advantage of. With the proliferation of faster network connections, such as fiber-optic and high-speed copper networks, around the world, collaboration has only one way to go—up. These improvements in network performance and the drop in prices for the high-quality hardware required to get the most out of data and video conferencing have helped increase the popularity of this feature, but don't expect any major earth-shattering improvements in this area for the foreseeable future.

In addition, you probably won't see any major advancements in text messaging; the field and its feature sets are pretty much fleshed out because it has been around in one form or another for many, many years. The only improvements left in this area are those that enhance cross-product interactions, which, given current conditions, could be a long way off.

Collaboration appears to be continuing to develop in a steady path, with an expected increase in usage of these features—the only tangible goal to date.

Chapter Summary

- Exchange 2000 offers a wide selection of user collaboration features, including Instant Messaging for instantaneous text messaging between users and text-based or graphical chats for discussions between two to thousands of users.
- Instant Messaging in Exchange 2000 allows for quick and easy messaging between IM users and provides additional benefits, including the ability to better determine the availability of other users based on their IM status and the ability to use the IM client both on local networks with other Exchange 2000 users and on the Internet with other IM servers.
- Instant Messaging uses the rendezvous protocol (RVP) to perform its communication between IM servers, other IM servers, and IM clients. RVP communicates over

HTTP port 80, allowing it to work through most firewall and proxy installations without any additional configuration or effort in changing settings on the firewall or proxy servers.

- IM requires DNS configuration to work properly on your local network; DNS configuration is also necessary if you decide to connect your IM service to the Internet so that users can communicate with other IM servers.
- Any problems with users logging on to the IM service can likely be traced back to a problem with the DNS configuration or operation. To save some time, check DNS configuration before delving into more troubleshooting. If the DNS configuration is correct, view the IIS 5 logs for the Web server that supports that particular IM server.
- The Exchange 2000 Chat services enable administrators to create their own IRC servers, complete with a Plain Text chat view and a Comic Strip view that adds a more personal touch to the chat experience. Chat services allow you to have large-scale conversations, meetings, and discussions with people all over the world in one place, and offer the ability for users to chat privately or in a group setting.
- When troubleshooting Chat services, little can go wrong with the service itself. Typically, if users cannot connect to the server, the Chat server has been stopped. Other than that, the biggest risk to a Chat server is attacks coming from the Internet, which can vary from annoying to debilitating. Protecting against these attacks is usually easy, requiring only a few simple changes to options in the Chat services.
- The Exchange 2000 Conferencing Server is installed as a separate product from the main Exchange 2000 installation. These advanced conferencing features allow users to collaborate in real time on the same document. In addition, the Exchange 2000 Conferencing Server offers the ability to chat and hold conferences with both video and audio, adding a more personal and high-tech flavor to your conferencing.

Key Terms

chat community — A virtual chat server that you can configure with the appropriate settings for that server. Under each chat community, you can create channels where users can chat on certain topics, or allow users to create their own topics.

Instant Messaging (IM) — A service through which users can exchange text messages in real time in your Exchange organization or with other IM servers on the Internet.

Internet Relay Chat (IRC) — A service that enables many people to connect to a server so that they can join channels with other users and chat with text messages in real time.

rendezvous protocol (RVP) — The extension to WebDAV protocol that works over HTTP port 80. RVP allows Instant Messaging to provide advanced features and functionality, including the ability to view the connection and availability status of other IM users.

Review Questions

1. The primary difference between Instant Messaging and e-mail is that IM users can send and receive text messages ______________.
2. In the following list of benefits, which one is not offered by Instant Messaging?
   a. reducing long-distance phone bills
   b. enabling users to determine the presence of other users they need to chat with
   c. allowing text chat with a conversation that looks like a comic strip
   d. providing a convenient, compact message interface for real-time messaging
3. Which of the following protocols is used by Instant Messaging and is an extension of the WebDAV protocol?
   a. NNTP
   b. RVP
   c. RCP
   d. CHAT
4. The Instant Messaging feature that allows users to determine when other users are online, connected, busy, out of the office, and so on is called the ______________ option.
5. Which port does IM use by default to communicate with other servers and users?
   a. HTTP port 800
   b. WebDAV port 80
   c. UDP port 80
   d. HTTP port 80
6. Describe the main benefit of IM when using the protocol and port configuration in Question 5.
7. A major drawback to using IM, especially over networks like the Internet, is that the text communications are unencrypted, and therefore open to being intercepted and read. True or False?
8. When designing your Instant Messaging implementation, Microsoft recommends that your IM setup mimic your ______________ implementation.
9. If you want to improve your Instant Messaging performance in a network that covers a wide geographic area and has slow network connections, which IM component should you install?
10. When designing your Instant Messaging implementation, what is the recommended ratio of users to IM home servers?
    a. one home server for every 10,000 users
    b. one home server for every 100,000 users

c. one home server for every 1500 users

d. one home server for every 15,000 users

11. According to Microsoft, what is the recommended ratio of users to IM routing servers?

a. one routing server for every 5000 users

b. one routing server for every 10,000 users

c. one routing server for every 15,000 users

d. one routing server for every 50,000 users

12. If you have the number of users mentioned in the correct answers for Questions 10 and 11, what are the Microsoft-recommended hardware requirements?

13. Instant Messaging cannot be installed to a particular server without Exchange 2000 being installed to that server first. True or False?

14. If you want to install Instant Messaging in an existing Exchange 5.5 domain, the two requirements are having the ________________ installed and Windows 2000 Server with AD enabled.

15. Describe the difference between addressing for an IM server and an e-mail server.

16. For Instant Messaging services to function properly once installed, you must have which service functioning and configured correctly?

a. Active Directory Connector (ADC)

b. Exchange 2000 Server

c. Domain Name System (DNS)

d. Hypertext Transfer Protocol (HTTP)

17. The most common error you see when users cannot log on to your IM server is the ________________ error code, which usually indicates that ________________ is not configured or functioning properly.

18. What is the name of the special protocol that Microsoft developed for its Chat service?

a. IRC

b. IRCX

c. CHAT

d. RVPX

19. If a user creates a channel on your Chat server, what type of channel is it?

a. registered

b. temporary

c. user

d. dynamic

20. How many channels are required for each chat community before users can start using the server?
    a. one
    b. none
    c. two
    d. one for each user
21. To create channels that support the extended Microsoft functionality for Chat servers, you have to add a ____________ symbol before the channel name.
22. Which of the following tabs in the Properties dialog box for a Chat channel is used to enable transcription for that channel?
    a. Security
    b. Modes
    c. Messages
    d. Extensions
23. To use the Chat service in Exchange 2000, you must have at least version ____________ of the Microsoft Chat software.
24. Which of the following attacks against a Chat server involves using up all available connections so that other users cannot connect?
    a. clone attack
    b. denial of Service
    c. flood attack
    d. client attack
25. The Exchange 2000 Conferencing Server feature that enables users to make notes and modifications on a common, shared image is called the ____________.

Hands-on Projects

If you have Instant Messaging already installed as part of your Exchange 2000 installation, you can start using it as soon as you create your first home server, set up DNS for the server, and then populate it with users. Creating your first home server is easy to do, and adding subsequent home and routing servers will be just as easy. By understanding how home servers are created, you can implement your IM service quickly and expand it in the future if needed. Project 11-1 forms the basis for every project that follows it in this chapter. In fact, it's recommended that you perform each project in order because the projects build on each other as you progress.

Project 11-1

This project requires a standard server with Windows 2000 Server with DNS services installed, Exchange 2000 Server installed and functioning with the Instant Messaging component installed, and Exchange administrator access to the server.

To install the first Instant Messaging home server:

1. Log on to your system using an account with Exchange administrative privileges.
2. To open the Exchange System Manager console, click **Start**, point to **Programs**, point to **Microsoft Exchange**, and then click **System Manager**.
3. Double-click **Servers**, double-click ***Server Name***, and then double-click **Protocols**. (If you have the display of administrative groups enabled, you might need to double-click Administrative Groups, and then First Administrative Group before you see the Servers folder.) Right-click the **Instant Messaging (RVP)** folder, point to **New**, and then click **Instant Messaging Virtual Server** on the shortcut menu to start the New Instant Messaging Virtual Server Wizard.
4. In the wizard's welcome window, click the **Next** button to proceed to the Enter Display Name window. For this project, type **Home Server** in the Display Name text box, and then click the **Next** button to proceed to the Choose IIS Web Site window.
5. In the Choose IIS Web Site window, you must select which IIS Web site will host your IM server. If all you have is the Default Web Site, then it is the only option displayed in the IIS Web Sites list box. If you have other sites, you can select them here if you have a particular preference (for instance, if you have a site that you want dedicated for OWA only). After making your selection, click the **Next** button to proceed to the Domain Name window.
6. Type the server's full domain name in the Domain Name text box (use the server name supplied by your instructor), and then click the **Next** button to continue to the Instant Messaging Home Server window.
7. The Instant Messaging Home Server window is where you specify whether this IM server will be a home server or a regular routing server. If you wanted a routing server, you would leave the Allow this server to host user accounts check box unchecked. For this project, however, you are setting up a home server, so click the **Allow this server to host user accounts** check box, as shown in Figure 11-12, and then click the **Next** button to proceed to the final step.

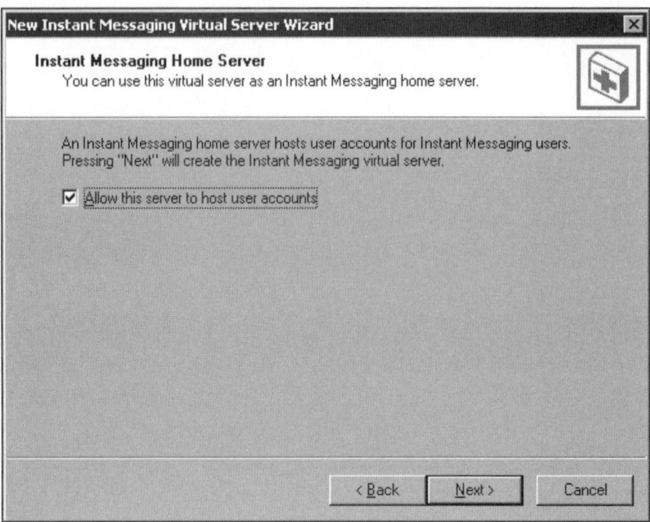

Figure 11-12 Setting up an IM home server in the New Instant Messaging Virtual Server Wizard

8. In the Completing the Virtual Server Wizard window; click the **Finish** button to complete the wizard and finish creating your first Instant Messaging home server.
9. Close any open windows, return to the Windows desktop, and leave the system at that state for the next project.

Project 11-2

The next step in your installation of Instant Messaging for your Exchange organization is to create the necessary DNS entries. If you do not create the proper DNS record, your users cannot authenticate with the IM server, and IM will fail to function correctly. The overall process is straightforward, especially if you have configured an entry in DNS before. This project assumes that you have completed Project 11-1.

To configure DNS for Instant Messaging:

1. Log on to your system using an account with Exchange administrative privileges. If you are continuing from Project 11-1, you can skip this step.
2. To open the DNS console, click **Start**, point to **Programs**, point to **Administrative Tools**, and then click **DNS**. Locate the DNS server you have configured previously for your AD domain. Double-click this entry, and then double-click the **Forward Lookup Zone** folder to show the entries underneath it.
3. Right-click the entry for your domain, and then click **Other New Records** on the shortcut menu to open the Resource Record Type dialog box. This dialog box has two sections: the Select a resource record type list and a text box underneath that describes the resource record you have selected. Scroll down the resource record type list, and click the **Service Location** option, as shown in Figure 11-13. Then click the **Create Record** button.

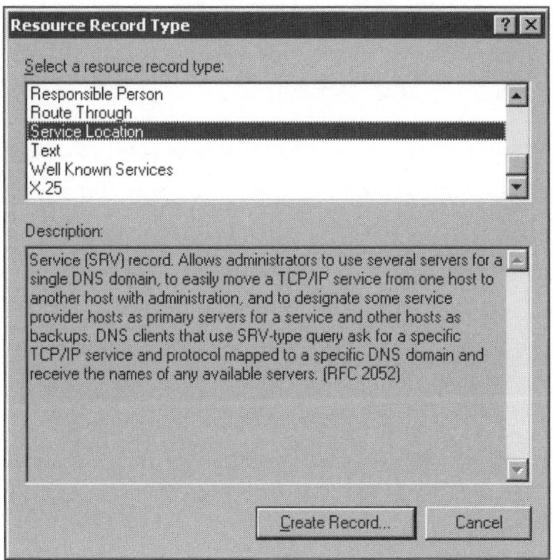

Figure 11-13 Selecting the DNS service location in the Resource Record Type dialog box

4. In the New Resource Record dialog box, there are several different text boxes and list boxes. In the Service list box, delete the default entry, and then type **_rvp**. In the Port number text box, delete the default entry, and then type **80**, as shown in Figure 11-14.

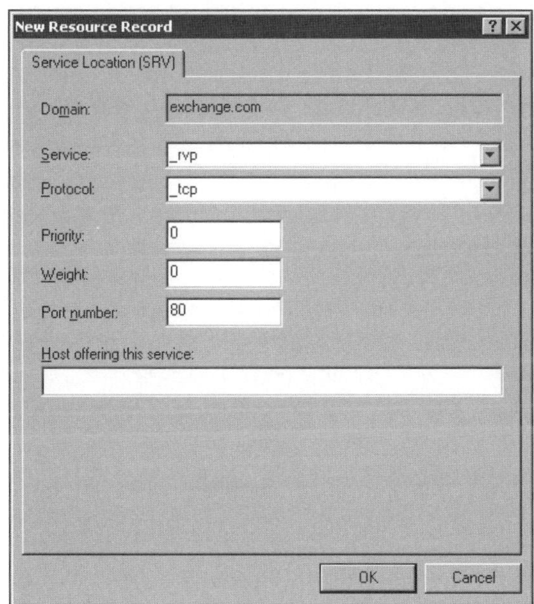

Figure 11-14 An example of the DNS resource record settings required for Instant Messaging

5. Click **OK** to finish creating your new DNS entry. Click **Done** in the Resource Record Type dialog box. Close the DNS console and return to the Windows desktop for Project 11-3.

As you learned earlier in this chapter, it can take several minutes for the DNS changes you made to replicate throughout the domain, so you should wait a few minutes before proceeding to the next project.

Project 11-3

You have created your first Instant Messaging home server, configured the necessary DNS entries, and allowed them to replicate throughout the domain; you are now ready to start setting up users for Instant Messaging. Then you can install the Instant Messaging client software and allow users to start sending messages. This project assumes that you have completed Projects 11-1 and 11-2.

To enable Instant Messaging for existing Exchange 2000 users:

1. Log on to your system using an account with Exchange administrative privileges. If you are continuing from Project 11-2, you can skip this step.
2. To open the Active Directory Users and Computers console, click **Start**, point to **Programs**, point to **Administrative Tools**, and then click **Active Directory Users and Computers**. Remember that you can also use the shortcut found under the Microsoft Exchange menu.
3. Navigate to and click the **Users** folder under your domain. In the Details pane, locate the Administrator account you are logged on as. Right-click the entry for the Administrator account, and then click **Exchange Tasks** on the shortcut menu to open the Exchange Task Wizard. In the Welcome window, click the **Next** button.
4. In the Select task to perform section of the Available Tasks window, click the **Enable Instant Messaging** radio button, and then click the **Next** button to proceed to the Enable Instant Messaging window. The Instant Messaging Domain Name text box should already have the default domain address for your IM server entered; if not, you should double-check your DNS configuration for IM or cancel the wizard and wait a bit longer for the DNS information to be replicated. Click the **Browse** button next to the Instant Messaging Home Server text box to open the Select Instant Messaging Server dialog box. In the Server Name field at the bottom, click **Home Server** (the server you created in Project 11-1), and then click **OK**.
5. In the Enable Instant Messaging window, your configuration should look similar to Figure 11-15. Click the **Next** button to proceed to the Completing the Exchange Task Wizard window, which shows a summary of the settings you configured during the wizard, and then click the **Finish** button to complete the wizard.

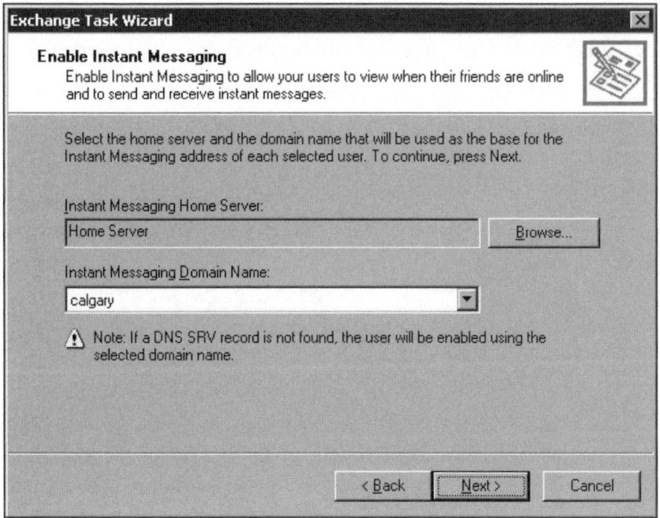

Figure 11-15 Enabling Instant Messaging in the Exchange Task Wizard

6. You have now enabled your first user to use Instant Messaging; feel free to enable additional users using the same steps. After you have finished, close any open windows, return to the Windows desktop, and leave the system in this state for Project 11-4.

Project 11-4

After you have finally completed all the necessary configuration on your Exchange 2000 server for your Instant Messaging service, you can start connecting users to it by using the MSN Messenger client software. This project shows you how to configure users to connect to and use your Exchange IM server, which is slightly different from the typical method you might be familiar with—connecting to the Internet. This project assumes that you have completed Projects 11-1, 11-2, and 11-3 and requires that MSN Messenger version 2.2 be installed. If you would like to use a higher version, you can install version 3.5 from the CD for the Exchange 2000 Service Pack 1. However, the steps for this project might be slightly different.

To connect a user to your IM server:

1. Log on to your system using an account with Exchange administrator privileges. If you left the system at the desktop from Project 11-3, you can skip this step.
2. To open MSN Messenger, click **Start**, point to **Programs**, and then click **MSN Messenger Service**. The Welcome to MSN Messenger Service! Window appears; click the **Next** button to proceed with the wizard.
3. The Provide Microsoft Exchange Instant Messaging information window opens. Click the **Use this program to talk to my Microsoft Exchange contacts** check box to configure the client to communicate with your Exchange server by default, instead of

the usual Internet connectivity. In the E-mail address text box, type the e-mail address for the user you have enabled IM for (for instance, *administrator@exchange.com*).

4. The Get a free Passport window opens, where you can create a Passport that is used with MSN Messenger to connect to IM servers on the Internet. Because you are not connecting to the Internet in this project, click the **Use Exchange Instant Messaging only** check box, and then click the **Next** button.
5. The Setup is now complete window appears; click the **Finish** button to complete the wizard and log on to the IM server. If everything has been configured properly in the previous projects, you should see the MSN Messenger Service client software and your contact list of users with no users in it. If you can't log on properly and the client says you do not have the authorization to log on, the problem likely is caused by one of two things: The DNS configuration is wrong or the information has not been replicated to the domain yet, or you are not logged on as the user you entered as the account for logging on to IM with. If this is the case, log off and log back on again with the appropriate user account, or enable the user account you are using for IM and try again. If you have logged on with no problems, click the **Add** button to open the Add a Contact Wizard.
6. In the first window of the Add a Contact Wizard, you select how you want to add the new contact. Click the **By e-mail address** radio button, and then click the **Next** button. In the next window, type the e-mail address for another IM-enabled user on your server or for the account you are currently logged on as in the text box provided. Click the **Next** button to proceed to the final window, where you see a message stating that your addition was successful. Click the **Finish** button to complete the wizard. (If you want to add another user, you can click the **Next** button to restart the wizard.)
7. You should now see your contact in the contact list of your client software, so you will be able to start sending messages and using IM. Close any open windows or applications, and return to the Windows desktop. Leave the system in this state for Project 11-5.

Project 11-5

Before your users can start using the Chat service on your Exchange 2000 server, you must first create a chat community (a Chat server) that holds the channels. Creating a chat community is very much like creating any other virtual protocol server, except that you will not be configuring a protocol. You can create more than one chat community if needed; understanding how they are created helps when you have to expand your Chat service. This project requires a standard server with Windows 2000 Server installed, Exchange 2000 Server installed and functioning with the Chat component installed, and Exchange administrator access to the server. Before you begin this project, the instructor should delete the default Chat server so that there's no existing chat community.

To create your first chat community:

1. Log on to your system using an account with Exchange administrative privileges. If you are continuing from Project 11-4, you can skip this step.

2. To open the Exchange System Manager console, click **Start**, point to **Programs**, point to **Microsoft Exchange**, and then click **System Manager**.
3. Under your Exchange server, right-click the **Chat Communities** folder, point to **New**, and then click **Chat Community** on the shortcut menu to open the New Properties dialog box. (If you have the display of administrative groups enabled, you might need to double-click Administrative Groups, and then First Administrative Group before you see the Chat Communities folder.) In the Name text box, type the name **Chat** for this community, and then click **OK** to finish creating the new chat community and return to the System Manager console.
4. In System Manager, right-click the **IRCX** entry under the Protocols folder, and then click **Properties** on the shortcut menu to open the IRCX Properties dialog box. Click the **Add** button to open the Add Community dialog box. In this dialog box, click the list arrow, click **Chat (First Administrative Group)** in the options list, and then click **OK**.
5. The Chat Properties dialog box opens. Click the **Enable server to host this chat community** check box, and then click **OK** to return to the IRCX Properties dialog box. Your Chat server should now be listed in the list of communities.
6. Close the IRCX Properties dialog box by clicking **OK**, and then close the System Manager console to return to the Windows desktop. Leave the system at this state for Project 11-6.

Project 11-6

After you have created your chat community, you must make at least one channel for that community for the Chat service to work. You can create as many as you like for your purposes, but for this project, you will create the first one necessary for operation of the Chat service. This project assumes that you have completed Project 11-5.

To create your first Chat channel:

1. Log on to your system using an account with Exchange administrative privileges. If you are continuing from Project 11-5, you can skip Steps 1–2.
2. To open the Exchange System Manager console, click **Start**, point to **Programs**, point to **Microsoft Exchange**, and then click **System Manager**.
3. Under your Exchange server, double-click the **Chat Communities** folder to show the communities hosted by the server (that should be the Chat server you created in Project 11-5). Double click the **Chat** folder to show the three folders underneath: Channels, Bans, and Classes. Right-click the **Channels** folder, point to **New**, and then click **Channel** to open the New Properties dialog box.
4. In the Name text box, type the name for this channel. For this project, type the name **%#main_channel**. In the Topic text box, type the topic of this particular channel. For this channel, type **Default Chat Channel**.
5. The rest of the text boxes are optional, but you must select one other option in the General tab. Click the **Create this channel when the service starts** check box (this forces the server to re-create this channel every time the server is

restarted, making the channel permanent), and then click **OK** to finish creating your first channel.

6. Close the System Manager console, and return to the Windows desktop. Leave the system in this state for Project 11-7.

Project 11-7

After you have created your chat community and created at least one channel for your users, you can allow users to connect to and start using your Chat service. You will probably use the Microsoft Chat 2.5 client, which is freely available from a number of different software archives on the Internet. Installing the software is very easy, so it is not covered in this project, but you will learn how to configure the initial server settings in the client to connect to your Chat server. This project assumes that you have completed Projects 11-5 and 11-6 and that you have Microsoft Chat 2.5 or higher installed on the server.

To configure the Microsoft Chat client to connect to your chat community:

1. Log on to your system using an account with Exchange administrative privileges. If you are continuing from Project 11-6, you can skip this step.
2. To open the Microsoft Chat 2.5 client, click **Start**, point to **Programs**, and then click **Microsoft Chat**. The Chat Connection dialog box opens to the Connect tab. In the Server text box, type the IP address for this server. (The local IP address of 127.0.0.1 will work if you are using the Chat client on the same server that is hosting the chat community.)
3. Click the **Show all available chat rooms** radio button. A window opens showing the different channels you can connect to, which is useful if your users don't know the exact spelling for the channel they want. Click **OK**.
4. The Message of the Day window opens. In the middle of this window you'll see the statistics for this server, including number of connected users, channels, and so on. This window can also hold any messages you care to enter in the properties for this chat community. Click **OK** to continue.
5. The Chat Room List window opens with a list of the available channels that the user can see (remember that you can configure channels to be hidden from certain users or to everyone). You can also use this window to perform advanced search functions, including topic searches, through the list of channels. In addition, you can create a dynamic channel by clicking the Create Room button. For this project, click the **Main_Channel** entry, shown in Figure 11-16, and click the **Join Room** button.

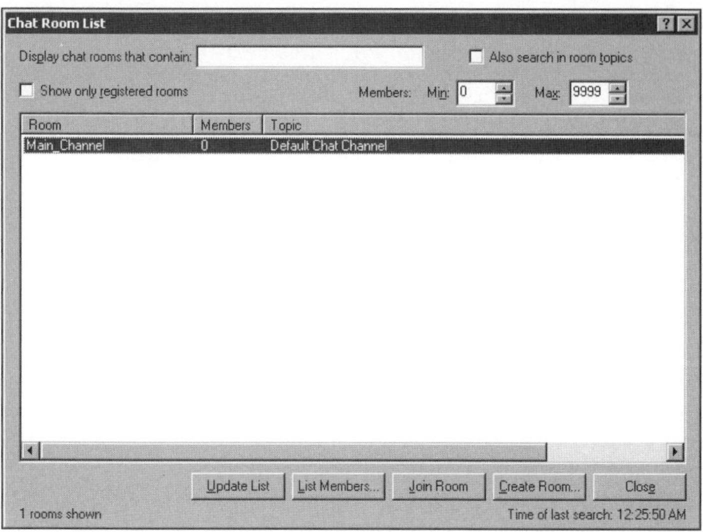

Figure 11-16 Selecting a channel in the Chat Room List window

6. You have now logged on to your chat channel and can send text messages. Feel free to have other users connect to your server (if they are on the same network) and to your chat channel. After you have finished experimenting, close Microsoft Chat, and return to the Windows desktop. Leave the system in this state for Project 11-8.

Project 11-8

Like any other object in Active Directory, each user has an address on the network. IM-enabled users are no different, except that they have additional address information that other users do not have. This project shows you how to view this information, which helps you troubleshoot your IM server and pinpoint the user's location on the server to assist in troubleshooting any problems with that particular user. This project assumes that you have completed Projects 11-1, 11-2, and 11-3.

To view Instant Messaging address information for an enabled user:

1. Log on to your system using an account with Exchange administrative privileges.
2. To open the Active Directory Users and Computers console, click **Start**, point to **Programs**, point to **Administrative Tools**, and then click **Active Directory Users and Computers**.
3. Navigate to and click the **Users** folder under your domain. In the Details pane, locate the user that you enabled Instant Messaging for in Project 11-3. Right-click the user, and then click **Properties** on the shortcut menu.
4. In the user's Properties dialog box, click the **Exchange Features** tab. In the Features list in the middle of this tab, you will see Instant Messaging and the

Status set to Enabled. If not, you should use another account that is enabled. Click the **Instant Messaging** entry, and then click the **Properties** button.

5. In the Instant Messaging dialog box, there are three different text boxes that you cannot modify. Each text box contains IM address information about the user and should look similar to Figure 11-17. Click **OK** to return to the Properties dialog box.

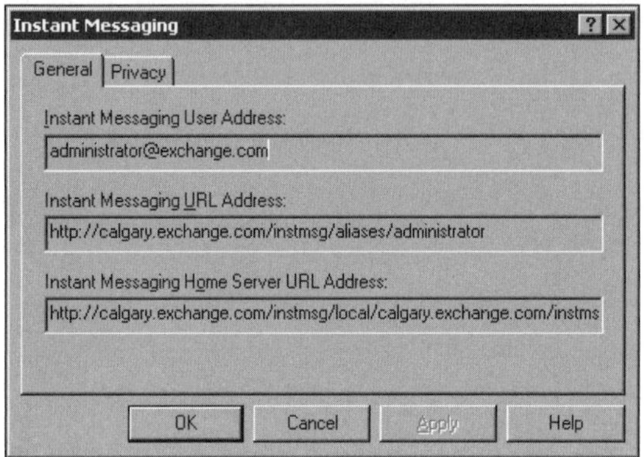

Figure 11-17 Address information for an IM-enabled user

6. Close the Properties dialog box, and then close the Active Directory Users and Computers console. Close any open windows or applications.

Case Projects

Case Projects Background

Charging Bull Inc. is an interior decorating company with locations all over North America. Each branch office has about 5000 employees in a variety of departments, including Sales, Accounting, Research, Clerical, Management, and Marketing. Branch offices are located in Calgary, Vancouver, Seattle, Los Angeles, Las Vegas, Phoenix, Austin, St. Louis, and Toronto. The head office in Philadelphia at last count had 12,000 employees, including the workers in Manufacturing, who each have access to a computer and e-mail to communicate with the Research, Clerical, and Management Departments. Each branch office has a fully optimized Exchange 2000 hardware configuration with server clustering and more than enough hardware for future expansion. Charging Bull currently runs Exchange 2000 Server with Exchange 2000 Service Pack 1 installed.

Charging Bull has had an established Exchange 2000 organization for some time and has been enjoying the features and integration with Active Directory. It now wants to take advantage of the collaboration features to increase user productivity.

Case 1

Charging Bull has heard about the Exchange 2000 collaboration features and has asked you to recommend and implement the services it needs. Charging Bull wants to hold regular open forum discussions and focus groups with its customers in a contained, moderated environment so that these customers can comment on new products. Previously, the only way to do this was to hold several costly focus group meetings in various locations and gather the data. Which Exchange 2000 collaboration service would you recommend implementing for this strategy, and how could Charging Bull retain the conversations from the open forum discussions and focus groups for later use?

Case 2

Many members of the Accounting Department have been complaining that because of viruses being spread through e-mail, they are getting deluged with junk mail and having other mail-related problems. These problems are slowing down productivity and responses to e-mail messages, and they want a faster way to communicate with each other when working on a large budget spreadsheet. When they were using the telephone to consult with other branch offices, their department manager forced them to stop using it for this type of work because the long-distance bills were too high. Which Exchange 2000 feature could you install to address their concerns and needs and to reduce the overall cost of communication for employees in this department?

Case 3

Charging Bull has decided to implement Instant Messaging for the entire company. You have been given the task of figuring out how many IM home and routing servers are needed. Charging Bull wants a worst-case scenario, assuming that employees will use IM frequently. Based on the user information in the background information, sketch out a basic IM infrastructure, listing where home servers should be placed and how many routing servers are needed. In addition, indicate good locations for these routing servers.

Case 4

You have finished discussing Charging Bull's needs and have decided to implement the components and configurations discussed in the three previous case projects. When you start implementing your recommendations, you realize that when the Exchange 2000 servers were installed, the components you need weren't installed. What will you have to do to get the components installed and ready to use?

CHAPTER

12

SECURITY AND ENCRYPTION IN EXCHANGE 2000 SERVER

After reading this chapter and completing the exercises, you will be able to:

- Understand security issues that relate directly to Exchange 2000 Server, including auditing, access control, Public Key Infrastructure, encryption, and certificate services
- Explain how the Key Management Services of Exchange 2000 function as a security measure for your servers, including how keys are managed, how public and private keys work, and how encryption is used
- Understand how to solve common security problems in Exchange 2000, including using user-issued keys for authentication
- Understand how firewall technology can affect your Exchange 2000 server and how to use your firewall and virtual protocol servers to control access to your network
- Understand advanced Exchange 2000 security issues, including Internet security, Exchange exploits, and use of security bulletins, and identify Exchange 2000 attacks that hackers might try to use against your servers

In Chapter 11, "Configuring Real-Time Collaboration in Exchange 2000 Server," you learned about the user collaboration features that Exchange 2000 Server offers, including Instant Messaging and Chat services. You also learned how these useful services enable instantaneous communication between your users and can be used to provide additional customer service. You also learned how the Exchange 2000 Conferencing Server can provide state-of-the-art video and audio communications and enable multiple users to simultaneously collaborate on a document in real time.

In this chapter, you learn the basics of security and Exchange 2000, with information on auditing Exchange 2000 and applying different methods of heightened security, such as key management or various levels of encryption used during authentication. In addition, you learn what to look for when troubleshooting your Exchange 2000 security implementation and see how firewall technologies can improve security (or sometimes cause problems) for your Exchange 2000 server. Finally, you learn about advanced Exchange 2000 security issues, such as encryption, hackers, and Internet use.

INTRODUCTION TO SECURITY ISSUES IN EXCHANGE 2000

In most organizations concerned with security, so much attention can be focused on securing network equipment, such as routers and firewalls, and ensuring that security policies are created and followed, that administrators don't take enough time to secure their Exchange 2000 servers. The plain truth is that securing your Exchange 2000 servers is critical for the following reasons, which some administrators might simply overlook:

- Exchange 2000 servers typically contain sensitive e-mail, such as company documents and other information, that could be useful to hackers.
- Exchange 2000 servers that are not properly secured can enable hackers or an e-mail spammer (a person who sends out unsolicited e-mails) to route messages through your Exchange 2000 server without your knowledge.
- If hackers intrude into an Exchange 2000 server or even capture a user account with Exchange 2000 access, they might manage to gain access to more secure accounts that could provide access to high-security areas of your network.

Exchange 2000 security is an important issue that goes beyond keeping hackers off your network or spammers from routing messages through your server. Not having the proper security could also cause downtime if a hacker manages to intrude into or attack your Exchange 2000 server and bring it down. As you have learned, most organizations find any amount of downtime unacceptable, especially when it pertains to e-mail access. Because of this, you should spend some time securing your Exchange 2000 server. Throughout this chapter, you will discover different features you can take advantage of to improve the security of Exchange 2000.

Auditing and Logging Exchange 2000 Server

A major security faux pas is not keeping accurate logs of activities on your servers *and* for services such as Web, newsgroup, OWA, and FTP servers. By keeping accurate logs with utilities such as the Windows EventViewer and enabling access logging in IIS-related services, you can monitor servers and services for unusual activity, catch problems before they start, or use the logged information to catch or stop an intruder. In addition, you can use this logged information to perform a **security audit**, in which you check the current security configuration for Exchange 2000 regularly to make sure it's up to date and nothing has happened to hamper security measures on your Exchange 2000 servers and services.

By default, Windows 2000 logs events and errors in software and services, including Exchange 2000, IIS, or the OS itself. However, it isn't until you start applying security policies on your domain and your Windows 2000 servers that you start gathering useful security-related information, such as failed access to objects in the domain, changes to the applied security policies, or modifications to user rights. By logging this information, you can best assess when possible attacks or questionable activities by hackers or even other staff members are taking place. Obviously, if Windows 2000 logs activity related to security policies and rights at 2 a.m. on a Saturday, and the IT staff isn't in at that hour, this event probably warrants more investigation on your part.

After you have determined a baseline for security by logging events, assessed your security needs and requirements, and then implemented your security through security policies, you can audit your Exchange 2000 servers. Unfortunately, as of this writing, there's no way to quickly and easily audit security on your Exchange 2000 servers. Any kind of auditing has to be done manually by inspecting your servers' configuration and activity and then comparing this data with your predefined security requirements. These comparisons are best accomplished with **security checklists**, documents that allow you to follow a set path and record information about components and settings for your servers (or network) that help you assess the current security status. Here is a sample pared-back security checklist for Windows 2000 and IIS 5:

Server Configuration

- Computer name: ______________________________
- Installed by: ______________________________
- Date installed: ______________________________
- Computer make/model: ______________________________
- Processor(s) make and speed: ______________________________
- Installed system RAM: ______________________________
- Network card(s): ______________________________
- Partitions formatted with NTFS? Yes or No: ______________________________
- Current Windows 2000 service pack installed: ______________________________
- Current hot fixes installed (Windows 2000): ______________________________
- Current hot fixes installed (IIS 5): ______________________________

- Telnet access disabled? Yes or No: ______________________
- Special notes about TCP services: ______________________

Unneeded Services Log—Determine whether services are running

- FTP Publishing: Yes ______ No ______
- NNTP Service: Yes ______ No ______
- SMTP Service: Yes ______ No ______
- Content Index: Yes ______ No ______
- Certificate Authority: Yes ______ No ______
- RPC Locator: Yes ______ No ______
- Server Service: Yes ______ No ______
- Routing and Remote Access Services: Yes ______ No ______
- Alerter: Yes ______ No ______
- NT Scheduler Service: Yes ______ No ______
- Computer Browser: Yes ______ No ______
- DHCP Client: Yes ______ No ______
- Instant Messaging: Yes ______ No ______
- Net Logon: Yes ______ No ______
- Network DDE: Yes ______ No ______
- Network Monitor Agent: Yes ______ No ______
- Simple TCP/IP Services: Yes ______ No ______
- NetBIOS Interface: Yes ______ No ______
- WINS Client (TCP/IP): Yes ______ No ______
- NWLink NetBIOS: Yes ______ No ______
- NWLink IPX/SPX: Yes ______ No ______

System Network Configuration

- IP addresses: ______________________
- Subnet address: ______________________
- Gateway address: ______________________
- DNS server: Yes ______ No ______
- DHCP server: Yes ______ No ______

- WINS server: Yes ________ No ________
- NAT server: Yes ________ No ________

Other notes about this server: ____

____

Using a security checklist, modified to include information targeted at Exchange 2000, can be handy for auditing the security of your Exchange 2000 servers and configurations. This kind of activity should be done on a regular basis; the schedule varies based on the organization's security requirements, but at least every six months is a good rule of thumb. You should use the sample checklist or a similar one to check the configuration of your Windows 2000 servers, including IIS services, which provide much of the OWA and other background services for Exchange 2000, and then use a modified version of the sample checklist to focus on Exchange 2000 issues, such as authentication, encryption, and Public Key Encryption—if you are using these features in your Exchange 2000 organization.

The key to effective auditing and logging of your Exchange 2000 servers is having a plan in place and carrying it out regularly. It's not enough to check your security situation and configuration only once in a while, given today's fast-changing and volatile environment of computer and network security—your security needs can change, so make sure you review and adjust them as needed.

Controlling Access to Exchange 2000 Server

As with overall network security, you do not want to provide access to every area of your Exchange 2000 organization, given the possibilities of hackers or other employees intruding into sensitive network areas by accident or on purpose. The best way to prevent these intrusions is to set the appropriate access rights to sensitive areas of your network.

Because Exchange 2000 is so tightly integrated with Windows 2000 and AD, you can take advantage of their inherent security features and capabilities to provide security for Exchange 2000. The core features and capabilities that Exchange 2000 can take advantage of include:

- *Active Directory integration*—The tightly woven integration between Exchange 2000 and AD allows you to use AD groups and rights management to assign rights for Exchange 2000 objects and features. In addition, this integration provides a unified directory to manage rights for users, objects, and data across the entire domain.
- *Kerberos authentication*—This new Windows 2000 feature provides more secure authentication methods for users connecting to Windows 2000 servers and for different Exchange 2000 services, such as OWA or SMTP e-mail.
- *Access control*—This flexible yet precise method of handling object security (working hand-in-hand with AD) enables you to provide high security for Exchange 2000 as well as Windows 2000.

- *Microsoft Certificate Services*—This security feature uses certificates to verify users' and servers' authenticity. Although not used as often with Exchange 2000, the services can still be used to help secure IM and Web services such as OWA.

Windows 2000 offers additional security features that do not directly influence security in Exchange 2000, but do provide better overall data and network security. These features include **IP Security (IPSec)**, which can provide network data security using encryption, the **Encrypting File System (EFS)** for encrypted file and data security, and the Security Configuration Analyzer, which is used to check your Windows 2000 security against preconfigured security policies on the domain.

Although detailed coverage of access control is beyond the scope of this chapter, in the following sections you will look at some different methods of securing authentication on your servers and network to give Exchange 2000 an extra level of security.

Public Key Infrastructure

Among the numerous Windows 2000 security improvements and features is Public Key Infrastructure (PKI). Basically, PKI uses the Key Management Services to configure both a public key and private key. When one system (for example, a server) communicates with another system, the systems exchange keys to see whether they match so that communications can proceed. PKI has several components that are used together to provide a more effective method of secure communications, including certificate services, digital certificates, certificate policies, Microsoft CryptoAPI, and certificate stores. You will learn about the ins and outs of each of these components in the upcoming sections on public and private keys and certificate services.

Public/Private Keys and Encryption

Encryption is both a valuable security feature and a misunderstood one. Many people think encryption is used to constantly secure communications between two systems; however, it's typically used to secure authentication methods between two systems and secure data, such as e-mail or files. To understand how encryption works with public and private keys, first you need to know how keys are used in a PKI configuration.

Two different types of keys can be used in a key exchange system like PKI: symmetric and asymmetric. **Symmetric keys** are encryption keys used between two systems for encrypting and decrypting data; both systems communicating with symmetric keys exchange the exact same key. This method, as you can imagine, is not that secure, given the possibility of a hacker intercepting a key and then using it to pretend to be a system with the appropriate key and access.

With **asymmetric keys**, two entirely different keys are exchanged (often called a "key pair"), one a public key and the other a private key. In an asymmetric key configuration (which is what Exchange 2000 uses), the public key is usually kept in an accessible place, such as a public folder or network share. The private key is typically not published, and it should be secured so that only its owner or administrator has access to it. When a key exchange takes place with an asymmetric pair, either the public key or the private key can encrypt (lock) or decrypt (unlock) the data, but only one can be used to perform either task. For instance, if a file is encrypted with the private key, only the public key can decrypt that file, and vice versa. When Exchange 2000 and Windows 2000 use asymmetric key exchange, the public key performs the encryption and the private key is used to decrypt the data. This arrangement offers the best overall security as long as you keep the private key as secure as possible and don't transfer it unsecured over a network medium, such as the Internet, where it could be intercepted.

Asymmetric keys are much easier to use with Exchange 2000 because you can give the public key to as many users as you want. They will never be able to decrypt data with that key; they can only encrypt with it. To help ensure that the sender is in fact the actual sender and the recipient is the actual recipient, you can use your public or private keys to sign the message. Receivers can then compare this signature (your key) with the key they have a record of, thereby verifying that this message did come from you (assuming, of course, that your system and key haven't become compromised).

Use Table 12-1 to clarify when private and public keys are used in Exchange 2000 with an asymmetric key pair.

Table 12-1 Exchange 2000 Asymmetric Key Usage

Action	Key Used	Message Signatures (Authenticity)
Send message	Sender uses public key to encrypt the message	Sender uses private signature key to write signature
Receive message	Recipient uses private key to decrypt the message	Recipient uses public signature key to open the sender's signature

Now that you have a basic grasp of how PKI works, you can start to make sense of how different methods of encryption work. Several different standards, methods, and strengths of encryption are currently available, and some are more popular than others for various reasons, including ease of use and compatibility. You will learn more about some of the popular encryption standards later in the "Advanced Security Issues" section of this chapter; for now, take a quick look at how encryption works and the common methods of encryption used to secure data and authentication.

Encryption is the process of applying a key (public or private) to a piece of information (for instance, an e-mail, a text file, or an authentication process), thus scrambling the information in the e-mail, text file, or authentication by using a mathematical formula. It is this mathematical formula that forms the core of the encryption method. You have likely seen the term **encryption strength** (sometimes called cipher strength) referred to in bits (for instance, 128-bit encryption). The encryption strength determines how difficult it is to crack the encryption keys. Only so many different keys can be generated for an encryption method, depending on its mathematical strength. The following list gives some examples of how many keys are possible for different encryption strengths:

- 8-bit key (very weak) = 256 possible keys
- 56-bit key (average strength) = 72,057,594,037,927,936 possible keys
- 128-bit key (very strong) = 3.4 × 10 to the 38th power possible keys

Based on current decrypting hardware, it would take an attack on 128-bit strength encryption by one system well over 10,819,926,705,615,920,821 years to break the key—unless, of course, the attacker had the mathematical algorithm used to create the encryption. Two important notes on 128-bit encryption: (1) It's been broken before using many powerful computers simultaneously, so it's not perfect. (2) The higher your encryption strength, the more resources attacking servers will need to effectively crack it. Given the performance increases in hardware these days, the impact on 128-bit encryption will be minimal, however.

Now that you have an idea what encryption does and what encryption strength means, take a look at the following list that shows some of the more common types of encryption standards:

- *CAST*—Short for "Carlisle Adams and Stafford Tavares," CAST is a 64-bit symmetric encryption method that encrypts a block, instead of a byte, of data at a time. It supports between 40-bit and 128-bit encryption keys.
- *DES*—Short for "Data Encryption Standard," this 64-bit symmetric encryption method encrypts blocks of data at a time, similarly to CAST, and is the most widely used encryption method today. It was developed by IBM for government use and uses 56-bit keys.
- *3DES*—Short for "Triple Data Encryption Standard," this encryption method is similar to DES, except that it encrypts the data three separate times.
- *MD2*—Short for "Message Digest," this 128-bit hash encryption method was developed by RSA (Rivest, Shamir, and Adleman). The hash algorithm produces a jumble of characters and numbers very similar to a standard encryption key.
- *MD4 and MD5*—These updated versions successively improve on the MD2 encryption method.
- *RC2*—Short for "Rivest's Cipher," RC2 is another RSA encryption method that uses a 64-bit symmetric key and processes a block of data at a time, as CAST and DES do.
- *RC4*—An update to the RC2 cipher, RC4 processes a byte, instead of a block, of data at a time. This encryption method can use variable-length encryption keys. The Microsoft version uses 40-bit or 128-bit keys.

- *RSA*—Another RSA encryption standard, RSA uses asymmetric encryption (public/private key).
- *SHA*—Short for "Secure Hash Algorithm," SHA uses a hash-type key like the MD encryption standards, except that it generates a 160-bit hash. This method is more secure, but slower than the others listed here.

As you can see, you'll encounter quite a few different types of encryption in your travels, and there are even more when you include the ones created by encryption enthusiasts and the government/military standards, which are supposed to be even stronger than those that are widely available.

Certificate Services

Although PKI can be a great boon to your network security, it has its shortcomings. The possibilities of keys being leaked, encryption being broken, or someone impersonating a server you are exchanging keys with are reason enough to suggest that PKI might not be the most solid, reliable security implementation for your Exchange 2000 organization. To improve on or add to PKI is a good idea; this is where certificate services comes in.

In Windows 2000, a **certificate authority (CA)** provides and manages certificate services. A CA is included in Windows 2000 (external, third-party CAs are also available), and administrators can issue and manage digital certificates for users wanting to connect securely to Windows 2000 (and Exchange 2000) services. AD supplies all the necessary information for the CA to issue certificates and control access. CAs require the following information:

- User and account names
- Group memberships
- Certificate templates (if any)
- Information on every CA installed in the domain

Digital certificates are very similar to an encryption key in that they present the information in a certificate format, showing that the identity of the person or server you are connecting to has been verified. Digital certificates were considered the utmost guarantee that the connection you had was with a legitimate host, until someone managed to obtain forged digital certificates for Microsoft. Presumably, these forged certificates could be used to falsely indicate to connecting users that the server was a legitimate Microsoft server and then potentially gain the users' trust and information. So, as with almost any other form of security, there can be security holes in digital signatures; therefore, it is always good to practice caution when using them.

Nearly every standard digital certificate issued by a CA (Windows 2000 or otherwise) conforms to the X.509 standard, which includes the following information in each certificate:

- Serial number of the certificate
- Version number
- Name of the person the certificate is issued to
- Expiration date of the certificate
- Public key information
- Issuer of the certificate's unique ID number
- Digital signature of the CA that issued the certificate

In Windows 2000, digital certificates don't try to carry the brunt of security on their own. The CA not only issues a digital certificate when required, but also sets a public/private key at the same time, providing two levels of security for users connecting to your services.

Issuing Certificates

When the CA issues a certificate (and keys), it signs each certificate with its private key to guarantee the certificate's validity because Windows 2000 can compare the public key to the private key to determine whether they match. Users could have multiple certificates from different CAs. In fact, by default, Web browsers include a few certificates of their own, which enables them to confirm certificates and provide secure connections to Web services such as OWA.

Most applications that make use of digital certificates have a way to manage them. For instance, in a Web browser, you can delete old certificates that aren't in use or have expired after a set period.

The task of issuing certificates falls on the CA, which has two ways of issuing them. The first way is manually, by having the certificate requests queue up in the CA manager as the administrator approves or denies them one at a time. The second way is automatically through the policy module. When a CA is set to manage certificate requests, it makes use of the policy module integrated within the CA and any available certificate templates. The policy module helps the CA determine whether the request should be automatically approved, automatically denied, or left for the administrator to decide. To perform its approval/denial procedure, the policy module references information in AD or external databases with user information to approve or deny the certificate request.

Another method of generating certificates is using certificate templates through the CA. CAs can issue different types of certificates based on templates that incorporate the security attributes you need. For example, these certificates can specify what the user is authorized to access, the encryption standards and strengths to use, and the certificate's life span. You can select from many different certificate templates, each geared toward a particular user or function. Some of these certificate types are described in Table 12-2.

Table 12-2 A Selection of Available Certificate Templates

Type of Certificate	Purpose
Administrator	Used for authenticating clients and for EFS
Authenticated Session	Used for authenticating clients
Basic EFS	Used for EFS functions
Computer	Used for authenticating clients and servers
Domain Controller	Used for authenticating domain controllers
EFS Recovery Agent	Used only for EFS recoveries of lost keys or data
Exchange Enrollment Agent (offline request)	Used by Exchange administrators who are requesting certificates for secure mail users
Exchange Signature Only (offline request)	Used by Exchange administrators who are obtaining certificates on behalf of secure mail users; used only for providing certificate signing of messages, not message encryption
Exchange User (offline request)	Used by the Exchange server for client authentication and secure mail (both message signing and message encryption)
IPSec	Used by Windows 2000 for IPSec authentication
User	Used for client authentication, use of services such as EFS, message signing, and message encryption
Web Server (offline request)	Used for authentication with a Web server

Generating and issuing certificates are tasks which are too complex to be outlined in this book, but this information should give you a starting point on how to issue certificates. For more information on how Windows 2000 handles certificate services, take a look at this Web site: *http://www.microsoft.com/WINDOWS2000/techinfo/reskit/en/Distrib/dsch_key_tnjk.htm*. In the "Hands-on Projects" section, you will learn how to manage certificate services with Exchange 2000.

Digest Authentication for Instant Messaging

As you learned in Chapter 11, Instant Messaging in Exchange 2000 uses the rendezvous protocol (RVP). RVP does not require users to authenticate directly with a home server. They can use two different methods of authentication: **Windows Integrated authentication (WIA)**, which is the default configuration that authenticates users based on the user account and password used for logging on to the domain, and Digest authentication, in which the systems that are communicating with each other share a private piece of information, such as a password. The difference is that the Digest authentication information passed between the systems is encrypted with keys that help keep the authentication information safe.

Although the WIA method is typically acceptable for most users who are connected to the same domain or physical network as the IM servers, users who are connecting from external messaging systems, such as UNIX or Macintosh systems, should use Digest authentication to ensure that they do not pass authentication information in clear text for anyone to capture and possibly exploit.

Certificate Trust Lists

Certificate services can provide a more direct approach to limiting access by unauthorized users. After you have PKI and a CA on your network, you can use a certificate trust list to specify which issuing CA your servers will trust. For instance, you can have a certificate trust configured to trust any certificates issued by VeriSign (a common issuer of certificates used on the Internet) and another trust configured to trust any certificates issued by your organization's business partners. Based on the certificates in the trust list, anyone connecting with a certificate from a listed CA issuer will be granted access; those with certificates from an issuing CA not in the trust list will be denied access. A brief but helpful article on creating and modifying certificate trust lists can be found at *http://www.microsoft.com/windows2000/en/advanced/iis/default.asp?url=/WINDOWS2000/en/advanced/iis/htm/core/iicarsc.htm*. You will learn how to find and manage certificate trust lists in the "Hands-on Projects" section of this chapter.

Overview of Key Management Services

Key Management Services (KMS) is a security tool included in Exchange 2000 that helps provide message and data security by using message encryption and digital signatures. KMS is not installed by default; however, you can install it during the initial Exchange 2000 installation or later. KMS provides a centralized service that mates Exchange 2000 with Windows 2000 certificate services to provide a PKI for Exchange 2000.

The Basics of Key Management Services Architecture

KMS can be thought of as the central hub between Exchange 2000 Server, Active Directory, and Windows 2000 certificate services. For KMS to function as it should, each of the main KMS components is required. KMS installs its own **Certificate Services Policy (CSP)**, which is similar to the certificate templates previously discussed in the "Certificate Services" section. This CSP stores users' private keys in the embedded Extensible Storage Engine (ESE) database, which is a central place for KMS to manage and keep track of private keys. The ESE serves two purposes. First, it allows you to keep all keys in one central place, making it easier to manage and encrypt keys. Second, it enables you to have a private key for every user in case an employee or an outside source (for example, the government) needs access to an encrypted message; you can then get the private key required for this access.

When a user requests a secure connection using the Key Management Services, KMS forwards the request to the certificate services on behalf of the user, as illustrated in Figure 12-1. Every certificate generated by the certificate services has the CA's certificate embedded within the user's certificate, which allows other users to automatically trust each other because they were all issued certificates from the same certificate authority. To help administer these KMS functions, when KMS is installed, it integrates with AD much as Exchange 2000 does by adding a Security tab to a user's Properties dialog box. By using this new tab, administrators have direct control over users' KMS status and can enroll users in KMS, revoke their privileges, and recover their key pairs (private or public) on an individual, as-needed basis.

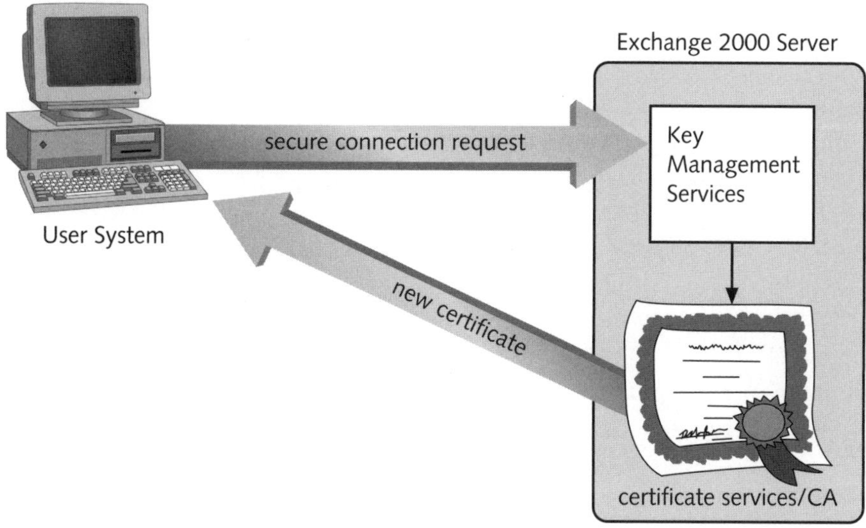

Figure 12-1 The user certificate request process

Although the different KMS components—including AD, the Certificate Services Policy, and Windows 2000 certificate services—all perform important functions in a KMS implementation, the real workhorse of the KMS is the actual client. The client system is in charge of the following important duties:

- Generating the signing key pair
- Storing users' keys
- Referencing Active Directory for other users' certificate information
- Encrypting and decrypting messages

To help keep the entire KMS architecture as secure as possible, one crucial task is performed not by the client system, but by the ESE working through the CSP: generating and storing users' encryption key pairs. This helps the KMS retain its security integrity, while taking some of the workload of client duties off the server. If you had thousands of users using KMS and all client duties were performed by the server, the server would have to be a supercomputer or buckle under the load.

Overview of Installing Key Management Services

Installing KMS can be an complex process because there are so many different subcomponents that make it all work. Before installing KMS, you must have at least one Windows 2000 server installed in the same domain as your Exchange 2000 organization. Note that your domain does not have to be running in native mode for KMS to work, so you can have Exchange 5.5 and Windows NT 4.0 servers in your domain. The different components and subcomponents must be installed or configured in the following order:

1. Install Windows 2000 Server.
2. Install Windows 2000 Certificate Services.
3. Install Exchange 2000 Server.
4. Install Exchange Certificate Templates.
5. Install Exchange 2000 Key Management Services.
6. Grant Manage permissions to Key Management Services.
7. Request a certificate from the certificate authority.

This list is simply a rudimentary set of steps to follow before KMS can be installed and ready to accept requests for keys from users. You will learn how to install and configure a KMS server in the "Hands-on Projects" section for this chapter.

Troubleshooting Security Issues in Exchange 2000 Server

When it comes to troubleshooting security issues in Exchange 2000, authentication problems are the most common—users trying to log on to a restricted area, trying to access data they do not have permissions for, or having problems with their keys. Because keys form the basis of high security in Exchange 2000, it stands to reason that they represent the bulk of your troubleshooting time with Exchange 2000 security, especially if you have PKI and KMS installed and functioning.

The main issues you run into when troubleshooting problems with user keys are often user-related, as described in the following examples:

- A user has been migrated from one KMS to another one that has a different configuration. In this case, issuing a new key pair from the new CA should solve the problem; however, the original key pair must still be imported to decrypt data that was encrypted using the old keys.
- A user has suffered a hardware failure, and the keys and other pertinent data have been lost. In this case, recovering the keys by using the CA will do the trick. When a user's keys are recovered, the CA creates a recovery token, which generates a new key pair for the user. The user can then encrypt data again, but the original key pair is also restored so that the user can continue accessing previously encrypted data.

- The user forgets the password, which has about the same result as a hardware failure. Recovering the key pair and issuing new ones can rectify this problem.

Keys can be recovered on a user-by-user or group basis by using the Advanced Security features in the Exchange System Manager console. You can access these features by right-clicking Key Manager, pointing to All Tasks, and then clicking Recover Keys. The Recover Users Selection dialog box allows you to recover keys for the user or group and confirms the keys you successfully recovered for the user or group. Other problems can occur when troubleshooting Exchange 2000 security; however, many of them require additional configuration or are not directly built into Exchange 2000, such as using Exchange 2000 with a firewall for added security.

FIREWALLS AND EXCHANGE 2000

In this age of increased threat of attack from hackers, the heightened use of firewalls to help protect networks and servers connected to the Internet is not surprising. Today, the use of a firewall is pretty much compulsory; a firewall can provide not only a great deal of security, but (in the more full-featured firewalls) also a great deal of information about exactly what is happening with data being sent between your network and the Internet. Firewalls used to be considered far too difficult for the entry-level administrator to configure, but with advances in the ease of use and setup wizards to get firewalls up to speed quickly, nearly everyone can install a firewall and enjoy its benefits. Unfortunately, this ease of use can cause some problems when you have a server such as Exchange 2000 installed behind the firewall.

Most configured firewalls allow SMTP and HTTP through, and although that's usually adequate for sending and receiving mail or using OWA and IM, sometimes those protocols are not enough. For instance, if you run an additional service like a chat community, or if you have IMAP4 or LDAP directory services running, the firewall's configuration might have closed the default ports these protocols and services typically communicate on. The solution is usually as simple as configuring the firewall to allow data to pass through on a certain port, but opening ports can present problems if you need to secure these protocols and services.

Unfortunately, if you must open the necessary ports for these services and leave them vulnerable on the Internet (and to anyone who might want to attack them), your best hopes are that your system is patched and updated with the latest security fixes and that you have an effective authentication method in place. In this chapter and previous ones, you have learned that many virtual protocol servers and collaboration services can take advantage of the stronger authentication methods, such as Digest authentication. Even enforcing a strong password policy for your users can be useful in securing authentication, if you do not have a PKI and CA configuration. Ultimately, when it comes to firewalls and Exchange 2000, the same policy applies as for any other server or network: Allow only required traffic in and out. Having additional ports open for services that aren't in use can cause more security-related problems than not having a firewall at all. In addition, make sure you have the best authentication and data encryption methods that your organization can manage and support because authentication can be the last line of defense between your servers and networks and the hackers trying to break in.

Ensure that systems you use as firewalls for your network are secured with the proper configuration, settings, and updates because if the server protecting your network isn't locked down, it does not do you much good when a hacker has control of it!

ADVANCED SECURITY ISSUES

As if the security-related configuration features, options, and issues discussed earlier in this chapter were not enough, there are some additional security issues you should be aware of. Because the security of your Exchange 2000 server often encompasses more than just improving the overall security of Exchange 2000, this section covers information on these security issues: general Internet security, known Exchange 2000 exploits that your servers could fall victim to, and security bulletins for updates that can affect not only your server and network security, but also Exchange 2000 in general.

Internet Security Issues

As you learned in the "Firewalls and Exchange 2000" section, firewalls are widely used to help protect networks. However, even a tightly designed and implemented firewall has holes and potential paths of intrusion, so you should be aware of certain guidelines when connecting any server (especially ones with sensitive information) to the Internet, whether it has a firewall or not.

Effective security for systems connected to the Internet starts with a plan; simply slapping a firewall on your server and putting it on the Internet isn't enough. When you're installing the operating system or other software, consulting information in the documentation, on the vendor's Web site, or in technical books can help you configure additional settings to improve security. Also, spending time regularly to review security-related Web sites, message forums, and mailing lists can help you discover potential vulnerabilities in your security measures before they are common knowledge. By keeping up to date on this information, you can download a fix or patch or make necessary configuration changes before the actual release date of a service pack.

Keeping on top of these new findings can mean the difference between a properly secured Exchange 2000 server and one that is prone to attacks from the Internet. Although there's no single silver bullet for security, when you combine your knowledge with that of others who are using and testing the software, you can start to develop a plan for applying more direct and forceful security. The plan should include a regular schedule for patching and applying hot fixes and auditing the server to glean additional information on its general use and on any virtual servers installed on it. Although some of the features you have learned about in this chapter can help improve your security, especially over the Internet, there are few replacements for good old-fashioned planning, particularly updating and researching security issues for your systems that are connected to the Internet. This research, in the end, is one of the most important elements of your security and protection against hackers and their exploits. An excellent site for security-related information on Microsoft products, including configuration information and updates, can be found at *http://www.microsoft.com/security*.

Another essential aspect of security for your network and Exchange 2000 is a well-designed and up-to-date antivirus solution for your servers and your workstations. Virus attacks have been steadily rising in the past couple of years, and the sophistication and capabilities of these new viruses are growing at an alarming rate. Viruses have gained abilities that weren't thought possible (such as the ability to self-mutate, allowing them to change and adapt to the environment they are in), and it can be almost a full-time job just keeping up on the latest virus findings and updating your servers and systems accordingly. In addition to implementing antivirus protection for your servers and workstations, you can take the following user-education steps:

- Educate users on the potential dangers of viruses and explain that antivirus software might not be enough protection against viruses—which spread more quickly than virus updates can be made available.
- Tell users that when they aren't using their e-mail accounts (for instance, at night), they should log off and close their e-mail applications, especially if they use their e-mail remotely through OWA or similar client software.
- Instruct users not to respond to e-mails from unknown sources from which they did not solicit e-mail. Replies to these e-mails can give potential hackers a target for attack once they know that users and an e-mail server exist at that address.
- Educate users on the potential risks of social engineering (see Table 12-3) and instruct them not to give out sensitive information to anyone, even typically trusted sources. Requests like this should be forwarded to the administrator for further investigation.

Potential Security Attacks Against Windows 2000 and Exchange 2000

There are many potential attacks that a hacker could level on your Windows 2000 or Exchange 2000 servers. Even attacks aimed at Windows 2000 can adversely affect Exchange 2000 because an unstable or compromised foundation in Windows 2000 can cause as much grief as an attack directly against Exchange 2000. Table 12-3 contains a basic list of different attacks or risks. Understanding the basics of these attacks can help you plan your security implementation by identifying potential vulnerabilities in your organization.

Table 12-3 Potential Attacks Against Windows 2000 and Exchange 2000

Attack	Description
Social Engineering	A hacker preys on users' typical social habits (not necessarily an attack in the truest sense). For instance, a hacker phones a user pretending to be a member of the IT staff and requests user name and password information to perform "maintenance" on his or her account.
Masquerading	A hacker manages to impersonate a valid system with a valid IP address on the network being attacked and, using this information, gains access based on the rights of the system being impersonated.
Replay	A hacker intercepts and records communications (such as authentication) between two systems, and then uses this information to impersonate one of the systems and gain access.
Man in the Middle	Similar to a replay attack, a hacker intercepts communication between two systems and captures information for a replay attack or simply captures information to use for other purposes, much like spying.
Manipulation	A hacker gains access to network communications via any of the above attacks and changes or corrupts the data being transferred to disrupt communication or cause network problems.
Virus	A multitude of viruses exist, ranging from minor annoyances to full-fledged attacks, that can be propagated through your network and damage your systems and servers. A solid, constantly updated antivirus solution for your network and servers is a must because of the vast number of new viruses continually appearing; this precaution is especially vital for any network running Microsoft products because their widespread use makes them a target for most viruses.
Denial of Service	A hacker floods a server or network with requests for information or with false, corrupted data that overwhelms the network or system resources. This attack is commonly used by hackers because of its relative ease of execution and, if done properly, its effectiveness. The flood causes a server to stop responding or crash entirely. A server crash sometimes offers an opportunity to intrude if the software the attack is focusing on leaves behind a remnant of software with system privileges when it crashes. Other attacks can then use these elevated privileges.
Abuse of Privileges	A user abuses his or her privileges to gain access to sensitive data or areas of the network, if given privileges or rights that aren't truly necessary. Even worse, this user-management issue could lead to more trouble if a hacker manages to gain access to one of these accounts through social engineering or a similar attack method.
Trojan Horse	A hacker can use these utilities, which are similar to viruses and quite plentiful, to gain nearly complete control over a server. In many cases, Trojan horses are installed similarly to viruses and can hide from even the most diligent administrators. Typically, a well-designed and up-to-date antivirus implementation can catch and stop the installation and use of Trojan horses on your servers.

Although defending against every form of attack is nearly impossible, reading up on the different types of attacks can better prepare you to combat them.

Another often forgotten element of security that doesn't necessarily involve the dangers of the Internet is physical attack. Many people do not think of the potential risk of unauthorized people gaining access to server equipment or possibly a free network jack to plug into their networks. All visitors to your organization should be checked in and not allowed to freely walk through the building; this precaution helps cut down on the number of people wandering around and accessing whatever they like. Remember, it's much easier to break into a server if you are sitting in front of it or are on the same network than it is to attack from the outside. In addition, any maintenance people brought in to do work on servers or equipment in a sensitive area, such as a server room or network wiring closet, should be accompanied and monitored by a staff member at all times. In addition to these steps, you should also physically secure your network equipment in server rooms with door locks, secure access cards, or lockable server cabinets.

Exchange 2000 Server Security Bulletins

Given its relatively young age (at the time of this writing), Exchange 2000 doesn't have as many product-related security issues as Windows 2000, which gets far more use than Exchange 2000 Server. Before you assume that Exchange 2000 (when properly configured) is very secure, however, you should be aware of the five security-related bulletins Microsoft released for Exchange 2000 (not including the security issues raised by its integration with Windows 2000). Table 12-4 summarizes these security bulletins. For more information on these and other Microsoft security bulletins, check this Web site: *http://www.microsoft.com/security*.

Table 12-4 Microsoft Security Bulletins for Exchange 2000 Server

Microsoft Bulletin	Date Issued	Details
MS00-088	November 16, 2000	This bulletin announces a patch to fix a potential Exchange user account vulnerability. Early copies of Exchange 2000 shipped with reconfigured passwords for sensitive user accounts, and a hacker could easily take advantage of this vulnerability if the passwords were not reset. This problem was fixed in later copies of Exchange 2000 Server.
MS01-014	March 1, 2001	This bulletin provides information about a possible denial-of-service attack against Exchange 2000 and IIS 5. A hacker could send specially formulated URLs to Web servers (including those hosting OWA) and cause a memory allocation error. This error causes IIS—and thus OWA, if hosted on this server—to fail.

Table 12-4 Microsoft Security Bulletins for Exchange 2000 Server (continued)

Microsoft Bulletin	Date Issued	Details
MS01-030	June 6, 2001	This bulletin addresses a flaw in the way a Web browser communicates with OWA on Exchange 5.5 and Exchange 2000. This flaw enables a hacker to trick OWA into running a script on the server by attaching the script as a URL to an e-mail of an OWA user. When the user opens the e-mail, the hacker uses the payload of the script to gain access to the server.
MS01-041	July 26, 2001	This bulletin describes a possible denial-of-service attack against not only Exchange 2000 servers, but also SQL servers and Windows NT 4.0 and 2000 servers. This attack sends an RPC request to the server with invalid data, thus potentially disrupting the operation of services or the server.
MS01-043	August 14, 2001	This bulletin deals with a denial-of-service vulnerability in the NNTP Service included in Windows NT 4.0, Windows 2000, and Exchange 2000. Because of a memory leak in the NNTP Service, when a message is posted, a bit of system memory is used and not released. Therefore, if hackers send a large number of messages to an NNTP server, they could cause the NNTP Service, or possibly the server, to fail.

There will probably be more security bulletins issued for Exchange 2000 Server; new vulnerabilities that these bulletins might address depend on three factors. The first factor involves increased deployment of Exchange 2000; as more organizations use it, they will no doubt discover new security issues that crop up during actual use. The second factor also has to do with increased use of Exchange 2000; as more organizations use a product, it becomes more of a target for hackers trying to find vulnerabilities and points of attack to exploit. On the other hand, increased use gives security researchers more opportunities to test for possible vulnerabilities and recommend solutions to address them. The third factor is potential errors in the software itself. Although Exchange 2000 Server is an excellent product, like any other software, problems caused by human error when coding software or bugs not being discovered during beta testing are always a possibility.

By using the tools, features, methods, and advice in this chapter—as well as information on Microsoft and third-party Web sites—you can develop a well-conceived plan to secure your Exchange 2000 server and related services.

CHAPTER SUMMARY

- Administrators and organizations often overlook the following reasons for securing their Exchange 2000 server: Servers house sensitive data and messages, e-mail spammers could use your servers as a launching point for their attacks, and compromised Exchange 2000 accounts could be used to gain access to other network resources.
- Auditing and logging activity on your Windows 2000 and Exchange 2000 servers is an essential component of your organization's security. The logged information can be critical in stopping or catching a hacker in the act. Auditing can help you confirm the current state of security and better assess changes to improve security.
- Both Windows 2000 and Exchange 2000 have logging tools, including the built-in Windows 2000 Event Viewer logs, which provide security-related information as well as information on the overall operation of servers and services. Exchange 2000 can also have logging enabled for its ancillary services, such as virtual protocol servers.
- Security checklists are a useful tool for auditing the security of your servers and network. By using a security checklist that you follow step by step, you can confirm the current configuration of your servers to assess security measures. You can then use this information to make configuration changes and update patches and security fixes on your servers, if needed.
- Access control is another vital security component. By taking advantage of the Exchange 2000 integration with Windows 2000 AD, you can more effectively manage user access to services and data.
- Public Key Infrastructure uses encrypted public and private keys to help provide a more secure way of authenticating users on your network. Because of the chance of keys being intercepted, however, consider implementing certificate services to add another level of authenticity to your user authentication process.
- The Key Management Services integrated into Exchange 2000 enables encryption of message information and communication by using PKI and certificate services. The KMS manages keys and certificates for users, taking some of the effort and learning curve out of the equation.
- When troubleshooting security issues in Exchange 2000, you'll find they usually boil down to two problems: users trying to gain access to resources they do not have the appropriate rights for, or losing passwords, keys, and certificates by accident or because of a hardware failure or other incident. Through AD, KMS offers a convenient, centralized place for administrators to rectify these problems by having access to users' properties information in AD.
- Firewalls are often useful in network security. For the most basic Exchange 2000 functionality, you do not need to worry about any special firewall configurations; however, for services such as IMAP4 or LDAP, you might need to open access to the ports these services use. As with any other server on the Internet, securing the firewall is crucial because if it becomes compromised, you could be in trouble.

12

- When your server is connected to the Internet, it's exposed to potential security issues. By understanding the different types of attacks, you can plan how to prevent falling prey to them. Education of your users and a well-thought-out security plan are your best methods of implementing and maintaining security on your network. In addition, an up-to-date antivirus software package is a requirement for network security.
- Although not many security bulletins are currently aimed at Exchange 2000, over time this number will undoubtedly grow. Keep apprised of these security bulletins and take action by changing your configuration or applying any patches specified in these bulletins to help ensure continued security.

KEY TERMS

asymmetric key — A type of encryption key used when two different keys—a public key and a private key—are exchanged. One key is used to encrypt and decrypt the data, and the other key is used only for decryption.

certificate authority (CA) — A central component of certificate services in which Windows 2000 and administrators can issue and manage digital certificates to users wanting to connect securely to servers.

Certificate Services Policy (CSP) — A certificate template in the certificate authority that uses specific user information to generate keys. It also stores users' private keys in the Extensible Storage Engine (ESE) database.

digital certificate — Very similar to an encryption key, a digital certificate presents the information in a certificate format, showing that the identity of the person or server you are connecting to has been verified.

Encrypting File System (EFS) — A Windows 2000 feature that can be used to encrypt files and folders for additional security.

encryption strength — A description of the security capabilities of encryption methods. Encryption strength describes how difficult it is to crack the keys for an encryption method.

IP Security (IPSec) — A Windows 2000 feature that allows you to secure TCP/IP network traffic by using encrypted keys.

security audit — A procedure for checking the current security configuration for Exchange 2000, using security checklists and information in the event logs. This audit should be performed regularly to ensure that your security is up to date and that nothing has happened to hamper the security of your Exchange 2000 servers and services.

security checklist — A document used to record information about components and settings for your servers (or network). This information can help you assess the current security status of your servers or network.

symmetric key — A type of encryption key used when both keys in the key pair are exactly the same.

Windows Integrated authentication (WIA) — The standard authentication method for Instant Messaging, in which authentication is based on the account name and password you use to log on to the Windows 2000 domain.

Review Questions

1. Which of the following are the two greatest concerns for Exchange 2000 adminisrators?
   a. viruses affecting the server
   b. Internet network outages
   c. unwanted messages routed through the server
   d. users leaving their systems logged on to Exchange 2000 or OWA
2. By not taking the time to secure your Exchange 2000 servers, you could be vulnerable to attacks by hackers, resulting in ______________ on your network, which for most organizations is unacceptable.
   a. failed hardware
   b. additional software bugs
   c. vulnerabilities
   d. downtime
3. The Windows 2000 utility for viewing important information on the general status of your system, including security-related information, is the ______________.
4. Your organization wants you to perform regular monthly audits of the servers on your network. What document can you use to ensure that the process goes smoothly and generates repeatable results?
5. Controlling access to Exchange 2000 resources is made easier by the Exchange 2000 integration with which of the following components/services?
   a. Public Key Infrastructure
   b. certificate authority
   c. Active Directory
   d. Domain Name System
6. Windows 2000 Public Key Infrastructure makes use of an encrypted ______________ and ______________ key pair to help secure authentication and data.
7. Which type of encrypted key configuration does PKI use?
   a. asynchronous
   b. synchronous
   c. asymmetric
   d. symmetric

8. With the type of encrypted keys that PKI uses to encrypt communications and messages, the sender of the message uses the ______________ key to encrypt the message.
9. Which of the following encryption strengths would produce the lowest workload on a system?
   a. 128-bit
   b. 8-bit
   c. 56-bit
   d. 160-bit
10. Your organization has implemented PKI and has been enjoying the benefits of increased security, although one user's key was intercepted by a hacker who tried to gain access to sensitive information with it. What solution would you recommend for this problem?
11. Which authentication method does Instant Messaging use by default when users log on with the client software?
    a. Kerberos
    b. Digest authentication
    c. Secure Password authentication
    d. Windows Integrated authentication
12. If you want to allow access only to users with certificates issued from a particular certificate authority, which feature could you use to accomplish this?
13. When you install Key Management Services, the KMS component that stores users' private keys is called the ______________ database.
14. In a Key Management Services implementation, which component performs the most work?
    a. client software and system
    b. Windows 2000 Server
    c. Active Directory
    d. Extensible Storage Engine
15. A user on your network had a hard drive failure on his workstation and lost all his data, so you built a new system for him. After he connects to the Exchange 2000 server, he realizes he can't open any messages that he could before. What could the problem be?
16. When deploying a firewall on a server to protect your network from attacks from the Internet, which security measure should you perform on the server?
    a. apply patches and updates
    b. close access to any open ports on the firewall
    c. place the firewall on a separate network
    d. place Exchange outside the firewall

17. Which factor is most important when implementing security on your network and servers?
    a. money in the budget
    b. a plan
    c. a firewall
    d. the latest updates and patches
18. A particularly dangerous attack that your organization can experience and likely will not recognize as a threat is a(n) ____________ attack.
19. What should you install on your servers and workstations to protect against the threat of a Trojan Horse attack?
    a. firewall
    b. certificate services
    c. antivirus software
    d. Public Key Infrastructure
20. A type of attack or method of intrusion that involves a hacker using trickery to get user names and passwords from unsuspecting users is called ____________.

Hands-on Projects

Project 12-1

The certificate services are required before you can install Key Management Services for Exchange 2000 and take advantage of its security features. Before you can install KMS, the certificate services must be installed and there must be at least one enterprise root certificate authority installed to the network.

After you install a new certificate authority on a server, it cannot change its name or be removed from the domain.

You must create three certificates after you have configured your first CA before you can move on to installing Key Management Services: Enrollment Agent (Computer), Exchange User, and Exchange Signature Only.

To install certificate services for Windows 2000:

1. Log on using an account with administrative rights, and insert your Windows 2000 CD-ROM.

2. Click **Start**, point to **Settings**, click **Control Panel**, and then double-click **Add/Remove Programs** to open the Add/Remove Programs utility. In the Add/Remove Programs dialog box, click the **Add/Remove Windows Components** button to open the Windows Components Wizard.
3. Click the **Certificate Services** check box in the Components text box to select this component. A message appears that warns you about the inability to rename the server once you install this component; click **Yes**, and then click the **Next** button to continue to the Certification Authority Type window shown in Figure 12-2.

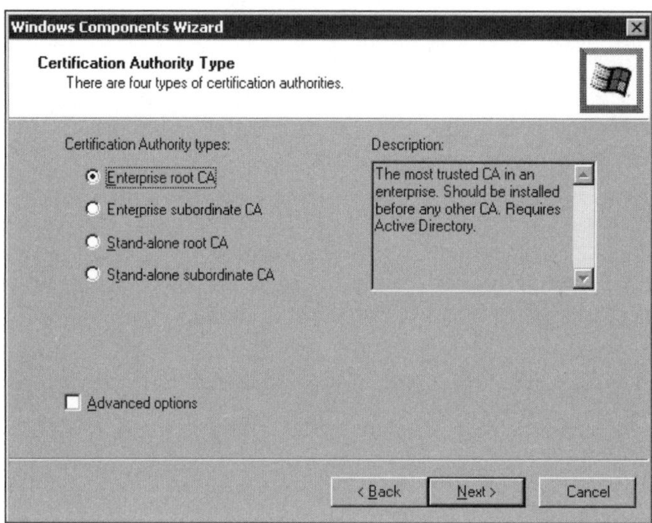

Figure 12-2 Selecting a CA to install

4. Click the **Enterprise root CA** radio button to select this option, and then click the **Next** button. The CA Identifying Information window opens, where you must enter the pertinent information about your organization. Type the requested information in the different text boxes (any information will do for this project). In the CA name text box, type **Exchange**. After you have finished, the window should look similar to Figure 12-3. Click the **Next** button to continue to the Data Storage Location window.

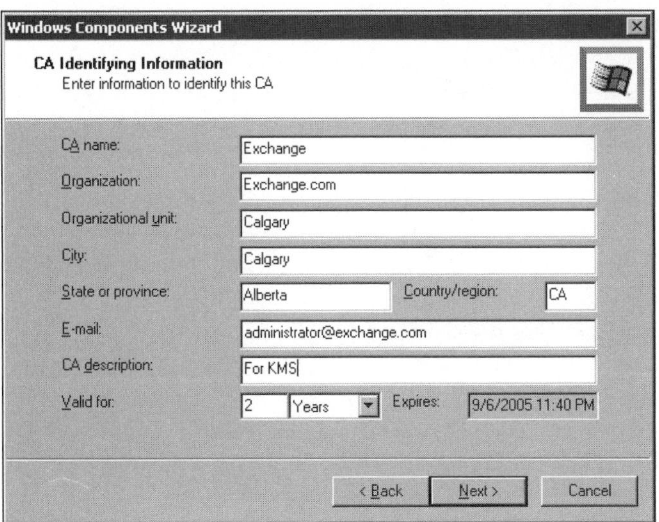

Figure 12-3 Entering identification information for a CA

5. Accept the default information in the Data Storage Location window by clicking the **Next** button. A message pops up warning you that IIS services are running and need to be shut down before installing certificate services. Click **OK** to clear this message, and continue to the Configuring Components window. The wizard starts copying files, and you can watch its progress in this window. After the file-copying process is finished, click the **Finish** button in the completion window to complete the wizard.
6. Close the Add/Remove Programs dialog box and any other open windows, and return to the Windows desktop. Next, you must configure the types of certificates that the new CA you just created will issue so that you can install KMS. To do this, open the Certification Authority console by clicking **Start**, pointing to **Programs**, pointing to **Administrative Tools**, and clicking **Certification Authority**.
7. Double-click the name of the CA you created in Step 5. In the list of folders that is displayed, right-click the **Policy Settings** folder, point to **New**, and then click **Certificate to Issue** to open the Select Certificate Template dialog box, as seen in Figure 12-4. Click the **Enrollment Agent (Computer)** option, and then click **OK**. You will be returned to the Certification Authority console. Repeat this step again for the other two required certificate templates: **Exchange User** and **Exchange Signature Only**.

Figure 12-4 Selecting a certificate template

8. Close any open windows or applications, and return to the Windows desktop. Leave the system at this state for Project 12-2.

Project 12-2

To install the Key Management Services component:

1. Log on using an account with administrative rights; if you are continuing from Project 12-1, you can skip this step.
2. Insert the Exchange 2000 Server installation CD-ROM, and then open the Add/Remove Programs utility by clicking **Start**, pointing to **Settings**, clicking **Control Panel**, and then double-clicking **Add/Remove Programs**. In the Add/Remove Programs dialog box, click **Microsoft Exchange 2000** in the Currently installed programs text box. Click the **Change/Remove** button to start the Microsoft Exchange 2000 Installation Wizard.
3. Click the **Next** button in the Welcome window to proceed to the Component Selection window. First, click the **Action** list arrow next to the Microsoft Exchange 2000 option, and then click **Change** in the available options. Do the same for the Microsoft Exchange Messaging and Collaboration Services option. Now click the **Microsoft Exchange Key Management Service** list arrow, and then click **Install** in the available options. After you are done, your Component Selection window should look similar to Figure 12-5.
4. Click the **Next** button to proceed to the Key Management Service Information window. To implement how you want to secure your Key Management Services, click the **Manual password entry** radio button. (You should make sure that either method of password entry you choose is kept secure—in a safe, for example.) Click the **Next** button to have the KMS give you a password.

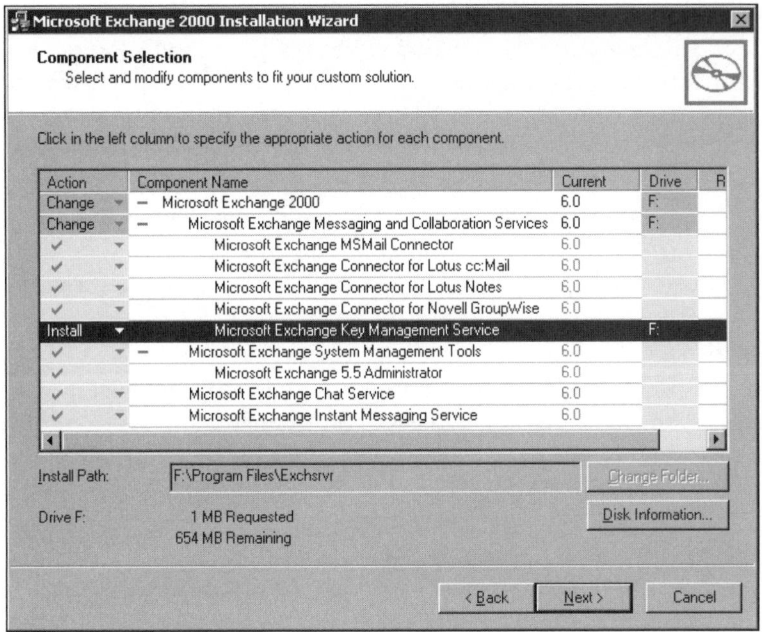

Figure 12-5 Installing the Key Management Service component

5. A new message appears informing you of your new password for the Key Management Service and reminds you that you have to enter it each time the service starts. Write the password down *exactly* as it's shown on-screen, and then double-check your notes! Click **OK** to continue to the Component Summary window. Click the **Next** button to start the copying process and install the Key Management Services. The Wizard Completion window then opens; click the **Finish** button to complete the wizard. (If you see a message box stating "Exchange Server had previously been updated by a Service Pack. Reinstall the Microsoft Exchange Server Service Pack," you can do so now.)
6. Close any open windows or applications, and return to the Windows desktop. Leave the system at this state for Project 12-3.

Project 12-3

This project demonstrates the next step in installing KMS, starting the Key Management Services. The Key Management server provides the backbone for the KMS implementation on your network. After you have the Key Management server in place and running, you can then start using KMS and all the security advantages it brings to your network. This project assumes that you have completed Projects 12-1 and 12-2.

To start the Key Management Services:

1. Log on using an account with administrative rights; if you are continuing from Project 12-2, you can skip this step.

2. To give the KMS the ability to manage the CA you created for it, open the Certification Authority console by clicking **Start**, pointing to **Programs**, pointing to **Administrative Tools**, and then clicking **Certification Authority**. Right-click the CA you created in Project 12-1, and then click **Properties** on the shortcut menu to open the Properties dialog box for that server. Click the **Security** tab.
3. Click the **Add** button to open the Select Users, Computers or Groups dialog box. Click the server where your CA is installed (the server you are working on now; if you don't see it listed, you can add it manually, using the fomat *domain-name\machinename*), click the **Add** button, and then click **OK** to return to the Properties dialog box.
4. To set the permissions this server will have, click the **Allow** check box next to the Manage option in the Permissions section to enable this server to manage the CA. When you are done, your Security tab should look similar to Figure 12-6. Click **OK** to return to the Certification Authority console.

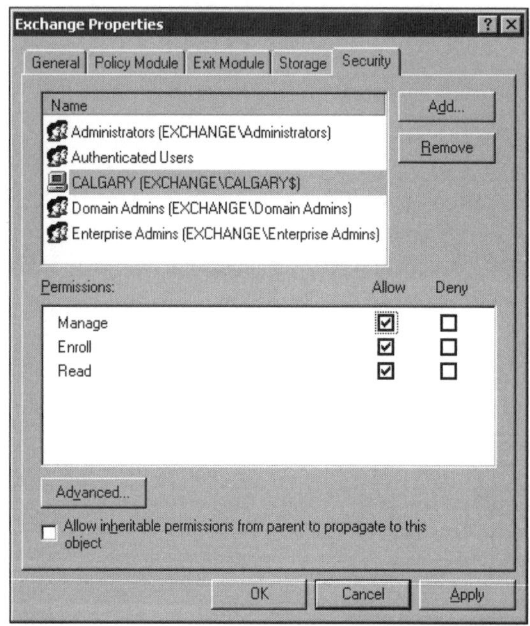

Figure 12-6 Setting permissions for the KMS server

5. To start the Key Management Services, click **Start**, point to **Programs**, point to **Microsoft Exchange**, and then click **System Manager**. When the Exchange System Manager console opens, click the **Advanced Security** folder in the Contents pane to display its contents in the Details pane. (If you have the display of administrative groups enabled, you might need to double-click **Administrative Groups** and then **First Administrative Group** before you see

the Advanced Security folder.) Right-click **Key Manager**, point to **All Tasks**, and then click **Start Service** on the shortcut menu.

6. The Service Start Up Password dialog box opens. In the text box, type the password you recorded when you first installed KMS in Project 12-2, and then click **OK**. If you typed the password correctly, the service starts.

Make sure you type the password as it was shown in Project 12-2 because it is case sensitive. For example, if the password was in all uppercase characters, make sure you enter it the same way!

7. Close any open windows or applications, and return to the Windows desktop. Leave your system at this state for Project 12-4.

Project 12-4

This project shows you how to quickly change the location of your KMS password if you selected the Read password from disk option when you installed the KMS. Although it is typically far more secure to have the password written down and put away in a safe place, by using a floppy you don't have to type a long password every time the service starts. The only downside to the floppy method is that floppies can get lost or corrupted. If you placed your password on a floppy disk, one option is to copy the Kmserver.pwd file from the disk to a folder on your server and have KMS use that file instead of the floppy when the service starts. This folder should be secured to the hilt, with the only access being by you or other KMS administrators. In addition, you can use the steps in this project to change your floppy or folder location so that KMS asks you for the password every time, just as though you had selected Manual password entry in the first place. This project assumes that Projects 12-1 through 12-3 have been completed.

12

To change the location of the Key Management Services password:

1. Log on using an account with administrative rights; if you are continuing from Project 12-3, you can skip this step.
2. To open the Registry Editor, click **Start**, click **Run**, type **regedit** in the Open text box, and then press **Enter**. The Registry Editor console opens with several folders displayed.
3. Navigate through the folders to the HKEY_LOCAL_MACHINE\Software\Microsoft\Exchange\KMServer folder. When you locate this folder, your screen should look similar to Figure 12-7.
4. Double-click the **MasterPasswordPath** entry in the Details pane to open the Edit String dialog box. In the Value data text box, type the name of the folder where you want to store your Kmserver.pwd file. For this lab, simply type **C:**, and then click **OK**. (Typically, using this folder location is a big security no-no.)

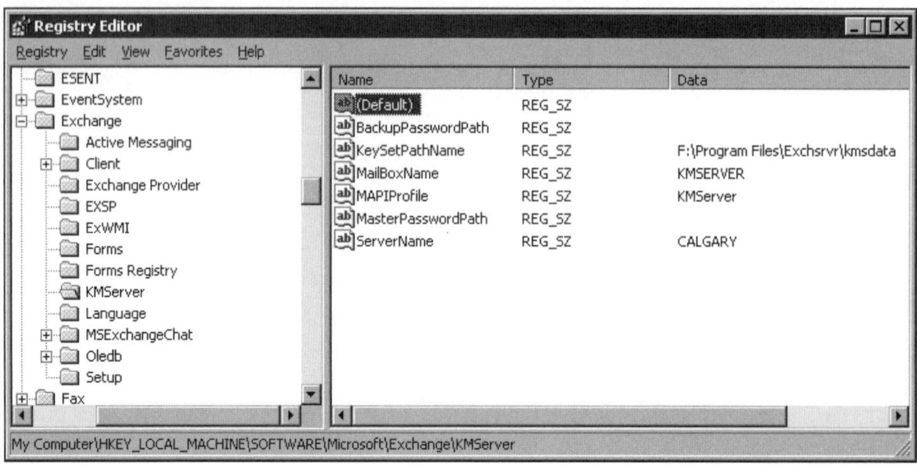

Figure 12-7 Modifying the KMS password location

5. You will now see the path where your .pwl file will be located listed in the Data column next to MasterPasswordPath. If you have a path listed here, but you want KMS to ask for a password to be typed every time, double-click this entry, delete any reference to any file, and leave the Value data text box blank. The next time you log on, you must type the password. (So make sure you have it written down if you plan to do this!)
6. Double-click the **MasterPasswordPath** entry, and return it to the same state it was in when you started this project (it should be blank by default). Click **OK**, and then close any open applications or windows and return to the Windows desktop. Leave your system at this state for Project 12-5.

Project 12-5

This method could also be used to remove organizations from your certificate trust list if needed.

This project assumes that you have a CA installed and functioning.

To add a certificate to your certificate trust list:

1. Log on using an account with administrative rights; if you are continuing from Project 12-4, you can skip this step.
2. Click **Start**, click **Run**, type **MMC** in the Open text box, and then press **Enter** to open a new MMC. Click **Console** on the menu bar, and then click **Add/Remove Snap-in** to open the Add/Remove Snap-in dialog box.

3. Click the **Add** button to open the Add Standalone Snap-in dialog box. Click the **Certificates** snap-in, and then click the **Add** button to open the Certificates snap-in dialog box, shown in Figure 12-8.

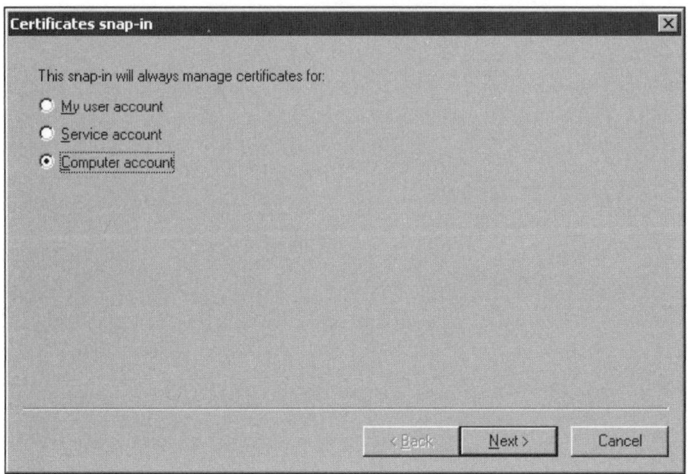

Figure 12-8 Selecting the type of certification to be managed in this snap-in

4. In the Certificates snap-in dialog box, click the Computer account radio button so that you can manage certificates for a computer in this console. Click the **Next** button to proceed to the Select Computer dialog box, where you can specify which computer this snap-in manages. Leave the default option (Local computer) selected, and click the **Finish** button to return to the Add Standalone Snap-in dialog box.

5. Click the **Close** button, and then click **OK** to return to the console you created; in the Contents pane, double-click the **Certificates (Local Computer)** folder to show its contents. Double-click the **Trusted Root Certification Authorities** folder, and then double-click the **Certificates** folder to show the currently trusted certificates for this domain. You will see a rather substantial list of certificates already listed, some from well-known companies, as shown in Figure 12-9.
6. Right-click the **Certificates** folder, point to **All Tasks**, and then click **Import** on the shortcut menu to open the Certificate Import Wizard. In the Welcome window, click the **Next** button to continue to the File to Import window.
7. To specify the actual filename for the certificate you want to import into your trust list, click the **Browse** button to open the Open dialog box, click the **Files of type** list arrow, and click **All Files (*.*)**. Navigate until you find your own certificate. It is usually in the root folder of the partition where you installed Windows 2000 (for example, C:\), and the icon looks like a small certificate. Click this certificate, click the **Open** button to place its path in the File name text box, and then click the **Next** button.

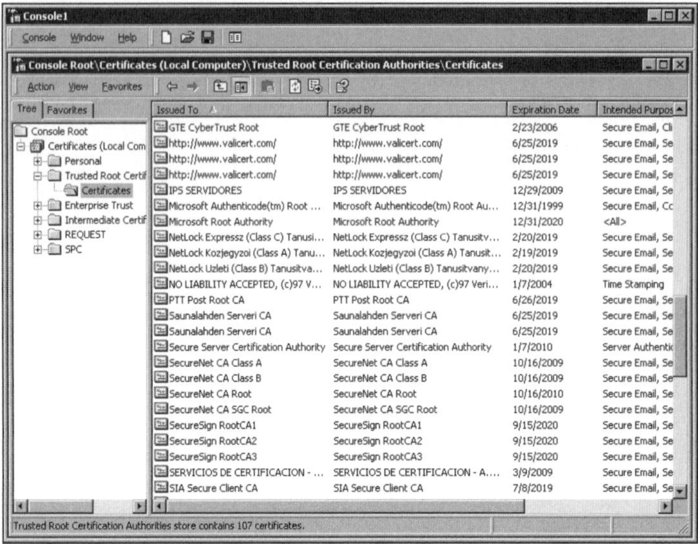

Figure 12-9 Displaying the default certificate trust list installed with KMS

8. In the Certificate Store window, you can leave the default option (Place all certificates in the following store) as is, and click the **Next** button to go to the Wizard Completion window. Click the **Finish** button to complete the wizard. A message pops up telling you that the import was successful; click **OK** to return to the Certificates snap-in console. (If a message box opens that asks whether you want to save console settings, click **No**.)
9. Close any open windows or applications, and return to the Windows desktop. Leave your system at this state for Project 12-6.

Project 12-6

To configure audit logging in Exchange 2000:

Enabling audit logging can drain system resources, especially when you have many users using the Exchange 2000 server you are logging. Unless you haven't had any major performance problems after enabling logging, you should leave logging disabled until you need it, such as when users complain about missing e-mail and other anomalies with their Exchange mailboxes. At that point, enable logging and view the information for possible activity that could pinpoint the problem with the users' mailboxes.

1. Log on using an account with administrative rights; if you are continuing from Project 12-5, you can skip this step.
2. To open the Exchange System Manager console, click **Start**, point to **Programs**, point to **Microsoft Exchange**, and then click **System Manager**.

3. Double-click the **Servers** folder, double-click the name of the server you have installed, double-click the **First Storage Group** folder, right-click the **Mailbox Store <*servername*>** folder, and then click **Properties** on the shortcut menu to open the Mailbox Store Properties dialog box. (If you have the display of administrative groups enabled, you might need to double-click **Administrative Groups** and then **First Administrative Group** before you see the Servers folder.)
4. Click the **Security** tab to show the available options for specifying security for the mailbox store. Click the **Advanced** button to open the Access Control Settings for Mailbox Store <*servername*> dialog box, and then click the **Auditing** tab to see the current auditing entries; this dialog box should look similar to Figure 12-10.

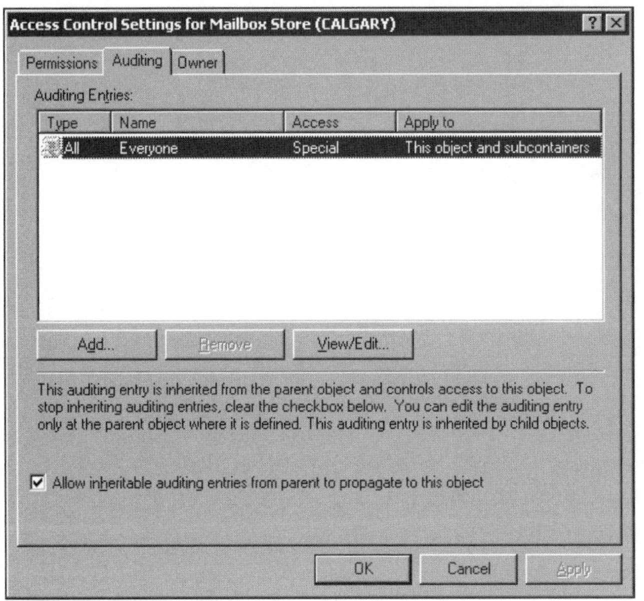

Figure 12-10 Configuring audit logging for a mailbox store in the Auditing tab

5. Click the **Add** button to open the Select User, Computer, or Group dialog box, and then double-click the account that corresponds to the account you logged on as (for example, administrator or exadmin) to open the Auditing Entry for Mailbox Store <*servername*> dialog box. Next, click the Successful and Failed check boxes next to the component you want to monitor. For this lab, click the **Failed** check boxes next to the Read and Write options and the **Successful** and **Failed** check boxes next to the Change permissions option. When you have finished applying these settings, your dialog box should look similar to Figure 12-11.

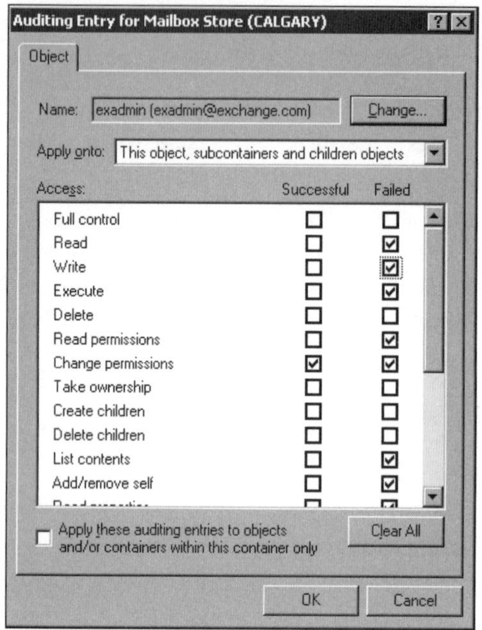

Figure 12-11 The auditing options available for objects in Exchange 2000

This configuration can help detect problems with a mailbox store because it reports only when read and write access to that mailbox store fails, which could indicate not only a security issue, but also a potential hardware problem. The Change permissions option can tell you whether users have escalated their permissions on their own; this could indicate that users—and possibly outside hackers—are poking around where they shouldn't be.

6. Click **OK**, and then click **OK** two more times to close any open windows and return to the Windows desktop.

Case Projects

Case Projects Background

Blue Heaven Motors is a large local dealership that specializes in selling nearly every type of domestic car on the market. Its growth in the past few years has been quite dramatic, and it has a very popular and profitable Web site where users can shop online and interact with other users in chat rooms. Blue Heaven has retained you to help with its Exchange 2000 security; because of its popularity, the number of attacks against its services has increased, especially against Exchange 2000, which supports its corporate e-mail and Chat services.

Even given its growth rate, Blue Heaven has only one Exchange 2000 server, which suits its 600 users perfectly. There haven't been any complaints about performance, but improving the security of the Exchange 2000 server and the network in general is very important to management. High security is especially essential when the Financing Department has to transfer contracts and other sensitive information between the dealership and a financial institution on the other side of the country.

Case 1

For your first task, Blue Heaven wants you to provide a basic assessment of its current security so that you can make the best recommendations on how to improve security measures. What would you do first before generating your assessment of Blue Heaven's security? After you have this information, how would you compare assessment information in the future with your original assessment?

Case 2

The Financing Department is concerned because of rumors that North Star Autos (across town) recently had sensitive customer contract information intercepted by a hacker when it was transferred to the same creditors that Blue Heaven deals with. What is the first thing you could do to help minimize the risk of data being captured and read by people who shouldn't have access to sensitive information? What additional features should you recommend to improve the security of this situation even more?

Case 3

Until recently, Blue Heaven Motors was test-piloting an Instant Messaging implementation on its local network so that users could chat and also use IM like a fast paging system. Because of potential security issues, Blue Heaven stopped using the services until you could assess them. What type of authentication do you recommend using with Instant Messaging? Is there any cause for concern if these services are used only on the local network and not connected to the Internet? If Blue Heaven does connect to the Internet with Instant Messaging, what would you recommend changing?

Case 4

You have finished making recommendations for Blue Heaven Motors and have been asked to provide a brief recommendation for its business partner, Axiom Parts Supply, on the three key steps any network can take to protect itself when it's connected to the Internet. What steps should you recommend to achieve the most impact on network security?

CHAPTER 13

EXCHANGE 2000 SERVER PUBLIC FOLDERS

After reading this chapter and completing the exercises, you will be able to:

- Understand how public folders are created, including the basics of public folder hierarchy and design, to best implement public folders for your organization
- Configure public folder properties so that you can secure access to your public folders and customize them to meet your needs
- Manage public folder stores, including replicating public folder information between different components of your public folder hierarchy
- Move and monitor the public folders installed in your Exchange 2000 organization for effective management and maintenance of your public folders
- Understand the use of public folders when you are disconnected from your Exchange 2000 server as well as the use of public folders via the Outlook Web Access client

In Chapter 12, "Security and Encryption in Exchange 2000 Server," you learned about securing Exchange 2000 using a variety of methods and features. These security features are included not only in Exchange 2000, but also in Windows 2000. You learned about the Exchange 2000 Key Management Services, which provide strong encryption techniques for user authentication and for message and data security. Key Management Services work with the two fundamental Windows 2000 security features: Public Key Infrastructure and certificate services. These features can be put to use with Exchange 2000, but can also be used on their own to help secure and protect your organization and its data. Finally, you learned about common security issues and recent security alerts pertaining to Exchange 2000 that you should be aware of to further secure your Exchange 2000 servers and organization.

In this chapter, you learn about Exchange 2000 and its public folder feature, including the creation and configuration of public folders on your Exchange 2000 servers. In addition, you learn about public folder stores and how they can benefit your organization. Certain management features and options are available in Exchange 2000, including moving, upgrading, and monitoring public folders. Finally, you learn how public folders work when you are not connected to an Exchange 2000 server and how you can use public folders through Outlook Web Access when connecting to your Exchange 2000 server over an Internet connection.

Introduction to Public Folders

Exchange 2000, like Exchange 5.5, offers public folder functionality that enables administrators to provide a centralized location for data storage for nearly any type of file, message, or other object (such as contacts and calendars). Public folders are often referred to as one of the main benefits of using Exchange 5.5 or 2000 over a competing messaging product. Most networks have some type of file storage on a network share for users to connect to and make use of. However, making this feature available can be difficult if you have users who reside outside the network. If you want your users to be able to access these shared files from outside the local network, it can require additional setup and configuration of the network infrastructure and servers to enable your users to connect and make use of the shared information in an efficient and, most important, secure fashion.

Exchange 2000 public folders can alleviate this problem, however. Using one of the clients that supports access to Exchange 2000 public folders—Outlook 2000, Outlook Web Access, and, in a limited fashion, Outlook Express—gives both remote and local users access to data stored in the Exchange 2000 public folders you have configured. Being able to gain access to a shared file repository can save a lot of time and effort for users and administrators.

Public folders in Exchange 2000 have been designed to offer the utmost ease of organization, creation, and management by using Outlook 2000. It might sound a bit odd to have users rather than an administrator manage an Exchange 2000 feature, but most users use Outlook 2000 as the interface for connecting to public folders, so this client is often the best way to manage public folders. In addition to using Outlook 2000 to manage the public folders, you can use the Exchange System Manager console for public folder maintenance. As you will see in the upcoming sections, public folders are designed from the start to be as scalable as you need, and users and administrators can easily use them to their fullest potential.

Each Exchange 2000 server has a public folder store installed by default. Any additional public folders created on your Exchange 2000 server are placed in the server's default public folder store. You can centrally manage the creation of additional public folder stores and public folders for different Exchange 2000 servers in your domain by using Exchange System Manager, thus simplifying administration and organization of this useful feature. Therefore, an Exchange 2000 server can host a variety of different folders in the original, default public folder store or in the additional public folder stores you create to facilitate management and organization of public folders, much as you would create additional mailbox stores to help manage user mailboxes.

Like any other feature implementation in Exchange 2000, if your organization plans to make widespread use of public folders over a few Exchange 2000 servers in different locations, you should design a plan to organize your public folders geographically. If this isn't practical or applicable for your organization, you should at least distribute the folders among your Exchange 2000 servers to minimize the performance impact for users with your public folders. If you have only one Exchange 2000 server, this does not apply to you, but take time to consider organizing your public folders logically by department or a similar layout. Creating public folders is fairly easy, and you will learn how to do it in the "Hands-on Projects" section later in this chapter.

The Public Folder Hierarchy

Any Exchange 2000 organization can host multiple public folder hierarchies called **public folder trees**. When you implement a public folder tree, any folders at the first level (or root of the tree) are called top-level public folders. Unless folder management is configured otherwise, both users and administrators can generate new public folders, but note that any user-created, top-level public folders are placed on the Exchange 2000 server where the user's mailbox resides. Any folders created inside a top-level public folder are automatically placed on the Exchange 2000 server where the top-level public folder was created. What complicates the situation is that any public folder in an Exchange 2000 organization can be replicated to any other Exchange 2000 server, so management of public folders becomes a nightmare. You will learn more about public folder replication later in the "Replicating Public Folders" section.

13

It is the **public folder hierarchy** that helps Exchange 2000 keep track of each folder in your Exchange 2000 organization. Each public folder tree's hierarchy is stored in and managed by Active Directory. Any new Exchange 2000 servers with one or more public folders added to the Exchange 2000 organization automatically have a new public folder hierarchy created for them in AD, and the hierarchy of these public folders is made available to every mailbox-enabled user in the organization (access permitting).

In Exchange 2000, a public folder has two parts. The first, and main, part is the folder's entry in the hierarchy, which includes the pertinent information the server must know (for example, name, location, and so on); the second part is the actual items stored in the folder.

If your public folders will see widespread, heavy use, it might be advisable to create a dedicated public folder server to ensure the best possible performance and accessibility to your public folder hierarchies. Exchange 2000 administrators can create dedicated public folder servers by installing Exchange 2000 on a dedicated server and then deleting, disabling, or removing all other services, such as the default virtual protocol servers and Outlook Web Access. In addition to removing these services, you should also delete any mailbox stores installed on the server. Remember, if you are deleting a mailbox store from a previously active server, any mailboxes residing on it will be deleted and lost as well. For this reason, make sure you have moved your users to a different server before you delete an active mailbox store. Next, create the public folder hierarchy on the dedicated public folder server and move any content from other Exchange 2000 servers to the dedicated public folder server. Finally, delete any remaining public folder stores on your other servers. Setting up a dedicated server for public folders enables the server to focus on providing storage for the data in public folders and to dedicate full network and system resources to filling users' requests for information.

Creating Public Folders

As mentioned earlier in this chapter, there are two different methods for managing public folders in your Exchange 2000 organization. The first, and most commonly used, method is through Outlook 2000; the second is through the Exchange System Manager console. With Exchange 2000 Server, public folders were designed to be easily managed from Outlook 2000, mainly because most users make use of this client to access public folders; however, any creation and administration you can do with Outlook 2000, you can also perform with Exchange System Manager. Using Outlook 2000 to create a public folder is a simple task. You will go through the required steps later in the "Hands-on Projects" section. In the meantime, take a look at the basic steps of creating a public folder using Outlook 2000.

First, double-click the Public Folders container in the Folder List section of your Outlook 2000 client to expand the current public folders you have access to, and then double-click the All Public Folders entry, as shown in Figure 13-1.

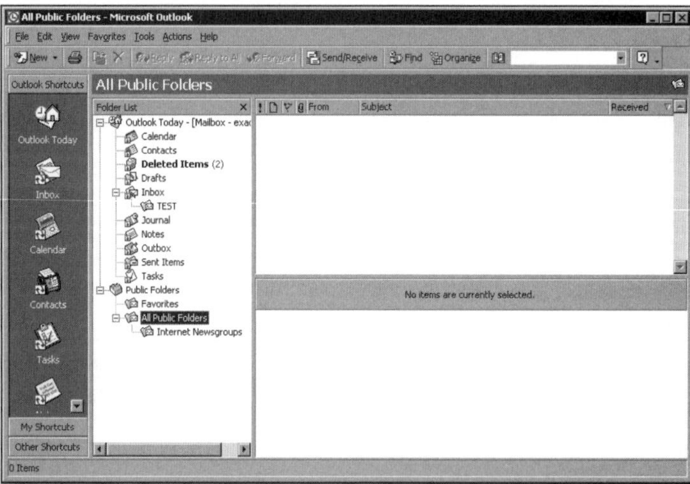

Figure 13-1 Using Outlook 2000 to display the public folders you currently have access to

Right-click the All Public Folders entry, and then click New Folder on the shortcut menu to open the Create New Folder dialog box. In this dialog box, simply type in a name for the folder you are creating, select the type of information the public folder will contain, and then select where you want to place the folder (that is, if you want to place it in a particular location in the public folder hierarchy). Different options are available to you when selecting what information will be stored in these folders:

- *Appointment Items*—Calendar entries for posting information on business or team meetings or details on booking dates and times for a shared meeting room
- *Contact Items*—Entries for user contact information and address books
- *Journal Items*—Journal entries that can be shared among team members working on the same project to keep a unified journaling implementation
- *Mail Items*—E-mail messages and messages with file attachments (any items usually kept in the Inbox)
- *Note Items*—Short messages that can be posted to share information; similar to Mail Items except that file attachments aren't included
- *Task Items*—Entries that team members can use for sharing to-do lists of tasks for a project (often used hand in hand with Appointment Items)

The type of information you choose to store in public folders affects how your users make use of them. In a small organization, configuring one of each type is probably adequate. Sometimes it's better to survey the users who manage or use the public folders the most so that you can gauge what types of folders you need to create. For instance, if your consulting firm holds several management training seminars, an Appointment Items folder would probably be useful to avoid conflicts in booking the meeting room. Of course, end users can set these options through Outlook 2000 if they are creating and managing these folders. Generally, it's a good idea to limit who can create and manage public folders on your Exchange 2000 server when you want to delegate the responsibility to other users. Delegation can help minimize the time and effort spent organizing your public folders. However, you must consider the security and legal ramifications of users posting inappropriate files or messages that your company could be held liable for.

After you have created a new folder, you can place information in it. The quick and easy way is to drag and drop messages, files, and items into the folder where you want to store them. Users or administrators could even configure Outlook 2000 to automatically transfer messages and the like to specific public folders, based on the subject, the sender, or other factors. Configuring these automatic transferrals can alleviate some of the time spent managing content for public folders.

You (as a user or administrator) don't have to wait for messages to be delivered to configure and move messages if you use the organize and sorting functionality of Outlook 2000. If there are a number of items from the same user or with a consistent keyword in the message subject, you could configure Outlook 2000 to sort messages based on this information. You can then have Outlook sort all your existing messages to quickly organize them—even if they have been sitting in your Outlook mailbox for years.

Configuring a public folder in the Exchange System Manager console is nearly identical, except that you do not select the type of information that will be held in the new public folder; the folder simply contains whatever you want to place in it. Typically, administrators use this method to create a new parent folder so that users can create their own folders underneath it by using Outlook 2000. Also, you have additional management options, including replication of the new public folder, as you will learn in the "Replicating Public Folders" section later in this chapter. You will learn how to create a new public folder in Exchange System Manager in the "Hands-on Projects" section.

You can create as many new public folder trees as you require; however, remember that you can have only one public folder tree accessible through Outlook 98 or Outlook 2000—the default All Public Folders. Any of the new public folder trees you create will be accessible, but only through other means, such as an Installable File System (IFS) share. For most organizations, this does not pose a problem because you can still create as many folders as you need in the default public folders tree, each with its own unique folder structure and access rights.

Configuring Public Folder Properties

As mentioned previously, additional public folder settings can be configured in Exchange System Manager, including the ability to replicate information from one public folder store to another on a different server. In addition, you can set storage limits for each public folder to manage how much space the folder uses. Setting storage limits can also encourage users to take a more active role in managing their own public folders. If your users tend to dump a lot of files in public folders and then forget about them, storage limits are a way to force users to clear out the mess to allow new files to be stored.

Another benefit of establishing storage limits is to remind administrators to back up the data when the public folder reaches a certain size. For instance, if the public folder hits its storage limit, the administrator could back up all old data, leaving only the past six months of data in the public folder; the rest could be archived to tape or CD backup. If a user needs some files from those backups, the administrator could restore the necessary files. Administrators have three main options for setting limits on public folders:

- *Storage limits*—Allows you to set the maximum amount of space the folder can use. You can also set a warning message that's sent (to whatever user you want) when the folder has reached a certain size.
- *Deleted item retention*—Allows you to set the number of days deleted items from a folder are retained. This option can give you some time to restore information if necessary. Keep in mind that retaining deleted items consumes hard drive space until the retention period runs out and the files are completely deleted.
- *Age limits*—Allows you to specify how many days a message posted in a public folder stays before it expires. If this option is not set, it takes on the default setting of the parent public folder store.

Another option that can be configured is the permissions for the folder, set in the Permissions tab. You use this option to specify who has access to the folder and what they can do in the public folder after they have logged on with the appropriate permissions. You will learn more about securing public folders in the next section of this chapter.

Any of these settings can be applied on a folder-by-folder, store-by-store basis; however, you can use System Manager to propagate settings from the parent folder to an entire folder tree.

Securing Public Folder Access

Securing public folder access is as simple as configuring security on any other type of folder. You can configure which users should have access to each folder and set what rights they have while working with that folder (create new folders, write, read, and so on). In almost every instance, you should configure the parent folder of a public folder tree to have the rights that users accessing folders in that particular tree need. If you need to set unique access rights for certain users, creating a new public folder tree or even a new public folder store makes it easier to manage those access rights. For example, if you want to have a special public folder configured just for the board of directors for your company, you could create a new public folder tree or public folder store called "Board of Directors" or "BOD," and then set access permissions to allow only administrators and members of the Board of Directors user group to access that public folder.

13

Setting security and access rights for a public folder is not limited to an administrator using Windows 2000 or Exchange 2000 tools; in fact, your users can take an active part in setting security for folders by using Outlook 2000, just as you can. Users and administrators alike can use the Permissions tab of a public folder's Properties dialog box to specify what role a user will have in the public folder. The permissions you can set for users include the following options:

- *Create Items*—The user can create new content for the folder (messages, contacts, and so on).

- *Read Items*—The user can open and read any content in the folder.
- *Create Subfolders*—The user can create new subfolders in the current folder.
- *Edit Items*—You can limit what content the user can modify in the folder. By setting this option to None, the user cannot modify anything; if it's set to Own, the user can edit items that he or she created. The All option enables the user to modify anything in the current folder.
- *Folder Owner*—The user can perform any management tasks in the folder, including assigning rights to other users of the folder.
- *Folder Contact*—The user receives copies of any status and nondelivery messages.
- *Folder Visible*—The user can see the folder in the public folder hierarchy.
- *Delete Items*—You can determine which items the user can delete. The options are the same as for Edit Items (None, Own, and All).

Recommending which access settings to configure for your public folders is beyond the scope of this book. These settings are unique to an organization, and can vary depending on the organization's intended use of public folders and its overall security policies. However, you should pay attention to the security of your public folders, just as you would for any other folder or software on your network or servers. Ensuring the best possible security across your network helps limit the potential for intrusion into public folders or other security incidents.

MANAGING PUBLIC FOLDERS

Management of public folders is a simple and straightforward affair. For example, you can move a public folder from one location to another within the same public folder tree by using the conventional cut-and-paste method or by dragging and dropping the folder from its current location to its new destination.

There is no way to move a folder outside its current public folder tree to another tree. Your only option is to create a matching directory structure in the new public folder tree and copy the contents you want to retain into the new public folder tree.

With the advanced administration options that users can have access to, much of the burden of folder creation and management is lifted from your shoulders. Lest you think you are out of the proverbial woods, however, there are some advanced management features that administrators shouldn't delegate to users. The following sections delve into the more advanced management and administration tasks you encounter when dealing with a public folder installation on your Exchange 2000 server.

Replicating Public Folders

By default, there is no replication of public folder items to other public folder stores in your Exchange 2000 organization. Replication can be set on a folder-by-folder basis or, like security, can be set on a parent folder so that subfolders can inherit the replication configuration. If you create a new folder under a parent folder that is set for replication, any new folders created under that parent folder are automatically configured for replication. You can, of course, change the replication configuration of a new folder after you create it, if needed.

Another useful feature of the Exchange 2000 public folder replication services is the ability to set limits for replicating data between public folder stores so that you can configure how Exchange 2000 handles this data. If your server has a high usage rate and stores a lot of files, you can configure folder replication to last for only a specified amount of time so that it doesn't affect performance or backups. For instance, if you have only two hours for folder replication after the office closes and before the scheduled server and network backup jobs run at their predefined times, you could set this option to cut off replication after two hours. If you are replicating public folder data over a WAN, however, you might want to use a bandwidth-limiting option instead of a time-based limitation. This way, you could set the transfer to be no more than 1 GB during a replication session to preserve as much bandwidth (which can cost money for use over a WAN) as possible when replicating data to other sites.

Managing the replication of public folders is made easy with the Exchange System Manager console. In the Properties dialog box for the folder, you can select which public folder stores you want to replicate the folder to. You can also use the Replication tab, shown in Figure 13-2, to set the schedule for folder replication, using the following schedule options:

- *Never run*—Disables replication for this folder
- *Always run*—Sets replication to run constantly for this folder (not advised as a permanent setting because of high system resource use)
- *Run every 1, 2, or 4 hours*—Enables replication to run at the set intervals
- *Use custom schedule*—Enables you to define a custom schedule for your specific needs and requirements
- *Use default schedule*—Sets this folder to follow the replication configuration settings configured for the parent public folder

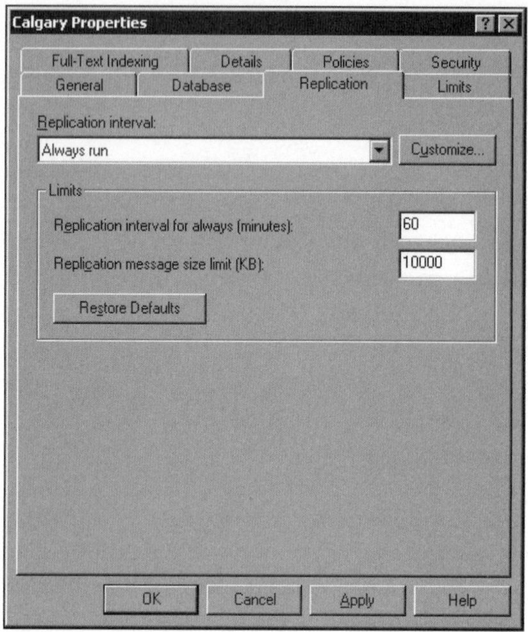

Figure 13-2 The replication options for a public folder

If there's one caveat to public folder replication in Exchange 2000, it is that after you have configured replication and replicated a folder to another public folder store, it's nearly impossible to tell the original folder from the one you replicated to another server.

Replicating the Entire Public Folder Hierarchy

In Exchange 2000, administrators don't need to take any action to have the public folder hierarchy replicated to other Exchange 2000 servers in the organization. By default, the public folder hierarchy is always replicated between Exchange 2000 servers in the Exchange organization. Even if you have disabled replication of public folders and any content in these folders, the hierarchy is always replicated automatically.

Replication of this information is handled internally on an Exchange 2000 server and between other Exchange 2000 servers in the organization by messages sent through the Message Transfer Agent (MTA). This function can be both good and bad. The advantage is that replicating the hierarchy is one less management task for administrators; on the other hand, it means that hierarchy replication messages are always being transmitted, potentially using bandwidth. However, if your public folder use is minimal, you probably will not have a hierarchy in place, so you won't have hierarchy replication information consuming bandwidth.

Replicating Individual Public Folders

So far, this chapter has focused on replicating all folders in a public folder tree to every other Exchange 2000 server in your organization. This method isn't always the best because it can take a fair amount of time to replicate all the data and information in a public folder tree. It's possible, however, to replicate only selected folders in a public folder tree by creating replicas of them on other servers. This process is best implemented by following these basic steps:

1. Create a new public folder tree and matching public store, or use an existing one.
2. Expand the folder hierarchy for the public folder tree you just created or are currently using.
3. Right-click the folder you want to replicate, and then click Properties on the shortcut menu.
4. Click the Replication tab, and then click the Add button.
5. Finally, select the Exchange 2000 server you want to replicate the folder to.

These are the basic steps for configuring individual folder replication, but after you have an established public folder tree and have populated it with folders, you can easily select which folders you want to replicate to any server you like. This flexibility makes public folder replication customizable to meet your organization's needs.

Troubleshooting Public Folder Replication

When replicating public folder information between servers, you can run into some errors, including the following problems:

- When trying to access a folder, you receive a "Public Folder cannot be opened" error. This error occurs mainly because the replication for this folder has not been completed or has failed to complete properly because the replication duration for that public folder has timed out. To rectify this problem, adjust the duration to allow more time for replication to take place. This situation can also occur if you have had to restore the public folder database files from a backup.
- A newly created public folder fails to replicate. This can occur if Active Directory has not yet had time to add the appropriate folder information to the domain, which causes the folder data being replicated to fail because the folder does not exist on the target servers yet. To rectify this, wait longer to allow AD to apply the new folder information or increase the amount of time your new public folder waits to replicate.
- Conflicts could occur if two versions of the same message are trying to replicate to a single server. Typically, Exchange 2000 handles replication conflicts; however, sometimes the messages aren't smoothly replicated. If this happens, Exchange 2000 leaves the two conflicting versions of the message in the replica, allowing you or the folder administrator to remove the incorrect version so that Exchange 2000 can replicate it properly.

There are a few other problems that can happen, but they usually involve replicating information from Exchange 2000 to Exchange 5.5, using the Active Directory Connector. In most cases, these problems can be fixed or avoided by waiting until the information has finished replicating or by configuring the Exchange 2000 replication duration for public folder information to match other replication configuration settings for Active Directory. Almost all errors logged during public folder replication have an entry in the Microsoft EventViewer. Information logged from these errors is usually kept in the Application or System logs. After you have located an error (either displayed onscreen or in the event logs), you should be able to find a solution for it on Microsoft TechNet by searching for that error or event ID.

Mail-Enabling Public Folders

It is possible to configure a public folder to appear as a mail-enabled user in Active Directory. By doing this, users can quickly send a regular e-mail message to the mail-enabled public folder, thus making it easier to post messages, files, and other objects to these folders. After you have mail-enabled a public folder, you can add it to any distribution list you like; in addition, you can allow users to see the folder in their address lists, or you can hide it from view (if, for example, you want to prevent users from choosing it by mistake when sending e-mails). Enabling folders' display in address lists allows users to post content to public folders that they cannot see through Outlook or OWA.

Configuring a folder to be mail-enabled is quick and easy; in System Manager, simply right-click the public folder you want to mail-enable, point to All Tasks, and then click Mail Enable on the shortcut menu. After being mail-enabled, that public folder will have three additional tabs in its Properties dialog box (see Figure 13-3): E-mail Addresses, Exchange Advanced, and Exchange General.

The three new tabs allow you to configure the options described in the following list, which are similar to ones you'd configure for any Exchange user:

- *E-mail Addresses*—Allows you to configure any e-mail addresses you like and to change the default address
- *Exchange Advanced*—Allows you to enter a simple display name (for instance, "Meetings Folder") and specify whether this folder can be viewed in Exchange address lists
- *Exchange General*—Allows you to specify delivery options and restrictions, such as forwarding addresses and inbound and outbound message size limits

As you can see, mail-enabling your public folders can make them more user-friendly, especially folders that are not visible when users are connected with Outlook 2000, OWA, or Outlook Express clients.

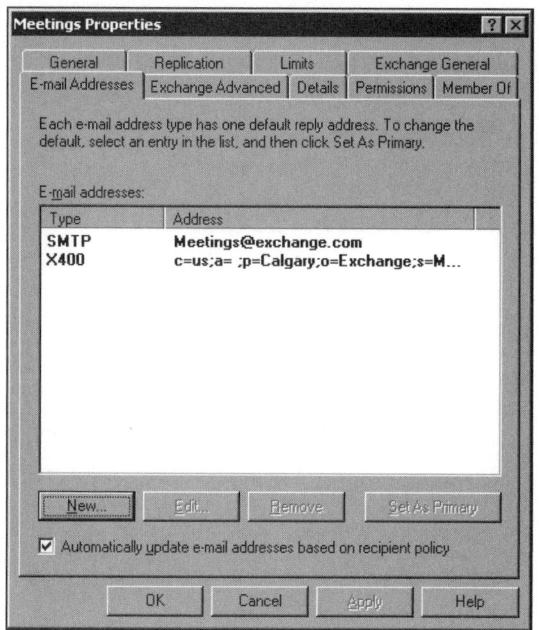

Figure 13-3 Additional tabs in a mail-enabled public folder's Properties dialog box

When a public folder is mail-enabled, the e-mail address that Exchange 2000 generates is usually based on the name of the folder. For instance, a folder called IT Department on the Exchange.com domain would have an e-mail address such as itdepartment@exchange.com. These addresses can be modified, and you can create additional ones as your situation warrants.

Monitoring Public Folder Usage

With Exchange 2000, you can quickly and easily determine how many users are logged on and which client they are connected with. This information can be handy when you are assessing server load or considering creating a dedicated public folder server for your users. To check this information, open the Logons folder under the public folder store you want to view (see Figure 13-4).

In Figure 13-4, you can see that one exadmin account is logged on through HTTP (Outlook Web Access) and that several system accounts are logged; these system accounts usually do not change and should be present in every active public folder store on your server, so do not be alarmed by them.

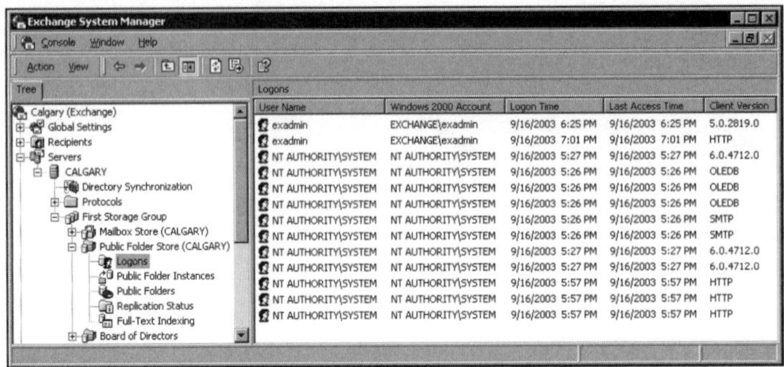

Figure 13-4 Public folder logon information in System Manager

In addition to this logon monitoring, you can also set up performance counters for Exchange 2000 public folders. There are several different counters you can activate under the MSExchangeIS Public performance object, including counters for client logons, folder opens per second, replication counters, and other public folder activities that you can use to gauge usage and performance statistics. In addition, if you have more than one public folder store, you can specify individual counters for each store, allowing you to get information for all stores rather than just one.

Configuring a performance counter for your Exchange 2000 public folder is exactly like configuring a performance counter for any other software. To open the Performance console, click Start, Programs, Administrative Tools, Performance. To add a new counter, right-click in an open area of the console's Details pane, and then click Add Counters on the shortcut menu. In the Add Counters dialog box, shown in Figure 13-5, click the appropriate object (MSExchangeIS Public) in the Performance object text box, and then select the counter you want to use in the Counters list. After you have selected the appropriate counter, click the Add button, and repeat this procedure until you have added all the counters you need. For more information on the different counters, simply select one and click the Explain button. After you have finished adding the counters, click the Close button to view the information being graphed. For more information on configuring a performance counter, refer to the Windows 2000 Help or the Microsoft Windows 2000 Server Resource Kit.

Making use of these features can help you get a handle on what exactly is going on with not only your Exchange 2000 server, but also your public folders. You can use the information to pinpoint problem areas and help you determine whether upgrades or configuration changes are needed.

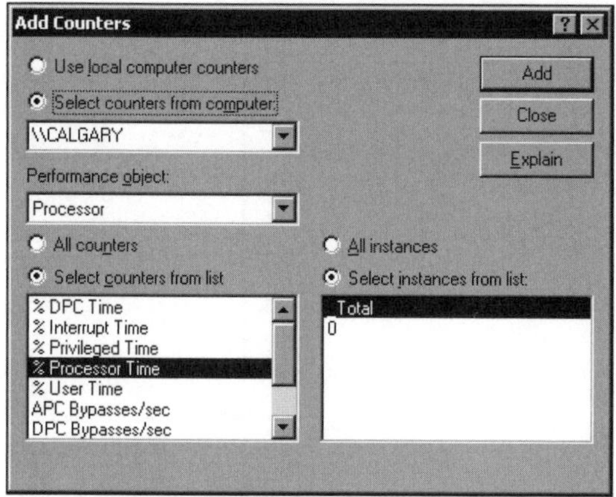

Figure 13-5 Selecting a counter in the Add Counters dialog box

Creating Public Folder Items Offline

It is not possible to make use of your public folders offline. You must be connected with one of the supported clients, such as Outlook 2000, OWA, or Outlook Express. Even in Outlook 2000, you cannot configure public folders for offline use with the offline synchronization features, as you would regular folders, such as Inbox or Sent Items.

The best way to work around this limitation is to have separate folders configured in Outlook 2000 for items you want to create offline. When you come back online, you can copy and paste or drag and drop the items you created offline to place them in their respective public folders. In addition, you could use the same folders or even another set of folders in Outlook 2000 to copy information in the public folders to take with you when you go offline. Even though you cannot manage your users' offline public folder usage as you would other information, you do have some options for offline use if your users need it.

Using Public Folders with Outlook Web Access

Using public folders with OWA is very easy and much like using them with Outlook 2000. By default, when you log on to Outlook Web Access, you see only the default folders (Inbox, Sent Items, and so on); to open the public folder view, you have to click the Folders button at the bottom of the left column in the OWA client. The left column changes to a folder view, the same as in Outlook 2000, as you can see in Figure 13-6.

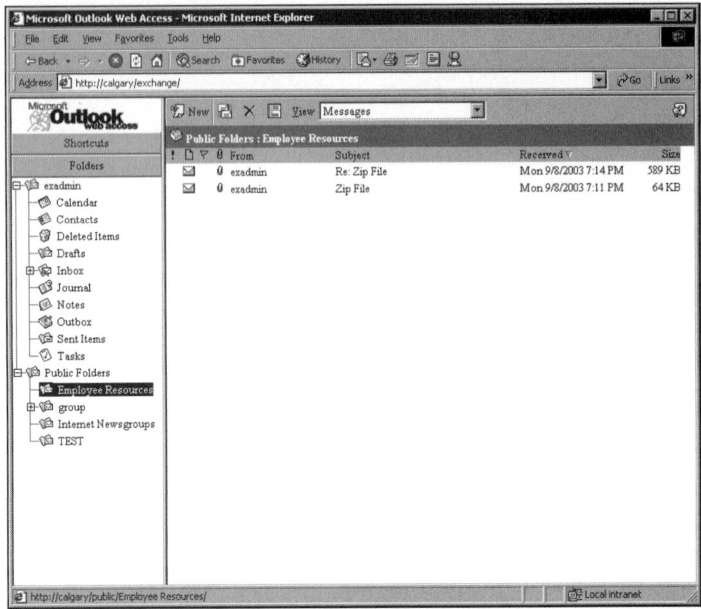

Figure 13-6 The default folder view in OWA

You can also open your public folders directly in OWA by connecting with the following URL: *http://<servername>/public*. Using this URL opens OWA, but you will see only the public folders listed in the left column (see Figure 13-7). Keep in mind that you cannot change your folder view if you log on using the "public" URL; your folder view is fixed like that unless you log on to OWA with the normal URL.

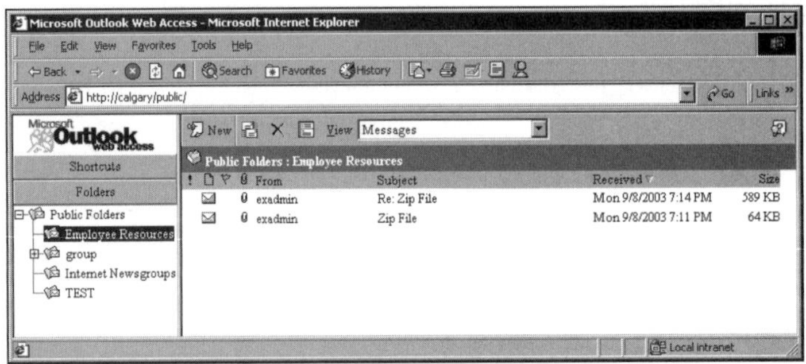

Figure 13-7 Viewing only public folders in OWA

CHAPTER SUMMARY

- Exchange 2000 provides public folders as centralized data storage for your users. With the varied access methods that are available, your users can quickly and easily gain access to the data and information they need.
- To help ease administrative tasks, end users with the appropriate access rights can easily create and manage public folders through Outlook 2000.
- Public folders are organized into a tree format with the parent folder as the basis for all other subfolders, making it easier to design and manage your public folders.
- The public folder hierarchy provides an easy-to-manage structure for your public folders and the information stored in them. Active Directory keeps a constant, up-to-date record of each hierarchy and enables hierarchy information for each public folder tree to be replicated to other Exchange 2000 servers in your Exchange organization.
- When creating new public folder stores, you can create as many as you want. However, only the default public folder store created when Exchange 2000 is installed can contain folders visible to users of Outlook (and similar clients). All other public folder stores are accessible, but only through IFS shares.
- Users can also play a role in securing access to public folders. Security can be applied to a public folder at many different levels, from simply blocking the folder from being seen to full control over the folder. Management of rights for public folders can be delegated to specific users or can be kept centralized for the Exchange administrator to manage.
- Replicating public folders spreads copies of the public folders around the domain so that the load is distributed more evenly; that way, more than one server is available for users to access information. Public folder replication can be configured for an entire folder tree or on a folder-by-folder basis.
- You can configure any public folder, even the default one, to be mail-enabled. This gives folders an e-mail address so that users can send messages to quickly and easily post information to mail-enabled public folders without needing direct access to them.
- Monitoring public folder usage can help you determine how your Exchange 2000 servers are handling the current load of your public folders and provide insight into locating potential problems.
- Using public folders offline is not supported in Outlook 2000. However, you can copy files from public folders that you need to use offline, and then upload files you have created offline to the public folders when you go back online. Using public folders through Outlook Web Access, however, is easy and nearly identical to using public folders through Outlook 2000, making remote access to public folders simple and user-friendly.

Key Terms

public folder hierarchy — The design of the public folder tree. It contains information on the public folders in the tree and helps keep track of every folder and piece of information in a public folder tree.

public folder tree — A collection of public folders organized into a tree-like file structure with a root folder and subfolders branching out from the root folder.

Review Questions

1. The department manager for the Human Resources Department at your company requests a centralized resource for the users in her department to access. She wants to be able to post work shift schedules, meeting requests, and contact information for members of her department. Can Exchange 2000 public folders be used for this purpose? Why or why not?
2. Which of the following clients can access public folders from your network when online? (Choose all that apply.)
   a. Outlook Express
   b. Outlook 2000
   c. any IMAP4-enabled third-party client software
   d. Outlook Web Access
3. Which of the following can users and administrators use to create public folders? (Choose all that apply.)
   a. Outlook 2000
   b. Outlook Web Access
   c. Exchange System Manager
   d. Installable File System
4. To improve access to and performance of your public folders, which of the following is the best option?
   a. combining all public folders on one fast server that offers other messaging services
   b. spreading the public folder stores among several servers in different geographical locations
   c. placing all user-managed public folders on one Exchange server with their related mailboxes and placing all administrator-managed public folders on another
   d. none of the above
5. Which of the following stores and manages public folder hierarchies?
   a. Active Directory
   b. the Registry

c. Exchange System Manager

d. Directory Services

6. When creating a dedicated public folder server, which of the following services must be removed from the Exchange 2000 server?

a. any collaboration features (Chat, Instant Messaging)

b. any mail services (IMAP4, SMTP, POP3)

c. any HTTP service (OWA)

d. all of the above

7. When creating a new public folder, which type of folder would you configure if you wanted your users to be able to post simple messages to other users?

8. For public folders that are not visible in Outlook and other client software, which Exchange 2000 feature would you use that allows you to share and view these folders?

a. Exchange System Manager

b. Information Store

c. Installable File System

d. none of the above

9. You can create as many different public folder stores as you require. Each of these stores can then contain folders to be viewed and accessed through Outlook 2000 and other clients. True or False?

10. When you create a new public folder, you can configure certain limits through Exchange System Manager. If you do not specify an age limit on the public folder, what happens?

11. When configuring user access rights for a given public folder, which permission would you set if you wanted the user to be able to receive status updates and non-delivery reports for the folder?

a. Read Items

b. Edit Items

c. Folder Contact

d. Folder Visible

12. If you mail-enable a public folder in Exchange 2000, which client program can you use to post new items to that folder?

a. Outlook 2000

b. Outlook Express

c. Outlook Web Access

d. any e-mail client software

13. Which of the following clients can make use of your public folders when offline? (Choose all that apply.)
    a. Outlook Express
    b. Outlook 2000
    c. any IMAP4-enabled third-party client software
    d. Outlook Web Access
    e. none of the above
14. Which of the following options are valid when scheduling folder replication? (Choose all that apply.)
    a. Never run
    b. Run when idle
    c. Run at off-peak hours
    d. Always run
15. Explain why you should consider setting a limit on the amount of data transferred instead of a limit on the replication duration when replicating over a WAN.
16. Is it possible to move folders between two different public folder trees? Yes or No?
17. When you are managing a mail-enabled public folder, which of the following tabs should you use to set a forwarding address for the folder?
    a. Details
    b. Exchange Advanced
    c. Exchange General
    d. Permissions
18. When a public folder is first mail-enabled, you must manually create e-mail addresses for the folder before any messages can be posted to it through an e-mail client. True or False?
19. When enabling a performance counter for monitoring your public folders, which of the following performance objects do you select?
    a. MSExchangeIS Public
    b. MSExchangeMTA
    c. MSExchangeNMC
    d. MSExchangeIS
20. When you are accessing your Exchange 2000 public folders through Outlook Web Access, is it possible to open an instance of Outlook Web Access that shows only the available public folders? Yes or No?

HANDS-ON PROJECTS

Project 13-1

This project shows you how to create a new public folder by using Outlook 2000. This project requires Outlook 2000 to be installed and configured with a user account on the Exchange 2000 server.

To create a public folder in Outlook 2000:

1. If necessary, log on to your Windows 2000 server and allow it to boot normally. When prompted, log on with the user account that you will use in Outlook 2000.
2. Double-click the **Microsoft Outlook** icon on the desktop, or click **Start**, point to **Programs**, and then click **Microsoft Outlook**. Outlook 2000 opens and you should see the regular folder view.
3. In the Folder list, locate and double-click **Public Folders** to display the folders underneath. Double-click **All Public Folders** to show the current folders in this public folder. The Internet Newsgroups folder appears, which is the default folder created when Exchange 2000 is installed. Right-click **All Public Folders**, and then click **New Folder** on the shortcut menu. The Create New Folder dialog box opens.
4. In the Name text box, enter a descriptive name for your new public folder. For this project, type **Employee Resources**. Click the **Folder contains** list arrow, and then click **Mail Items** from the available options. Because this is the first folder you are creating, you should place it in the root of All Public Folders (the default option when you right-clicked the All Public Folders entry to create a new folder). After you have entered the information and settings, your Create New Folder dialog box should look similar to Figure 13-8. Click **OK** to create the new folder. If you are prompted to add a shortcut to the Outlook bar, click **No**. You should now see the new folder listed with the Internet Newsgroups under the All Public Folders entry.
5. Perform Steps 3–4 again, creating two more folders—one named **Payroll** and one named **Company Contacts**. Set the Payroll folder to be a **Mail Items** folder and the Company Contacts folder to be a **Contact Items** folder. Create both of these folders as subfolders under the Employee Resources folder you just created. After creating your two new folders, your Outlook 2000 screen should look similar to Figure 13-9. Notice how the icons for each folder change to represent the type of items stored in the folder.

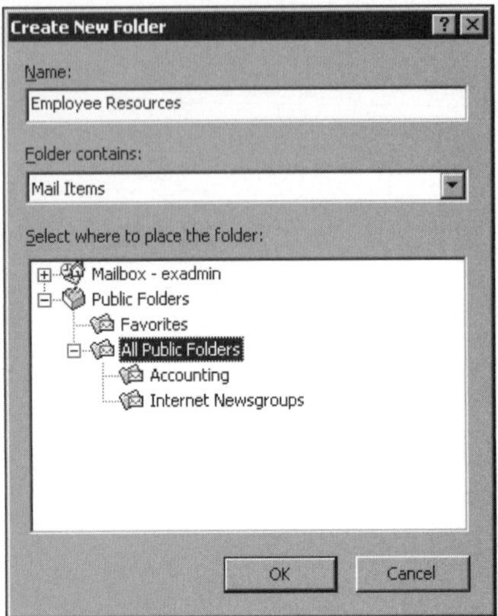

Figure 13-8 Configuring a new public folder

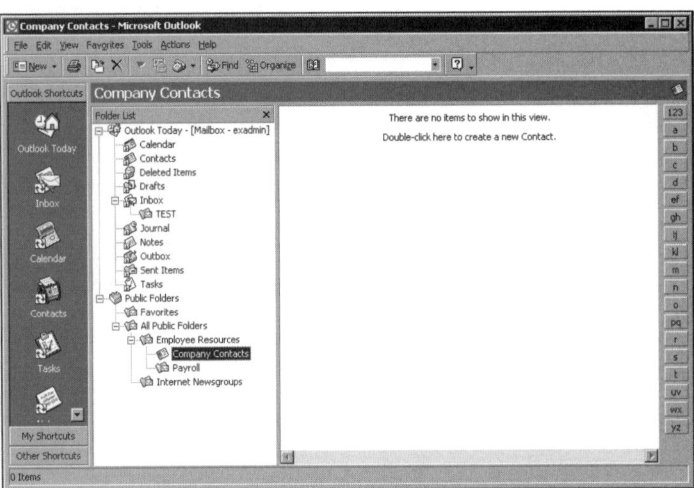

Figure 13-9 Additional folders displayed in Outlook 2000

6. Leave your system in this state with Outlook 2000 open for Project 13-2.

Project 13-2

This project shows you how to manage user rights to a folder by using Outlook 2000. You will be setting user access rights for two of the new folders you created in Project 13-1; therefore, it is assumed that you have completed Project 13-1 and are using the same system and/or configuration.

To configure public folder permissions in Outlook 2000:

1. If necessary, log on to your Windows 2000 server. When prompted, log on with the user account that you will use in Outlook 2000. If you are continuing from Project 13-1, you can skip Steps 1–2.
2. Double-click the **Microsoft Outlook** icon on the desktop, or click **Start**, point to **Programs**, and then click **Microsoft Outlook**. Outlook 2000 opens, and you should see the regular folder view.
3. Right-click the **Employee Resources** folder you created in Project 13-1, and then click **Properties** on the shortcut menu to open the Employee Resources Properties dialog box.
4. To set permissions, click the **Permissions** tab. By default, you should see three entries in the Name and Role section at the top of the dialog box. Click the **Anonymous** entry, and then click the **Read items** and **Folder visible** check boxes to enable these rights. After you have completed this step, your dialog box should look similar to Figure 13-10.

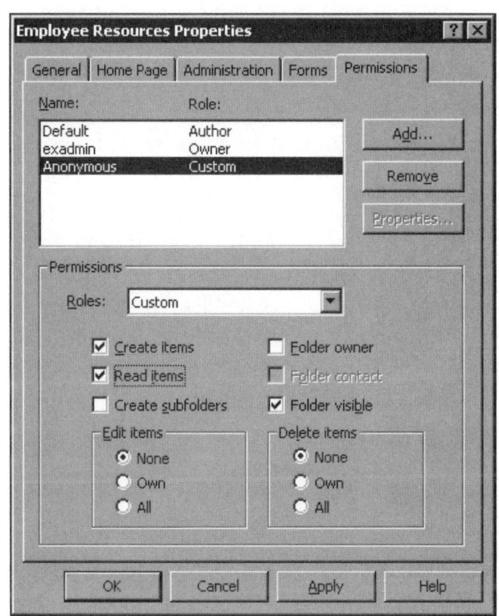

Figure 13-10 Setting permissions and roles for a public folder

5. After setting the rights for this folder, click **OK** to return to Outlook 2000. Right-click the **Payroll** public folder, and then click **Properties** on the shortcut menu to open the Payroll Properties dialog box. Click the **Permissions** tab, click the **Anonymous** entry in the Name and Role section, and then click the **Remove** button. By removing Anonymous access, you can stop anonymous users from accessing this folder.

13

6. Still in the Payroll Properties dialog box, click the **Add** button to open the Add Users dialog box. In the left side of the dialog box, click the **Administrator** account, click the **Add** button, and then click **OK**. (Note: If the permissions in this step have already been applied, you can skip to Step 7.) Back in the Payroll Properties dialog box, click the **Administrator** account (if not already selected), and then click the **Create subfolders** and **Folder contact** check boxes to enable these options. Next, click the **All** radio button in both the Edit items and the Delete items sections at the bottom. If you set these options correctly, you will notice that the role of the Administrator account (in the Roles list box) has changed to Publishing Editor.
7. Click **OK** to return to Outlook 2000, and then close any open windows or applications to return to the Windows desktop. Leave the system in this state for Project 13-3.

Project 13-3

Creating a new folder by using the Exchange System Manager console is similar to creating a new folder in Outlook 2000, except that you do not have the option to set which items will be stored in the folder. Even though you do not have this option, you do have some other options you can set, such as replication and folder limits.

If at any time during these projects you encounter the inability to access or expand the Folders entry in the Exchange System Manager console, you might have to make some changes to the Default Web site in Internet Information Services. This is a known problem with Exchange 2000. If you are having problems, set the IP address for the Default Web site to the IP address of the NIC in the server, instead of the All Unassigned setting. After you have set the IP address, restart IIS and open the Exchange System Manager console. This method should fix any problems you are having; if not, you should perform a search on Microsoft TechNet for additional troubleshooting information.

To create a public folder in Exchange System Manager:

1. If necessary, log on to your Windows 2000 server. If you are continuing from Project 13-2, you can skip this step.
2. To open the Exchange System Manager console, click **Start**, point to **Programs**, point to **Microsoft Exchange**, and then click **System Manager**.
3. Double-click the **Folders** folder in the Contents pane to show the currently installed public folders. (If you have enabled viewing administrative groups, you might need to double-click **Administrative Groups** and then **First Administrative Group** before you see the Folders folder.) Right-click the **Public Folders** entry, point to **New**, and then click **Public Folder** on the shortcut menu to open the Properties dialog box. Click the **General** tab if it isn't selected by default.

4. In the Name text box, type **Accounting** for this public folder. In the Public folder description text box, type **Special announcements from Accounting Dept.** for the description. After you have entered this information, your dialog box should look similar to Figure 13-11.

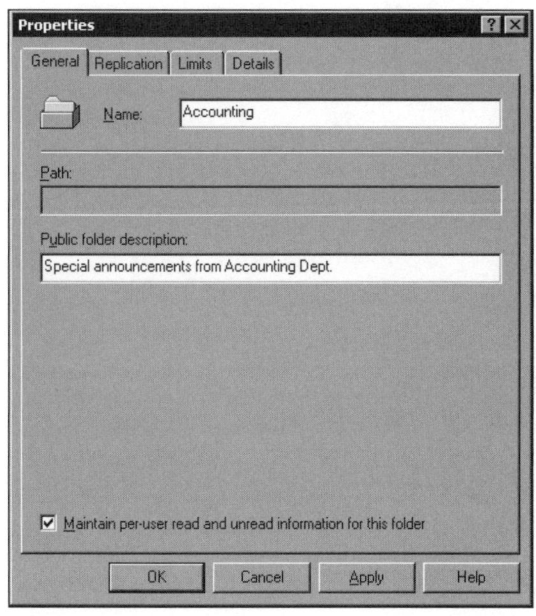

Figure 13-11 Creating a new public folder in Exchange System Manager

13

5. While still in the Properties dialog box, click the **Limits** tab to show the contents of this tab. Click the **Issue warning at (KB)** check box to enable this option, and in the text box next to this option, type **50000**. Click the **Maximum item size (KB)** check box, and in the text box next to this option, type **1000**.
6. Click the **Use public store defaults** check box in the Age limits section to deselect this option. This enables the Age limit for replicas (days) text box; type **30** in that text box. When you are finished, your Limits tab should look similar to Figure 13-12.
7. After you have finished configuring these settings, click **OK** to return to the Exchange System Manager console. Double-click the **Public Folders** entry to display the new public folder you just created. Leave the system in this state for Project 13-4.

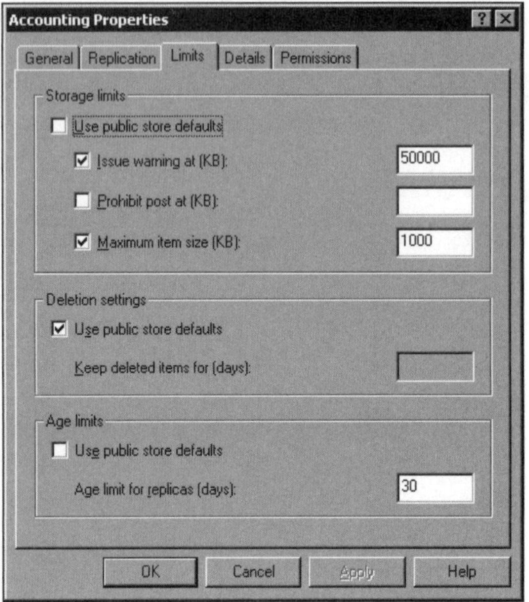

Figure 13-12 Setting limits for a public folder in Exchange System Manager

Project 13-4

This project shows you how create a new public folder tree in the Exchange System Manager console. To host the new public folder tree, you'll need to create a new public folder store. As you learned in this chapter, new public folder trees are not visible through regular client software, such as Outlook 2000.

To create and configure a new public folder tree:

1. If necessary, log on to your Windows 2000 server. If you are continuing from Project 13-3, you can skip Steps 1–2.
2. To open the Exchange System Manager console, click **Start**, point to **Programs**, point to **Microsoft Exchange**, and then click **System Manager**.
3. Right-click the **Folders** entry in the Contents pane (Remember to first double-click **Administrative Groups** and then **First Administrative Group** if you have enabled viewing administrative groups.), point to **New**, and then click **Public Folder Tree** on the shortcut menu to open the Properties dialog box.
4. In the Name text box, type **NorthWest** to name this new tree, and then click **OK** to create a new public folder tree.
5. Next, you must create a matching public folder store to support this tree. In System Manager, double-click the **Servers** folder in the Contents pane, and then double-click your Exchange server.
6. Right-click the **First Storage Group**, point to **New**, and then click **Public Store** on the shortcut menu to open the Properties dialog box. In the Name text box, type **NorthWest** to name this store. (Note that it's not necessary for the

store's name to match the public folder tree's name; the same name is used in this project just for simplicity's sake).

7. Click the **Browse** button to open the Select a Public Folder Tree dialog box. In the Available public folder trees text box, click **NorthWest**, and then click **OK**. Your General tab should now look similar to Figure 13-13.

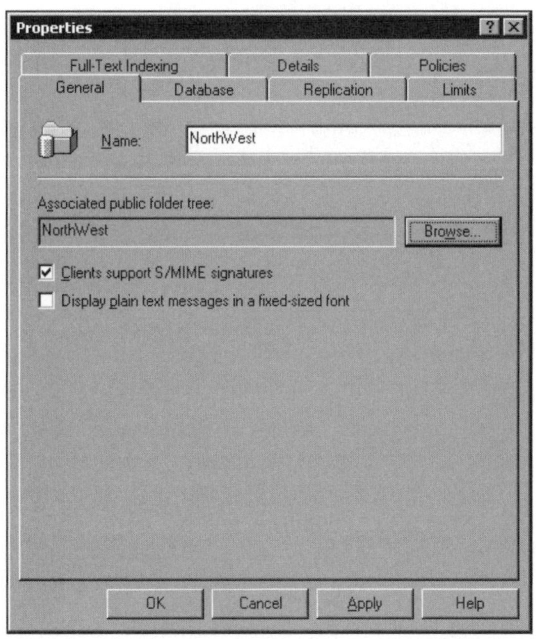

Figure 13-13 Configuring a new public folder store

8. Click the **Replication** tab to show the available options. Click the **Replication interval** list arrow, and then click **Run every 4 hours** in the listed options. In the Replication message size limit (KB) text box, type **5000**.

9. Click the **Limits** tab. Click the **Prohibit post at (KB)** check box, and in the text box next to this option, type **1000000**. In the Keep deleted items for (days) text box, delete the 0 and type **7**. These settings stop users from posting to this store when the size reaches 1 GB, and retains deleted items for only seven days.

10. Click **OK** to return to the Exchange System Manager console; a message appears letting you know the new store was created and asking if you want to mount it now. Click **Yes**. After a minute or two, your new store will be created. A message appears letting you know the store was mounted successfully; click **OK**.

11. Finally, right-click the **NorthWest** public folder tree you created in Step 4, and then click **Connect to** on the shortcut menu to open the Select a Public Store dialog box. Click the **NorthWest** entry, and then click **OK**.

Sometimes the Connect to menu option is grayed out. If this happens, simply close the Exchange System Manager console, and then open it again. After it has reloaded, navigate back to the public folder tree you just created and try again. This is a known bug in the console.

12. After you have finished the previous steps, leave the system in this current state for Project 13-5.

Project 13-5

Deleting a public folder tree is not as simple as just clicking and deleting it because the tree is connected to a few different components of Exchange 2000. This project assumes that you have completed Project 13-4.

To delete a public folder tree in Exchange System Manager:

1. If necessary, log on to your Windows 2000 server. If you are continuing from Project 13-4, you can skip Steps 1–2.
2. To open the Exchange System Manager console, click **Start**, point to **Programs**, point to **Microsoft Exchange**, and then click **System Manager**.
3. Double-click the **Servers** folder in the Contents pane (Remember to first double-click **Administrative Groups** and then **First Administrative Group** if you have enabled viewing administrative groups.), double-click your Exchange server, and then double-click the **First Storage Group**.
4. Right-click the **NorthWest** public folder store you created in Project 13-4, and then click **Delete** on the shortcut menu. A warning message opens recommending that any replicas be removed from this store prior to deleting. If there were any replicas, you should delete them first, but because this is not the case, click **Yes** to continue. In the second confirmation message box, click **Yes** again.
5. Another message box appears, informing you that the store has been removed and that you must manually remove the database files for this server. (To completely recover any space used by this store, it is a good idea to remove those files). Click **OK** to clear the message.
6. Next, double-click the **Folders** entry in the Contents pane, right-click the **NorthWest** public folder tree, and then click **Delete** on the shortcut menu. A confirmation message box appears, asking if you do in fact want to delete the tree; click **Yes**. The public folder tree and store are now gone.
7. As an optional step, you can delete the database files (there should be two). If you did not change the database location when you created the store, you can find the folder (named after the name of the store) at C:\Program Files\Exchsrvr\mdbdata\ <*foldername*> (*foldername* is the name of the public folder you just deleted). Note that the pathname could vary if you upgraded to Exchange 2000 from Exchange 5.5.
8. Leave the system in this state for Project 13-6.

Project 13-6

This project shows you how to configure the permissions settings for a folder by using the Exchange System Manager console. This procedure is similar to the one in Outlook 2000, except that you do not set roles.

To configure public folder permissions in Exchange System Manager:

1. If necessary, log on to your Windows 2000 server. If you are continuing from Project 13-5, you can skip Steps 1–2.
2. To open the Exchange System Manager console, click **Start**, point to **Programs**, point to **Microsoft Exchange**, and then click **System Manager**.
3. Double-click the **Folders** entry in the Contents pane (again, you might need to expand administrative group folders first if you have enabled viewing them), and then double-click the **Public Folders** tree to show the currently installed public folders. Right-click **Accounting**, and then click **Properties** on the shortcut menu to open the Accounting Properties dialog box.
4. Click the **Permissions** tab. Click the **Client permissions** button to open the Client Permissions dialog box so that you can view the roles and other permissions that you can set for this public folder, as you did in Project 13-2. Click **OK** to return to the Permissions tab. Next, click the **Administrative rights** button to open the Permissions for Accounting dialog box shown in Figure 13-14.

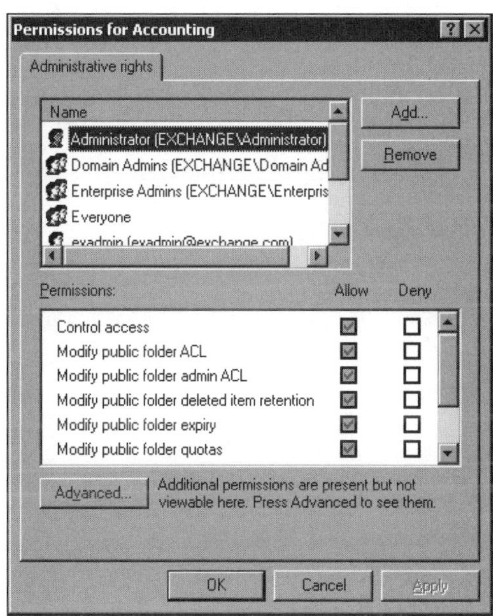

Figure 13-14 Setting public folder permissions in Exchange System Manager

5. This dialog box is similar to the one for applying rights to a folder in Windows 2000, except that it has additional permissions geared specifically to public folders. Click the **Everyone** group in the Name list box. In the Permissions list box, click the **Deny** check box next to the Administer information store, the View Information store status, and the Control access options.
6. Click **OK** to return to the Accounting Properties dialog box, and then click **OK** again to return to System Manager. Leave the system in this state for Project 13-7.

Project 13-7

This project assumes that you have completed Projects 13-1 through 13-3.

To move a public folder in Exchange System Manager:

1. If necessary, log on to your Windows 2000 server. If you are continuing from Project 13-6, you can skip Steps 1–2.
2. To open the Exchange System Manager console, click **Start**, point to **Programs**, point to **Microsoft Exchange**, and then click **System Manager**.
3. Double click the **Folders** entry in the Contents pane. Double-click the **Public Folders** entry, and then double-click the **Employee Resources** folder to expand the contents of that folder tree.
4. To drag the folder, simply click the **Payroll** public folder, hold down the mouse button, and then drag the folder to the **Accounting** public folder and release the mouse button. If you click the Accounting folder, you will now see your Payroll public folder underneath it.
5. To cut and paste, right-click the **Payroll** public folder, and then click **Cut** on the shortcut menu. Next, right-click the **Employee Resources** folder, and then click **Paste** on the shortcut menu. The Payroll public folder is now back in its original place.
6. Remember, you cannot move a public folder outside its public folder tree. As an optional step, to see this in action, you can create a new public folder tree as you did in Project 13-3, and then repeat Steps 4–5 to see how the other public folder tree stops you from dropping or pasting the public folder anywhere in the new public folder tree.

CASE PROJECTS

Case Projects Background

Bouncing Baby Wear has used Novell NetWare for its corporate network and Novell GroupWise for its e-mail client for many years. Bouncing Baby Wear has seen its clothing line expand and has opened clothing factories all over the world, including Thailand and the Philippines, so it has decided to move to Microsoft Exchange 2000 to take advantage of its new collaboration and management features. Your consulting company has already spent the past six months putting the new network in place; however, the use of public folders was not in the original plans. The head of the IT Department has been reading about public folders, and he wants to take advantage of this feature. You, as the public folder expert, are called in to make suggestions and recommendations for a public folder implementation.

The network consists of six different Exchange 2000 servers spread all over the world: two in North America (one on each coast), one in London, one in Thailand, one in the Philippines, and one in Mexico. There are approximately 2000 users at each location, with four major departments (Accounting, Management, Sales, and Manufacturing). Outlook 2000 is the primary client being used; however, some users also take advantage of the OWA services.

Case 1

Bouncing Baby Wear wants to get some basic public folders up and running right away for its different departments to try out and make suggestions on how they should be set up. What basic configuration would you recommend, given the current network configuration? What could you recommend to allow their departmental heads to create a mock folder organization before the official public folder rollout takes place?

Case 2

After seeing the potential of public folders, all the department heads want to move forward with planning and implementing their public folder services. Some technically savvy users have a few questions and concerns about the new public folder services, however. They want to know if there will be any way to quickly restore items that are accidentally deleted; in addition, they want to know if they will be able to make use of the public folders while offline and on the road. What answers can you supply for these questions?

Case 3

You have progressed through the public folder implementation, and users are already taking advantage of public folders. Unfortunately, there has been a snag. Users in Mexico want to be able to quickly and easily gain access to the public folders in the North America West Coast branch office for design documents and notes that are being passed back and forth, and they find the group forum aspect of public folders more appealing than using e-mail for this project. What feature could you implement to help this situation? What settings could you change for this feature to provide the most up-to-date information possible? If money and ongoing costs are a concern, what could you do to help limit some of the costs associated with your solution?

Case 4

You have implemented extensive public folder services for Bouncing Baby Wear that encompass all its locations. During the course of your implementation, you ended up deciding to create individual public folder trees and stores for each department at each location. However, the users are now complaining that they find it difficult to quickly and efficiently post messages and other data to the folders in the new dedicated public folder trees. What is the cause of this problem, and what can you do to make public folder access more efficient and convenient for users in the different locations?

CHAPTER

14

MAINTAINING AND MONITORING EXCHANGE 2000 SERVER

After reading this chapter and completing the exercises, you will be able to:

- Understand key concepts that can help you determine a plan for maintenance and Exchange 2000 optimization methods that can affect your maintenance plan
- Maintain Exchange 2000 Server database files, including the Information Store, recover space no longer being used by Exchange 2000, and maintain circular logging files to provide useful logging information without consuming all your disk space
- Configure notifications and alerts by using the Exchange System Manager console to retrieve information on the events and status of your Exchange 2000 server
- Use the Exchange 2000 Server Message Tracking Center to gain insight into how your server is functioning and how messages are flowing
- Use the Windows 2000 Performance console to assess your server's performance and ensure that it meets the performance levels your organization requires
- Understand how to use Exchange 2000 utilities for troubleshooting your server, including the Message Transfer Agent Checker and ESEUTIL to check your Exchange 2000 databases for corruption and help fix them

In Chapter 13, "Exchange 2000 Server Public Folders," you learned about the advantages that public folders can offer your organization. Public folders provide an easily organized and manageable file structure that users outside your network can access remotely. These folders can include not only e-mail messages with or without file attachments, but also contacts, notes, and other useful information. Public folders are certainly not new to the Exchange product line, but Exchange 2000 brings a few improvements—including the ability to create more than one public folder tree. Each public folder tree can be configured with different folders and a different design, but only the default public folder tree and store can be viewed and accessed through clients such as Outlook 2000 and Outlook Web Access. Finally, you learned about the management and maintenance of public folders in Exchange 2000.

In this chapter, you learn about different concepts you can apply to maintaining your Exchange 2000 server, including preventive maintenance and how to optimize your Exchange 2000 server for performance and reliability. You also learn about maintaining Exchange 2000 databases, including advanced logging options that can give you more information when monitoring and maintaining your Exchange 2000 server. Finally, you learn about various Exchange 2000 utilities and features that enable advanced monitoring and maintenance of your server, including the Message Tracking Center, the MTACheck utility, and ESEUTIL, as well as Windows 2000 utilities, such as the Network Monitor and the Performance console, which can be used for server monitoring and maintenance. All of these features and concepts come together to ensure the best possible monitoring of your server and enable you to maintain your installation for performance and reliability.

MAINTENANCE CONCEPTS

Maintaining Exchange 2000 is much like maintaining any other piece of software or operating system in that some general concepts apply across the board. Among these concepts are preventive maintenance and the optimization of Exchange 2000. Both are equally important in the grand scheme of maintaining Exchange 2000 so that it performs to the best of its abilities; however, often these tasks are not given enough consideration until it's too late, and either the server has failed or its performance has degraded to the point where it takes less time and effort to rebuild the server than to correct the problem.

Preventive Maintenance and Optimization

As any experienced system administrator will tell you, performing preventive maintenance is far better than resorting to reactive maintenance. Preventive maintenance consists of taking active steps to maintain your systems and network before any real problems have occurred to help keep your server running in a stable state. You can think of preventive maintenance as being similar to regularly changing the oil in your car. Although your car could probably run fine for a while longer without the oil change, it benefits from your keeping fresh oil in the engine. The same concept applies to your servers and networks; regular maintenance keeps them running in the best condition possible.

Reactive maintenance consists of responding to problems as they arise instead of heading them off before they occur. Although many people prescribe to this form of maintenance, it is far from the optimal solution because if you're forced to fix a problem, often your server or network is either not functioning or performing at a less than useful level.

In most organizations, having your server or network down for maintenance is often unacceptable unless it is during off hours (which might not be feasible in, for example, companies that run round-the-clock shifts). Unfortunately, some problems require your immediate attention and, according to Murphy's Law, these problems never happen during off hours, which can be the single best reason to perform preventive maintenance. Of course, preventive maintenance isn't the be-all-end-all solution; problems can still occur even if you have been diligent in taking preventive maintenance steps. Preventive maintenance does help cut down on potential problems, however.

Keeping your Exchange 2000 server functioning at peak performance is part and parcel of maintaining your Exchange 2000 server, almost another step in preventive maintenance. If your system is not maintained properly, this can lead to poor performance, even total failure. To help prevent maintenance problems, therefore, keep your Exchange 2000 server in peak operating condition. Even seemingly small tasks such as regular defragmentation of your server's hard drives can help keep your Exchange 2000 server optimized. Never underestimate the potential impact of optimizing your server's configuration and performance, in addition to regular preventive maintenance of your servers and network.

There are many aspects of optimizing your Exchange 2000 server (including keeping databases uncluttered and orderly and considering organizational factors in your server maintenance plans), but unfortunately there isn't a single big red button to optimize your server. Monitoring your system before performing any optimization or maintenance tasks can give you an idea of where time and money would be best spent in managing and upgrading your servers to keep them running smoothly. As you will learn later in the "Other Maintenance and Monitoring Tasks" section of this chapter, a wealth of information can be gathered by using the Windows 2000 Performance Monitor utility to monitor not only Exchange 2000, but also the server and its operating system.

MAINTAINING EXCHANGE 2000 SERVER DATABASES

Maintaining your Exchange 2000 server is essential to ensuring its long-term performance and the availability of its messaging services. One of the most important aspects of server maintenance is maintaining the databases used by Exchange 2000 in the course of its duties, including the Information Store (which you will learn about in the next section). Remember, any store on your computer (the Information Store, mailbox stores, or public folder stores) requires regular maintenance, including recovering space that's no longer being used in the Exchange 2000 databases. As information is created and removed, database space ends up being wasted, resulting in three potential problems. First, larger databases take longer to access; second, larger databases take up more hard drive space; and third, larger databases take longer to back up and restore. Running out of disk storage space could cause your server to crash; if that happens, space must be freed up for the server to operate properly again.

In addition to database management, you are most likely logging database and server events. Although the default logging techniques usually work fine, when your server activity grows, so do the logs. When this occurs, you should adjust how the logs are updated and how additional log files are created by modifying the Exchange 2000 logging configuration. You will learn more about these maintenance issues in the next few sections of this chapter.

Maintenance of Exchange 2000 Databases

Maintenance of your Exchange 2000 databases (stores) is of paramount importance because the databases hold all the data for your Exchange 2000 installation. Even the server being shut down abnormally (the power cord being disconnected accidentally while the server is running, for example) or a failed hard drive can have a dramatic effect on the database files, varying from corruption to all-out loss. Maintaining the Exchange 2000 stores helps limit the possibility of losing your data entirely; you should pay particular attention to the Information Store because it typically holds the most critical data.

Utilities can be run on your Exchange 2000 server that help check the integrity of database files and perform repairs on or recoveries of them. The ESEUTIL utility is useful even if your server appears to be in working order because it detects and helps fix anomalies that even you or your users haven't noticed. The ESEUTIL utility is included with Exchange 2000; you will learn how to use this tool in the "Hands-on Projects" section in this chapter.

Another maintenance step that applies not only to the Information Store, but also to any other server component, is performing regular backups and ensuring their reliability so that when you need to restore a database, you have complete information to work with. With the backup software built into Windows 2000, there is little excuse for not performing regular backups. Although the Microsoft backup software included with Windows 2000 is adequate, some administrators opt for a more expensive backup solution, such as Backup Exec or NetBackup by Veritas Software (found at *http://www.veritas.com/*), that can offer better performance, customization, and flexibility than the Microsoft backup software. Whichever backup software you decide to use, a reliable backup can be a lifesaver if something happens to your server.

When it comes to backups, simply making a backup isn't enough. You have to invest some time verifying that your backups have worked properly and that the data stored in these backups is valid and safe to restore to your computer. When developing a plan for your backup solution, you should also consider where the backup media is stored because the data on backups is usually of a sensitive nature (so you don't want the backup tapes falling into the wrong hands). You must consider the possibilities of a fire or other natural disaster happening where your backups are stored. Being able to restore your data quickly can make or break your organization. Many companies specialize in safe, secure solutions for storing your tapes. These offsite storage sites can provide a perfect environment to ensure that your tapes don't suffer water or heat damage, which can destroy useful data. Even if you have a trusted secretary take the backup media home for offsite storage, there's the potential for loss. For instance, if your secretary's home burns down with a week's worth of information on backup tapes—and this is the only offsite storage you had arranged—you are left without the data from the backups. If secure offsite storage is not an option (because of cost or availability of that service in your community), other solutions include using a fireproof safe to store your tapes and placing full monthly backups in a safety deposit box. Do not underestimate the need for reliable, available backups of your server's information, and don't limit yourself to backing up just the Information Store.

If a natural disaster causes total loss of a company's network equipment and data and the company doesn't get up-to-date data restored within seven days, it's quite possible the company could go out of business. Many companies rely on the data on their network and servers to conduct their business, so if this information is permanently lost, they often must start over from scratch.

In addition to using database maintenance utilities and performing regular backups, there are some integrated maintenance procedures that Exchange 2000 Server runs to keep the Information Store and other databases in peak condition. One is the Information Store Maintenance Schedule, an automated schedule that can be configured to run whenever you choose (typically, after hours is the most logical choice so that it doesn't disrupt users' work). The Information Store Maintenance Schedule performs the tasks described in Table 14-1.

Table 14-1 Information Store Maintenance Schedule Tasks

Task	Description
Index Aging	Deletes user-created database indexes that haven't been used for a certain amount of time (default is eight days).
Message Expiration	Deletes any messages older than a specified time from public folders.
Update Server Versions	Updates the current versions of installed and connected Exchange servers. As servers in the organization are updated, version information is updated as well. Updates can include upgrades from Exchange 5.5 to Exchange 2000 or even a service pack installation.
Tombstone Maintenance	Packs down deleted message information that has been used to direct replication of data through the public folders.
Age Folder Tombstones	Similar to Tombstone Maintenance, packs down deleted folder information that has been used to direct replication of data through the public folders.

14

Most of the tasks in the preceding table are performed in the background, so unless something goes wrong with the Information Store Maintenance Schedule, you probably won't see any messages or activity to indicate it's happening. In addition to these maintenance tasks, the operating system or Exchange 2000 performs several other maintenance tasks automatically on a regular schedule or an as-needed basis. Generally, the administrator doesn't configure or manage these tasks, which are outlined in the following list:

- *Background cleanup*—This background cleanup process reclaims lost space from deleted folders, messages, and attachments in Exchange 2000. Although administrators can't directly control this process, they can configure a few Registry settings that dictate how often the cleanup is performed and whether to log errors or events in the Windows event logs. For more information on the Registry settings for this task, search for article Q159306 on the Microsoft TechNet site.
- *Database compacting*—The JET database engine in Windows 2000 handles compacting the Exchange 2000 databases and reallocating and cleaning up unused space. If the event ID 63 appears in the Windows event logs, defragmenting the Exchange 2000 databases is required. To do this, run the Edbutil.exe utility from a command prompt and use the /d option for both Exchange 2000 database files (Priv.edb and Pub.edb).
- *Background activities*—These activities always run at 10-minute intervals, in the following sequence:
  - Reread Information Store quotas and update information accordingly.
  - Flush information to the database.
  - Flush cached Exchange Server directory information.
  - Reread individual user quotas and update information accordingly.
  - Perform other miscellaneous Information Store functions, such as replicating public folder information (if scheduled).

As you can see, beyond the utilities and software used to maintain, back up, and optimize your Information Store and other databases, Exchange 2000 and Windows 2000 do quite a bit to help keep your Information Store running in peak condition. However, even with these automated maintenance features, you should run your own maintenance procedures to supplement the preexisting ones.

Recovering Space in Exchange 2000 Information Store Databases

As mentioned, the ESEUTIL utility can be used to search for and repair problems with your Exchange 2000 database files. In addition, you can use it to recover space in your databases, check their integrity, and repair them. ESEUTIL will certainly be the foundation for much of your maintenance and troubleshooting efforts. When an Exchange 2000 database is created in the Information Store, it starts out empty; like your hard drive, though, over time as information is added, moved, and deleted, it can get fragmented. The only way to sort out and recover the unused space is to defragment the database files by using ESEUTIL. Although Exchange 2000 performs defragmentation and minor cleanup of the databases while the server is online, these automatic online utilities do nothing to actually recover lost space. Therefore, you need to use the offline ESEUTIL utility (when the Exchange 2000 Server services are stopped) to recover lost space.

Although very useful, the ESEUTIL should not be run every day or even every week. Rather, you should use it only when your servers need it (for instance, after deleting or purging a lot of mailbox and public folder data from the server) or if there appears to be a genuine problem with the database. However, periodic tests of the integrity of your Exchange 2000 database files with ESEUTIL's integrity-checking component (explained in the following list) is certainly a good preventive maintenance measure.

ESEUTIL is run from the command prompt, and by adding a command-line switch after the executable, you can perform the following key maintenance tasks:

- *Defragmentation*—Use the /d switch to compact the database's fragmented sections into solid blocks of information. After the defragmentation, any left-over unused space is deleted from the database. When the database file is being defragmented, a temporary copy of the original database is made and the defragmentation runs on the temporary file, which then replaces the original database file. Microsoft recommends making a full backup of your database files after a defragmentation because any restoration data you had before is of little use after restructuring the database.
- *Repair*—Use the /r switch to check for and repair broken links in the database's table of contents and the information it points to. This task runs very slowly and its ability to repair a damaged database is not guaranteed, so Microsoft recommends running it only as a last resort if nothing else has worked. If this switch does uncover errors in the database, ESEUTIL returns one of three errors: 1018, 1019, or 1022. These errors can have several different causes, so the best plan of attack is to search for the error number on Microsoft TechNet to find possible causes and fixes.
- *Integrity*—Use the /g switch to check the integrity of the database file (see Figure 14-1). This task does not make any changes to the file itself; it simply makes a temporary copy of the original database, checks it, and finds any pertinent information that can be supplied to Microsoft tech support for troubleshooting purposes.

As you can see, ESEUTIL is a useful addition to your Exchange 2000 troubleshooting toolkit. It helps keep your Information Store databases from getting bloated and causing problems that affect the performance of Exchange 2000.

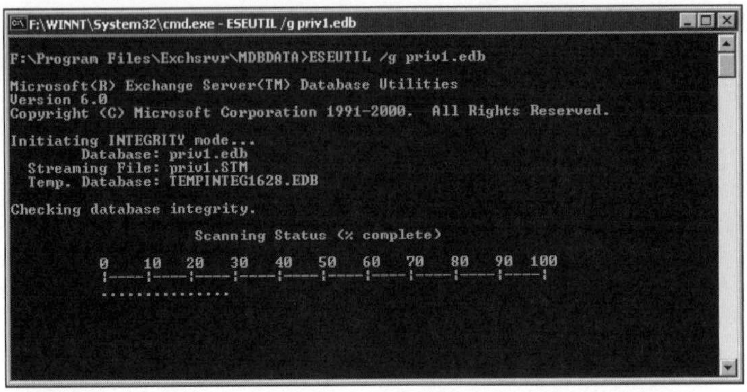

Figure 14-1 Checking database integrity with ESEUTIL

Maintaining Log Files with Circular Logging

When a transaction occurs in the Exchange 2000 databases, the event is written to a log file and then eventually to a separate database. When the log file reaches its size limit, a new log is created and the previous log is renamed. The result is that you start to accumulate a set of leftover log files that store records of the activities in your Exchange 2000 databases. This set of log files can be used to rebuild the databases if there's a server failure or crash.

This default logging method has one downside, however; it can take a considerable amount of space to store the log files generated by your servers, especially in large networks with multiple mailbox and public folder stores. To reduce the amount of space these logs use, Exchange 2000 offers the option to enable circular logging. **Circular logging** reuses the first log file generated after its contents have been written to the database. This method allows you to reuse existing space instead of creating another log file and taking up more space. By default, circular logging is disabled, and in a typical Exchange 2000 deployment, Microsoft recommends that it remain disabled because you cannot use circular logging files to rebuild databases if your system fails or crashes. In circular log files, the original log files aren't retained, so your database restore won't be complete and up to date. If you do decide to enable circular logging, you should regularly make a properly functioning, full backup of your databases to help ensure a more complete restore if something should go wrong. You will learn how to enable and disable circular logging in the "Hands-on Projects" section, later in this chapter.

Other Maintenance and Monitoring Tasks

You can take advantage of several utilities when maintaining your Exchange 2000 server. In this section, you will learn about some of the advanced monitoring and maintenance features in Exchange 2000 and Windows 2000, including tracking activity on your server and using the Performance Monitor to assess your servers' performance so that you can decide whether you need to upgrade hardware to accommodate the needs of Exchange 2000 and your users. You can also make use of many other logging and troubleshooting utilities in Exchange 2000 to keep your installation running as smoothly as possible.

Windows 2000 Event Viewer

As discussed in previous chapters, the Windows Event Viewer can be a useful troubleshooting tool. In many cases, it is the only indication from your server and the installed software of any problems. Event Viewer keeps three log files (described in Table 14-2), which can be saved for future use to help in your troubleshooting efforts.

Table 14-2 Event Viewer Log Files

Log File	Function
Application	Records events generated by applications installed on the server, including any Exchange 2000 services. It provides the most useful and critical information when troubleshooting your Exchange 2000 installation.
Security	Records security-related events (either successes or failures), based on the security auditing configuration for the server or domain.
System	Records system-level errors, particularly device driver and network connectivity failures.

In addition to these three key logs, when you install DNS and AD, logs are added to the Event Viewer for DNS and Directory Services; you can check these logs for errors, warnings, and general information on these services. These logs might not supply any direct troubleshooting information for Exchange 2000, but you could use them to help detect underlying problems plaguing Exchange 2000 as well as the entire network.

Configuring Notifications in Exchange System Manager

It is unlikely that even the most dedicated network administrators are constantly hovering over their servers to notice every single problem that occurs. For that reason, Microsoft has included a notification feature in Exchange 2000 that alerts the appropriate people to problems with the server.

You have a great deal of flexibility in configuring notifications in Exchange System Manager. For instance, you can configure the server to notify you of certain events or let you know when the server starts a particular task, such as a database flush. In addition, you can specify sending an e-mail to certain users to notify them of an event. When you configure Exchange 2000 to send notifications via e-mail, you can monitor activity on and set notification options for the following five resources:

- CPU utilization
- Free disk space
- SMTP queue growth

- Windows 2000 services
- X.400 queue growth

Figure 14-2 shows an example of the Properties dialog box for e-mail notifications. In the Servers and connectors to monitor list, you have the option of enabling notifications for a resource to be sent when it reaches a warning state (typically nothing has failed yet, but there's a potential problem) or a critical state (a service or component has failed or a system resource is depleted). In addition, you can configure which server should monitor the server for which you are configuring e-mail notifications. Microsoft does not recommend that you set up a server to monitor itself (but you certainly can)—mainly because if there's a critical problem, the server might not be able to send out notifications to alert users.

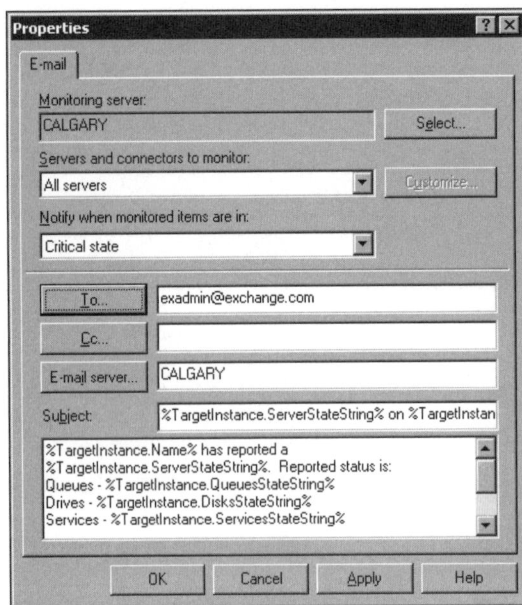

Figure 14-2 The Properties dialog box for e-mail notifications

You can also have Exchange 2000 start a preconfigured script file that performs a series of commands, such as copying and renaming log files when they exceed a certain size or shutting down Exchange 2000 services if available hard drive space sinks below a specified amount. To create a new script notification, simply right-click the Notifications folder in the Exchange System Manager console, point to New, and then click Script Notification on the shortcut menu. When configuring a script to run when a particular notification occurs, you can specify the server you are monitoring, at what event level (warning or critical) the script will be started, and, naturally, the path to the script file you want to start. Figure 14-3 shows an example of the Properties dialog box for script notifications.

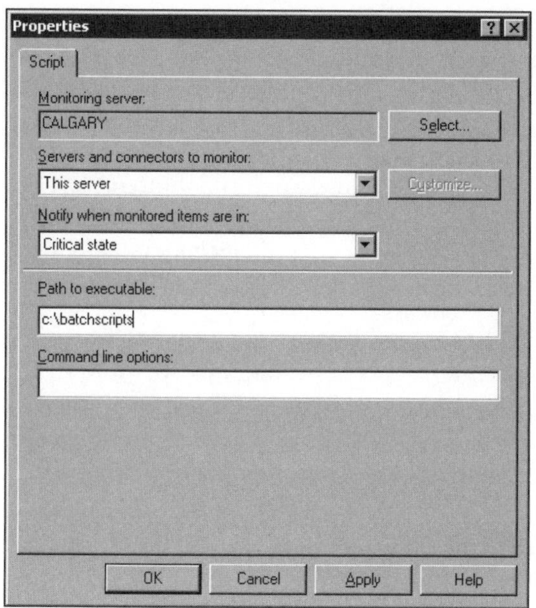

Figure 14-3 The Properties dialog box for script notifications

Configuring notifications on your servers helps you catch problems before they get out of control and can give you the opportunity to fix problems before they cause lengthy downtime for your servers and users. This feature can be especially handy if, for instance, you configure e-mail notifications to be sent to an e-mail address that's relayed to a pager carried by an IT staff member who is on call during evenings and weekends when IT staff aren't usually on site. Also, you can configure both an e-mail notification and a script notification for the same server and the same warning level if you want to simultaneously notify the administrator and run a script. You will learn how to configure an e-mail notification in the "Hands-on Projects" section.

Using Message Tracking in Exchange System Manager

As you have learned, in Exchange 2000, administrators can track messages sent to and from the server. When message tracking is enabled, Exchange 2000 keeps logs of all messages sent and received, allowing you to perform detailed searches for particular keywords, recipients, subjects, and more. This feature can be a great boon to administrators—especially for locating a message to determine whether it was, in fact, delivered. You can also use message tracking to ferret out inappropriate messages. For instance, you can search for messages with certain keywords on subjects prohibited in your network environment, such as software piracy, pornography, or other topics that most organizations typically don't allow. Being able to search for messages sent with these subjects makes it easier to locate and warn offending users to stop these activities.

In addition, you can use the Message Tracking Center to help you troubleshoot Exchange 2000 Server message delivery. For instance, you have a user who is not receiving messages, even though other users on the same network are sending messages to the user's correct assigned e-mail address. In this case, you can perform a message track on the messages being sent to that one user and find out where they are going. Message tracking can also help you determine whether a user's assigned e-mail address has been mistyped by one character so that messages are going to the wrong mailbox. Performing a message track allows you to see where messages are going, adding to the tools you have for maintaining and monitoring your Exchange 2000 installation.

Before you can take advantage of the message-tracking functionality in Exchange 2000, you must enable message tracking in the Properties dialog box for your Exchange 2000 server so that it can start logging messages, as shown in Figure 14-4. Enabling subject logging and display in this dialog box gives you a broader range of information (such as a message's subject line) from your message-tracking searches.

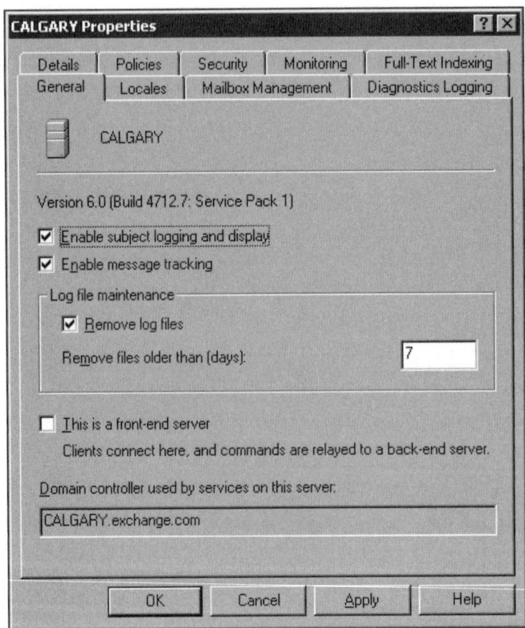

Figure 14-4 Enabling message tracking and subject logging and display in the server's Properties dialog box

After you have enabled tracking, you can use the Message Tracking Center (under the Tools folder in Exchange System Manager) to perform a search. Simply right-click the Message Tracking Center folder, and then click Track Message on the shortcut menu. The Message Tracking Center dialog box opens, through which you can enter senders, recipients, servers the message was sent through, date and time, and configure advanced features, such as searching for a particular message ID. After you have located the message for which you want more information, click it, and then click the Message History button to have Exchange 2000 generate a basic message history, as shown in Figure 14-5.

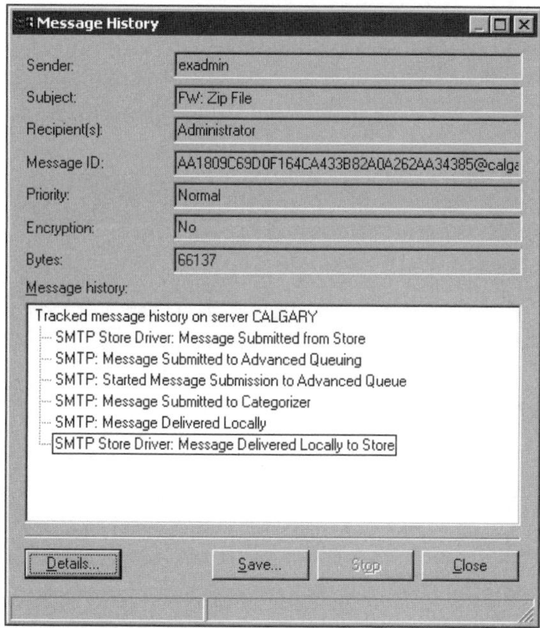

Figure 14-5 The message history of a message tracked through the Message Tracking Center

Monitoring Message Queues and System Resources

When you first install Exchange 2000 Server, it creates monitors for tracking various features of Exchange 2000, such as SMTP and X.400 message queues. By viewing these message queues, you can determine whether data being transferred on these protocols is backing up and view the overall activity of your messaging system. In addition to monitoring message queues, Exchange 2000 provides built-in monitors for connector links and other system-level resources, such as:

- CPU utilization
- Free disk space
- Available virtual memory on the server
- Windows 2000 services

In the Tools folder in the Exchange System Manager console, you can view the default installed queues by double-clicking the Monitoring and Status folder and then clicking the Status folder. You should see something similar to Figure 14-6.

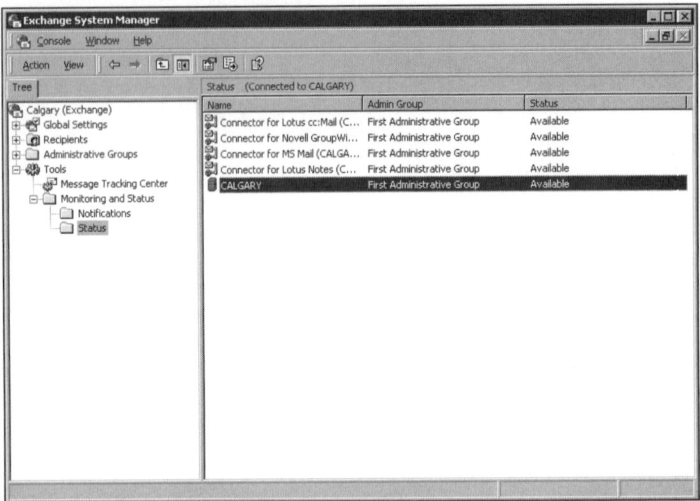

Figure 14-6 The default Exchange 2000 connector monitors

You can quickly and easily add monitors for services, queue sizes (SMTP and X.400), and system resources and specify at which state the server will warn you. For instance, you can set the server to warn you when the CPU usage reaches a critical level (for instance, 80% constant usage) or the free hard disk space goes below 10%.You must monitor free hard disk space, especially for Exchange servers, because if the server runs out of room, you could have complete server failure, not to mention the potential for losing data that you cannot recover.Therefore, you should configure these monitors not only for your message queues and their usage, but also for system resources.You will learn how to install some of these additional monitors in the "Hands-on Projects" section.

Using the Performance Console

A vital part of monitoring, maintaining, and tuning the performance of your Exchange 2000 server is actually part of the Windows 2000 operating system. When configured properly, the Performance console can supply a wealth of useful information about the operating system, Exchange 2000, and its respective resources, connectors, and stores.You have learned a little about the Performance console in previous chapters; in this chapter, you will take a closer look at this useful monitoring utility, including the Exchange-specific performance counters and how to install them. In addition, you will learn about configuring logs and alerts based on information supplied by the Performance console.

The Performance console has two main components: the System Monitor and the Performance Logs and Alerts. Each performs a special function, described in more detail in the following sections. In System Monitor, you can add performance counters for a wide variety of operating system and software components. The Performance Logs and Alerts component enables you to create alerts based on information in the performance counter logs.

System Monitor

The System Monitor component of the Performance console is the bread and butter of this utility and can be found by clicking Start, Programs, Administrative Tools, Performance. System Monitor allows you to monitor four key elements of your Windows 2000 server: hard drives, memory, processors, and network hardware. Each element can have a few different types of data collected. The basic information generated in System Monitor is the **counter**, a record of the information that's measured and stored for the monitored element. Each counter can measure different objects that define where the data is collected from, including the processor, memory, network connections, and even Exchange 2000. For each object, you can apply 10 or more different counters. Note that each counter can measure more than one object; when you have multiple objects, each one is called an **instance**. For example, if you are measuring CPU performance on your server and you have two processors to monitor, each processor is an instance of the processor object being measured by the CPU performance counter. In the Add Counters dialog box, you can select which instances you monitor, as shown in Figure 14-7.

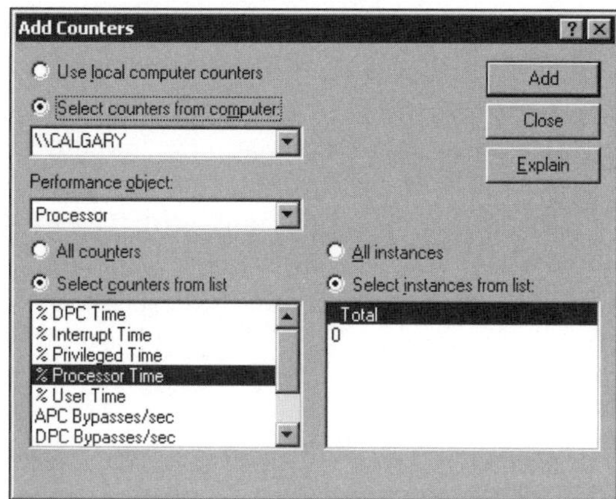

Figure 14-7 The Add Counters dialog box

In addition to monitoring your local server, you can use the Performance console to connect to and monitor other servers without having to be directly in front of them, allowing easier management of remote servers. The next four sections outline the main components of Windows 2000 that should be monitored with System Monitor.

Memory Usage System memory can make or break the performance and stability of your servers and their software, so any logging of its performance should be done over an extended period of time, such as an entire week. Logging for just a few minutes does not produce accurate results. Rather, you need information gathered over time to take into account varying usage rates at different times of the day, for example, to get valid user activity numbers that accurately reflect typical memory usage on your server. In System Monitor, these are the three main memory counters:

- *Memory\Pages/sec*—Shows the rate at which data is flowing between RAM and the server's hard drives. The recommended goal is to keep this value under 20.
- *Memory\Available Bytes*—Shows the amount of installed memory (RAM) in the server and how much of it is being used. Microsoft recommends that at least 4000 KB should be available.
- *Paging File(_Total)\% Usage*—Shows how much of the Windows 2000 paging file is in use. If this number is consistently high, you might want to add more system memory. Microsoft recommends keeping this counter at 75% or lower.

You should not be alarmed if the counters hit at or above the recommended limits; it's normal to see spikes in the information being gathered. However, you should be concerned if the counters are consistently out of range or are spiking frequently.

Processor Usage Like system memory, excessively high usage of your processor leads to sluggish performance on your server. If your server is exhibiting this sluggishness, you can apply the following counters to help determine whether your processor is being overworked. If these counters are consistently out of range, upgrading the currently installed processor or adding processors will help improve your server's performance.

- *Processor\% Processor Time*—Shows the percentage of elapsed time it is taking the processor to carry out instructions. Microsoft recommends keeping this value below 80%.
- *System\Processor Queue Length*—Shows how many threads (sets of instructions) are queued up for the processor to handle. The recommended limit for this counter is 2 or fewer. Typically, if the % Processor Time counter is high, this number is also high.

Disk Usage Disk usage monitoring encompasses counters that monitor the hard drives installed on the server, including the logical partitions. Just as with the previous two server components, a few key counters can be used to monitor and evaluate the performance of your server's hard drives. Take a look at the more important counters you might want to use to gauge your hard drive's performance:

- *PhysicalDisk\Avg. Disk Sec/Transfer*—Averages the rate for how fast data is being moved in seconds. Although no guidelines from Microsoft are available, keep an eye out for consistently high numbers in this counter; it could indicate that data is backing up.
- *PhysicalDisk\Avg. Disk Queue Length*—Similar to processor queue length, this counter averages how many data requests are queued up by the hard drive. Microsoft recommends keeping it below 2.

- *PhysicalDisk\Disk Bytes/sec*—Indicates the rate at which bytes of data are being transferred. This is the primary counter for measuring hard drive performance.
- *PhysicalDisk\Disk Transfers/sec*—Shows how much the hard drives are being utilized based on read and write requests per second. If you see values in the range of 50% or higher, you could have a problem with your hard drive.

Some factors can limit the performance of your hard drives even if you have up-to-date, fast hardware, including:

- A fragmented hard drive is causing the drive to work harder to locate data.
- You are using a RAID 1 hard drive mirror, meaning that the system has to write two copies of everything.
- You use file compression software, such as Disk Space, on your computer (not a good idea on a server because it can take additional CPU time to decompress the data if it's needed).
- You use encryption to secure documents and folders on your hard drives. (Encrypting/decrypting information takes time and resources.)

Network Usage There are two ways to monitor network usage and performance information on a Windows 2000 server. The first is through System Monitor, using the counters outlined in the following list. The second method is to use the Network Monitor tool, which you will learn about in the "Network Monitor" section of this chapter. Even if you do not have any current problems with network performance, monitoring network usage gives you a better overall picture of your server performance. Another reason to monitor network usage is to check what happens to the usage rate when you log information, which can help you decide whether money should be spent on network infrastructure upgrades. Take a look at just a few of the counters you can use for monitoring network usage and performance with System Monitor:

- *Network Segment\% Network Utilization*—Shows the percentage of total network bandwidth being used for that network segment. The lower this number, the better, especially on an Ethernet network that uses hubs because collisions are more frequent on those networks.
- *TCP\Segments Retransmitted/sec*—Shows the rate at which network segments are retransmitting data. If this counter is high, there might be too many users for the network to handle, or there could be a hardware problem on a NIC or other device, such as a network switch.
- *Redirector\Network Errors/sec*—Counts serious network errors that indicate whether a server is having difficulty communicating with other systems on the network.

In addition to the server-related counters, System Monitor has counters for monitoring SMTP, POP3, IMAP4, and even OWA that you can configure just as easily. Configuring counters in System Monitor is much easier when you know what the different counters do; in the Add Counter dialog box, you can click the Explain button to get more information on a particular counter.

Performance Logs and Alerts

In addition to System Monitor, you can use the Performance Logs and Alerts component of the Performance console to create counter logs, in which you can combine groups of counters that you have configured in System Monitor into one log that you can start and stop as needed. You can then take the information logged in these performance counters to create alerts, such as for counters that have exceeded a specified range. After selecting what you will configure alerts for, you specify how you want to send the alert. By default, a log entry is added to the Application event log, but you can also send a network message to a particular computer or even run a program or batch file. Figure 14-8 shows the dialog box for configuring these options (note that the name of this dialog box varies, depending on the name you give to the counter log).

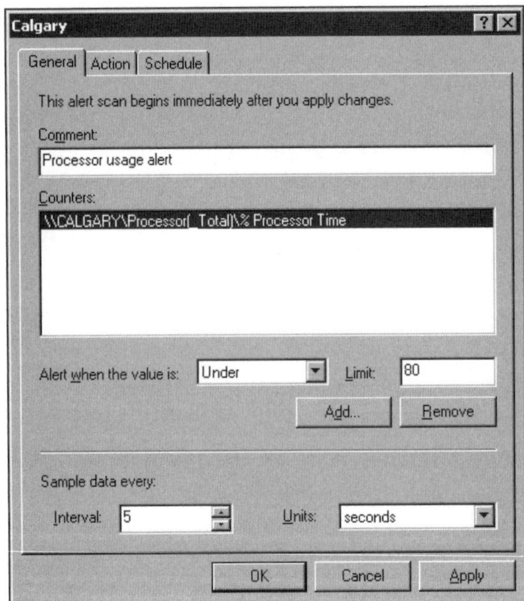

Figure 14-8 Configuring an alert

Much like notification of events and alerts in Exchange System Manager, configuring alerts in the Performance console can notify you of issues with your server before they become problems. In addition, alerts can notify you of performance-related problems if you're out of the office and can't directly monitor the server and its information. Configuring alerts and sets of performance logs is just as easy as creating counters in

System Monitor, which you will learn more about in the "Hands-on Projects" section; when in doubt, access the Exchange 2000 Help by pressing F1.

Network Monitor

There is more than one way to skin the proverbial network usage–monitoring cat. The first method, outlined previously, is using counters in the System Monitor component of the Performance console. The second is through the Windows 2000 Network Monitor, which is accessed by clicking Start, Programs, Administrative Tools, Network Monitor. This basic utility, shown in Figure 14-9, can capture network statistics, such as network traffic, data flow information, and network utilization.

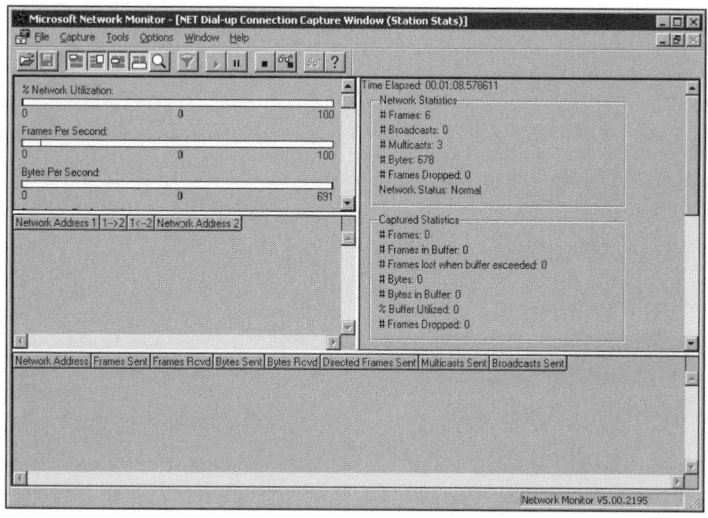

Figure 14-9 The Windows 2000 Network Monitor utility

This utility can be far more useful than System Monitor for gathering information on network usage because you get hard numbers instead of just graphs, and it is dedicated to network monitoring, so you don't have to sort through extraneous data. With Network Monitor, you can even capture network traffic frames on the connection by clicking the Play button on the toolbar. You can then view the captured packets to check for any network traffic information. Although there are certainly better third-party software packages that can do everything Network Monitor can and more, Network Monitor can handle your basic network-monitoring needs.

You can purchase other monitoring tools for your Windows 2000 servers that offer a much wider range of options and features. One such tool is built into Microsoft SMS (Server Management Software), which can be an indispensable software package for closely monitoring and managing your servers.

Troubleshooting and Maintenance Utilities for Exchange 2000

So far, you have learned about the wide array of utilities, features, and background services that can help you maintain, monitor, and even troubleshoot your Exchange 2000 installation. In this section, you will learn about other useful utilities, with a focus on what each utility can be used for in your Exchange 2000 installation.

Message Transfer Agent Check (MTACheck)

As you know, the Message Transfer Agent (MTA) is what transfers all messages for the X.400 Connector in Exchange 2000; it is also responsible for all message transfers in Exchange 5.5. The MTA creates and maintains a separate message queue for each X.400 Connector installed on your server. Like any other file, these queues can be corrupted over time or by more direct means, such as powering off the server right in the middle of writing to the file. The MTACheck utility is designed to fix MTA X.400 queues and their contents. All MTA queues are kept in .dat files, usually stored in the Program Files\Exchsrvr\Mtadata directory on the hard drive where you installed Exchange 2000.

MTACheck is a command-line utility (Mtacheck.exe) in the Program Files\Exchsrvr\Bin directory on your Exchange 2000 Server Installation CD-ROM. You can use the command-line switches in Table 14-3 to control the behavior of MTACheck.

Table 14-3 MTACheck Command-Line Switches

Command-Line Switch	Function
/f *filename*	Writes the status information of the MTA files into the file and path specified in the *filename* portion of the switch
/v	Enables verbose logging of information (use with /f), which gives you more readable information
/rd	Removes queued directory replication messages
/rp	Removes queued public folder replication messages

You will learn how to run the MTACheck utility in the "Hands-on Projects" section.

Information Store Integrity Checker (ISINTEG)

ISINTEG is a command-line utility that can be used to find and remove errors in Exchange 2000 public and private stores. Microsoft does not recommend ISINTEG as a regular Information Store maintenance utility; rather, it should be used only when there is a problem with the store's database files. For instance, if one of the files has become corrupt and refuses to allow the stores to be mounted, you should run ISINTEG.

This utility is on the same hard drive where you installed Exchange 2000 Server, in the Program Files\Exchsrvr\Bin directory.

Use of ISINTEG is fairly straightforward; simply run it at the command line to perform a check of your database files. If you specify the -fix command-line switch, ISINTEG tries to fix any errors it finds. Table 14-4 describes additional command-line switches you can use with ISINTEG.

Table 14-4 ISINTEG Command-Line Switches

Command-Line Switch	Function
/?	Displays help information for command-line switches
-pri	Tests the private Information Store
-pub	Tests the public Information Store
-detailed	Forces the ISINTEG tool to run a full battery of tests on the database (be aware that this option can take a considerable amount of time on a large database)

ISINTEG can provide another useful tool to add to the utilities and features at your disposal. If you want more information on the ISINTEG tool, take a look at this site: *http://www.microsoft.com/technet/treeview/default.asp?url=/TechNet/prodtechnol/exchange/reskit/ex55res/exc07.asp*.

Remote Procedure Calls Ping Utility (RPC Ping)

The Remote Procedure Calls (RPC) protocol is used to allow one system to run an application remotely on a second system. If you have routing groups in Exchange 2000, you already make use of RPC. The RPC Ping utility tests the RPC connection between two systems, thus ensuring that the two systems are communicating properly through RPC. This command-line utility is on the Exchange 2000 Server installation CD-ROM in the \Support\Rpcping folder.

There are two parts to the RPC Ping utility: the server and the client software. The server (Rpings.exe) software must be run before you connect with the client software. It remains running until you cancel it by typing in the @q command and pressing Enter on the RPC Ping server system. The RPC client is also in the same directory and can be run by using Rpingc.exe. After the client is running, specify which server you are checking, and click Start. You should, after a few moments, see information on the server, verifying that it's present and accounted for and that the RPC connection is working.

Chapter Summary

- There are two main forms of maintenance: preventive and reactive. Although both can achieve the same results, preventive maintenance is the more logical plan of attack for maintaining your servers and network. With reactive maintenance, problems aren't fixed until they reach a critical state and you are potentially dealing with a failed server. With preventive maintenance, you perform ongoing steps to help ward off major failures and catch minor ones before they become serious problems.

- There is no single solution to optimizing the performance of your Exchange 2000 server. However, regular maintenance and simple tasks, such as defragmenting your server's hard drives, can produce tangible performance benefits for your Exchange 2000 server and its users.
- Regular maintenance of the Exchange 2000 databases is essential to overall performance and maintenance. Although Exchange 2000 performs some of its own maintenance on its database files in the background, utilities such as ESEUTIL can perform additional maintenance tasks that Exchange 2000 can't perform on its own, such as compacting the database files and recovering unused space.
- Regular, reliable backups of your Exchange 2000 databases are critical to the long-term functioning of your Exchange 2000 services. If you lack complete backups, you might not be able to restore lost data if your servers crash. You should also retain offsite copies of your backups in case of a fire, flood, or other disaster.
- If your server is low on available hard drive space, you might want to enable circular logging, which allows Exchange 2000 to reuse old log files generated from the transactions that occur on your server. If you enable circular logging, however, you cannot rebuild databases from the log files; if you do go this route, make doubly sure you have reliable, full, frequent backups of your databases.
- The Windows Event Viewer is the single best troubleshooting utility for locating information on your server's current status. The three main event logs (Application, Security, and System) contain valuable information on errors occurring on your server. Nearly all Exchange 2000–related errors appear in the Application log, but often the System log supplies error information on the Windows 2000 operating system, pointing the way to other problems on your server.
- In Exchange 2000, you can have notifications sent to selected users via e-mail when certain events occur. When Exchange 2000 enters a warning or critical state, it can send an e-mail message to specified users reporting the problem. E-mail notifications can be particularly handy if you don't have IT staff constantly available. You can also configure Exchange 2000 to run a script when the server enters a warning or critical state, allowing certain tasks to be performed automatically.
- You can use the Exchange 2000 Message Tracking Center to search for messages to and from selected users, on a given server, and even by date and time. After messages have been found, you can generate a message history to see when the messages were transmitted into or out of the server, allowing you to determine where problems (if any) might lie.
- Both Exchange 2000 and Windows 2000 have useful utilities for monitoring your server's performance and services. Exchange 2000 includes a group of monitors to check SMTP and other messaging queues and key system performance monitors to

gauge how the server is performing. System Monitor, in the Windows 2000 Performance console, enables you to configure custom sets of counters for monitoring almost every aspect of your Windows 2000 server.

- Several other utilities included on the Exchange 2000 installation CD-ROM can be useful for troubleshooting and maintaining your Exchange 2000 server, such as MTACheck, which can be used to check and repair X.400 messaging queues. You can also take advantage of RPC Ping, which tests the RPC connectivity between two servers with connectors configured between them, and ISINTEG, which checks the integrity of your Information Store database files.

Key Terms

circular logging — A logging option in Exchange 2000 that reuses the first transaction log file that's created for new transaction entries after its contents have been written to the database that stores the log information.

counter — The software used in System Monitor that is configured to measure and store information on the object being monitored.

instance — Each of the objects that's measured when a counter measures multiple objects (such as multiple processors in a server).

Review Questions

1. If you do not take any maintenance steps until your server exhibits problems or fails, you are performing ________________ maintenance.
2. Which of the following Exchange 2000 components is most likely to occupy the majority of your maintenance time and effort?
   a. managing databases
   b. monitoring performance
   c. managing transaction log files
   d. creating and managing notifications
3. Which of the following utilities can you run to free up space in the Information Store?
   a. MTACheck
   b. ISINTEG
   c. RPC Ping
   d. ESEUTIL
4. The organization you work for has a backup policy that requires full backups of your Exchange 2000 databases twice per week and regular backups of any other changed data every other day. What recommendation should you make to management to ensure that these backups are as safe as possible, but still readily available?

5. Which of the following locations offers the safest storage for your data backups? (Choose all that apply.)
   a. in the same room as the server
   b. at an offsite storage facility
   c. in a fireproof safe
   d. at an employee's house
6. When the database files for your Exchange 2000 storage groups grow larger, what are two potential problems you might encounter?
   a. slower access time when users are searching for data
   b. data in the database becomes corrupt
   c. Exchange 2000 takes longer to open when first booting the server
   d. increased time to back up and restore databases
7. If you want to allow Exchange 2000 to conserve hard drive space and overwrite the files used to record events, you should enable which of the following options or utilities?
   a. ISINTEG
   b. event notifications or alerts
   c. circular logging
   d. ESEUTIL
8. Which of the following log files in the Windows 2000 Event Viewer contains information that's most pertinent to Exchange 2000?
   a. Directory Services
   b. System
   c. Security
   d. Application
9. Which of the following methods can you use to configure Exchange 2000 to respond to problems on your Exchange 2000 server? (Choose all that apply.)
   a. run a script file
   b. shut down the server
   c. e-mail a specified user
   d. disable Exchange 2000 services
10. Is it possible to configure the correct methods in Question 9 on the same server and for the same event level? Yes or No?

11. To display a broader range of information on the messages you search in the Message Tracking Center, which of the following options should you enable?
    a. subject logging and display
    b. enhanced logging
    c. message subject display
    d. verbose logging
12. Which Windows 2000 utility in the Performance console is used to gauge how your server and Exchange 2000 are performing?
    a. Exchange Monitor
    b. System Information
    c. System Monitor
    d. Performance Graphing
13. When monitoring the server where Exchange 2000 is installed, it is important to monitor CPU, network, memory, and ________________ performance.
14. By default, the Information Store Maintenance Schedule runs automatically but can be configured to run whenever you like. Typically, when is the best time to run these maintenance tasks?
    a. hourly
    b. during off hours
    c. continuously
    d. immediately after a backup
15. Which of the following utilities would you use if you wanted to inspect and repair X.400 message queues?
    a. MTACheck
    b. ESEUTIL
    c. ISINTEG
    d. RPC Ping
16. Which two command-line switches would you use if you wanted the ISINTEG utility to perform an intensive full set of tests on your mailbox store databases?
    a. /?
    b. –pri
    c. –pub
    d. –detailed

17. Which of the following protocols do you use if you want to remotely manage another computer from your server?
    a. SMTP
    b. RPC
    c. TCP/IP
    d. IMAP4
18. The Exchange 2000 self-maintenance tasks cannot compact databases and free up unused space. True or False?
19. In System Monitor, what do you add to measure information on a component or system service?
    a. object
    b. counter
    c. log
    d. alert
20. Why is it a good idea to monitor your system using System Monitor over an extended period of time, such as an entire week?

HANDS-ON PROJECTS

Project 14-1

This project assumes that you have a standard system with Windows 2000 Server and Exchange 2000 Server installed and functioning, as well as a preconfigured e-mail account and administrative access to the server.

To configure a notification with Exchange System Manager:

1. If necessary, log on to your system using an account with administrative privileges.
2. To open the Exchange System Manager console, click **Start**, point to **Programs**, point to **Microsoft Exchange**, and then click **System Manager**.
3. Double-click the **Tools** folder, double-click the **Monitoring and Status** folder, right-click the **Notifications** folder, point to **New**, and then click **E-mail notification** to open the <*servername*> Properties dialog box for your notification.
4. Click the **Select** button to open the Select Exchange Server dialog box (see Figure 14-10). Click the server you want to configure the notification for, and then click **OK** to return to the *servername* properties dialog box.

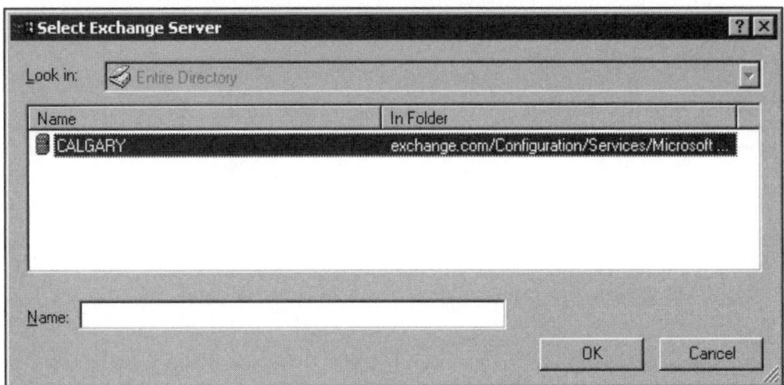

Figure 14-10 Selecting the server to monitor for notifications

5. Click the **To** button to open the Select Recipient dialog box. Click the account to which you want to send the e-mail notifications, and then click **OK**. After configuring your new e-mail notification, it should look similar to Figure 14-11.

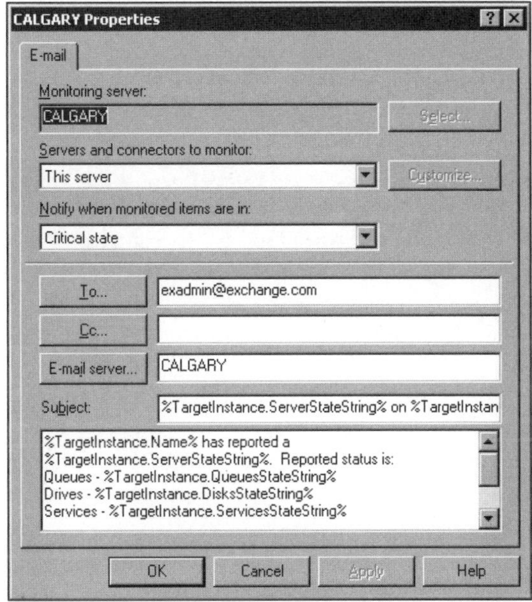

Figure 14-11 Configuring an e-mail notification

6. Click **OK** to return to the System Manager console; you should see the new notification you created in the Details pane, as shown in Figure 14-12.

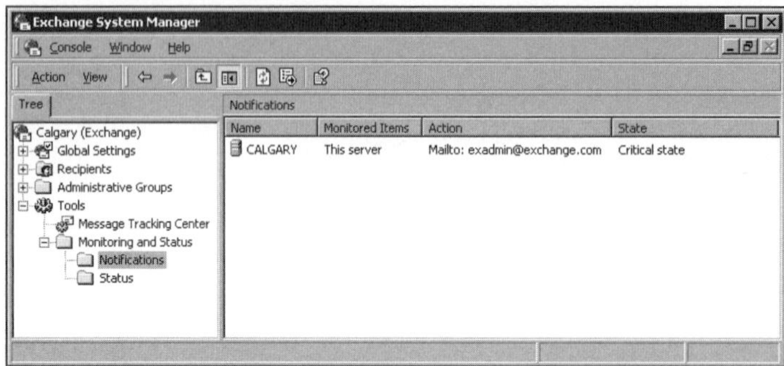

Figure 14-12 Displaying a new e-mail notification in Exchange System Manager

7. Leave the system in this state for the next project.

Project 14-2

To configure a CPU Utilization Server Monitor in Exchange System Manager:

1. If necessary, log on to your system using an account with administrative privileges. If you are continuing from Project 14-1, you can skip Steps 1–2.
2. To open the Exchange System Manager console, click **Start**, point to **Programs**, point to **Microsoft Exchange**, and then click **System Manager**.
3. Double-click the **Tools** folder, double-click the **Monitoring and Status** folder, and then double-click the **Status** folder to show the contents. Right-click the server in the Details pane, and then click **Properties** on the shortcut menu to open the <*servername*> Properties dialog box to the Monitoring tab. Click the **Add** button to open the Add Resource dialog box (see Figure 14-13). Click the **CPU Utilization** option in the Resources list box, and then click **OK** to open the CPU Utilization Thresholds dialog box.

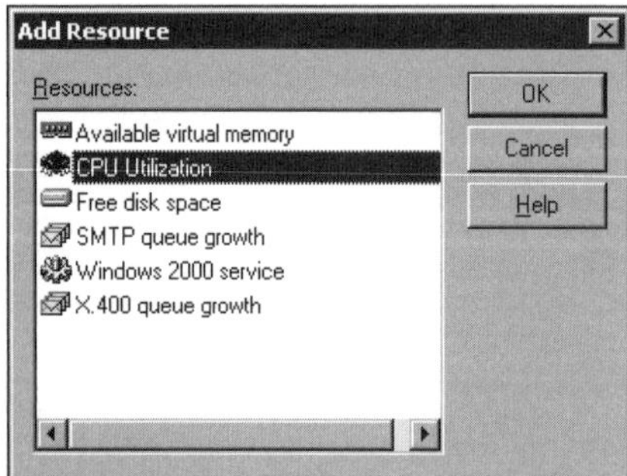

Figure 14-13 Selecting a monitor in the Add Resource dialog box

4. In the CPU Utilization Thresholds dialog box, type **5** in the Duration (minutes) text box. Click the **Warning state (percent)** check box, click the list arrow that's enabled, and then click **40** in the list of options. Click the **Critical state (percent)** check box, click the list arrow that's enabled, and then click **80** in the list of options. After you are finished, your CPU Utilization Thresholds dialog box should look similar to Figure 14-14.

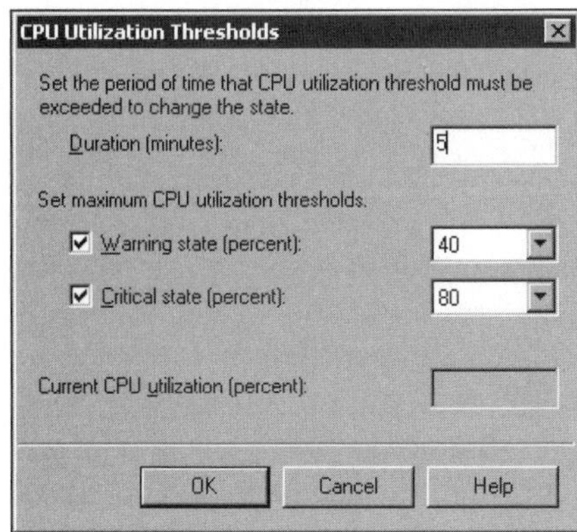

Figure 14-14 Configuring the monitor in the CPU Utilization Thresholds dialog box

5. Click **OK** to finish creating the monitor; you will be returned to the Monitoring tab of the <*servername*> Properties dialog box, where you will see the new monitor you just created. Click the new monitor, and then click the **Detail** button; you will see the information you configured and in the Current CPU utilization (percent) text box, you will see your server's current utilization rate.
6. Click **OK**, and then click **OK** again to return to the Exchange System Manager console. Close the Exchange System Manager console, and leave your system in this state for the next project.

Project 14-3

By using counter logs, you can record performance-related information in log files rather than graphs, giving you more detailed information that's useful for reports.

To create a counter log by using Performance Logs and Alerts:

1. If necessary, log on to your system using an account with administrative privileges. If you are continuing from Project 14-2, you can skip this step.
2. To open the Performance console, click **Start**, point to **Programs**, point to **Administrative Tools**, and then click **Performance**.
3. Double-click the **Performance Logs and Alerts** folder in the Contents pane, and then double-click the **Counter Logs** object to display the default log in the Details pane.

4. Right-click the **Counter Logs** folder, and then click **New Log Settings** on the shortcut menu to open the New Log Settings dialog box. Type a name for this new counter log in the Name text box (for this lab, use **Sample**), and then click **OK**. The Sample dialog box opens, where you can configure the counter log.
5. Click the **Add** button to open the Select Counters dialog box. If it is not selected already by default, click the **Performance object** list arrow, and then click **Processor** in the list. Click the **Select counters from list** radio button, and then click **% Processor Time** in the list. Click the **Add** button. Repeat this process, but click **Memory** in the Performance object list, and in the **Select counters from list** text box, click **Pages/sec**. Click the **Add** button, and then click the **Close** button.
6. In the Counters text box in the General tab, you should now see the two counters you added in Step 5. Click the **Schedule** tab, and then click the **Manually (using the shortcut menu)** radio button to allow you to start the logging when you want to. Click the **Log Files** tab, click the **Log file type** list arrow, and then click **Text File – CSV** in the available options.
7. Click **OK** to return to the Performance console. (If a message box appears stating that the C:\PerfLogs folder cannot be found, click **Yes** to create it.) In the Details section, you will see the default counter log and the new counter log you just created with a red icon next to it (see Figure 14-15).

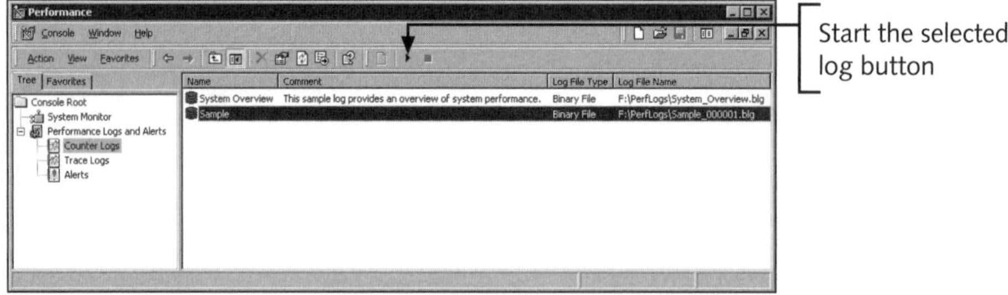

Figure 14-15 A newly created, stopped counter log in the Performance console

8. Click the **Sample Counter Log** you created in the previous steps, and then click the **Start the selected log** button on the main toolbar to start logging this counter log. You can also start logging by right-clicking the counter log and then clicking **Start** on the shortcut menu.
9. As an optional step, you can go to the directory path specified in the Log File Name column and open the log file to view its contents. After you have finished the previous steps, close the Performance console to return to the Windows desktop. Leave your system in this state for the next project.

Project 14-4

Circular logging can be useful for conserving hard disk usage, but you cannot use the transaction logs to rebuild databases. If you use this feature, make sure you have current, full backups available.

To enable and disable circular logging in Exchange System Manager:

1. If necessary, log on to your system using an account with administrative privileges. If you are continuing from Project 14-3, you can skip this step.
2. To open the Exchange System Manager console, click **Start**, point to **Programs**, point to **Microsoft Exchange**, and then click **System Manager**.
3. Double-click the **Servers** folder (if you have the display of administrative groups enabled, you might have to double-click Administrative Groups and then the First Administrative Group folder before you see the Servers folder), and then right-click the **First Storage Group** in the Details section. Click **Properties** on the shortcut menu to open the First Storage Group Properties dialog box, as shown in Figure 14-16.

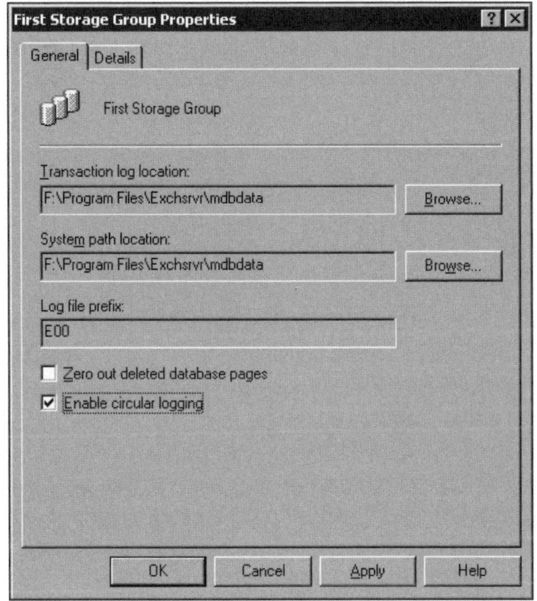

Figure 14-16 Enabling circular logging for a storage group

4. If necessary, click the **Enable circular logging** check box to enable this option. Click **OK** to close the dialog box and return to the Exchange System Manager console. A warning message appears, letting you know about the inability to use the log files to restore databases; click the **Yes** button to continue.

5. Perform Steps 3–4 again, but this time, click the **Enable circular logging** check box to remove the check mark to disable circular logging. Click **OK** to return to the Exchange System Manager console, and leave the system in this state for the next project.

Project 14-5

A protocol log can provide valuable information on how the protocol is functioning, what commands are being sent to it, and any problems with the protocol. This project assumes that you have access to Outlook Express or another SMTP-enabled e-mail client configured to use SMTP on the Exchange 2000 server.

To create and view an SMTP protocol log in Exchange System Manager:

1. If necessary, log on to your system using an account with administrative privileges. If you are continuing from Project 14-4, you can skip Steps 1–2.
2. To open the Exchange System Manager console, click **Start**, point to **Programs**, point to **Microsoft Exchange**, and then click **System Manager**.
3. Double-click the **Servers** folder (if you have the display of administrative groups enabled, you might have to first double-click Administrative Groups and then the First Administrative Group folder), double-click the **Protocols** folder, and then click the **SMTP** folder to show the Default SMTP Virtual Server in the Details section.
4. Right-click the **Default SMTP Virtual Server**, and then click **Properties** on the shortcut menu to open the Default SMTP Virtual Server Properties dialog box. Click the **General** tab, if necessary. At the bottom of the General tab, click the **Enable logging** check box. Click **OK** to return to the Exchange System Manager console, and then close this console.
5. Navigate to the location of the log files (by default, ***X*:\WINNT\system32\LogFiles**; *X* represents your hard drive) by using My Computer or Windows Explorer. The log files used for the SMTP server are typically in the SMTPSVC1 folder. Double-click this folder to show the log files.

If you do not see the folder, you might need to have some SMTP activity on the server first. If this is the case, open Outlook Express (or any other SMTP-enabled e-mail client software), and send some e-mail messages to different e-mail accounts on the server to start logging SMTP activity.

6. After you have the SMTPSVC1 folder open, double-click a text file in the folder; you should see several lines of logged information, as shown in Figure 14-17. This logged information shows the time, the IP address (source), the command sent to the virtual server, and a status number of the command (250 typically means the command was issued properly). After you have finished reading this information, close the log file and any open windows or applications to return to the Windows desktop. Leave your system in this state for the next project.

```
ex030926 - Notepad
File  Edit  Format  Help
#Software: Microsoft Internet Information Services 5.0
#Version: 1.0
#Date: 2003-09-26 06:15:41
#Fields: time c-ip cs-method cs-uri-stem sc-status
06:15:41 192.168.162.1 HELO - 250
06:15:41 192.168.162.1 MAIL - 250
06:15:41 192.168.162.1 RCPT - 250
06:15:41 192.168.162.1 DATA - 250
06:15:41 192.168.162.1 QUIT - 0
```

Figure 14-17 Viewing logging information in the SMTP protocol log

Project 14-6

This project demonstrates using the MTACheck utility to check the status of an X.400 Connector queue on your Exchange 2000 server for errors that need your attention.

To use the MTACheck utility:

1. If necessary, log on to your system using an account with administrative privileges. If you are continuing from Project 14-5, you can skip this step.
2. To open the Services console, click **Start**, point to **Programs**, point to **Administrative Tools**, and then click **Services**. Click the **Microsoft Exchange MTA Stacks** entry in the Details section, and then click the **Stop service** button on the main toolbar to stop the MTA service. It could take a minute for the service to stop. After it's stopped, close the Services console.
3. Open the **Mtadata** folder for this Exchange 2000 installation using My Computer or Windows Explorer. The default path is *X*:\Program Files\Exchsrvr\Mtadata; *X* is the location of the drive where you installed Exchange 2000 Server.
4. Locate and select any files with the filename **DB*.dat** (for instance, DB000001.dat). After you have selected these files as a group by using Ctrl+click, right-click the group of files, and then click **Copy** on the shortcut menu. Right-click in an open area of the same folder, and then click **Paste** on the shortcut menu to create a backup copy of the .dat files in case something goes wrong with the MTACheck utility (you can never be too careful).
5. After copying the files, close any open windows or applications and return to the Windows desktop. Next, you will run the MTACheck utility from a command prompt. Click **Start**, click **Run**, type **cmd.exe** in the Open text box, and then press **Enter**. In the command-prompt window, navigate to **X:\Program Files\Exchsrvr\Bin**.
6. Type the command **MTACHECK /?** (case is not important), and then press **Enter** to see a list of command-line switches for this utility. Next, type **MTACHECK /f C:\mtalog.txt**, and then press **Enter** to run the MTACheck utility and log the results to the Mtalog.txt file on your C:\ drive. You should see

an output displayed in the command-prompt window showing that the database was clean and no errors were detected. Close the command prompt by typing **exit**, and then pressing **Enter**.

7. As an optional step, navigate to your **C:** drive using My Computer or Windows Explorer, and then double-click the **Mtalog.txt** file you created in Step 6. You should see the same output in this text file as you did in the command-prompt window; however, if there were errors, this file would be a great way to log them for future investigation and troubleshooting.
8. After you have completed the previous steps, close any open windows or applications and return to the Windows desktop. Leave your system in this state for the next project.

You can restart the Microsoft Exchange MTA Stacks service in the Services console after you have completed this project by performing the reverse of Step 2. Instead of clicking the Stop service button on the main toolbar, click the Start service button.

Project 14-7

By defragmenting your databases, you can keep the database running in peak condition. In addition, performing a manual defragmentation with ESEUTIL can compact files and recover free space in the database to keep its size in check.

To use the ESEUTIL utility to defragment a database:

1. If necessary, log on to your system using an account with administrative privileges. If you are continuing from Project 14-6, you can skip this step.
2. To open the Exchange System Manager console, click **Start**, point to **Programs**, point to **Microsoft Exchange**, and then click **System Manager**.
3. Double-click the **Servers** folder (if you have the display of administrative groups enabled, you might have to first double-click Administrative Groups and then the First Administrative Group folder), double-click your server, and then click the **First Storage Group** to show its contents in the Details section.
4. Right-click the **Mailbox Store**, and then click **Dismount Store** on the shortcut menu to have Exchange 2000 stop accessing this store while you work on the defragmentation. A warning appears, advising that users will not be able to access this store if you dismount it; click the **Yes** button to continue. After a few seconds, the store will be stopped. Close the Exchange System Manager console.

Although a large mailbox store database often hampers backing up the file before defragmenting it, it's still a good idea to do so before running this utility. To do this, follow Step 4 in the previous project, but copy the Priv1.edb file in the *X*:\Program Files\Exchsrvr\Mdbdata directory.

5. Open a command prompt to run ESEUTIL. To do this, click **Start**, click **Run**, type **cmd.exe** in the Open text box, and then press **Enter**. In the command-prompt window, navigate to ***X*:\Program Files\Exchsrvr\Bin**.

6. At the command prompt, type **eseutil /d *X*:\program files\exchsrvr\mdbdata\priv1.edb** (remember to replace *X* with your drive letter), and then press **Enter**. (If the command doesn't work, try it again eith the path *x*:\Exchsrvr\mdbdata\priv1.edb. If that fails, issue the command with the filename priv.edb rather than priv1.edb.) The ESEUTIL utility starts and shows a rudimentary progress bar to help you gauge how long the defragmentation will take (see Figure 14-18). When the defragmentation is finished, the utility lets you know it was completed successfully and in how many seconds. After you see this message, type **exit**, and then press **Enter** to close the command prompt.

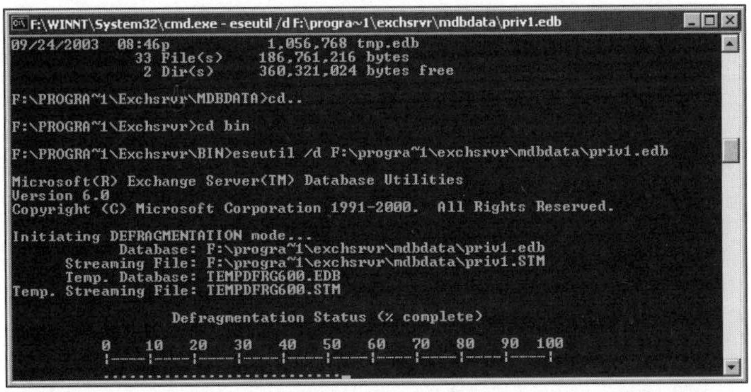

```
F:\WINNT\System32\cmd.exe - eseutil /d F:\progra~1\exchsrvr\mdbdata\priv1.edb
09/24/2003  08:46p           1,056,768 tmp.edb
              33 File(s)    186,761,216 bytes
               2 Dir(s)     360,321,024 bytes free

F:\PROGRA~1\Exchsrvr\MDBDATA>cd..

F:\PROGRA~1\Exchsrvr>cd bin

F:\PROGRA~1\Exchsrvr\BIN>eseutil /d F:\progra~1\exchsrvr\mdbdata\priv1.edb

Microsoft(R) Exchange Server(TM) Database Utilities
Version 6.0
Copyright (C) Microsoft Corporation 1991-2000.  All Rights Reserved.

Initiating DEFRAGMENTATION mode...
            Database: F:\progra~1\exchsrvr\mdbdata\priv1.edb
      Streaming File: F:\progra~1\exchsrvr\mdbdata\priv1.STM
      Temp. Database: TEMPDFRG600.EDB
Temp. Streaming File: TEMPDFRG600.STM

                  Defragmentation Status (% complete)

          0    10   20   30   40   50   60   70   80   90  100
          |----|----|----|----|----|----|----|----|----|----|
          ...........................
```

Figure 14-18 Checking the progress of the defragmentation in the ESEUTIL utility

7. Proceed to remount the mailbox store you dismounted in Step 4. Instead of clicking Dismount Store on the shortcut menu, click **Mount Store**. Then close any open windows or applications.

14

CASE PROJECTS

Case Projects Background

Mini Mites Moving has a nationwide network to support its moving business. Included in this network are several Exchange 2000 servers that have been running for some time, but the administrator who originally set up, configured, and maintained them left over a year ago for greener pastures, leaving Mini Mites Moving without a skilled Exchange 2000 administrator. For this past year, it has been relying on the regular network manager, who has been able to manage the account and public folder management. However, Mini Mites is having some problems with the installation and has contacted your company to bring an Exchange 2000 administrator out to help them.

The two Exchange 2000 servers just barely exceed the minimum hardware requirements for Exchange 2000. Each server has only one public folder store and one mailbox store (one server's store is used for the East Coast and the other is used for the West Coast). The servers were upgraded from Exchange Server 5.5 and performed fine; lately, however, users have complained of sluggish performance when accessing their mailboxes on the network and over the Internet using OWA. Each server supports approximately 1000 users, who frequently send quotes to customers in the form of small Microsoft Word documents.

Case 1

Upon arriving at Mini Mites Moving, you are asked to give management a state- of-the-servers report, including how the servers are performing. What is the first thing you should do to find the information you need to give to the management committee? What could you do to the servers and Exchange 2000 that would help increase the servers' general responsiveness and performance before reporting to management?

Case 2

After you have logged performance information for a week and informed management of the servers' poor performance state, the committee has decided to spend additional funds to upgrade server hardware. Management has left it in your hands to determine where upgrades are necessary to get the best performance results. Based on your findings, the CPU utilization rate was frequently in the 60–70% range; hard drive transfers were at 50% nearly all the time, memory utilization was at 5%, and network utilization was at 10%. What would you upgrade immediately if you had the budget to upgrade only one server component? Given the high percentage for hard drive transfers, if the hard drive is a high-performance model, what could be causing this problem?

Case 3

After taking your recommendations and upgrading the necessary components to get the Exchange 2000 servers running better, Mini Mites Moving's IT Department has expressed some concern about the servers' reliability because of a severe crash three months ago; it took them three days to find out about the server failure because it was a holiday weekend. When everyone returned on Tuesday morning, there was no e-mail service and business was interrupted. What should you recommend that would help Mini Mites avoid this situation in the future?

Case 4

Many months have passed since you assisted Mini Mites Moving with its maintenance and performance needs. The company has contacted you again, complaining that the Exchange 2000 servers have been running out of hard drive space. The culprit appears to be the rather expansive transaction log files for the mailbox stores. The company has no money in the budget for further IT hardware upgrades for another two months. Is there something you can recommend Mini Mites do in the meantime? If the company follows your recommendation, is there anything else you can advise it to do?

CHAPTER

15

EXCHANGE 2000 SERVER DISASTER RECOVERY

After reading this chapter and completing the exercises, you will be able to:

- Understand how to develop a disaster recovery plan for your organization, focusing on factors that affect your Exchange 2000 server
- Design and implement a backup strategy that will help you effectively protect your organization from data loss in the event of a disaster, such as server failure or database corruption
- Understand how to back up the Exchange 2000 database files, the Exchange 2000 configuration, and the system state so that you can restore your server after a disaster
- Understand how to restore and recover data from your backups to your Exchange 2000 server, how to restore your backups to an entirely different server, and how to restore a single mailbox
- Solve a few common problems that you might encounter during Exchange 2000 backups and restorations

In Chapter 14, "Maintaining and Monitoring Exchange 2000 Server," you learned about principle maintenance concepts, including the importance of performing preventive maintenance rather than reactive maintenance. You also learned how preventive maintenance and optimization of your Exchange 2000 server can improve services for your users and help ensure your server's long-term stability. In addition, you learned about maintaining your Exchange 2000 databases by using the included Exchange 2000 tools and how you can use the Windows 2000 Performance console to determine your server's health and overall performance to catch problems before they occur. You also learned how to use e-mail notifications to alert you to problems or warnings and how to use maintenance utilities to help fix Exchange 2000 components, including the Exchange 2000 database stores.

In this chapter, you learn about disaster recovery concepts, including the development and implementation of a disaster recovery plan for your Exchange 2000 servers as well as your entire organization. In addition, you learn about implementing a solid backup strategy and performing backups of critical Exchange 2000 components, such as the stores' database files. Finally, you learn about restoration and recovery of Exchange 2000 and of single mailboxes, if needed.

DEVELOPING A DISASTER RECOVERY PLAN FOR YOUR ORGANIZATION

Each organization should develop its own disaster recovery plan to suit its particular needs. With organizations' growing dependence on data and information, having an effective plan to back up, store, and then quickly restore your data and network infrastructure is imperative. When most people think of disaster recovery, they think of floods, fire, tornadoes, and other acts of nature; however, disasters can encompass several other possibilities, including loss of data from viruses, human error, or hacker attack. The essence of a good disaster recovery plan is considering all potential disasters, particularly those that are likely in your environment. It is these unknown potential disasters relating to your environment that can't be accounted for in a one-size-fits-all disaster recovery plan. This is the primary reason that *your* disaster recovery plan will be different from that of any other organization.

It is difficult to outline in this chapter exactly what a disaster recovery plan should look like when it is finished. Rather, this chapter supplies the information you need to fill in the key components of a plan. There are many resources available from Microsoft and third parties on the Internet that can provide detailed outlines of a disaster recovery plan.

Outside influences can affect how your disaster recovery plan is put together. Obviously, natural disasters must have a spot in your disaster recovery plan. You should protect against events such as a building fire, but there are other disasters you should protect against:

- *Data loss from user error*—This type of data loss can certainly be classified as a disaster in that it doesn't matter how the data is lost; if it's important and you can't get it back, it's a disaster.
- *Hacker intrusion or attack*—If hackers manage to infiltrate your network, they can wreak all kinds of havoc, ranging from stealing information to deleting sensitive data or critical operating system/application files required for the server to function.
- *Virus infection*—Viruses are getting smarter and more dangerous; many of them can now propagate on their own, infecting operating systems and other data at random. If you have a good disaster recovery plan in place, you can attempt to recover from the damaging effects of viruses.

- *Hardware or operating system failure*—Remember that server and operating system hardware can fail (typically software fails more often than hardware), so you should take this possibility into account in your disaster recovery plan. However, you have a better chance of spotting hardware or operating system failure than you do of detecting the other problems in this list.

The only way to quickly and effectively deal with a hardware failure on your network is to have spare parts on hand (not always an option with some of the more expensive and exotic servers on the market) or have a customer response policy with the vendor or reseller; this policy should specify having spare parts on hand and quick turnarounds for replacing them if necessary. Many of the larger vendors, such as Hewlett-Packard or Compaq, guarantee a four-hour turnaround for parts in certain areas of North America, which means you don't have to worry about storing parts on site.

Of course, there will always be events you can't plan for. For example, a staff member could trip over a power cable and accidentally power off a piece of equipment. Accidents like this can cause considerable grief, especially if you don't have a way to get back up and running quickly. Even though you can't control accidents, you can take steps to account for random or accidental power outages in addition to your regular planning.

Data loss can be crippling for your organization, especially if it is loss of e-mail data and even e-mail services. Keep in mind that even if you have methods for backing up your data and keeping it safe, without an effective plan to restore the data after the disaster, downtime will still occur, and this can cause almost as much trouble as losing the data. Therefore, you must ensure that your disaster recovery plan has at least three essential elements: a data backup plan, a data restoration plan, and personnel to implement and manage these plans. Although these three elements are paramount and what you will be focusing on in this chapter, considering all potential disasters and problems will make your disaster recovery plan that much better.

An essential piece of your disaster recovery plan—disaster avoidance—can be performed before you even complete the plan. For example, you should consider protecting your server room from water damage (for instance, turning off fire sprinklers in the room that houses your servers) and installing adequate air-conditioning units to make sure the equipment stays cool and doesn't overheat. You could also check out installing a fuel-powered backup generator in the building where your network equipment is housed so that if you have an electrical outage, you can use backup power to keep your equipment running. It is this basic planning that helps you avoid potential disasters, especially those caused by human error. Keep in mind your network equipment's environment when you are considering your disaster recovery options because if your server room is a disaster area in itself, putting any kind of recovery plan into action will be even more difficult.

Later in this chapter, you learn about backup and restoration concepts and strategies that you can integrate into your disaster recovery plan, but having someone to manage and carry out disaster recovery is a straightforward matter. This person should be the IT staff member who's most familiar with the organization's inner workings. You don't have to appoint just one person, however; in fact, you might need to include a large cross-section of the staff to implement and manage your disaster recovery plan, especially in large organizations. If you appoint a team for your disaster recovery plan, make sure that each team member has a specific role in how the plan comes together. Their roles should reflect their areas of expertise or experience with the network to help ensure your plan's success. The remainder of this chapter deals mainly with backup and restoration, as the effects of outside disasters have been covered in previous chapters; for instance, Chapter 14 covered ways to handle virus attacks.

At a minimum, you should have a short document for a disaster recovery plan that outlines your backup schedule, the steps you have taken to secure your backups, the restoration process for your data and services, and the people in charge of implementing this plan. Although the more information you have in this plan the better, it doesn't necessarily have to be long and wordy to be effective. Having a simple plan available while you develop a more detailed one is better than having none at all. A simple disaster recovery plan could be as straightforward as the following list:

Backups

- Run full backups of Server 1 and Server 2 every Sunday at 10 a.m.
- Run incremental backups of Server 1 and Server 2 every workday at 8 p.m.
- Store backup data offsite in a fireproof safe at the IT manager's home.

Restoration

- Data must be restored in full only if servers have been completely rebuilt or all data has been lost. Otherwise, restore just the data that needs to be restored.

Other Considerations

- Battery backup units must be installed for each major server in the server room, including network equipment such as routers. Battery backup units must be tested once a month to ensure that they are running properly.
- All visitors who will be working in and around network equipment and servers must be monitored and accompanied by a member of the IT staff.
- An exact replica of each of the two servers must be kept onsite for hardware swaps in case one of the systems fails.

Personnel

- John is responsible for starting and managing data backups.
- Harry is responsible for taking the backup tape media home and storing it in a fireproof safe.
- Nicole is responsible for testing the battery backups every month to make sure they are working and for maintaining the hot-swap replacement hardware for the servers.

DESIGNING AN EFFECTIVE BACKUP STRATEGY

As with building a good disaster recovery plan, there are several smaller parts of the overall backup strategy that can help make your plan successful. As the saying goes, you must walk before you run, and the same applies here; before you can even think of a restoration strategy, you must plan your backup strategy. Without knowing how your backups are scheduled, which data is backed up, and where your backups are eventually stored (onsite or offsite), you won't be able to bring that data back into play when you need to. During your backup strategy planning, you should also keep in mind the amount of time data restoration will require, both for a single mailbox and for a complete system restoration. This chapter assumes that you know the basic fundamentals of how data backup works with Windows 2000. Exchange 2000 isn't any different when it comes to backing up data; however, there are some guidelines to keep in mind for backing up mailboxes and Exchange 2000 configuration data.

Several basic backup concepts and required information should be included in any backup recovery plan:

- *Create daily backups*—Performing daily backups is a good idea and highly recommended by anyone who has lost data, even if your Exchange 2000 server and network don't experience a lot of use; any gaps in your backup schedule could prove to be a problem when the time comes to restore data.
- *Verify backup integrity*—After backing up your data, you should perform a verification of the data to ensure that it is correct and intact. (This option is available when you first start a backup job.) It's also a good idea to verify data integrity by trying a test restoration after a period of time (for instance, a month after the data was originally backed up) to ensure that the data is still valid and can be restored.
- *View backup logs religiously*—Many tape backup drives automatically show a green light if the backup job was good and a red light if the backup job was bad; however, don't rely on these indicators alone because they can be inaccurate. Backup software always keeps a log of the backup process; reading these logs (for instance, first thing in the morning after the backup is completed) can give you the best indication of the results.
- *Select the type of data you will back up*—Depending on the needs of your organization, you may decide to back up only user mailboxes and public folder information instead of backing up everything, including the operating system and Exchange 2000. This is a decision you will have to make based on your organization's needs. You will learn more about backing up individual mailboxes and Exchange 2000 configuration information later in this chapter.
- *Decide where the data will be stored*—Selecting an appropriate location for your data backups is essential. Typically, it's unwise to leave your tapes in the same location as the data you have backed up, especially when you take into

account the risks from fire, flood, and so on. Keeping offsite secure backups of data is a smart idea, and the popularity of services that provide environmentally controlled, secure, offsite storage for your data backups is growing rapidly. For more information on these services, refer to Chapter 14.

- *Schedule your backups for an appropriate time of day*—Backup jobs can take a considerable amount of time and server performance as they copy files to the backup media. This can lead to not only a server slowdown (if users access this server, they typically notice a sluggish response), but also a network slowdown if you are copying your data across the network from a remote server to the backup drive. Usually, a company should run backups during off-peak hours. This is, again, at your discretion, depending on the needs of your organization.

In addition to these general concepts, you must address issues specific to Exchange 2000, such as deciding which data to back up—just mailboxes and other user data, or the entire Exchange 2000 setup and its configuration information, which you will learn about in the following section.

Selecting the Type of Data to Back Up

Major services such as Exchange 2000 Server can generate a lot of data, including mailboxes, public folders, log files, and other configuration information. As you learned previously, when you are generating your backup strategy, you should consider how long it will take to back up *and* restore the data you need. This time factor often causes a change in your overall backup strategy that affects what you back up or when you perform the backups. If your Exchange 2000 server consumes a lot of space with user mailboxes and the like, it could take longer than your window of opportunity to perform your backup—and often far longer to restore your data. Because of this, you should choose your priorities carefully.

Typically, the most important data that should be backed up is the Exchange 2000 stores, including the mailbox stores and public folder stores. In addition, transaction logs, which record everything that goes on inside your Exchange 2000 database stores, can be useful when you need to restore your Exchange 2000 server. The stores and their respective databases should be considered your first priority when planning your backup because they are the most likely components to contain critical information; in addition, they are usually updated constantly, making regular daily backups that much more important. When performing backups, it is possible to back up a single mailbox or an individual public folder, but to do this, you usually need a third-party backup software package with an add-on geared for Exchange 2000. Windows 2000 offers a simple yet effective backup solution that can back up wholesale amounts of data (such as entire mailbox or public folder stores and other critical system configuration information), but it lacks the backup customization features of more expensive software packages. Even with this limitation, it is certainly better than nothing, and if backing up individual mailboxes and public folders isn't that important to you, it can provide adequate backup services.

In addition to mailboxes, you should consider backing up the current state of the server on which Exchange 2000 is installed. Unlike Exchange 5.5, Exchange 2000 does not keep its own directory information; it is kept in AD. So it can be to your benefit to back up AD as well as the operating system's Registry because it contains essential Exchange 2000 configuration information. The Windows 2000 Backup utility has the option of backing up your System State folder that allows you to select which system components you want to back up, including Active Directory, system boot files, the system Registry, and the operating system itself. Backing up all this data can take a lot of time, but if you must replace Exchange 2000 on a failed server with as little reconfiguration as possible, this information can be invaluable.

Finally, the third bit of data you should consider backing up is the Exchange 2000 files and folders on the server. Backing up the folder to which you installed Exchange 2000, including all its subfolders, can help back up Exchange 2000 system files that include configuration and message-tracking information. Without this data, restoring Exchange 2000 to the state it was in before the server failed can take additional time. At a minimum, you should back up the user data in mailboxes and public folders, and then back up the operating system and Exchange 2000 files as time allows. If you have a large Exchange 2000 installation and you need to regularly back up all this information, you should ensure that you have a quick backup device. Even in a small Exchange 2000 organization, you shouldn't overlook the advantages of having a fast backup device because it makes the restore process quicker.

Most likely, you will have to make a compromise; instead of constantly backing up everything, consider backing up just the mailbox and public folder stores daily. Then perform a full backup (with the critical user data and the operating system and Exchange 2000 files required for a full backup of all your data and configuration) after hours, when you have more time to do it. Any missing information that is not backed up translates into additional time and effort on your part when it's time to rebuild your failed Exchange 2000 server. Balancing time, space, and the data you need to back up can be a difficult part of designing your backup strategy. Only careful consideration of the data you need to back up and the amount of available time will help you figure out the best plan of action.

Backing Up Exchange 2000 Database Information

The Windows 2000 Backup utility has the capability to back up individual databases in a storage group. For instance, if you want to back up your mailboxes but not the information in the public folders, you can simply back up the mailbox store rather than the entire storage group or server. However, Microsoft recommends backing up the entire storage group because if you back up multiple databases in the same storage group, each time you back up an individual database, you back up all the transaction log files for that storage group, which takes up quite a bit of extra time and hard disk space.

Deciding what to back up requires balancing what information you really need, how much space you have (hardware limitations), and how much time you have to back up the data. If you have trouble establishing how much data you can back up because of space limitations or time restrictions, you might have to consider distributing your backups to accommodate your available time and backup space. Often, the best plan in this situation is to run daily backups of the most critical information (for instance, your mailbox stores), and then run full backups on the weekend when you typically have more time to back up information (assuming that most users are not working on weekends).

If you do decide to back up individual databases, Microsoft recommends that you download the latest service pack for Exchange 2000 Server (although installing the latest service pack should be a given because of the fixes and improvements it brings to your systems). The latest service pack (any version) contains the most up-to-date Windows 2000 Backup configuration and add-ons for backing up Exchange 2000 databases and components. The latest service pack for Exchange 2000 can be found at *http://www.microsoft.com/exchange*. You learn how to perform a backup of an individual database file in the "Hands-on Projects" section later in this chapter.

As you learned in Chapter 14, although circular logging helps save space used by transaction logs, it can effectively cripple your disaster recovery efforts if you need to rebuild a database and one of the files has been corrupted or is missing. Microsoft recommends not enabling circular logging so that you can take advantage of as many data recovery options as possible.

Online and Offline Backups

There are two different approaches to backing up your Exchange 2000 data beyond your regular choices (full, differential, incremental, and so on): online and offline backups. **Offline backups** occur when the server's services have been stopped and the server is not accepting new information or currently processing anything. For many applications, this is the only way to get all the information backed up properly, but it isn't necessarily the case for Exchange 2000. **Online backups** in Exchange 2000 enable you to back up your Exchange 2000 server, including information that hasn't been written to the databases yet, while the server is still processing information. This might seem impossible, but given how Exchange 2000 makes use of the transaction logs and database files, it works rather well. As you learned in Chapter 14, activity in a database file is recorded in the transaction logs until the information is moved into the database files; therefore, if you back up the database file and information is queued in the transaction logs, nothing is lost because the information can be written from the transaction logs to the database files after the backup is finished.

Exchange 2000 is designed for online backups because, as you know, taking down the servers for any length of time is impossible for many organizations. Using online backups, you can retrieve backups of current information and information that might still be in a processing stage without taking down your server. Exchange 2000 uses a smart feature for online backups: the patch file. When information is sent to the server while the database is being backed up, it is sent to the transaction logs and then is eventually destined for the database. However, if your database has already been backed up (sans the new data),

Exchange 2000 ends up writing this "homeless" information into a patch file, which can later be used to help restore the missing information to the database. Think of it as a mini-database that contains only information processed during or after the database is backed up online. The information in the patch file is eventually written to the database through the transaction logs; however, the patch file can be used to help in restoration if you do not have a new backup complete with the previously missing information.

After you have finished your online backup of your Exchange 2000 database files, the information recorded in the patch file will also be written to tape to ensure that it is backed up and secure. After the patch file is backed up, the original file on the server is deleted to conserve space and minimize the clutter of having patch files on your server. As you can see, Exchange 2000 has effective online backup methods that almost completely negate the need for offline backups.

Backing Up Exchange 2000 Configuration and System State Information

Although the entire process of creating different types of backup jobs is explained in the "Hands-on Projects" section later in this chapter, in this section you learn how Exchange 2000 handles the backup of two useful pieces of data: the Exchange 2000 configuration information and the system state information. These two pieces of information contain system data that can be critical to getting a failed server back up and running quickly. Windows 2000 Backup allows for quick and easy backups of Exchange system data and information in the System State folder, which includes the ever-useful Registry configuration.

The advantage of Windows 2000 Backup is that it enables you to quickly and easily select the configuration and system state information you want to back up, just as you would any other file or folder on your server. Using this feature is much easier than hunting down each component separately and trying to keep track of what you have already backed up and what still needs to be backed up. Windows 2000 Backup takes the guesswork out of the process and makes it easy to select this important data. You simply place a check mark next to the Microsoft Exchange installation folder (typically *X*:\Program files\Exchsrvr) and the System State folder (which already contains the operating system information mentioned) in Windows 2000 Backup, as shown in Figure 15-1.

The Windows 2000 Backup software is quite good (considering it is included free with the operating system), with its ability to back up entire Exchange 2000 servers or just a single database while online and still provide services to your users. In addition, the ability to back up the System State folder is a handy feature to help provide additional disaster recovery information for restoring your server. The importance of backing up your entire Exchange 2000 server's installation directory on occasion (preferably at least once a week) cannot be stressed enough. Without the information in this directory, including message-tracking data and configuration files, the job of restoring your Exchange 2000 installation becomes that much harder and more time consuming.

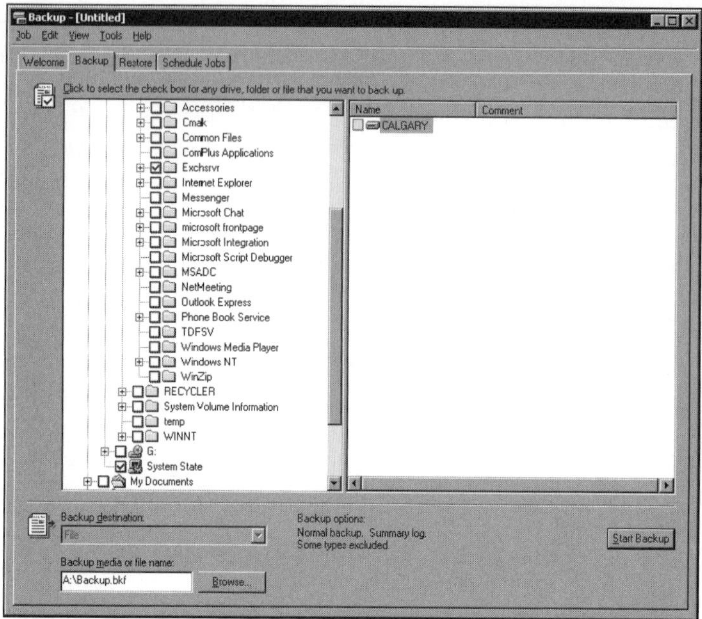

Figure 15-1 Selecting the System State and Exchange installation folders to back up

RESTORING AND RECOVERING EXCHANGE 2000 DATA

Restoring data to your Exchange 2000 server isn't difficult as long as you have good backups of your data and you have a clear idea of what you want to restore. Windows 2000 Backup (and most third-party backup software) shows you all your previous backup jobs, allowing you to select the one you want to restore from (assuming that you still have the backup media and you didn't overwrite the data on that media). You have a lot of flexibility when performing an Exchange 2000 data restore; you can select individual components and databases to restore, and you can restore the data to the original location, to a different folder, or even to a different server.

The next few sections of this chapter outline complete server restorations, restorations of data to different locations, and restoration of individual mailboxes.

Prerequisites for Restoration

Before you perform any type of data restoration on your Exchange 2000 server, there are a few issues you should address. First, if you are restoring data to an Exchange 2000 server that is a member of a domain, make sure AD is running for that domain. In addition, to avoid problems such as the domain's schema information being corrupted, make sure a server object is registered in AD before continuing. If you are performing a full restoration to a replacement server or a rebuilt server, make sure you have completed the required preinstallation tasks for Exchange 2000, including having AD and DNS installed and functioning. Second, by the same token, if you are restoring Exchange 2000 data to a domain controller in an AD domain and you are essentially rebuilding the server, ensure that AD and DNS are installed.

Just as you would for your backups, having a restoration strategy in place is a good idea. The rules for backups also apply for restorations; the more data and tapes you have in your backup strategy, the more time it takes to back up and restore. The time it takes to restore your data should be considered both in backup and restoration plans. If it takes longer to restore your data than what's considered acceptable by your organization, you might need to revise your backup strategy to ensure that you can perform restorations as quickly as needed and with the correct data. Ultimately, a full daily backup offers the best balance between backed up data and ease of restoration, but with the obvious time penalties when backing up the data. If you want to take advantage of the easier-to-manage and quicker-to-restore data in a full daily backup and you have a lot of data to back up, consider purchasing one of the new high-speed, high-capacity tape backup drives or even **DVD-RW**, a new backup standard in which you can write your backups to DVDs. Keep in mind, however, that the size limits for DVD are far lower (typically around 6–8 GB) than the largest tape backup drives available (some ranging into hundreds of gigabytes).

As you know, the more tapes used for your backup, the more are required for your restore. The following list outlines how many tapes you might need for your restore, depending on the backup method:

- *Daily full backup*—Typically performed only if all the data fits on one tape, although it is possible to switch tapes if needed to carry data onto additional tapes. This restoration is often the quickest and easiest to manage because you usually have only one tape to deal with and all your data is in one place.
- *Weekly full backup with differential data backed up*—The next-best plan to a daily full backup of your information, a full data backup is typically performed on the weekend, and backups are run daily for files that have changed from the original backup. The changed data is updated every day so that it is the most current, but will definitely expand in size as the week wears on. Restoring with this method should require the use of only two tapes: the original full backup from the weekend and the latest differential backup tape.
- *Weekly full backup with incremental daily backup*—Requires the most tapes to back up and restore because tapes are used every day to back up data that changed from the last session. This method requires restoring the weekly full backup tape and every daily incremental tape to fill in blank spots in your data.

To give you the best idea of how your restorations work and how much time they will take, consider performing practice disaster recovery restorations of your Exchange 2000 data. To effectively test your recovery plans, try restoring data under a multitude of different circumstances (such as individual database and full restorations) to give you a better idea of what to expect when the time comes to put your plan into action.

Periodically performing these test restorations helps ensure that you know what to do; in addition, you can confirm that your data can be restored successfully—taking the guesswork out of whether your restoration will succeed when you need it the most.

Using a spare system as a recovery server can also be useful in restoration management. With the recovery server, you can restore information, such as individual mailboxes, to the server and then move or access the data you need. You can also use the recovery server to give you the opportunity to make sure the date is not corrupted before you restore it to the production server. You can also make sure you don't accidentally overwrite or damage otherwise good data on your production server, which could certainly require a lot more time and effort, and cause frustration.

Restoring a Full Backup to the Production or Recovery Server

As mentioned in the previous section, you can perform full restorations of your data both to recovery and production servers. When restoring your entire Exchange 2000 installation (assuming that you backed up everything, including system state information) to the production or recovery server, make sure you rebuild the server as though you were going to do a fresh installation of Exchange 2000. The following list is a broad outline of the basic steps you should follow when installing to a server you have rebuilt after a failure.

1. Reinstall Windows 2000 Server with service packs to the same drive and path as your original installation.
2. Install DNS but leave your system configured as a workgroup; the Active Directory information will be restored with the system state restoration.
3. Perform a restoration of the system state data to restore the appropriate Registry, Active Directory, and other operating system configuration information.
4. Reinstall Exchange 2000 with the same options as before, including service packs, to the same drive and path as your original installation.
5. Restore your Exchange 2000 data, including databases and other information from the original Exchange 2000 installation directory.
6. Test your server as much as possible to help ensure that there are no surprises when you put it back into production (an optional step, but a highly recommended one). To test it, try sending mail to and from the server from various sources. If you have connectors set up, make sure they work, and have a user (or yourself) use your primary client to see whether public folders and other functions are working as they should.

The previous steps also apply if you are restoring data to a recovery server; however, when you are restoring data to a recovery server (if it has Exchange 2000 installed already), you should follow these Microsoft guidelines:

- The recovery server must be on a different Windows 2000 domain forest from the production server.

- If you are restoring a database, the storage group that you are restoring to must have the same name as the one you are restoring from.
- When restoring databases, the organization name and the administrative groups (if you are using them) must be the same as the original databases' server.

After you have followed these steps and restored the data to a recovery server, you can then move the data and individual mailboxes as necessary, as you will read about in the next section.

Restoring a Single Mailbox

Although it is possible with Windows 2000 Backup to restore a single mailbox that has been deleted or lost, you must take a slightly roundabout route. First, you need to restore your data to a recovery server, and then you can move the mailbox around as needed. If you have a third-party backup software package with the appropriate Exchange 2000 capabilities or add-on (Exchange 2000 is typically an add-on module for most backup software), you can quickly and easily restore an individual mailbox to the original production server. Even though the Windows 2000 Backup software is good, it does have certain limitations, such as the mailbox restoration issue. You will learn how to restore a single mailbox later in the "Hands-on Projects" section of this chapter.

If you delete users from Active Directory, their mailboxes are retained for 30 days before Exchange 2000 sets them for deletion. If you accidentally delete users, you should reconnect their mailboxes as soon as you can by creating new users in Active Directory (or selecting other preexisting ones), and then use the Exchange System Manager console to configure which user is connected to a particular mailbox.

Another useful option in Exchange 2000 is configuring a mailbox store's deleted mailbox-retention settings. As with configuring your deleted message-retention settings, you can specify how many days you want a deleted mailbox to hang around. If you have lost or accidentally deleted a mailbox and you have configured mailbox-retention settings, you can recover the mailbox within that set time period without having to restore it from backup. You learn how to set this handy option in the "Hands-on Projects" section later in this chapter.

Restoring Online and Offline Backups

When you restore data from an online backup, you can restore it to recovery servers. The key is to make sure you have restored any transaction logs needed for the databases you have restored, thus ensuring that any data not written to the database is complete and the databases function properly. This can be accomplished because the transaction logs contain records of all traffic for a database, so you can use the transaction logs to restore any information missing from the database. If you are rebuilding a server using online backups, you should first make sure there is a computer account in AD with the same name as the server you're restoring to ensure that the server is a member of the domain; otherwise, there could be problems with the server communicating with the objects in your AD domain.

Contrary to what you may think, restoring data from an offline backup can require more time and be a bit more finicky than restoring from an online backup. You might run into the following problems when restoring from an offline backup:

- Exchange 2000 services must be taken offline to perform the backup (hence the name "offline backup") and when you restore the services to write the data, which prevents any use by end users.
- Database information is not checked as it is restored, which can lead to data corruption.
- Using your log files to re-create databases and fill out unwritten data from your logs is not supported.

Lest you think there aren't any benefits to restoring from an offline backup, there is at least one useful benefit that you should know about. You can move a restored database file without more information being written to the file during the move that must be added in later. After the Exchange 2000 services are offline, no information can be added to the databases. Overall, however, online methods allow for the most seamless backup and restoration processes. They enable your organization to carry on its business with as little downtime as possible, an important consideration when using Exchange 2000 and its services.

Additional Exchange 2000 Recovery Options

Some Exchange 2000 recovery options don't involve data restoration. For instance, you might not have lost any Exchange 2000 data, such as a mailbox, but another program or virus could have modified your Exchange 2000 installation, or some of the installation files might have been deleted by accident. For these situations, it may be more practical to use Exchange 2000 utilities and features to repair or recover from the damage caused to your server and databases.

One of the main recovery utilities is ESEUTIL, which you learned about in Chapter 14; however, you can also take advantage of the Exchange 2000 disaster recovery option, which is performed through the Exchange 2000 Installation Wizard. In addition to its regular maintenance duties, ESEUTIL can replay transactions (insert missing data) to help stabilize a database that has been determined to be inconsistent with the transaction logs. If ESEUTIL determines that a database file is consistent, Microsoft recommends that you move all database files as one unit, including their log files. Microsoft also recommends that you never move, rename, or delete files in the database folders, especially if you do not know what they do; often Exchange 2000 uses several smaller files and if you do not have them, you can cause a database failure or loss of data. In addition to the ESEUTIL utility, you can use the ISINTEG utility (also covered in Chapter 14) to inspect the integrity of your Information Store and check for any database inconsistencies. Both of these utilities are invaluable when restoring information or trying to recover from a server crash.

If your Windows 2000 server is still functioning and your Exchange 2000 installation has simply failed or had files deleted, you can run the Exchange 2000 Installation Wizard to reinstall the files you need for Exchange 2000 to function again. If you already had Exchange 2000 installed on this server and it has failed, you can take advantage of the /disasterrecovery switch when you run the wizard. The /disasterrecovery switch runs through the Exchange 2000 installation, replacing files and system settings without tampering with the preexisting Active Directory configuration and data. In addition, this switch reinstalls Exchange 2000 with its previous configuration (assuming that some of the files for the previous configuration are intact), saving you the time required to reconfigure the server to its previous settings. After your Exchange 2000 installation is running again, you can restore your database and other information from your data backups (if you lost the files when your server failed). You learn how to perform a disaster recovery enabled installation in the "Hands-on Projects" section.

If you want to read more about some of the advanced restoration options, including how to restore data to clustered Exchange 2000 servers or even how to restore Key Management Services databases, you can purchase the Microsoft Exchange 2000 Server Resources Kit in book form or view it online at *http://www.microsoft.com/exchange/techinfo/reskit/default.asp.*

CHAPTER SUMMARY

- Developing an effective disaster recovery plan should be an essential element of your overall network management plan. When developing your disaster recovery plan, think of potential problems beyond natural disasters, such as fires, floods, or tornadoes.
- Many disasters, such as viruses, hackers, and even hardware or operating system failures, involve factors that are often within your control. Even though these problems can occur without warning, you can at least take preventive measures and use an early warning mechanism, such as the Windows Event Viewer.
- You should have at least a short disaster recovery plan that outlines the basics of what will happen in certain emergencies while you develop a more detailed custom disaster recovery plan. Having a plan to work from, no matter how short, is certainly better than not having one at all.
- Data backup represents a vast amount of time and effort in your disaster recovery plans. Keeping data secure and available is of paramount concern for most organizations, and loss of sensitive data can cripple a network if it cannot be recovered.

- When developing your backup plan, you must consider which data you are going to back up and where it will be stored. You should locate a secure, environmentally managed facility to store your data backups in case a fire or similar incident destroys your onsite data; this precaution ensures that you don't simultaneously lose your servers and your backed up data.
- You can selectively back up certain data on your server or back it all up. It is advisable to occasionally perform full backups of your Exchange 2000 and other system configuration information so that you stand a better chance of recovering your servers if necessary. Often, you have to prioritize which data to back up because of limitations in time or backup media storage space. If you simply do not have the time to back up everything, you might have to schedule periodic full backups during off-peak hours to ensure that you get a full set of data backed up.
- As with planning your backup strategy, planning your restoration strategy must be well thought out. Keep in mind how long it takes to restore the data you have backed up and how you will go about restoring it to get your servers and data functioning again. To determine your restoration method and the time involved, periodic test restorations of your data are highly recommended.
- A few steps are required to ensure a smooth data restoration to both the production and recovery servers. If you are restoring after a complete server failure, you must make sure that you install Windows 2000 to the point just before you would normally reinstall Exchange 2000, except for your system state data. This is necessary because the system state data can help rebuild the AD configuration for that server after Exchange 2000 has been reinstalled. If performed correctly, you will be able have your system up and running quickly.
- You can restore individual Exchange 2000 mailboxes, but not directly through the Windows 2000 Backup software. Most third-party backup software packages with the appropriate Exchange 2000 add-on components can restore an individual mailbox to the server it was deleted from.
- In addition to backups and restorations, you can also use Exchange 2000 utilities and configuration options to help repair a damaged installation. Utilities such as ESEUTIL and ISINTEG can help you repair or rebuild damaged database files in Exchange 2000 so that you don't have to restore the files from a backup. The Exchange 2000 Server Installation Wizard includes a command-line switch that can perform a recovery installation on Exchange 2000 and not disturb Active Directory or preexisting Exchange 2000 configuration information, thus allowing you to safely retain your previous configuration.

Key Terms

DVD-RW — A new backup standard in which you can back up your data onto DVD media, which can hold much more data than CDs, but often less than the more traditional tape backup media.

offline backup — A backup performed when the server's Exchange 2000 services have been stopped and the server is not accepting new information or processing current information; this allows data at an exact point in time to be backed up without worrying about new information being sent during the backup.

online backup — A backup performed on your Exchange 2000 server while it is running and processing new information. Data being processed during the backup will be stored in an additional patch file that can later be integrated into the appropriate database if a restoration is necessary.

Review Questions

1. Besides natural disasters, which of the following are external factors for which you should try to plan? (Choose all that apply.)
   a. virus infection
   b. hardware or operating system failure
   c. users tripping over power cords to servers
   d. hacker intrusion
2. When developing your backup strategy, you must keep in mind the timeline you will have to both ________________ and ________________ your data.
3. Which of the following are an effective means to help mitigate the effects of a hardware failure? (Choose all that apply.)
   a. Routinely reboot the hardware (server).
   b. Keep a selection of spare parts on hand.
   c. Establish a hardware service agreement with the vendor.
   d. Implement a well-designed backup strategy.
4. To provide all the necessary information for backups, data restoration, hardware failure, and other problems, you should generate a ________________.
5. You have a full Exchange 2000 Server backup scheduled to run at 2 a.m. on Saturday morning. Users who are coming in on Saturday morning at about 9 a.m. are complaining that it is taking too long for Outlook 2000 to retrieve and send e-mail, and they are getting frustrated. What could be the possible cause of this problem?
6. Describe what you can do to rectify the problem in Question 5 and get users' e-mail working again.
7. It is generally advisable to store your server's backup media ________________ to minimize the potential for total loss of your data in a disaster.

8. Which of the following folders contains the current Active Directory, Registry, and other operating system configuration data that can be backed up with the Windows 2000 Backup software?
   a. Exchsrvr
   b. Winnt
   c. System State
   d. Program Files
9. If you do not have enough time to back up all your data, or you lack enough storage space on your backup media, which of the following backup strategies should you consider performing to get a reliable and complete set of data quickly?
   a. Do a full backup on Sunday; back up system state and databases every night.
   b. Do a full backup on Saturday or Sunday with system state backed up every night.
   c. Back up database files every night.
   d. Back up system state and databases every Sunday; back up Exchange 2000 installation directory every night.
10. When you back up your database files, Microsoft recommends that you back up your entire storage group rather than just the individual database files. This is to ensure that you back up the ______________ files, which can be used to help restore missing data.
    a. event log
    b. system state
    c. Exchange installation
    d. transaction log
11. If you are planning to back up just individual database files by using the Windows 2000 Backup software, you must install the latest Exchange 2000 ______________ because it contains the most recent updates for Exchange 2000 data backups.
12. During an online Exchange 2000 data backup, any transactions and information destined for the databases being backed up are stored in the ______________ file.
13. If you want to ensure that you retain a backup of your message-tracking logs, you should back up the System State folder. True or False?
14. Which of the following is the easiest Exchange 2000 backup method to restore?
    a. full daily backup
    b. weekly full backup with incremental daily backup
    c. weekly full backup with differential daily backup
    d. monthly full backup with weekly differential daily backup

15. Microsoft recommends that you perform periodic ______________ of data to confirm that your backup media can be restored, and to determine how long it takes to restore the data.
16. If you are using Windows 2000 Backup software and you want to restore an individual mailbox, you will have to restore that data to a recovery server before moving it to the server it belongs on. True or False?
17. If you are restoring a full backup of Exchange 2000 to a recovery server, you must ensure that some information from the old system is configured the same way on the new system. Which of the following options must be the same on both systems?
    a. forest domain name
    b. organization name
    c. administrative account password
    d. storage group name
18. How many days are deleted mailboxes retained by Exchange 2000?
    a. 7
    b. 14
    c. 21
    d. 30
19. It can take more time and effort to restore an offline backup than an online backup. True or False?
20. Which of the following command-line switches can you use to install Exchange 2000 without affecting the previous Exchange 2000 installation configuration or AD?
    a. \recovery
    b. \disasterrecovery
    c. \repair
    d. \restoreexchange

Hands-on Projects

Project 15-1

Backing up an entire storage group allows you to back up not only its databases (both public folder and mailbox databases) but also any associated transaction logs. Although you could back up just the individual database files, Microsoft recommends backing up the entire storage group to ensure that you retain the transaction logs, which can be used to recover information not written to the database files during the backup. This project requires Windows 2000 Backup software to be installed.

To use Windows 2000 Backup to back up an Exchange storage group:

1. If necessary, log on to your system using an account with administrative rights.
2. To open the Windows 2000 Backup software, click **Start**, point to **Programs**, point to **Accessories**, point to **System Tools**, and then click **Backup**. The Welcome tab of the Backup utility appears, as shown in Figure 15-2.

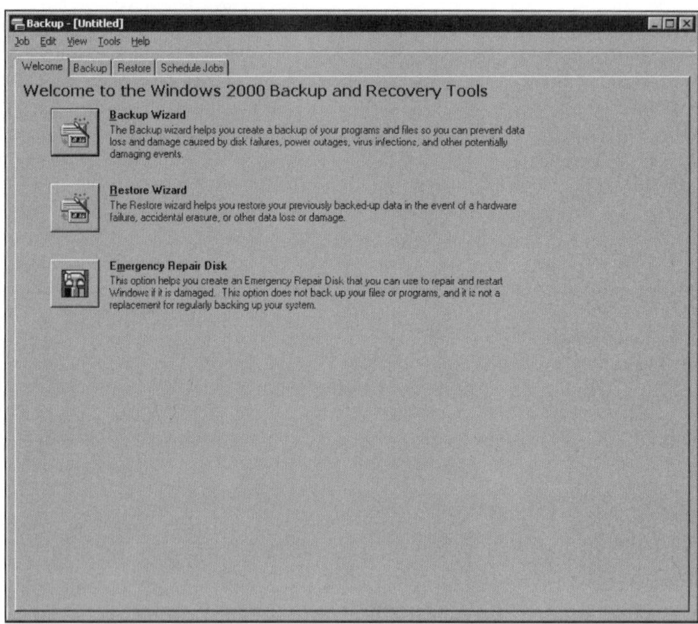

Figure 15-2 The Windows 2000 Backup utility

3. Click the **Backup** tab to show the folder list on your computer. In the folder view, you will see your various drives, the System State folder, and the Microsoft Exchange Server folder. Click the plus symbol next to the Microsoft Exchange Server folder to show the Exchange 2000 server you are connected to (the local server; in this project's figures, it is Calgary).
4. Double-click this server icon to show the Microsoft Information Store folder underneath it. (If needed, you can select just this folder to back up the entire Information Store and its storage groups.) Next, double-click the **First Storage Group** folder. After you have navigated to this folder, you will see the mailbox and public folder stores listed in the Details pane, as shown in Figure 15-3.
5. Click the **First Storage Group** check box to select this storage group and the databases listed underneath. When you click this check box, any databases in this storage group are automatically selected as well.

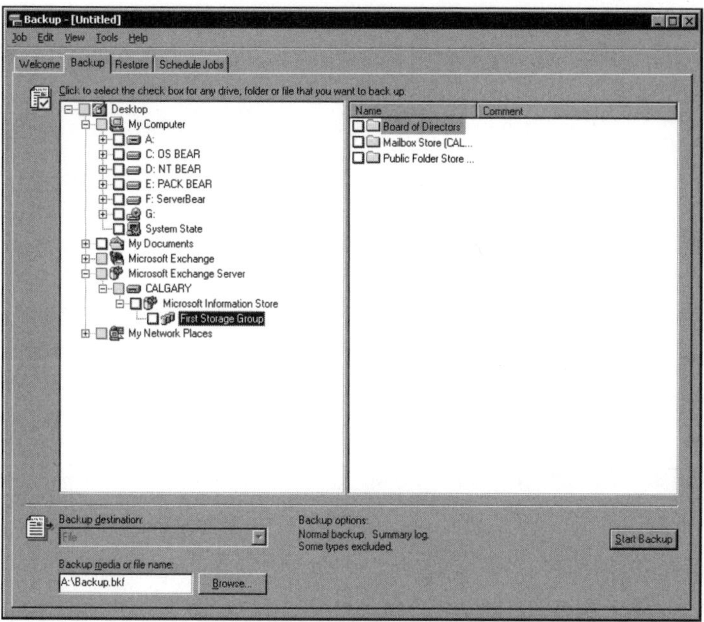

Figure 15-3 Selecting storage groups to back up in the Backup tab

If you do not want to back up a certain folder, you can simply click the check box next to its folder in the Details pane of the Backup software to remove the check mark and prevent it from being backed up.

6. Typically, you back up your data to a tape backup drive, but for this project, you can back up this information to your Windows desktop. On the bottom of the Backup tab, you will see the Backup destination and Backup media or file name text boxes where you can specify where the backup will go. Click the **Browse** button to open the Open dialog box. Navigate to the **Desktop** folder, and in the File name text box, type in **storagegroup**. Your Open dialog box should look similar to Figure 15-4. Click the **Open** button to return to the Backup tab.
7. After you have specified the destination, you are ready to start the backup. To do this, click the **Start Backup** button to open the Backup Job Information dialog box shown in Figure 15-5. In the Backup description text box, the date and the time of the backup job will be entered as the job's description by default. You can change this description to be more specific if you want. For this project, delete the information in this text box, and then type **Storage Group backup on *Today's Date*** (replace *Today's Date* with the actual date). Then click the **Start Backup** button to create the backup of your data.

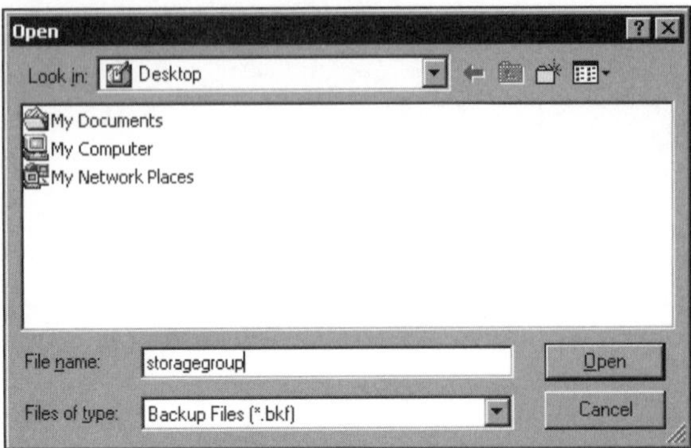

Figure 15-4 Creating a backup file in the Open dialog box

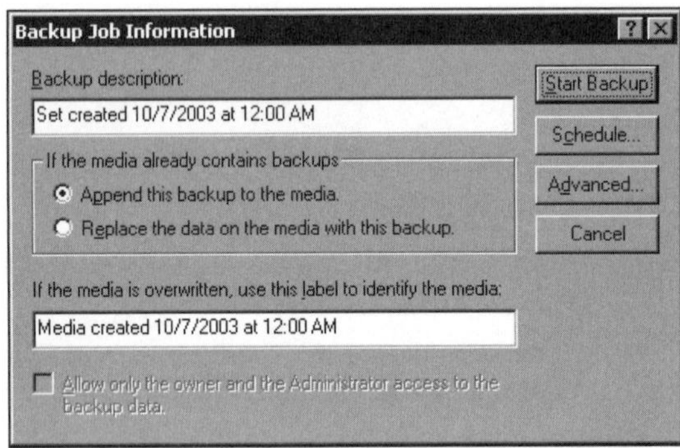

Figure 15-5 The Backup Job Information dialog box

8. After your backup has started, you will see the Backup Progress window outlining the backup's progress, similar to Figure 15-6.
9. When the backup is finished, the Backup Progress dialog box changes to indicate that the backup is complete and displays information about the backup, such as how long it took and the total amount of data written (see Figure 15-7). Click **Close** to complete the backup and return to the Windows 2000 Backup program. Leave your system in this state for the next project.

Project 15-2

This project shows you how to back up the System State folder and the Exchange 2000 installation folder to ensure that you retain the important system and Exchange 2000 installation configuration information for your server. You also learn how to set a few important advanced backup options, including verification of your backed up data after the backup is complete. This project requires Windows 2000 Backup software to be installed.

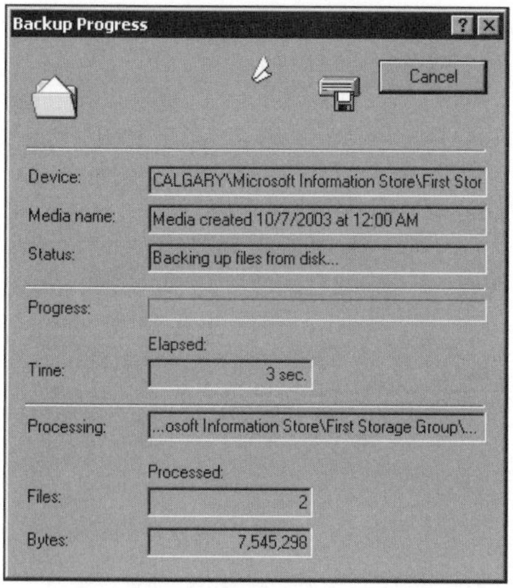

Figure 15-6 The Backup Progress dialog box

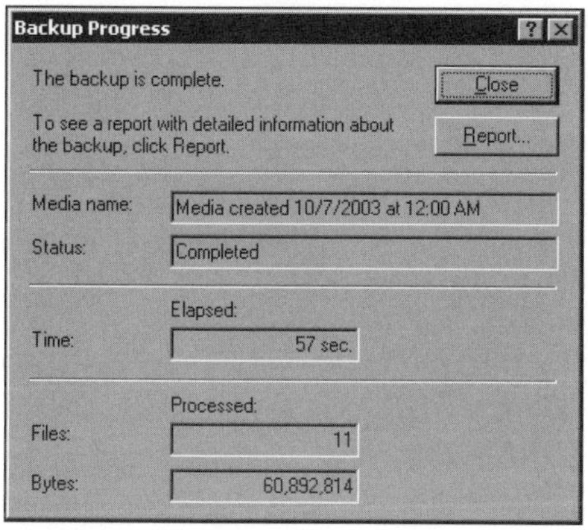

Figure 15-7 Backup information displayed after the backup is finished

To back up the System State and Exchange 2000 installation folders:

1. If necessary, log on to your system using an account with administrative rights. If you are continuing from Project 15-1, you can skip Steps 1–3.
2. To open the Windows 2000 Backup software, click **Start**, point to **Programs**, point to **Accessories**, point to **System Tools**, and then click **Backup**. The Welcome tab of the Backup Utility appears.
3. Click the **Backup** tab to show the folder list on your computer. In the folder view, you will see your various drives, the System State folder, and the Microsoft Exchange Server folder. Click the plus symbol next to the Microsoft Exchange

Server folder to show the Exchange 2000 server you are connected to (the local server; in this project's figures, it is Calgary).

4. Click the **System State** folder's check box to select this folder for your backup. Then navigate through the folder tree above the System State folder, locate your Exchange 2000 installation folder (typically **C:\Program Files\Exchsrvr**), and then locate the *Servername*.log folder underneath this folder (*Servername* is the name of your Exchange 2000 server). Next, click the check box next to this folder (you can select the entire Exchsrvr folder, but it will be larger than what's needed for this project).Your Backup tab should look similar to Figure 15-8.

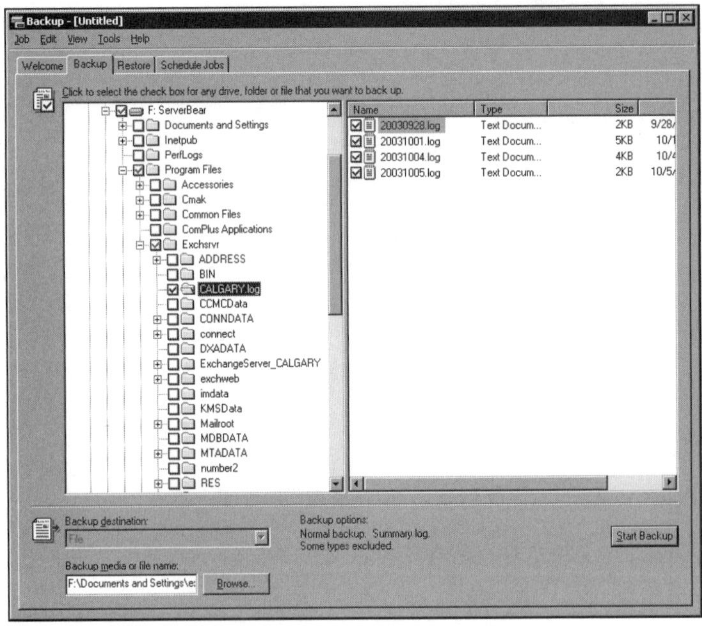

Figure 15-8 Selecting an Exchange 2000 folder for backup

5. At the bottom of the Backup tab, click the **Browse** button to open the Open dialog box. In the File name text box, type **systemstate**, and then click the **Open** button.

The System State folder can be rather large, so make sure the drive you select for saving your backup file has enough space.

6. After selecting the folders and the destination for the backup file, click the **Start Backup** button to open the Backup Job Information dialog box. In the Backup description text box, delete the default information, and then type **System state – *Today's date*** (replace *Today's date* with the actual date). Click the **Advanced** button to open the Advanced Backup Options dialog box.

7. In the Advanced Backup Options dialog box, you want to enable the backup to verify the data after the backup is complete. To do this, simply click the **Verify data after backup** check box. Your dialog box should look similar to Figure 15-9. Click **OK** to return to the Backup Job Information dialog box.

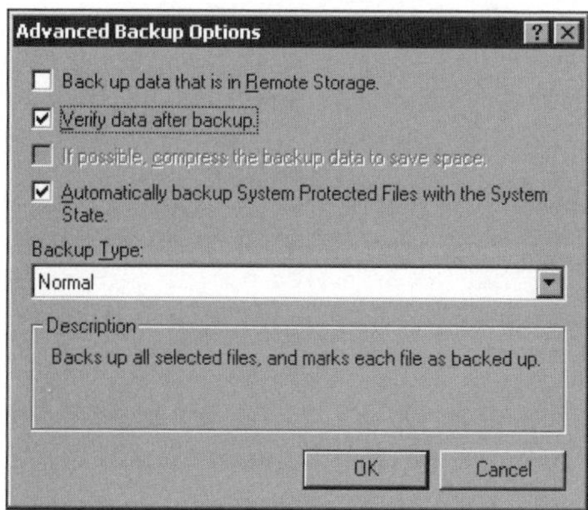

Figure 15-9 Enabling the option to verify the data after backup

8. Click the **Start Backup** button to get the backup running. This backup can take a few minutes; after the backup is finished writing the data, the Backup Progress dialog box lets you know the backup is complete. Click the **Close** button to finish the backup. Note that during the actual backup, the data was verified to ensure its validity; there is no additional process after the data is actually written that you will see.
9. Close Windows 2000 Backup to return to the Windows desktop. Leave your system in this state for the next project.

Project 15-3

15

This project shows you how to configure Exchange 2000 to retain a deleted user mailbox so that you can keep this information (as you would for a deleted message or other object) for a set number of days. By default, if you delete the user account associated with a mailbox, Exchange 2000 retains that user's mailbox for 30 days before it is deleted to give you time to re-create that user's mailbox if the deletion was a mistake. By enabling Exchange 2000 to retain a deleted mailbox, you are essentially enabling the same feature except that it helps protect against accidental deletion of mailboxes rather than user accounts and their data.

In addition, you can also set Exchange 2000 to not delete a mailbox before you have performed a backup of that mailbox. This option does not allow any data to be completely deleted from the server without being backed up first—a great failsafe to ensure that you get the data you need backed up in case you made a mistake and deleted the wrong mailbox. Even if the set amount of days for Exchange 2000 to retain that mailbox has expired, the data will stay on the server. If you have backed it up already, you can still restore it from backup after the retention days have run out.

To set deleted mailbox-retention settings:

1. If necessary, log on to your system using an account with administrative rights. If you are continuing from Project 15-2, you can skip this step.
2. To open the Exchange System Manager console, click **Start**, point to **Programs**, point to **Microsoft Exchange**, and then click **System Manager**.
3. Double-click the **Servers** folder, double-click your Exchange 2000 server, and then double-click the **First Storage Group** folder. (If you have the display of administrative groups enabled, you might have to first double-click the **Administrative Groups** folder and then the **First Administrative Group** folder).
4. Right-click the **Mailbox Store (*Servername*)** object (*Servername* is the name of your Exchange 2000 server), and then click **Properties** on the shortcut menu to open the Mailbox Store (*Servername*) dialog box. Click the **Limits** tab to show the available options.
5. Locate the Deletion settings section near the bottom of the tab. In the Keep deleted mailboxes for (days) text box, delete the contents (if any) and then type **14**. This tells Exchange 2000 to retain the mailbox for two weeks, which should be more than enough time to determine whether the mailbox is still needed. Finally, click the **Do not permanently delete mailboxes and items until the store has been backed up** check box. Your Limits tab should now look similar to Figure 15-10.

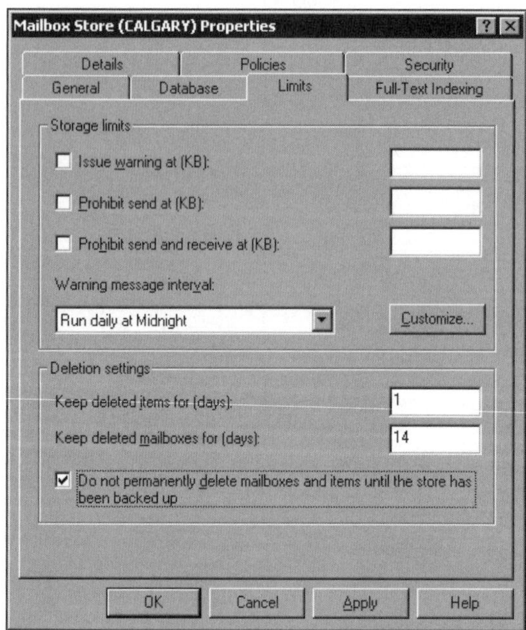

Figure 15-10 Configuring mailbox-deletion settings

6. Click **OK** to close the Properties dialog box and return to the Exchange System Manager console. Close the Exchange System Manager console to return to the Windows desktop. Leave your system in this state for the next project.

Project 15-4

This project shows you how to restore a database file backed up from your Exchange 2000 server to the same Exchange 2000 server. The backups you performed in Project 15-1 and 15-2 are both online backups, allowing you to back up the data without having to shut down Exchange 2000. Performing this restore while the server is online shows you how quick and easy restoring database files can be, with as little downtime as possible. This project assumes that you have completed Project 15-1.

To use Windows 2000 Backup to restore a database to the original server:

1. If necessary, log on to your system using an account with administrative rights. If you are continuing from Project 15-3, you can skip this step.
2. To make this project easier, you should first dismount the public folder store to facilitate a clean and easy restoration of your data. To do this, open the Exchange System Manager console (click **Start**, point to **Programs**, point to **Microsoft Exchange**, and then click **System Manager**). Navigate through the folders, locate and right-click the **Public Folders Store** folder, and then click **Dismount Store** on the shortcut menu. After a few seconds, the folder is disabled.
3. To open the Windows 2000 Backup software, click **Start**, point to **Programs**, point to **Accessories**, point to **System Tools**, and then click **Backup**. The Welcome tab of the Backup Utility appears.
4. Click **Tools** on the menu bar, and then click **Options** to open the Options dialog box. Click the **Restore** tab to see the options available to you when restoring. For this project, click the **Always replace the file on my computer** radio button, and then click **OK**.
5. Click the **Restore** tab to show the recent backup jobs that you have performed with this backup software. Your **Restore** tab should look similar to Figure 15-11, with the File object on the left and a few backup jobs on the right.
6. Double-click the backup jobs listed in the Details pane of the Windows 2000 Backup software. This shows the contents of this backup; locate and click the check box next to the one folder that's available in that backup job, locate the backup job with the storage groups listed, and then click the check box next to the listing with the newest date (if you have run this software more than once). After you have done this, the Windows 2000 Backup software should look similar to Figure 15-12.

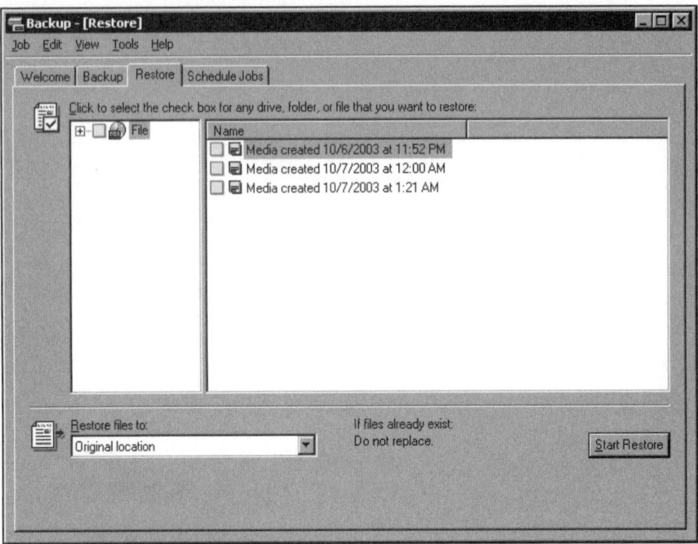

Figure 15-11 Viewing recent backups in the Restore tab

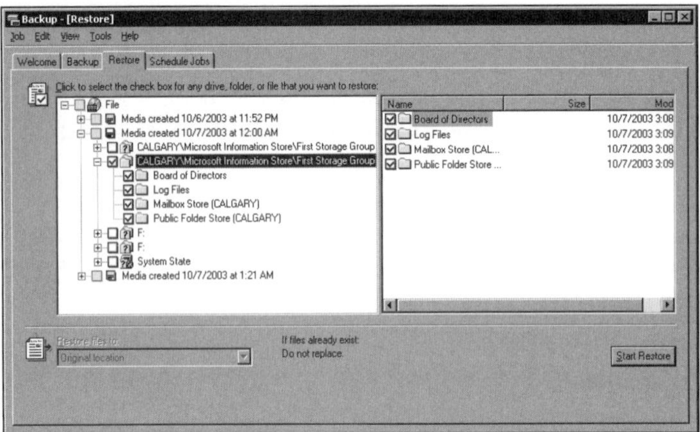

Figure 15-12 Selecting files to restore

7. Next, click the **Start Restore** button to open the Restoring Database Store dialog box. In this dialog box, you can set the server you want to restore to and the path for saving log files. For this project, leave the information in the Restore To text box at its default configuration. You must specify a location for log and patch files before attempting a restore. In the Temporary location for log and patch files text box, type **c:\exch2000**. Click the **Last Backup Set** check box, and then click the **Mount Database After Restore** check box when this option becomes enabled. Your Restoring Database Store dialog box should look similar to Figure 15-13.

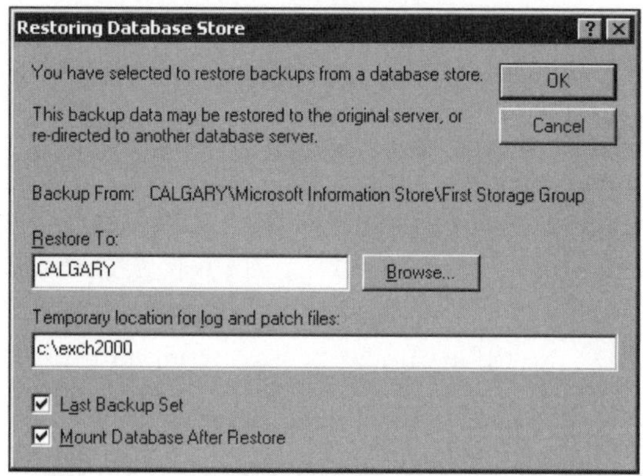

Figure 15-13 Configuring restoration settings in the Restoring Database Store dialog box

You do not want to select the Last Backup Set option if you are not restoring from a full backup. If you are restoring additional data from an incremental backup, leave this option unchecked. Otherwise, if the backup data you are restoring initially is all you will be restoring, you want this option enabled so that Exchange 2000 knows that no additional data will later be written to the databases.

8. When you have finished configuring this dialog box, click **OK**. If the Enter Backup File Name dialog box is displayed again, make sure that the correct location for the backup file you created in Project 15-1 is listed in the Restore from backup file text box, and then click **OK** to start the restore.
9. After the restore is finished, click the **Close** button on the Restore Progress dialog box, and then close the Windows 2000 Backup software. Also, don't forget to remount the Public Folder Store before closing the Exchange System Manager console. When you're back at the Windows desktop, leave your system in this state for the next project.

Project 15-5

This project shows you how to delete a user's mailbox and then reconnect it to the appropriate user account. Exchange 2000 allows you to reconnect a mailbox to a user account as a safety precaution to protect you from losing valuable information in a mailbox if you accidentally delete it or you need to associate a mailbox with another user. This project requires creating an additional user named "Test Mailbox" with an Exchange 2000 mailbox and having a user and mailbox that existed before the backups in Projects 15-1 and 15-2.

To use Exchange System Manager to reconnect a deleted mailbox to a user:

1. If necessary, log on to your system using an account with administrative rights. If you are continuing from Project 15-4, you can skip this step.

2. To open the Exchange System Manager console, click **Start**, point to **Programs**, point to **Microsoft Exchange**, and then click **System Manager**.
3. Double-click the **Servers** folder, double-click your Exchange 2000 server in your lab (for instance Calgary), double-click the **First Storage Group** folder, and then double-click the **Mailbox Store (Servername)** folder. (If you have the display of administrative groups enabled, you might have to first double-click the **Administrative Groups** folder and then the **First Administrative Group** folder).
4. Click the **Mailboxes** folder to show the mailboxes on your server. Ensure that the Test Mailbox object is in the Details pane of the console. Then minimize the Exchange System Manager console and open the Active Directory Users and Computers console by clicking **Start**, pointing to **Programs**, pointing to **Administrative Tools**, and clicking **Active Directory Users and Computers**.
5. When the console is open, double-click your domain, and then click the **Users** folder. Locate and right-click the **Test User** object, and then click **Exchange Tasks** on the shortcut menu to open the Exchange Task Wizard.
6. At the Welcome to the Exchange Task Wizard window, click the **Next** button to proceed to the Available Tasks window. Click the **Delete Mailbox** item, and then click the **Next** button to proceed to the Delete Mailbox window, which simply warns you about deleting the mailbox. Click the **Next** button to finish deleting the mailbox and continue to the Completing the Exchange Task Wizard window; click the **Finish** button to complete the wizard.
7. Return to the Exchange System Manager console, right-click an empty area of the Details pane, and click **Run Cleanup Agent** on the shortcut menu. This refreshes the mailbox store, and your Test Mailbox object will now be displayed with a red X through it. This red X indicates that it is marked for deletion and will be deleted when the time limit you set for deleted mailbox retention expires.
8. Right-click the **Test Mailbox** object, and then click **Reconnect** on the shortcut menu to open the Select a new user for this mailbox dialog box. Scroll through the list and click the **Test Mailbox** user, and then click **OK** to reconnect this mailbox. A message appears letting you know the operation was a success. Click **OK** to clear this message. If you see a message about replication to the destination server, click **OK**.
9. Back at the mailbox view, right-click an empty area of the Details pane, and then click **Run Cleanup Agent** on the shortcut menu. This refreshes the mailbox store, and your Test Mailbox object will now be displayed without the red X, indicating that the mailbox has been reconnected.
10. Close the Active Directory Users and Computers console and the Exchange System Manager console to return your system to the Windows desktop. Leave your system in this state for the next project.

Project 15-6

The disaster recovery option allows you to reinstall Exchange 2000 to a server that has failed without affecting Active Directory or any preexisting Exchange 2000 configuration.

To run Exchange 2000 installation in disaster recovery mode:

1. If necessary, log on to your system using an account with administrative rights. If you are continuing from Project 15-5, you can skip this step.
2. To open a command-prompt window, click **Start**, click **Run**, type **cmd.exe** in the Open text box, and then press **Enter**. At the command prompt, navigate to the Exchange 2000 Server Installation CD-ROM, type **setup.exe /disasterrecovery**, and then press **Enter**.
3. After a few seconds, the Exchange 2000 Installation Wizard opens and you are presented with the Welcome to window. Click the **Next** button to continue to the Component Selection window, as shown in Figure 15-14.

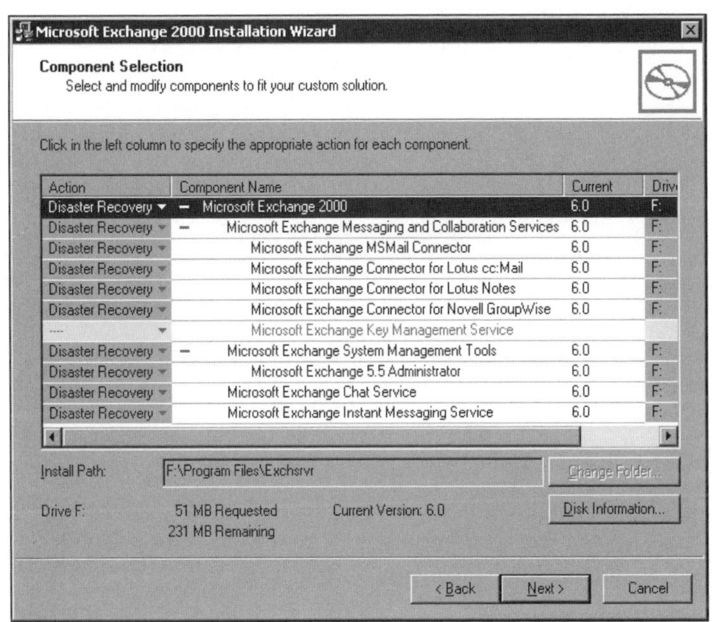

Figure 15-14 The Component Selection window showing Disaster Recovery as the action

4. As you can see in Figure 15-14, the Action column for every component is set to Disaster Recovery; if you do not see this, exit Setup and restart, making sure that you entered the command-line switch properly. If you do see this, click the **Next** button to start the installation; the Component Progress window will appear, showing the installation's progress at reinstalling Exchange 2000 in disaster recovery mode. You might see a message partway through the installation,

asking you to ensure that there is a server object in Active Directory for the server you are recovering. Click **OK** to clear this message and continue with the installation.

5. When the installation gets to the point of copying files to replace certain components of Exchange 2000, the Confirm File Replace window appears, asking if you want to overwrite files on your server. Normally, if you were having problems with your installation that appeared to be the result of file corruption or you lost parts of your Exchange 2000 installation directory, you would click Yes for any files you wanted to replace; in this project, click the **No to All** button because this is not the case. This message will appear when the installation process gets to each major Exchange 2000 component; click **No to All** any time it appears in this project.
6. After a few minutes of copying, a message appears, indicating that after the installation is complete, you should restart the system and then restore your databases from backup. After the installation is finished, you'll see the wizard completion window indicating that the installation was successful. Click the **Finish** button to complete the wizard and return to the Windows desktop. At the Windows desktop, close any open windows or applications and reboot your server; when it has restarted, proceed to Step 7.
7. Wait a couple of minutes for the server to finish loading Exchange 2000 components, and then use the Exchange System Manager console to mount your mailbox and public folder stores as you have in previous projects. They are disabled by the disaster recovery installation to enable you to restore the databases without having to worry about dismounting them before you try restoring the data. After you have remounted the stores, try using Outlook 2000 to make sure e-mail is being delivered. When you have done this, shut down and power off your server.

Case Projects

Case Projects Background

Mega Money Savings and Loan is a local bank that specializes in retaining vast amounts of money and providing investment-planning information and proposals for its clients. Mega Money S&L recently had a server crash, which affected a large section of its ongoing investment-tracking documents for clients and a selection of essential user documents stored in a public folder mounted on that server. The loss of this information has left Mega Money S&L's management committee and some clients alarmed because there were no reliable backups of the company's data. This unease has caused Mega Money S&L to bring in your consulting company to help them establish a reliable backup plan for their Exchange 2000 servers.

Mega Money S&L's network consists of two Exchange 2000 servers with two mailbox and two public folder stores on each server. The second server is the one that failed; however, the IT Department has rebuilt it to its previous configuration, without the data. Each server's mailbox store is organized into management and staff users, with 10 in the Management mailbox store and 30 in the Staff mailbox store. At the time of the failure, the servers were being backed up manually whenever the staff remembered to do it (usually about twice a month). In addition, when IT staff members tried to restore the data from the last few backup tapes, they found that the tapes were damaged because they were placed too close to a window in direct sunlight. They have since replaced the antiquated tape backup drive with a new, up-to-date 40-GB DLT tape backup drive on each of the two servers, with 40 tapes for each drive.

Case 1

When you first arrive at Mega Money S&L, the management committee wants recommendations on what to do first to help them avoid a similar situation in the future. Per your recommendations, they want to have a written disaster recovery plan. What three key pieces of information should you include in this disaster recovery plan? Also, what do you recommend as a first step to make sure they get consistent backups of their information?

Case 2

You have finished your initial recommendations for Mega Money S&L and you are now working on filling out the basic disaster recovery plan you created for the bank. In this disaster recovery plan, the bank should include backing up and restoring the Exchange 2000 and other important information on the network. In addition to this information, should information be included about other potential issues?

Case 3

Mega Money S&L wants to have a couple of different recommendations on which backup strategies you think will work the best. What do you recommend as the optimum backup solution that's easy and quick to restore? If you cannot perform this type of backup, what is your second choice? Why is this second method not your first choice?

Case 4

Several months after you were at Mega Money S&L, you receive a phone call from its IT Department. Since you were there, they had a flood, which caused a server to fail, and the company lost the data on its hard drives. The IT staff members have been backing up information regularly, but when they tried to restore the information to the server, the tapes weren't working. They have been storing their backup tapes in the same spot as before. What should they do to prevent this problem from happening again, and what should you recommend they do between backups and restorations?

APPENDIX A

EXAM OBJECTIVES TRACKING FOR MCSE CERTIFICATION EXAM #70-224: INSTALLING, CONFIGURING, AND ADMINISTERING MICROSOFT EXCHANGE 2000 SERVER

INSTALLING AND UPGRADING EXCHANGE 2000 SERVER

Primary references are highlighted in bold.

Objective	Chapter: Section
Install Exchange 2000 Server on a server computer.	Chapter 5: **Installation of the First Exchange 2000 Server (Starting the Installation)**
Diagnose and resolve failed installations.	Chapter 5: **Troubleshooting Failed Installations** (all subsections)
Upgrade or migrate to Exchange 2000 Server from Exchange Server 5.5.	Chapter 6: **Upgrading Exchange Server 5.5 to Exchange 2000 Server** (all subsections)
Diagnose and resolve problems involving the upgrade process.	Chapter 6: **Troubleshooting Exchange Upgrading and Migrating Issues** (all subsections)
Manage coexistence with Exchange Server 5.5. • Maintain common user lists. • Maintain existing connectors. • Move users from Exchange Server 5.5 to Exchange 2000 Server. • Configure the Exchange 2000 Active Directory Connector to replicate directory information.	Chapter 3: **Understanding Coexistence and Migration Issues** (all subsections) Chapter 4: **Deploying Active Directory with Exchange Server 5.5 and Exchange 2000 Server** (all subsections) Chapter 6: **Using the Active Directory Connector in a Mixed-Mode Environment** (all subsections) Chapter 10: **Using Exchange 2000 Connectors** (Legacy Exchange 5.5 Connectors)

Objective	Chapter: Section
Diagnose and resolve Exchange 2000 Active Directory Connector problems.	Chapter 4: Deploying Active Directory with Exchange Server 5.5 and Exchange 2000 Server (**Deploying the Active Directory Connector, Deploying Connection Agreements,** Troubleshooting Active Directory Connectors and Connection Agreements)
Perform client deployments. Clients include Microsoft Outlook 2000, Outlook Web POP3, IMAP4, and IRC. • Configure Outlook Web Access. • Configure client access protocols.	Chapter 7: **Installation of Outlook 2000** (all subsections), **Configuring Outlook 2000,** (all subsections), **Configuring Messaging Profiles** Chapter 8: **Outlook Web Access** (all subsections)

Configuring Exchange 2000 Server. Types of Servers Include Mailbox, Public Folder, Gateway, Virtual, Chat, and Instant Messaging.

Objective	Chapter: Section
Configure server objects for messaging and collaboration to support the assigned server role. • Configure information store objects. • Configure multiple storage groups for data partitioning. • Configure multiple databases within a single storage group. • Configure virtual servers to support Internet protocols. • Configure Exchange 2000 Server information in the Windows 2000 Active Directory. • Configure Instant Messaging objects. • Configure Chat objects.	Chapter 2: **Active Directory Planning and Design** (The Active Directory Schema) Chapter 8: **Overview of Internet Protocols** (all subsections) Chapter 9: **Managing Exchange 2000 Server Resources** (all subsections) Chapter 11: **A Detailed Look at Instant Messaging** (all subsections), A Detailed Look at Chat Services (all subsections)
Create and manage administrative groups.	Chapter 4: **Deploying Administrative Groups, Routing Groups** (all subsections)
Configure separate Exchange 2000 Server resources for high-volume access. Resources include stores, logs, and separate RAID arrays.	Chapter 9: **Managing Exchange 2000 Server Resources** (Managing Administrative Groups; all subsections)

Objective	Chapter: Section
Diagnose and resolve Exchange 2000 Server availability and performance problems. • Diagnose and resolve server resource constraints. Resources include processor, memory, and hard disk. • Diagnose and resolve server-specific performance problems.	Chapter 14: **Other Maintenance and Monitoring Tasks** (all subsections)
Configure Exchange 2000 Server for high security. • Configure Exchange 2000 Server to issue v.3 certificates. • Enable Digest authentication for Instant Messaging. • Configure Certificate Trust Lists. • Configure virtual servers to limit access through firewalls. • Configure Key Management Service (KMS) to issue digital signatures.	Chapter 12: **Introduction to Security Issues in Exchange 2000** (all subsections), Overview of Key Management Services (all subsections), Firewalls and Exchange 2000
Create, configure, and manage a public folder solution. • Configure the Active Directory object attributes of a public folder. • Configure the store attributes of a public folder. • Configure multiple public folder trees.	Chapter 13: **Introduction to Public Folders** (all subsections)
Configure and manage system folders.	Chapter 13: **Introduction to Public Folders** (all subsections), Managing Public Folders

Managing Recipient Objects

Objective	Chapter: Section
Configure a user object for messaging. • Configure a user object for e-mail. • Configure a user object for Instant Messaging. • Configure a user object for Chat.	Chapter 9: **Managing Exchange 2000 Recipients** (all subsections) Chapter 11: **A Detailed Look at Instant Messaging** (all subsections), A Detailed Look at Chat Services (all subsections)
Manage user and information store association. • Configure user information stores.	Chapter 9: **Managing Exchange 2000 Server Resources** (Managing Growth of Message Stores and Messaging Traffic)
Diagnose and resolve problems that involve user and information store placement. Problems include security, performance, and disaster recovery.	Chapter 12: **Troubleshooting Security Issues in Exchange 2000 Server** (Advanced Security Issues; all subsections)

Objective	Chapter: Section
Create and manage address lists. • Create security groups. • Create distribution groups.	Chapter 9: **Managing Exchange 2000 Server Resources** (all subsections)
Diagnose and resolve Recipient Update Service problems.	Chapter 9: **Managing Exchange 2000 Recipients** (all subsections)

Monitoring and Managing Messaging Connectivity

Objective	Chapter: Section
Manage and troubleshoot messaging connectivity. • Manage Exchange 2000 Server messaging connectivity. • Manage connectivity to foreign mail systems. Connectivity types include X.400, SMTP, and Internet messaging connectivity. • Diagnose and resolve routing problems. • Diagnose and resolve problems reported by non-delivery report messages.	Chapter 10: **Planning Routing Groups** (all subsections), Using Exchange 2000 Connectors (all subsections), Troubleshooting Messaging Connectivity (all subsections)
Manage messaging queues for multiple protocols.	Chapter 8: **Overview of Internet Protocols** (all subsections) Chapter 10: **Using Exchange 2000 Connectors** (all subsections)
Monitor link status. • Monitor messages between Exchange 2000 Server computers. • Monitor messages between Exchange 2000 systems and foreign systems.	Chapter 10: **Managing Link State Information**
Configure and monitor client connectivity. Clients include Outlook 2000, Outlook Web Access, POP3, IMAP4, and IRC.	Chapter 7: **Installation of Outlook 2000** (all subsections), Configuring Outlook 2000 (all subsections) Chapter 8: **Overview of Internet Protocols** (all subsections), Outlook Web Access (all subsections)
Diagnose and resolve client connectivity problems. Problems include DNS structure, server publishing structure, DS Proxy/DS Access, address resolution, Instant Messaging clients, various connection protocols, and non-Windows 2000 environments.	Chapter 7: **Reviewing Different Types of Clients** (Selecting Your Client Software) Chapter 8: **Overview of Internet Protocols** (all subsections) Chapter 10: **Using Exchange 2000 Connectors** (all subsections), Troubleshooting Messaging Connectivity (all subsections)

Objective	Chapter: Section
Manage public folder connectivity. • Configure and monitor public folder replication. • Diagnose and resolve public folder replication problems.	Chapter 13: **Managing Public Folders** (all subsections)

MANAGING EXCHANGE 2000 SERVER GROWTH

Objective	Chapter: Section
Monitor services use. Services include messaging, Chat, public folder access, Instant Messaging, and calendaring. • Monitor the Information Store service. • Monitor server use by configuring server monitors. • Monitor Instant Messaging by using System Monitor.	Chapter 14: **Other Maintenance and Monitoring Tasks** (all subsections)
Manage growth of public and private message store databases.	Chapter 14: **Maintaining Exchange 2000 Server Databases** (all subsections)
Manage growth of user population and message traffic.	Chapter 14: **Other Maintenance and Monitoring Tasks** (Monitoring Message Queues and System Resources)
Monitor the growth of client use. Clients include Outlook 2000, Outlook Web Access,` POP3, IMAP4, and IRC.	Chapter 14: **Other Maintenance and Monitoring Tasks** (Monitoring Message Queues and System Resources)
Manage recipient and server policies.	Chapter 9: Configuring Servers Using System Policies (Configuring System Polices for Servers), **Managing Exchange 2000 Recipients** (Managing Exchange 2000 Using Recipient Policies; all subsections)
Diagnose and resolve problems that involve recipient and server policies.	Chapter 9: Configuring Servers Using System Policies (Configuring System Polices for Servers), **Managing Exchange 2000 Recipients** (Managing Exchange 2000 Using Recipient Policies; all subsections)
Optimize public folder and mailbox searching. • Configure the public folder store or mailbox store for full-text indexing. • Perform full-text indexing.	Chapter 9: **Managing Exchange 2000 Recipients** (Managing Full-Text Indexing in Exchange 2000; all subsections)

RESTORING SYSTEM FUNCTIONALITY AND USER DATA

Objective	Chapter: Section
Apply a backup and restore plan.	Chapter 15: **Developing a Disaster Recovery Plan for Your Organization**, Designing an Effective Backup Strategy (all subsections), Restoring and Recovering Exchange 2000 Data (all subsections)
Diagnose and resolve backup and restore problems.	Chapter 15: **Designing an Effective Backup Strategy** (all subsections), Restoring and Recovering Exchange 2000 Data (all subsections)
Restore user data and System State data. • Recover deleted mailboxes. • Recover deleted items.	Chapter 15: **Restoring and Recovering Exchange 2000 Data** (Restoring a Full Backup to the Production or Recovery Server, Restoring a Single Mailbox)
Restore information stores.	Chapter 15: **Restoring and Recovering Exchange 2000 Data** (Restoring a Full Backup to the Production or Recovery Server, Restoring a Single Mailbox)
Configure a server for disaster recovery. Configurations include circular logging, backup, and restore.	Chapter 14: **Maintaining Exchange 2000 Server Databases** (all subsections) Chapter 15: **Developing a Disaster Recovery Plan for Your Organization**, Designing an Effective Backup Strategy (all subsections), Restoring and Recovering Exchange 2000 Data (all subsections)
Diagnose and resolve security problems that involve user keys.	Chapter 12: Overview of Key Management Services (all subsections), **Troubleshooting Security Issues in Exchange 2000 Server**

APPENDIX

B

EXCHANGE RESOURCES

There is a wealth of valuable resources available through the Microsoft Web site and its various resources and in Exchange 2000-related texts. These materials and Web links are only a small part of the many resources you may find useful in your exam preparation and in further development of your Exchange 2000 skills. When the time comes to troubleshoot a problem or implement a more involved feature of Exchange 2000, these resources will help provide the foundation and the direction to successfully complete your task.

PRINTED MATERIALS

English, Bill, and Linda Vittori. *MCSE Microsoft Exchange 2000 Server Administration Readiness Review Exam 70-224.* Redmond, Wash.: Microsoft Press, 2001 (ISBN 0735612439).

English, Bill, and Nick Cavalancia. *Exchange 2000 Server Administration: A Beginner's Guide.* McGraw-Hill Professional Publishing, 2001 (ISBN 0072131195).

Glenn, Walter J., and Bill English. *Microsoft Exchange 2000 Server Administrator's Companion.* Redmond, Wash.: Microsoft Press, 2000 (ISBN 0-7356-0938-1).

Microsoft Press. *Microsoft Exchange 2000 Server Resource Kit.* Redmond, Wash.: Microsoft Press, 2000 (ISBN 0-7356-1017-7).

Schein, Phillip G., and Evan Benjamin. *MCSE Exchange 2000 Administration Exam Prep: Exam 70-224.* Coriolis, 2001 (ISBN 1576109194).

ONLINE/ELECTRONIC MATERIALS

TechNet online version: *http://www.microsoft.com/technet/* (also available monthly on CD from Microsoft by subscription, starting at $299.95 per year)

RFC.Net (Request For Comments reference site): *http://www.rfc.net*

Chapter 2 Web References

For more information on Microsoft Project, visit *http://www.microsoft.com/office/project/default.htm.*

To review some of the technical documents about Active Directory and organizational units, visit the TechNet Web site at *http://www.microsoft.com/technet.*

For more information about DNS and Windows 2000, visit *http://www.microsoft.com/TechNet/win2000/dnsover.asp.*

For more information about DNS innovations, check Microsoft TechNet at *http://www.microsoft.com/technet/treeview/default.asp?url=/TechNet/itsolutions/network/domain.asp.*

Chapter 4 Web References

For more information about server scalability and messaging benchmarks used to choose appropriate hardware, check *http://www.microsoft.com/exchange/techinfo/planning/2000/mmb2desc.asp* for details.

For information about optimizing resources on domain controllers or Global Catalog servers, visit the Microsoft site at *http://support.microsoft.com/support/kb/articles/Q244/3/68.asp.*

For more details about using the Move Server Wizard, visit *http://support.microsoft.com/support/kb/articles/Q196/4/13.asp.*

Chapter 5 Web References

For the latest service packs for Exchange 2000 Server, check the Microsoft Exchange Web site at *http://www.microsoft.com/exchange/downloads/2000/SP1.asp.*

For more information on event IDs or error codes, enter them in the Search text box at *www.microsoft.com/technet* to search for articles related to those errors and codes.

For information on the Exchange 2000 Server Setup Troubleshooter, visit *http://support.microsoft.com/support/tshoot/exch2ksetup.asp.*

The Microsoft Knowledge Base is available at *http://support.microsoft.com/default.aspx?prs.kbinfo&.*

For more information on server clustering technologies, you can visit *http://www.microsoft.com/windows2000/technologies/clustering/default.asp.*

For more information about minimum requirements for Exchange 2000 Server, go to *http://www.microsoft.com/exchange/evaluation/sysreq/default.asp.*

Chapter 6 Web References

For more information about the Hardware Compatibility List, visit *http://www.microsoft.com/hcl/default.asp*

For information on upgrading to Windows 2000, consult the Microsoft Web site at *http://www.microsoft.com/windows2000/server/howtobuy/upgrading/*.

For more information on the DS/IS Consistency Adjuster and to remove any unused ACL entries, please visit *http://support.microsoft.com/support/kb/articles/Q156/7/05.asp*.

For more information on the LDP.exe utility, you can visit *http://support.microsoft.com/support/kb/articles/Q252/3/35.asp*.

Chapter 7 Web References

For more information on Outlook 2002 and its new features, go to *http://www.microsoft.com/office/outlook/evaluation/guide.htm*.

A free version of the Digital Dashboard Resource Kit is available at: *http://msdn.microsoft.com/downloads/default.asp?URL=/code/sample.asp?url=/MSDN-FILES/027/001/584/msdncompositedoc.xml*.

For more details on Outlook 2000 hardware requirements, visit *http://www.microsoft.com/office/previous/outlook/2000Tour/SysReqs.htm*.

For more information on Outlook 2002 hardware requirements, check out *http://www.microsoft.com/outlook/evaluation/sysreq.htm*.

For information on the Office Custom Installation Wizard, visit *http://www.microsoft.com/office/ork/2000/appndx/toolbox.htm*.

Chapter 8 Web References

For more detailed information on the inner workings of LDAP, take a look at *http://www.microsoft.com/windows2000/techinfo/howitworks/activedirectory/ldap.asp*.

To keep apprised of the latest and greatest in IIS security, check out this Web site: *http://www.microsoft.com/technet/treeview/default.asp?url=/technet/itsolutions/security/default.asp*.

For a sample chapter of the *Exchange 2000 Server Resource Kit* that deals specifically with OWA, go to *http://www.microsoft.com/technet/treeview/default.asp?url=/TechNet/prodtechnol/exchange/reskit/ex00res/deploygd/part5/c25owa.asp*.

For articles that outline LDAP troubleshooting steps, visit Microsoft TechNet at *http://www.microsoft.com/technet/*.

For additional reading on securing IIS and other Microsoft products, go to *http://www.Microsoft.com/technet/security*.

Chapter 9 Web References

For information about the effects of a large amount of system memory on an Exchange 2000 server, visit *http://support.microsoft.com/support/kb/articles/Q266/0/96.asp*.

Chapter 10 Web References

For information on creating and registering events, visit *http://msdn.microsoft.com*.

For information on status codes, visit *http://www.faqs.org/rfcs/rfc821.html*.

For information on enhanced status codes, visit *http://www.faqs.org/rfcs/rfc1893.html*.

Chapter 11 Web References

For information on Yahoo! Messenger, visit *www.yahoo.com*.

For more information on large-scale planning for IM, perform a search on *http://www.microsoft.com/exchange* for the *Microsoft Exchange 2000 Server Resource Kit* or Instant Messaging. For more information, refer to the TechNet Web site at *http://www.microsoft.com/technet* and perform a search for instant messaging DNS, or look up the TechNet article ID 266643.

For more information on the Conferencing Server, visit Microsoft TechNet and perform a search for Exchange 2000 Conferencing Server Datasheet. You can also check the information at this site: *http://www.microsoft.com/Exchange/techinfo/conferencing/default.asp*.

To download Microsoft Chat, a free download, go to *www.tucows.com*. Simply enter a search for Microsoft Chat or Comic Chat, and you should see the most current version available for download.

Chapter 12 Web References

For more information on how Windows 2000 handles certificate services, take a look at this Web site: *http://www.microsoft.com/WINDOWS2000/techinfo/reskit/en/Distrib/dsch_key_tnjk.htm*.

A brief but helpful article on creating and modifying certificate trust lists can be found at *http://www.microsoft.com/windows2000/en/advanced/iis/default.asp?url=/WINDOWS2000/en/advanced/iis/htm/core/iicarsc.htm*.

An excellent site for security-related information on Microsoft products, including configuration information and updates, can be found at *http://www.microsoft.com/security*.

Chapter 14 Web References

For information on Backup Exec by Veritas Software, visit *http://www.veritas.com/*.

For more information on the ISINTEG tool, take a look at this site: *http://www.microsoft.com/technet/treeview/default.asp?url=/TechNet/prodtechnol/exchange/reskit/ex55res/exc07.asp*.

Chapter 15 Web References

The latest service pack for Exchange 2000 can be found at *http://www.microsoft.com/exchange*.

The *Microsoft Exchange 2000 Server Resource Kit* can be purchased in book form as an offline reference or it can be viewed online at *http://www.microsoft.com/exchange/techinfo/reskit/default.asp*.

Other Exchange Resources

For a handy site that highlights virus alerts, downloads, recent updates, and other miscellaneous information, visit *http://www.msexchange.org/*.

For an interesting site where you can get free answers to your technical questions as though you were talking to a support technician, go to *http://www.freeanswers.com*.

To visit the Outlook and Exchange Solutions Center, visit *http://www.slipstick.com*.

To find answers to frequently asked questions about Exchange Server, Outlook, and more, visit *http://windows2000faq.com*.

Try out *http://exchange.devx.com/* to find more information about Exchange.

For information on troubleshooting Exchange 2000, visit *http://www.labmice.net/Exchange2000/troubleshooting.htm*.

For information on sharing with Exchange public folders and mailbox folders, visit *http://www.slipstick.com/exs/pfshare.htm*.

For security tips with Exchange 2000, visit *http://www.wsd2d.com/wsD2D/Tips/Security/*.

For information on configuring an X.400 Exchange Connector, visit *http://www.windows2000faq.com/Articles/Index.cfm?ArticleID=13668*.

Outlook 2002 Resources

To order an Outlook 2002 Evaluation CD-ROM, visit *http://www.microsoft.com/Office/Outlook/evaluation/default.htm*.

Tips for using Outlook 2002 can be found at *http://www.microsoft.com/Office/using/tips/archives/outlooktips.htm*.

Information on upgrading to Outlook 2002 is at *http://www.microsoft.com/technet/treeview/default.asp?url=/TechNet/prodtechnol/office/reskit/officexp/part5/c20uou02.asp*.

To view the handy Outlook 2002 Performance Tuning White Paper, go to *http://www.microsoft.com/Office/Outlook/evaluation/performance.htm*.

The Microsoft Outlook 2002 Attachment Security presentation can be viewed at or downloaded from *http://support.microsoft.com/servicedesks/Webcasts/WC081701/wcblurb081701.asp*.

The Microsoft Knowledge Base article "OL2002: Administrator Information About E-Mail Security Features" is available at *http://support.microsoft.com/support/kb/articles/Q290/4/99.asp*.

APPENDIX

C

COMMON TROUBLESHOOTING SCENARIOS

SCENARIO 1

Situation

You are providing network support for a startup company that has recently moved into a new office and decided to upgrade its infrastructure. Before the move, employees worked out of their homes. They accessed files via FTP servers and received e-mail through POP3 servers. The company has decided to take the next step and move all its formerly external resources to a centralized location in its new office. You have completed your first installation of Exchange 2000 Server. To make sure the installation went smoothly, you created and followed a checklist of the proper steps and made sure all prerequisites were met. You also made sure that the company's system met the minimum hardware requirements, and you established a format for naming schemes. The new server has been added to the domain and at first seemed to be working well. Almost immediately, however, Outlook began locking up on users' machines.

Problem

What steps should be taken to ascertain what caused the new installation to fail, and what steps could have been taken to prevent Outlook from locking up at system startup?

Suggested Answer

Although the initial problem seems to be user systems not being able to access Exchange, the server is still the primary culprit because all the users are having the same problem. To diagnose this system, there are several steps you can take. First, examine the Event Viewer in Administrative Tools, and scan its logs to see whether there are any event IDs you can check for more information. Second, view any available queues to search for message stacking and backlogging. Third, if the system fails completely, you should consider possible hardware failure. Swap in new memory, try installing another hard drive, or even try the installation on a different system. Keep in mind that sometimes system failures simply can't be prevented; acts of nature and flukes do exist. One strong recommendation, however, is to keep a new system in a test environment for several days before you use it in a live network. Attach some spare PCs to the server and run Exchange as you would in a network. Send test e-mails with large file attachments to ascertain the efficiency of the new server. You should be completely confident of the system's performance before you move it back to the live network.

SCENARIO 2

Situation

You are the network administrator of a small business that's currently running Exchange Server 5.5 in a Windows NT 4.0 environment with Service Pack 2 installed. You are upgrading a single server from Exchange Server 5.5 to Exchange 2000 Server, but the server is not functioning properly. What factor could be contributing to this problem, and how can you overcome it?

Problem

What basic steps should you take to prevent initial problems with installing Exchange 2000 Server in this upgrade scenario?

Suggested Answer

First, you should create a detailed list, outlining the installation process, that includes all software and hardware prerequisites for using Exchange 2000 Server. After checking this list, it should be obvious that the problem with this installation is that you are running Windows NT Server 4.0. Exchange 2000 Server must be installed with at least Windows 2000 Server because it works hand in hand with Active Directory, which falls under the umbrella of Windows 2000.

SCENARIO 3

Situation

You are in charge of maintaining a diverse network infrastructure that includes systems running Windows as well as UNIX/Linux. An Exchange 2000 server provides the primary mail service. Outlook is still the main client used for the obvious reason that it was designed specifically for use with Exchange and its features can be used to their fullest with Exchange. However, Outlook was created for a Windows platform, which makes it incompatible for the few UNIX users. There are compatible MAPI clients, but none that could take full advantage of what Exchange 2000 Server has to offer. Although most users will continue to use Outlook, you decide that the best solution for your remote users is Outlook Web Access, because those users can simply open a Web browser (whether they use Windows or UNIX) and enter a domain name and password to have access to e-mail. You set up OWA as the e-mail client for your remote users, who usually access e-mail in the office, but occasionally log on from home. However, users complain that mail already opened while they were in the office is no longer accessible from OWA.

Problem

Why can't remote users view e-mail messages at home through OWA that they were able to view previously in the office?

Suggested Answer

More than likely, the office desktop, which is linked to the Exchange 2000 Server via a local client, is not configured to leave mail on the server. Mail retrieved by that system is stored on that system. To remedy this problem, from the user's office system, click Start, Settings, Control Panel, and then double-click Internet E-mail. Enable the option to leave all messages on the Exchange 2000 server.

SCENARIO 4

Situation

You are the network administrator for a securities company with 100 users. You have recently deployed Exchange 2000 Server as your core mail delivery service. Although most of the users work in the office during trading hours, some of them travel to other cities and even other countries, and others contribute many hours of work from their homes. Therefore, you have several remote users who need access to common resources to do their work efficiently. They rely on e-mail for current news and information on clients, investments, and so forth. They also rely on full-time access to important files and applications. You are looking for a common solution to provide e-mail and file access to all of your users, no matter where they're located.

Problem

Considering the time it would take to assess possible problems with remote locations, what would be the most convenient and efficient method of providing e-mail and file access to remote users?

Suggested Answer

Internet Information Server (IIS) 5, installed by default with Exchange 2000 Server, incorporates the Outlook Web Access and Web Storage System services. OWA is a Web-based utility that allows users to access their e-mail through an Internet browser, which saves the time of configuring Microsoft Outlook on each user's home system for mail service from the office. This in turn prevents e-mail problems for the remote user. By configuring the Exchange server to allow Web-based access to its resources, any issues that come up can be dealt with on the server's end.

Scenario 5

Situation

Recently, you have decided to implement an Exchange 2000 server in your network environment. Because it is a fairly new package, you deploy it while still using an Exchange 5.5 server as your core e-mail system. Both servers are configured for interoperability so that users on both systems can receive mail from each other and from the Internet. However, you notice that the Exchange 2000 users can send and receive mail within their own group, but are getting no mail from the Internet and cannot send and receive e-mail messages to and from their Exchange 5.5 co-workers. Users on the Exchange 5.5 system are still able to send and receive mail among themselves and can get mail from the Internet, but cannot send or receive e-mail messages to or from the Exchange 2000 users. Because of the mixed-mode environment, the Message Transfer Agent (MTA) transport stacks in Exchange 2000 use the X.400 Connector, which was initially used for communications between Exchange and non-Exchange systems. This connector now links the Exchange 5.5 and Exchange 2000 servers for compatibility.

Problem

What is causing the e-mail problem between Exchange 5.5 and Exchange 2000 users? How could this problem have been prevented? If the situation could not have been avoided, what could you have done to catch the problem before it progressed to its current level?

Suggested Answer

If you check the logs in Event Viewer on the Exchange 2000 server, you will notice that the MTA Service has locked up, thus preventing the transfer of mail between Exchange 2000 and Exchange 5.5. This bottleneck results in mail messages being stacked up in the MTA Service queues of each server. In all likelihood, this problem could not have been prevented. The MTA Service must be stopped and restarted. Instead of waiting for a problem like this to occur and persist, take advantage of your system's resources. You have access to monitoring tools, such as Performance Monitor, Insight Manager, and Event Viewer, that can provide alerts for many problems, including message stacking in queues and stopped services.

Scenario 6

Situation

Your WAN consists of offices in several geographical locations, named A, B, and C. Each has its own internal network, which includes an Exchange 2000 server. All three networks are linked by a high-speed connection. You notice that mail from A is not getting to B, and vice versa. Both are still able to make contact with C.

Problem

What short-term measure can you take to fix the problem until you can reestablish the failed link?

Suggested Answer

Setting up routing groups is integral to efficient delivery. You can configure routing groups in Exchange 2000 at any time, not just during installation. The configuration can include setting up alerts to the administrator when a link is down or broken in a group of servers. If a sending server is correctly set up in Exchange 2000, it can reroute mail on a different path to get to the recipient's destination, acting much like a physical router. So, if the link between A and B isn't working, your configurations should have prompted the sending server to push messages through the closest functioning server (which in this case is C) as a short-term solution, thus linking it back to B until you can fix the problem and reestablish the link.

SCENARIO 7

Situation

You are responsible for implementing a mail solution for your company's users that will allow them to access the Exchange 2000 collaboration features. You decide to install the Exchange 2000 Conferencing Server. Users start to take advantage of audio and video conferencing and file transferring, but Instant Messaging and Chat aren't working.

Problem

Why are Instant Messaging and Chat not working, and what can be done to fix the problem?

Suggested Answer

Instant Messaging and Chat are products that are separate from the Exchange 2000 Conferencing Server, so you must install Exchange 2000 for these products to work. Until the Conferencing Server can incorporate these features, administrators will have to rely on third-party solutions, such as Yahoo! Messenger or ICQ, or dedicate other servers to provide IM and Chat services.

SCENARIO 8

Situation

Viruses and hackers attacking across the Internet are common problems that any network administrator faces. To prevent intrusions into the network, whether they're destructive viruses or just someone out for a cyber joyride, administrators must run a tight ship. You have had some fairly mild virus attacks through e-mail messages on your Exchange 2000 server. Upon further investigation, you trace some of the mail back to a source server.

Problem

Although no solution is foolproof, what actions can you take to prevent infected file infiltrations and unwanted mail in general?

Suggested Answer

Exchange can be an unknowing participant in the spread of viruses. These infected files frequently hide their true nature by assuming a common file extension, such as .exe. Virus scanning is always an obvious choice, but you can also take some steps in Exchange 2000 to address the problem. Known spam mail servers can be blocked by adding their IP addresses to rejection lists, thus stopping their mail from getting through. If any undesired mail does manage to get through, you can use filters to remove mail based on specified criteria.

SCENARIO 9

Situation

You are a senior administrator of a large network consisting of approximately 2500 users. You have decided to take advantage of the Information Store and create several public and private databases on a single Exchange 2000 server for your users. You also use the default Exchange 2000 mailbox quotas. You soon start to notice lagging on the system. The Exchange server processes are running full tilt, and the system's CPU is consistently running at almost 100%. Users have noticed the slowdown and are starting to complain. Backups of the database are now taking up the entire weekend, instead of just Friday night. Although you have not reached your user limit, bottlenecking has already occurred.

Problem

How can you ascertain what's causing the decrease in speed, and what can be done to remedy the situation?

Suggested Answer

An efficient network administrator always uses the tools at hand. Check the transaction log files (the .edb and .stm files), which monitor many users' actions. Try to assess who the culprits might be, and design a plan of action. If database use is excessive, the system will undoubtedly slow down. First, consider partitioning. Break up the larger databases and spread them over a cluster of servers, if possible. Second, in Exchange 2000, mailbox size is restricted only by the amount of disk space. You have set no additional quotas on mailbox size, so you should set some limits on their size. Third, consider partitioning for the mailboxes to distribute the load that's currently on one server among several servers. This distribution also provides a measure of fault tolerance. By spreading the load, single points-of-failure won't cripple the entire system, which makes problems easier to troubleshoot.

SCENARIO 10

Situation

Your organization has decided to use the full benefits of the Exchange 2000 Server tools and has implemented a database on the Compaq-built Exchange 2000 server. System backups are scheduled for Saturday nights. The Information Store soon becomes a popular function, and you run complete backups regularly as a failsafe. However, it takes 15 hours to run a backup and at least that long to restore the database. As use of the Information Store increases, you are alerted by monitoring tools in the system that the hard disk is near its capacity, and it is time to look at other options. You had configured monitoring alerts to notify you at 75% capacity, so you assume that you have time to rectify the problem. Almost immediately, however, you are alerted by Compaq's Insight Manager utility that the hard disk on your Information Store server has failed. Luckily for you, it's Sunday morning.

Problem

What proactive steps should you have taken to prevent this problem from happening, or at least to make it less critical? How could the backup procedure have been improved?

Suggested Answer

To lessen the effects of hardware failure, try to use more servers so that you can distribute data into multiple storage groups and databases. This way, only partial data can be lost, resulting in a much shorter restore time. Remember, you can choose what needs to be restored. Exchange 2000 Server is quite flexible in that respect. Disk mirroring is another option. Redundancy doesn't get much easier than having a server switch paths from a failed hard disk to an identical, functioning hard disk. As a last resort, Exchange 2000 Server

Setup does come with a switch intended to reinstall the system with the last working configuration, but certain stipulations do apply. For example, Active Directory must reside on another domain controller. After you start Setup with the /disasterrecovery switch, all that needs to be done is to restore the database.

SCENARIO 11

Situation

You have recently migrated from Exchange Server 5.5 to Exchange 2000 Server. Several users complain that public folders on the older version of Exchange Server are no longer accessible or even visible. It turns out that these folders aren't visible in any Outlook client. Several mailboxes which migrated to the new system belong to users who no longer exist. Also, the missing public folders are visible in the Exchange System Manager console.

Problem

What can be done to make these folders accessible, and what measures could have been taken to prevent this problem?

Suggested Answer

The easiest fix is to open the Properties dialog box for the public folders in Exchange System Manager and remove the permissions of users who are no longer valid. Migrating users can frequently corrupt permissions on public folders. To keep this situation from happening, you must keep up to date with the addition and subtraction of users. By letting this task slip by, you risk taking on an enormous amount of organizational work. Proper planning is the best tool an administrator has. Using it effectively saves time and, ultimately, money.

APPENDIX

D

OUTLOOK 2002, OUTLOOK EXPRESS 6, AND EXCHANGE 2000 SERVER

After reading this appendix, you will be able to:

- Identify new and improved features found in Outlook 2002 and Outlook Express 6, which ship with the XP versions of Microsoft Office and Microsoft Windows, respectively
- Use Exchange 2000 to modify default security settings in Outlook 2002 to improve security and better protect your organization from e-mail viruses
- Support users who want to use the new and improved group scheduling and calendaring features of Microsoft Outlook 2002
- Allow users to communicate in real time from Outlook 2002 by using MSN Instant Messenger
- Support the workflow enhancements, such as the new Built-In Review Cycle, in Outlook 2002
- Use the new Mailbox Cleanup dialog box in Outlook 2002 to help users maintain their mailboxes
- Understand and support Outlook 2002 performance improvements in remote access
- Take advantage of the improved synchronization and offline files features of Outlook 2002
- Support users who want to take advantage of the new full-text indexing and searching capabilities of Outlook 2002
- Use the new antivirus features of Outlook Express 6

In Chapter 7, "Configuring MAPI Clients in Exchange 2000 Server," you learned about several Microsoft client software packages for accessing e-mail and the Internet, including Outlook 98 and 2000. In this appendix, you learn about Outlook 2002, the latest version of Outlook, which ships with all the Microsoft Office XP program suites. In particular, this appendix focuses on new features of interest to Exchange 2000 Server administrators. You also learn about the improved virus protection in Outlook Express 6, which comes with the Microsoft Windows XP operating system.

Overview of Outlook 2002 Improvements

As you might expect, many of the new features and improvements in Outlook 2002 apply to all users, not just those who use Outlook with Exchange 2000 Server. You can find a quick summary of the Outlook 2002 improvements and enhancements in the "Outlook 2002 Product Guide" available online at *http://www.microsoft.com/Office/Outlook/evaluation/guide.htm*. This appendix focuses mostly on improvements that are relevant to Exchange 2000 administrators and users, as summarized in the following list:

- Improved security against e-mail viruses and the ability for Exchange 2000 administrators to impose security policies
- Enhancements to calendaring and group scheduling capabilities
- Workflow enhancements
- New instant messaging features
- Mailbox management improvements
- Offline file and remote access performance improvements
- Document storage improvements

Many of these new features require Exchange 2000 Service Pack 1. If you haven't already done so, you can download the service pack or order it on CD-ROM from *http://www.microsoft.com/exchange/downloads/2000*. You might also want to visit the Windows Update Web site at *http://www.windowsupdate.com* and the Microsoft Outlook Web site at *http://www.microsoft.com/office/outlook* to see if any additional updates have been made available since the publication of this book.

See also *http://support.microsoft.com/support/kb/articles/Q303/8/ 25.asp?id=kb;en-us;Q303825* for an article on Outlook 2002 public updates dated August 16, 2001. The page includes updates for clients as well as administrators.

New and Improved Security and Virus Protection

Perhaps one of the most important improvements in Outlook 2002, from an Exchange 2000 administrator's perspective, is the improved security in blocking and preventing the spread of viruses. Viruses are the bane of many administrators. As you probably know, many viruses are spread through e-mail attachments. After a virus infects a computer, it can use Outlook's e-mail capabilities to replicate and send itself to people in the Outlook address book.

Microsoft Outlook 2002 combats viruses on two fronts. On the receiving end, it blocks attachments that could potentially contain viruses. When an Outlook 2002 user receives a message with possibly unsafe content, the InfoBar above the message displays a warning, as in the example shown in Figure D-1.

This HTML message contains script, which Outlook cannot display. This may affect how the message appears.
Outlook blocked access to the following potentially unsafe attachments: readme.exe.
From: info@netobjective.com To: alan@coolnerds.com
Subject: Xautorepapptaskt01_131at01_134 Cc:

Figure D-1 The InfoBar for an Outlook 2002 message that contains blocked content

The default settings for incoming attachment file types that Outlook 2002 blocks are divided into two categories, Level 1 and Level 2. Any file type that might have script or code associated with it is categorized as Level 1 by default. Access to Level 1 attachments is blocked and cannot be changed by the user. File types that fall into the Level 1 category by default are listed in Table D-1.

Table D-1 Level 1 Attachment File Types

File Extension	Contents of File	File Extension	Contents of File
.ade	Microsoft Access project extension	.js	JScript script file
.adp	Microsoft Access project	.jse	JScript-encoded script file
.bas	Microsoft Visual Basic class module	.lnk	Shortcut
.bat	Batch file	.mda	Microsoft Access add-in
.chm	Compiled HTML Help file	.mdb	Microsoft Access application
.cmd	Microsoft Windows NT Command Script	.mde	Microsoft Access MDE database
.com	Microsoft MS-DOS command	.mdz	Microsoft Access database wizard
.cpl	Control Panel extension	.msc	Microsoft Common Console Document
.crt	Security certificate	.msi	Microsoft Windows Installer package
.exe	Executable program	.msp	Windows Installer patch
.hlp	Help file	.mst	Visual Test source files
.hta	HTML application	.pcd	Microsoft Visual Test compiled script or Photo CD image
.inf	Setup Information	.pif	MS-DOS program information file
.ins	Internet Naming Service	.reg	Registry entries
.isp	Internet Communication settings	.scr	Screen saver

Table D-1 Level 1 Attachment File Types (continued)

File Extension	Contents of File	File Extension	Contents of File
.sct	Windows script component	.vbs	VBScript script file
.shs	Scrap object	.wsc	Windows Script Component
.url	Internet shortcut	.wsf	Windows Script file
.vb	VBScript or Visual Basic source file	.wsh	Windows Script Host Settings file
.vbe	VBScript-encoded script file		

Level 2 attachments are initially blocked as well. However, recipients get a warning that the attachment might contain hazardous code and still have the option to save the attachment to their hard disk. (Users cannot open the attachment directly.) By default, there are no file types in the Level 2 category. As you'll see, however, an Exchange administrator can categorize any file type as Level 2.

On the sending side, Outlook 2002 can display an alert when a program tries to send a message or access an address book *programmatically* (without the user's intervention) via the Outlook object model (functionality that Outlook 2002 makes available to programmers so that they can send messages from within program code). When a program attempts to send a message or access the address book, a dialog box like the example shown in Figure D-2 appears on the user's screen. The user can allow or disallow the action.

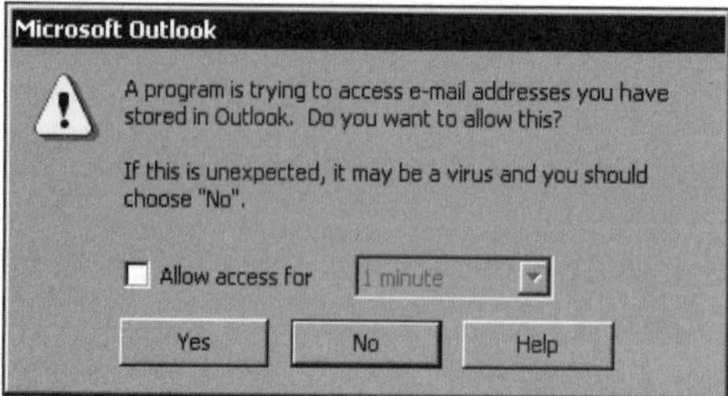

Figure D-2 An Outlook 2002 warning that a program is attempting to access a user's address book

In a standalone environment, users have some control over their own security levels via the Options command on the Outlook 2002 Tools menu. Clicking Tools, Options on the Outlook menu bar opens the Options dialog box. In the Security tab, users can make general selections for encryption, digital signatures, secure receipts, scripts and active content in HTML messages, and digital IDs (certificates), as shown in Figure D-3.

In an administered environment, an Exchange 2000 administrator should customize the Outlook 2002 security settings and impose security policies, provided that users are using Outlook 2002 with Exchange Server and have either offline folders (OST) or the mailbox (MDB) as the default e-mail delivery location.

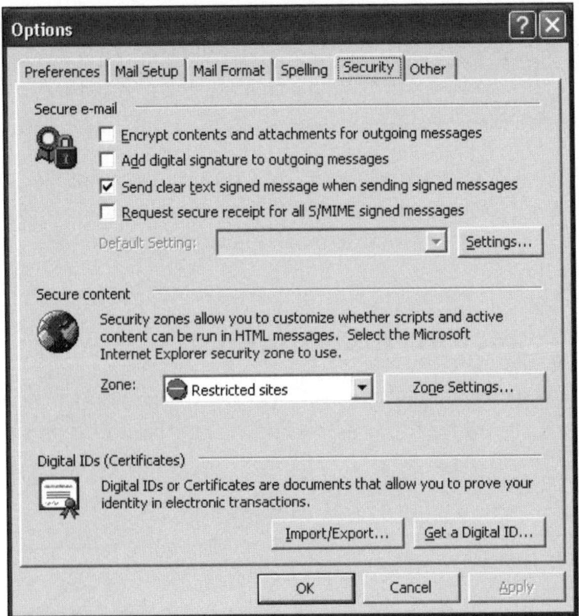

Figure D-3 An Outlook 2002 user's security options

If the administrator's and user's security settings conflict, the setting that provides the highest security takes precedence.

The administrative tools for Outlook security are available in the Outlook Security Features Administrative Package (AdmPack.exe), which is part of the Microsoft Office XP Resource Kit. AdmPack.exe is a self-extracting executable that, when run, produces four files for customizing Outlook 2002. They can be placed in any working directory of your choosing on any computer running Windows 2000. To extract the files, run AdmPack.exe from the \Files\PFiles\ORKTools\ORK10\Tools\Admpack folder on the Office XP Resource Kit CD. Optionally, you can download AdmPack.exe from *http://msdn.microsoft.com/library/default.asp?url=/library/en-us/xpreskit/html/appa11.asp*, and then run it from your own computer. The four files extracted to the working directory are described in the following list:

- *Readme.doc*—A document that supplies step-by-step instructions for installing, registering, and deploying files and security settings via Exchange Server
- *OutlookSecurity.oft*—The Outlook template with options for customizing security settings on the Microsoft Exchange server

- *Comdlg32.ocx*—An ActiveX control required to display the Trusted Code tab in the Default Security Settings dialog box described later in this appendix
- *Hashctl.dll*—The DLL that provides the user interface for the Trusted Code tab described later in this appendix

In the sections that follow, you'll look at the general procedures for defining new security settings via Exchange 2000. Should you encounter any problems along the way, or need additional information for your particular work environment, be sure to read the Readme.doc file.

Installing and Registering Security Components

The first step is to install and register the Comdlg32.ocx and Hashctl.dll files because they provide access to the Trusted Code tab of the security template. Follow these steps:

1. Copy the Comdlg32.ocx and Hashctl.dll files from the working directory to your operating system folder (typically \Winnt\System32).
2. Click Start, click Run, and type "regsvr32 hashctl.dll" in the Open text box.
3. Press Enter or click OK; you'll see a message indicating that the installation was successful. Click OK.
4. To install the other file, click Start, click Run, and type "regsvr32 comdlg32.ocx" in the Open text box.
5. Press Enter or click OK. Once again, click OK in the feedback dialog box that opens.

Creating a Public Folder for Security Settings

The next phase requires creating a public folder on the Exchange server. This folder must be created by the administrator, and named either Outlook Security Settings or Outlook 10 Security Settings. The folder must be placed in the root folder of the public folder tree. Set the permissions for the All items in the folder to Read for all users. If you want multiple users to be able to create or change security settings, create a security group that includes all those users and give them Owner permissions for the folder.

Defining Security Settings

After you've created the public folder and assigned permissions, you can use the Outlook Security template to modify the default settings on Exchange Server. On a computer that's running Outlook 2002, open the OutlookSecurity.oft file from the working directory where you stored it. Initially, you'll see a Select Folder dialog box. Choose the Outlook Security Settings (or Outlook 10 Security Settings) public folder, and click OK to open the security template.

On the template's menu bar, click Tools, Forms, Publish Form. In the Publish Form As dialog box that opens, type "Outlook Security Form" in the Form Name text box, and then click the Publish button. The template is published in the Security Settings folder. You can then close the security template. If asked whether you want to save the changes, click No.

Next, open Outlook 2002, click the list arrow on the New button in the toolbar, and click the Choose Form option. In the Choose Form dialog box that opens, navigate to the Outlook Security Form template you created in the preceding paragraph, and then click the Open button. The security template opens once again, as shown in the example in Figure D-4. Now you're ready to start customizing security settings.

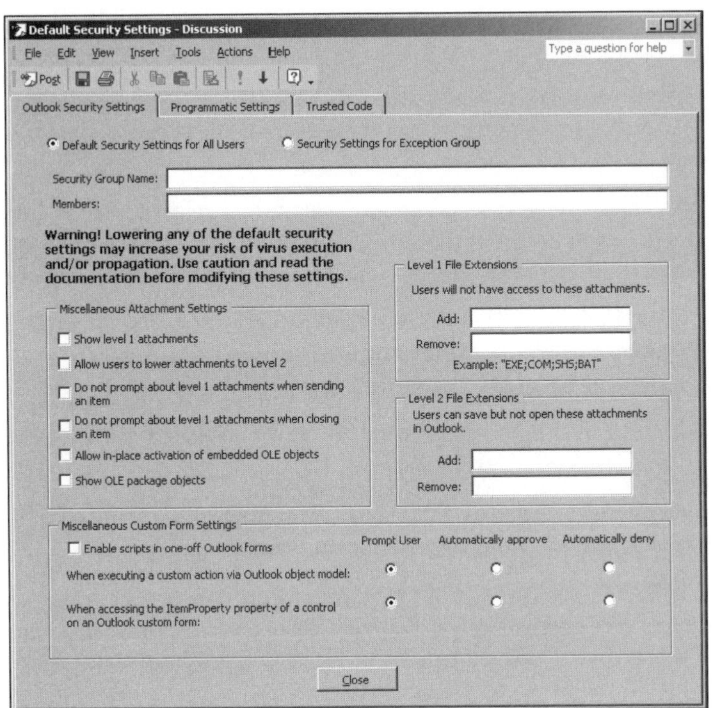

Figure D-4 Configuring a security template in Outlook 2002

In the Outlook Security Settings tab (see Figure D-4), you can first choose to whom you want to apply your new settings. Click the Default Security Settings for All Users radio button to set up settings for all users, or the Security Settings for Exception Group radio button if you want to configure settings for a specific group of users. If you select the latter option, enter a name in the Security Group Name text box that describes the group and list the names of users for this group in the Members text box.

You can use the two panes on the right side of the dialog box to categorize file types as Level 1 or Level 2, based on their extensions. To add extensions to a category, click the

Add button and type the file type extensions, without the periods. Separate multiple extensions with semicolons, as follows:

```
EXE;BAT;COM
```

You can use the following options under Miscellaneous Attachment Settings to further refine how attachments are handled:

- *Show level 1 attachments*—If selected, users can view attachments you've defined as Level 1.
- *Allow users to lower attachments to Level 2*—If selected, users can convert a Level 1 attachment to a Level 2, and thereby save it to their hard disk.
- *Do not prompt about level 1 attachments when sending an item*—If selected, users can send Level 1 attachments without being prompted.
- *Do not prompt about level 1 attachments when closing an item*—If selected, users do not see a warning message when they close a message or appointment with a Level 1 item attached.
- *Allow in-place activation of embedded OLE objects*—If selected, users can open embedded OLE objects, such as Excel worksheets, by double-clicking them. (If users are using Microsoft Word as their e-mail editor, the item opens when it's double-clicked.)
- *Show OLE package objects*—If selected, OLE objects that have been placed in a package icon will be visible in messages.

You can use the following options under Miscellaneous Custom Form Settings to control security settings for Outlook custom forms:

- *Enable scripts in one-off Outlook forms*—If selected, you can run scripts within Outlook forms, provided that the script and form layout are both contained in the message.
- *When executing a custom action via Outlook object model*—You can create custom actions to reply to a message and circumvent the programmatic send protections. This option allows you to determine what happens when a program attempts to run an action from the Outlook object model. The user can be prompted, the action can happen automatically without prompting, or the action can be disabled without prompting.
- *When accessing the ItemProperty property of a control on an Outlook custom form*—This option specifies what happens when a user binds a control in a custom form to an Address Information field. The security risk is that the code can retrieve the value of the Address Information field. As with the preceding option, you can have the user prompted or explicitly allow or disallow access to Address Information fields.

The Programmatic Settings tab, shown in Figure D-5, is where the administrator can configure tight control over security settings having to do with the spread of viruses. This tab has options that apply to items that use script or code and the Outlook object model to programmatically send mail and manipulate data stored in Outlook folders. These items include Collaboration Data Objects (CDO), used to implement collaboration and messaging in custom applications, as well as Simple MAPI, which is used to add basic message sending and receiving to custom applications. The administrator can allow or disallow such items, or have the user be prompted to make his or her own decision.

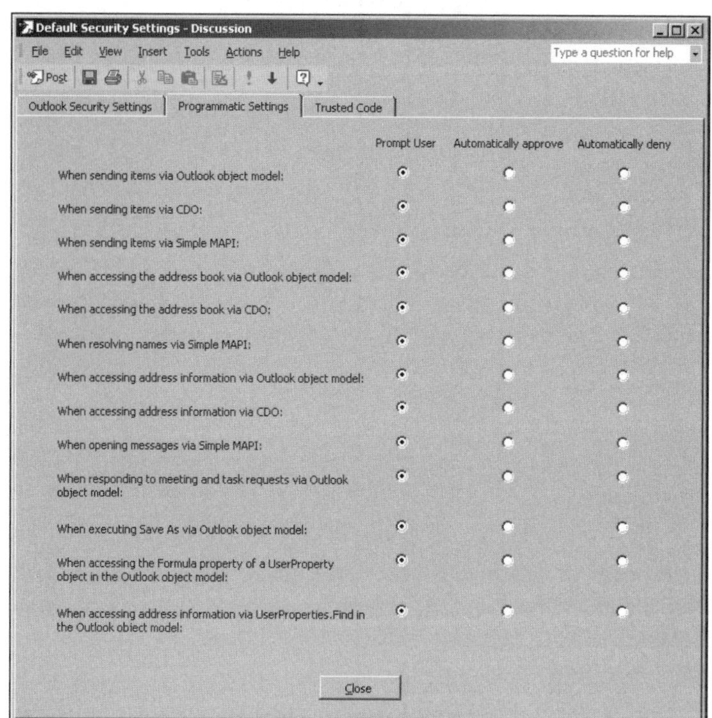

Figure D-5 Configuring virus-related security settings in the Programmatic Settings tab

The options are summarized as follows:

- *When sending items via Outlook object model*—Determines what happens when a program attempts to send mail through the Outlook object model
- *When sending items via CDO*—Determines what happens when an application attempts to use CDO to send mail through Outlook 2002
- *When sending items via Simple MAPI*—Specifies what happens when a program tries to send mail using Simple MAPI

- *When accessing the address book via Outlook object model*—Determines what happens when an application program tries to access an address book through the Outlook object model
- *When accessing the address book via CDO*—Specifies what happens when an application attempts to access an address book using CDO
- *When resolving names via Simple MAPI*—Specifies what happens when a program attempts to gain access to an address book when using Simple MAPI
- *When accessing address information via Outlook object model*—Specifies what happens when a program attempts to access a recipient field, such as To, via the Outlook object model
- *When accessing address information via CDO*—Determines what happens when a program tries to access a recipient field via CDO
- *When opening messages via Simple MAPI*—Specifies what happens when a program attempts to use Simple MAPI to access a recipient field
- *When responding to meeting and task requests via Outlook object model*—Determines what happens when a program tries to send mail by using the Respond method on task requests and meeting requests
- *When executing Save As via Outlook object model*—Determines what happens when a program tries to use File, Save As attempts to save an item to the hard disk
- *When accessing the Formula property of a UserProperty object in the Outlook object model*—Determines what happens when a user attempts to bind an Address Information field to a Combination or Formula custom field on a custom form
- *When accessing address information via UserProperties.Find in the Outlook object model*—Determines what happens when a program tries to search mail folders for address information via the Outlook object model

Finally, in the Trusted Code tab, the administrator can determine which COM add-ins can be run. To specify a trusted add-in, the administrator needs to copy the file used to load the COM add-in to a location where the administrator has access to the file. The file must be the same one that's used on the client computers. When the COM add-in is accessible to the administrator, she can click the Add button on the Trusted Code tab, select the name of the file to add, click to select the file, and click the Close button. The trusted add-in will run without prompting the user.

As discussed in the Readme.doc file, if Office XP is deployed with system policies, the Outlk10.adm file automatically passes customized security settings to client computers at logon. If Office is deployed without system policies, you need to make changes to the Registry manually. Settings and procedures are covered in the Readme.doc file.

OUTLOOK 2002 CALENDARING ENHANCEMENTS

Outlook 2002 users with access to Exchange 2000 gain some improvements in the areas of calendaring and group scheduling. A group leader or project manager can create a public folder and subfolders in which to store all group-related items. For example, in Figure D-6 the team leader has created a new public folder named Project X that contains Mail and Post items. Within that folder, the leader has created folders named Group Calendar, Group Contacts, Group Tasks, Milestones, and Post Documents Here, which members can use for a variety of communication and scheduling jobs, as you'll learn next.

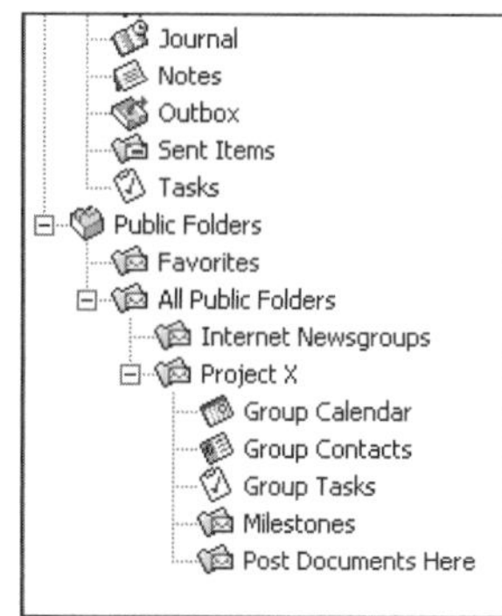

Figure D-6 A new public folder created for a team

Next, the team leader can create a contact record for each team member in the Group Contacts folder. For example, in Figure D-7 you can see where the team leader is creating a contact record for Ashley Martinez. Setting up a list of contacts in this manner simplifies communications with group members.

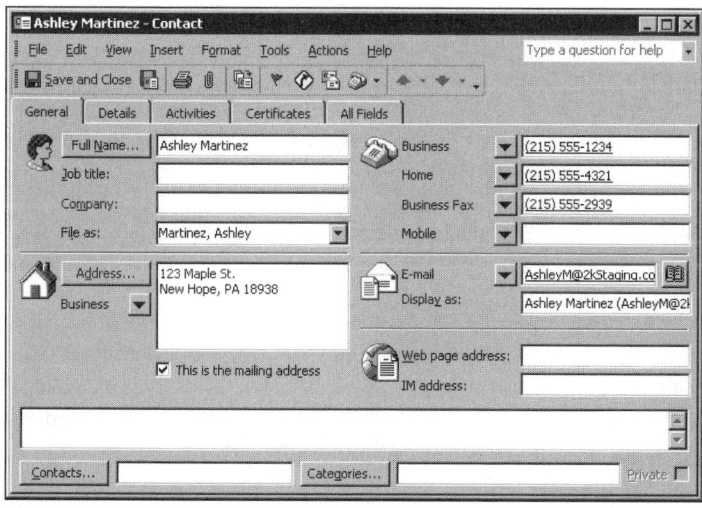

Figure D-7 Creating a contact record for a team member

The team leader can then control access to folders by assigning permissions. For example, the leader might allow all users to be able to post documents to the Post Documents Here folder, but grant only Read access to the Milestones folder so that other team member can view, but not change, the contents of that folder. To assign permissions to a folder, the team leader simply needs to right-click the folder, click Properties, and then click the Permissions tab of the Properties dialog box for the folder (see Figure D-8). In this figure, you can see that the team leader has assigned the Reviewer permission level to a couple of members, allowing them to view, but not change, the contents of the Milestones folder.

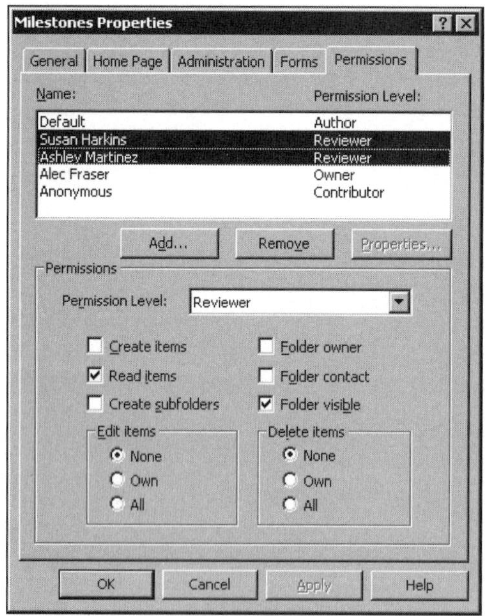

Figure D-8 Setting permissions for a group folder

Group members who do have permissions to change the contents of a folder can post their documents there from any Microsoft Office XP application. For example, suppose that all users are granted Author permissions to the Post Documents Here subfolder, and that a group member wants to put a Word document in the folder. To do so, the member can click File, Send To, Exchange Folder on the Microsoft Word menu bar, click the folder, as shown in Figure D-9, and then click OK.

Creating a group schedule is easy in Outlook 2002. The team leader simply needs to click the Group Calendar public folder, click the Schedules button, enter a name for the schedule, and then click OK. A window with the schedule name opens. To select members from the address book to add to the schedule, the team member clicks the Add Others button. For example, in Figure D-10 the team leader has added three group members to the Planning Phase schedule.

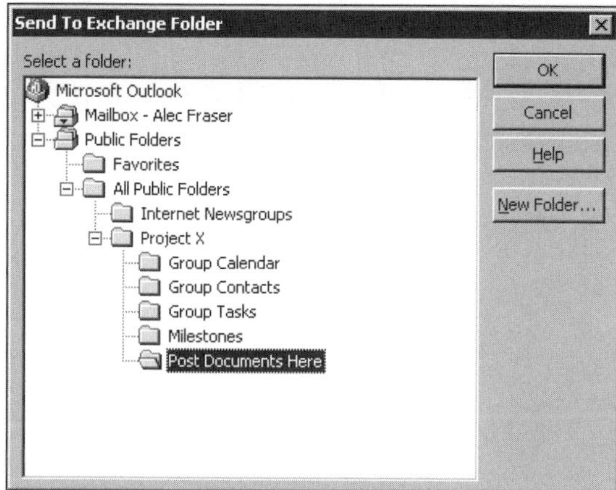

Figure D-9 Posting a document to a public folder from a Microsoft Office XP application

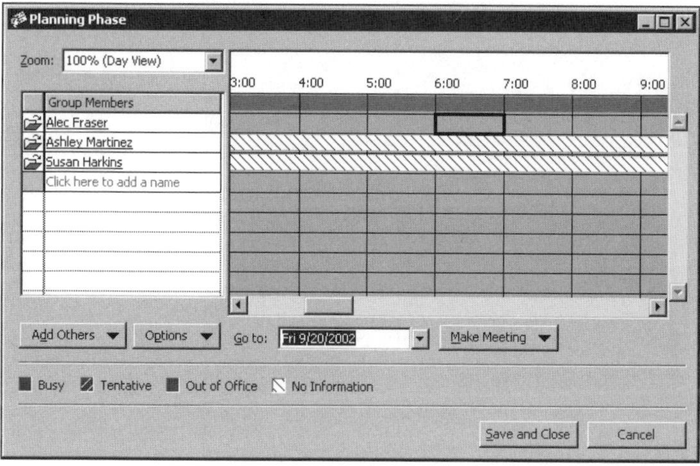

Figure D-10 Scheduling a meeting

Clicking the Make Meeting button enables the team leader to create a message that's automatically sent to all members. When recipients click the message in their Outlook 2002 Inboxes, they have the option to accept or decline the meeting, to tentatively accept, or to propose a new time, as shown in Figure D-11.

Clicking the Propose New Time button displays the group schedule, where the group member can propose a different time if he or she is unable to make the scheduled meeting time. Note the AutoPick Next button, visible in Figure D-12. That handy button automatically locates the next available time when all meeting attendees are free. This feature is especially useful because it prevents potential attendees from proposing new times that conflict with other members' schedules.

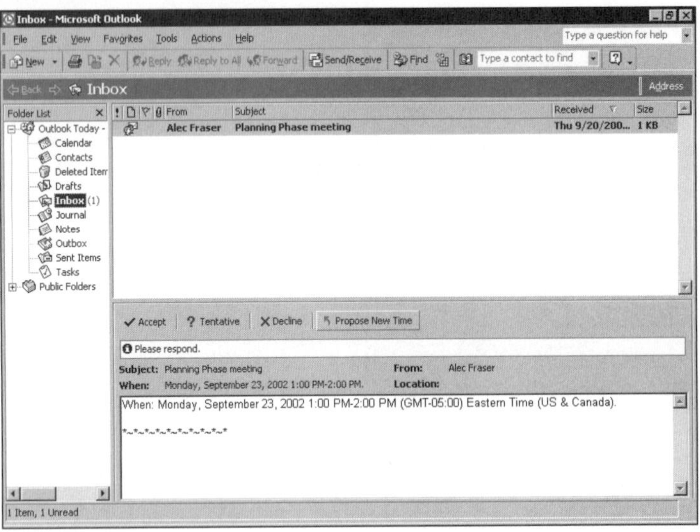

Figure D-11 Options for responding to a meeting request

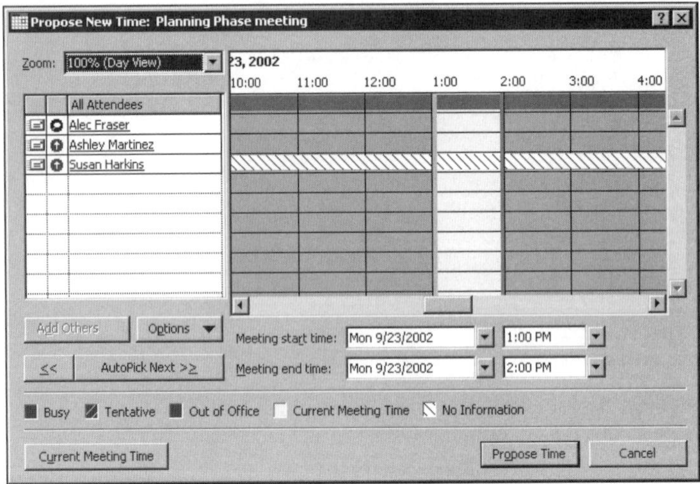

Figure D-12 The new Propose New Time dialog box includes an AutoPick Next button to avoid scheduling conflicts

Outlook 2002 also has a new means of sharing free and busy times with other users. This feature works even without Exchange 2000, allowing users to share schedules over any network, including the Internet. To publish free and busy times, an Outlook 2002 user simply needs to click Tools, Options, Calendar Options on Outlook's menu bar. The

Free/Busy Options dialog box, shown in Figure D-13, opens, where the user can publish up to 36 months of free/busy times on the Microsoft Office Internet Free/Busy Service server (*http:freebusy.office.microsoft.com*) or on a local server.

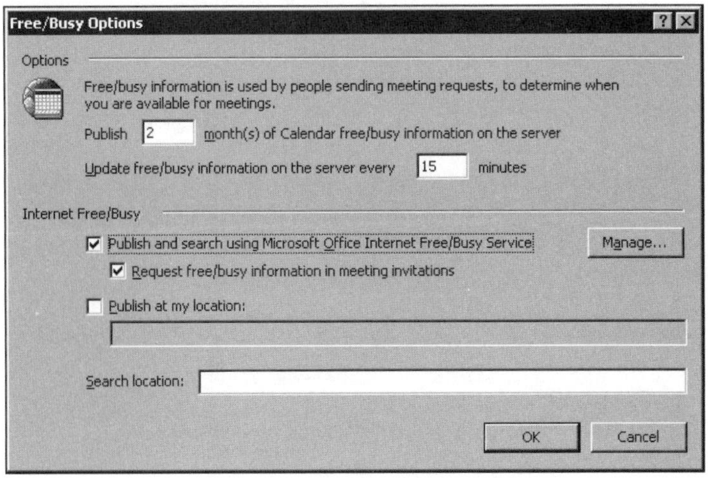

Figure D-13 The Free/Busy Options dialog box

Outlook 2002 also uses a new unified Reminders window that displays all upcoming and past-due events in a single window, as shown in Figure D-14. This is an improvement over previous versions of Outlook, which displayed each reminder in a separate window, cluttering up the screen.

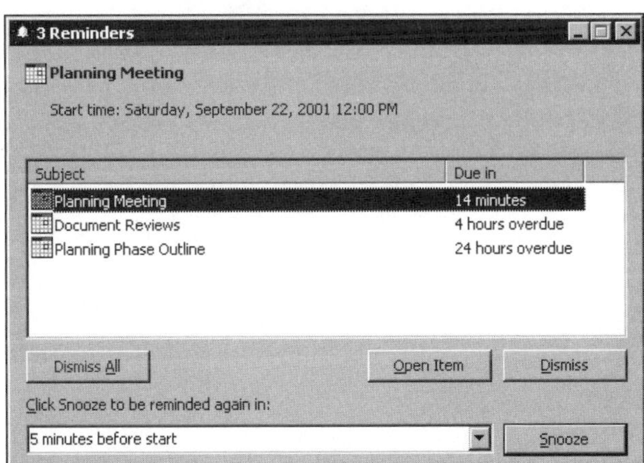

Figure D-14 Multiple reminders are listed in a single Reminder window

Color-coding is yet another handy new feature of the Outlook 2002 calendar, particularly with busy group calendars that might show the schedules of dozens of people. When creating a new calendar item or editing an existing item, you can use the Label list box to define a label and color for the item, as shown in Figure D-15.

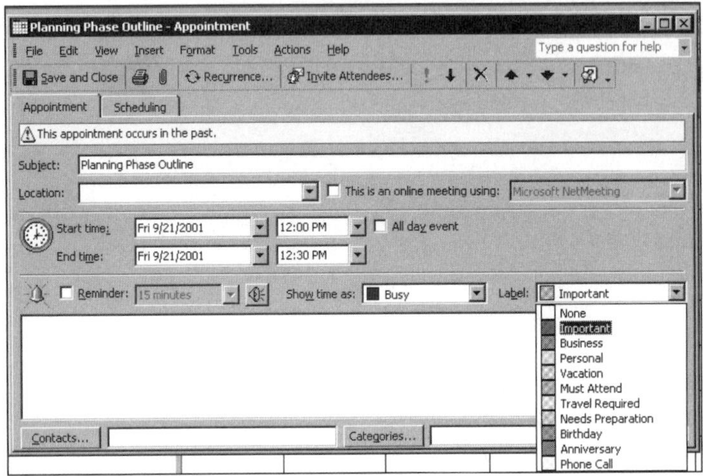

Figure D-15 Color-coding calendar items

USING MSN MESSENGER

Combining Exchange 2000 with Service Pack 1, Outlook 2002, and MSN Messenger (or Windows Messenger from Windows XP) allows group members to communicate in real time by chatting or voice (or video, in the case of Windows Messenger). To enable instant messaging for a user, the Exchange Server administrator needs to open Active Directory Users and Groups, select Users in the console tree, right-click the user's name, and then click the Exchange Features tab in the Properties dialog box that opens. If the Instant Messaging option is disabled, clicking the Enable button turns that feature on.

In the Options dialog box, click the Accounts tab, shown in Figure D-16, to use Exchange to communicate with other group members. When viewing a contact in Outlook 2002, you'll see the InfoBar with the contact's name followed by "…is online. Click here to send an instant message," as shown in Figure D-17. Clicking the InfoBar opens an Instant Message window where the users can start chatting.

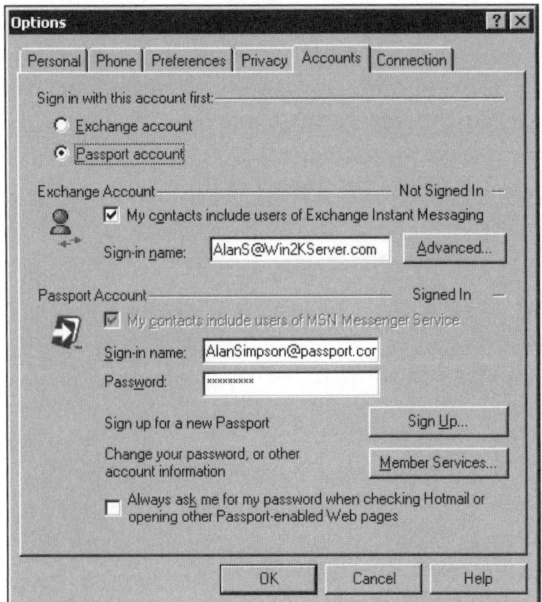

Figure D-16 Configuring a sign-in account in the Options dialog box

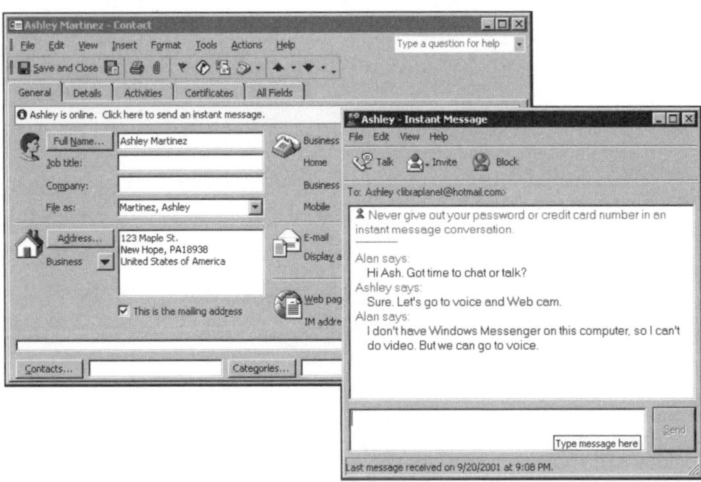

Figure D-17 Chatting in an MSN Messenger instant message window

A .NET Passport is required to use MSN Messenger or Windows Messenger on the Internet. The Sign Up button in the Options dialog box allows you to get a Passport on the spot.

MSN Messenger and Windows Messenger provide simple alternatives to using NetMeeting for holding a quick online meeting. By clicking the Invite button, either user can invite other members to join the conversation. By the time you read this, the Windows Messenger program, which comes with Windows XP, might contain the Whiteboard, Application Sharing, and other NetMeeting features. (These features have been included in beta test software, but haven't been released to the public as of this writing.)

Workflow Enhancements

Outlook 2002 improves collaboration and workflow processes for all of the Microsoft Office XP applications. For example, the author of a Word document or Excel worksheet (who we'll refer to as the owner of the document) might want to distribute a document to one or more reviewers. Using Outlook 2002 and Exchange Server, the owner can route the document through several reviewers to get their comments. Each reviewer can make changes or comments, and then return the document to the owner. When the owner receives the reviewers' documents, she can then opt to automatically merge the document's new versions with the original versions.

Although routing was available in earlier versions of Office, Outlook 2002 incorporates a new capability dubbed the Built-In Review Cycle. Using this method, the document owner clicks File, Send To, Mail Recipient for Review on the application's menu bar. An e-mail message form opens with the document already attached. The owner can type recipient names or select them from an address book, as shown in Figure D-18.

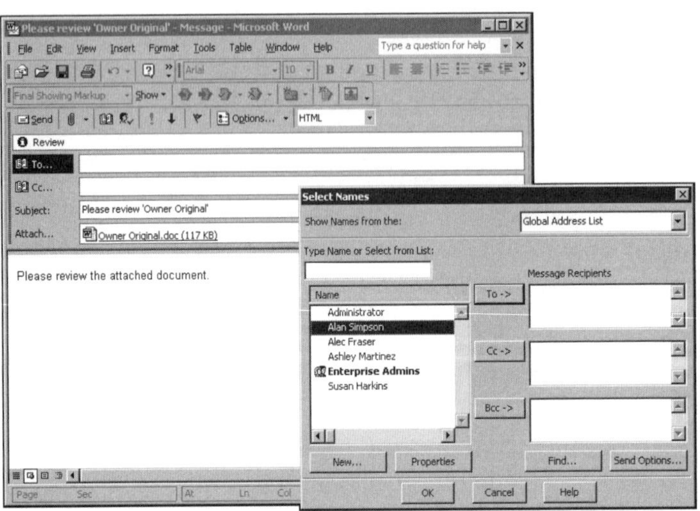

Figure D-18 Selecting reviewers for an attached document

When the recipient opens the document for review, the standard tools for tracking revisions are turned on automatically. The reviewer can make changes and add comments, and then click the Reply with Changes button that appears in a toolbar above the edited document. When the owner receives and opens the reviewed document, a prompt appears asking whether the reviewer's changes should be merged into the document. Clicking Yes opens the documents with revision tools turned on and the reviewer's changes clearly marked for easy acceptance or rejection. A toolbar above the merged document includes an End Review button, which the owner can click to end the review cycle and stop accepting reviewing feedback.

MAILBOX MANAGER IMPROVEMENTS

Mailbox Manager is an Exchange program that originally shipped with Exchange 5.5 Service Pack 3, but was missing from the original release of Exchange 2000. Exchange 2000 Service Pack 1 brings back the Mailbox Manager, which Exchange administrators can use to define recipient policies, such as setting age and size limits on folders. You can use the Mailbox Manager Settings (Policy) tab of a recipient policy to automatically send notifications to recipients when their mailboxes are approaching their limits, as shown in Figure D-19.

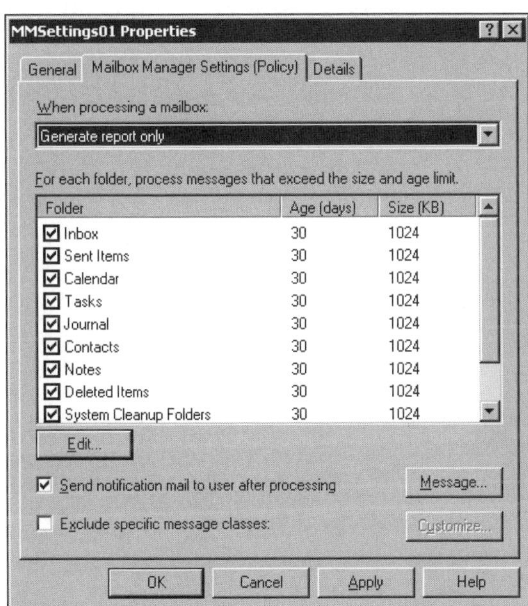

Figure D-19 Defining a recipient policy in Mailbox Manager

The new Outlook 2002 Mailbox Cleanup dialog box, shown in Figure D-20, provides tools that enable users to manage their own mailboxes. To open the dialog box, the user simply chooses Mailbox Cleanup on the Tools menu in Outlook 2002. The topmost button is used to view the size of each subfolder in a mailbox to determine which folders are consuming the most space.

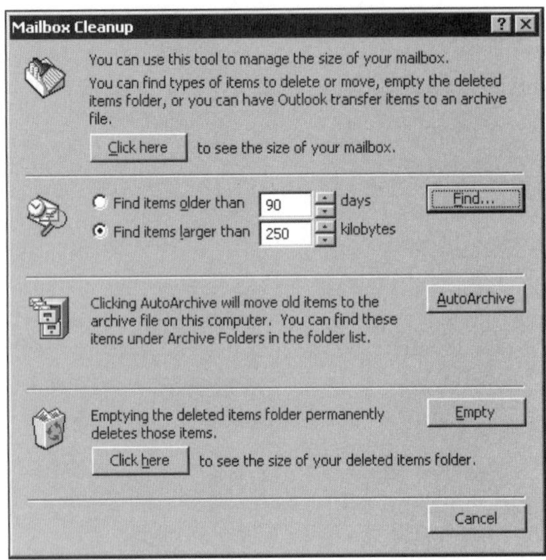

Figure D-20 The Outlook 2002 Mailbox Cleanup dialog box

Users can click the Find button to locate items based on their size or age. Choosing a criterion and clicking the Find button lists all matching items in an Advanced Find dialog box. Users can then delete any or all items in that dialog box to quickly recover space. The AutoArchive and Empty buttons make it easy for users to archive and delete items in their mailbox.

IMPROVEMENTS TO REMOTE ACCESS

Outlook 2002 users who dial into a remote computer running Exchange 2000 Server will find several performance improvements. Send and receive operations transmit less overhead data and use fewer remote procedure calls, thereby speeding up these processes. Users can send and receive e-mail using multiple accounts and multiple folders, and can configure different accounts, each with its own Dial-Up Networking settings. Furthermore, Outlook 2002 users can activate or deactivate background send and receive tasks and can configure them to operate independently for maximum performance.

The new Requesting data from Microsoft Exchange Server dialog box that appears during a remote procedure call can now notify the user of any delays. The user has two options for dealing with the delay. One option is to minimize the dialog box and continue working while waiting for the connection to be made. The other option is to click the new Cancel button to terminate the connection. Either way, the user is no longer required to wait idly for the call to complete.

SYNCHRONIZATION PERFORMANCE IMPROVEMENTS

Outlook 2002 users who use offline files (synchronization) now have the option to turn off automatic synchronization during an online session, thereby eliminating the delays that often occur with slow connections. The new version uses larger packets for MAPI synchronization, which helps reduce transfer times.

Multiple e-mail accounts can be organized into groups, and each group can be assigned unique settings. Each group can contain any combination of HTTP, POP3, IMAP, and Exchange accounts. All options are available in the Send/Receive Groups dialog box, shown in Figure D-21, which the user can access by clicking Tools, Send/Receive Settings, Define Send/Receive groups.

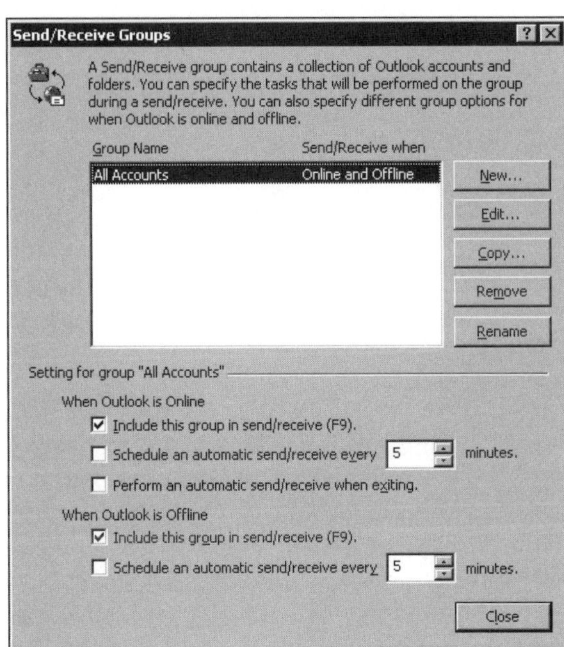

Figure D-21 The Send/Receive Groups dialog box

Users have several options for determining how a group sends and receives messages, including the following:

- *Include this group in send/receive (F9)*—If selected, all accounts in the group are updated when the user initiates a Send/Receive command.
- *Schedule an automatic send/receive every x minutes*—If selected, the user can determine how frequently automatic send/receive commands are initiated.
- *Perform an automatic send/receive when exiting*—If selected, a send/receive operation is started automatically when the user exits Outlook 2002.

FULL-TEXT INDEXING AND SEARCHING

Administrators can use the Exchange full-text indexing feature to create an index of every word in every message and every document stored in a folder. Outlook 2002 can use this database to speed users' searches for information in the folders. Users aren't limited to searching for messages; they can use queries in Outlook 2002 to find matching items in calendars, documents, attachments, contacts, tasks, and collaboration data. To find information about these items, users can use the Advanced Find dialog box in Outlook 2002 to search on a huge number of properties, as shown in Figure D-22.

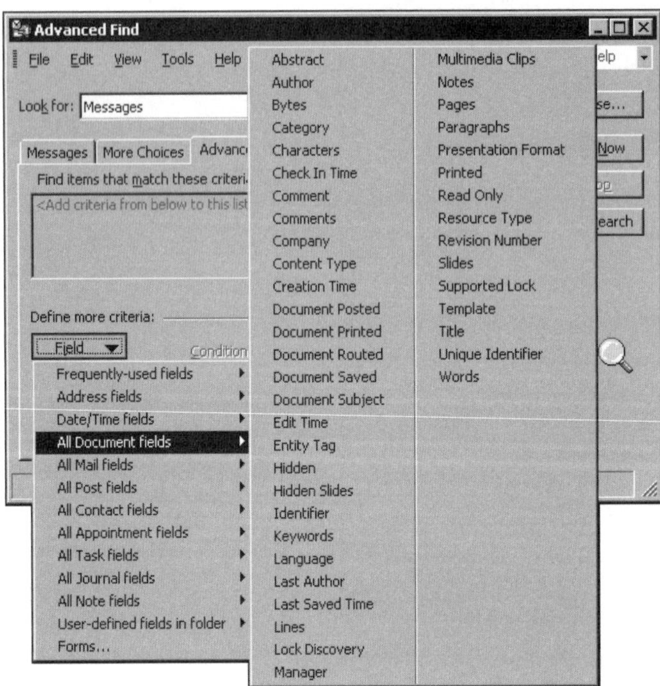

Figure D-22 Specifying search criteria in the Advanced Find dialog box

Outlook Express 6

Windows XP comes with Microsoft Internet Explorer 6, which in turn brings you Outlook Express 6. You won't find any significant changes in the new Outlook Express, and it's still largely incompatible with Exchange, except through standard protocols such as IMAP and SMTP. The main new feature of Outlook Express 6 is that the user can now block incoming messages that might contain viruses and be notified when a program attempts to send e-mail programmatically, as shown in Figure D-23.

D

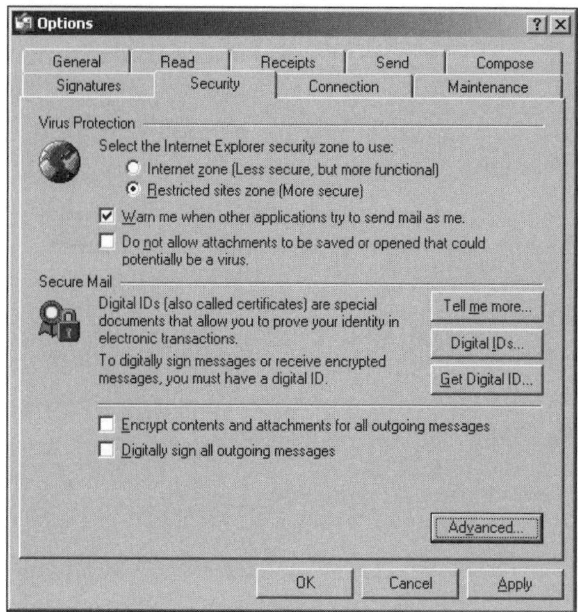

Figure D-23 Security settings in Outlook Express 6

These new options, obviously, correspond to the new security options in Outlook 2002. However, an administrator cannot use Exchange to change the default settings of Outlook Express 6. So if you're trying to use Outlook Express 6 in an administered environment, settings will have to be made on a per-machine basis rather than centrally through a server.

Chapter Summary

This appendix has covered new and improved features of Outlook 2002, which comes with all the Microsoft Office XP suites, as well as Outlook Express 6, which comes with all versions of Windows XP.

Outlook 2002 offers Exchange 2000 administrators new and improved tools for managing e-mail security:

- By default, Outlook 2002 blocks virtually all types of e-mail attachments that could potentially contain a virus. The Outlook Security Features Administration Pack allows administrators to change the default settings.
- To help prevent the spread of viruses, Exchange 2000 administrators can also use the Outlook Security Features Administration Pack to control the types of code that are allowed to access the Outlook 2002 address book and send e-mail through Outlook 2002.
- New calendaring features in Outlook 2002 make it easier for groups of users to schedule meetings.
- Outlook 2002 now supports instant messaging among Exchange users, via MSN Messenger or Windows Messenger (which comes with Windows XP).
- Outlook 2002 offers some workflow enhancements, such as the new Built-In Review Cycle, to simplify routing documents among reviewers for changes and suggestions.
- Outlook 2002 users have a new Mailbox Cleanup dialog box, which helps them to better manage their mailboxes without administrator intervention.
- Remote access, offline files, and synchronization have all been made more efficient, and simplified for users, in Outlook 2002.
- Indexing and full-text searching is now supported in Outlook 2002, allowing users to search for a word or phrase in message bodies and attached documents.
- Although Outlook Express 6 doesn't offer much for the Exchange 2000 administrator, it does give users improved security options, such as the ability to block attachments and programmatic sending of messages.

Glossary

16-bit clients — Older client software packages created for 16-bit operating systems, such as Windows 3.1 or Windows 3.11 for Workgroups. Windows NT and Windows 2000 are both 32-bit operating systems that support 16-bit applications for backward-compatibility. Although 16-bit clients function on 32-bit operating systems, they tend to not perform as well as 32-bit clients.

access control lists (ACLs) — Security settings placed on objects that dictate what users and other systems can do in relation to the object.

Active Desktop — A useful feature that enables the Windows desktop to display HTML information and pages, including JPEG images as background files and active content such as the digital dashboard.

Active Directory (AD) — A new domain management structure introduced with Windows 2000. AD uses the Domain Name System to perform naming resolution and is much more flexible and expandable than previous Windows domain management methods.

Active Directory Connector (ADC) — A Microsoft utility that helps provide temporary coexistence between Exchange 5.5 and Exchange 2000 and then helps ease the migration to the final Exchange 2000 deployment. Basically, the ADC enables Active Directory to support the older directory design in Exchange 5.5.

active server — The server in a cluster that maintains complete control over the shared disk subsystem and anything else managed by the cluster. The active server performs all necessary processing; if it fails, a passive server switches to an active server to fill this role.

address space — A filter identifying a set of recipients that can be routed through a connector. You can build an address space with any level of granularity, identifying single recipients, groups of recipients, or all recipients of a specific address type (SMTP, X.400, cc:Mail, and so on).

administrative group — A group that helps define your company's organizational structure and helps define separate groups of administrators who are responsible for distinct servers spread throughout the organization. This group is equivalent to an Exchange 5.5 site in a mixed-mode organization.

advanced queuing engine (AQE) — A primary component in the extended SMTP Service of IIS, involved in the Exchange 2000 Transport Architecture. Governs the internal processing and categorization of messages, identifies next-hop information, and calls custom event sinks.

application service providers — A new type of business service in which a provider operates a server farm that hosts published applications for a company, which connects to the service using client software. None of the software is managed from the client end, and data is typically stored at the provider's site. The application service providers also ensure that the services are maintained and backed up, relieving the cost and burden of maintenance for the client.

asymmetric key — A type of encryption key used when two different keys—a public key and a private key—are exchanged. One key is used to encrypt and decrypt the data, and the other key is used only for decryption.

back-end — Represents the actual Exchange 2000 servers that provide the bulk of the processing. The front-end server forwards requests from the client software to the back-end servers for processing.

backup domain controller (BDC) — For redundancy and network performance, BDCs can perform backup authentication on the network in case the primary domain controller fails, or if the PDC is busy, the BDC can authenticate requests.

Berkley Internet Name Domain (BIND) — An open-source set of services that is considered a very reliable set of Domain Name System services. It is commonly found under Linux, but can be used with Windows 2000 and Exchange 2000.

beta testing — A phase in software development and testing during which users test for functionality and bugs in the software and provide feedback to the software publisher to help resolve user issues and bugs in the software.

bridgehead server — An Exchange 2000 server that has one or more connectors linking multiple Exchange sites or providing connections to the Internet for Exchange servers. These servers are typically set to be bridgehead servers by the Exchange administrator.

Categorizer (Phatcat.dll) — A series of event sinks, called by the AQE, that perform AD lookups to resolve message recipients to their associated SMTP addresses. Removes redundant recipients and enforces transport-level quotas.

certificate authority (CA) — A central component of certificate services in which Windows 2000 and administrators can issue and manage digital certificates to users wanting to connect securely to servers.

Certificate Services Policy (CSP) — A certificate template in the certificate authority that uses specific user information to generate keys. It also stores users' private keys in the Extensible Storage Engine (ESE) database.

chat community — A virtual chat server that you can configure with the appropriate settings for that server. Under each chat community, you can create channels where users can chat on certain topics, or you can allow users to create their own topics.

circular logging — A logging option in Exchange 2000 that reuses the first transaction log file that's created for new transaction entries after its contents have been written to the database that stores the log information.

client-server messaging system — A network architecture that involves processing work on a dedicated machine, known as the server, which processes client requests. Clients normally talk to servers by using translation mechanisms called protocols.

configuration connection agreement — A read-only connection agreement that transfers two-way configuration information. This CA cannot be changed, but you can view configuration information using the Active Directory Connector Management tool that's installed when you first configure the ADC. This CA replicates configuration information specific to Exchange 2000 between the Exchange 5.5 directory and AD.

connection agreement — An object that establishes a relationship between an existing Exchange 5.5 site and Active Directory by replicating recipient objects and configuration information between AD and the Exchange 5.5 directory service. You can define multiple connection agreements for each instance of the Active Directory Connector that you configure in Exchange 2000.

connector — Any routine or service that provides message, scheduling, and/or directory synchronization between Exchange 2000 routing groups or between an Exchange 2000 organization and an external messaging system. Although third-party connectors can be developed, Exchange 2000 Server provides native connectors for SMTP, routing groups, Lotus Notes and cc:Mail, and Novell GroupWise.

connector cost — An administrator-assigned value between 1 and 100 that identifies the relative preference for a connector (lowest cost preferred). When routing messages, Exchange uses the path with the lowest total cost to transport messages.

counter — The software used in System Monitor that is configured to measure and store information on the object being monitored.

Delivery Status Notification (DSN) — An automatically generated e-mail notifying a user of a message delivery problem. DSNs generally refer to a delay message, although NDR notifications also fall into this category. A DSN (delay) message indicates that the initial attempt at sending a message failed, and Exchange will continue trying.

digital certificate — Very similar to an encryption key, a digital certificate presents the information in a certificate format, showing that the identity of the person or server you are connecting to has been verified.

digital dashboard — A high-tech HTML document that allows you to include active content from various sources, such as other Web pages, Outlook, and similar Microsoft Office applications. An example of a digital dashboard is the Outlook Today interface.

Directory Information Tree (DIT) — A selection of information on various objects held in the directory. Each object in the database has attributes, such as a name or an address, and the DIT retains this information. To search this data, users use directory access servers connected with LDAP.

Directory Service Proxy (DSProxy) — A dynamic link library in Exchange 2000 Server that allows a MAPI client, such as Microsoft Outlook 2000, to access the Active Directory database on a Windows 2000 Server computer. It sends all client directory requests using a Name Service Provider Interface (NSPI).

Disk Defragmenter — A system utility that analyzes a hard drive or partition and then defragments it. When the defragmentation software defragments a hard drive or partition, it rearranges the various bits of data on the hard drive into the proper order to optimize data retrieval.

distinguished name (DN) — The unique name given to each object in the directory. The DN is built by taking the information in the Directory Information Tree leading up to the object in hierarchical order, starting from the topmost entry in the directory and moving down in order to the name of the object.

Domain Name System (DNS) — A commonly used service that translates IP addresses into readable English names. Active Directory uses DNS to handle all name translation requests from the clients and other services that use DNS.

domain tree — A grouping of domains, usually by a common organizational structure or naming scheme.

DVD-RW — A new backup standard in which you can back up your data onto DVD media, which can hold much more data than CDs, but often less than the more traditional tape backup media.

Encrypting File System (EFS) — A Windows 2000 feature that can be used to encrypt files and folders for additional security.

encryption strength — A description of the security capabilities of encryption methods. Encryption strength describes how difficult it is to crack the keys in an encryption method.

event sink — An indicator of the registered process called at a predefined point in processing a message. The three categories of event sinks are storage events, transport events, and protocol events.

Exchange 2000 Transport Architecture — A functional description of the logic in Exchange 2000 and IIS that routes the messages within a single Exchange server.

Exchange Development Kit (EDK) — A set of development tools from Microsoft that enables programmatic connectivity to the Exchange organization through the MTA. The EDK is used primarily for developing connectors to external messaging systems.

Exchange Interprocess Communication (ExIPC) layer — A message-queuing layer between the IIS process (Inetinfo.exe) and the Web Storage System in Exchange 2000 Server that facilitates fast data exchange between these two components. The IIS process hosts all Exchange 2000 protocols, whereas the Web Storage System is a structured database that manages items such as e-mail messages or Web pages.

Extensible Storage Engine (ESE) — A component that manages the physical databases necessary for storing and retrieving messages.

forest — The collection of domain trees that is usually the boundary of the main domain structure. Exchange 2000 can work only within its own forest, not with domains outside that forest.

front-end — The server that the client software typically connects to. A common example of a front-end server is OWA. The front-end server rarely controls information or fulfills requests for the client; rather, it sends the users' requests to the back-end servers.

full-text indexing — A Windows 2000 service that allows users to perform searches for messages, documents, or attachments. This is done by integrating the query engine component of the Information Store with the Microsoft Search service, which is installed as part of the Exchange 2000 Setup program.

gateway connector — Connector used in Exchange 2000 Server to connect to external computer systems, such as IBM mainframes running other operating systems, or to external programs that supply features such as fax or voicemail.

global address list — A central depository for all objects and users in the Active Directory domain. For instance, users access the global address list when sending an e-mail to someone else in the domain; they can type a name instead of a full e-mail address. Active Directory searches for the name entered and sends it to the appropriate user if possible.

global catalog (GC) — A centralized clearinghouse of information, similar to a phone book, that stores information about every object that could exist in a Windows 2000 domain or forest. Users query the global catalog when searching for objects stored in Active Directory. At least one server in each Windows 2000 domain must function as the Global Catalog server, which holds a copy of the global catalog.

HTTP with WebDAV — The protocol that Outlook Web Access uses to communicate with the back-end services on an Exchange 2000 server.

Information Store — The Exchange 2000 database that maintains information on user data, such as e-mail messages or public folder information. It is run as one file, known as Store.exe, and separates mail messages into private mailbox stores and public data into public folder stores.

Installable File System (IFS) — A service that enables direct access to Exchange data, including mailboxes and public folders. With this direct access, a user can map a shared folder to a mailbox or public folder and access it as though it were a directory on a server's hard drive.

instance — Each of the objects that's measured when a counter measures multiple objects (such as multiple processors in a server).

Instant Messaging (IM) — A service through which users can exchange text messages in real time in your Exchange organization or with other IM servers on the Internet.

Internet Information Server (IIS) — A set of services included with Windows 2000 that provides various Internet services, including the ability to host FTP and Web sites. Exchange 2000 uses IIS to provide Outlook Web Access services.

Internet Mail Service (IMS) — The system-level service that Microsoft Exchange uses to transfer information to and from external message systems that use SMTP. IMS dictates how the server uses SMTP, DNS, and TCP/IP to perform the required message transfer services.

Internet Messaging Access Protocol version 4 (IMAP4) — A messaging protocol that allows users to retrieve e-mail from a server without directly downloading it to their local disks. Users access e-mail information or public folder information as though it were stored locally on their computers.

Internet Relay Chat (IRC) — A system that uses a set of rules and conventions to allow users to chat with text messages in real time. It is one form of client-server communication and uses TCP/IP on port 6667.

IP Security (IPSec) — A Windows 2000 feature that allows you to secure TCP/IP network traffic by using encrypted keys.

Kerberos — Named after the three-headed dog from Greek mythology, this authentication protocol has three main components to its design: the key distribution center, the client user, and the server.

Kerberos version 5 authentication — The client authentication method that uses the Kerberos protocol, a fundamental security protocol in Windows 2000 Server. This mechanism issues tickets containing encrypted information so that clients can access network services; for example, the Kerberos service issues Exchange service tickets to clients who need access to the Exchange 2000 server.

Key Management Service (KMS) — A set of services integrated with Microsoft Certificate Services, which is included with Windows 2000. KMS provides message and data security by generating keys for encrypting and decrypting e-mail sent to and from Exchange 2000.

Lightweight Directory Access Protocol (LDAP) — A distributed directory services protocol that can be used to gain access to directory services on other operating systems. It is an industry standard described in RFC 1777 and uses TCP/IP for client-server communication to build directories based on object information.

list server — A service that enables users subscribing or posting to a mail list to receive, at preset intervals, the information that the e-mail server sends out.

mailbox store — A database that is part of the Information Store and holds user mailboxes or provides mailbox information to clients using a protocol such as the MAPI specification. You can have up to five mailbox stores per storage group to provide the level of customization and optimization you need.

member server — A Windows 2000 computer that has joined a Windows 2000 domain, but does not handle any authentication or logon validation for users wanting to access the domain. A member server can be changed to a domain controller at any time by using the Active Directory Installation Wizard or Dcpromo.exe.

message — Also known as electronic messaging, it refers to the creation, storage, and management of various forms of data, including text, images, voice, and e-mail, over some form of communications network. It is an exchange of specially formatted data describing some event or a request to a messaging server.

message header — The part of the document that contains the pertinent message information, such as senders, recipients, and their addresses.

Message Tracking Center — A tracking and troubleshooting tool that tracks messages in an Exchange organization from their point of entry to their point of departure.

Message Transfer Agent (MTA) — An agent that provides X.400-based connectivity with remote X.400 servers and communicates directly with EDK-based connectors.

Messaging Application Programming Interface (MAPI) — An industry standard for writing e-mail messages used by Exchange 2000 and other similar messaging systems. It is also the interface that allows you to attach a Windows application to an e-mail note.

messaging server — A message exchange program for client programs. It is a middleware program that handles messages sent for use by other programs using a MAPI. Messaging servers usually prioritize and queue messages sent to them.

Microsoft Solutions Framework (MSF) — A set of guidelines developed by Microsoft to help establish a reliable path for implementing infrastructure projects efficiently and properly.

mixed-mode environment — The condition that exists when an Exchange 5.5 server is used in an Exchange 2000 Server or when an organization running Exchange 2000 server is introduced into an Exchange Server 5.5 organization. In this setting, the Exchange 5.5 server cannot distinguish between separate administrative groups or routing groups, so each Exchange 2000 administrative group appears as an Exchange 5.5 site.

multi-master replication — An Active Directory feature that ensures that any changes to a domain controller or Global Catalog server in a Windows 2000 forest are copied to all other domain controllers in the same domain. These changes include configuration changes made to Exchange 2000 Server.

naming contexts — Components that outline which naming information is stored in the naming databases Active Directory uses to organize the domain.

native-mode environment — The optimal state of operations for Exchange 2000 Server. All servers are running Exchange 2000 Server, with no communication whatsoever with previous versions of Exchange. You have full flexibility in using routing and administrative groups, so that routing groups can now contain servers from different administrative groups. This setup cannot happen in a mixed-mode environment.

NetBIOS name — The system name given to a system or server for easier identification over a network. Make sure you apply an appropriate name when setting up Active Directory because the name will stay; if it's hard to understand or doesn't mean anything (for instance, K37T110 or ASDFJGL), it could become difficult to efficiently manage naming on the domain.

Network News Transport Protocol (NNTP) — The main protocol used by computers for administering messages posted on Usenet newsgroups on the Internet; it is slowly replacing the UNIX-to-UNIX Copy Protocol (UUCP). The protocol allows distribution, retrieval, and posting of news articles using a stream-based transmission of news among the Internet community. NNTP is a client-server protocol. An NNTP server manages all Usenet newsgroups, and an NNTP client is included with most browsers so that users can download messages posted to newsgroups.

Non-Delivery Report (NDR) — A type of Delivery Status Notification, indicating that a permanent error has occurred while attempting to deliver a message.

offline backup — A backup performed when the server's Exchange 2000 services have been stopped and the server is not accepting new information or processing current information; this allows data at an exact point in time to be backed up without worrying about new information being sent during the backup.

online backup — A backup performed on your Exchange 2000 server while it is running and processing new information. Data being processed during the backup will be stored in an additional patch file that can later be integrated into the appropriate database if a restoration is necessary.

organization — A logical object used in Exchange 5.5 and Exchange 2000 to represent the highest level in a hierarchy of objects. This object defines a boundary for other objects used by Exchange (such as server objects).

Outlook Web Access (OWA) — An Exchange service that enables Internet Explorer users to connect to their Exchange mailboxes and any public folders for which they have access. The interface is similar to Microsoft Outlook client software.

passive server — A server that is a member of a server cluster but is not currently active. Passive servers sit in a standby state, waiting for the active server in the cluster to fail or go offline; when one goes down, one of the passive servers in the cluster activates and becomes the active server.

Post Office Protocol version 3 (POP3) — A standard Internet protocol allowing a client to download e-mail from a server. It differs from IMAP4 in that messages are managed locally on the client's computer, not on the server, as with IMAP4. Users cannot directly manipulate messages stored on a server, nor can they access public folders on a server using POP3. POP3 offers much less functionality than IMAP4.

pre-categorization queue — A queue that temporarily holds messages awaiting processing by the Categorizer. In System Manager, it is the Messages awaiting directory lookup queue of an SMTP virtual server.

pre-routing queue — A queue that temporarily holds categorized messages awaiting next-hop information from the routing engine. In System Manager, it is the Messages waiting to be routed queue of an SMTP virtual server.

primary domain controller (PDC) — The main domain controller on the network. The PDC contains the master list of users and their rights on the network and replicates the data as necessary. PDCs are used only in Windows NT 4.0 domains, but can still be present in Active Directory mixed-mode networks.

protocol engine — A component of SMTP that directly connects to remote SMTP servers to send and receive messages.

protocol stub — A protocol-specific interface between IIS and Exchange. Protocol-specific commands and requests are sent between IIS and Exchange through their respective protocol stubs, related data (such as an e-mail message body) is placed in a shared memory heap, and a reference to it is placed in the protocol stub.

public folder hierarchy — The design of the public folder tree. It contains information on the public folders in the tree and helps keep track of every folder and piece of information in a public folder tree.

public folder store — A database residing on an Exchange 2000 server that holds information stored in public folders, which become accessible to entire communities of users at one time. Users can access public folders using a MAPI client, such as Outlook 2000, or using Internet protocols, such as HTTP and IMAP4. It is possible to replicate information in public folder stores, which are part of the Information Store in Exchange 2000.

public folder tree — A collection of public folders organized into a tree-like file structure with a root folder and subfolders branching out from the root folder.

public folder — A separate file system in Exchange where users can create folders and place documents, such as calendars and contact lists, that can be accessed by anyone in the network. Although these folders are called "public," security settings are available for the data if needed.

recipient policy — An Exchange 2000 Server feature that controls the generation of e-mail addresses. It is similar to the site addressing concept found in Exchange Server 5.5. Recipient policies allow administrators to assign more than one SMTP address to a user so that external addresses can be maintained for users in an organization.

Registry — A database repository in Windows 2000 that contains most of the information relating to the hardware and software configuration of a Windows 2000 computer. Adding new keys or values to it can sometimes cause problems; therefore, you need to back up the entire database structure and export it to remote storage locations before you make any changes.

Remote Procedure Calls (RPC) — A communication mechanism operating at the Application layer of the Open Systems Interconnect (OSI) model and used by Exchange 2000 Server components for Interprocess Communication. A machine uses RPC to request a service from a program found on another machine. It represents a synchronous operation, which suspends the requesting program until all results of the remote procedure have been returned.

rendezvous protocol (RVP) — The extension to WebDAV protocol that works over HTTP port 80. RVP allows Instant Messaging to provide advanced features and functionality, including the ability to view the connection and availability status of other IM users.

Routing and Remote Access Services (RRAS) — The services that allow remote users to connect to servers via a modem or another connection method, such as ISDN, to provide networking connections over the Internet or phone lines.

routing connector — A component of Exchange 2000 Server that connects two or more routing groups. The two major types of connectors include those that bypass the Message Transfer Agent and use SMTP directly and those that use the Message Transfer Agent and the X.400 protocol directly. The three connectors used in Exchange 2000 are the Routing Group Connector, the SMTP Connector, and the X.400 Connector.

routing engine — A component that manages and uses link state information to identify next-hop information for message routing on behalf of the AQE.

routing group — A group of Exchange 2000 servers that share permanent and high-bandwidth connections and communicate via SMTP. In a default installation of Exchange 2000 Server, all servers are added to a default routing group known as the First Routing Group. Servers in one routing group can belong to more than one administrative group.

routing group master (RGM) — The server in a routing group assigned the task of maintaining that routing group's link state table. Initially, it is the first server added to a routing group, but this can be changed in System Manager.

routing group topology — The design that indicates the architecture used to logically connect routing groups. The basic routing group topologies are hub-and-spoke, linear, ring, and full-mesh. Generally, the topology is a hybrid of the basic routing group topologies.

schema — An object or component, such as a user object, that controls the attributes maintained by the Active Directory service in Windows 2000 Server. The schema is the group of classes that represent directory objects, such as computers and groups. Installing Exchange 2000 Server automatically adds new object classes to the existing schema structure.

security audit — A procedure for checking the current security configuration for Exchange 2000, using security checklists and information in the event logs. This audit should be performed regularly to ensure that your security is up to date and that nothing has happened to hamper the security of your Exchange 2000 servers and services.

security checklist — A document used to record information about components and settings for your servers (or network). This information can help you assess the current security status of your servers or network.

security hot fix — A software patch for operating systems and other software that focuses entirely on security-specific issues.

security principal — A user object in Windows 2000 and AD that is capable of logging on to a domain. Some mail-enabled objects, such as contacts, are not considered security principals in AD, but most mailbox-enabled users and groups are.

server cluster — A pair or group of servers used for load balancing or for providing redundancy for your servers. In a server cluster, if one server goes down, another member of the cluster should automatically pick up where the other left off, allowing functionality to continue uninterrupted.

service pack — A collection of patches, hot fixes, and other preexisting service packs that can perform wholesale system patching. To save time, service packs are used instead of installing each individual hot fix or patch because often hundreds of these patches are included in a service pack.

shared-file messaging system — A system that uses a centralized location to process incoming mail for users. The centralized location is referred to as a post office, and each user has one mailbox in the post office. An example of a shared-file system is Microsoft Mail for PC Networks. The alternative to a shared-file system is a client-server architecture.

Simple Mail Transport Protocol (SMTP) — A protocol used for sending e-mail messages. It is often used with POP3 and IMAP4 because it is limited in its ability to queue messages at the receiving station. These other protocols allow users to download mail from a server. SMTP, described in RFC 821, is implemented over TCP/IP port 25. SMTP can transfer messages across low-speed connections and is used to transfer messages between servers in a routing group.

site — A logical representation of a collection of Exchange 5.5 servers that may or may not be in close proximity. All servers in a site use Remote Procedure Calls to communicate with each other.

Site Replication Service (SRS) — A component that works with the Active Directory Connector to provide interoperability with legacy Exchange sites running Exchange Server 5.5. It directly communicates with the Exchange Server 5.5 directory service using Remote Procedure Calls. SRS contains some of the same executable code that ran previous versions of the Exchange Directory Service. This helper service is activated when you install your first Exchange 2000 server in a site or when you upgrade a directory replication bridgehead server. It consists of the Srsmain.exe executable, a site consistency checker that creates replication links, and the Srs.edb database, which contains Exchange Server 5.5 directory data.

storage groups (SGs) — An Exchange 2000 feature used to organize a collection of mailbox stores, public folder stores, and transaction log files into one group. This grouping feature can ease management and offer better organizational control.

store drivers (Ntfsdrv.dll, Drviis.dll) — Ntfsdrv.dll uses the local file system to temporarily hold outgoing messages pending delivery by the protocol engine and incoming messages pending processing by the AQE. Drviis.dll is the IIS method of accessing the Information Store via ExIPC.

symmetric key — A type of encryption key used when both keys in the key pair are exactly the same.

System Attendant (SA) — The service that controls the Information Store in Exchange 2000. This component (Mad.exe, in the \Exchsrvr\Bin directory by default) is responsible for monitoring services and connectors. The SA communicates directly with Active Directory to generate e-mail addresses for new users and also updates the configuration repository for IIS known as the metabase.

system policy — An Exchange 2000 Server feature that allows administrators to apply configuration settings to a collection of server objects at the same time. There are three types of system policies: for server objects, for mailbox store objects, and for public folder store objects.

Systems Management Server (SMS) — A specialized Microsoft application that enables large-scale deployment of software and configuration over networks.

transaction log — A file on the hard disk that stores all changes made to Exchange 2000 Server database files. These files store a history of all operations performed in memory and are used in case of disaster to restore transactions that have already been committed to disk. The log files should never exceed 5 MB because this is a sure sign of corruption. Log files and database files should always remain on separate physical hard drives for optimum performance of Exchange 2000 Server.

Transmission Control Protocol/Internet Protocol (TCP/IP) — This basic communication language of the Internet is a suite of protocols broken down into two basic layers. The upper layer manages assembling packets for transmission over the Internet or a private network, and the lower layer manages the addressing of each data packet to ensure that it reaches its intended destination. TCP/IP is an example of the client-server model of communication and uses a point-to-point mechanism so that each communication between computers is from one distinct host computer to another distinct host computer. As a suite, TCP/IP contains other higher-layer protocols, such as HTTP, FTP, and SMTP.

Uniform Resource Locator (URL) — The address of a resource that is accessible over the public Internet. It contains the name of the protocol used to access the resource, a domain name specifying a unique computer on the Internet, and the path description of the file location on the computer. For example, the following is a valid example of a URL: *http://www.microsoft.com/exchange*. The protocol used is HTTP, the domain name specifying the computer name is *www.microsoft.com*, and the directory or file path for the requested files is */exchange*.

universal distribution group (UDG) — A type of group in Windows 2000 used for nonsecurity purposes, such as sending e-mail messages to a group of users simultaneously.

universal security group (USG) — A type of group created in Windows 2000 Server that's used to assign network permissions to group members. This group can be mail-enabled via an SMTP proxy address, which allows the group to function as a distribution list. Security groups are also used to assign permissions to public folders in Exchange 2000.

user connection agreement — An object you create in Exchange System Manager that's used with the ADC to replicate recipient objects and their properties between the Exchange 5.5 directory and AD. The Active Directory Connector Management console displays these CAs, showing their names and the direction of replication.

virtual protocol server — A server created and managed through the Exchange System Manager console that can allow a single Exchange 2000 server to simultaneously have many different servers, each with its own unique configuration.

Web Distributed Authoring and Versioning (DAV) Protocol — An extension to HTTP version 1.1, WebDAV is a communications-related protocol that provides an interface to the Web Storage System in Exchange 2000 Server. It allows access to all databases in Exchange 2000 Server.

Web Storage System — A file-based system that integrates the Store.exe service of Exchange 2000 Server with the protocols hosted by the IIS process (Inetinfo.exe) of Windows 2000 Server. Many features of Exchange 2000, including Outlook Web Access, are based on this new system of accessing information in the Information Store. Most items in the Web Storage System can be accessed using common URL notation.

Web Store — An Exchange service that allows users of OWA to connect to WebDAV-enabled directories configured with IIS 5 services and access these directories as any other user accesses files in the public folders.

Windows Integrated authentication (WIA) — The standard authentication method for Instant Messaging, in which authentication is based on the account name and password you use to log on to the Windows 2000 domain.

Windows Internet Naming Service (WINS) — A Windows naming service that allows for NetBIOS name translation to TCP/IP addresses. Typically, a WINS server helps cut down on TCP/IP traffic by providing name-resolution services with less broadcast traffic on the network.

Windows Sockets Application Programming Interface — The Microsoft implementation of a communication mechanism that was instituted by BSD UNIX; it is an interface for accessing underlying protocols used for network communications, such as TCP/IP. A socket is normally thought of as the endpoint in a network connection, but it can also be used for communication between processes within the same computer.

Index

Special Characters

3DES (Triple Data Encryption Standard) encryption, 512
7-bit character sets, 312
8-bit character sets, 312
16-bit clients, 293

A

AbandonRequest LDAP command, 318
Abuse of Privileges attacks, 522
access control, 509
access rights and OUs (organization units), 60
ACLs (access control lists), 56, 68
  DN (distinguished name), 318
  removing unused errors, 224
Active Desktop, 266, 293
Active Directory Connector Management snap-in, 100, 229
Active Directory Sites and Services MMC snap-in, 237
Active Directory Users and Computers console, 130, 184, 219, 236, 290, 365–366, 379
Active Messaging, 21
active messaging servers, 3–4
active server, 94, 103
Active Server Pages, 332
active-active clustering, 21
AD (Active Directory), 6–7, 17, 68, 170
  Account Cleanup Wizard (ADClean.exe), 130, 184, 231, 233
  Chat Services, 19
  configuration data, 58
  configuration events, 371
  deploying, 122–125
  domain forest, 52
  domain structures, 51, 123
  DSProxy (Directory Service Proxy) DLL service, 125
  GC (Global Catalog) servers, 7, 59, 124–125
  Installation Wizard, 217
  integration, 509
  manager, 44
  manually initiating replication, 237
  naming contexts, 61–62
  network and DNS issues, 237
  OUs (organization units), 59–60, 123
  planning and design, 50–63
  populating, 231–233
  public folder as mail-enabled user, 554–555
  public folder trees, 545
  replication, 123–124
  ReplMon (Replication Monitor), 226
  schema, 6, 58
  SMTP (Simple Mail Transport Protocol), 18
  synchronization, 123–124
  trust relationships, 56–58
  unable to modify, 236
  viewing and modifying databases, 131
ADC (Active Directory Connector), 10, 11, 103, 120, 123, 218
  basics, 228–230
  coexistence, 100, 228
  configuration connection agreement, 229
  connection agreements, 128–130, 225, 229–230
  deploying, 126–133
  domain controller, 229
  Exchange 2000 Server, 126, 229
  installing and configuring, 227
  instance of, 225
  LDAP (Lightweight Directory Access Protocol), 100, 127, 230
  low-bandwidth WAN links, 131
  member server, 229
  migration, 100
  mixed-mode environments, 126, 228–234
  populating AD (Active Directory), 231–233
  replication, 229–230, 236
  RPC (Remote Procedure Calls), 230
  SRS (Site Replication Service), 127–128
  troubleshooting, 130–131, 236
  type of server to install on, 129
  user connection agreement, 229
  Windows 2000, 229
  Windows 2000 Server, 126
ADC servers, 130
Adcadmin.ext (Active Directory Connector Management tool), 128
Add Bridgehead Server dialog box, 426
Add Request LDAP command, 318
Add/Remove Programs utility, 190, 369, 470
AddResponse LDAP command, 318
address book views, 381, 382
Address List Service, 380
address lists, 381–382
address space, 444
Address Templates folder, 360
administration, centralized, 358–361
Administrative Group container, 362
administrative groups, 17–18, 23
  adding and removing servers, 373–374
  administering routing groups, 419–420
  assigning objects to, 133
  assigning permission, 135
  centralized model, 373
  deploying, 134
  design of, 136
  Distributed model, 373
  environment, 140
  Hybrid model, 373
  integrating with routing groups, 136–137
  managing, 372–374
  mixed-mode environment, 134, 372
  native-mode environment, 134, 372
  number of, 372
  permission management, 372
  renaming, 374
  roles, 135–136
  system policies, 362
  System Policies container, 362
Administrative Groups folder, 359, 362, 374
administrator digital certificates, 515
AdminSch account, 431
AdmPack.exe (Outlook Security Features Administrative Package), 669

ADMT (Active Directory Migration Tool), 120, 231–232
advanced security features, 177
Age Folder Tombstones task, 579
AIM (AOL Instant Messenger), 464, 469
alerts, 370, 592–593
All Conferencing address list, 382
All Contacts address list, 382
All Global Address Lists folder, 360
All Groups address list, 382
All Tasks, Update Now command, 131
All Users address list, 382
anonymous access, 332
Anonymous authentication, 334
antivirus software, 181, 226–227
APPEND IMAP4 command, 316
Application event log, 592
Application log file, 583
application logs, 370–371
application service providers, 87, 103
application sharing, 485
applications
  managing, 366–368
  removing, 369
  unloading or uninstalling, 175
Appointment Items folder, 547
AQE (advanced queuing engine), 411, 444
  courier for, 413
  message categorizer component, 13
  per-destination-domain queue, 414
  pre-categorization queue, 413–414
  pre-routing queue, 414
  routing engine, 414
  viewing queues, 414–415
Archive folder, 429
ARPA (Advanced Research Projects Agency), 1
ARPANET, 1
ARTICLE 123 NNTP command, 322
assumptions, 42–43
asymmetric keys, 510–511, 526
asynchronous events, 416
auditing, 506–509
AUTHENTICATE IMAP4 command, 316
authenticated session digital certificates, 515
authentication, optimizing with shortcut trusts, 58
authentication control, 332
Authentication Methods dialog box, 332–333
auto-generated connection agreements, 230

B

back-end environments, 95–97
  OWA (Outlook Web Access), 335–337
back-end servers, 95–97, 103
  Basic authentication, 336
  deployment, 142–143
  guidelines, 143–144
  load-balancing, 337
  mailboxes and public folder information, 337
  moving mailboxes between, 144
  processing, 337
  unified OWA existence, 337
background activities, 580
background cleanup, 580
Backup Exec, 578
Backup utility, 617–618
backups, 578–579, 614
  configuration information, 619
  current state of server, 617
  daily, 615
  daily full, 621
  database information, 617–618
  effective strategy, 615–619
  Exchange 2000 files and folders, 617
  mailbox stores, 616
  offline, 618–619
  online, 618–619
  public folder stores, 616
  scheduling, 616
  selecting type of data for, 615, 616–617
  of server in current state, 179
  storing data, 615–616
  of system settings, 179
  system state information, 619
  verifying integrity, 615
  viewing logs, 615
  weekly full with differential data backup, 621
  weekly full with incremental data backup, 621
Basic authentication, 334, 336
basic EFS digital certificates, 515
BDCs (backup domain controllers), 50, 51, 68, 217
beta testing, 261, 293
BIND (Berkley Internet Name Domain), 63–64, 68, 81–82
Boot.ini file, 379
bridgehead servers, 89–92, 103
  configuration connection agreements, 128
  connectors linking multiple Exchange sites, 89
  design, 90–91
  Exchange 5.5, 230
  exchange connector issues, 91
  funneling messages through, 407
  GC (global catalog), 90
  Internet connections, 89
  Lotus Notes Connector, 428
  mail transfer between servers, 89
  replication, 89, 90
  RGCs (Routing Group Connectors), 138, 426
  SMTP Connector, 138
  transport stack, 91–92
  X.400 Connectors, 138
buddy list, 20

C

calendar, 264
CAPABILITY IMAP4 command, 316
CAs (certificate authorities), 513–515, 526
CAST (Carlisle Adams and Stafford Tavares) encryption, 512
Categorizer (PhatCat.dll), 414, 444
cc:Mail, 428
cc:Mail Connector Queue, 428
cc:Mail Connector Service, 428
CDO (Collaboration Data Objects), 21
CDONTS programming model, 415
centralized administration, 358–361
centralized management approach, 137
centralized model, 373
Certificate authentication, 334
certificate services, 513–516
channel operators, 475
channels, 20
  accessible, 478
  chat community, 477–479
  Chat services, 475
  creation of, 477–479
  dynamic, 477
  enabling transcription, 479–481
  limiting users, 478
  logging conversations, 479
  modes, 479
  naming, 477–478
  passwords, 478
  permanent, 478
  profanity filter, 479
  security, 479
  subject matter or purpose, 478

temporary, 477, 478
welcome and good-bye message, 479
Channels folder, 477
character sets, 312
Chat clients, 481–484
Chat Communities folder, 360, 477
chat community, 476–479, 489
Chat Connection window, 481
Chat services, 10–11, 19–20, 475, 481–484
AD (Active Directory), 19
attacks, 484–485
channel creation, 477–479
channel operators, 475
channels, 475
chat community, 476
client attacks, 485
clone attacks, 484
configuring, 477–484
enabling transcription for channel, 479–481
event logs, 484
flood attacks, 484
installation, 476–477
IP addresses, 476–477
IRCX, 475
sysop, 475
troubleshooting, 484–485
Choose Form dialog box, 671
Choose Profile window, 285
cipher strength, 511–512
circular logging, 582, 597
client attacks, 485
clients
16-bit, 272–273, 293
access problems after upgrade, 237
e-mail clients, 261
Eudora 5.x, 261
Microsoft Mail (Exchange Client), 272–273
Outlook 97/98, 261, 266
Outlook 98, 260
Outlook 2000, 260, 262–266, 273
Outlook 2000/2002, 261
Outlook Express, 260, 261, 267–270
Outlook for Macintosh, 261
Outlook Web Access, 261
OWA (Outlook Web Access), 270–272
Schedule+, 272–273
selecting, 273
type to use, 118
types, 260–274
client-server configurations, 118
client-server messaging systems, 2–5, 23
clone attacks, 484
CLOSE IMAP4 command, 316
cluster configurations, 93–95
clustering, 177–178
coexistence
ADC (Active Directory Connector), 100, 228
issues, 99–102
mixed-mode environment, 212, 227–228
SRS (Site Replication Service), 233–234
strategies, 127
collaboration
Chat, 464
Data and Video Conferencing, 464
future of, 488
IM (Instant Messaging), 464, 465–466
real-time, 464–465
Comdlg32.ocx file, 670
command-line switches, 278
common naming context, 62
communication stream, 12
company requirements, 80
CompareRequest LDAP command, 318
CompareResponse LDAP command, 318
Component Progress window, 183
Component Selection window, 190
components
Active Directory Connector, 11
backward-compatibility, 10
Chat service, 10–11
connectors, 11
custom installation mode, 181
directory service integration, 6–7
essential, 8–10
Exchange 2000 Conferencing Server, 10
Exchange Server 5.5, 15–17
functions of, 182–183
IM (Instant Messaging) service, 10–11
installation, 181–183
integration of essential, 5–8
interaction between, 11–12
KMS (Key Management Service), 11
message flows, 11–13
minimum installation mode, 181
MTA (Message Transfer Agent), 11
optional, 10–11
predefined, 5
SRS (Site Replication Service), 11
typical installation mode, 181
unattended installation, 192
uninstalling, 190
computer digital certificates, 515
Computer Management snap-in, 366–368, 370
conferences, 10
Conferencing folder, 360
conferencing forests, 218
Conferencing Server, 485–487
configuration CAs and SRS (Site Replication Service), 233
configuration connection agreements, 128–130, 228, 229, 239
configuration information and replication, 228
configuration naming contexts, 61, 216
connection agreements, 141, 146
ADC (Active Directory Connector), 225, 229–230
auto-generated, 230
configuration, 128–130
deploying, 128–130
endpoints, 129
low-bandwidth WAN links, 131
multiple, 131
one-way, 225
primary, 230
troubleshooting, 130–131
two-way, 225
user, 128–130
connectivity overview, 404–407
Connector and the SNADS (Systems Network Architecture Disbribution System) Connector, 16
connector costs, 433, 444
connector servers, 92–93
connectors, 11, 404, 424–425, 444
comparing, 138–139
Exchange Server 5.5, 16
fault tolerance, 138
levels of messaging traffic, 139
native, 404
proprietary, 425
routing groups, 120
standards-based, 425
troubleshooting routing problems, 440–443
value-added, 404
Connectors subcontainer, 420
Contact Items folder, 547
contacts, 264, 379, 381
containers and address lists, 382
content indexing, 382–383
COPY IMAP4 command, 316
corporate infrastructures, 40

cost of hardware, 116
counter logs, 366, 592–593
counters, 589, 597
CPU utilization notification, 583
CREATE IMAP4 command, 316
Create Items permission, 549
Create New Folder dialog box, 547
Create Subfolders permission, 550
CreateTimestamp attribute, 317
/createunattend filename.ini option, 192
CreatorsName attribute, 317
critical system services, 366
cryptography, 11
CSP (Certificate Services Policy), 516, 526
Current Sessions subcontainer, 405
current system, optimizing performance, 174–176
custom installation mode, 181
custom installations, 280
custominstall.ini file, 192, 193
customizable security, 290

D

daily backups, 615
daily full backups, 621
data
  corruption, 188
  decrypting, 511
  encrypting, 511
  loss from user error, 612
  selecting type for backups, 615, 616–617
  storing backup, 615–616
data conferencing, 20–21
data conferencing services, 20–21
data files, configuring, 377
DATA SMTP command, 312, 442
Database property page, 364
databases, 85
  backing up information, 617–618
  checking integrity of files, 578
  compacting, 580
  defragmentation, 581
  deleted database pages, 375
  integrity, 581
  log files with circular logging, 582
  maintenance, 577–582
  managing, 86, 376–379
  multiple, 377, 378
  placement, 377
  recovering space in, 580–581
  removing deleted entries, 375
  repairing, 581
DB8 (Post Office Database Version 8)-type Lotus Notes post offices, 428
Dcpromo.exe utility, 54
decrypting data, 511
dedicated
  mailbox servers, 378
  public folder hierarchies, 545
  public folder servers, 378
default
  address lists, 382
  protocols, 310
  public folder store, 98
  recipient policies, 380–381
  routing groups, 120
  SMTP virtual server, 404, 439
  storage groups, 374
  Telnet client, 442
Default SMTP Virtual Server container, 439
Default Web Site container, 368
Default-Chat-Community, 476, 477
defragmentation, 186, 581
DELE POP3 command, 314
DELETE IMAP4 command, 316
Delete Items permission, 550
deleted database pages, 375
Deleted Items folder, 288, 290
DelRequest LDAP command, 318
DelResponse LDAP command, 318
Denial of Service attacks, 522
deploying phase, 49–50, 121–122
deployment scenarios, 137
DES (Data Encryption Standard) encryption, 512
Details Templates folder, 360
developing phase
  developing test environment, 115
  requests for features, 48
  technical user testing, 47–48
  test environment, 115–116
  testing all possible scenarios, 116–117
  testing e-mail clients, 118–119
  testing routing groups, 119–120
  testing storage groups, 119
  testing third-party connectors, 117–118
  testing upgrade scenarios, 120–121
  user testing, 48, 115
  validating design, 114–115
development/engineering group, 41
DHCP (dynamic host configuration protocol) server, 66
dial-up connection and Outlook 2000, 283
Digest authentication, 334
digital certificates, 513–515, 526
digital dashboard, 265–266, 293
directories, 11
  names, 223
  replication and MS Mail, 431
  schemas, 317
  synchronization, 128
  user access to information, 124
directory replication bridgehead server, 16
directory replication events, 371
directory service integration, 6–7
Directory Service Locator, 225
directory service log, 371
directory service structure, 11
Dir.edb file, 234
DirSync Requestors, 431
DirSync Server, 431
disaster recovery plan, 612–614
Disk Defragmenter, 175, 194
disk usage, 590–591
display names, 223
distributed management approach, 137
Distributed model, 373
distribution lists and Exchange 5.5, 222–223
DIT (Directory Information Tree), 317–318, 339
DN (distinguished name), 317–318, 339
DNS (Domain Name System), 68, 171–172
  domain name and external e-mail users, 142
  domain-naming conventions, 64
  existing, 81–82
  non-windows-based, 66–67
  overview, 63
  planning and design, 63–67
  problems with configuration, 237
  records, 64–65
  reliance on, 65–66
  secure dynamic updates, 66
  zones, 64
DNS database, 63
DNS Manager snap-in utility, 144
DNS namespace, 63
DNS server log, 371
DNS servers, 63–67
DNS services, 82
documents, indexing, 368
Domain Administrators group, 179
Domain Admins account, 234
Domain Admins group, 472
domain controller digital certificates, 515

domain controllers, 51, 54–55, 123, 217–218
ADC (Active Directory Connector), 229
adding, 55
BDCs (backup domain controllers), 217
Domain Name System name, 55
managed by, 55
monitoring, 125
security policies, 226
sending schema changes to, 226
Windows 2000, 216
Windows 2000 SP1, 222
Windows NT 4.0, 215
domain forests, 52
Domain Name System names, 54
domain names
IM (Instant Messaging), 472–473
selection of, 55
domain naming context, 171–172, 216
domain structures, 123
Exchange 5.5, 221
Exchange 2000 Server, 221
preparing for upgrade, 221–227
replication, 123–124
synchronization, 123–124
upgrading, 221
Windows 2000, 221–227
domain tree, 53–54, 68
DomainPrep command, 226
DomainPrep switch, 192, 221–222, 228, 234
domains
adding domain controllers, 55
boundaries, 51
current configuration, 54
data and naming contexts, 61
domain controller, 51, 54–55
limiting number of, 122
migrating, 52
mixed-mode, 51, 223
naming context, 228
native-mode, 51, 222–223
optimal design, 62–63
preparing for upgrade, 226
RUS (Recipient Update Service), 133
security, 176
structure, 51
transition, 223
trust relationships, 56–58, 176
Windows NT 4.0, 215
Drviis.dll store driver, 12, 13, 413–414
DS (Directory Service), 15
DS/IS Consistency Adjuster, 224
DSN (Delivery Status Notification), 437–438, 444
DSN (delay) message, 437
DSProxy (Directory Service Proxy), 7, 23, 125
dual-node active clustering, 94
DVD-RW, 626
dynamic channels, 477

E

.edb file, 374
Edit Items permission, 550
EDK (Exchange Development Kit), 404, 444
EFS (Encrypting File System), 510, 526
EFS recovery agent digital certificates, 515
e-mail
access over Internet, 142
company guidelines on inappropriate usage, 81
company requirements, 80
delay notifications, 405
global list of unwanted senders, 406
groups, 366
message filtering, 406–407
nondelivery reports, 405
notifications of errors, 583–585
optional information, 310
Outlook Express, 268
required information, 310
searching common fields, 383
sensitive, 506
spam, 506
types of messages or attachments searched for, 383–384
uptime, 93
users, 366
e-mail clients
MAPI (Messaging Application Programming Interface), 262
Outlook 2000, 262–266
Outlook Express, 267–270
POP3 or IMAP4 support, 261
searching for object, 125
testing, 118–119
UNIX/Linux operating systems, 261
e-mail servers, 93
e-mail service connectors, 93
emergency repair disk, 179
encryption
3DES (Triple Data Encryption Standard), 512
CAST (Carlisle Adams and Stafford Tavares), 512
data, 511
DES (Data Encryption Standard), 512
front-end/back-end design, 142–143
MD4 and MD5, 512
operation of, 511–512
public/private keys and, 510–513
RC2 (Rivest's Cipher), 512
RC4, 512
RSA, 513
security, 336
SHA (Secure Hash Algorithm), 513
standards, 512–513
encryption strength, 511–512, 526
End-User License Agreement window, 181
Enterprise Administrators group, 61, 179
Enterprise Admins account, 234
environment, 140
envisioning phase, 41–43, 78
error codes, 188–189
error message box, 187
error messages when editing text, 333
ESE (Extensible Storage Engine), 19, 376, 412–413, 413, 444, 516
ESEUTIL utility, 578, 580–581, 624–625
ESMTP (Extended SMTP commands), 313
Eudora 5.x, 261
event handling, 415–416
event IDs, 188–189
event logging, 474
event logs, 188–190, 370–371
Chat services, 484
checking after installation, 185
Event Properties dialog box, 189
event sinks, 415–416, 444
EventViewer, 188–189, 366, 370–371, 583
events, 370–371
Exadmin folder, 326
EXAMINE IMAP4 command, 316
Exchange 5.5 servers
antivirus software, 226–227
maintenance mode, 236
user information, 126
Exchange 2000 Conferencing Server, 10, 20–21, 485–488
Exchange 2000 folder, 183
Exchange 2000 mailbox folder (Mbx), 326
Exchange 2000 Server, 182
AD (Active Directory), 17
ADC (Active Directory Connector), 126, 229

administrative groups, 17–18
architecture, 85–89
attempting to restart server, 236
auditing, 506–509
back-end configuration, 95–97
backward-compatibility, 92
bridgehead servers, 89–92
Chat feature, 464
Chat Services, 19–20, 192
cluster configurations, 93–95
coexistence with Exchange Server 5.5, 126
company requirements, 80
comparing Exchange Server 5.5 to, 14–17
complexity, 5
components, 5, 85–89
configuring, 646–647
connector servers, 92–93
controlling access to, 509–510
current network infrastructure requirements, 81–85
data conferencing services, 20–21
database maintenance, 578–580
dedicated multiple servers, 116
developing and deploying project plan, 114–122
digital dashboard starter kit, 266
display names, 223
domain structure, 221
enhanced status codes, 442
essential components, 8–10
forests, 52–53
front-end configuration, 95–97
IM (Instant Messaging) services, 20
indexing process, 383–384
Information Store, 85–87
installation, 645–646
installation of first, 179–184
integration of essential components, 5–8
logging, 506–509
mailbox servers, 97–98
mailbox stores, 87–88
management tools, 236
managing growth, 649
messaging model, 5–13
migration, 211–218
minimum configuration, 116
minimum hardware configuration, 116
mixed-mode environment, 213–214
multiple-forest infrastructure, 52–53
naming contexts, 61–62
native-mode environment, 213–214
new features, 17–21
optional components, 10–11
Organization, 185, 226
OUs (organizational units), 60
permission assignments, 226
physical memory, 384
potential attacks against, 521–523
public folder servers, 98–99
real-time collaboration services, 19
requirements, 79–85
resources, 372–379
restarting services that do not exist, 235
routing groups, 18
security bulletins, 523–524
server roles, 221
service packs, 174
setting retention time for deleted items, 289
Setup program, 221
SGs (storage groups), 88–89
site design, 89–99
SMTP (Simple Mail Transport Protocol), 18, 313
SMTP and X.400 addresses, 380
storage groups, 19
system component events, 371
tools for server management, 358–365
troubleshooting routing problems, 439
uninstalling, 190–191
upgrading, 645–646
upgrading Exchange 5.5 Server to, 219–227
user requirements, 79
WANs (wide area networks), 82–85
Windows 2000 management tools, 365–372
Windows NT 4.0, 213
Exchange 2000 Server CD key, 181
Exchange 2000 Server CD-ROM defects, 188
Exchange 2000 Server installation CD-ROM, 180
Exchange 2000 Server Resource Kit, 471
Exchange 2000 Server Setup Troubleshooter Web site, 190
Exchange 2000 servers
acting as many different servers, 308
remotely managing, 358
sensitive e-mail, 506
subsequent installation of, 184–185
Exchange 2000 Setup program, 127–128
ForestPrep option, 225–226
/unattendfile filename.ini option, 193
Exchange 2000 System Manager program, 141
Exchange 2000 Transport Architecture, 410–416, 439, 444
Exchange Administration Delegation of Control Wizard, 135, 136
Exchange Administration Delegation Wizard, 372
Exchange Administrator account, 178, 179
Exchange Administrator program, 141, 224
Exchange Administrator role, 135–136
Exchange Admins group, 472
Exchange Advanced Configuration tab, 286
Exchange Chat Service, 183
Exchange Domain Servers global security group, 226
Exchange enrollment agent digital certificates, 515
Exchange Enterprise Servers group, 226
Exchange folder, 326
Exchange Full Administrator role, 135–136
Exchange Organization, 183
Exchange Organization Selection window, 183, 185
Exchange Properties dialog box, 330–333
Exchange Server 5.5, 14
address book views, 382
basic components, 15–17
bridgehead server, 230
CDO (Collaboration Data Objects), 21
Chat Services, 19, 20
connectors, 16
consolidating organizations, 218
directory replication bridgehead server, 16
Directory Service, 17
distribution lists, 222–223
domain structure, 221
DS (Directory Service), 15
ESE (Extensible Storage Engine) component, 19
Exchange Administrator program, 127, 141
GAL (global address list), 15
IM (Instant Messaging), 471
independent directory database, 16
Information Store, 15
installed on domain controller, 223
Internet Mail Connector, 117
LDAP port number, 223, 235
mailboxes, 221
member servers, 215
Move Server Wizard, 218

MTA (Message Transfer Agent), 15, 410
Organization, 226
PROFS (Professional Office System) Connector, 117–118
replication, 124
SA (System Attendant), 15
separate addressing rules for each site, 380
server location, 16
server roles, 221
Service Pack 3, 220–221
Service Pack 4, 221
Site Connector, 117
SMTP and X.400 addresses, 380
transaction log files, 16
unique SMTP addresses, 16
upgrading to Exchange 2000 Server, 219–227
Exchange Server Administrator program, 235
Exchange Server clients
IP addresses, 368
operating system integration, 7
Exchange Server Setup Progress.log file, 189
Exchange Service account, 178
Exchange signature only digital certificates, 515
Exchange System Manager MMC (Microsoft Management Console), 13, 135, 212, 309
Exchange user digital certificates, 515
Exchange View Only Administrator role, 135–136
Exchange-to-GroupWise queues, 429
Exchmem.dll file, 235
Exchweb folder, 326
executive advisory member, 41
ExIPC (Exchange Interprocess Communication), 13, 411
ExIPC (Exchange Interprocess Communication) layer, 8, 12, 23
ExIPC.dll file, 13
EXPN SMTP command, 312
EXPUNGE IMAP4 command, 316
Extensions dialog box, 480

F

failed installations, troubleshooting, 187–191
fault tolerance, 55, 66–67, 130–131
connectors, 138
RAID (redundant array of independent disks), 88
RAID 1, 377
RAID 5, 377
SGs (storage groups), 88
features, 43
FETCH IMAP4 command, 316
File Replication Service, 371
files, troubleshooting, 366
firewalls, 519–520
IM (Instant Messaging), 467, 473
OWA servers, 335
First Administrative Group, 133, 134, 373
First Routing Group, 120, 420
First Storage Group, 374
Floodgate-1
Folder Contact permission, 550
Folder Owner permission, 550
Folder Visible permission, 550
Folders folder, 360
ForestPrep, 192, 227
installation, 183
before reinstalling Exchange 2000 Server, 191
ForestPrep switch, 58, 221–222, 225–226, 234
forests, 68
conferencing, 218
directory replication events, 371
Exchange 2000 Server, 52–53
first domain configured for, 55
instant messaging, 218
Internet interaction, 55
multiple Windows 2000, 218
name of, 55
preparing for upgrade, 221–227
public folders in other, 218
security principal, 218
synchronizing information between, 218
Windows 2000, 221–227, 225–226
formally assigning control, 121–122
front-end environments, 95–97, 335–337
front-end servers, 95–97, 103
additional level of security, 337
authentication for users, 337
Basic authentication, 336
behind firewall, 144
common namespace, 97
configured inside firewall, 143
deployment, 142–143
guidelines, 143–144
Information Store, 144
load-balancing connections, 143
ports, 144
redundancy, 96–97
referring external clients to proper public folder locations, 143
separate DNS entries for, 144
full-mesh topology, 421, 422
full-text indexing, 119, 146
best practice recommendations, 384–385
catalog, 384
gather files, 385
high priority, 384
low priority, 384
managing, 382–385
Maximum priority, 384
minimum priority, 384
monitoring, 385
populating with data, 385
property store, 384–385
resource intensive, 383
scheduled basis, 383
temporary files, 385
Full-Text Indexing property page, 364
functional specification, 43
functional specification design, 44–45

G

GAL (global address list), 15, 52, 68, 128, 382
gateway connectors, 117, 146
Gateway Services for NetWare, 428, 429
gateway virus protection, 416
gather files, 384, 385
GC (Global Catalogs), 23
bridgehead servers, 90
role in upgrading, 216–217
GC (Global Catalog) servers, 7, 59, 82, 124–125, 216–217
MAPI-based clients, 118
monitoring, 125
referred to, 118
Windows 2000 SP1, 222
General property page, 364
global list of unwanted senders, 406
Global Settings folder, 358, 359
Global Settings root container, 406
GPs (group policies), 59–60
graphics, 326
GROUP A.B NNTP command, 322
grouping mailbox stores, 97
groups
e-mail, 366
mailbox-enabled, 379
mail-enabled, 379

matching particular criteria, 381
permissions, 234
GroupWise Connector and advanced troubleshooting steps, 443
.gthr extension, 384

H

H.323 protocol suite, 20–21
hacker intrusion or attack, 612
hackers, 506
hard drives
adequate space for upgrade, 224–225
defragmenting, 186
Disk Defragmenter, 175
free disk space notification, 583
maintaining and monitoring configurations, 384
for operating system, 175
RAID 5 hard drive array, 175
Windows pagefile, 175
hardware
cost, 116
failure, 613
minimum requirements, 173–174
testing, 115–116
unreliable, 188
upgrade method, 219
hardware RAID implementation, 377
Hashctl.dll file, 670
HCL (Hardware Compatibility List), 116, 215
HELO SMTP command, 312, 442
HELP NNTP command, 322
HELP SMTP command, 312
helper service, 127
home servers, 470
HTTP (Hypertext Transfer Protocol), 20
HTTP virtual servers, configuring, 368
HTTP (Hypertext Transfer Protocol) with WebDAV (Web Distributed Authoring and Versioning), 310, 319, 339
hub-and-spoke topology, 421
hub-ring hybrid topology, 422
hybrid hub-and-spoke topology, 422
Hybrid model, 373

I

IBM OfficeVision/VM (PROFS), 432–433
ICQ, 464, 468–470
IFS (Installable File System), 99, 103
IFS (Installable File System) driver, 313
IHAVE NNTP command, 322
IIS (Internet Information Server), 7–8, 24, 411
application environment, 323
authentication methods, 334–335
configuring OWA, 330
ExIPC (Exchange Interprocess Communication) layer, 324
improvements, 323
main window, 325–326
management, 323
reliability and performance, 323
Reliable Restart, 323
security, 323
version 5, 177, 322–323
Web site, 325
Web Storage System, 323–324
IIS servers, 325–326
IM (Instant Messaging), 10–11, 20, 183, 192, 464, 465–466, 489
address list, 467
addressing and naming, 471–472
AIM (AOL Instant Messenger), 469
benefits, 466
client software, 472
commands, 468
comparing Microsoft and third-party products, 468–470
configuring, 472–473
dedicated administrative group, 471
digest authentication, 515–516
domain names, 472–473
Exchange 5.5, 471
firewalls, 467, 473
forests, 218
high usage, 467–468
home servers, 467, 470, 472
HTTP (Hypertext Transfer Protocol), 20
ICQ, 468–469, 470
installation, 470–471
lack of encryption, 469
management of users, 470
managing, 472–473
minimal impact on network resources, 467
MSN Messenger, 469
passwords, 474
presence information, 20
protocols, 466–468
proxies, 467
proxy servers, 473
routers, 470
RVP (rendezvous protocol), 515
_rvp SRV resource record, 473
servers using, 470–471
service configuration, 470
slow network connections, 471
troubleshooting, 473–474
watcher, 467
Yahoo! Messenger, 469
IM servers, 473–474
IM virtual server and replication, 474
IMAILMSG object, 12
IMAP (Internet Messaging Access Protocol), 98
IMAP 4 servers, 315
IMAP4 (Internet Messaging Access Protocol Version 4), 7, 24, 118, 310, 314–317
commands and functions, 316
IMS (Internet Mail Service), 10, 103
InBound protocol events, 416
Index Aging task, 579
Inetinfo.exe file, 8–9, 12
information
gathering, 44, 45
holding point for, 323–324
Information Store, 8, 12, 15, 23, 85–87, 103, 186, 411
components for storing and retrieving messages, 412
databases, 16
front-end servers, 144
limiting number of people with permission to log, 377–378
mailbox store, 8
managing, 376
multiple, 378
planning and maintenance, 86
public folder store, 8
recovering database space, 580–581
SA (System Attendant), 9
SGs (storage groups), 8
single-instance storage design, 86
size and draining resources, 86
storage groups, 86, 87
transaction logging, 86
virtual address space, 378–379
WSS (Web Storage System), 411
Information Store driver, 12
Information Store Maintenance Schedule, 579
.ini files, 193, 279
in-place upgrade, 101, 120, 219–220, 222–227
installation
antivirus software, 181

Auto Run, 180
Chat services, 476–477
from command prompt, 192
command-line switches, 278
components, 181–183
custom, 280
custom mode, 181
Exchange 2000 Conferencing Server, 486–488
Exchange 2000 Organization, 183, 185
Exchange 2000 Server, 645–646
Exchange 2000 Server CD key, 181
first Exchange 2000 server, 179–184
ForestPrep, 183
gathering information for, 173
IM (Instant Messaging), 470–471
KMS (Key Management Services), 518
license agreement, 181
minimum mode, 181
Outlook 2000, 274–280
OWA (Outlook Web Access), 325–330
progress of, 183
restarting computer after, 185
service packs status after, 186
service status after, 186
shutting down unnecessary software, 181
special accounts required for, 178–179
starting, 180–184
subsequent Exchange 2000 servers, 184–185
troubleshooting failed, 187–191
typical mode, 181
unattended, 192–193
Windows 2000 server, 180
Windows 2000 support tools, 225
Installation Wizard, 180–183
instances, 589, 597
Instant Messaging folder, 359
Integrated Windows (Kerberos) authentication, 335
integration of Windows 2000, 170–172
Internet
connection to, 172
security issues, 520–521
Internet browsers, 118–119
Internet clients and front-end/back-end design, 143
Internet Email Properties dialog box, 283
Internet Explorer, 118–119
Internet Mail Connector, 117
Internet Message Formats folder, 359
Internet message stream format, 374
Internet protocols, 308
HTTP (Hypertext Transfer Protocol) with WebDAV (Web Distributed Authoring and Versioning) extensions, 319
IMAP4 (Internet Messaging Access Protocol Version 4), 314–317
LDAP (Lightweight Directory Access Protocol), 317–319
NNTP (Network News Transport Protocol), 320–322
POP3 (Post Office Protocol version 3), 313–314
security, 139
SMTP (Simple Mail Transport Protocol), 309–313
Interprocess Communication facility, 411
intrinsic full-mesh routing topology, 407
IP addresses
Chat services, 476–477
Exchange clients, 368
resolving readable names, 63
virtual servers, 309
IPC (Interprocess Communication) path, 12
IPSec (IP Security), 510, 526
IPSEC digital certificates, 515
IRC (Internet Relay Chat), 19–20, 24, 475, 489
IRC channels, 477
IRC clients, 481
IRCX, 20, 475
IRCX channels, 477
IRCX Properties dialog box, 476
IRCX server, 480, 484
ISINTEG (Information Store Integrity Checker), 594–595

J

JET database engine, 580
Journal Items folder, 547
journals, 264

K

KCC (Knowledge Consistency Checker), 223–224
Kerberos version 5 authentication, 65, 68, 119, 146, 336, 509
KMS (Key Management Service), 11, 177, 183, 194, 510, 516–518
Knowledge Base, 190, 237

L

LDAP (Lightweight Directory Access Protocol), 12, 24, 65, 68, 125, 317–319
ADC (Active Directory Connector), 100, 127, 230
commands, 318
DIT (Directory Information Tree), 317–318
DN (distinguished name), 317–318
Outlook Express, 270
port number, 230
LDAP Synchronization Utility, 53
LDAP Viewer (LDP.exe), 131, 236
leapfrog upgrade, 101, 219–220
legacy
Exchange 5.5 Connectors, 432–433
messaging systems, 11
license agreement, 181
Limits property page, 364
linear (or ring) topology, 421
link monitors, 227
link state
information, 139
managing information, 433–436
routing groups, 139
link state table, 433–434
Linux and OWA (Outlook Web Access), 272
LIST IMAP4 command, 316
LIST NNTP command, 322
LIST POP3 command, 314
list servers, 320, 339
load-balancing, 131
back-end servers, 337
cluster, 94–95
Local Administrator account, 234
local computers, managing, 366–368
local Path directory rights, 331–332
log files
with circular logging, 582
reusing for new transactions, 376
viewing, 366
logging, 506–509
LOGIN IMAP4 command, 316
logistics manager, 42
LOGOUT IMAP4 command, 316
Lotus cc:Mail Import and Export programs, 428
Lotus Notes Connector and bridgehead servers, 428
Lotus Notes organization, linking to, 428
LSUB IMAP4 command, 316

M

Macintosh
  operating systems, 261
  users, 178
MAIL FROM SMTP command, 442
Mail Items folder, 547
MAIL SMTP command, 312
Mailbox Manager, 683
mailbox object, 366
mailbox servers, 97–98
mailbox store policies, 362, 364
mailbox stores, 8, 24, 86, 87–88, 103, 368
  backups, 616
  boundary limits, 374–376
  conflicting policies, 364
  default size limit, 87
  grouping, 97
  independently stopping and starting, 87
  multiple, 87
  special-needs, 87
  storage limits, 364
mailboxes
  associated with only one user account, 130
  available to non-e-mail client software, 99
  configuring delivery restrictions, 380
  Exchange 5.5, 221
  IFS (Installable File System), 99
  index of all text, 383
  managing, 365–366, 379
  moving, 380
  multiple users permissions, 286
  restoring, 623
  single-instance message storage, 219
  supported by OWA server, 331–332
mail-enabling public folders, 554–555
maintenance
  background activities, 580
  background cleanup, 580
  backups, 578–579
  concepts, 576–577
  database compacting, 580
  database integrity, 581
  databases, 577–582
  defragmentation, 581
  Exchange 2000 databases, 578–580
  Information Store Maintenance Schedule, 579
  preventative, 576–577
  reactive, 576
  repairing databases, 581
  setting cycles, 364
  stores, 578–580
Man in the Middle attacks, 522
Manipulation attacks, 522
MAPI (Messaging Application Programming Interface), 24, 98, 262, 293, 374
MAPI clients, 8
  DSProxy (Directory Service Proxy), 125
  front-end/back-end design, 143
  GC (Global Catalog) server, 118
Masquerading attacks, 522
master index, 383
master project plan, 43
Mbx folder, 99
MCSE Certification Exam #70-224, 645–650
MD4 and MD5 encryption, 512
MDBOnShutDown event, 416
MDBOnStartUp event, 416
MDI (multiple-document interface) applications, 365
meetings, 10
member servers, 214, 239
  ADC (Active Directory Connector), 229
  BDCs (backup domain controllers), 217
  demoting servers to, 217
  Exchange Server 5.5, 215
Members subcontainer, 420
memory usage, 589–590
Memory\Available Bytes counter, 590
Memory\Pages/sec counter, 590
Message Delivery folder, 359
Message Expiration task, 579
message flows, 11–13
message header, 310–311, 339
message queues, monitoring, 587–588
message routing, 413–415
  concepts, 407
  routing groups, 409–410
  technical overview, 407–410
message stores, 376–376, 383
Message Tracing Center folder, 361
message tracking, 585–587
Message Tracking Center, 440, 441, 444, 586
message transport services, 170–171
messages, 2, 24
  filtering, 406–407
  guaranteeing delivery, 12
  managing growth of traffic, 376–376
  message transport or storage, 413
  retrieval, 412–413
  routing, 410–416
  storing, 410–416
  transaction logging, 413
messaging
  future of, 21–22
  managing growth, 377–378
Messaging and Collaboration Services, 181, 182, 192
messaging connectivity
  DSN (Delivery Status Notification), 437–438
  managing, 648–649
  monitoring, 648–649
  NDR (Non-Delivery Report), 437–438
  resolving routing problems, 439–443
  troubleshooting, 437–443
messaging servers, 24
  active, 3–4
  passive, 3–4
  types, 2–5
messaging services, connecting to external, 11
messaging systems
  behavior, 2–5
  client-server, 2–5, 23
  components, 2
  connecting to, 11
  legacy, 11
  routing mechanism, 18
  shared-file, 2–5, 24
  transport protocol, 18
MEx2GW folder, 429
MEx2GWa folder, 429
Microsoft Certificate Services, 510
Microsoft Chat, 481
Microsoft Chat client, 464
Microsoft Exchange Connector for Lotus cc:Mail, 182
Microsoft Exchange Connector for Lotus Notes, 182
Microsoft Exchange Connector for Novell GroupWise, 182, 429
Microsoft Exchange Web site, 174
Microsoft Mail, 4
Microsoft Mail (Exchange Client), 272–273
Microsoft Mail for AppleTalk Networks, 178
Microsoft Outlook Setup Wizard, 285
Microsoft Project, 47

Microsoft tech support phone line, 188
Microsoft Web site, 19, 125, 188, 221
migration
  ADC (Active Directory Connector), 100
  domains, 52
  Exchange 2000 Server, 211–218
  goal of, 220
  in-place upgrade, 101
  issues, 99–102, 140–141
  leapfrog upgrade, 101
  mailbox transition, 100–101
  maintaining existing users, 100–102
  mixed-mode operation, 102
  move mailbox upgrade, 101
  strategies, 127
  troubleshooting, 234–237
  versus upgrading, 212
  users, 121
  Windows 2000 Server, 211–218
Migration Wizard, 184
minimum installation mode, 181
mixed-mode domains, 223
mixed-mode environment, 17–18, 24, 140
  ADC (Active Directory Connector), 126, 228–234
  administrative groups, 134, 372
  coexistence, 212, 227–228
  deployment guidelines, 140
  Exchange 2000 Server, 213–214
  managing resources, 141–142
  migration, 102
  public folders, 141
MMC (Microsoft Management Console) snap-in, 365
MODE READER NNTP command, 322
modifiersName attribute, 317
ModifyDNRequest LDAP command, 318
ModifyDNResponse LDAP command, 318
ModifyRequest LDAP command, 318
ModifyResponse LDAP command, 318
modifyTimestamp attribute, 317
modules, predefined, 5
monitoring, 371–372
Monitoring and Status folder, 361
MouseDown (left) event, 415
MouseDown (right) event, 415
move mailbox upgrade, 101, 219–220
MS Mail, 430–431
MS Mail Connector, 430–432
MS Mail Connector Interchange, 431
MS Mail Connector MTAs, 431
MS Mail Connector post office, 431
MSExchangeGWRtr (Microsoft Exchange Router for Novell GroupWise), 429
MSExchangeIS performance object, 370
MSExchangeIS Public performance object, 556
MsExchReplicateNow attribute, 129
MSF (Microsoft Solutions Framework), 40, 68
  deploying phase, 49–50, 121
  developing phase, 47–48, 114–121
  envisioning phase, 41–43, 78
  flexibility, 78
  phases, 40–50
  planning phase, 43–47, 78
MSMail Connector, 182
MSN Messenger, 469, 680–682
MTA (Message Transfer Agent), 11, 15, 138, 410, 444, 552, 594
MTACheck (Message Transfer Agent Check), 223–224, 594
MTS_OUT queue, 429
multi-master replication, 123, 146
multiple-domain AD model, 58
MX (Mail Exchange) records, 311

N

name resolution services, 125
naming contexts, 61–62, 68
  domains, 228
  role in upgrading, 216
native connectors, 404
native MAPI Store, 412
native-mode environment, 18, 24, 227
  administrative groups, 134, 372
  domains, 222–223
  Exchange 2000 Server, 213–214
  Windows 2000, 213–214
NDR (Non-Delivery Report), 437–438, 445
NDR message, 440
nesting OUs (organizational units), 59
NetBackup, 578
NetBIOS name, 176, 194
NetMeeting, 485
network diagrams, 81
Network Load Balancing service, 143
Network Monitor, 593
Network Segment\%Network Utilization counter, 591
networks
  current infractructure requirements, 81–85
  design of, 81
  existing DNS (Domain Name System), 81–82
  fault tolerance, 55
  performance, 83
  problems preventing Exchange 2000 Server installation, 234
  problems with configuration, 237
  redundancy, 83
  shared information, 366
  statistics, 593
  usage, 591–592, 593
New Instant Messaging Virtual Server Wizard, 472
New Policy dialog box, 362
New Properties dialog box, 477
newsgroup servers, 320–322
newsgroups, 267, 269–270, 320–321
Nltest, 225
NNTP (Network News Transport Protocol), 7, 24, 171
  commands, 321, 322
  commands and functions, 322
  IIS version 5.0, 177
  Outlook Express, 270
  response codes, 321
  starting before installation, 177
  storing posts and information on central server, 320
  verifying installation, 226
non-transitive trust, 56–57
non-windows-based DNS systems, 66–67
NOOP IMAP4 command, 316
NOOP POP3 command, 314
NOOP SMTP command, 312
Note Items folder, 547
notes, 264
Notes Mail Router database, 428
Notes router mailbox, 428
Notes.ini configuration file, 428
notifications of errors, 583–585
Notify IM command, 468
Novell Group Wise servers, 429
Novell GroupWise Connector, 429–430
nslookup utility, 64
NT 4.0
  domain and trust relationship, 141
  domain structure, 50–51
Ntds.dit file, 6
Ntfsdrv.dll store driver, 12, 13, 413–414

O

ObjectClass attribute, 317
objects
  directory names, 223
  display names, 223
  managing permissions, 134
  mandatory attributes, 317
  performance counters, 370
  read-only permissions, 236
  replication, 225–226
Office 2000, 275
Office 2000 Resource Kit Web site, 280
Office Custom Installation Wizard, 280
Offline Address Lists folder, 360
offline backups, 618–619, 623–624, 627
Offline Folder File Settings dialog box, 282
Offline Folder Settings command, 281
Offline Folder Settings dialog box, 282
OLE (object linking and embedding) messaging, 21
OnDelete event, 416
one-way connection agreements, 225
one-way replication, 126, 129
one-way trust relationships, 56
online backups, 618–619, 627
  before upgrading, 224–225
  restoring, 623–624
  temporary files, 375
online/electronic materials, 651–655
OnMessagePostCategorize event, 416
OnMessageSubmission event, 416
OnSave event, 416
OnSyncDelete event, 416
OnSyncSave event, 416
OnTime event, 416
operating system
  failure, 613
  service packs causing problems, 187
optimal domain design, 62–63
optimization, 576–577
Options dialog box, 285
Organization container, 420
Organization object
  assigning permission, 135
  msExchMixedMode attribute, 141
OrganizationName (Local delivery) queue, 414
organizations, 14, 24
  consolidating Exchange 5.5, 218
  duplicate accounts, 233
  Exchange 5.5, 226
  Exchange 2000, 226
  lack of status updates, 52
  valid display names, 223
OUs (organizational units), 59–60, 123
OutBound protocol events, 416
Outlook, 263
Outlook 97/98, 261, 266
Outlook 98, 260, 266
Outlook 2000, 260, 273
  account information for users, 277
  activity tracking for contacts, 264
  Advanced Find feature, 383
  appearance, 281
  calendar, 264
  command-line switches, 278
  component installation, 275
  configured as Internet e-mail only client, 283
  configuring, 280–284
  configuring messaging profiles, 284–287
  contacts, 264
  Corporate or Workgroup mode, 276, 277
  correct user name and server information, 277
  Deleted Items folder, 288
  dial-up connection, 283
  e-mail clients, 262–266
  e-mail configuration options, 276
  forcing to request profile, 287
  functioning offline, 283
  hard drive space, 274
  important features added, 264–265
  installation, 274–280
  installation program, 274
  Internet Only mode, 276, 277
  journals, 264
  Mail configuration menu, 281
  Mail Merge, 265
  managing public folders, 546
  minimum requirements, 274
  No E-mail mode, 276
  notes, 264
  Office Custom Installation Wizard, 280
  offline, 281
  offline folders, 281–282
  operation of, 281
  Options menu, 281
  Outbox, 281
  Outlook Startup Wizard, 276
  Outlook Today, 265
  permissions-related issues, 290
  problems synchronizing data, 290–291
  profile selection dialog box, 284
  profile setup dialog box, 285
  protocols and services support, 265
  public folders, 290
  recovering deleted items, 288–289
  remote access, 283
  setup information file, 279
  shortcuts, 265
  simple-step publishing of calendar to Web page, 264
  synchronization error log file, 290
  synchronized folders, 281–282
  tasks, 264
  time-saving features, 278–280
  troubleshooting, 288–291
  user profiles, 284–287
  VPN (virutal private network), 283
  Windows Installer application, 275–276
Outlook 2000 installation CD-ROM, 274
Outlook 2000/2002, 261
Outlook 2002, 263
  administered environment, 668
  attachment files, 666–668
  calendar enhancements, 675–680
  COM add-ins, 674
  Comdlg32.ocx file, 670
  core components, 263
  defining security settings, 670–674
  full-text indexing and searching, 686
  Hashctl.dll file, 670
  installing and registering security components, 670
  managing mailboxes, 684
  OutlookSecurity.oft file, 669, 670
  public folder for security settings, 670
  Readme.doc file, 669
  refining attachment handling, 672
  remote access improvements, 684–685
  resources, 655–656
  security, 666–674
  security settings for custom forms, 672
  standalone environment, 668
  synchronization performance improvements, 685–686
  user interface, 263
  virus protection, 666–674
  workflow enhancements, 682–683
Outlook clients and native MAPI Store, 412
Outlook Express, 260, 261, 321
  contact and directory services, 270
  custom e-mail rules, 268
  e-mail, 268
  e-mail clients, 267–270
  information not available to, 270

interface, 267
introductory start screen, 267
LDAP (Lightweight Directory Access Protocol), 270
limited access to public folder content, 270
multiple profiles, 268
newsgroup reader, 269
newsgroups, 267, 269–270
NNTP (Network News Transport Protocol), 270
protocols, 268
Outlook Express 6, 687
Outlook for Macintosh, 261
Outlook Security Form template, 671
Outlook Security Settings public folder, 670
Outlook Startup Wizard, 276
Outlook Today, 265–266
OutlookSecurity.oft file, 669–670
OWA (Outlook Web Access), 81–82, 95, 103–104, 142, 172, 261, 324–325
anonymous access, 332
authentication control, 332
back-end environments, 335–337
Calendar view, 327–328
configuration options, 329
Contacts view, 328
domain name restrictions, 333
features, 325
Folders view, 328–329
front-end environments, 335–337
IIS version 5.0, 177
installation, 325–330
IP address restrictions, 333
limitations in connectivity with Exchange 2000, 271–272
Linux, 272
logging on and validating accounts, 271
main screen, 327
non-Windows operating systems, 324
Options window, 329
public folders, 557–558
remote users, 272
secure communications, 333
security, 334–335
testing functionality, 327
Web site, 325
WebDAV (Web Distributed Authoring and Versioning), 319
OWA clients, 118–119
OWA servers, 95
configuring, 330–334
firewalls, 335
mailboxes supported by, 331–332
multiple, 330

P

Paging File (_Total)\% Usage counter, 590
partial-mesh topology, 422
partitions
defragmenting, 186
Disk Defragmenter, 175
PASS POP3 command, 314
passive servers, 3–4, 94, 104
passwords
channels, 478
IM (Instant Messaging), 474
patches, 174
PDCs (primary domain controllers), 50, 51, 68, 216
per-address-space queues, 415
per-destination-domain queue, 414
Performance Console
Performance Logs and Alerts, 588
System Monitor, 588, 589–592
Performance console, 370, 385
performance counters
monitoring, 370
public folders, 556
performance data, real-time, 370
Performance Logs and Alerts, 588, 592–593
Performance utility, 370
permanent channels, 478
permissions
conflicting, 135–136
groups, 234
incorrect, 235
managing, 133, 372
multiple users, 286
problems with, 135–136
users, 234
personnel, 614
Phatcat.dll, 12, 13
PhysicalDisk\Avg. Disk Bytes/Sec counter, 591
PhysicalDisk\Avg. Disk Queue Length counter, 590
PhysicalDisk\Avg. Disk Sec/Transfer counter, 590
PhysicalDisk\Disk Transfers/Sec counter, 591
PKI (Public Key Infrastructure), 510–513
planning phase, 78
functional specification, 43
master project plan, 43
project plan generation, 46
project schedule, 43, 46–47
proof of concept testing, 45
resource identification, 46
POP3 (Post Office Protocol version 3), 7, 24, 118, 310, 313–314
ports and front-end servers, 144
POST NNTP command, 322
postinstallation steps, 185–187
pre-categorization queue, 413–414, 414, 445
predefined components, 5
predefined modules, 5
pre-destination queues, 415
preinstallation steps, 172–173
backup of system settings, 179
final tasks, 226–227
gathering information for installation, 173
patches, 174
security hot fixes, 174
service packs, 174
special accounts required for installation, 178–179
verifying hardware meets requirements, 173–174
verifying system protocols and services availability, 176–177
pre-routing queue, 414, 445
preventative maintenance, 576–577
primary connection agreements, 230
private keys, 510–513
private SMTP virtual servers, 405
private stores, 412, 594–595
Priv.edb database, 16
procedures for unattended installation, 192
processor usage, 590
Processor\% Processor Time counter, 590
profile setup dialog box, 285
PROFS (Professional Office System) Connector, 16, 117–118
program manager, 41
project manager, 41
project team
assumptions, 43
development/engineering group, 41
executive advisory member, 41
functional specification design, 44–45

information gathering, 44, 45
logistics manager, 42
organization, 41–42
planning phase, 44
program manager, 41
project manager, 41
realistic goals for functionality, 45
testing, 47
testing/quality assurance manager, 42
user requirements, 79
user training team, 42
validating design, 47
projects
company requirements, 80
completion and evaluation, 49–50
conceptual design layout, 43
deploying phase, 49–50, 121
developing and deploying plan, 114–122
developing phase, 47–48, 114–121
developing test environment, 115
envisioning phase, 41–43
features, 43
functional specification, 43
functional specification design, 44–45
master project plan, 43
MSF model phases, 40–50
plan generation, 46
planning phase, 43–47
project schedule, 43
realistic goals for functionality, 45
requests for features, 48
requirements, 42
resource identification, 46
resources, 43
schedule, 43
schedule generation, 46–47
scope, 42–43
steps in deploying, 121
technical user testing, 47–48
test environment, 115–116
user migration, 49
user requirements, 79
user testing, 48, 115
validating design, 47, 114–115
vision, 42–43
Properties dialog box, 420
property store and full-text indexes, 384–385
Propfind IM command, 468
Proppatch IM command, 468
proprietary connectors, 425
protected messaging environment, 11
protocol conflicts, 235
protocol engine, 413, 445
protocol events, 416
protocol stub, 414, 445
protocols
default, 310
IM (Instant Messaging), 466–468
Outlook Express, 268
verifying availability, 176–178
Protocols container, 235
proxy servers and IM (Instant Messaging), 467, 473
.pst file, 282
Pub.edb database, 16
public folder hierarchy, 560
public folder servers, 98–99
public folder store policies, 362, 365
public folder stores, 8, 24, 86, 98, 368, 544
backups, 616
indexes of all text, 383
limiting data replication, 551
public folder trees, 545–546, 560
public folder/newsgroups folder, 326
public folders, 8, 98, 104, 326, 378, 544–545
access security, 549–550
age limits, 549
available to non-e-mail client software, 99
configuring properties, 548–549
creation of, 546–548
deleted item retention, 549
hierarchies, 98, 545–546
IFS (Installable File System), 99
IFS (Installable File System) driver, 313
item-level security, 141
mail-enabling, 379, 554–555
managing, 326, 379, 550–558
mixed-mode environments, 141
monitoring usage, 555–556
naming, 547
offline item creation, 557
in other forests, 218
Outlook 2000, 290
OWA (Outlook Web Access), 557–558
performance counters, 556
permissions, 549–550
placing information in, 547
publishing documents as Web pages, 98–99
replicating, 551–552
replicating hierarchy, 552
replicating information between, 548
replication intervals, 365
replication limits, 365
searching Subject field, 383
storage limits, 548–549
troubleshooting replication, 553–554
type of information stored in, 547
Public Folders address list, 382
Public Folders container, 546
Public Folders folder, 99
public keys and encryption, 510–513
public SMTP virtual servers, 405
public stores, 412
boundary limits, 374–376
finding and removing errors, 594–595
Publish Form As dialog box, 671
publishing documents as Web pages, 98–99

Q

Queues subcontainer, 405
QUIT POP3 command, 314
QUIT SMTP command, 312, 442

R

RAID (redundant array of independent disks), 88
RAID 1, 377
RAID 5, 175, 377
RC2 (Rivest's Cipher) encryption, 512
RC4 encryption, 512
RCPT SMTP command, 312
RCPT TO SMTP command, 442
reactive maintenance, 576
Read Items permission, 550
real-time collaboration, 19, 464–465
real-time performance data, 370
recipient objects, 366
domain-naming context, 131
mailbox-enable, 366
mail-enable, 366
managing, 647–648
managing after replication, 130
updating address information, 131–132
updating merged or migrated, 131–133
recipient policies, 380–381, 386
recipients, managing, 379–385
Recipients container, 380
Recipients folder, 358, 360, 381
Recipients Policies folder, 360
Redirector\Network Errors/Sec counter, 591
Recover Deleted Items From dialog box, 288–289
redundancy, 93–94, 96–97, 177
REG_BINARY Registry value, 369

REG_DWORD Registry value, 369
Regedit.exe, 368–369
Regedt32.exe, 368–369, 377
REG_EXPAND_SZ Registry value, 369
Registry, 386
backing up before editing, 378
configuring audit policy, 371
configuring Exchange 2000-specific information, 369
editing, 368–370
hives, 369
keys, 369
names of users who can access Information Store, 378
removing or deleting programs, 369
Registry Editor, 368–370, 377
REG_MULTI_SZ Registry value, 369
REG_SZ Registry value, 369
remote access and Outlook 2000, 283
remote administration, 237
remote computers, 366–368
remote users
connecting to servers, 172
OWA (Outlook Web Access), 272
RENAME IMAP4 command, 316
Replay attacks, 522
replication, 123–124
AD (Active Directory), 124
ADC (Active Directory Connector), 229–230, 236
bridgehead servers, 89, 90
checking status, 226
configuration information, 228
defining schedules, 225
direction of, 225
Exchange Server 5.5, 124
IM virtual server, 474
increasing efficiency, 126
manually initiating, 237
multi-master, 123
objects, 225–226
one-way, 126, 129
public folder hierarchy, 552
public folders, 551–552
single-master, 123
two-way, 126, 129
user object information, 228
Windows 2000 Server, 124
Replication property page, 365
ReplMon, 237
Res1.log file, 376
resource records and events, 371
resources, 43
identifying, 46
managing, 372–379
managing in mixed-mode environment, 141–142
monitoring, 587–588
online/electronic materials, 651–655
Outlook 2002, 655–656
printed materials, 651
transitive trusts and, 58
troubleshooting, 187–190
restoring
daily full backups, 621
data, 614, 650
ESEUTIL utility, 624–625
full backup, 622–623
mailbox, 623
online and offline backups, 623–624
prerequisites, 620–622
storage groups, 119
strategy, 621
system functionality, 650
RETR POP3 command, 314
RGCs (Routing Group Connectors), 117, 120, 121, 138–139, 407, 425–426
automatic load-balancing, 425
bridgehead servers, 138, 426
redundancy, 425
RPC over X.400, 426
schedules, 425
SMTP (Simple Mail Transport Protocol), 426
unidirectional nature, 421
use of different protocols, 426
RGM (routing group master), 139, 434, 445
roles and administrative groups, 135–136
routers and IM (Instant Messaging), 470
routing connectors, 117, 146
routing engine, 139, 414, 445
Routing Engine Service, 186
Routing Group Connectors, 52
routing group topology, 420–424, 445
routing groups, 11, 18, 24, 83, 136, 418
administering, 419–420
bandwidth, 417
comparing connectors, 138–139
connecting, 420–424, 427–428
connecting servers, 425–426
connectors, 120
creating, 420
default, 120
environment, 140
geographical areas, 417–418
integrating with administrative groups, 136–137
link state, 139
message routing, 409–410
messages, 407
naming, 420
network latency, 417
number needed, 120
number of, 372
planning, 417–424
populating, 420
routing connectors, 117
SMTP (Simple Mail Transport Protocol), 18
spanning administrative groups, 420
testing, 119–120
transferring messages, 120
troubleshooting routing problems, 439–440
Routing Groups container, 420
Routing Groups folder, 359, 360
RPC (Remote Procedure Calls), 7, 11, 12, 24, 595
ADC (Active Directory Connector), 230
limiting deployment issues, 18
SRS (Site Replication Service), 127
RPC Ping (Remote Procedure Calls Ping), 595
RRAS (Routing and Remote Access Services), 172, 194
RSA encryption, 513
RSET POP3 command, 314
RSET SMTP command, 312, 442
RUS (Recipient Update Service), 131–133, 380, 382
RVP (rendezvous protocol), 466–467, 489
IM (Instant Messaging), 515
minimal impact on network resources, 467
_rvp SRV resource record, 473

S

SA (System Attendant), 9, 15, 26
sample upgrade scenario, 215–218
scalability, 21–22
schedule, 43
Schedule+, 272–273
Schedule+ Connectors, 430–432
Schedule+ Free/Busy Connector, 431–432
scheduling backups, 616
Schema Administrators group, 61, 179
Schema Admins account, 234

schema naming context, 61, 216
schemas, 24
  AD (Active Directory), 58
  directories, 317
  expanding, 58
  making changes to, 58
  ms-Exch-attributes, 216
  rebooting after updating, 191
  sending changes to domain controllers, 226
  unable to update, 187
  updates, 227
SEARCH IMAP4 command, 316
Search service, 384
Search service (Mssearch.exe), 383
SearchRequest LDAP command, 318
SearchResultDone LDAP command, 318
SearchResultEntry LDAP command, 318
SearchResultReference LDAP command, 318
secure communications, 333
secure dynamic updates, 66
security, 11, 506
  AD (Active Directory) integration, 509
  administrator accounts, 179
  advanced features, 177
  advanced issues, 520–524
  anonymous access, 332
  auditing, 506–509
  authentication control, 332
  back-end servers, 96
  baseline, 507
  certificate services, 513–516
  channels, 479
  controlling access to Exchange 2000 Server, 509–510
  customizable, 290
  dedicated accounts for administration, 178
  DN (distinguished name), 318
  domain name restrictions, 333
  domains, 176
  encryption, 336
  firewalls, 519–520
  front-end servers, 96
  IIS (Internet Information Server), 323
  Internet issues, 520–521
  IP address restrictions, 333
  Kerberos authentication, 509
  KMS (Key Management Services), 516–518
  logging, 506–509
  Microsoft Certificate Services, 510
  OUs (organizational units), 60
  Outlook 2002, 666–674
  OWA (Outlook Web Access), 334–335
  PKI (Public Key Infrastructure), 510–513
  potential attacks against Windows 2000 and Exchange 2000 Server, 521–523
  public folder access, 549–550
  public/private keys and encryption, 510–513
  secure communications, 333
  security checklists, 507–509
  security policies, 507
  troubleshooting, 518–519
  virus attacks, 521
  Windows 2000, 510
security audit, 507, 526
security checklists, 507–509, 526
Security Configuration Analyzer, 510
security events, 370–371
security hot fixes, 174, 194
Security log file, 583
security logs, 370–371
security policies, 507
security principal, 218, 239
Security Settings folder, 671
SELECT IMAP4 command, 316
server clusters, 93–94, 104
server policies, 361–362
Server Policy Properties dialog box, 362–363
server roles, 221
server-based lists, 382
servers
  adding and removing from administrative groups, 373–374
  Chat clients, 481
  configuring notifications, 583–585
  configuring system policies, 362–364
  configuring with system policies, 361–365
  controlling flow of messages between, 120
  disabling or removing monitors, 227
  enabling message tracing, 363–364
  equipment diagrams, 81
  hardware configuration, 173
  intended role, 173
  limiting number of logons, 378
  logical group, 372–374
  management tools, 358–365
  message tracking, 585–587
  mixed-mode environment, 17–18
  monitoring state and health of, 370
  NetBIOS name, 176
  permissions, 223
  restoring full backup, 622–623
  routing messages within, 410–411
  scalability and messaging benchmarks, 116
  storage groups, 374
Servers folder, 360
Service Pack 2, 222
Service Pack 3, 220–221
Service Pack 4, 221
service packs, 174, 186–187, 194
services, 171–172
  listing configured, 368
  managing, 366–368
  shutting down, 9
  starting, 9
  status after installation, 186
  troubleshooting, 366
  unloading or uninstalling, 175
  verifying availability, 176–178
Services and Applications container, 366
Services and Applications\DHCP subcontainer, 368
Services and Applications\Exchange subcontainer, 368
Services and Applications\Indexing Service subcontainer, 368
Services and Applications\Internet Information Services subcontainer, 368
Services and Applications\Services subcontainer, 368
session, 12
Set as Master command, 139
Setup, 228
  DomainPrep switch, 226
  failure, 235
  incomplete routines, 234
  information file, 279
  troubleshooting issues, 234–236
Setup.exe file, 180, 279
Setup/ForestPrep command, 225
Setup.ini file, 279
SGs (storage groups), 8, 19, 26, 86, 87, 104, 143, 368, 412
  accidentally deleting database files, 376
  allocating resources, 89
  default, 374
  Enable circular logging property, 376
  fault tolerance, 88
  level of organization, 89
  limitations, 19
  location-specific design, 89
  Log file prefix property, 375
  managing, 374–376
  multiple, 377

optimal distribution, 119
placement, 377
planning backup schedules, 119
Properties dialog box, 375
restoring, 119
System path location property, 375
testing, 119
transaction log files, 19, 88, 374
Transaction log location property, 375
Zero out deleted database pages property, 375
SHA (Secure Hash Algorithm) encryption, 513
shared folders, 366
Shared Folders subcontainer, 366
shared information, 366
shared-file messaging systems, 2–5, 24
shortcut trusts, 58
shortcuts to tools, 183
showInAddressBook attribute, 382
single-instance message storage, 219
single-master replication, 123
Site Connector, 117, 138
Site Consistency Checker, 128
Site Replication Service, 10
Site Replication Services folder, 361
sites, 14, 26, 129, 223
SMP (Symmetric Multiprocessing) systems, 115
SMS (Systems Management Server), 280, 293
SMTP (Simple Mail Transport Protocol), 7, 13, 26, 81, 139, 170–171
AD (Active Directory), 18
address spaces, 427
advanced queuing engine, 9–10
advanced troubleshooting steps, 441–442
character sets, 312
commands, 311–312
Exchange 2000 Server, 139, 313
extending functionality, 9
inbound message flow, 12–13
message header, 310–311
MX (Mail Exchange) records, 311
native connectors, 404
as open protocol, 311
optional information, 310
as preferred protocol, 310
protocol stub, 414
queue growth notification, 583
required information, 310
RGCs (Routing Group Connectors), 426
routing groups, 18
transporting messages, 311
verifying installation, 226
virtual servers, 313, 404–406
SMTP Connector, 52, 117, 120, 121, 138–139, 427
SMTP mail, 139
SMTP Service, 10, 13, 413
SMTP Virtual Server Properties dialog box, 406
SMTP virtual servers, 405–406
Smtpsvc.dll, 12, 13
SNADS, 432
Social Engineering attacks, 522
software RAID implementation, 377
sorting newsgroups, 320
spam, 506
special accounts required for installation, 178–179
special-needs mailbox stores, 87
SRS (Site Replication Service), 11, 26
coexistence, 233–234
configuration CAs, 233
default configuration connection agreement, 129
mixed-mode administrative group, 233
RPC (Remote Procedure Calls), 127
Site Consistency Checker, 128
Srsmain.exe file, 128
standalone computer, 214
standalone servers, 217
standard indexing, 383
standards-based connectors, 425
Start button event sink, 415
STAT POP3 command, 314
STATUS IMAP4 command, 316
.stm file, 374
Storage container, 366
storage events, 415–416
store drivers, 413, 445
STORE IMAP4 command, 316
Store.exe file, 8, 12, 13, 86, 223, 237
stores, maintenance of, 578–580
Streaming Store, 412
subdomains, limiting number of, 122
Subscribe IM command, 468
SUBSCRIBE IMAP4 command, 316
swing method, 219
symmetric keys, 510, 526
synchronization, 123–124
directories, 128
error log file, 290
problems with, 290–291
Synchronize command, 281, 282
synchronizing information between forests, 218
synchronous events, 415–416
sysop, 475
System Attendant process, 131
System Attendant Service, 186
system events
monitoring, 366
viewing, 370–371
System log file, 583
system logs, 371
System Management tools, 181, 183, 192
System Manager, 184, 358–361, 374, 380, 477, 544, 548
Address Templates folder, 360
Administrative Groups container, 133, 135, 362
Administrative Groups folder, 374
Administrative Groups (or Routing Groups) folder, 359
Advanced Security features, 519
All Global Address Lists folder, 360
Chat Communities folder, 360
Conferencing folder, 360
configuring notifications, 583–585
Details Templates folder, 360
Folders folder, 360
Global Settings folder, 358, 359
Instant Messaging folder, 359
Internet Message Formats folder, 359
managing public folders, 546
Message Delivery folder, 359
message tracking, 585–587
Message Tracking Center folder, 361
Monitoring and Status folder, 361
monitoring message queues and system resources, 587–588
Offline Address Lists folder, 360
Recipient Policies list, 381
Recipients container, 131
Recipients folder, 358, 360, 381
Recipients Policies folder, 360
Routing Groups folder, 360
Servers folder, 360
Site Replication Services folder, 361
System Policies container, 362
System Policies folder, 360
Tools folder, 359
System Monitor, 370, 588
counters, 589
disk usage, 590–591
instances, 589

memory usage, 589–590
network usage, 591–592
processor usage, 590
system policies, 386
administrative groups, 362
configuring, 362–364
configuring servers, 361–365
message tracking, 363–364
properly configured, 376
server policies, 361
System Policies container, 362
System Policies folder, 360
system protocols, verifying availability, 176–178
system resources, monitoring, 587–588
system settings, defining, 380
System Tools container, 366
System Tools\Event Viewer subcontainer, 366
System Tools\Local Users and Groups subcontainer, 366
System Tools\Performance Logs and Alerts subcontainer, 366
System\Processor Queue Length counter, 590
Sysvol folder, 371

T

T.120 standard, 20
Task Items folder, 547
Task Manager, 371–372
tasks, 264
TCP/IP (Transmission Control Protocol/Internet Protocol), 7, 26
configured and functioning properly, 177
X.400 Connector, 139
TCP\%Segments Retransmitted/Sec counter, 591
TechNet Web site, 60, 67, 190, 318, 337, 471
technical requirements, 79
technical user testing, 47–48
Telnet, 321
Telnet client, 442
temporary channels, 477, 478
test environment, 115–116
test installation, 188
testing
all possible scenarios, 116–117
e-mail clients, 118–119
hardware, 115–116
relevant software or operating systems, 116
routing groups, 119–120
storage groups, 119
third-party connectors, 117–118
upgrade scenarios, 120–121
testing/quality assurance manager, 42
text-based messaging standards, 20
third-party connectors, testing, 117–118
ToGWise folder, 429
Tombstone Maintenance task, 579
tools, shortcuts to, 183
Tools container, 440
Tools folder, 359
Tracking.log files, 441
transaction log files, 8, 16, 26
ESE (Extensible Storage Engine), 413
Information Store, 86
local directory path, 375
name of active, 375
SGs (storage groups), 88
storage groups, 19, 374
transition domain, 223
transitive trust, 56–58
transport events, 416
Transport Layer Security, 139
transport protocols, 7–8
trees, 52
Trojan Horse attacks, 522
troubleshooting, 371–372
ADC (Active Directory Connector), 130–131, 236
Chat services, 484–485
connection agreements, 130–131
error codes, 188–189
event IDs, 188–189
failed installations, 187–191
files, 366
IM (Instant Messaging), 473–474
messaging connectivity, 437–443
migration, 234–237
Outlook 2000, 288–291
public folder replication, 553–554
resources, 187–190
scenarios, 657–664
security, 518–519
services, 366
setup issues, 234–236
test installation, 188
upgrade errors, 223–224
upgrading, 234–237
trust relationships
domains, 176
limiting, 57–58
NT 4.0 domain, 141
one-way, 56
two-way, 56–57
Windows 2000 domain, 141
TScript transcription extension, 479–480
TUCOWS Web site, 481
TURN SMTP command, 312
two-way connection agreements, 225
two-way replication, 126, 129
two-way trust relationships, 56–57
typical installation, 181, 470

U

UBE (unsolicited broadcast e-mail), 405
UDG (universal distribution group), 141, 223, 239
Unable to contact remote host error message, 440
Unable to resolve remote host error message, 440
unattended installation, 192–193
uninstalling
components, 190
Exchange 2000 Server, 190–191
unique SID (security identifier), 231–232
UNIX/Linux operating systems, 261
Unsubscribe IM command, 468
UNSUBSCRIBE IMAP4 command, 316
Update Server Versions task, 579
upgrading
adequate disk space, 224–225
BDCs (backup domain controllers), 217
domain structure, 221
Exchange 2000 Server, 645–646
Exchange Server 5.5 to Exchange 2000 Server, 219–227
global catalogs role, 216–217
goal of, 220
in-place upgrade, 101, 219–220, 222–227
leapfrog upgrade, 101, 219–220
versus migrating, 212
move mailbox upgrade, 101, 219–220
multiple Windows 2000 forests, 218
naming contexts role, 216
online backup, 224–225
preparing domains for, 226
preparing Windows 2000 environment for, 225–227
progressing as planned, 223–224
sample upgrade scenario, 215–218
server permissions, 223
server roles, 221
Service Pack 3, 220–221
swing method, 219

testing scenarios, 120–121
troubleshooting, 234–237
troubleshooting errors, 223–224
unused ACL (access control list) entries, 224
Windows 2000 Server, 214–215
URLs (Uniform Resource Locators), 8, 27
user accounts, 178
Administrator permission, 235
duplicate, 233
incorrect permissions, 235
managing, 365–366, 379
modifying or deleting, 380
not having appropriate rights, 290
special features, 380
user connection agreements, 128–130, 229, 239
user digital certificates, 515
user information, 231
user mailbox, 14
User Manager for Domains, 130
user migration, 49
user objects
Exchange-specific attributes, 231
information and replication, 228
USER POP3 command, 314
user profiles, 284–287
user requirements, 79
user testing, 48, 115
user training team, 42
users
access to directory information, 124
connections, 55
e-mail, 366
mailbox-enabled, 379
mail-enabled, 379
matching particular criteria, 381
migrating, 121
modifying aliases or display names, 379
not having appropriate rights, 290
permissions, 234
unique SID (security identifier), 231–232
USG (universal security group), 223, 239

V

value-added connectors, 404
verifying backup integrity, 615
VeriSign, 516
video conferencing, 10, 20–21
Video Conferencing Provider, 10
View Only permission, 134
virtual memory, 378–379
virtual protocol servers, 308–309, 339
virtual servers, 97
access controls, 368
IMAP4 (Internet Messaging Access Protocol Version 4), 315
IP addresses, 309
POP3 (Post Office Protocol version 3), 314
SMTP (Simple Mail Transport Protocol), 313, 404–406
virus
infection, 612
protection and Outlook 2002, 666–674
virus attacks, 521, 522
voice conferencing, 20–21
VPN (virtual private network), 283
VRFY SMTP command, 312

W

WANS (wide area networks)
network architecture diagram, 83–85
requirements and structure, 82–85
watcher, 467
Web browsers and digital certificates, 514
Web pages, default, 332
Web server digital certificates, 515
Web sites
content information, 333
event logging, 474
IIS (Internet Information Server), 325
OWA (Outlook Web Access), 325
remote file system viewing and modifying, 319
WebDAV-enabled folder, 319
Web Store, 319–320, 323–324, 339
WebDAV (Distributed Authoring and Versioning), 8, 27
WebDAV (Web Distributed Authoring and Versioning), 118, 319
WebDAV-enabled folder, 319
weekly full backup with differential data backup, 621
weekly full backup with incremental data backup, 621
WIA (Windows Integrated authentication), 515–516, 526
Windows 2000, 44
Active Directory Users and Computers console, 365–366
AD naming structure, 62
AD (Active Directory) service, 6–7
ADC (Active Directory Connector), 229
Computer Management utility, 366–368
delegating administrative duties, 60
displaying object classes or attributes, 7
DNS (Domain Name System), 171–172
domain and trust relationship, 141
domain controllers, 51, 54, 216
domain name structure, 54
EFS (Encrypting File System), 510
Event Viewer, 370–371, 583
forests, 225–226
installing support tools, 225
integration, 5–8, 170–172
IPSec (IP Security), 510
logging events and errors, 507
management tools, 236
native-mode environment, 213–214
Network Load Balancing service, 143
NNTP (Network News Transport Protocol), 171
nslookup utility, 64
patches, 174
Performance console, 370
potential attacks against, 521–523
preparing environment for upgrade, 225–227
preparing forest and domain structure for upgrade, 221–227
protocols, 170–171
Registry Editor, 368–370
RRAS (Routing and Remote Access Services), 172
security, 510
Security Configuration Analyzer, 510
security hot fixes, 174
Service Pack 2, 222
services, 171–172
services notification, 584
SMTP (Simple Mail Transport Protocol), 170–171
system component events, 371
Task Manager, 371–372
tools for Exchange Server management, 365–372
UDG (universal distribution group), 223
user profiles, 286
USG (universal security group), 223
Windows 2000 Advanced Server, 7, 378
dual-node active clustering, 94
IM Server, 20
Windows 2000 forests, 218
Windows 2000 Server, 213, 221
ADC (Active Directory Connector), 126
clustering, 177–178
IIS (Internet Information Server), 7–8

IM Server, 20
installation, 180
migration, 211–218
replication, 124
SMP (Symmetric Multiprocessing) systems, 115
upgrading to, 214–215
Windows 2000 SP1, 222
Windows clients and dynamic DNS updating, 66
Windows EventViewer, 506
Windows Installer application, 275–276
Windows NT 4.0, 44
delegating administrative duties, 60
domain controllers, 54, 215
domains, 215
Exchange 2000 Server, 213
multiple-master domain model, 57
upgrading domains, 130
upgrading network, 215
user profiles, 286
WINS (Windows Internet Naming Service), 81
Windows operating systems and MAPI (Messaging Application Programming Interface), 262
Windows pagefile, 175
Windows Sockets, 12
Windows Sockets API (Application Programming Interface), 7, 27
WinRoute.exe, 433
WINS (Windows Internet Naming Service), 81, 104
Workflow Designer for Exchange, 21
workflow enhancements, 682–683
workflow management, 21
workgroup management, 21
WSS (Web Storage System), 8, 27, 323–324, 411, 413
WWS (Web Storage System), 415–416

X

X.25 and X.400 Connector, 139
X.400 Connector, 52, 120, 138–139, 427–428
bridgehead servers, 138
queue growth notification, 584
TCP/IP (Transmission Control Protocol/Internet Protocol), 139
X.25, 139
X.400 messaging system, connecting to, 427–428
X.400 transport stack, 427–428
XML (eXtensible Markup Language), 119

Y

Yahoo! Messenger, 469

Z

zone files and events, 371